EARLY WESTERN AUGUSTA PIONEERS

Including the Families
of
Cleek, Gwin, Lightner and Warwick

And Related Families
of
Bratton, Campbell, Carlile, Craig,
Crawford, Dyer, Gay, Givens, Graham,
Harper, Henderson, Hull, Keister,
Lockridge, McFarland, and Moore

CLEARFIELD

Originally published
Staunton, Virginia, 1957

Reprinted for
Clearfield Company, Inc. by
Genealogical Publishing Co., Inc.
Baltimore, Maryland
1992, 1993, 1995, 1999, 2000, 2001

Library of Congress Catalogue Card Number 57-11495
International Standard Book Number: 0-8063-4522-5
Made in the United States of America

To
The Cherished Memory
of
My Father and Mother
George Washington Cleek
and
Malcena Catherine (Lightner) Cleek

TABLE OF CONTENTS

PREFACE

In 1875 my father, George Washington Cleek, at the age of forty, began to record on the walls of his grist and flour mill the important events of the Cleek's Mill community located on Jackson River between Warm Springs, Bath County and Monterey, Highland County, Virginia. He recorded births, marriages and deaths of his community and county. He began with the death of Polly Gwin on November 5, 1875, a relative. He recorded the height of the river, the first killing frost, house burnings and when the first automobile passed the mill on September 9, 1903. He maintained this record for thirty five years - until his death on January 1, 1910. The mill also served for a time as the community post office and voting precinct. These recordings were naturally the subject of much "cracker-barrel" conversation while the mill visitors waited for their grain to be ground or the mail to arrive.

As I look back, I believe these recordings by my father on the white pine planks of the old mill (built in 1848) were the beginnings of my interest in history and genealogy which has continued until the present day, almost fifty years.

This liking for the subject, I think, is born of a sincere interest in my fellowman and a great respect for the pioneers who founded and built our present civilization. Over the years, I have collected a great mass of data, much of it from older settlers of old western Augusta, who have long since departed this earth. Most of this information has never been formally recorded, at least in a manner or at a place where it will be permanently preserved. To preserve this data for posterity is my sole objective in undertaking this task.

Many friends have urged me to write an accompanying history of the area but I feel that this has already been recorded - and well done - over the past fifty years. I have therefore limited myself to a brief review of the reasons why the Germans and the Scotch-Irish happened to settle the area -- this largely for the information of the younger generations.

I have also gathered a great mass of data from books and records referred to in the bibliography included herein. I invite those who would do further research to consult the books listed. They will be well rewarded.

The data herein (other than the references listed) has been obtained, I will repeat from old family and court records and letters and testimony of creditable persons and from every source considered reliable, by long and patient search. There are, no doubt, some errors and I would appreciate being advised of these when they are detected. In a work of this kind I do not believe perfection is possible or can be expected. The human element enters to such a large degree; however all matters set forth as facts are known or

believed to be true from substantial evidence. This manuscript
is submitted to the kind and charitable judgment of the families
included and their friends; and pardon is asked for shortcomings
and imperfections. It is hoped that it may be interesting
enough to cause them to overlook its faults and that they may
be inspired by their ancestors to be more worthy ancestors
themselves.

The compiler is grateful to the many people who have
assisted him over the years in gathering this data. He is
particularly grateful to his daughter, Malcena Cathrine Cleek
Mann, and her husband, Robert Neville Mann, who assisted him
in searching records and in the final preparation of this
manuscript.

Geo. W. Cleek
Staunton, Virginia
May 1, 1957

FOREWORD

This manuscript is divided into twenty (20) parts, and each part is numbered by the following system. The emigrant or earliest known member of the family of the name is given the number 1. His children are numbered 2, 3, 4, 5, 6, etc., in the order of birth, if known. The children are listed immediately following the parents. If any child is the ancestor of a line to be followed further or a more detailed picture of that individual is to be given, a cross (+) is typed in the manuscript opposite his or her name. His or her number will be found numerically further on in the text. The number in parenthesis, (7), after the subject individual's name, indicates his or her generation with respect to the emigrant or earliest known ancestor in that particular family line.

This system, it is believed, is the easiest to follow of the various systems used in genealogy.

The index of this manuscript includes names only. Places and events are not indexed. The page number where an individuals name is first listed is given, as well as the page number where supplementary information is given.

THE GERMAN FAMILIES OF AUGUSTA

One might ask what caused the German families of Augusta to leave their native Vaterland and undertake such a hazardous adventure as a trip across the ocean to America in the early 1700's. The answer lies in the culminating factors of almost constant recurring warfare, the constant drain of taxation imposed by their royal rulers to keep up with the grandeur of the court of Louis XIV in France, the incessant struggle of the Catholic element against the Protestants, and not the least, that the entire valleys of the Rhine, the Neckar, and the Main Rivers had been set aflame by the fiery speeches of William Penn preaching the new religion of brotherly love, and the glories and the abundance of freedom in the New World.

They had witnessed years filled with oppression and taxation by petty but strong rulers; years filled with bloody religious strife; the incessant pillaging by armies of conquest; the years filled with the sights of the Palatinate laid waste many times by the sword by day and the torch by night. This, of course, was not conducive to a spirit of daring but a few were and took the adventuresome step. They constantly sent messages back telling of the wonders in the land of William Penn - all that country on the frontier north of Philadelphia where the colony of Womelsdorf had been established in the Tulpenhocken territory and reaching eastward into the established colony of Oley where there was a direct "high road" into Philadelphia. Oley was the northern terminus of this road. The town of Oley is older than Reading, which was founded in 1748. A German Lutheran and Reformed group had begun a settlement of small farms at Oley about 1710. (Reading and Berks County, Cyrus T. Fox, Vol. I, page 15). Some historians say a beginning was made at Oley in 1704. This settlement was Pennsylvania's frontier. It was often attacked by Indians until after the French and Indian War. The first church was established here by John Caspar Stoever in 1730. It was known as "St. Josephs" or the "Hill Church" and was one of the ten charter member congregations of the Ministerium of Pennsylvania. Historians say it is perhaps one of the oldest churches in Pennsylvania. The writer visited this church in June 1951 on a rainy afternoon and found three cornerstone dates, 1747, 1753, and 1786.

To continue with our narrative about the early German emigrants - there was nothing but praise for settling in Pennsylvania, while there was nothing but condemnation against settling in New York. The way that England had practiced the boldest deception and intrigues upon the early emigrants who were landed on Governor's Island and later transferred to Livingston Manor was soon broadcast throughout the entire Palatinate. As a result the German emigration to New York State soon came to a halt.

The section of Germany known as the Palatinate lies along the Rhine, the Neckar, and the Main Rivers. In 1700 its principal cities were Pforzheim, Heidelberg, Mannheim, Frankenthal, Worms, Spire, Alzey, Baccarach, Bretten, Lauteren, Masbach Newstadt, Oppenheim, Simmeren, Stromberg, and Ladenberg.

7

The Palatinate was composed of two states: Upper or Bavarian Palatinate, and the Lower or The Palatinate of the Rhine, bounded on the east by Wurttemburg and Baden, on the south by Baden and Lorraine, and on the west by Alsace and Lorraine. It extended as far north as Treves and Mainz. East to west, the Palatinate extended over one hundred miles and about sixty miles from north to south. The capitol was Heidelberg.

The Palatinate was first mentioned in history about the middle of the tenth century, A.D. We know, however, that there existed during the fourth century B.C. a large number of tribes of people on the shores of the Baltic Sea. Further, that during the second century B.C. several of these tribes descended upon the Roman provinces in Germany. Then began the bitter contest between the German tribes and the Romans which lasted over a period of five hundred years, and which resulted in the disintegration of the Roman Empire and the immediate seizing of all territory as far south as Switzerland by the German tribes.

By the time of the beginning of the fourth century A.D. all tribal names had disappeared except four - Goths, Franks, Saxons, and Alemanni. The Alemanni are supposed to have settled in the region of the upper Rhine. The Romans regarded the Alemanni as the largest and most formidable of all the German tribes. (The Story of the Pennsylvania Germans, William Beidelman).

The Palatinate was founded during the twelfth century with Conrad Hohenstauffer as its first Prince. As a sovereign state it continued until it was merged in 1801 - over a period of almost seven hundred years.

In 1547 Charles V led his forces against the Protestant League at Muhlberg. For sixteen hundred years petty wars had followed one another in recurring cycles and by 1618 the universal bitterness which had become engendered among surrounding countries and Germany culminated in the catastrophe that almost decimated the Palatinate - the Thirty Years War. By the time of the close of the war in 1648, the Palatinate was completely exhausted. Most of the population of the country districts had been killed.

The fertile lands of the Palatinate were the envy of all neighboring powers. The country along the Rhine and the Neckar was the garden spot of Europe. No sooner had the Thirty Years War come to a close in 1648 than the Palatinate was again visited by the ravages of war. After the war in Holland in 1674, Marshal Turrene of France overran the Palatinate, sparing nothing of value and showing no mercy.

The impoverished remnants of the Palatinate had scarcely drawn a breath of relief before clouds of war again obscured their hopes of peace. Louis XIV of France wanted the Palatinate as a gift for his sister-in-law, the Duchess of Orleans, and in 1681, without declaration of war, sent his army to seize Strasbourg. In 1688, to vent his hatred against the Protestants, the French under Melac attempted to usurp the Palatinate. For nine years the entire Palatinate was overrun, burned and pillaged.

By 1697, when peace was declared, the population of the area had been reduced from 500,000 to a mere 50,000 - ninety per cent of the population had been destroyed.

War again broke out in 1701 and lasted until 1713. It was the War of Spanish Succession. The Palatinate again was sucked into the boiling cauldron. Marshal Villars of Frances let his armies into the Palatinate and again nothing was left but scorched earth.

During these grievous times when the Palatinate again and again had been bathed in blood and tears, there was an upsurge of hope that was drifting across the impoverished Palatinate. An enthusiastic young Englishman was proclaiming his new religion of Brotherly Love. He was a fluent German scholar and made frequent pilgrimages up and down the Rhine and Neckar Rivers making many converts to his new religious sect, the Quakers. Where dispair had smothered the minds of men, he set them aflame with the comforts of his religion and the glories of life in the "Promised Land." William Penn was a Godsend to the Palatinate. He was a compelling force which kindled the craving of the Palatinate to leave their homes and seek refuge in America.

Will Penn was the son of Admiral William Penn of the English Navy. His mother was German. He was born in 1644 and died in 1718, having lived through the turbulent times of the Palatines since the Thirty Years War. At the age of 27 in 1671, he made his first preaching venture in the Palatinate, proclaiming the tenets of his religion. He made frequent visits thereafter. The people, weary of warfare and oppression, were a fertile field for Penn to receive recruits.

England owed Admiral Penn 16,000 pounds and in settlement of the debt, King Charles II in 1681 granted to William Penn a total of 40,000 square miles of land in Pennsylvania. Being well known in the Palatinate, Penn combined his religious preachings with pleas to colonize his newly acquired land in Pennsylvania. He issued pamphlets, "The Golden Book," and circulated these throughout the Palatinate. He was fluent, he was convincing, he was honest, he painted inspiring pictures of freedom and easy life in a land of plenty - the Utopia in his colony.

He kindled the fire which soon was to set all aflame. Emigration was slow to start, but once in motion, the exodus was to continue unabated until the American Revolution. Penn had been pleading for rain but he had coaxed on a flood. Over 13,000 fled the Palatinate in 1709 alone.

Wars followed wars and when there was any respite the old bitter feeling of Protestant against Catholic would break out among the ruling class and engulf the entire Palatinate. In

1708 a desperate condition was reached. The people of the Palatinate were so desperate they sent an appeal to Queen Anne of England to come to their rescue. She extended asylum to them in England but her hospitality soon proved a nightmare. What to do with the ever growing thousands who emigrated to England taxed the best minds of her country.

Now (1708) was the time for William Penn to come to the rescue. England needed these sturdy Germans on the frontiers in America as buffers against the Indians, but Penn had gotten into financial difficulties and was thrown into prison in 1708 through the sharp practice of former friends. At the time his help was most needed, he himself was helpless.

The thousands who fled to London were dispersed over a period of years by sending them to Ireland, Jamaica, New York, and North Carolina. Those sent to New York for the most part made their way overland and settled in the Tulpenhocken area, about seventeen miles west of where Reading, Pennsylvania is today. The relations with the Indians was friendly and in 1732 the entire Tulpenhocken district was purchased from them.

The experiences through which the emigrants to New York had passed was so discouraging that it was relayed back to the Palatinate and thereafter arrivals at New York ended and the great masses of Palatines fleeing Germany landed at Philadelphia, Pennsylvania. Pennsylvania might well be considered the central point of emigration from Germany, France and Switzerland from 1682 to 1776. In the first period of twenty years, 1682 to 1702, comparatively few Germans arrived: not over two hundred families - they located principally at Germantown, near Philadelphia. The period from 1702 - 1727 marks an era in the early German emigration. Between forty and fifty thousand left their native country and came to the Quaker colony.

In Professor I. Daniel Rupp's collection, "Thirty Thousand Names of German, Swiss, Dutch, and French Immigrants," first published in 1856, we have the names of many of the people that landed at Philadelphia from 1727 to 1776, together with other facts of the country from which they came, the vessels in which they sailed, etc. The original lists of signatures were taken by requirement of the laws of the colony and generally contain only the names of men over sixteen years of age. It is estimated that over fifty thousand emigrated during this period.

The names of practically all the German families of the Shenandoah Valley are to be found in Rupp's collection. From 1727 to 1739 each ship load of arrivals are designated "Palatines" almost without exception. During the years 1740 and 1741 they are also called "Palatines" except that one ship load, registered on September 23, 1740, are labeled "Palatines and Switzers." From 1742 to 1748 "Foreigners" is the designation used. In 1749 there are "Foreigners," "Wirtembergers," "Palatines," etc. From 1750 to 1753 the emigrants are not identified with respect to

residence, but they are sometimes identified with respect to religion as "Calvanists," "Mennonites," "Catholics," etc. In 1754
places of former residence are usually given: Alsace, Lorraine,
Franconia, the Palatinate, Wirtemberg, Darmstadt, Zwebrucken,
Hesse, Westphalia, Hanau, Switzerland, Hamburg, Hanover, Saxony.
From 1755 to 1775 they are not identified as to place of birth,
a few shiploads are identified with respect to religion;but in
nearly every case from 1727, the name of the ship, the ship master,
and the names of the foreign ports from which the ship last sailed
are given. It will be observed, from the foregoing that the great
majority of emigrants of the 18th century were from South Germany.

The Rhine was the highway along which the refugees fled the
Palatinate, and it became clogged with every type of vessel that
could boast a mast and a sail. The exodus down the Rhine lasted
for the six months from May through October each year. The trip
down the Rhine to Rotterdam in the Netherlands lasted from three
to six weeks. They had to pass some twenty to thirty customhouses
on their way down and each one exacted its fee. The resources of
many were exhausted by the time Rotterdam was reached. They were
sometimes held in the Netherlands for one to two months. From
Dutch ports they were transferred to some English port, where they
usually experienced another delay sometimes lasting several months,
while waiting to be passed by the customhouse or waiting for suitable winds.

The ships that brought over these people were small sailing
vessels "from sixty-three feet to less than one hundred feet long.
Their tonnage was from one hundred to three hundred tons." (German
Immigration into Pennsylvania, Frank Reid Diffendeiffer). Some
of the ships carried as many as four hundred people. The voyage
to America took up to three months or longer to reach Philadelphia.
Upon arrival in Philadelphia there was usually another long delay
before they took the Oath of Allegiance to the Crown of England
before the city council.

The great majority of these Germans first settled in the
counties of Lancaster, Lebanon, Berks, York, and those immediately
surrounding Philadelphia. When the land was all taken up they
moved southward. The Germans in the Valley of Virginia came across
the Potomac above Harper's Ferry from Maryland and Pennsylvania.
The narrow neck of western Maryland was soon traversed, and the
Shenandoah Valley lay next beyond. In addition to the great body
from Pennsylvania, there were a few who came from New Jersey and
New York and a few came from the east Virginia counties of Spottsylvania, Orange, and Madison; and also a few, doubtless, from the
German settlements in North Carolina.

During the latter part of the Revolution and immediately
following that struggle, a considerable number of Germans belonging to the religious body known as Dunkers came to the Shenandoah
Valley, and established homes. But they, too, were from Pennsylvania, almost without exception; and did not differ materially in
racial or social qualities from the earlier emigrants.

11

The German element of the Shenandoah Valley is chiefly made
up of the descendants of early emigrants: families who, for the
most part, came into this country prior to the year 1800, who
bought land and established homes, and handed their growing
possessions down from father to son. The great influx of Germans
to the United States during the last century and a half scarcely
touched the Shenandoah Valley. Most of these individuals went
into the North and West so that comparatively few new families
have come into the Valley during the last four or five generations.

The causes that brought the German people from Pennsylvania
to Virginia were no doubt chiefly economic, though race pre-
judice growing out of the close association of heterogeneous
nationalities and real or fancied neglect on the part of the
Pennsylvania government may have contributed to the cause. But
the Pennsylvania Germans having passed the stressful period of
their history wanted land for their children: good land, cheap
land, much land. William Beverly, writing April 30, 1732, to a
friend in Williamsburg concerning lands on the Shenandoah, says:
"Ye northern men are fond of buying land there, because they can
buy it, for six or seven pounds pr: hundred acres, cheaper than
they can take up land in pensilvania and they don't care to go
as far as Wmsburg." Therefore, after the best farms in Pennsylvania had been taken, and the narrow breadth of Maryland had
been occupied, the next and most natural thing was to go across
the Potomac into the Shenandoah Valley. There they found a free,
open, and fertile new land; and there they chose to invest their
savings and build their dwellings.

In summary, the fact is emphasized that the Germans of the
Valley of Virginia are descended almost entirely from the emigrants of the early eighteenth century; people who left the
Fatherland, not for economic reasons alone, but largely because
of religious persecution, political oppression, or military out-
rages. Such forces always move the best classes - people who at
such times are seeking most of all liberty of conscience, health
of the state, and safety for the morals of home and family. The
German pioneers of the Valley, like their neighbors the Scotch-
Irish, were such a people.

THE SCOTCH-IRISH FAMILIES OF AUGUSTA

Since many of the people included in this manuscript are of Scotch-Irish ancestry an attempt has been made to give a sketch of the origin and history of the people so-called and what induced them to leave their native land and come to America.

The name Scotland was never applied to that country, now so designated, before the tenth century, but was called Alban, Albania, Albion. At an early period Ireland was called Scotia, exclusively so before the tenth century. Scotia was then a territorial or geographical term, while Scotus was a race name or generic term, implying people as well as country. The generic term of Scoti embraced the people of that race whether inhabiting Ireland or Britain. The name in its Latin form of Scotia was transferred from Ireland to Scotland in the reign of Malcolm, the Second, who reigned from 1004 to 1034.

A strong emigration took place from the north of Ireland to the western parts of Scotland prior to the year 1000. The inhabitants of Ireland and the Highlands of Scotland were but branches of the same Keltic stock and their language was substantially the same. There were frequent migrations between the two countries however the history of the Scotch-Irish since 1600 is necessarily a history of the troubles they suffered on account of their religion. In this connection, it must be remembered that the great principle of religious liberty was not recognized in the seventeenth and the early part of the eighteenth centuries. The opinion prevailed that it was the duty of the civil government to maintain the Church; and, the Church being divided into various sects, nearly every sect was striving to obtain governmental recognition and support, to the exclusion of every other. In nearly all European countries some one church was established by law, and nonconformity to it was regarded as disloyal and punishable; and no doubt some good men believed they were doing God service by trying to crush out all those who did not follow them.

Ulster, the most northern province of Ireland, is composed of the following nine counties: Antrim, Armagh, Cavan, Donigal, Down, Fermanagh, Londonderry, Monaghan, and Tyrone.

In consequence of rebellions in Ireland during the latter years of the reign of Queen Elizabeth, large portions of the land held by titled proprietors were confiscated, and many new settlers were introduced from England. At the time James came to the throne, the country enjoyed peace, which was due to the desolations the land had suffered. The province of Ulster was almost depopulated. With the exception of a few fortified cities, the towns and villages were destroyed; and scarcely any buildings remained except the castles of the English conquerors. Early in the reign of James I, several of the landed proprietors in Ulster engaged in a conspiracy to dethrone the King. The plot was discovered, and the Lords taking part in the plot flew from the country, and their lands were confiscated by the Crown. Thus about 500,000 acres were at

13

the disposal of the King. These lands were parcelled out to
favorites of the King, English and Scotch, as rewards for services rendered or expected. The natives of the soil were treated
with little consideration, being relegated to the more rugged or
barren areas of the province.

In the autumn of 1609, commissioners started from Dublin
accompanied by a military force to survey the confiscated lands
and assign the allotments to the new owners. Previous to this,
however, there had been a rush of people from the Highlands of
Scotland. Some years afterward there was another migration of
Highlanders numbering over ten thousand.

This volunteer emigration became annoying to the authorities of Ireland, and a warrant was issued "to stay the landing
of these Scotch that came without a certification." It is un-
likely that all the Scotch took root and remained in Ulster;
there was much coming and going for many years; but the Highlanders who came and remained account for the many 'Macs' who
constitute so large a part of the Scotch-Irish group.

From 1609 and on, a poor but more staid class of people
from the lowlands of Scotland were introduced by the new proprietors. The lands of Ulster yielded the new comers abundant
harvests, and others of their countrymen sold out in Scotland
and crossed over to Ireland.

Further, King James, being dissatisfied by the progress
made by the Scotch, interested the Corporation of London in the
plantation of Ulster; accordingly the whole county of Coleraine
was assigned to the Londoners, who changed the name to Londonderry, and founded the town of Derry. These people also migrated
with the Scotch-Irish to America.

The Scotch did not degenerate in Ulster, nor did they mingle
by intermarriage with the natives; but with their intelligence,
industry and thrift soon transformed the country.

Charles I came to the throne in 1625 and for some years Ireland enjoyed peace. Archbishop Land became the dominant power
in England and in 1632 ordered the trial of certain alleged
"fanatical disturbers of the peace." Four Scotch ministers in
Ireland were chosen for their refusal to conform to the Church
of England. All four were deposed from the ministry and prohibited from preaching. Dispairing of relief for themselves, and
discovering the storm which was gathering around others, the deposed ministers began to look for some place of refuge where religious liberty might be enjoyed. They considered New England
but were prevented from going there when they reached London. As
a result of the oppressions suffered the Ulster Scotch were deter-
mined to seek religious liberty in America. They built a ship,
the Eaglewing, and on September 9, 1636, one hundred and forty of
them set sail for New England. This venture failed, however, and
they were forced to turn back. They continued to preach and to

14

escape arrest they fled to Scotland. The non-conforming laity also fled to avoid the fines and other punishments. Many who did not flee were committed to prison.

In May 1639 all residents of Ulster above the age of fifteen, male and female, except Catholics, were required by proclamation to take what was known as the "Black Oath" binding them to yield an unconditional obedience to all royal commands, civil or religious, just or unjust. Many of the people refused to take the oath and on these the heaviest penalties of the law, short of death, were inflicted. Multitudes fled to Scotland, leaving their homes to go to ruin; while so many of the farmers abandoned the country it was scarcely possible to carry on the work of the harvest.

After Land and the King were deposed, Ireland, for a time, enjoyed peace and prosperity. In 1641, however, the native Irish rose in rebellion. The insurrection was speedily converted into a religious war, carried on with fury and savage ferocity. Many were ruthlessly slaughtered. The brunt of the conflict fell upon people of English origin.

The Presbyterians, as a body, suffered less by the rebellion than any other class. Many of them had retired to Scotland to escape the tyranny of the Bishop and were thus preserved. Troops arrived from Scotland and during the year 1642 the rebellion was put down. Few of the English clergy, and not one prelate, remained in Ulster. The people of Scottish birth or descent, who had left the province, gradually returned, and this class became a majority of the population.

During the existence of the Commonwealth, the Presbyterians in Ulster, were for a time not molested by the government. The motion of "bringing home the King," Charles II, first made by ministers of the Church of Scotland, was a grave error, as they demanded no guarantees for civil and religious liberty. He was proclaimed King on May 8, 1660, and it was not long until he repudiated all his promises. He declared in favor of Prelacy, refused toleration to Non-conformists, and named Bishops for all the dioceses in Ireland.

It was during the seven preceding years that the Presbyterian Church in Ulster gathered strength to withstand the storms to arise. In 1653, not more than a half dozen ministers remained in the country. In 1660, however, there were about seventy regularly settled ministers, having eighty congregations, embracing a population of about one hundred thousand.

The Irish Parliament met on the eighth of May 1660, the House of Lords being composed largely of the Bishops. A declaration was put forth establishing the former ecclesiastical laws, and forbidding all to preach who would not conform. The dissenting ministers remained among their people and the oppressions of the ecclesiastical courts and the exorbitant demands of the established clergy for tithes, constituted their principal grievance.

At this time the people of Scotland were suffering the most intolerable persecution, and the Ulster Scotch lived in comparative peace. Their ministers, the Scotch, preached in barns and administered the sacraments in the night. Even at the burial of their dead, they were hardly permitted to conduct the services according to their own usages. But throughout, the trouble to which the Dissenters were subjected, was not caused so much by the civil as by the ecclesiastical authorities.

The battle of Bothwell Bridge in Scotland occurred on June 22, 1679. An old account of this battle says 250 were banished to America. A list of these men reads like a roll of Augusta County people: Anderson, Bell, Brown, Craig, Campbell, Hutchison, Hamilton, Reid, Scott, Walker, Wilson, and others.

For observing a fast day in 1681 four ministers were sentenced to pay a fine of twenty pounds each or be imprisoned, and were confined for more than eight months. Thereupon the meeting houses in Ulster were closed and public worship prohibited. This state of affairs continued for many years and many of the ministers declared their intention to emigrate to America, but were induced to remain, hoping for better times.

James II came to the throne in February 1685, and then the clergy and members of the established Church began to feel the brunt of persecution. Every favor was shown by the King to Roman Catholics, and to gain the support of Dissenters, he issued his "Declaration for liberty of conscience." This afforded relief to the Presbyterians, and the fears of the established clergy for their own safety induced them to relax in their severities towards Non-conformists. In this hour of peril, the Presbyterians forgot their recent sufferings and made common cause with the Episcopalians in opposition to the despotic and bigoted monarch. They were the first to hail the arrival of William, Prince of Orange. The native Irish rose in behalf of King James, and a general massacre of Protestants was threatened.

In 1688, the Earl of Antrim, a partisan of James, was approaching Londonderry to occupy it with his regiment, but a number of resolute youths, encouraged by the bulk of the inhabitants, seized the keys and closed the gates against the Earl. The small town of Derry thus became the only refuge of the Protestants of Ulster. Thirty thousand Protestants of both sexes and of every age were crowded behind the bulwarks of this City of Refuge. The seige of the town lasted more than three miserable months. Finally a frigate and two provision ships came in and Derry was saved. Seldom has an unfortified and ill-supplied place been defended with such obstinate valor. On July 31 the seige was raised.

The duke of Schomberg and his army arrived in August and secured comparative peace and safety to the inhabitants. Soon thereafter King William wrote to Schomberg, recommending the Ulster Scotch to his protection.

The law prohibiting Presbyterian ministers from officiating
in public was still in force, and Presbyterians were still legally
incapable of holding any public office. The first step which King
William caused to be taken for the relief of the Irish Presbyterians
was the abolition of the oath of supremacy. The English Parliament
passed an act in 1691 abolishing the oath, and substituting another
which the dissenters did not object to taking, and thereby all
public employments were opened to them.

King William was anxious to obtain from the British Parliament
the abolition of tests,and to secure for his dissenting subjects
in England ample toleration, but his plans were defeated by the
High Church party. The same influence arrested his measures for
the protection of the Irish Presbyterians.

The matter of marriages by Presbyterian clergymen was again
brought forward. The ministers were "libeled" in the Bishop's
courts for celebrating the marriages of their own people, and
heavy penalties were imposed upon them; and the parties married
were condemned, either publicly to confess themselves guilty of
sinful cohabitation, or to pay heavy fines to the officers of the
courts; while the marriages of those who refused to submit were
declared void, and their children pronounced illegitimate. No
attempt was made, however, by the established clergy to have the
validity of such marriages tested in the civil courts for the
reason that they had been held to be valid contracts even though
irregularly entered into.

During the time of Cromwell, a number of French Protestant
refugees settled in Ireland, and afterwards, upon the revocation
of the Edict of Nantes, many more came over. Being of the same
religious faith as the Ulster Presbyterians, they affiliated with
them, and thus it is that some French names appear among the
Scotch-Irish.

King William died in March 1702, all his efforts to obtain
parliamentary relief and protection for the Dissenters in Ireland
having failed. Queen Anne immediately placed herself under the
guidance of the High Church Tories, and from the beginning of her
reign the series of anti-popery laws began. The Sacramental Test
Act was now enacted by which all non-conformists, Protestants,and
Catholics, were excluded from public office.

In addition to the oppressions on account of their religion,
the industry and commerce of the people of Ulster were system-
atically repressed by the English government. Twenty thousand
people left Ulster on the destruction of their woolen trade in
1698. Many more were driven away by the passage of the Test Act.
The wonder is that the whole people did not leave the country,
and seek rest elsewhere from their intolerable harrassments.
Their industry and thrift enabled them to survive, and to some
extent flourish, in the midst of the oppressive measures of government. Moreover they were constantly buoyed up by the hope of
relief.

In 1711, the Tory party of England again came into power, and this political revolution was the signal of a fresh outburst of High Church zeal against Dissenters. A new Lord Lieutenant having come into office, some of the ministers of Ulster laid before him a statement of their grievances, and said they contemplated going to America that they might in a wilderness enjoy the quiet which was denied them in their native country.

The accession of George I to the throne in 1714, arrested the career of the High Church party, and gave some relief to the Irish Presbyterians. Several leading members of the late English ministry were arraigned for high treason. The Ulster people lost no time in appealing to the King, who showed a liberal spirit toward them.

The Act of Toleration was passed in 1724, and by it liberty of worship was granted to the Presbyterians, but other grievances were left unredressed. Presbyterians were still subject to frequent prosecutions and expensive litigation in the ecclesiastical courts for the marriages celebrated by their clergy.

George I died, and was succeeded by his son, George II in June 1727. The highest authorities in the Irish church and State were generally favorable to the Presbyterians. The Episcopal primate was a friend to toleration and disposed to relieve Dissenters of their grievances, except those arising out of tithes and church dues. As leases of lands expired, the proprietors began to raise their rents, and as the rents increased, the tithes payable to the established clergy increased in proportion. In addition, the three successive harvests after 1724 were unfavorable. These discouragements, with the Test Act and other civil disabilities, caused the Presbyterians in 1728 to look to America as a country for the investment of capital and labor, and where religious liberty might be enjoyed. In 1718, six ministers and many of their people came to America. The passage of the Toleration Act and the hope of further relief checked the spirit of emigration for a season. It revived in 1724, and by 1724 grew to such proportions as to attract the attention of the government. Archbishop Boulton sent to the Secretary of State in England a "melancholy account", as he calls it, of the state of the North. He says the people who go complain of the oppressions they suffer, as well as the dearness of provisions. Writing in March 1729, he says: "There are now seven ships at Belfast, that are carrying off about 1000 passengers thither" - to America. In 1729, nearly 6,000 Irish, nearly all Presbyterians, came to America, landing at Philadelphia. Before the middle of the century nearly 12,000 arrived annually for several years. Almost all who came to America were Presbyterians. Protestant Episcopalians did not have the same motive for emigration, and the tide of Irish Catholic emigration from Ireland did not begin until after the Revolution.

The emigrants first came to Pennsylvania, because they had heard of it as a province where civil and religious liberty were enjoyed. But jealousies arose in the minds of the original settlers of Pennsylvania, and restrictive measures were adopted by the proprietary government against the Scotch-Irish and German emigrants. The Pennsylvania Quakers are said to have especially disliked the Presbyterians. Hence this led many of the Presbyterians in 1732, and afterwards to seek homes within the limits of Virginia, and run the risk of the church establishment there. Many of these soon found their way into the wilderness of Augusta County.

Yielding to her fears in a time of national peril in 1780, England repealed the Test Act; and in 1782, an act was passed declaring the validity of all marriages celebrated among Protestant Dissenters by their own ministers. It was then too late, the damage had been done; the American Colonies had been wrested from the control of England in a large measure by the prowess of the people she had driven away.

PART I

CLEEK FAMILY

The Cleek family came from Germany to America about 1732. The name is found in records as Glück, Glick, Cleak, Cleck, Click, Clerk, and Cleek. After many years of research and study, the compiler believes that Baltas Click, aged 33, who arrived in America in 1732 is the father of the four brothers named Michael, Mathias, Palser, and Jacob Cleek. Baltas Click, sailed from Rotterdam with his family in 1732. However, the voyage proved to be too much for him and he became ill and died. Thirty Thousand Names of Immigrants by Prof. I Daniel Rupp lists the following on page 82:

> September 26, 1732. Palatines imported in the Ship Mary, of London, John Gray, Master, from Rotterdam, last from Cowes.
> ### Dead -- Baltas Click, 33

1. Baltas Click (1), was born in Germany in 1699, sailed from Rotterdam in 1732 in the Ship Mary, arrived in America on September 26, 1732 - dead, aged 33. His four sons were:

   2. i. Michael Cleek (2). No further information.
   3. ii. Mathias Cleek (2), married Margaret _____. He served as a soldier in the French and Indian Wars. (List of Colonial Soldiers of Virginia, H. J. Eckenrode, page 29). He finally settled in Tennessee and his descendants still live in Tennessee, Kentucky, West Virginia, and Texas. On November 10, 1772, Mathias Cleek and Margaret, his wife, sold land on the north branch of the James River, Botetourt County, Virginia to John Little. (Botetourt County, Deed Book 1, pages 439 and 440). On August 9, 1774, Mathias Cleek purchased land in Botetourt County, formerly Augusta County, from John and Isabel Summers. Witnesses were James Gilmore, Hugh Barclay and Jacob Cleek. (Botetourt County, Deed Book 2, pages 148 and 149).
   + 4. iii. Palser Cleek (2).
   + 5. iv. Jacob Cleek (2), born 1725.

The four brothers settled in Lancaster County, Pennsylvania, but soon moved to the Valley of Virginia, in Rockbridge County near Natural Bridge. Virginia Tax Payers, 1782-87 (other than those published by the U.S. Census Bureau) by Augusta R. Fothergill and John Mark Naugle, lists the following:

Tax Payer	Poll	Slaves	County
Cleck, Jacob	1	-	Rockbridge
Cleck, Mathias	1	-	Rockbridge
Cleck, Michael	1	-	Rockbridge
Cleck, Palser	1	-	Rockbridge

4. Palser Cleek (2), died in 1803 in Botetourt County, Virginia; married Sophia _____. On September 5, 1797, Palser

20

Cleek sold land in Arnold's Valley to Geo. Roads. (Rockbridge County, Deed Book C, page 440). On September 24, 1801, Palser Cleek of Rockbridge County, Virginia bought land in Botetourt County, Virginia from Patton Anderson of Fayette County, Kentucky. (Botetourt County, Deed Book 7, page 700). Recorded in Botetourt County, Virginia, Will Book B, page 47, is a will translated from the original will which was written in German which the compiler believes to be the will of Palser Cleek. It reads as follows:

In the name of God Amen Whereas I Boldas (or Palser?) Cleek now living in a low condition of health but perfect in mind and understanding Therefore calling to mind that it is appointed for all Men once to die I think it necessary and a great part of my duty to settle my world affairs with as much Justice as possible I can and to give and bestow my hole Estate as it pleaseth me. In the first place I recommend my Soul to God that gave it and my Body to the Earth to be Buryed in a christian manner by my Executor. In the next place I give and Bestow to Sophie my Beloved wife two Horse Beasts and Two cows and calfs with all my Houseing Furniture as her own to possess forever. Then to John Cleek my Son and Margaret Cleek and Christeanah Cleek my Daughters I give and Bestow the sum of five shillings each to be paid to them out of my Estate. Then to my son Jacob Cleek I give and Bestow one Horse Beast and two cow beasts and half of the Hogs and Sheep and my Daughter Elizabeth Cleek I give and Bestow the other part of the Hogs and Sheep and one young Mare also to Jacob my son I leave one Rifle Gun and my Plantation I leave to be rented for Eight years and the rent thereof to be yearly and Equally divided Between Jacob and Elizabeth my Son and Daughter then the Land to be Sold and the price equally divided between the sd Jacob and Elizabeth my Son and Daughter. Also I give and Bestow to my Grandson, John Cleeks oldest son one cow Beast a Heifer and I do appoint and constitute Cord (?) Brady Executor for me to Act for the Legatees in my stead and behalf. In Witness whereof I acknowledge this to be my last Will and Testament and have affixed my hand and Seal the 26th of September one thousand Eight Hundred and Three.

Teste: Boldas (or Palser?)
Archd Thomas   Cleek (SEAL)
Frederick Michael

Recorded at the December Court 1803 in Botetourt County, Virginia.

Children: 5 (as given in will)

+   6.   i.   John Cleek (3), born October 12, 1772.
     7.   ii.   Margaret Cleek (3). No further information.
     8.   iii.   Christeanah Cleek (3). No further information.
     9.   iv.   Jacob Cleek (3), died in 1825 in Rockbridge County, Virginia, apparently unmarried. His will was recorded in Rockbridge County in Will Book 5, page 511. It was dated November 26, 1824 and recorded May 2, 1825. It mentioned his mother, Sophia Cleek; "my part of a plantation in Botetourt County, Virginia; and sister, Elizabeth Cleek, deceased. Executrix - mother. Witnesses: John Croddy, James Glasgow, and Peter Salling. Securities of

Sophia Cleek, executrix, were Joseph Glasgow and Christopher Croddy. His estate was appraised and recorded in Will Book 6, page 25 on April 27, 1826. The appraisal was made by James Greenlee, John Croddy, and John Salling.

     10.   v.   Elizabeth Cleek (3), died before November 26, the date of her brother's will (see above).

     5. Jacob Cleek (2), was born in 1725 on the Rhine River, Germany; died in 1813 in Bath County, Virginia and was buried in the Jacob Cleek Cemetery approximately ten miles north of Warm Springs, Virginia on U.S. Route 220; married in 1764, Christina Croddy, born 1739; still living in 1812 (the date of her husband's will); buried by the side of her husband, a daughter of John Croddy.

    John Croddy had the following children:
     1.   John Croddy, born 1725; died 1808. He served in the Colonial Wars. His children were:
          a.   John Croddy, Jr., married February 15, 1822 in Rockbridge County, Virginia by Rev. Samuel Houston, Polly Shaver.
          b.   Margaret Croddy, married January 4, 1810 in Rockbridge County, Virginia by Rev. Samuel Houston, Garrett Peck.
          c.   Elizabeth Croddy, married November 1, 1804 in Rockbridge County, Virginia, by Rev. Samuel Houston, Charles Roach.
     2.   George Croddy.
     3.   Christina Croddy, born 1739; died after 1812; married in 1764, Jacob Cleek.
     4.   William Croddy, married Polly _____.
     5.   Ann Croddy, married Samuel Ginger and they are the ancestors of the Ginger family in Bath County, Virginia.

    Jacob Cleek (2) came to America in 1732, and settled first in Pennsylvania, then moved to Rockbridge County, Virginia near Natural Bridge about 1755, and finally settled on Jackson River in what is now Bath County, Virginia in 1790. On March 10, 1790, Jacob Cleek and Christina, his wife, of Rockbridge County, Virginia, sold 120 acres on the south side of James River opposite the mouth of Cedar Creek in Rockbridge County to Jacob Barringer. (Rockbridge County, Deed Book B, page 123). On February 20, 1792, Alexander McFarland of Green County, North Carolina, by virtue of a power of attorney from his father, Duncan McFarland, sold 319 acres of land on Jackson River, Bath County, Virginia to Jacob Cleek. (Bath County Deed Book 1, pages 66 and 68). The land which Jacob Cleek purchased is approximately ten miles north of Warm Springs, Virginia on U.S. Route 220.

    Jacob Cleek served as a soldier in the French and Indian Wars and there is a government marker at his grave inscribed as follows:

"Jacob Cleek
Byrd's Co. 2nd Va. Regt. Ind. War
1725-1813"

List of the Colonial Soldiers of Virginia, H. J. Eckenrode, gives the following on page 29: "Cleek, Jacob, French and Indian Bounty Warrants, 1, 142." Virginia Colonial Militia 1651-1776 by William Armstrong Crozier, gives the following on page 21: "Jacob Cleet soldier under command of Col. Byrd in 2d Va. Regt. in 1760, Rockbridge Co., Dec. 7, 1779."

Abstracts from the Records of Augusta County, Virginia, Lyman Chalkley, Vol. II, page 133, gives the following: "Evans vs Cleak -- O.S. 162; N.S. 57 -- Bill, 1809. Orator, Abraham Evans, became security for his brother, John Evans, to Jacob Cleak for purchase of land in Kenawha. John removed to Fluvanna County. Suit was brought against orator in Pendleton."

The Jacob Cleek Family Bible was burned when William Henderson Cleek's residence on Knapp's Creek, Pocahontas County, West Virginia, was destroyed by fire in the 1890's.

Jacob Cleek's will was recorded in Will Book 2, page 9, Bath County, Virginia at the July Court 1813. It reads as follows:

In the name of God Amen I Jacob Cleek of the County of Bath and State of Virginia Being Sick and weak in body but sound in mind considering the certainty Death and the uncertainty of the time thereof and being Desirous to settle my worldly affairs and thereby be better prepared to leave this world when it shall please God to call me hence do therefore make this my last will and Testament in the manner and form following that is to say First and priseble(?) I commit my Soul to God that gave it and my Body to the Earth to be decently Buried at the Discretion of my Executors hereafter mentioned and after my Debts funeral charges are paid I devise and bequeath as followeth - First I give and bequeath to my beloved wife Cristenah all my moveables as Bonds and cash after the payment of Debts and the Legacies hereafter mentioned. I also bequeath to my wife my part of the salt peter cave. I also give and bequeath to my sons Micah, John, Matthias two Dollars Each and I give and bequeath to my Daughters Rebeccah McGlaughlin, Peggy Pots and Eve Fuller two Dollars each. I also give and bequeath to my five grandsons that is to say John, Jacob, William, Henry, Isaac Hartman and William Hartman my son in law one Dollar Each. I also give and bequeath to my sons Petter and George four Hundred acres of Land lying in the County of Kananay to be equally divided between them. My son George to pay twenty three Dollars the Half of the Costs of recovering said land and lastly I do hereby constitute and appoint my son Petter Cleek to be my sole Executor of this my last will and testament revoking and annulling all former wills by me heretofore made. Ratefying and confirming this and none other to be my last Will and Testament. In testimony whereof I have hereunto set my hand affixed my seal this 13th day of December in the year of our Lord one Thousand eight Hundred and twelve.

Signed sealed and published in
the presence of us
Robert Given   John McGlaughlin
Samuel Given   Samuel Given, Jr.
John Berry

his
Jacob (JC) Cleek (SEAL)
mark

Children: 10

+	11.	i.	Michael Cleek (3).
+	12.	ii.	Peter Cleek (3).
+	13.	iii.	George Washington Cleek (3).
+	14.	iv.	Mathias Cleek (3), born 1782.
+	15.	v.	John Cleek (3), born 1777.
+	16.	vi.	Margaret Cleek (3).
+	17.	vii.	Rebeccah Elizabeth (Hetty) Cleek (3).
+	18.	viii.	Sophia Cleek (3).
	19.	ix.	Eve Cleek (3), married __Fuller__. No further

information.
    20.   x.   Jacob Cleek (3). Will Book 1, page 267, Bath County, Virginia, gives the appraisal of the property of Jacob Cleek, deceased. The appraisal was made July 22, 1803 and recorded at the September Court 1803. He apparently died unmarried.

    6. John Cleek (3), son of Palser Cleek (2) and Sophia _____, was born October 12, 1772; died October 22, 1835 in Boone County, Kentucky and was buried at Beaver Lick Cemetery; married February 23, 1797 in Rockbridge County, Virginia by Rev. Samuel Houston, Elizabeth Jacobs, born February 25, 1777; died January 6, 1864. In 1803, John Cleek and Elizabeth, his wife, sold land in Arnold's Valley on the waters of Elk Creek, a branch of the James River, in Rockbridge County, Virginia to George Goode of Rockbridge. (Rockbridge County, Deed Book F, page 23). He was listed in the tax books of Boone County, Kentucky in 1808. The 1810 Census for Boone County, Kentucky, gives the following: Cleek, John, males 10 to 16 - 2; males 45 and up - 1; females 10 to 16 - 1; females 45 and up - 1; 7 slaves. The following was extracted from a letter addressed to John Cleek, Esq, Cleeks Mills, Va. from George W. Cleek of Council Grove, Kansas, dated January 23, 1874: "My Grand Father John Cleek emigrated to Boone Co., Ky. in an early day from Vir. and left behind the only Brother Jacob. He at that time was an old batchelor and Grandfather never heard from him after they came to Ky. Grandfather married Miss Nancy Jacobs of Culpeper County. They had 4 sons and 3 daughters. John, Ben, Esau, and Jacob. My uncles are all dead except Jacob who lives near the old home near Beaver Lick, Boone County, Ky. My father a twin brother of Jacob's, died Oct. 13, 1873. His name Esau. . . . . Father lived in Boone County until 1871 when he came to this country . . . . ."

Children: 8

+	21.	i.	John Jacobs Cleek (4), born December 28, 1800.
	22.	ii.	Benjamin Cleek (4). He took a land grant in

northern Illinois where descendants still live.
    23. iii.   Mary Anne Cleek (4), married _____ Osserman. No further information.

+	24.	iv.	Esau Cleek (4), a twin to Jacob.
+	25.	v.	Jacob Cleek (4), a twin to Esau.
	26.	vi.	Julia Cleek (4). No further information.
	27.	vii.	Margaret Cleek (4), married _____ Finnell.

No further information.
    28. viii. Eliza Cleek (4), married _____ Peek. No further information.

24

11. Michael Cleek (3), son of Jacob Cleek (2) and Christina Croddy; died in 1834 in Pocahontas County, West Virginia; married Margaret Henderson Crawford, daughter of William Crawford and Margaret Henderson of Dry Branch. (See Crawford and Henderson Family Histories.) They lived at first on a part of his father's land on Jackson River, Bath County, Virginia. They then moved to Pocahontas County, now in West Virginia, and was one of the first settlers of Knapps Creek near Minnehaha Springs. He was the first man to cross the Allegheny Mountain with a wagon drawn by a team of oxen. His will was dated December 12, 1833 and was recorded March 1834 in Pocahontas County, West Virginia, Will Book 1, page 353. It mentions wife, Margaret; sons, William and John Cleek; and daughter, Elizabeth Hull. Executors - sons, John and William Cleek. Witnesses were Joseph Moore and George Gay.

Children: 6

29. i. William Cleek (4), born August 1, 1803; died June 20, 1880, unmarried. His will was dated March 4, 1880 and was recorded July 6, 1880 in Pocahontas County, West Virginia, Will Book 4, page 172. It mentions nephews, Peter L. Cleek, William H. Cleek, Jesse Hull, and Andrew Hull; nieces, Margaret H. McDermott, Mary A. Hull, Margaret Ward, Alcinda Dever, Adaliza Fleshman, Alcinda Hull, and Charlotte Hull; Margaret Fleshman, orphan of Eveline Fleshman, deceased; Butler Lockridge, Augustus Lockridge, and Lee Lockridge, children of niece Caroline Lockridge, deceased. Executor - Sherman H. Clark. Witnesses were Jas. T. Lockridge and Wm. Curry.
+ 30. ii. Elizabeth Cleek (4), born 1807.
+ 31. iii. John Cleek (4), born July 19, 1809.
  32. iv. Jacob Cleek (4), died in infancy.
  33. v. Barbara Cleek (4), died in infancy.
  34. vi. Violet Cleek (4), died in infancy.

12. Peter Cleek (3), son of Jacob Cleek (2) and Christina Croddy, married (1) Jennie Corbett; married (2) May 27, 1815 in Bath County, Virginia, Elizabeth McGuffin. They migrated west.

Children: 1 - first marriage

+ 35. i. James Hickman Cleek (4).

13. George Washington Cleek (3), son of Jacob Cleek (2) and Christina Croddy, died December 1, 1851 in Iowa City, Iowa; married in 1805, Catherine Peck. He settled on part of his father's farm on Jackson River, Bath County, Virginia and lived there more than a decade. He then sold his farm to Jere Starr and took up the western march, finally settling in Iowa City. Nothing further is known of the descendants of this branch of the family except that he had three children.

36. i. Jane Cleek (4), married James Robert Conklin.
37. ii. Moses Cleek (4).
38. iii. Jacob Cleek (4).

14. Mathias Cleek (3), son of Jacob Cleek (2) and Christina Croddy, was born in 1782; died August 15, 1855 in Bath County, Virginia; married May 9, 1815 in Bath County, Virginia, Elizabeth Sitlington Crawford, born May 9, 1787; died December 6, 1852, a daughter of Nathan Crawford and Elizabeth Sitlington. They settled on part of his father's land, building their cabin on the site of the old Cleek home, overlooking the Jackson River in Bath County, Virginia. His will was dated March 31, 1855 and was recorded September 1855 in Bath County, Virginia, Will Book 6, page 45. It mentions sons, Samuel C. Cleek, Jacob Cleek, William C. Cleek, and Andrew S. Cleek; and daughters, Mary Jane Matheny and Christina Matheny. Executor - son, William C. Cleek. Witnesses were George Gillett and S. A. Porter.

Children: 8

+ 39. i. Andrew Sitlington Crawford Cleek (4), born March 10, 1817.
   40. ii. John Crawford Cleek (4), born May 5, 1818 in Bath County, Virginia; died March 23, 1842 at the home of Henry Givens in Bath County, Virginia, unmarried.
   41. iii. Martha Cleek (4), born January 15, 1820; died October 14, 1823.
+ 42. iv. Christina Croddy Cleek (4), born May 15, 1821.
+ 43. v. William Crawford Cleek (4), born March 23, 1823.
   44. vi. Samuel Crawford Cleek (4), born May 25, 1825 in Bath County, Virginia; died November 30, 1903; married April 24, 1877 in Bath County, Virginia, Elizabeth Gillett, born May 12, 1834; died June 28, 1917 in Whitewright, Texas, daughter of George Gillett and Alban Oliver Starr. He left the land of his birth to seek his fortune in the far west in the gold rush of 1849. He returned to Virginia in 1877 when he was married. Geo. W. Cleek of Staunton, Virginia, has a watch, the case of which was made from silver mined by Samuel Crawford Cleek who used them as long as he lived. No children.
+ 45. vii. Jacob Crawford Cleek (4), born May 17, 1827.
+ 46. viii. Mary Jane Cleek (4), born August 15, 1831.

15. John Cleek (3), son of Jacob Cleek (2) and Christina Croddy, was born in 1777 in Rockbridge County, Virginia; died April 16, 1848 in Bath County, Virginia and was buried at the George Cleek Cemetery in Bath County, Virginia; married in 1800 in Bath County, Virginia, Jane Gwin, born July 1, 1780 in Bath (now Highland) County, Virginia; died October 16, 1856 in Bath County, Virginia and was buried by the side of her husband, a daughter of Captain David Gwin and his first wife, Jane Carlile. (See Gwin Family.) Like his brother, Mathias Cleek, he settled on part of his father's estate on the east side of Jackson River. Later he moved his home farther up the river on land given them by his father-in-law, David Gwin. A part of this property is now known as Mill Run Farm. He served in the War of 1812 in Todd's Company, 2nd Pennsylvania Militia. He had gone to Lancaster County, Pennsylvania with a drove of cattle that belonged to his father-in-law hoping to sell them on the Philadelphia market,

but he was inducted into service in the War of 1812 while on this trip. A government marker has been placed at his grave.

Children: 1

+ 47. i. John Cleek, II (4), born May 12, 1803.

16. Margaret Cleek (3), daughter of Jacob Cleek (2) and Christina Croddy, married June 12, 1792 in Bath County, Virginia, Benjamin Potts, Jr., son of Benjamin Potts who came from Wales. He was in the iron business in New York. He later moved to Pottstown, Pennsylvania. Benjamin Potts, Jr. was born in Pottsville, Pennsylvania and later moved to Maryland. He and his wife first lived on part of the land which her father bought from the McFarland family in Bath County, Virginia. Later, they migrated to Pocahontas County, now in West Virginia, near Stony Bottom to spend their last days near their children.

Children: 8

48. i. Sophia Potts (4), married in 1814, William Townsend, son of Ezekiel Townsend and Frances McAvoy. Frances McAvoy was a daughter of James McAvoy.
49. ii. Jonathan Potts (4), married (1) Elizabeth Burns; married (2) Carlotta Arbogast, daughter of Benjamin Arbogast. They lived in Upshur County, West Virginia.
50. iii. John Potts (4), married _____ Vess.
51. iv. Jacob Cleek Potts (4), married March 5, 1822 in Bath County, Virginia, Elizabeth Wiley, daughter of James Wiley and Agnes Crawford. (See Crawford Family.)
52. v. Samuel Potts (4), died unmarried.
53. vi. Jane Potts (4), married (as his first wife) Rheuben Buzzard, son of Rudolph Buzzard and Susanna Zickafoose.
54. vii. Christina Potts (4), married July 11, 1822 in Bath County, Virginia, Joseph Burns, Jr.
+ 55. viii. Mathias Potts (4), born March 16, 1806.

17. Rebeccah Elizabeth (Hetty) Cleek (3), daughter of Jacob Cleek (2) and Christina Croddy, married in 1795 in Bath County, Virginia, (as his first wife) Daniel McGlaughlin, son of John McGlaughlin. They lived in Bath County, Virginia. After the death of his first wife, Daniel McGlaughlin married (2) Mary Carpenter and moved to Pocahontas County, now in West Virginia.

Children: 7 - first marriage

56. i. Anne McGlaughlin (4), married James Burns. No children.
57. ii. Margaret McGlaughlin (4), married George Wilfong.
58. iii. Mary McGlaughlin (4), married Andrew Ratcliffe.
59. iv. Catherine McGlaughlin (4), died unmarried.
60. v. Nancy McGlaughlin (4), married (as his first wife) John Townsend. He married (2) Mary Ryder.
61. vi. Jacob Cleek McGlaughlin (4), married Margaret Doyle.
+ 62. vii. Jane McGlaughlin (4).

Children: 5 - second marriage (not Cleek descendants)

   viii. David McGlaughlin married Jane Wanless, daughter of William Wanless.
   ix. Abigail McGlaughlin married A. Jackson Moore.
   x. Mary Elizabeth McGlaughlin married George Sutton.
   xi. John M. McGlaughlin married Mary Jane Moore.
   xii. Margaret J. McGlaughlin married Morgan Grimes.

18. Sophia Cleek (3), daughter of Jacob Cleek (2) and Christina Croddy, married in 1801, William Hartman. He was killed in the War of 1812.

Children: 5

63. i.   John Hartman (4).
64. ii.   Jacob Hartman (4).
65. iii. William Hartman (4).
66. iv. Henry Hartman (4).
67. v.   Isaac Hartman (4).

21. John Jacobs Cleek (4), son of John Cleek (3) and Elizabeth Jacobs, was born December 28, 1800; died August 28, 1859; married Martha Finnell, born May 15, 1805; died June 6, 1854, daughter of Robert and Frances Finnell. They lived in Boone County, Kentucky. Robert Finnell was born September 12, 1776 and died July 18, 1841. His wife, Frances, was born March 22, 1781 and died April 27, 1845.

Children: 11

68. i.   Elizabeth Cleek (5), born February 4, 1824.
69. ii.   Robert Finnell Cleek (5), born November 26, 1825.
70. iii.   Benjamin W. Cleek (5), born March 27, 1828.
71. iv.   Lamira Jane Cleek (5), born June 18, 1830.
72. v.   John Dudley Cleek (5), born July 28, 1832; died July 7, 1848.
73. vi.   Esau Cleek (5), born July 1, 1835; died November 18, 1889.
74. vii.   Frances Ann Cleek (5), born September 3, 1838.
75. viii. Martha Mildred Cleek (5), born November 7, 1841.
76. ix.   Thomas Jefferson Cleek (5), born March 4, 1845.
77. x.   John Jacobs Cleek, Jr. (5), born July 2, 1848; died January 26, 1927; married January 28, 1875, Kittie Stansifer, born February 3, 1853. They lived in Boone County, Kentucky.
78. xi.   Margaret Julia Cleek (5), born May 9, 1851.

24.. Esau Cleek (4), son of John Cleek (3) and Elizabeth Jacobs, a twin to Jacob, moved to Kansas in 1871 from Boone County, Kentucky. He married November 14, 1836 in Boone County, Kentucky, Elizabeth MacMamama and died in Kansas on October 13, 1873. They had nine children, four sons and five daughters, two of whom were:

79. i.   George W. Cleek (5), born March 6, 1848 in Boone County, Kentucky; married in Kansas, May 18, 1881 _____. They lived in Council Grove, Kansas. They had a son, George W. Cleek (6), born in 1888; died in St. Louis, Missouri.

80. ii.   Mattie Cleek (5), married in Kansas, November
24, 1880, _____.

25. Jacob Cleek (4), son of John Cleek (3) and Elizabeth
Jacobs, a twin to Esau, married Sally Polly of Boone County,
Kentucky. They lived in Boone County, Kentucky.

Children: 8

81. i.   John J. Cleek (5), married Jennie Sleet.
82. ii.   Emily Cleek (5), died unmarried.
83. iii.   James W. Cleek (5), married Martha Fry.
84. iv.   George Omer Cleek (5), married Molly Hume.
85. v.   Ben Cleek (5), died unmarried.
86. vi.   Frank Cleek (5), married Fanny Gordon.
87. vii.   Walter Cleek (5), died unmarried.
88. viii. Joe Cleek (5), married Marceline (called Marce)
Osserman. They lived in Boone County, Kentucky. They had one
child, Anna Cleek (6) who married J. E. McCabe.

30. Elizabeth Cleek (4), daughter of Michael Cleek (3) and
Margaret Henderson Crawford, was born in 1807; died in 1879; married
in 1827, Jesse Hull, born 1801; died 1875, son of George Hull and
Hannah Keister. (See Hull and Keister Families.) George Hull was
a Revolutionary Soldier.

Children: 9

89. i.   Margaret Hull (5), born 1828; married in 1875,
_____ McDermott. They lived on Anthony's Creek, Greenbrier
County, West Virginia.
+ 90. ii.   William Crawford Hull (5), born 1830.
91. iii.   John Hull (5), born 1833. He served in Company
B, Edgar's Battalion, 26th Infantry, CSA, and died at Christians-
burg, Virginia in 1862.
+ 92. iv.   Evelina Hull (5), born 1835.
93. v.   James Silas Hull (5), born 1836; died 1837.
94. vi.   Alcinda Frances Hull (5), born 1838; died
October 1918; married 1884, Augustus Tyler Stephenson, born 1838;
died January 1, 1900, son of Adam Stephenson and Charlotte Wilson.
Adam Stephenson was the first Clerk of Highland County, Virginia.
95. vii.   Jesse A. Hull (5), born 1841. He served in
Taylor's Company, 22d Virginia Infantry, CSA. Migrated to
Washington state.
+ 96. viii. Andrew Hull (5), born 1850.
97. ix.   Charlotte Hull (5), born 1854; died 1883;
married _____ Fertig. They lived on Anthony's Creek, Greenbrier County, West Virginia.

31. John Cleek (4), son of Michael Cleek (3) and Margaret
Henderson Crawford, was born July 19, 1809; died June 27, 1859;
married March 11, 1834 in Pocahontas County, West Virginia,
Phoebe Ann Lightner, born February 26, 1813; died September 26,
1885, daughter of Peter Lightner and Annis Harper. His will was
recorded in Will Book 3, page 217, Pocahontas County, West Virginia.

Children: 8

98. i. Mary Ann Cleek (5), born 1837; married November 16, 1854 in Pocahontas County, West Virginia (1) Josiah Herold, died c. 1863, son of Christopher Herold and Elizabeth Cook; married (2) in 1867, William Crawford Hull (5), born 1830, son of Jesse Hull and Elizabeth Cleek.
+ 99. ii. Peter Lightner Cleek (5), born February 5, 1840.
100. iii. William Henderson Cleek (5), born on Knapps Creek, Pocahontas County, West Virginia; died in 1898; married Margaret Jane Fleshman (5), daughter of Benjamin Franklin Fleshman and Evelina Hull.
+ 101. iv. Carolina Elizabeth Cleek (5).
+ 102. v. Alcinda Susan Cleek (5).
+ 103. vi. Margaret Eveline Cleek (5).
+ 104. vii. Adaliza Martha Cleek (5).
105. viii. Sheldon Washington Cleek (5), born February 22, 1858; died May 27, 1859.

35. James Hickman Cleek (4), son of Peter Cleek (3) and Jennie Corbett, was born in Bath County, Virginia; married Isabel (Ibby) Freeman. They lived in Thorny Draft, Bath County, Virginia.

Children: 8

+ 106. i. John Cleek (5).
+ 107. ii. Jacob Cleek (5).
+ 108. iii. James Cleek (5), born 1832.
109. iv. Thomas Cleek (5), born December 24, 1834; died April 24, 1867; married Sarah Walton, daughter of William Walton. Sarah Walton Cleek married (2) September 4, 1869, George Hively, son of Michael Hively.
+ 110. v. Eli Cleek (5), born January 28, 1840.
+ 111. vi. Jennie Cleek (5).
112. vii. Nancy Cleek (5), born 1842; married May 5, 1863 in Bath County, Virginia, Thomas J. Hively, born 1839, son of George and Elizabeth Hively.
113. viii. Sarah J. Cleek (5), married May 1, 1851 in Bath County, Virginia, Tazewell Gibson.

39. Andrew Sitlington Crawford Cleek (4), son of Mathias Cleek (3) and Elizabeth Sitlington Crawford, was born March 10, 1817 in Bath County, Virginia; died July 2, 1879 in California; married January 28, 1842, Mary Virginia Corder. He joined the western march and crossed the Alleghenies to Missouri, where he was married. Shortly after his marriage he crossed the plains and Rockies and reached California early in 1850. He returned to Missouri and went again to California in 1863, where his descendants still live.

Children: 4

114. i. John William Cleek (5), born April 2, 1843 in Warren, Missouri; died October 1860 in Calusa County, California.

+   115. ii.   Vincent Corder Cleek (5), born October 27, 1844.
+   116. iii.   Ann Elizabeth Cleek (5), born March 7, 1847.
     117. iv.   Eliza Jane Cleek (5), born December 23, 1856 in
Bethel, Shelby County, Missouri; died February 21, 1935 at Willows,
California; married March 18, 1880, James Ewing Mitchell, born
1830 in Roane County, Tennessee; died 1926 at Willows, California.
No children.

     42. Christina Croddy Cleek (4), daughter of Mathias Cleek (3)
and Elizabeth Sitlington Crawford, was born May 15, 1821 in Bath
County, Virginia; died December 8, 1893; married June 12, 1841 in
Bath County, Virginia, Robert B. Matheny, born near Valley Center,
Highland County, Virginia, son of Levi Matheny and Mary Hazlett.
Robert B. Matheny served as Sheriff of Bath County, Virginia.

     Children: 9

     118. i.   Carolina Matheny (5), married Adam L. Varner.
     119. ii.   Crawford Matheny (5).
     120. iii.   Brown Matheny (5).
     121. iv.   Nancy Matheny (5), married _____ Chittum.
     122. v.   Arminta Matheny (5).
     123. vi.   Elizabeth Matheny (5), married Andrew Brinkley.
They lived in Greenbrier County near Frankford, West Virginia.
     124. vii.   Lula Matheny (5).
     125. viii. Scott Matheny (5).
     126. ix.   Millard Filmore Matheny (5), died at age 37 in
Kanawha County, West Virginia.

     43. William Crawford Cleek (4), son of Mathias Cleek (3) and
Elizabeth Sitlington Crawford, was born March 23, 1823 in Bath
County, Virginia; died February 26, 1907 in Nebraska; married
August 8, 1844 in Pocahontas County, West Virginia, Martha Dilley
of Pocahontas County, West Virginia; died 1892 in Virginia,
daughter of Martin Dilley and Hannah Moore. They settled on the
Cowpasture River near Windy Cove Church, Bath County, Virginia.

     Children: 9

+   127, i.   Mary Anne Cleek (5), born 1848.
+   128. ii.   Andrew Martin Cleek (5).
     129. iii.   Martha Elizabeth Cleek (5), born 1851; died July
11, 1866, aged 15.
+   130. iv.   Sarah Virginia Cleek (5), born 1854.
     131. v.   William H. Cleek (5), born 1855; died September
14, 1862, aged 7.
     132. vi.   Alice B. Cleek (5), born September 14, 1857;
died October 4, 1862.
     133. vii.   Hanson Cleek (5), born July 15, 1859; died
September 30, 1862.
+   134. viii. Charles Edward Cleek (5), born October 23, 1860.
     135. ix.   Laura Ellen Cleek (5), born April 8, 1862; died
unmarried.

31

45. Jacob Crawford Cleek (4), son of Mathias Cleek (3) and Elizabeth Sitlington Crawford, was born May 17, 1827 in Bath County, Virginia; died April 1, 1900; married February 1, 1855, Margaret Thompson, born July 5, 1837; died April 18, 1925, daughter of Benjamin Thompson and Emmeline Johnson.

Children: 12

136. i. Alban Gillett Cleek (5), born March 31, 1857; died June 25, 1931 in Pendroy, Montana; married March 27, 1884 (as his second wife) David Gwin Cleek (5), born November 23, 1831; died March 29, 1901, son of John Cleek, II and Sarah Kimes-Givens.
+ 137. ii. Victoria Samuel Cleek (5), born April 15, 1859.
+ 138. iii. Annie Virginia Cleek (5), born December 4,1861.
+ 139. iv. Louisa Benjamin Cleek (5), born January 8,1864.
+ 140. v. Bias Ashby Cleek (5), born February 19, 1866.
141. vi. Lillie Jane Cleek (5), born May 6, 1868; died March 1935; married October 3, 1906 (as his second wife) Anderson F. Stephenson, born February 22, 1850; died September 1925, son of David Stephenson and Esther R. (Hettie) Gwin. (See Gwin Family).
142. vii. Rachel Price Cleek (5), born November 12, 1869; married December 25, 1896, Alfred Simpson (6), died July 14, 1919, son of George W. Simpson and Mary Anne Cleek.
+ 143. viii. Jacob Crawford Cleek (5), born December 12,1871.
144. ix. William Andrew Cleek (5), born November 10,1873; died in childhood.
+ 145. x. Cordelia E. Cleek (5), born August 29, 1875.
146. xi. Mary B. Cleek (5), born November 25, 1877; died in childhood.
147. xii. Sally Hopkins Cleek (5), born June 5, 1880; married October 31, 1908, W. Oscar Hodge, born December 1872, son of Reuben Hodge and Emmeline Stephenson. No children.

46. Mary Jane Cleek (4), daughter of Mathias Cleek (3) and Elizabeth Sitlington Crawford, was born August 15, 1831 in Bath County, Virginia; died February 16, 1893; married January 4, 1855 in Bath County, Virginia, John Garwin Matheny, son of Levi Matheny and Mary Hazlett and a brother of Robert B. Matheny who married Christina Croddy Cleek.

Children: 4

+ 148. i. Ida Ella Josephine Matheny (5).
+ 149. ii. Edward Lee Matheny (5), born June 27, 1863.
150. iii. Register Matheny (5), died in childhood.
151. iv. Arminta Matheny (5), died in childhood.

47. John Cleek, II (4), son of John Cleek (3) and Jane Gwin, was born May 12, 1803 in Bath County, Virginia; died July 28, 1887 in Bath County, Virginia; married July 14, 1825 in Bath County, Virginia, Sarah Kimes-Givens, born March 3, 1807 in Bath County, Virginia; died March 20, 1885 in Bath County, Virginia, daughter of Abraham Kimes and his first wife, Mary O'Hare.

32

Abraham Kimes was a son of Henry Kimes and Catherine _____.
On June 9, 1798, Henry and Catherine Kimes of Bath County, Virginia
appointed their son, Valentine Kimes, their attorney to convey land
in Rockbridge County, Virginia to William Cooper of Rockbridge.
This land had been purchased by Henry Kimes from Evan Brannon.
(Bath County, Will Book 1, page 111.) The will of Henry Kimes was
dated December 17, 1799 and was recorded July 1802 in Will Book 1,
page 229, Bath County, Virginia. It mentions wife, Catherine Kimes;
sons, Valentine Kimes and Abraham Kimes; other children, Conrad Kimes,
Christina Martingood, Catherine Deale, Lisey Ryerson, Jacob Kimes,
and Molly Kimes; and "land whereon Stephen Ryerson formerly lived."
Witnesses were Chas. Cameron, Thomas L. Lewis, Anthony Mustoe, and
Samuel Gay. Henry Kimes was a soldier in the Revolution. (Historical Register of Virginians in the Revolution, John H. Gwathmey,
pages 435 and 438). The surname Kimes is found in records as Keem,
Keim, Kem, Kyme, Kein, and Kimes.

Abraham Kimes and his first wife, Mary O'Hare had three
children:
1. Abraham Kimes, born September 15, 1805; married October
   11, 1838, Louisa Vermille. They had two children, Robert
   Kimes and Harriett Kimes. They lived in Meigs County, Ohio.
2. Sarah Kimes, born March 3, 1807; married John Cleek, II.
3. Harriett Kimes, born September 27, 1808 in Bath County,
   Virginia; married November 23, 1826, Robert Solomon
   Carner Bradley, born July 4, 1790; died March 9, 1860,
   son of William Bradley (born 1759; died 1839) and Mary
   Elizabeth Susan Carlock (married 1789 in Rockbridge
   County, Virginia, born 1770; died 1840). William Bradley
   served as Sergeant in the 7th Virginia Regiment in the
   Revolution and received a pension for his services.
   Robert Solomon Carner Bradley served in the War of 1812.
   Harriett Kimes and Robert Solomon Carner Bradley had the
   following children:
   a. Nancy Given Bradley, born November 22, 1827; died
      April 16, 1910, unmarried.
   b. Adam Given Bradley, M.D., born August 17, 1830;
      died February 24, 1895; married Betty Noel____.
      They had a son, Waldo Bradley, buried at El Paso,
      Texas.
   c. Martha Ann Bradley, born May 26, 1832; died July
      17, 1922, unmarried.
   d. Sarah Jane Bradley, born May 1, 1834; died October
      23, 1871, unmarried.
   e. John David Cleek Bradley, born July 3, 1836; died
      October 10, 1915.
   f. James Solomon McDaniel Bradley, born March 24, 1838;
      killed in 1862 while serving in the Liberty Hall
      Volunteers, CSA.
   g. William Abraham Kime Bradley, born March 14, 1840;
      died July 16, 1858.
   h. Mary Elizabeth Susan Bradley, born August 26, 1842;
      died August 21, 1926, unmarried.
   i. Harriett Alice Cavendish Bradley, born May 22, 1845;
      died November 11, 1923, unmarried.

j. Margaret Virginia Columbia Bradley, born December
5, 1847; died November 7, 1867, unmarried
All of this Bradley family are buried on the family farm 14 miles
north of Covington, Virginia. There is a government marker at
the grave yard.

Abraham Kimes married (2) March 20, 1810 in Bath County,
Virginia, Nancy Evans (orphan). Sureties were Abraham Evans
and Abraham Kimes. Witnesses were James McGuffin and Adam Givens.
They had three children:
1. John Kimes, born December 27, 1814; married September
   10, 1840 in Meigs County, Ohio, Effa Green.
2. Jacob Kimes, born January 7, 1817; married in 1836,
   Leodicea Coleman.
3. Mary Ann Kimes, born February 4, 1818; died March 23,
   1834.

Sarah Kimes and her sister, Harriett Kimes, were adopted by
Adam Givens and his wife, Nancy McGuffin in 1814. The adoption
papers read as follows:

This Indenture made the _____ day of _____, 1814, between
Abraham Kimes of Meigs County, Ohio, party of the first part, and
Adam and Nancy Givens his wife, parties of the second part.
WHEREAS, the said party of the first part has two daughters,
Sallie Kimes and Harriett Kimes born 1807 and 1808 respectively,
and whereas the said parties of the second part are willing to
adopt the said children, provided they use the names Sallie Kimes-
Givens and Harriett Kimes-Givens and are subject to the conditions
here-in-after contained. Now this indenture witnesseth that the
said parties covenant and agree as follows, that is to say:
1. The said parties of the second part shall adopt the said
Sallie and Harriett Kimes and shall, until the said children
shall respectively attain the age of twenty-one years, or marry
under that age, maintain, board, lodge and clothe them in a
manner suitable to their station, and as if they were lawful
children of the parties of the second part.
2. The said party of the first part shall not himself nor
shall any person or persons claiming under him, or acting under
his authority, at any time or in any manner interfere with the
training or management of the said children, or either of them,
or with their or her moral, intellectual or religious instruction.
3. If the said part of the first part shall not perform and
observe all and every of the stipulations herein contained and on
his part to be performed and observed then and in every such case
it shall be lawful for the said parties of the second part and the
survivor of them, by notice in writing under their, his or her
hand or hands, and addressed either to the party of the first part
or to the person setting up such claim or demand or so interfering
as aforesaid, to put an end to the agreement hereby expressed to
be made, and thereupon the same shall absolutely cease and deter-
mine; provided that in such event the said party of the first part,
or his estate, shall be liable to pay and satisfy all debts and
liabilities incurred by or in any wise for the benefit of said

children, or either of them which at the time of such determination of this agreement shall not have been paid and satisfied.

In witness whereof we have this _____ day of _____ 1814, set our hands and seals.

Abraham Kimes
Adam Givens
Nancy (X her mark) Givens.

Abraham Kimes and his second wife migrated to Meigs County, Ohio. His will was recorded in Meigs County, Ohio in Vol. I, page 212. It was probated November 1840 and reads as follows:

In the name of the Benevolent Father of All;

I, Abraham Kimes of Olive Township, Meigs County and State of Ohio, Do make and Publish this my Last Will and Testament:

Item First: I give and devise to my beloved wife, in lieu of her dower, the farm on which we now reside, situate in the County and State aforesaid in Range Eleven, Town Three, one hundred acre Lot Homestead, one hundred and twenty nine supposed to contain one hundred acres with the exception of about one acre and three-fourths of an acre out of the South West corner contracted and bargained to Samuel Sutton; during her natural life and all the household goods, furniture, provisions and all the stock, viz; horses, cattle, sheep and hogs with the exception of one sorrell horse five years old last spring; one sorrell mare colt three years old last spring; one red heffer two years old last spring and one other two year old heffer white and red; and all other goods and chattels, which may be thereon at the time of my decease, during her natural life as aforesaid; she however, selling so much thereof as may be sufficient to pay my just debts. At the death of my said wife, the real estate aforesaid and such part of the said personal property or the proceeds thereof, as may then remain unconsumed and unexpended, I give and devise to my sons, Abraham Kimes, John Kimes and Jacob Kimes to be sold at Public Sale and after paying to Hannah Topping a girl now residing with us Thirty Dollars which sum I will and bequeath to her; the balance of the proceeds of such sale to be divided equally among my aforesaid three sons Abraham, John and Jacob Kimes and their heirs; if however either of my said three sons should die before the decease of my said wife leaving no children living at the decease of my said wife, then the share of said property above devised to such deceased son is hereby devised and bequeathed to my surviving sons or son and his or their heirs. If my said wife should not survive me then I devise and bequeath the property aforesaid to my said three sons Abraham Kimes, John Kimes and Jacob Kimes after paying the aforesaid sum of thirty dollars to Hannah Topping as aforesaid to be sold at public sale as aforesaid and equally divided and to their heirs as aforesaid forever.

Second: I devise and bequeath to my son Abraham Kimes one sorrel mare three years old last spring and one red heffer two years old last spring and his heirs the said property as heretofore excepted.

Third: I devise and bequeath to my son John Kimes one white and red heffer two years old last spring as heretofore excepted.

Fourth: I hereby devise and bequeath to my son Jacob Kimes one sorrell horse five years old last spring the said horse heretofore excepted.

Fifth: I do hereby nominate and appoint my beloved wife Nancy Kimes executor of this my Last Will and Testament hereby authorizing and empowering her to compromise, adjust, release and discharge in such manner as she may deem proper the debts and claims due me. I also authorize and empower her if necessary to sell at private sale or otherwise as she may think proper any of my personal property to pay and discharge my debts. I do hereby revoke all former wills made by me.

IN TESTIMONY WHEREOF, I have hereunto set my hand and seal this the twenty-fourth day of July in the year of our Lord one thousand eight hundred and forty.

Abraham (X his mark) Kimes (SEAL)
Signed, acknowledged by Abraham Kimes as his last will and testament in our presence and signed by us in his presence.
Major Reed
Samuel Sutton
Jasper Branch.

The following has been extracted from a letter written to John Cleek by Abraham and Nancy Kimes, from Long Bottom, Meigs County, Ohio, date November 19, 1836:
"Our children since my last marriage, are John and Jacob - boys; and Mary Ann a daughter. She lives with us on earth no more. She died a Christian on the 23rd of March 1834. . . . . Jacob was married a short time since to a Miss Leodicea Coleman, and lives about 3/4 of a mile from us. John is yet single and so is Abraham, your own brother. . . . ."

The following marriages were taken from the records of Meigs County, Ohio:
John Kimes to Elizabeth Wilbarger, December 18, 1828.
Thomas Kimes to Eliza Shumway, May 24th, 1829.
Elias Kimes to Sarah Wilbarger, April 1, 1830.
Abraham Kimes to Louisa Vermille, October 11, 1838.
John Kimes to Effa Green, September 10, 1840.
George W. Kimes to Emily Williamson, September 23, 1839.
Samuel Kimes to Jane McIntyre, April 8, 1841.

The following is a copy of the marriage bond of John Cleek and Sarah Kimes:
"Know all men by these presents that we John Cleek and Adam Given are held and firmly bound unto James Pleasants esquire, Governor of Virginia in the sum of one hundred and fifty Dollars to which payment will and truly be made to the said Governor or his Successor we bind ourselves our heirs, exrs and adrs jointly and Severally firmly by these presents Sealed with our Seals and dated this 25 day of June 1825.
The condition of the above obligation is such that whereas there is intended to be had and solemnized a marriage between the above bound John Cleek and Sarah Kime now if there be no

lawful cause to obstruct the said marriage then the above obligation to be void else to remain in full force.

John Cleek (SEAL)
Adam Givens (SEAL)."

John Cleek, II served as a justice of Bath County and was a
member of the Board of Equalization. As one of the justices, his
picture hangs in the Courthouse of Bath County, at Warm Springs,
Virginia. He was also purchasing agent for the Confederacy and
as a result lost large land holdings in Missouri, Illinois, and
Iowa which were confiscated by the federal government during the
War Between the States.

A post office called Cleek's Mill was established in 1840,
and was discontinued in 1900 with the extension of rural mail de-
livery. John Cleek, II was the first postmaster of this post
office, and it was named for an old tub mill built by John Cleek,
the father of John Cleek, II. John Cleek, II built a grist and
flour mill powered by an overshot wheel below the site of the old
tub mill in 1848. This grist and flour mill was condemned by the
highway department in 1936 and removed.

In 1830, John Cleek, II journeyed to Fort Dearborn (now
Chicago) to inspect lands inherited from his father, John Cleek
and his grandfather, Captain David Gwin, which they had received
for service in the Revolutionary War and the War of 1812. He
returned from Fort Dearborn by way of Muskinghum River, Meigs
County, Ohio, where he visited his father-in-law, Abraham Kimes.
He was accompanied by his cousin, William Lockridge, and the return trip to Bath County, Virginia from Fort Dearborn was made
on foot in thirty days.

The following was copied from the Family Bible of John Cleek,
II. This Family Bible was published in 1832 and is now in the
possession of Geo. W. Cleek, Staunton, Virginia (1957).

Family Record

Marriages	Marriages
Sally Kimes and John Cleek Jr. was Married July 14th 1825	A.G. Cleek married on the 11th day of October 1849
Sarah Ann Cleek married on the 24th day of July 1866	John Cleek was married 31th of October 1854
Nancy G. Cleek married on the 24th day of October 1866	David G. Cleek was married 19th day of June 1855
Harriet Cleek married on the 25th day of October 1866	George W. Cleek married on the 26th of November 1867 By Wm. T. Price
Mary Jane Cleek married on the 14th day of October 1873	John Cleek, Jr. married 2nd time September 28, 1868.

Marriages

David G. Cleek 2
married March 27/84

Births	Deaths
A.G. Cleek born the 30th day of April 1826	--Died on Saturday Feb. 16th 1901
John Cleek was born September the 28th 1827	--Died Apr 27 1910
Nancy G. Cleek was born July 23rd 1829	--Died 31st Dec 1907
David G. Cleek was born November 23rd 1831	--David G. Cleek died 29th March 1901 Annie Cleek wife of D.G. Died February the 7th 1880
William Cleek was born September 1st 1833	--Died on the 23rd of August 1835
George Washington Cleek was born the 3rd day of June 1835	--Geo.W. Cleek died on Saturday, January 1, 1910 at 4:35 p.m.
Harriet Cleek was born April the 5th 1837	--Died May 21st 1921
Mary Jane Cleek was born the 11th day of October 1839	--Died Oct. 22nd 1919
Sarah Ann Cleek was born January the 9th 1842	--Died 26th January 1899
Andrew Jackson Cleek was Born the 20th of January 1845	--A.J. Cleek died on the 9th of October 1846
Martha Elisabeth Cleek born the 1st day of October 1847	--Martha Elisabeth Cleek died on the 25th of February 1850
John Cleek was Born May the 12th 1803	--Died 28th July 1887
Sally Kime was Born March the 3rd 1807	--Died March the 20th 1885 The wife of John Cleek,Sr. Being 78 years & 17 days old

Children of A. G. Cleek
Sarah Jane Cleek was
born Septr 13th 1850

Rhuhamy A. Cleek born
December the 15th 1850

Births	Deaths
John Cleek was born May the 15th 1855	John Cleek Senr died on the 16th day of April 1848 in the 71st year of his age
Emma Cleek was born 2nd day of September 1855 (This is a daughter of John Cleek, Jr. and Rebecca A. Sitlington)	Jane Cleek died 16 October 1856 76 years 3 - 16 old
Jane Gwin Born July 1st 1780 married to John Cleek	William Cleek son of Michael Died on June the 20th 1880 in the 77th year of his age Being 76 years 10 m and 19 D
Children: 11	

+ 152. i. Adam Given Cleek (5), born April 30, 1826.
+ 153. ii. John Cleek, Jr. (5), born September 28, 1827.
+ 154. iii. Nancy Givens Cleek (5), born July 23, 1829.
+ 155. iv. David Gwin Cleek (5), born November 23, 1831.
  156. v. William Cleek (5), born September 1, 1833; died August 23, 1835.
+ 157. vi. George Washington Cleek (5), born June 3, 1835.
+ 158. vii. Harriet Cleek (5), born April 5, 1837.
  159. viii. Mary Jane Cleek (5), born October 11, 1839 in Bath County, Virginia; died October 22, 1919; married October 14, 1873, John Robert Warwick, born October 29, 1843; died May 30, 1915, son of Robert Craig Warwick and Esther Hull. (See Hull and Warwick Families.) They lived at Green Bank,West Virginia.
+ 160. ix. Sarah Anne Cleek (5), born January 9, 1842.
  161. x. Andrew Jackson Cleek (5), born January 20, 1845; died October 9, 1846.
  162. xi. Martha Elisabeth Cleek (5), born October 1, 1847; died February 25, 1850.

55. Mathias Potts (4), son of Benjamin Potts and Margaret Cleek (3), was born March 16, 1806; died February 1, 1882; married October 24, 1833 in Bath County, Virginia, Rachael Warwick McCabe, born October 30, 1803; died March 23, 1881.

Children: 6

163. i. B. Franklin Potts (5), born August 13, 1834; married (1) September 25, 1856, Mary Elizabeth Ann Mathews, died May 16, 1860; married (2) in 1865, Mary Susan Hartman.
164. ii. James Newton Potts (5), born September 14, 1838; died January 10, 1931; married June 27, 1867 in Bath County, Virginia, Margaret M. A. Stewart, daughter of Henry and V. C. Stewart. He was a Lieutenant in the CSA.
165. iii. Lanty Gatewood Potts (5), born August 5, 1841; died February 18, 1925; married (1) October 1867, Mrs. Martha Dinkle Wood, died 1872; married (2) in 1876, Anna Waugh, died March 1, 1937 near Elkins, West Virginia, daughter of John Waugh and Martha Moore. He served in Company G, 18th Virginia Cavalry, CSA.

39

166. iv. Eliza Potts (5), born 1843; died 1861.
167. v. Mathias Porter Hamilton Potts (5), born 1847;
died December 1, 1931; married (1) October 2, 1872, Martha
Elizabeth Logan, died 1886; married (2) in 1886, Margaret A.
Baxter, died 1907; married (3) in 1926, Mary Moore Logan. He
served in the 20th Virginia Cavalry, CSA. James Edwin Potts,
born August 22, 1910; married September 2, 1933, Elizabeth Lee
Booker, born October 7, 1911, and lives at 1029 Lyndhurst Road,
Waynesboro, Virginia, is one of the descendants of Mathias Porter
Hamilton Potts and his first wife, Martha Elizabeth Logan.
168. vi. Warwick Potts (5), died in 1861.

62. Jane McGlaughlin (4), daughter of Daniel McGlaughlin
and Elizabeth Cleek (3), married in 1824, John McAvoy, son of
James McAvoy.

Children: 3

169. i. Elizabeth McAvoy (5), married Taylor Townsend,
son of Ezekiel Townsend.
170. ii. Rosa McAvoy (5), married James _____.
171. iii. Marguerite McAvoy (5), married Samuel Carpenter.
They were the parents of Martha Carpenter (6) who married Joseph
Burns. They lived in Wilson's Little Valley, south of Bolar,
Virginia.

90. William Crawford Hull (5), son of Jesse Hull and
Elizabeth Cleek (4), was born in 1830 on Anthony's Creek, Greenbrier County, West Virginia; married in 1867 (as her second husband) Mary Ann Cleek (5), born 1837, daughter of John Cleek and
Phoebe Ann Lightner.

Children: 2

172. i. Lillian Hull (6), married Paterson Poage.
173. ii. Utokia Hull (6), married George Hannah.

92. Evelina Hull (5), daughter of Jesse Hull and Elizabeth
Cleek (4), was born in 1835; died 1869; married (as his first
wife) Benjamin Franklin Fleshman, born March 1829; died August
14, 1909.

Children: 1

174. i. Margaret Jane Fleshman (6), married (1) William
Henderson Cleek (5), son of John Cleek and Phoebe Lightner; married
(2) December 11, 1900, Adam Given Cleek (5), son of John Cleek, II
and Sarah Kimes-Givens. No children by either marriage.

96. Andrew Hull (5), son of Jesse Hull and Elizabeth Cleek
(4), was born in 1850; married in 1875, Emmaline Walkup, born
1852 near Frankford, Greenbrier County, West Virginia, daughter
of Joseph Walkup and Ann Elliot.

Children: 8

174.	i.	Maude Hull (6).
176.	ii.	Lucy Hull (6), married John Ayers.
177.	iii.	Virginia Hull (6).
178.	iv.	Margaret Hull (6), married _____ Fore.
179.	v.	Verna Hull (6).
180.	vi.	Willie Hull (6), married _____.
181.	vii.	John Hull (6), married _____.
182.	viii.	Grace Hull (6).

99.   Peter Lightner Cleek (5), son of John Cleek (4) and
Phoebe Ann Lightner, was born February 5, 1840 on Knapps Creek,
Pocahontas County, West Virginia; died June 3, 1916 in Pocahontas
County, West Virginia; married September 12, 1876 in Pocahontas
County, West Virginia, Effie May Amiss, born August 1, 1855 in
Pocahontas County, West Virginia; died December 21, 1938, daughter
of Andrew Dyer Amiss and Evelina McNeel. He served in the CSA as
a member of the 19th Virginia Cavalry. His will was recorded in
Will Book 7, page 175, Pocahontas County, West Virginia. The will
of Effie May Amiss Cleek was recorded in Will Book 10, page 436,
Pocahontas County, West Virginia.

Children: 7

+   183.   i.   John Andrew Cleek (6), born June 3, 1877.
    184.   ii.   Evelyn Belle Cleek (6), born December 8, 1878
on Knapps Creek, Pocahontas County, West Virginia; married (1)
John A. McDaniels, died January 6, 1932; married (2) June 6, 1942,
George Neely, born 1874; died July 29, 1948.
    185.   iii. Mabel Lillian Cleek (6), born July 1, 1881,
unmarried.
    186.   iv.   Annie May Cleek (6), born March 4, 1883;
married May 2, 1917 in Pocahontas County, West Virginia, William
Chapman Cleek (7), born August 6, 1884, son of John Henry Wise
Cleek and Nannie Mayse.
    187.   v.   Pinckney Lightner Cleek (6), born September 30,
1885; died June 3, 1886.
    188.   vi.   Mary Susan Cleek (6), born April 14, 1888,
unmarried.
    189.   vii. William Ward Cleek (6), born May 3, 1890;
married Mrs. Icie (Malcolm) Shinaberry Lantz, widow of John
Harman Lantz, who died July 1, 1951.

101.   Carolina Elizabeth Cleek (5), daughter of John Cleek
(4) and Phoebe Ann Lightner, married December 26, 1854 in Pocahontas County, West Virginia, Lancelot Lockridge, Jr., son of
Lancelot Lockridge and Elizabeth Benson. (See Lockridge Family).
They settled at Ord, Nebraska.

Children: 3

190.	i.	Lee Lockridge (6).
191.	ii.	Augustus Lockridge (6).
192.	iii.	Butler Lockridge (6).

102. Alcinda Susan Cleek (5), daughter of John Cleek (4)
and Phoebe Ann Lightner, married April 24, 1866 in Pocahontas
County, West Virginia, Hugh Dever, son of John Dever. They
migrated to Kansas.

Children: 3

193.	i.	Frank Dever (6).
194.	ii.	Benton Dever (6).
195.	iii.	John Dever (6).

103. Margaret Eveline Cleek (5), daughter of John Cleek (4)
and Phoebe Ann Lightner, married October 2, 1866 in Pocahontas
County, West Virginia, Renick S. Ward of Randolph County, West
Virginia.

Children: 1

196.	i.	John Ward (6).

104. Adaliza Martha Cleek (5), daughter of John Cleek (4)
and Phoebe Ann Lightner, married September 25, 1872 in Pocahontas
County, West Virginia (as his second wife) Benjamin Franklin
Fleshman, born March 1829; died August 14, 1909.

Children: 1

197. i. Annie Fleshman (6), married George Stephenson.
They lived in Houston, Texas.

106. John Cleek (5), son of James Hickman Cleek (4) and
Isabel Freeman, married Sarah Hinton, daughter of William Hinton
and Catherine Karns.

Children: 7

+	198.	i.	Mary Jane Cleek (6).
+	199.	ii.	Clarissa (Clara) Cleek (6), born 1846.
+	200.	iii.	James W. Cleek (6), born 1850.
+	201.	iv.	John Lewis Cleek (6), born April 13, 1853.
	202.	v.	Thomas Cleek (6).
	203.	vi.	Henry G. Cleek (6), born August 4, 1857;

married Mrs. _____ Cason.
| | 204. | vii. | Maria Cleek (6), died young. |

107. Jacob Cleek (5), son of James Hickman Cleek (4) and
Isabel Freeman, married March 27, 1853 in Bath County, Virginia,
Nancy Stonestreet. He was a volunteer in the Confederate Army to
which cause he gave his life. He was buried at Moorefield, West
Virginia. Their children lived at Beverly, West Virginia.

Children: 5

205.	i.	Mary E. Cleek (6), born June 1, 1854.
206.	ii.	Sarah J. Cleek (6), born March 7, 1855.
207.	iii.	James Cleek (6), born February 7, 1857.

208. iv.   George H. Cleek (6), born December 17, 1858.
209. v.   William Cleek (6).

108.   James Cleek (5), son of James Hickman Cleek (4) and
Isabel Freeman, was born in 1832; married September 17, 1868 in
Bath County, Virginia, Mary Rebecca Walton, born 1850, daughter
of Andrew and Catherine Walton.

Children: 4

210. i.   Martha A. Cleek (6), born July 16, 1869;
married (as his second wife) Perry Matheny. They lived on
Cowpasture River, Bath County, Virginia. No children.
211. ii.   Elizabeth Cleek (6), married George Hoover.
No children.
212. iii.   Virginia Cleek (6), married William J. Lloyd
of Charlottesville, Virginia.
+   213. iv.   Benjamin Harrison Cleek (6).

110.   Eli Cleek (5), son of James Hickman Cleek (4) and
Isabel Freeman, was born January 28, 1840; died October 17, 1902;
married November 17, 1864 (1) in Bath County, Virginia, Elizabeth
H. Kincaid, born 1842; died March 6, 1890, daughter of Willis
Kincaid and Margaret Rhea; married (2) June 10, 1891 in Bath
County, Virginia, Martha Smith, born 1843, daughter of William
Smith and Patsy Williams. (See Lockridge Family.)

Children: 3 - first marriage

+   214. i.   Floyd L. Cleek (6), born August 2, 1866.
+   215. ii.   Margaret J. Cleek (6), born May 15, 1869.
216. iii.   Allie Cleek (6), married in Indiana, _____
Kimble.

111.   Jennie Cleek (5), daughter of James Hickman Cleek (4)
and Isabel Freeman; married _____ Huddleston.

Children: 2

217. i.   Susie Huddleston (6), married Thallis Wilcox.
218. ii.   William Huddleston (6), married Mollie _____.

115.   Vincent Corder Cleek (5), son of Andrew Sitlington
Crawford Cleek (4) and Mary Virginia Corder, was born October 27,
1844 at Warren, Marion County, Missouri; died July 1909 in
Sebastopol, California; married November 20, 1871, Julia Celestia
Richelieu. When five years of age he went to California with his
parents in an oxen train, and arrived in Sacramento on August 1,
1850. The family made their way up the valley and settled on the
river in the vicinity of Hamilton City. Here his father opened a
store and a hotel. Suffering from poor health, his family was sent
back to the old home in Missouri via Panama. Andrew Sitlington
Crawford Cleek remained in California and continued in the business he had started, and also engaged in farming and stock raising
with M. A. Reager as partner. In 1852 he joined his family in

43

Missouri and remained there for ten years; after which he and his family returned to California and settled again in the same place where he engaged exclusively in farming. At the outbreak of the War Between the States, Vincent Corder Cleek enlisted in the CSA. Upon his return to California, he went to work on his father's farm. When he was about 25 years of age, he homesteaded the quarter section east of Orland, and made a comfortable home which he still owned when he died. They had eleven children, but four died in early childhood.

Children: 7

+ 219. i. Andrew William Cleek (6).
+ 220. ii. Jeb Stuart Cleek (6).
  221. iii. Hadassah Cleek (6), died in 1945; married John Hamilton, died in 1950.
+ 222. iv. Vincent Carlyle Cleek (6).
+ 223. v. John Leslie Cleek (6), born 1882.
  224. vi. Samuel Perry Cleek (6), married Ruby Snow. They had one son who was killed in an automobile accident.
+ 225. vii. James Corder Cleek (6).

116. Ann Elizabeth Cleek (5), daughter of Andrew Sitlington Crawford Cleek (4) and Mary Virginia Corder, was born March 7, 1847 in Warren, Marion County, Missouri; died November 1, 1910; married December 30, 1863, William M. Hood.

Children: 4

226. i. Jennie Monette Hood (6), married Homer A. Hicks of Bakersfield, California.
227. ii. John W. Hood (6).
228. iii. Minnie Hood (6), married Fred E. Perkins of San Francisco, California.
229. iv. _____ Hood (6), died in childhood.

127. Mary Anne Cleek (5), daughter of William Crawford Cleek (4) and Martha Dilley, was born in 1848; married October 16, 1866 in Bath County, Virginia, George W. Simpson, born 1839; died December 18, 1910, son of Reason Simpson and Mary Jane Keyser. He was one of the early educators in Bath County, Virginia, and was for years a teacher and superintendent of schools.

Children: 9

+ 230. i. Alfred Simpson (6).
  231. ii. Mary Virginia Simpson (6), died 1940; married December 25, 1895, Jacob Crawford Cleek (5), born December 12, 1871; died March 4, 1956, son of Jacob Crawford Cleek and Margaret Thompson.
+ 232. iii. Aldine Simpson (6).
+ 233. iv. Reese Simpson (6).
+ 234. v. Edward Simpson (6).
+ 235. vi. Howard Simpson (6).

+ 236. vii. Marvin Simpson (6).
+ 237. viii. Ruth Simpson (6).
+ 238. ix.   Andrew Milton Simpson (6), born September 5, 1886.

128. Andrew Martin Cleek (5), son of William Crawford Cleek (4) and Martha Dilley, married Cordelia McKnight. They lived in Missouri.

Children: 2

239. i.   Rose Cleek (6), married Perry Cochran. They had two children.
240. ii. Leonard Cleek (6).

130. Sarah Virginia Cleek (5), daughter of William Crawford Cleek (4) and Martha Dilley, was born in 1854; married April 21, 1875 in Bath County, Virginia, William S. Simpson, born 1847, son of Reason Simpson and Mary Jane Keyser.

Children: 4

241. i.   Lena Simpson (6), married Henry Brooks.
242. ii.   Mattie Simpson (6), married Dill Neff. They had one daughter.
243. iii. Gertrude Simpson (6), married Leonard Rowe.
244. iv.   Wilbur Simpson (6), died unmarried. He was a school teacher.

134. Charles Edward Cleek (5), son of William Crawford Cleek (4) and Martha Dilley, was born October 22, 1860; died July 27, 1940 in Bryantsburg, Indiana; married (1) Emma Nice of Indiana, died in 1902; married (2) in 1903, Clara Mellott Harrison. He first moved to Nebraska and then to Indiana.

Children: 5 - first marriage

245. i.   Ralph Cleek (6), born August 6, 1890 at Broken Bow, Nebraska; died October 12, 1956, unmarried.
246. ii.   Earl Edwin Cleek (6), died in World War I, unmarried.
247. iii. Leola Merle Cleek (6), married Joe Weeks. No children.
+ 248. iv. Charles Lloyd Cleek (6).
249. v.   Wayne Forrest Cleek (6).

Children: 4 - second marriage

+ 250. vi.   Ruth Vivian Cleek (6).
+ 251. vii. Bernard Cleek (6), born October 27, 1906.
+ 252. viii. Leila Cleek (6).
+ 253. ix.   Ethel Mildred Cleek (6).

137. Victoria Samuel Cleek (5), daughter of Jacob Crawford Cleek (4) and Margaret Thompson, was born April 15, 1859; died

45

September 1915; married December 24, 1895, Robert Lee Lindsay, born November 10, 1870; died September 10, 1936, son of John Alexander Lindsay and Sarah Thompson.

Children: 1

254. i.   Samuel Lee Lindsay (6), born September 1896; married (1) Lucy Eckard, daughter of Job Eckard and Ruhama Gwin; married (2) Pauline Ogden. No children.

138. Annie Virginia Cleek (5), daughter of Jacob Crawford Cleek (4) and Margaret Thompson, was born December 4, 1861; died June 30, 1938; married February 21, 1899 (as his second wife) Valentine Franklin Harouff, born November 27, 1852; died October 3, 1950, son of Christian Hupman Harouff and Harriet Katherine Burns.

Children: 4

255. i.   Jessie Virginia Harouff (6), born March 19, 1900; married June 27, 1951 (as his second wife) Ira Thornton Ritenour, born November 13, 1884, son of Thornton Ritenour and Eliza Catherine Boyer. No children.
256. ii.   Frank Cleek Harouff (6), born 1904; married Melvina Newman. They have one son, Billy Harouff (7).
257. iii.   Jacob Christian Harouff (6), born April 9, 1906.
258. iv.   (Infant) Harouff (6), died.

139. Louisa Benjamin Cleek (5), daughter of Jacob Crawford Cleek (4) and Margaret Thompson, was born January 8, 1864; died July 1903; married August 20, 1885, John W. Baldwin, born October 16, 1859; died July 27, 1900, son of Peter Baldwin and Anne Woodzell.

Children: 2

259. i.   Harry Tucker Baldwin (6), born 1890; married (1) Ruby Willey; married (2) Bertha Harnt.
260. ii.   John W. Baldwin (6), born August 25, 1900; married Eva Terry. They have a foster daughter, Virginia Baldwin.

140. Bias Ashby Cleek (5), son of Jacob Crawford Cleek (4) and Margaret Thompson, was born February 19, 1866; died March 16, 1942; married (1) October 22, 1890, Allie F. Baldwin, born March 1, 1870; died April 14, 1904, daughter of Peter Baldwin (born September 10, 1827) and Anne Woodzell (born September 17, 1828, married 1850); married (2) May 29, 1912, Georgia Lee Goul Bratton, born May 27, 1879; died May 6, 1955, daughter of John Feamster Bratton and Cornelia Goul. (See Bratton Family.)

Children: 2 - first marriage

261. i.   Bessie Lee Cleek (6), born September 25, 1892; married January 22, 1922, Harry Robert Lightner, born September

46

24, 1890, son of Robert Warwick Lightner and Augusta H. Bird.
(See Lightner Family.)
+   262.   ii.   Dewey Suddarth Cleek (6), born January 26, 1899.

Children: 3 - second marriage

+   263.   iii.   Mabel Gray Cleek (6), born July 2, 1913.
     264.   iv.   Allie Virginia Cleek (6), born March 12, 1915;
married (1) Dr. Charles W. Reavis; married (2) Benjamin Tucker.
They live in Richmond, Virginia. No children.
     265.   v.   Phyllis Audrey Cleek (6), born February 24,
1918; died from burns in 1923.

143. Jacob Crawford Cleek (5), son of Jacob Crawford Cleek
(4) and Margaret Thompson, was born December 12, 1871 in Bath
County, Virginia; died March 4, 1956 in Bath County, Virginia;
married December 25, 1895, Mary Virginia Simpson (6), born 1872;
died 1940, daughter of George W. Simpson and Mary Anne Cleek.

Children: 6

+   266.   i.   Brownie Campbell Cleek (6), born December 25,
1896.
+   267.   ii.   Roy Moffett Cleek (6), born February 20, 1898.
+   268.   iii.   Ernest Simpson Cleek (6), born October 20, 1899.
     269.   iv.   Otis Aubrey Cleek (6), born June 1901; married
Virginia D. Sively, born November 10, 1901. No children. Mrs.
Cleek is Clerk of Bath County, Virginia.
     270.   v.   Raymond Gray Cleek (6), born 1904; married (1)
Helen Schmidt; married (2) _____.
+   271.   vi.   Ruth Corrinne Cleek (6), born 1912.

145. Cordelia E. Cleek (5), daughter of Jacob Crawford
Cleek (4) and Margaret Thompson, was born August 29, 1875; died
January 20, 1916; married at Hively, Bath County, Virginia,
March 3, 1903 (as his second wife) Charles Jasper Williams, born
December 1, 1859; died April 4, 1928 and was buried at Woodland
Cemetery, Bath County, Virginia, son of Dr. Robert Williams (born
November 21, 1826) and Mary Magdaline McNeel (married August 27,
1850, born February 26, 1832; died February 12, 1912).

Children: 9

+   272.   i.   Charles Hubert Williams (6), born 1904.
+   273.   ii.   Jacob Herbert Williams (6), born 1904, twin to
Charles Hubert.
+   274.   iii.   Ernest Moffett Williams (6).
+   275.   iv.   Margaret McNeel Williams (6).
+   276.   v.   Otho Alexander (Bob) Williams (6).
+   277.   vi.   Glenn Crawford Williams (6).
     278.   vii.   Elizabeth Cabell Williams (6), married James
Straub.
+   279.   viii.   Roberta Virginia Williams (6).
+   280.   ix.   Richard Cleek Williams (6).

148. Ida Ella Josephine Matheny (5), daughter of John Garwin Matheny and Mary Jane Cleek (4), died February 24, 1902; married May 11, 1882 at Valley Center, Virginia (as his first wife) Charles Jasper Williams, born December 1, 1859; died April 4, 1928, son of Dr. Robert Williams and Mary Magdaline McNeel.

Children: 8

281. i.   Otto Garwin Williams (6), died February 7, 1883, an infant.
+   282. ii.   Forest Cleveland Williams (6), born February 26, 1884.
+   283. iii.   Mary Edith Williams (6).
+   284. iv.   Harry Lee Williams (6).
+   285. v.   DeWitt Talmadge Williams (6).
    286. vi.   Betsy Williams (6), died in infancy.
    287. vii.   Lucy Blanche Williams (6), unmarried. She is a teacher in the public schools of Virginia.
    288. viii. Carl Jasper Williams (6), born April 9, 1898; died January 3, 1920, unmarried.

149. Edward Lee Matheny (5), son of John Garwin Matheny and Mary Jane Cleek (4), was born June 27, 1863; died November 5, 1905; married Cuba Wade, born 1868, daughter of David Wade and Mahala Bird.

Children: 1

+   289. i.   Hazel Matheny (6).

152. Adam Given Cleek (5), son of John Cleek, II (4) and Sarah Kimes-Givens, was born April 30, 1826 in Bath County, Virginia; died February 16, 1901 in Bath County, Virginia and was buried at Woodland Cemetery, Bath County, Virginia; married (1) October 11, 1849, Mary Jane Miller, born December 25, 1829 in Bath County, Virginia; died June 27, 1896 in Bath County, Virginia and was buried by the side of her husband, daughter of Morrell Miller and Jane Cauley; married (2) December 11, 1900, Margaret Jane (Fleshman) Cleek (6), daughter of Benjamin Franklin Fleshman and Evelina Hull, and the widow of William Henderson Cleek. Adam Given Cleek served for three years in Company K, 52d Virginia Infantry, CSA, and he had two brothers in the service. The battles in which he took part were McDowell, Winchester, Cross Keys, Port Republic, Chancellorsville, Fredericksburg, Mechanicsville, Seven Pines, Cedar Mountain, Second Manassas, Sharpsburg, Antietam, Monocacy, Gettysburg, and Harpers Ferry. His father was justice of Bath County, Virginia for 30 years. Adam G. Cleek lived in the Williamsville District of Bath County, Virginia and rode as Sheriff of Bath County for over 16 years. He also filled the offices of Clerk of the Circuit and County Courts for twenty years. He became Clerk in July 1, 1875.

Children: 9 - first marriage. No children second marriage.

+   290. i.   Sarah Jane Cleek (6), born September 13, 1850.

291. ii.   Ruhamy A. Cleek (6), born December 15, 1852;
died September 6, 1939; married December 25, 1873, John Lewis
Cleek (6), born April 15, 1853; died 1927, son of John Cleek and
Sarah Hinton.
+   292. iii.   John Henry Wise Cleek (6), born May 15, 1855.
+   293. iv.   Mary Elizabeth Virginia Cleek (6), born December
21, 1857.
+   294. v.   Cornelia Harriett Cleek (6), born February 5,1861.
+   295. vi.   George Lee Cleek (6), born September 23, 1865.
+   296. vii.   Lillah Bell Cleek (6), born March 19, 1867.
+   297. viii.   Susan Byrd Cleek (6), born October 11, 1870.
     298. ix.   Ella Florence Cleek (6), born February 13, 1873;
died October 9, 1873 and was buried at the Gatewood grave yard,
Mountain Grove, Bath County, Virginia.

153. John Cleek, Jr. (called Jack) (5), son of John Cleek, II(4)
and Sarah Kimes-Givens, was born September 28, 1827 in Bath County,
Virginia; died April 27, 1910 in Bath County, Virginia; married (1)
October 31, 1854, Rebecca A. Sitlington, died 1863, daughter of
William Sitlington and Mary Dorothy McClung (married 1816). His
first wife and four young children: Emma Cleek (6), born September
2, 1855; Mary Cleek (6); Sallie Cleek (6); and an infant son, all
died with diphtheria in 1863. He married (2) September 28, 1868,
Rachel McNiel Myers, born March 17, 1846 in Pocahontas County,
West Virginia; died January 21, 1924 at Lexington, Kentucky and
was buried in Bath County, Virginia, daughter of _____ Myers
and Abigail Moore. John Cleek, Jr. was a business partner of his
brother, George Washington Cleek, before the War Between the States
at Millboro Springs and Williamsville, Bath County, Virginia. He
was also Sheriff of Bath County, Virginia for a number of years.

Children: 4 - second marriage

299. i.   Fannie Moore Cleek (6), born May 17, 1871; died
April 17, 1893. She graduated from the State Normal School, Farmville, Virginia, and was a teacher in Rockbridge County, Virginia
schools.
300. ii.   Harriett Cleek (6), born September 14, 1878; died
May 28, 1954 and was buried in Bath County, Virginia. She was a
graduate of the Good Samaritan Hospital School of Nursing, Lexington, Kentucky. She specialized as an anesthetist, taking her
training in Philadelphia, Cleveland, and Boston, and became the
first woman anesthetist in the world. She was a veteran of World
War I, in which she served with Base Hospital Unit No. 40, known
as the Barrow Unit. She was a member of the First Presbyterian
Church, Lexington, Kentucky, American Legion, United Daughters of
the Confederacy, and the Daughters of the American Revolution.
She served as president of the Kentucky Nurses Association and
for many years served as a member of the board of nurse examiners.
301. iii.   Infant Son (6), died in infancy.
+   302. iv.   John (Jack) Cleek (6), born March 7, 1881.

154. Nancy Givens Cleek (5), daughter of John Cleek, II (4)
and Sarah Kimes-Givens, was born July 23, 1829; died December 31,

49

1907; married October 24, 1866 (as his second wife) Thomas Brown Wallace, born June 10, 1812; died July 28, 1898, son of Matthew Wallace (born February 5, 1772; died October 5, 1848) and Sarah Brown (born November 8, 1775; died March 30, 1853). They made their home near Williamsville, Bath County, Virginia, on a large farm which was part of the Thomas Feamster estate.

Children: 2

+   303.   i.   Dr. John William Wallace (6), born 1867.
+   304.   ii.   George Washington Wallace (6), born June 17, 1869.

155. David Gwin Cleek (5), son of John Cleek, II (4) and Sarah Kimes-Givens, was born November 23, 1831; died March 29, 1901; married (1) June 19, 1855, Annie Maria Louisa Weldon, born September 11, 1833; died February 7, 1880, daughter of William J. Weldon (born August 20, 1796; died June 24, 1864) and Nancy Temple; married (2) March 27, 1884, Alban Gillett Cleek (5), born March 31, 1857; died June 25, 1931 in Pendroy, Montana, daughter of Jacob Crawford Cleek and Margaret Thompson. The Weldon family migrated to Texas soon after the War Between the States and finally settled in Fannin County, Texas. Temple, Texas, was named for Mrs. William J. Weldon (Nancy Temple). David Gwin Cleek served in Company F, 11th Virginia Cavalry, CSA, and was wounded in the battle of the Wilderness.

Children: 10 - first marriage

305.   i.   Eva Virginia Cleek (6), died in childhood.
306.   ii.   Cordelia Price Cleek (6), died in 1915 and was buried in Washington, D. C.
+   307.   iii.   George Washington Cleek (6), born 1863.
308.   iv.   Charles Weldon Cleek (6), died in childhood.
+   309.   v.   Robert Edward Cleek (6), born August 27, 1869.
310.   vi.   James Thomas Cleek (6), died July 27, 1870, aged 3 years, 8 months, and 12 days.
311.   vii.   Nancy Carolina Cleek (6), born 1871; died November 20, 1918; married in 1898, Jesse Lee Warwick, died July 21, 1939, son of Peter Hull Warwick and Sarah Caroline Matheny. (See Warwick Family).
312.   viii.   John David Cleek (6), died in childhood.
+   313.   ix.   Sallie Byrd Cleek (6), born 1875.
314.   x.   Annie Weldon Cleek (6), born December 26, 1878; died January 25, 1955; married in 1896, George Craig Warwick, son of William Fechtig Warwick and Phoebe Anthea Pray. (See Warwick Family).

Children: 1 - second marriage

+   315.   xi.   Mary Ethel Cleek (6), born December 12, 1893.

157. George Washington Cleek (5), son of John Cleek, II (4) and Sarah Kimes-Givens, was born June 3, 1835 in Bath County, Virginia; died January 1, 1910 in Bath County, Virginia; married

November 26, 1867 in Bath County, Virginia, Malcena Catherine Lightner, born February 22, 1844 in Bath County, Virginia; died December 15, 1937 in Bath County, Virginia, daughter of Jacob Lightner and Nancy Jane Warwick. (See Lightner and Warwick Families). George Washington Cleek enlisted at Warm Springs, Virginia on May 15, 1862 in Company F, 11th Virginia Cavalry (known as the Bath Grays), Hampton's Division, Rosser's Brigade, CSA. He was made a corporal, and participated in both battles of Manassas, Gettysburg, Wilderness, Chancellorsville, and Sharpsburg. He was wounded in the battle at Upperville, Virginia. He was captured at Martinsburg, Virginia (now West Virginia), also shown as Darksville, September 7, 1862, was imprisoned at Camp Chase, Ohio, was transferred to Cairo, Illinois, where he was admitted to the General Hospital on October 10, 1862 with typhoid fever, and was received at the Federal prison at Jackson, Mississippi, for a year, was then exchanged and returned to his old command. His public service in Bath County, Virginia included Deputy Surveyor, Deputy Sheriff, and Surveyor from 1894 to his death in 1910. He also operated the grist and flour mill located at the post office, Cleek's Mill, Bath County, Virginia, which had been built by his father, John Cleek, II. He was the second and last post master of Cleek's Mill.

Children: 6

316. i.   Charles Henry Cleek (6), born August 21, 1868; died January 26, 1935; married on October 17, 1906, Mrs. Esther (Warner) Phares, born March 10, 1871; died November 24, 1914 and was buried at the Warner grave yard in Pendleton County, West Virginia, near Route 33, daughter of John Warner and Ellen Bland. He was a cadet at VPI and a veternarian of rare skill. He held the office of Commissioner of Revenue of Bath County, Virginia for twenty years. He was a member of the fraternal organization of Odd Fellows. No children.
+   317. ii.   Andrew William Cleek (6), born May 10, 1871.
+   318. iii. John Robert Cleek (6), born November 23, 1873.
     319. iv.   Mary Virginia Cleek (6), born May 21, 1876; died December 6, 1937, unmarried. She was a member of the United Daughters of the Confederacy and the Society of the Daughters of the American Revolution.
+   320. v.   Wade Hampton Cleek (6), born July 24, 1880.
+   321. vi.   George Washington Cleek (6), born August 19, 1889.

158. Harriet Cleek (5), daughter of John Cleek, II (4) and Sarah Kimes-Givens, was born April 5, 1837 in Bath County, Virginia; died May 21, 1921; married October 25, 1866, Henry Harrison (Tip) Revercomb, born September 6, 1840; died April 8, 1915, son of George Archer Revercomb and Rebecca Griffith, and grandson of Abel Griffith.

Children: 2

+   322. i.   Mary Emma Revercomb (6), born September 15, 1867.
     323. ii.   Sallie Rebecca Revercomb (6), born May 15, 1871; died February 5, 1900. She was a teacher of public schools in Bath County, Virginia.

160. Sarah Anne Cleek (5), daughter of John Cleek, II (4) and Sarah Kimes-Givens, was born January 9, 1842 in Bath County, Virginia; died January 26, 1899; married July 24, 1866, Charles Francisco Revercomb, born November 17, 1842; died February 14, 1933, son of George Archer Revercomb and Rebecca Griffith. Both are buried at Woodland Cemetery, Bath County, Virginia. He was Sheriff of Bath County, Virginia.

Children: 5

+ 324. i. George Archie Revercomb (6), born January 24, 1868.
325. ii. Eva Harris Revercomb (6), born 1870; died October 17, 1950 and was buried at Woodland Cemetery, Bath County, Virginia. She was a teacher in the public schools.
326. iii. Nannie Jane Revercomb (6), born May 6, 1873; died February 12, 1912 and was buried at Woodland Cemetery, Bath County, Virginia. She was a teacher in the public schools.
+ 327. iv. John Cleek Revercomb (6), born 1876.
328. v. Charles Wallace Revercomb (6), born 1879; died 1938; married in 1903, Lelia Lowman. He was buried at Windy Cove Cemetery (new), Bath County, Virginia.

183. John Andrew Cleek (6), son of Peter Lightner Cleek (5) and Effie May Amiss, was born June 3, 1877 on Knapps Creek, Pocahontas County, West Virginia; died January 29, 1952; married November 24, 1897 in Pocahontas County, West Virginia, Fannie Grace Harper, born March 25, 1876; died April 20, 1929, daughter of Preston M. Harper.

Children: 2

329. i. Hazel Gray Cleek (7), married November 26, 1919 in Pocahontas County, West Virginia, Herbert C. Criser. They have one son, Edward Criser (8).
330. ii. Jewell Alma Cleek (7), died November 11, 1934; married November 28, 1923 in Pocahontas County, West Virginia, Claude Gay Malcolm.

198. Mary Jane Cleek (6), daughter of John Cleek (5) and Sarah Hinton, married Charles D. Thomas.

Children: 6

+ 331. i. Newton Thomas (7).
+ 332. ii. Gordon Ellsworth Thomas (7), born May 5, 1867.
333. iii. Andrew Thomas (7), married (1) Bessie Gibson (7), daughter of John Lewis Nicholas Gibson and Clarissa (Clara) Cleek; married (2) Bettie Garth, Marlinton, West Virginia.
+ 334. iv. Annie Thomas (7).
+ 335. v. Houston H. Thomas (7).
+ 336. vi. Malcena Thomas (7).

199. Clarissa (Clara) Cleek (6), daughter of John Cleek (5)

and **Sarah Hinton**,born in 1846; married March 8, 1866 in Bath County, Virginia, **John Lewis Nicholas Gibson**, born 1844, son of Tazewell M. Gibson and Sophronia _____.

Children: 9

337. i.   Virginia Josephine Gibson (7), born April 14, 1875 in Bath County, Virginia; died July 6, 1954; married March 8, 1892, Gordon Ellsworth Thomas (7), born May 5, 1867 at Clarksburg, West Virginia; died February 15, 1953 in Bath County, Virginia, son of Charles D. Thomas and Mary Jane Cleek.
338. ii.   Clara Gibson (7), married _____ Cannon.
339. iii.   Alice Gibson (7), married Benjamin Sharp, Frost, West Virginia.
340. iv.   Bessie Gibson (7), married (1) Andrew Thomas (7), son of Charles D. Thomas and Mary Jane Cleek; married (2) Wheeler Gladwell.
341. v.   John D. Gibson (7), married _____ in Kansas.
342. vi.   Garnett Gibson (7), died in Kansas.
343. vii.   _____ Gibson (7), married James Nelson.
344. viii.   Henry Gibson (7), died in Kansas.
345. ix.   Earl Gibson (7), lived in Kansas.

200.   James W. Cleek (6), son of John Cleek (5) and Sarah Hinton, was born in 1850; married December 23, 1874 in Bath County, Virginia, Amelia Rowan, born 1857 in Randolph County, West Virginia; died April 17, 1929, daughter of George W. Rowan. They lived in lower Bath County, Virginia.

Children: 3

+ 346. i.   Ella B. Cleek (7).
   347. ii.   Myrtle Cleek (7), born February 15, 1880; died January 8, 1951 at Mt. Sidney, Virginia; married Houston H. Thomas (7), died 1929, son of Charles D. Thomas and Mary Jane Cleek.
   348. iii.   Carrie Cleek (7), married (1) William Wingfield; married (2) J. E. Enders, Farmville, Virginia. He was the first Public Health Officer employed by Bath County, Virginia. She is buried in Thornrose Cemetery, Staunton, Virginia.

201.   John Lewis Cleek (6), son of John Cleek (5) and Sarah Hinton, was born April 13, 1853; died 1927; married December 25, 1873, Ruhamy A. Cleek (6), born December 15, 1852; died September 6, 1939, daughter of Adam Given Cleek and Mary Jane Miller. They moved to Oklahoma in 1903 and later to LaJunta, Colorado, where they were buried.

Children: 8

+ 349. i.   Annie Pleasant Cleek (7), born January 30, 1875.
+ 350. ii.   Bettie Cleek (7), born February 9, 1878.
+ 351. iii.   Walter L. Cleek (7).
+ 352. iv.   Charles Massey Byrd Cleek (7).

353. v.   Mary Cleek (7), died in infancy.
354. vi.   Clarence Cleek (7), died in infancy.
355. vii. Ruth Cleek (7), died in infancy.
356. viii. (Infant) Cleek (7), died.

213. Benjamin Harrison Cleek (6), son of James Cleek (5)
and Mary Rebecca Walton, died December 5, 1950; married (1) Mrs.
Willie (McFadden) Vass; married (2) Bertha Gum.

Children: 2 - second marriage

357. i.   Lucille Cleek (7), married _____ Hill.
358. ii.   Virginia Cleek (7), married _____ Smith.

214. Floyd L. Cleek (6), son of Eli Cleek (5) and Elizabeth
H. Kincaid, was born August 2, 1866; died January 6, 1943 and was
buried at Woodland Cemetery, Bath County, Virginia; married Emma
V. McFadden Trimble, born October 14, 1844.

Children: 3

359. i.   Dorothy L. Cleek (7), born July 11, 1910; died
May 6, 1937 and was buried at Woodland Cemetery, Bath County,
Virginia. She was a R. N.
360. ii.   Mary Cleek (7), twin to Dorothy L, born July 11,
1910; married Charles Bryant.
361. iii. Floyd L. Cleek, Jr. (7).

215. Margaret J. Cleek (6), daughter of Eli Cleek (5) and
Elizabeth H. Kincaid, was born May 15, 1869; died October 17,
1941; married May 18, 1893 in Bath County, Virginia, Edgar L.
Smith, born 1868, son of Isaac Smith and Martha _____.

Children: 5

362. i.   Benton Smith (7).
363. ii.   Harman Smith (7).
364. iii. Hobert Smith (7).
365. iv.   Fannie Smith (7), married _____ McComb.
366. v.   Nellie Smith (7), married _____ Hefner.

219. Andrew William Cleek (6), son of Vincent Corder Cleek
(5) and Julia Celestia Richelieu, married Nellie Grear. This family lives in Chico, California.

Children: 3

367. i.   Mildred Cleek (7).
+ 368. ii.   Irving Cleek (7).
369. iii. Hadassah Cleek (7).

220. Jeb Stuart Cleek (6), son of Vincent Corder Cleek (5)
and Julia Celestia Richelieu, married Ethel Moon.

Children: 1

+ 370. i.   Stuart Cleek (7).

222. Vincent Carlyle Cleek (6), son of Vincent Corder Cleek (5) and Julia Celestia Richelieu, married Myra Norris, who died May 2,1952. His home is at Orland, California.

Children: 2

371. i.   Thelma Cleek (7), married Emerson Foltz. They have an adopted son, Glenn Foltz who married Lorraine Booth.
+ 372. ii.   Norris Cleek (7).

223. John Leslie Cleek (6), son of Vincent Corder Cleek (5) and Julia Celestia Richelieu, was born in 1882; married (1) Elizabeth Wallace, who died May 1936; married (2) Mrs. Kate Duigman. Their home is at Vallejo, California.

Children: 3 - first marriage

+ 373. i.   John Vincent Cleek (7), born 1905.
+ 374. ii.   Sidney Richelieu Cleek (7).
+ 375. iii. George Wallace Cleek (7).

225. James Corder Cleek (6), son of Vincent Corder Cleek (5) and Julia Celestia Richelieu, married Louise J. Arnold.

Children: 7

376. i.   Henry Cleek (7), married Audrey _____.
+ 377. ii.   Carroll Cleek (7).
378. iii. Everett Cleek (7).
379. iv.   Robert Cleek (7).
380. v.   Donald Cleek (7), was killed in a school accident in 1950.
381. vi.   Richard Cleek (7).
382. vii. Anita Louise Cleek (7).

230. Alfred Simpson (6), son of George W. Simpson and Mary Anne Cleek (5), died July 14, 1919; married December 25, 1896, Rachel Price Cleek (5), born November 12, 1869, daughter of Jacob Crawford Cleek and Margaret Thompson.

Children: 3

383. i.   Jesse Simpson (7), married Violet Williams. They had one child, Houston Simpson (8), that died young.
+ 384. ii.   George Simpson (7).
385. iii. Mary Margaret Simpson (7).

232. Aldine Simpson (6), son of George W. Simpson and Mary Anne Cleek (5), married (1) Emma Thorn; married (2) Mary _____. They lived in Kentucky.

Children: 3 - first marriage

386. i.   George Simpson (7).
387. ii.   William Simpson (7).
388. iii. Hazel Simpson (7).

233. Reese Simpson (6), son of George W. Simpson and Mary Anne Cleek (5), married Sophia Feaster. They lived in Grant County, West Virginia.

Children: 9

389. i.   Thelma Simpson (7).
390. ii.   Gladys Simpson (7).
391. iii.   Fred Simpson (7).
392. iv.   Roy Simpson (7).
393. v.   Clyde Simpson (7).
394. vi.   James Simpson (7).
395. vii.   Lois Simpson (7).
396. viii. Alice Simpson (7).
397. ix.   Elizabeth Simpson (7).

234. Edward Simpson (6), son of George W. Simpson and Mary Anne Cleek (5), married Ella Keplinger. They lived in Grant County, West Virginia.

Children: 10

398. i.   Ronald Simpson (7).
399. ii.   Lee Simpson (7).
400. iii.   Charlie Simpson (7).
401. iv.   Ralph Simpson (7).
402. v.   Carl Simpson (7).
403. vi.   Houston Simpson (7).
404. vii.   Glenn Simpson (7).
405. viii. Opal Simpson (7).
406. ix.   Sarah Simpson (7).
407. x.   Ruby Simpson (7).

235. Howard Simpson (6), son of George W. Simpson and Mary Anne Cleek (5), married Virginia Shell. They lived in Grant County, West Virginia.

Children: 5

408. i.   Hugh Simpson (7).
409. ii.   Frank Simpson (7), married Opal Ryder.
410. iii. Homer Simpson (7).
411. iv. Earl Simpson (7).
412. v.   Helen Simpson (7).

236. Marvin Simpson (6), son of George W. Simpson and Mary Anne Cleek (5), married (1) Cora Turner; married (2) Belle Keplinger.

Children: 7 - second marriage

413. i.   Esten Simpson (7), a son.
414. ii.   Helen Simpson (7).
415. iii. Pauline Simpson (7).
416. iv.   Carl Simpson (7).
417. v.   Virgil Simpson (7).
418. vi.   Doyle Simpson (7).
419. vii. Lyne Simpson (7).

237. Ruth Simpson (6), daughter of George W. Simpson and Mary Anne Cleek (5), married James Edward Utz.

Children: 3

420. i.   Sarah Edna Utz (7).
421. ii.   Nina Ruth Utz (7).
422. iii. James Edward Utz (7).

238. Andrew Milton Simpson (6), son of George W. Simpson and Mary Anne Cleek (5), was born September 5, 1886; married December 25, 1906, Lula Feaster, born June 26, 1887.

Children: 14

+   423. i.   Mary Dorothy Simpson (7), born April 10, 1908.
+   424. ii.   Charlotte Ruth Simpson (7), born October 26,1909.
+   425. iii. Paul Edwin Simpson (7), born September 23, 1911.
+   426. iv.   Lewis Francis Simpson (7), born July 12, 1913.
᾿   427. v.   Elvin Blair Simpson (7), born August 3, 1915;
died February 2, 1944; married Violet Turner. No children.
+   428. vi.   William Wood Simpson (7), born July 22, 1917.
+   429. vii. Grace Estelle Simpson (7), born June 5, 1919.
+   430. viii. Roy Milton Simpson (7), born May 25, 1921.
    431. ix.   Mark Bailey Simpson (7), born February 9, 1923;
died March 30, 1923.
+   432. x.   Quinton Brown Simpson (7), born February 23, 1924.
    433. xi.   Kenneth Moffit Simpson (7), born February 23,
1924, a twin to Quinton, married Edith Ultis.
+   434. xii. Darrell Austin Simpson (7), born October 10, 1926.
+   435. xiii. Marvin Craft Simpson (7), born August 25, 1929.
    436. xiv. Phyllis Lee Simpson (7), born February 3, 1931;
married Clyde Warnick.

248. Charles Lloyd Cleek (6), son of Charles Edward Cleek (5) and Emma Nice, died 1930; married Catherine Kaeff of Gary, Indiana.

Children: 2

+   437. i.   Robert Charles Cleek (7).
+   438. ii.   Howard Melvin Cleek (7).

250. Ruth Vivian Cleek (6), daughter of Charles Edward Cleek

57

(5) and Clara Mellott Harrison, married (1) in 1925, Byron Vestal;
married (2) Gaynor Glascock.

Children: 2 - first marriage

+   439. i.   Lillian Vestal (7).
+   440. ii.   Bernard William Vestal (7).

251. Bernard Cleek (6), son of Charles Edward Cleek (5) and
Clara Mellott Harrison, was born October 27, 1906; married Rae
Solomon.

Children: 1

441. i.   Mary Kay Cleek (7).

252. Leila Cleek (6), daughter of Charles Edward Cleek (5)
and Clara Mellott Harrison, married Gordon Buchanan.

Children: 6

442. i.   Richard Eugene Buchanan (7), born May 1934.
443. ii.   Dennis Dean Buchanan (7).
· 444. iii.   Jerry Cleek Buchanan (7).
445. iv.   James Edward Buchanan (7).
446. v.   Roger Allen Buchanan (7).
447. vi.   John Evan Buchanan (7).

253. Ethel Mildred Cleek (6), daughter of Charles Edward
Cleek (5) and Clara Mellott Harrison, married Laurence Cooley.

Children: 1

+   448. i.   Charles Omer Cooley (7).

262. Dewey Suddarth Cleek (6), son of Bias Ashby Cleek (5)
and Allie F. Baldwin, was born January 26, 1899; married Mary
Edith Gum, born May 10, 1906, daughter of Robert F. Gum and
Mary V. Bonner.

Children: 1

+   449. i.   Robert Suddarth Bias Cleek (6), born June 20,
1926.
263. Mabel Gray Cleek (6), daughter of Bias Ashby Cleek (5)
and Georgia Lee Goul Bratton, was born July 2, 1913; married
August 1934, Raymond Sandy of Stephens City, Virginia.

Children: 2

450. i.   Raymond Sandy, Jr. (7).
451. ii.   Ann Sandy (7).

266. Brownie Campbell Cleek (6),daughter of Jacob Crawford
Cleek (5) and Mary Virginia Simpson (6), was born December 25,

1896; married (1) April 20, 1935, Joseph Frank Clarke; married (2) November 11, 1942, Harper Turner.

Children: 1 - first marriage

452. i. Jacob Frank Clarke (7). He served in the U.S. Air Force after World War II.

267. Roy Moffett Cleek (6), son of Jacob Crawford Cleek (5) and Mary Virginia Simpson (6), was born February 20, 1898; married Carey Knopp.

Children: 2

453. i. Helen Gray Cleek (7), married Willard Hicks, son of Horace Franklin Hicks and Cornelia Ruth Warwick. (See Warwick Family).
454. ii. Roy Moffett Cleek, Jr. (7).

268. Ernest Simpson Cleek (6), son of Jacob Crawford Cleek (5) and Mary Virginia Simpson (6), was born October 20, 1899; married Clarice Wine.

Children: 3

455. i. Audrey Ernestine Cleek (7).
456. ii. Ronald Lloyd Cleek (7), married November 21, 1949, Ruth Lynelle Hodge.
457. iii. Lyndon Crawford Cleek (7), married July 31, 1951, Joyce Eleanor Withrow.

271. Ruth Corrinne Cleek (6), daughter of Jacob Crawford Cleek (5) and Mary Virginia Simpson (6), was born April 5, 1912; married Dr. Jack Grizzard.

Children: 3

458. i. Gwendolyn Grizzard (7), married John B. Smith.
459. ii. Jack C. Grizzard (7).
460. iii. Richard C. Grizzard (7).

272. Charles Hubert Williams (6), son of Charles Jasper Williams and Cordelia E. Cleek (5), was born in 1904; married September 3, 1929, Ruby Fay Stracher.

Children: 2

461. i. Margaret Virginia Williams (7), born May 24,1931.
462. ii. Charles Hubert Williams, Jr. (7).

273. Jacob Herbert Williams (6), son of Charles Jasper Williams and Cordelia E. Cleek (5), a twin to Charles Hubert, was born in 1904; married (1) Mary _____; married (2) Mildred Horner.

Children: 4 - second marriage

463. i.   Jimmie Williams (7).
464. ii. Richard Williams (7).
465. iii. Lynne Williams (7).
466. iv. Gary Wayne Williams (7).

274. Ernest Moffett Williams (6), son of Charles Jasper
Williams and Cordelia E. Cleek (5), married April 9, 1940, Anna
D. Mulligan.

Children: 2

467. i.   Nancy Lee Williams (7), born August 30, 1941.
468. ii. Laura Jane Williams (7), born December 24, 1948.

275. Margaret McNeel Williams (6), daughter of Charles
Jasper Williams and Cordelia E. Cleek (5), married Frank
Armentrout.

Children: 3

469. i.   Marion Armentrout (7), married _____ Fitzgerald.
470. ii. Barbara Armentrout (7).
471. iii. Joe Anne Armentrout (7).

276. Otho Alexander (Bob) Williams (6), son of Charles
Jasper Williams and Cordelia E. Cleek (5), married Gladys (Polly)
Heizer.

Children: 4

472. i.   Betty Joe Williams (7).
473. ii. Peggie Lee Williams (7).
474. iii. Lucy Page Williams (7). She is a student nurse
at C & O Hospital Nursing School, Clifton Forge, Virginia.
475. iv. Otho Alexander Williams, Jr. (7).

277. Glenn Crawford Williams (6), son of Charles Jasper
Williams and Cordelia E. Cleek (5), married Virginia Miles.

Children: 3

476. i.   Glenn Crawford Williams, Jr. (7).
477. ii. Dennis Williams (7).
478. iii. Forest Wayne Williams (7).

279. Roberta Virginia Williams (6), daughter of Charles
Jasper Williams and Cordelia E. Cleek (5), married Tracy Peters.

Children: 1

479. i.   Carrie Elizabeth Peters (7).

60

280. Richard Cleek Williams (6), son of Charles Jasper
Williams and Cordelia E. Cleek (5), married Sarah Sensabaugh.

Children: 3

480. i.   Richard Lee Williams (7).
481. ii.   Wanda Loretta Williams (7).
482. iii. Mary Juanita Williams (7).

282. Forest Cleveland Williams (6), son of Charles Jasper
Williams and Ida Ella Josephine Matheny (5), was born February
26, 1884; died May 8, 1954; married Ida Pearl Elliott.

Children: 2

483. i.   Ina Marie Williams (7).
484. ii.   Bobbie Elliott Watson Williams (7), married
Mary Della Hoops.

283. Mary Edith Williams (6), daughter of Charles Jasper
Williams and Ida Ella Josephine Matheny (5), married Fred P.
Armentrout.

Children: 7

    485. i.   James Frederick Armentrout (7).
+   486. ii.   Patsy Josephine Armentrout (7).
    487. iii. Ruth Cleveland Armentrout (7).
+   488. iv.   Lucy Virginia Armentrout (7).
+   489. v.   Charlotte Williams Armentrout (7).
+   490. vi.   Frances Winn Armentrout (7).
+   491. vii. Jane Porter Armentrout (7).

284. Harry Lee Williams (6), son of Charles Jasper Williams
and Ida Ella Josephine Matheny (5), married Bessie M. Wheeler.
They live in New Jersey.

Children: 4

+   492. i.   Harry Truman Williams (7).
+   493. ii.   Dorothy Mae Williams (7).
+   494. iii. Marian Edith Williams (7).
    495. iv.   Clide Talmadge Williams (7).

285. DeWitt Talmadge Williams (6), son of Charles Jasper
Williams and Ida Ella Josephine Matheny (5), married Inez Mackey.

Children: 3

496. i.   Harriet Ann Williams (7), married James Fix.
497. ii.   Mary Mackey Williams (7).
498. iii. Charles Williams (7).

289. Hazel Matheny (6), daughter of Edward Lee Matheny (5)
and Cuba Wade, married in 1909, Charles Reed.

Children: 2

499. i.   Elizabeth Reed (7), married David Wolfenbarger.
She is a teacher in Augusta County, Virginia schools.
500. ii.   Kathleen Reed (7), married Carl Brown. She is
a teacher in Augusta County, Virginia schools.

290. Sarah Jane Cleek (6), daughter of Adam Given Cleek (5)
and Mary Jane Miller, was born September 13, 1850; died March 20,
1934; married March 12, 1873, Charles Vance, born August 14, 1843;
died August 8, 1894. Charles Vance was a direct descendant of
Lieutenant Colonel Samuel Vance, who built Fort Vanse, near
Mountain Grove, Bath County, Virginia.

Children: 5

+   501. i.   Vivian Sievers Vance (7), born December 20,
1873.
502. ii.   John Cleek Vance (7), born April 16, 1875;
married in 1928 (as her second husband) Ada McGlaughlin, born
November 1875; died February 6, 1952, daughter of Ewing A.
McGlaughlin and Sarah Elizabeth Hite. Her first husband was
William A. G. McGlaughlin. (See Crawford Family). No children.
+   503. iii.   Mary Elizabeth Vance (7), born October 31, 1877.
504. iv.   George William Vance (7), born August 8, 1879;
died   June 20, 1902.
505. v.   Sallie W. Vance (7), born October 11, 1892; died
August 16, 1906.

292. John Henry Wise Cleek (6), son of Adam Given Cleek (5)
and Mary Jane Miller, was born May 15, 1855; died 1924 in Hillsboro, West Virginia; married January 2, 1879, Nannie Mayse; died
August 24, 1928, daughter of Anderson Mayse and Rebecca _____ .

Children: 4

506. i.   Michael Given Cleek (7), born December 10,
1879; died October 1, 1952.
+   507. ii.   Lillie Grace Cleek (7), born August 24, 1882.
+   508. iii.   William Chapman Cleek (7), born August 6,1884.
+   509. iv.   Jane Cleek (7), born August 1, 1891.

293. Mary Elizabeth Virginia Cleek (6), daughter of Adam
Given Cleek (5) and Mary Jane Miller, was born December 21,1857;
married (1) George Mayse; married (2) in 1893, John H. Gardner.

Children: 4 - first marriage

510. i.   Fred Mayse (7), died in early manhood from re-
sults of an accident caused by a runaway horse.
+   511. ii.   Edna Mayse (7), born June 25, 1880.
512. iii.   Nellie Mayse (7), born 1885; married Edward
Thomas Hathaway, born 1888; died 1948 and was buried in Woodland
Cemetery, Bath County, Virginia.
+   513. iv.   Gratton Mayse (7).

Children: 2 - second marriage

514. v. J. Scott Gardner (7), born 1894.
515. vi. Virginia Gardner (7).

294. Cornelia Harriett Cleek (6), daughter of Adam Given
Cleek (5) and Mary Jane Miller, was born February 5, 1861; died
April 6, 1939; married October 20, 1881, Joseph Samuel Smith,
born March 17, 1859; died May 10, 1926, son of William Smith
(born October 1812; died January 25, 1892) and Patsy Williams.

Children: 8

+ 516. i. Elliot Hopkins Smith (7), born June 5, 1883.
   517. ii. Waldo Cleaveland Smith (7), born August 3,1885;
died October 24, 1918 in Ohio in the influenza epidemic, unmarried.
+ 518. iii. Stella Lee Smith (7), born May 24, 1887.
+ 519. iv. Joseph Tucker Smith (7), born June 28, 1889.
+ 520. v. Flora Richardson Smith (7), born September 12,1891.
   521. vi. Cornelia Jane Smith (7), born December 8, 1899;
married Raymond Myers. No children.
· 522. vii. Orra Wallace Smith (7), born July 16, 1896; died
July 3, 1904.
+ 523. viii. Carol Independence Smith (7), born July 4, 1902.

295. George Lee Cleek (6), son of Adam Given Cleek (5) and
Mary Jane Miller, was born September 23, 1865; died April 5, 1939
and was buried in Woodland Cemetery, Bath County, Virginia; married
December 22, 1892, Ida V. Taylor, born August 24, 1870, a sister
of Russell Beard and daughter of James F. Taylor and Martha A.
Jordan.

Children: 3

524. i. Leslie Cleek (7), married October 8, 1932,
Virginia Watson. No children.
525. ii. Arlie B. Cleek (7), married May 2, 1924, Leola
Russmeisel. No children.
526. iii. James A. Cleek (7), married October 30, 1942,
Gladys L. Reed, R.N. They had two daughters.

296. Lillah Bell Cleek (6), daughter of Adam Given Cleek
(5) and Mary Jane Miller, was born March 19, 1867; died February
28, 1949; married November 13, 1884, Floyd Lee LaRue, born
October 24, 1859; died April 18, 1924, son of Robert S. LaRue
and Rebecca R. Brinkley. He served as Deputy Clerk under Adam
Given Cleek, Superintendent of Schools and Clerk of the Courts,
Bath County, Virginia.

Children: 9

+ 527. i. Clyde Hall LaRue (7), born August 4, 1885.
+ 528. ii. Harry Brooks LaRue (7), born 1887.

63

529. iii. Madie M. LaRue (7), R. N., born 1889; married
Howard Jewett, Lexington, Kentucky. He was Kentucky State Ento-
mologist. No children.
530. iv. Anna LaRue (7), died early in life.
+ 531. v. Lillie Cleek LaRue (7), born 1896.
532. vi. Virginia Ruth LaRue (7), died early in life.
+ 533. vii. Clara Baxter LaRue (7), born May 10, 1899.
+ 534. viii. Floyd L. LaRue (7), born February 14, 1902.
+ 535. ix. Ralph Scott LaRue (7), born September 1907.

297. Susan Byrd Cleek (6), daughter of Adam Given Cleek (5)
and Mary Jane Miller, was born October 11, 1870; died June 27,
1953; married James A. Cauley, born November 8, 1867; died June
2, 1955. Both were buried in Woodland Cemetery, Bath County,
Virginia.

Children: 4

+ 536. i. Restie Nickell Cauley (7).
537. ii. Mary E. Cauley (7), married Lynch Fulwider.
+ 538. iii. Blanche A. Cauley (7).
+ 539. iv. James A. Cauley, Jr. (7).

302. John (Jack) Cleek (6), son of John Cleek, Jr. (5) and
Rachel McNiel Myers, was born March 7, 1881 in Bath County, Virginia;
died April 18, 1933 in High.County, Virginia; married February 8,
1906 at Washington, D. C. by Justice O'Neil, Elizabeth Agnes Gwin,
born March 28, 1886, daughter of David Franklin Gwin and Minnie
Herman Lockridge. (See Gwin Family).

Children: 8

540. i. Harriett F. Cleek (7), born 1906; died 1907.
541. ii. Katherine Cleek (7), born 1907; died 1908.
542. iii. Mary Lydia Cleek (7), born June 7, 1909;
married June 27, 1938 in Lexington, Kentucky, Henry Philip Orem,
February 28, 1910 at Campbellsburg, Kentucky. Mrs. Orem attended
the University of Kentucky where she received her B.S. and M.S.
degrees. Mr. Orem received a B.S. in Industrial Chemistry from
the University of Kentucky in 1932 and a M.S. from the University
of Kentucky in 1934. He also did two and one half years of additional work at the Pennsylvania State College toward a Ph.D.
under Dr. F. C. Whitmore. At the University of Kentucky, he held
a graduate assistantship in physical chemistry and at Pennsylvania
he held a graduate scholarship. He is now employed by United
States Pipe and Foundry Company, Birmingham, Alabama in the Chemical Research and Development Department. He is a member of Alpha
Chi Sigma (Professional Chemistry), Sigma Xi (research), American
Chemical Society, American Institute of Chemical Engineers, and
the Alabama Section of the American Chemical Society, of which
he is Secretary. No children.
543. iv. Dorothy McNiel Cleek (7), born February 1, 1913;
married September 30, 1944 at Lexington, Kentucky, James Ruble,
D.D.S. Mrs. Ruble attended the University of Kentucky where she
received a Ph.D. No children.

544. v.   John (Jack) Wilson Cleek (7), born December 22,
1914. He attended the University of Kentucky and Washington and
Lee University. He served in the Marine Corps in the South Pacific
in World War II.
+   545. vi.   Ralph Allen Cleek (7), born June 13, 1917.
    546. vii.   Robert Austin Cleek (7), born December 1919.
    547. viii.   Russell Carlisle Cleek (7), born February 9,
1930; married November 23, 1955, Joanne Jones. He attended
Augusta Military Academy, Fort Defiance, Virginia. He served
three years in the Army of Occupation in Germany after World War II.

303. Dr. John William Wallace (6), son of Thomas Brown
Wallace and Nancy Givens Cleek (5), was born in 1867; died 1930;
married (1) Anna Seward, died June 24, 1917; married (2) Mrs. Amy
Williams Wright, born 1865; died 1920; married (3) Irma Robinson,
R.N.
Children: 2 - first marriage

548. i.   Nannie Laura Wallace (7), married Benjamin C.
Moomaw.
549. ii.   John William Wallace, Jr. (7), married Robbie
Lee Rainey.

304. George Washington Wallace (6), son of Thomas Brown
Wallace and Nancy Givens Cleek (5), was born June 17, 1869; died
December 31, 1931; married (1) in 1894 Virginia Bragg, born
December 17, 1869; died April 1, 1904; married (2) September 18,
1906, Frances Sieg McClung, born January 2, 1878, daughter of
Louis Martin McClung and Sudie Elizabeth Reamer. (See Gwin Family).

Children: 2 - first marriage

550. i.   Frank Brooks Wallace (7), born December 8,
1895; died October 15, 1940, unmarried.
.   551. ii.   Ruth Bagley Wallace (7), married (1) in 1922,
Benjamin Hooper, an attorney; married (2) Dr. Lionel Hooper, a
brother of Benjamin Hooper.

Children: 3 - second marriage

552. iii.   Lewis McClung Wallace (7), born and died in
June 1907.
+   553. iv.   Virginia Blair Wallace (7), R. N., born March
7, 1909.
554. v.   Thomas Reamer Wallace (7), born July 6, 1912;
married August 19, 1939, Elizabeth Lee McGuffin, born September
14, 1914, daughter of John Crawford McGuffin (born November 18,
1858; died July 6, 1942) and Burta Lee Wright, born July 21, 1883.
(Hamilton Genealogy, page 40).

307. George Washington Cleek (6), son of David Gwin Cleek
(5) and Annie Maria Louisa Weldon, was born in 1863; married (1)
Annie O'Burta; married (2) _____. They lived in Oklahoma and Texas.

Children: 3 - first marriage

555. i. David O'Burta Cleek (7).
556. ii. Frank Shaw Cleek (7).
557. iii. George Washington Cleek (7), died young.

309. Robert Edward Cleek (6), son of David Gwin Cleek (5) and Annie Maria Louisa Weldon, was born August 27, 1869 in Bath County, Virginia; died December 27, 1952 at Fredericksburg, Virginia; married June 7, 1893, Texie May Harlow, daughter of Joshua Moses Harlow and Henrietta Larkin.

Children: 7

558. i. David Harlow Cleek (7), born May 31, 1894; married in 1946, Mrs. Laura Bell. No children.
+ 559. ii. Forrest Andrew Cleek (7).
+ 560. iii. Wilfred Ernest Cleek (7).
+ 561. iv. Charles Edward Cleek (7), born November 11,1901.
+ 562. v. Wilbur Jesse Cleek (7).
563. vi. Woodrow Wilson Cleek (7), married Lucile Haley. No children.
564. vii. Robert Turner Cleek (7), married Camilla Pettigoe. No children.

313. Sallie Byrd Cleek (6), daughter of David Gwin Cleek (5) and Annie Maria Louisa Weldon, was born in 1875; died July 1909; married October 10, 1906 in Pocahontas County, West Virginia (as his first wife) Lothian Roy Bowers.

Children: 2

+ 565. i. Millard Price Bowers (7).
+ 566. ii. Jesse Cleek Bowers (7).

315. Mary Ethel Cleek (6), daughter of David Gwin Cleek (5) and Alban Gillett Cleek (5), was born December 12, 1893; died August 2, 1932; married June 30, 1926 (as his first wife) Ira Thornton Ritenour, born November 13, 1884, son of Thornton Ritenour and Eliza Catherine Boyer.

Children: 2

+ 567. i. Margaret Katherine Ritenour (7), born March 28, 1928.
+ 568. ii. Rose Mary Ritenour (7), born May 2, 1932.

317. Andrew William Cleek (6), son of George Washington Cleek (5) and Malcena Catherine Lightner, was born May 10, 1871 in Bath County, Virginia; died February 8, 1938 in Bath County, Virginia; married October 18, 1899, Clara Belle Siple, born August 26, 1870; died August 10, 1927, daughter of George W. Siple and Hannah Rebecca Warwick. (See Warwick Family.)

66

Children: 2

+ 569. i. Elizabeth Graham Cleek (7), born October 18, 1900.
+ 570. ii. Andrew William Cleek (7), born February 5, 1909.

318. John Robert Cleek (6), son of George Washington Cleek (5) and Malcena Catherine Lightner, was born November 23, 1873 in Bath County, Virginia; died June 8, 1950 in Bath County, Virginia; married January 16, 1907, Ruth Ann Gillett, born April 17, 1884, daughter of William Roffe Gillett (born June 10, 1831) and Rosetta Jane Baldwin,(born 1858).

Children: 4

+ 571. i. Gladys Adelaide Cleek (7), born March 18, 1908.
572. ii. Harriett Evelyn Cleek (7), born August 30, 1910; married April 3, 1930, Glenn Criser, born February 17, 1907; died July 11, 1946. He served in World War II. No children.
+ 573. iii. Charles Edwin Cleek (7), born April 18, 1914.
574. iv. John Robert Cleek, Jr. (7), born February 6, 1917; married October 7, 1950, Ernestine Payne, born April 28, 1914, daughter of Ernest Edward Payne and Harriet Melissa Agner. He served in World War II as a sergeant. He entered service on April 3, 1942 at Camp Lee, Virginia and served in Company C, 306th Infantry, 77th Division in the Pacific Theatre in the Central Pacific Area. He was wounded on August 8, 1944 at Guam, again on December 23, 1944 at Leyete, and was wounded a third time on May 13, 1945 at Okinawa. He was promoted to Sergeant on December 13, 1943 and was discharged on May 7, 1946 at Camp Upton, Long Island, New York. He received the Purple Heart, two Oak Leaf Clusters, and the Bronze Star for his services. Mrs. Cleek is Deputy Commissioner of Revenue of Bath County, Virginia. No children.

320. Wade Hampton Cleek (6), son of George Washington Cleek (5) and Malcena Catherine Lightner, was born July 24, 1880 in Bath County, Virginia; died October 26, 1951 in Bath County, Virginia; married March 9, 1904, Stella Pearl Lockridge, born December 8, 1880, daughter of Stephen A. Lockridge and Laura Ervine. (See Gwin and Warwick Families).

Children: 2

+ 575. i. Constance Virginia Cleek (7), born December 29, 1904.
+ 576. ii. George Washington Cleek (7), born November 5, 1906.

321. George Washington Cleek (6), son of George Washington Cleek (5) and Malcena Catherine Lightner, was born August 19, 1889 in Bath County, Virginia; married June 1, 1915 at Maurertown, Shenandoah County, Virginia by Dr. William C. White, Seraphine Catherine Ritenour, born March 3, 1889 in Shenandoah County,

Virginia, daughter of Thornton Ritenour and Eliza Catherine Boyer. He attended the schools of Bath County, Virginia, his instructors being Rev. George L. Brown, Miss Margaret Bratton, S. B. Rexrode, and Miss Isabel Goss. Later he was a student at Monterey High School, where he won a Washington and Lee University scholarship, and after a year at Washington and Lee (where he won a scholarship in Physics) he spent a year (1910) at the University of Virginia specializing in mathematics and science. He taught school in Bath County, Virginia and at Strasburg High School, Strasburg, Virginia. He also devoted time to farming on Springway Farm, Bath County, Virginia, which was the original farm of John Cleek, II. He was Deputy Commissioner of Revenue and Deputy Clerk of the Court of Bath County, Virginia. Mrs. Cleek graduated from Eastern College, Front Royal, Virginia, and received a B.A. degree from Valparaiso University, Valparaiso, Indiana. She also did graduate work at Columbia University, New York City. Before her marriage, she taught school at Strasburg, Virginia.

The original research on the families included in this manuscript has been compiled by Geo. W. Cleek during the past 50 years. Mr. Cleek obtained much of his information from original sources now unobtainable, such as Family Bibles, wills, legal documents, and personal interview with older inhabitants of the valley. In addition, Mr. Cleek is the possessor of a large and varied historical, biographical, and genealogical library.

He became a Mason on his 21st birthday. He is also a member of the Stonewall Jackson Camp No. 161, Sons of Confederacy, and the Virginia Society of the Sons of the American Revolution. He is also a member of the fraternal organization of Odd Fellows.

In 1938, Mr. and Mrs. Cleek moved from Springway Farm, Bath County, Virginia, to Staunton, Virginia, where they now reside.

Children: 5

+ 577. i. Given Wood Cleek (7), born November 6, 1916.
+ 578. ii. Thornton Ritenour Cleek (7), born June 24, 1919.
 579. iii. Malcena Cathrine Cleek (7), born May 1, 1921; married May 14, 1949 at Staunton, Virginia, Robert Neville Mann, born November 3, 1904, son of Eugene Turner Mann and Lola Josephine Williamson. She attended Mary Washington College, a branch of the University of Virginia at Fredericksburg, Virginia. Mrs. Mann entered the War Department shortly before the outbreak of World War II where she was promoted rapidly. She advanced through various administrative and executive assignments in the Office of Chief Signal Officer to the Office of the Chief of Staff of the Army. At the time of her resignation on April 1, 1949 to be married, she was Chief of the Administrative Area Section, Office of the Chief of Staff. She was awarded the War Department's Meritorious Civilian Service Badge and Citation by the Chief of Staff for her services in that office. Mrs. Mann, since her marriage, has been much interested in history and genealogy, and has written a number of books in this field. She is a member of the

Society Daughters of Colonial Wars, the Daughters of the American Revolution, and United Daughters of the Confederacy. Mr. Mann attended the Alabama Polytechnic Institute at Auburn, Alabama and did graduate study in Economics at Columbia University, New York City for two years. Until his retirement for physical disability in 1954 he was employed by the New York Telephone Company as executive in charge of Revenue and Financial Matters. Mr. Mann served as a Lieutenant Colonel in World War II from February 28, 1942 to June 15, 1946 in the Office of the Chief Signal Officer of the Army in Washington, D. C. He wrote the book, The Efficient Utilization of Officer Personnel in the Signal Corps. This plan was adopted subsequently by the entire Army, Air Force, and the Navy. For his services he was awarded the Legion of Merit in 1945. For his services in World War II, he also was awarded the New York State Conspicuous Service Cross by Governor Thomas E. Dewey in 1946. Mr. Mann is a member of the New York Society of Colonial Wars and the Tennessee Society Sons of the American Revolution. He is a former member of the New York Society Military and Naval Officers, The Commonwealth Club, The City Club of New York, The University Club of New York, and The University Club of Washington, D.C. He is a member of the Official Board of the First Methodist Church, Cedar Bluff, Alabama.

+ 580. iv. George Kime Cleek (7), born August 27, 1926.
581. v. John Andrew Cleek (7), born July 25, 1932.

322. Mary Emma Revercomb (6), daughter of Henry Harrison (Tip) Revercomb and Harriet Cleek (5), was born September 15, 1867; died November 4, 1942; married December 28, 1905, Charles Hunter McCormick, born May 25, 1862; died April 23, 1947, son of Alfred McCormick and Elizabeth McClintic. She was a graduate of Bridgewater College, Bridgewater, Virginia, and a teacher in the public schools of Bath County, Virginia.

Children: 2

+ 582. i. Charles Revercomb McCormick (7), born 1907.
583. ii. Sallie Elizabeth McCormick (7), born 1910; married in 1938, Ted S. Farrar.

324. George Archie Revercomb (6), son of Charles Francisco Revercomb and Sarah Anne Cleek (5), was born January 24, 1868; died September 1, 1916 and was buried at Woodland Cemetery, Bath County, Virginia; married (1) Emma Armentrout; married (2) Virginia Hollinbeck of New Mexico. He served as Sheriff of Bath County, Virginia.

Children: 1 - first marriage

584. i. Lula Revercomb (7), died June 20, 1913 at Southern Pines, North Carolina; married J. C. Fulford. They had one son.

327. John Cleek Revercomb (6), son of Charles Francisco Revercomb and Sarah Anne Cleek (5), was born in 1876; married Annie Halk.

Children: 2

585. i.　Virginia Revercomb (7).
586. ii.　Annie Hill Revercomb (7), married Randolph
Merrill.

331. Newton Thomas (7), son of Charles D. Thomas and Mary
Jane Cleek (6), married Teresa Page.

Children: 2

+ 587. i.　Raymond Thomas (8).
　588. ii.　Charles Thomas (8), married _____ Jones.

332. Gordon Ellsworth Thomas (7), son of Charles D. Thomas
and Mary Jane Cleek (6), was born May 5, 1867 at Clarksburg,
West Virginia; died February 15, 1953 in Bath County, Virginia;
married March 8, 1892, Virginia Josephine Gibson (7), born April
14, 1875 in Bath County, Virginia; died July 6, 1954, daughter of
John Lewis Nicholas Gibson and Clarissa (Clara) Cleek.

Children: 8

+ 589. i.　Harper Thomas (8).
　590. ii.　Mary Thomas (8).
　591. iii.　Mabel Thomas (8).
+ 592. iv.　Hycie Thomas (8).
　593. v.　Maxine Thomas (8), married Roy Dever.
　594. vi.　Edgar Thomas (8), a daughter, unmarried.
　595. vii.　Edith Thomas (8), unmarried.
+ 596. viii.　Paralee Thomas (8),

334. Annie Thomas (7), daughter of Charles D. Thomas and
Mary Jane Cleek (6), died February 26, 1954; married Charles J.
Richardson of West Virginia.

Children: 7

597. i.　Charles Richardson (8), married Elizabeth
McElwee.
598. ii.　Pleas Richardson (8), married Roy Campbell, son
of William Price Campbell and Annie L. Ruckman. (See Campbell
Family).
599. iii.　Craig Richardson (8), married Gertrude Golding.
600. iv.　Jack Richardson (8), married Vivian Musgrave.
601. v.　Mary Richardson (8), married Reed Davis.
602. vi.　Anna Richardson (8), unmarried.
603. vii.　Frank Richardson (8), unmarried.

335. Houston H. Thomas (7), son of Charles D. Thomas and
Mary Jane Cleek (6), died in 1929; married Myrtle Cleek (7), born
February 15, 1880; died January 8, 1951 at Mt. Sidney, Virginia,
daughter of James Cleek and Amelia Rowan.

Children: 4

+ 604. i.   Homer Thomas (8).
+ 605. ii. Allenne Thomas (8).
+ 606. iii. Hugh Thomas (8).
  607. iv. Helen Thomas (8), married Larry Lawrence. They
live in New York.

336. Malcena Thomas (7), daughter of Charles D. Thomas and
Mary Jane Cleek (6), married Lewis Page.

Children: 2

608. i.   Della Page (8), married George William Campbell,
born June 1889; died June 14, 1949, son of Filmore T. Campbell
and Mary Ada Sively. No children. (See Campbell Family).
609. ii. Harry Page (8), married (1) Lillie Carpenter
Green; married (2) Annie Brinkley, daughter of Troy Brinkley and
Lula Robinson.

346. Ella B. Cleek (7), daughter of James Cleek (6) and
Amelia Rowan, married (1) Andrew Wright; married (2) February 1,
1904 in Pocahontas County, West Virginia, Joe H. Lantz.

Children: 2 - first marriage

610. i.   Henderson Wright (8).
611. ii. Frances Wright (8).

Children: 2 - second marriage

  612. iii. Cecil Dane Lantz (8), married Ida Morrison.
+ 613. iv. Veva Lantz (8).

349. Annie Pleasant Cleek (7), daughter of John Lewis Cleek
(6) and Ruhamy A. Cleek (6), was January 30, 1875; died December
13, 1955 at Fresno, California and was buried at Spokane, Washington; married October 18, 1893 in Pocahontas County, West
Virginia, Frank Conrad Moore, born December 20, 1875; died
January 19, 1931, son of Rev. James E. Moore and Luemma Harper.
They lived at Spokane, Washington.

Children: 3

+ 614. i.   John Grady Moore (8), born December 8, 1894.
  615. ii. Emma Grace Moore (8), born November 29, 1896;
married George Krous. He is supervising principal at the schools
of Fresno, California and she is the music supervisor.
  616. iii. Clarence Albert Moore (8), born March 2, 1900;
married _____.

350. Bettie Cleek (7), daughter of John Lewis Cleek (6) and
Ruhamy A. Cleek (6), was born February 9, 1878; died October 1926;
married in Pocahontas County, West Virginia on January 30, 1901,
Marshall L. Isbell.

Children: 2

617. i.   Frank K. Isbell (8), married Frances _____.
They live in Dallas, Texas.
618. ii.   Lillah Cleek Isbell (8), married (1) Gordon
Booze; married (2) _____.

351. Walter L. Cleek (7), son of John Lewis Cleek (6) and
Ruhamy A. Cleek (6), married (1) Dovie Wiley; married (2) Goola
May Talley.

Children: 1 - first marriage

+   619. i.   Hermit C. Cleek (8).

Children: 3 - second marriage

+   620. ii.   Virginia Cleek (8), born August 1921.
+   621. iii.   Elizabeth Cleek (8), born September 1924.
     622. iv.   Betty Jean Cleek (8), born November 1927;
married John Martin.

352. Charles Massey Byrd Cleek (7), son of John Lewis Cleek
(6) and Ruhamy A. Cleek (6), married (1) Anna Van DeVeer; married
(2) Mrs. Cora (Giles) Hunter. They live in Olympia, Washington.

Children: 1 - first marriage

+   623. i.   Edward Vaughn Cleek (8).

368. Irving Cleek (7), son of Andrew William Cleek (6) and
Nellie Greer, married Donna Due.

Children: 2

624. i.   Carolyn Cleek (8).
625. ii.   John Cleek (8).

370. Stuart Cleek (7), son of Jeb Stuart Cleek (6) and
Ethel Moon, married Bettey Danner. They live at Orland, California.

Children: 1

626. i.   Betty Lee Cleek (8).

372. Norris Cleek (7), son of Vincent Carlyle Cleek (6) and
Myra Norris, married Helen Seiersen. Their home is at Orland,
California.

Children: 4

627. i.   Joan Cleek (8).
628. ii.   Vincent Cleek (8).
629. iii.   Gerald Cleek (8).
630. iv.   Eugene Cleek (8).

373. John Vincent Cleek (7), son of John Leslie Cleek (6) and Elizabeth Wallace, was born in 1905; married Lillian Stevens. They live at Santa Rosa, California.

Children: 2

631. i. Richard Stevens Cleek (8), born 1942.
632. ii. Jean Valerie Cleek (8), born 1945.

374. Sidney Richelieu Cleek (7), son of John Leslie Cleek (6) and Elizabeth Wallace, married Guinevere Loughery. They live at Santa Rosa, California.

Children: 2

633. i. Sydney Ann Cleek (8), born 1936.
634. ii. Harold Leslie Cleek (8), born 1938.

375. George Wallace Cleek (7), son of John Leslie Cleek (6) and Elizabeth Wallace, married Lillian Napier. They live at Santa Rosa, California.

Children: 2

635. i. William Wallace Cleek (8), born 1936.
636. ii. Susan Cleek (8), born 1946.

377. Carroll Cleek (7), son of James Corder Cleek (6) and Louise J. Arnold, married (1) Dorothy _____; married (2) ____ _____.

Children: 1

637. i. Paul Cleek (8).

384. George Simpson (7), son of Alfred Simpson (6) and Rachel Price Cleek (5), married Mary Wiley, daughter of Robert Wiley and Elizabeth Woods. (See Crawford Family).

Children: 3

638. i. Betty Lou Simpson (8).
639. ii. Georgia Price Simpson (8).
640. iii. Alfred Simpson (8).

423. Mary Dorothy Simpson (7), daughter of Andrew Milton Simpson (6) and Lula Feaster, was born April 10, 1908; married Lester Hardy. She is a R.N.

Children: 5

641. i. Shirley Hardy (8).
642. ii. John Milton Hardy (8).
643. iii. David Hardy (8).
644. iv. Richard Hardy (8).
645. v. Nancy Lynn Hardy (8).

424. Charlotte Ruth Simpson (7), daughter of Andrew Milton Simpson (6) and Lula Feaster, was born October 26, 1909; married Ralph M. Pullin, born May 16, 1905, son of Edward L. Pullin and Maude Rodgers. (See Gwin Family).

Children: 1

+   646. i.   Alma Ruth Pullin (8).

425. Paul Edwin Simpson (7), son of Andrew Milton Simpson (6) and Lula Feaster, was born September 23, 1911; died November 6, 1938; married Bertha Zembower.

Children: 1

647. i.   Zola Naomi Simpson (8), married October 26, 1956, Roy Chaney.

426. Lewis Francis Simpson (7), son of Andrew Milton Simpson (6) and Lula Feaster, was born July 12, 1913; married February 27, 1937, Ann Mongon.

Children: 1

648. i.   Dwight Francis Simpson (8), born February 1938.

428. William Wood Simpson (7), son of Andrew Milton Simpson (6) and Lula Feaster, was born July 22, 1917; married Ravell Luttrell.

Children: 4

649. i.   Paul David Simpson (8).
650. ii.   William Simpson (8).
651. iii.   Gary Simpson (8).
652. iv.   Ronald Simpson (8).

429. Grace Estelle Simpson (7), daughter of Andrew Milton Simpson (6) and Lula Feaster, was born June 5, 1919; married Avery Chedester.

Children: 1

+   653. i.   Julia Ruth Chedester (8).

430. Roy Milton Simpson (7), son of Andrew Milton Simpson (6) and Lula Feaster, was born May 25, 1921; married Virginia Mosser.

Children: 4

654. i.   Roy Milton Simpson (8), died young.
655. ii.   Richard Simpson (8).
656. iii.   Stephen Simpson (8).
657. iv.   Jackie Lynn Simpson (8).

432. Quinton Brown Simpson (7), son of Andrew Milton
Simpson (6) and Lula Feaster, was born February 23, 1924; married
Dorothy Hite.

Children: 3

658. i.   James Edward Simpson (8).
659. ii.   Quinton Blair Simpson (8).
660. iii.   Kenneth Simpson (8).

434. Darrell Austin Simpson (7), son of Andrew Milton
Simpson (6) and Lula Feaster, was born October 10, 1926;
married Eleanor Michael.

Children: 4

661. i.   Royce Simpson (8), a twin to Joyce.
662. ii.   Joyce Simpson (8), a twin to Royce.
663. iii.   Elvin Simpson (8).
664. iv.   Connie Simpson (8).

435. Marvin Craft Simpson (7), son of Andrew Milton Simpson
(6) and Lula Feaster, was born August 25, 1929; married Ruth Ella
Rice.

Children: 2

665. i.   Robert Simpson (8).
666. ii.   Edward Simpson (8).

437. Robert Charles Cleek (7), son of Charles Lloyd Cleek
(6) and Catherine Kaeff, married in 1947, Gertrude Dellman of Gary,
Indiana.
Children: 1

667. i.   Charles Lloyd Cleek (8).

438. Howard Melvin Cleek (7), son of Charles Lloyd Cleek
(6) and Catherine Kaeff, married Rose _____ of Gary, Indiana.

Children: 2

668. i.   Jerry Cleek (8).
669. ii.   Kenneth Allen Cleek (8), born March 14, 1954.

439. Lillian Vestal (7), daughter of Byron Vestal and Ruth
Vivian Cleek (6), married Freddie Monroe.

Children: 2

670. i.   Johnny Monroe (8).
671. ii.   Jimmy Monroe (8).

440. Bernard William Vestal (7), son of Byron Vestal and

75

and Ruth Vivian Cleek (6), married Hazel Hutsell.

Children: 2

672. i.   Melvin Vestal (8).
673. ii.   Ruth Ellin Vestal (8).

448. Charles Omer Cooley (7), son of Laurence Cooley and
Ethel Mildred Cleek (6), married Mary Newton.

Children: 1

674. i.   Charlasu Cooley (8).

449. Robert Suddarth Bias Cleek (7), son of Dewey Suddarth
Cleek (6) and Mary Edith Gum, was born June 20, 1926; married
Delores Snead.

Children: 2

675. i.   Patty Lynn Cleek (8).
676. ii.   _____ Cleek (8), a son.

455. Audrey Ernestine Cleek (7), daughter of Ernest Simpson
Cleek (6) and Clarice Wine, married May 30, 1946, Rodney Francis
Brecht.

Children: 1

677. i.   Gregory Lyndon Brecht (8).

486. Patsy Josephine Armentrout (7), daughter of Fred P.
Armentrout and Mary Edith Williams (6), married David Lawrence
Glick. She is a teacher. He is athletic instructor at Effinger
High School, Rockbridge County, Virginia.

Children: 3

678. i.   Patricia Ann Glick (8).
679. ii.   David Lawrence Glick, Jr. (8).
680. iii.   Betty Lou Glick (8).

488. Lucy Virginia Armentrout (7), daughter of Fred P.
Armentrout and Mary Edith Williams (6), married (1) Clarence
Krider; married (2) March 1957, Lloyd H. Weaver.

Children: 1 - first marriage

681. i.   Frederick Murray Krider (8).

489. Charlotte Williams Armentrout (7), daughter of Fred
P. Armentrout and Mary Edith Williams (6), married William
Harold Dietz.

Children: 2

682. i.   Charlotte Beatrice Dietz (8).
683. ii.   William Harold Dietz, Jr. (8).

490. Frances Winn Armentrout (7), daughter of Fred P.
Armentrout and Mary Edith Williams (6), married Edward McGuire
Daniels.

Children: 2

684. i.   Mary Margaret Daniels (8).
685. ii.   Phillip Edward Daniels (8).

491. Jane Porter Armentrout (7), daughter of Fred P.
Armentrout and Mary Edith Williams (6), married Meredith Shanks.

Children: 2

686. i.   James Meredith Shanks (8).
687. ii.   Richard Shanks (8).

492. Harry Truman Williams (7), son of Harry Lee Williams
(6) and Bessie M. Wheeler, married Rachel Sensabaugh.

Children: 1

688. i.   Harry Truman Williams, Jr. (8).

493. Dorothy Mae Williams (7), daughter of Harry Lee
Williams (6) and Bessie M. Wheeler, married A. W. Newton.

Children: 1

+   689. i.   Palmer Ann Newton (8).

494. Marian Edith Williams (7), daughter of Harry Lee
Williams (6) and Bessie M. Wheeler, married Wesley White.

Children: 1

690. i.   DeWitt Talmadge White (8).

501. Vivian Sievers Vance (7), daughter of Charles Vance
and Sarah Jane Cleek (6), was born December 20, 1873; died
February 6, 1906; married (as his second wife) Sheppe Gilliland.

Children: 3

+   691. i.   Emil Gilliland (8).
+   692. ii.   Carrie Gilliland (8).
    693. iii. Garland Gilliland (8), married _____.

503. Mary Elizabeth Vance (7), daughter of Charles Vance

and Sarah Jane Cleek (6), was born October 31, 1877; died July 6, 1952; married Joseph L. Tate.

Children: 8

694. i.   Blanche Tate (8), married Noland Stevens, Lovingston, Virginia.
695. ii. Edna Tate (8), married Robert Williams. Divorced. She is a R. N. Huntington, West Virginia.
696. iii. Raleigh Tate (8), married _____ in Boston, Massachusetts.
697. iv. Mildred Tate (8), married Garland Blair, Portsmouth, Virginia.
698. v.   Dorothy Tate (8), married Ben Dougherty, Portsmouth, Virginia.
699. vi. Kenneth Tate (8), married Margaret Akins, Clifton Forge, Virginia. No children.
700. vii. M. Elizabeth Tate (8), married Robert L. Stevens, Charlottesville, Virginia. No children.
701. viii. Katherine Tate (8), married Kenneth Banfield, St. Petersburg, Florida.

507. Lillie Grace Cleek (7), daughter of John Henry Wise Cleek (6) and Nannie Mayse, was born August 24, 1882; married May 1, 1910 in Pocahontas County, West Virginia, Cecil Hiner, died August 1938 of Lewisburg, West Virginia.

Children: 2

702. i.   Katherine Hiner (8), born February 7, 1911; married February 1, 1934 (1) Charles Colborn; married (2) Warren DeLay, an X-Ray Technician at Jefferson Hospital, Roanoke, Virginia.
+ 703. ii. Julian Craig (Buddy) Hiner (8), born October 10, 1912.

508. William Chapman Cleek (7), son of John Henry Wise Cleek (6) and Nannie Mayse, was born August 6, 1884; married May 2, 1917, Annie May Cleek (6), born March 4, 1883, daughter of Peter Lightner Cleek and Effie May Amiss.

Children: 2

+ 704. i. Audrey Mabel Cleek (8), born February 1, 1919.
+ 705. ii. Ward Chapman Cleek (8), born August 20, 1922.

509. Jane Cleek (7), daughter of John Henry Wise Cleek (6) and Nannie Mayse, was born August 1, 1891; died April 30, 1933 at Hinton, West Virginia; married April 30, 1912, Fred G. Hannah of Renick, West Virginia.

Children: 1

+ 706. i.   Ruth Hannah (8).

511. Edna Mayse (7), daughter of George Mayse and Mary Elizabeth Virginia Cleek (6), was born June 25, 1880; married Russell Beard Taylor, born January 10, 1884; died June 18, 1955, and was buried in Woodland Cemetery, Bath County, Virginia, a brother of Ida V. Taylor who married George Lee Cleek, and son of James F. Taylor and Martha A. Jordan.

Children: 3

```
+   707.  i.    Louis Taylor (8).
    708.  ii.   Constance Taylor (8), married Clyde Hanley.  She
is a R.N.
+   709.  iii.  Lydia Taylor (8).
```

513. Gratton Mayse (7), son of George Mayse and Mary Elizabeth Virginia Cleek (6), married Maysie Frances Stuart.

Children: 3

```
    710.  i.    Frances McClintic Mayse (8), married C. Gustave
Agreen.
    711.  ii.   Dorothy Mayse (8), died June 26, 1932.
    712.  iii.  Stuart Mayse (8), married _____.
They have one child, Gratton Mayse (9).
```

516. Elliot Hopkins Smith (7), son of Joseph Samuel Smith and Cornelia Harriett Cleek (6), was born June 5, 1883; died October 2, 1955; married (1) Lillie Carpenter; married (2) Mary Higgombottom.

Children: 3 - first marriage

```
    713.  i.    Clarence Smith (8), died young.
+   714.  ii.   Elva Smith (8).
+   715.  iii.  Wilbert Smith (8).
```

518. Stella Lee Smith (7), daughter of Joseph Samuel Smith and Cornelia Harriett Cleek (6), was born May 24, 1887; married Henry Pole Hoover, son of William Hoover and Virginia Smith of Maryland.

Children: 5

```
    716.  i.    Agnes Smith Hoover (8), born August 17, 1906;
married _____ Givens. No children.
+   717.  ii.   Eugene Hoover (8), born February 21, 1909.
+   718.  iii.  Melvin Hoover (8), born February 25, 1911.
+   719.  iv.   Victor Dow Hoover (8), born April 20, 1920.
+   720.  v.    Robert June Hoover (8), born June 23, 1922.
```

519. Joseph Tucker Smith (7), son of Joseph Samuel Smith and Cornelia Harriett Cleek (6), was born June 28, 1889; married Fannie Donovan.

Children: 1

+ 721. i. Jesse Smith (8).

520. Flora Richardson Smith (7), daughter of Joseph Samuel Smith and Cornelia Harriett Cleek (6), was born September 12, 1891; married Russell Carpenter.

Children: 2

+ 722. i. Nelson Blair Carpenter (8).
  723. ii. Virginia Carpenter (8), married _____ Ward.
No children.

523. Carol Independence Smith (7), daughter of Joseph Samuel Smith and Cornelia Harriett Cleek (6), was born July 4, 1902; married William O. Campbell.

Children: 2

+ 724. i. Osborn Campbell (8).
  725. ii. Willard Campbell (8).

527. Clyde Hall LaRue (7), son of Floyd Lee LaRue and Lillah Bell Cleek (6), was born August 4, 1885 in Jamestown, Ohio; married December 26, 1906, Cornelia McGuffin Bonner, born July 15, 1886, daughter of John A. Bonner and Mary E. Revercomb. He served as Deputy Clerk of Bath County, Virginia.

Children: 1

+ 726. i. Clyde Bonner LaRue (8).

528. Harry Brooks LaRue (7), son of Floyd Lee LaRue and Lillah Bell Cleek (6), was born in 1887; married Blanche Gum, born February 13, 1887; died March 22, 1952, daughter of John Ervin Gum and Mary Beverage.

Children: 2

+ 727. i. Virginia LaRue (8).
  728. ii. Gladys La Rue (8), married (1) Robbie West; married (2) Don Kreckel. No children.

531. Lillie Cleek LaRue (7), daughter of Floyd Lee LaRue and Lillah Bell Cleek (6), was born in 1896; married April 30, 1914, Walter Ricks.

Children: 4

+ 729. i. Helen Erma Ricks (8).
  730. ii. Grace Ricks (8), R.N., Superintendent of Nurses, C&O Hospital, Clifton Forge, Virginia.
+ 731. iii. Betty Lee Ricks (8).
+ 732. iv. Anne Ricks (8).

533. Clara Baxter LaRue (7), daughter of Floyd Lee LaRue and Lillah Bell Cleek (6), was born May 10, 1899; married Darrell G. Jarrett.

Children: 1

733. i.   Darrell G. Jarrett, Jr. (8), married _____ Parks. They have one child.

534. Floyd Lee LaRue (7), son of Floyd Lee LaRue and Lillah Bell Cleek (7), was born February 14, 1902; married in 1931, Lenora Hipes.

Children: 2

734. i.   Mary Katherine LaRue (8), married Joel Simon Sonnabend. She is a R.N. They have two children.
735. ii.   Dorothy LaRue (8).

535. Ralph Scott LaRue (7), son of Floyd Lee LaRue and Lillah Bell Cleek (6), was born September 1907; married Anne Frye.

Children: 2

736. i.   Patricia Ann LaRue (8).
737. ii.   Ralph Scott LaRue, Jr. (8).

536. Restie Nickell Cauley (7), son of James A. Cauley and Susan Byrd Cleek (6), married May 18, 1920, Lucy May Samples, born September 5, 1889, daughter of James Hughart Samples and Annie Laurie Gilliland.

Children: 2

+ 738. i.   Ruth Cleek Cauley (8), born April 7, 1930.
+ 739. ii.   Restie Nickell Cauley, Jr. (8), born December 7, 1931.

538. Blanche A. Cauley (7), daughter of James A. Cauley and Susan Byrd Cleek (6), married Gratton Williams.

Children: 1

740. i.   Dallas Lee Williams (8), married Janet Webb.

539. James A. Cauley, Jr. (7), son of James A. Cauley and Susan Byrd Cleek (6), married Ruby Pangle.

Children: 3

741. i.   Helen Louise Cauley (8).
742. ii.   Paul Curtis Cauley (8).
743. iii. Susan Belle Cauley (8).

545. Ralph Allen Cleek (7), son of John (Jack) Cleek (6) and Elizabeth Agnes Gwin, was born June 13, 1917; married November 28, 1946, Katherine James. He attended VPI, Blacksburg, Virginia where he received a B.S. in Agronomy. He served as Captain in the Chemical Warfare Service in the 80th Division of the Army in World War II.

Children: 2

744. i.   Dorothy Ann Cleek (8), born 1947.
745. ii.   Mary Susan Cleek (8), born 1949.

553. Virginia Blair Wallace (7), daughter of George Washington Wallace (6) and Frances Sieg McClung, was born March 7, 1909; married October 26, 1935, George Wilkins Ruppersberger of Baltimore, Maryland, son of George Gustav Ruppersberger, Jr. and Marguerite Wilkins. She is a R. N.

Children: 3

746. i.   Linda Lucy Ruppersberger (8), born April 9, 1940.
747. ii.   Susan Ann Ruppersberger (8), born November 29, 1943.
748. iii. George William Ruppersberger (8), born October 17, 1945.

559. Forrest Andrew Cleek (7), son of Robert Edward Cleek (6) and Texie May Harlow, married Louise McGuire.

Children: 3

749. i.   Dorothy Lee Cleek (8).
750. ii.   Mary Lou Cleek (8).
751. iii. Forrest Andrew Cleek, Jr. (8).

560. Wilfred Ernest Cleek (7), son of Robert Edward Cleek (6) and Texie May Harlow, married Mrs. Thelma Minor Fenwick.

Children: 2

752. i.   Wilfred Edward Cleek (8), died at age 19 months.
753. ii.   Betty Ann Cleek (8).

561. Charles Edward Cleek (7), son of Robert Edward Cleek (6) and Texie May Harlow, married Elizabeth Baker.

Children: 1

754. i.   June Cleek (8).

562. Wilbur Jesse Cleek (7), son of Robert Edward Cleek (6) and Texie May Harlow, married Margaret Haley.

Children: 3

755. i.   Barbara Lee Cleek (8).

756. ii.   Phyllis Cleek (8).
757. iii.   Nancy Cleek (8).

565. Millard Price Bowers (7), son of Lothian Roy Bowers and
Sallie Byrd Cleek (6), married (1) Rosie Marie Moskey; married (2)
Grace Helms.

Children: 1 - first marriage

758. i.   Carol Marie Bowers (8).

566. Jesse Cleek Bowers (7), son of Lothian Roy Bowers and
Sallie Byrd Cleek (6), married Dorothy Gorrie.

Children: 1

759. i.   Jesse Cleek Bowers, Jr. (8).

567. Margaret Katherine Ritenour (7), daughter of Ira
Thornton Ritenour and Mary Ethel Cleek (6), was born March 28,
1928; married August 20, 1950, Vernon Eugene Sylvester, born
May 29, 1924.

Children: 2

760. i.   James Thornton Sylvester (8), born October 27,
1953.
761. ii.   Virginia Katherine Sylvester (8), born July 8,
1955.

568. Rose Mary Ritenour (7), daughter of Ira Thornton
Ritenour and Mary Ethel Cleek (6), was born May 2, 1932; married
October 20, 1951, Robert Z. Snodgrass.

Children: 2

762. i.   Robert Z. Snodgrass, II (8), born May 2, 1953.
763. ii.   Marlene Ethel Snodgrass (8), born August 18, 1954.

569. Elizabeth Graham Cleek (7), daughter of Andrew William
Cleek (6) and Clara Belle Siple, was born October 18, 1900;
married October 22, 1919, Thomas Burr.

Children: 2

764. i.   Augusta Catherine Burr (8), born in 1920; died
in infancy.
765. ii.   Thomas Love Burr (8), born July 23, 1921;
married Agnes McNamara. They have three children. He served in
World War II as a Second Lieutenant in the Army Air Corps, and
was a prisoner of war in Germany for 20 months.

570. Andrew William Cleek (7), son of Andrew William Cleek
(6) and Clara Belle Siple, was born February 5, 1909; married

April 28, 1932, Frances (Criser) Stinnett.

Children: 1

766. i.   Urban Olin Cleek (8), born January 7, 1933;
married January 23, 1954, Marie Fry. He served in the Armed
Forces after World War II.

571. Gladys Adelaide Cleek (7), daughter of John Robert
Cleek (6) and Ruth Ann Gillett, was born March 18, 1908; married
June 10, 1933, Albert McHone, born December 29, 1909. She is a
R.N.

Children: 3

+   767. i.   Owen Heywood McHone (8), born November 3, 1934.
    768. ii.   Nolan Wilson McHone (8), born February 18, 1945.
    769. iii.   James Clayton McHone (8), born August 6, 1951.

573. Charles Edwin Cleek (7), son of John Robert Cleek (6)
and Ruth Ann Gillett, was born April 18, 1914; married January
26, 1936, Lucy Criser, born January 27, 1910.

Children: 1

770. i.   Chester Cleek (8), born December 11, 1936.

575. Constance Virginia Cleek (7), daughter of Wade Hampton
Cleek (6) and Stella Pearl Lockridge, was born December 29, 1904;
married October 22, 1925, John Lee Thompson, born May 29, 1897;
died May 6, 1932, son of John Lee Thompson and Lina Wilson. Mrs.
Thompson graduated from Madison College, Harrisonburg, Virginia
and teaches school in Bath County, Virginia. Mr. Thompson graduated
from VPI, Blacksburg, Virginia.

Children: 3

+   771. i.   Constance Lee Thompson (8), born July 29, 1927.
+   772. ii.   Carol Marie Thompson (8), born November 15,
1928.
    773. iii.   Johnnie Lou Thompson (8), born September 29,
1932 after the death of her father. She graduated from Madison
College, Harrisonburg, Virginia, and teaches school.

576. George Washington Cleek (7), son of Wade Hampton
Cleek (6) and Stella Pearl Lockridge, was born November 5, 1906;
married February 14, 1942, Margaret Matheny, born May 18, 1910,
daughter of Wade Hampton Matheny and Belle Liggett. He served
from March 28, 1942 to November 29, 1945 as Mail Man 1st Class
in the U.S. Navy and spent 8 months in North Africa. He has the
American Theatre, European-African-Middle Eastern, Victory, and
Good Conduct Medals. He was also in the Army Reserve, Quarter-
master Corps for 18 months after World War II. He attended VPI,
Blacksburg, Virginia and did graduate work at Westinghouse,
Pittsburg, Pennsylvania. He was postmaster at Warm Springs,
Virginia for 16 years. He was appointed Treasurer of Bath County

on December 21, 1956 by Judge Earl Abbott.

Children: 1

774. i.   Elizabeth Ann Cleek (8), born June 24, 1944.

577. Given Wood Cleek (7), son of George Washington Cleek
(6) and Seraphine Catherine Ritenour, was born November 6, 1916 in
Bath County, Virginia; married December 11, 1941 at Spartanburg,
South Carolina, Dorothy Virginia Healy, born March 3, 1916 at
Baltimore, Maryland, daughter of Maurice Cornelius Healy (born
April 7, 1884 at Lynchburg, Virginia; died February 14, 1941 at
Baltimore, Maryland) and Edna Frances Dillehunt (born November
20, 1889 at Baltimore, Maryland; died November 25, 1943 at El
Paso, Texas) and granddaughter of John Healy and Marie McCormick.
Mrs. Cleek received a B.S. degree in education from Maryland State
Teachers College, Towson, Maryland, and taught school before her
marriage. Mr. Cleek attended Washington and Lee University, Lex-
ington, Virginia and received a B.S. degree from George Washington
University, Washington, D.C. He is employed at the Bureau of
Standards, Washington, D.C. and is listed in the current edition
of American Men of Science and Chemical Who's Who. He enlisted
in the District of Columbia National Guard in October 1937 and
was inducted into Federal Service with the 260th CA (AA) as a
First Lieutenant on January 6, 1941 with station at Fort Bliss,
Texas. He served in the Western Defense Command from December
1941 to March 1943 with station in the vicinity of Seattle,
Washington, as Captain and Major. He was reassigned to Fort
Bliss, Texas in April 1943 and served in various staff jobs until
April 1944, when he was transferred to Camp Haan, California. He
was transferred with the 734th AAA Gun Battalion to the 14th AAA
Command, SW Pacific Theatre in November 1944 with station in New
Guinea and Luzon, P.I. He returned to the U.S. in October 1945
and was separated from the service in December 1945 as a Lieutenant
Colonel. He has the American Defense Service Medal, American
Service Medal, Asiatic Pacific Service Medal with combat star,
World War II Victory Medal, and Philippine Liberation Medal. He
reactivated the 260th AAA Gun Battalion, District of Columbia
National Guard as the commanding officer (Major) in November 1946
and was promoted to Lieutenant Colonel in 1947. He served as
Battalion Commander until his retirement for physical disability
as Colonel in September 1949. He is an elder in the Washington,
D.C. Church of God.

Children: 3

775. i.   George Andrew Cleek (8), born February 9, 1943
in Everett, Washington.
776. ii.   Jane Katherine Cleek (8), born January 6, 1950
in Washington, D. C.
777. iii.   Linda Ann Cleek (8), born September 28, 1953
in Washington, D. C.

578. Thornton Ritenour Cleek (7), son of George Washington

Cleek (6) and Seraphine Catherine Ritenour, was born June 24, 1919 in Bath County, Virginia; married December 25, 1943 at Dillon, South Carolina, Dorothy Elizabeth Rich, born January 25, 1922, daughter of Thomas Egbert Rich (died June 5, 1945) and Beulah Mae Melvin. He graduated from Washington and Lee University, Lexington, Virginia in 1939 with a B.A. degree. He then taught mathematics and science in Mt. Vernon High School, Fairfax County, Virginia. He entered military service on January 6, 1941 with the 260th CA (AA) Battalion, District of Columbia National Guard. He was commissioned Second Lieutenant on July 17, 1942. He served overseas in the Pacific Theatre from April 6 to December 19, 1945 and was discharged from the service on March 6, 1946. He has the American Defense Service Medal, Asiatic Pacific Service Medal with combat star (Luzon), American Theatre Ribbon, World War II Victory Medal, and the Philippine Liberation Medal with one star. He attended the Medical College of Virginia, Richmond, and received a M.D. degree on June 6, 1950. He interned at Brooke Army Hospital, Fort Sam Houston, Texas in 1950-51, and has been practicing medicine in Asheboro, North Carolina from 1951 to present. He is a member of the American Academy of General Practice, American Medical Association, North Carolina State Medical Society, Theta Kappa Psi, Tau Kappa Iota, B.P.O.E. - Lodge Number 1694, North Carolina, Masons - Balfour Lodge Number 188 A.F. & A.M., and is a deacon of the Asheboro Presbyterian Church. He holds a commission as Captain, US Army Reserve in the Medical Corps.

Children: 1

778. i. Thomas Rich Cleek (8), born October 13, 1944 at Durham, North Carolina.

580. George Kime Cleek (7), son of George Washington Cleek (6) and Seraphine Catherine Riternour, was born August 27, 1926 in Bath County, Virginia; married July 31, 1948 at Richmond, Virginia, Ileta Marian Brooks, born January 22, 1927, daughter of Ervin P. Brooks and Nellie Ward. Mrs. Cleek graduated from Mary Washington College, University of Virginia, Fredericksburg, Virginia. Mr. Cleek graduated from VPI, Blacksburg, Virginia and received a B.S. in Chemistry in 1948. He is now employed with Allied Chemical and Dye Corporation as a research chemist. He is listed in American Men of Science. He served as Electronics Technician 3rd Class, U.S. Navy, in World War II. He is a member of Phi Lambda Upsilon. He is an elder of the Presbyterian Church at Hopewell, Virginia.

Children: 2

779. i. Sara Ann Cleek (8), born June 3, 1949 at Hopewell, Virginia.
780. ii. George Ervin Cleek (8), born October 3, 1950 at Hopewell, Virginia.

582. Charles Revercomb McCormick (7), son of Charles Hunter McCormick and Mary Emma Revercomb (6), was born in 1907; married

Elsie Shinaberry. He has been a member of the Board of Supervisors of Bath County, Virginia from the Williamsville District since 1956.

Children: 1

781. i.   Charles David McCormick (8).

587. Raymond Thomas (8), son of Newton Thomas (7) and Teresa Page, married Irene Griffith.

Children: 1

782. i.   Newton Thomas (9).

589. Harper Thomas (8), son of Gordon Ellsworth Thomas (7) and Virginia Josephine Gibson (7), married Anna Armentrout.

Children: 1

+   783. i.   Tappan Thomas (9).

592. Hycie Thomas (8), daughter of Gordon Ellsworth Thomas (7), and Virginia Josephine Gibson (7), married George Callison.

Children: 2

784. i.   Joe Cameron Callison (9), married Alfred Dilley.
785. ii.   Harper Thomas Callison (9).

596. Paralee Thomas (8), daughter of Gordon Ellsworth Thomas (7) and Virginia Josephine Gibson (7), married Ralph Pace, died April 19, 1954.

Children: 2

786. i.   Alice Pace (9), married Ben Jones.
+   787. ii.   Nancy Pace (9).

604. Homer Thomas (8), son of Houston H. Thomas (7) and Myrtle Cleek (7), married Martina Allen.' He died in 1949.

Children: 2

788. i.   Julian Thomas (9).
789. ii.   Anita Thomas (9).

605. Allene Thomas (8), daughter of Houston H. Thomas (7) and Myrtle Cleek (7), married T. F. Hoffman in Texas.

Children: 1

790. i.   Theodore Hoffman (9).

606. Hugh Thomas (8), son of Houston H. Thomas (7) and Myrtle Cleek (7), married Virgie Hanger.

Children: 5

791.	i.	Hugh Thomas (9), married Evelyn Fultz.
792.	ii.	Mary Lee Thomas (9), married Ray Landes.
793.	iii.	James Harper Thomas (9).
794.	iv.	Ray Thomas (9), a twin to Jay.
795.	v.	Jay Thomas (9), a twin to Ray.

613. Veva Lantz (8), daughter of Joe H. Lantz and Ella B. Cleek (7), married William E. Puffenbarger.

Children: 10

796.	i.	Hubert Puffenbarger (9), married Geraldine Dean.
797.	ii.	Mildred Puffenbarger (9), married William Swab.
798.	iii.	Anna Grace Puffenbarger (9), married Jack Rase.
799.	iv.	Julian Puffenbarger (9), married Betty Anne Scott.
800.	v.	Samuel Puffenbarger (9).
801.	vi.	Caroll Puffenbarger (9).
802.	vii.	Dock Puffenbarger (9).
803.	viii.	Loraine Puffenbarger (9).
804.	ix.	Billy Puffenbarger (9).
805.	x.	Dotty Lou Puffenbarger (9), married February 1957, Summers Price Poage, Jr.

614. John Grady Moore (8), son of Frank Conrad Moore and Annie Pleasant Cleek (7), was born December 8, 1894; married (1) Leta Hill; married (2) _____.

Children: 2

| 806. | i. | Jack Pershing Moore (9), killed in World War II. |
| 807. | ii. | Virginia Moore (9). |

619. Hermit C. Cleek (8), son of Walter L. Cleek (7) and Dovie Wiley, married May Jones.

Children: 1

| 808. | i. | Shirley Cleek (9), born November 1924. |

620. Virginia Cleek (8), daughter of Walter L. Cleek (7) and Goola May Talley, was born August 1921; married Paul Cooper, Kansas City, Missouri.

Children: 1

| 809. | i. | Mike Cooper (9). |

621. Elizabeth Cleek (8), daughter of Walter L. Cleek (7)

and Goola May Talley, was born September 1924; married Kenneth Schermer.

Children: 1

810.   i.   Shirley Schermer (9).

623.   Edward Vaughn Cleek (8), son of Charles Massey Byrd Cleek (7) and Anna Van DeVeer, married Lola Steadman.

Children: 3

811.   i.   Romona Cleek (9), born 1934.
812.   ii.   Judy Cleek (9), born 1936.
813.   iii.   Dennis Cleek (9), born June 1, 1938.

646.   Alma Ruth Pullin (8), daughter of Ralph M. Pullin and Charlotte Ruth Simpson (7), married July 30, 1949, Byron Haines.

Children: 3

814.   i.   Mary Ruth Haines (9).
815.   ii.   Larry Montgomery Haines (9).
816.   iii.   Blaine William Haines (9).

653.   Julia Ruth Chedester (8), daughter of Avery Chedester and Grace Estelle Simpson (7), married James Twigg.

Children: 2

817.   i.   Sally Lou Twigg. (9).
818.   ii.   Carol Raye Twigg (9).

689.   Palmer Ann Newton (8), daughter of A. W. Newton and Dorothy Mae Williams (7), married William T. Cochran.

Children: 3

819.   i.   William T. Cochran, Jr. (9).
820.   ii.   Arthur Wilford Cochran (9).
821.   iii.   Sharon Lee Cochran (9).

691.   Emil Gilliland (8), son of Sheppe Gilliland and Vivian Sievers Vance (7), married Mattie Pullin.

Children: 3

822.   i.   Vivian Gilliland (9). She is a R.N.
823.   ii.   Emil Gilliland, Jr. (9), called Jack.
824.   iii.   Rosemary Gilliland (9).

692.   Carrie Gilliland (8), daughter of Sheppe Gilliland and Vivian Sievers Vance (7), married Lawrence Curtis.

Children: 4

825. i. Elsie Curtis (9).
826. ii. Mary Curtis (9).
827. iii. Louise Curtis (9).
828. iv. Earl Curtis (9).

703. Julian Craig (Buddy) Hiner (8), son of Cecil Hiner and Lillie Grace Cleek (7), was born October 10, 1912; married Nellie Maria Renick, born March 9, 1912. She is a R.N.

Children: 2

829. i. Helen Craig Hiner (9), born January 4, 1941.
830. ii. Dorothy Ann Hiner (9), born July 13, 1943.

704. Audrey Mabel Cleek (8), daughter of William Chapman Cleek (7) and Annie May Cleek (6), was born February 1, 1919; married April 11, 1936 in Pocahontas County, West Virginia, Dale Loury.

Children: 4

831. i. Phylis Sue Loury (9), born September 1, 1938; married _____ Johnson.
832. ii. Judith Ann Loury (9), born 1936.
833. iii. David Dale Loury (9), born 1943.
834. iv. Sandra Lynn Loury (9), born September 13, 1956.

705. Ward Chapman Cleek (8), son of William Chapman Cleek (7) and Annie May Cleek (6), was born August 20, 1922; married Rachel Curry.

Children: 1

835. i. Ronald Paul Cleek (9), born 1944.

706. Ruth Hannah (8), daughter of Fred G. Hannah and Jane Cleek (7), married (1) Kearney Moore; married (2) Dr. Charles Martin.

Children: 1 - second marriage

836. i. Charles Martin, Jr. (9).

707. Louis Taylor (8), son of Russell Beard Taylor and Edna Mayse (7), married Alma Merican.

Children: 2

837. i. Robert Taylor (9), U.S. Navy.
838. ii. Constance Taylor (9).

709. Lydia Taylor (8), daughter of Russell Beard Taylor and

Edna Mayse (7), married Ernest Brandt.

Children: 1

839. i.   David Brandt (9).

714. Elva Smith (8), daughter of Elliot Hopkins Smith (7) and Lillie Carpenter, married Decater (Dick) Keyser.

Children: 2

+ 840. i.   Betty Keyser (9).
+ 841. ii.   June Keyser (9).

715. Wilbert Smith (8), son of Elliot Hopkins Smith (7) and Lillie Carpenter, married Kitty McClosky.

Children: 1

842. i.   Dianna Smith (9).

717. Eugene   Hoover (8), son of Henry Pole Hoover and Stella Lee Smith (7), was born February 21, 1909; married Minnie Moock.

Children: 3

843. i.   Billy Hoover (9).
844. ii.   Brenda Hoover (9).
845. iii. Darlene Hoover (9).

718. Melvin Hoover (8), son of Henry Pole Hoover and Stella Lee Smith (7), was born February 25, 1911; married (1) Sara Grey; married (2) Faye Webb.

Children: 1 - second marriage

846. i.   Sidney Hector Hoover (9), died in infancy.

719. Victor Dow Hoover (0), son of Henry Pole Hoover and Stella Lee Smith (7), was born April 20, 1920; married (1) Mae Lester; married (2) Phyllis Altizer.

Children: 1- first marriage

847. i.   Infant son, died.

Children: 1 - second marriage

848. ii.   Hazel Ann Hoover (9).

720. Robert June Hoover (8), son of Henry Pole Hoover and Stella Lee Smith (7), was born June 23, 1922; married (1) Viola Cogsdale; married (2) Helen McElwee.

Children: 1 - second marriage

849. i.   Jeffrey Hoover (9).

721. Jesse Smith (8), son of Joseph Tucker Smith (7) and
Fannie Donovan, married _____.

Children: 2

850. i.   Barry Smith (9).
851. ii.   Jimmy Smith (9).

722. Nelson Blair Carpenter (8), son of Russell Carpenter
and Flora Richardson Smith (7), married Marie Flint.

Children: 2

852. i.   Nelson Blair Carpenter, Jr. (9).
853. ii.   Eleanor Ann Carpenter (9).

724. Osborn Campbell (8), son of William O. Campbell and
Carol Independence Smith (7), married Mary Miller.

Children: 2

854. i.   Gary Campbell (9).
855. ii.   Dennis Campbell (9).

726. Clyde Bonner LaRue (8), son of Clyde Hall LaRue (7)
and Cornelia McGuffin Bonner, married Margaret Hubbard Hansel,
born April 30, 1908.

Children: 1

856. i.   Clyde Bonner LaRue, Jr. (9).

727. Virginia LaRue (8), daughter of Harry Brooks LaRue
(7) and Blanche Gum, married William Russell Croson.

Children: 2

857. i.   Juinita Croson (9), married Harvey Dudley.
858. ii.   Helen Jean Croson (9).

729. Helen Erma Ricks (8), daughter of Walter Ricks and
Lillie Cleek LaRue (7), married (1) Jack Fanning; married (2)
Frank Lagodica; married (3) Charles H. Whittaker. No children
second marriage.

Children: 1 - first marriage

859. i.   Patricia Ann Fanning (9).

Children: 1 - third marriage

860. ii. Virginia Marie Whittaker (9).

731. Betty Lee Ricks (8), daughter of Walter Ricks and Lillie Cleek LaRue (7), married Charles E. Holloway.

Children: 1

861. i. Betty Sue Holloway (9).

732. Anne Ricks (8), daughter of Walter Ricks and Lillie Cleek LaRue (7), married (1) Thomas J. Robinson; married (2) Robert M. North.

Children: 1 - second marriage

862. i. Robert Walter North (9).

738. Ruth Cleek Cauley (8), daughter of Restie Nickell Cauley (7)and Lucy May Samples, was born April 7, 1930; married Raymond Bussard.

Children: 2

863. i.   Carrie Ann Bussard (9).
864. ii. Christy Ruth Bussard (9).

739. Restie Nickell Cauley, Jr. (8), son of Restie Nickell Cauley (7) and Lucy May Samples, was born December 7, 1931; married Stella Lunsford.

Children: 1

865. i. Laura Ann Cauley (9).

767. Owen Heywood McHone (8), son of Albert McHone and Gladys Adelaide Cleek (7), was born November 3, 1934; married January 4, 1954, Beverley Derrer. He served in the Army after World War II.

Children: 1

866. i. Ginger McHone (9).

771. Constance Lee Thompson (8), daughter of John Lee Thompson and Constance Virginia Cleek (7), was born July 29,1927; married October 9, 1954, William Smith Peebles, III. She graduated from Madison College, Harrisonburg, Virginia and from the School of Nursing, Medical College of Virginia, Richmond, Virginia.

Children: 2

867. i.   William Smith Peebles, IV (9), born August 14, 1955.
868. ii. Constance Palmer Peebles (9), born November 21, 1956.

93

772. Carol Marie Thompson (8), daughter of John Lee Thompson and Constance Virginia Cleek (7), was born November 15, 1928; married October 18, 1952, Dr. Charles F. Wingo, a graduate of the Medical College of Virginia at Richmond. She graduated from Madison College, Harrisonburg, Virginia and from the School of Nursing, Medical College of Virginia, Richmond, Virginia.

Children: 1

869. i. Carol Lockridge Wingo (9), born April 20,1956.

783. Tappan Thomas (9), son of Harper Thomas (8) and Anna Armentrout, married Sue Ann McElwee.

Children: 2

870. i. Anna Sue Thomas (10).
871. ii. Carla Thomas (10).

787. Nancy Pace (9), daughter of Ralph Pace and Paralee Thomas (8), married _____ Richmond.

Children: 1

872. i. Mike Richmond (10).

840. Betty Keyser (9), daughter of Decater (Dick) Keyser and Elva Smith (8), married Hugh Stanley.

Children: 2

873. i. Hal Stanley (10).
874. ii. Donna Jean Stanley (10).

841. June Keyser (9), daughter of Decater (Dick) Keyser and Elva Smith (8), married Walter Fails.

Children: 1

875. i. Rebeckia Fails (10).

PART II

GWIN FAMILY

The Gwin Family is of ancient Welsh origin, and the name in Welsh means "white" or "candid." The Gwin coat-of-arms bears the legend, "vim vi pellere licet" --"It is permissible to oppose force with force." The name Gwin is found in records as Guinne, Guin, Guinn, Gwinn, Gwinne, Gwyn, Gwynn, and even Gowan. This name has often been confused with the name of Given, sometimes spelled Givin.

Different emigrants bearing this name appeared at various times in early Virginia. We are concerned with the descendants of the emigrant bearing the name of Robert Gwin.

1. Robert Gwin (1), the progenitor of this branch of the Gwin Family, came to Virginia before 1744. He was born in Orange County, Wales. In 1746 he was appointed Constable at the head of the Great Calfpasture River in Augusta County, Virginia. (Abstracts from the Records of Augusta County, Virginia, Lyman Chalkley, Vol. I, page 18.) He was allowed a certificate for land as a result of military services, which shows he participated in the early Colonial Wars in Captain Wm. Preston's Company of Rangers, 1758. (Ibid., Vol. I, page 212.) In 1744, he bought 544 acres of land lying on both sides of the Calfpasture River from James Patton and John Lewis. In 1762, for five shillings, he deeded to his son, Robert Gwin, Jr., 241 acres of land. Robert Gwin married Jean (or Jane) Kincaid, daughter of David Kincaid and Winnifred _____ of Albemarle County, Virginia.

The Kincaid (also found as Kinkead) family is of the Scottish Clan. David Kincaid, brother of the then Laird, took part in the unsuccessful Stuart Rebellion in 1715, and was in consequence forced to leave Scotland. He came to Spotsylvania County, Virginia, where he took up land with George Robinson; later moved to Albemarle County, thence to Augusta County; and finally died in Bath County. He arrived in America shortly after 1715, and was an early settler in Orange County, Virginia and reared a large family. He built the first Augusta County jail. Among his children were Jean (or Jane) Kincaid who married Robert Gwin, and Isabella Kincaid who married James Lockridge.

Four nephews of David Kincaid, sons of his brother, Alexander Kincaid, came to America in 1746 and first settled in Augusta County, Virginia. They were Samuel Kincaid, died c. 1780; George Kincaid, killed by the Indians in 1756; Robert Kincaid; and James Kincaid, who migrated south. There were two other Kincaid families that came to Augusta County, Virginia from Pennsylvania at an early date. One of these families was that of Thomas Kincaid, who came from Ireland to Pennsylvania and then to Augusta County, Virginia. The other family was that of John Kincaid. All of these Kincaids left a large number of descendants.

The Kincaid Family is very difficult to trace due to the
similarity of given names and the fact that the families often
intermarried. (Dr. Herbert Clarke Kincaid, member of the
National Genealogical Society, Washington, D. C.)

Robert Gwin (1) had three brothers: John Gwin whose wife's
name was Alice _____; William Gwin; and Patrick Gwin whose
wife's name was Janet _____. (Abstracts from the Records of
Augusta County, Virginia, Lyman Chalkley, Vol. III, pages 526
and 533.)

Children: 9

+   2.   i.   Joseph Gwin (2).
    3.   ii. Robert Gwin, Jr. (2), married Sally Lockridge,
daughter of Samuel Lockridge and Elizabeth _____. (Ibid.,
Vol. I, page 536.) They migrated to Kentucky. (See Lockridge
Family).
+   4.   iii. David Gwin (2), born 1742.
    5.   iv. Thomas Gwin (2), married April 8, 1800, Eliza-
beth Lockridge, daughter of Samuel Lockridge and Elizabeth _____.
They migrated to Kentucky. (Ibid., Vol. I, page 536 and Vol. II,
page 339). (See Lockridge Family).
    6.   v.   Simon Gwin (2), married Elizabeth (Lockridge)
Gay, daughter of Andrew Lockridge and Jean Graham, and widow of
Robert Gay. (See Lockridge Family).
+   7.   vi. James Gwin (2).
+   8.   vii. Samuel Gwin (2).
    9.   viii. Agnes Gwin (2), married William Lockridge. (See
Lockridge Family).
    10. ix. Nell Gwin (2).

    2. Joseph Gwin (2), son of Robert Gwin (1) and Jean (or
Jane) Kincaid; died 1817 in Bath County, Virginia; married Mary
Jane Kincaid. They lived in Highland and Bath Counties, Virginia.
He served as First Lieutenant in Captain Hicklin's Company in the
Revolution. (Ibid., Vol. II, pages 496 and 497). His will was
dated August 17, 1817 and recorded October 1817 in Will Book 2,
page 156, Bath County, Virginia. It mentions wife, Mary Gwin;
sons, John, Moses, Robert, Wm. Kinkead, and Joseph Gwin; grand-.
daughters, Sarah, Elizabeth, Mary, Margaret, and Jean Stuart;.
daughter, Elizabeth and Andrew Kinkead. Executors - Joseph,
John, and Moses Gwin. Witnesses were Charles Erwin, James
Stewart, and James Stewart, Jr.

    Children: 9

    11. i.   John Gwin (3), married Mary (Pickens) Callahan,
widow of William Callahan.
    12. ii. Joseph Gwin (3).
+   13. iii. Moses Gwin (3).
+   14. iv. Mary Elizabeth Gwin (3).
+   15. v.   William Kinkead Gwin (3).
    16. vi. Robert Gwin (3).

17.   vii.   Elizabeth Gwin (3), married January 7, 1812 in Bath County, Virginia, Andrew Kincaid, son of Thomas Kincaid and Isabell (nee) Kincaid.
18.   viii.   Jane Gwin (3), married December 15, 1795, John Law. (Ibid., Vol. II, page 318).
19.   ix.   Virginia Gwin (3), married William Stuart.

4.   David Gwin (2), son of Robert Gwin (1) and Jean (or Jane) Kincaid, was born in 1742 in Orange County, Wales; died in 1822 at Clover Creek, Highland County, Virginia; married (1) in 1768, Jane Carlile, born November 26, 1746; died 1787 and was buried on Jackson River, Bath County (now Highland County), Virginia, daughter of James Carlile, Jr. and Rachel Campbell; married (2) November 11, 1790, Viola (or Violet) Crawford, buried at Clover Creek, Highland County, Virginia, daughter of William Crawford and Margaret Henderson of Dry Branch of Jackson River near Mustoe, Highland County, Virginia. (Ibid., Vol. II, page 288 gives marriage bond for his second marriage). (See Carlile and Crawford Families).

Augusta County records show that David Gwin purchased the farm of John Peoples, Sr. from his two sons, John and Thomas Peoples in 1805. John and Thomas Peoples moved to Kentucky and Missouri respectively. This land was originally patented by Captain Wallace Estill in 1746 and John Peoples, Sr. purchased it in 1772 from Captain Wallace Estill.

David Gwin served as Lieutenant and Captain in the Revolutionary War. He commanded a company at the battle of Guilford Court House. (Ibid., Vol. I, pages 199 and 204; Vol. II, pages 494 and 495; A History of Highland County, Oren F. Morton, pages 193 and 222; Annals of Bath County, Virginia, Oren F. Morton, pages 95 and 96; Virginia Militia in the Revolutionary War, J. T. McAllister, Sections 33, 58, 76, 92, and 253; Annals of Augusta County, Virginia, Jos. A. Waddell, page 281; and Historical Register of Virginians in the Revolution, John H. Gwathmey, page 334). The South Branch Valley Chapter of the Virginia Daughters of the American Revolution placed a memorial marker over his grave, together with a government marker on August 14, 1936. The government marker was secured through the efforts of Geo. W. Cleek, Staunton, Virginia, a descendant of Captain David Gwin.

David Gwin amassed a sizeable fortune which he disposed of in his will dated April 18, 1820 and recorded in Will Book 2, page 416 on January 1822 in Bath County, Virginia. The will reads as follows:

In the name of God, Amen:
I, David Gwin, of the county of Bath, State of Virginia, being advanced in years but of sound mind and disposing memory and calling to mind the uncertainty of human life and the numerous inconveniences which might arise from my dying intestate have thought proper to make this my last will and testament hereby revoking and annulling all former wills by me made:

97

In Primus: I direct my executors hereinafter named as soon as may be after my decease, to pay my funeral expenses and all my just debts. Item: I give and bequeath to my son David Gwin all the lands I purchased of John and Thos. Peoples whereon I now live including the mountain tract to him and his heirs forever, but as my death may happen before my said son David Gwin arrives at lawful age, in case of such an event, it is my will and desire that the property before devised be managed by my executors or rented out at their discretion until my said son arrives at full age and the proceeds thereof be applied at their discretion to the support and maintenance of such of my daughters as may then be unmarried and the maintenance and education of my said son David Gwin and his heirs forever one thousand pounds in money which I hereby direct my executors to pay over to him when he shall arrive at the age of twenty one years. I also give and bequeath to my son David Gwin and his heirs forever my rifle gun, my desk and bookcase, my four tables, all my chairs, my bed and furniture and three chests, all which property I direct my Executors to have good care taken of and delivered over to my said son on his arriving at age aforesaid.

Item: I give and bequeath to my grandson David Gwin Kincaid, son of Thos. Kincaid the lands allotted to him by Adam Lightner, James Campbell lying on the waters of Jackson's River in the County of Bath, being the same land whereon the said Thomas Kincaid now lives to him and his heirs forever, but it is my will and desire that the said Thomas Kincaid and his wife Sally and the longest liver of them shall have the right and privelege to live on and enjoy the whole of land during their natural lives upon condition they continue to reside on the same, but if they should, at any time, remove from said land then the benefits intended them by this devise shall cease and terminate and from the date of such removal the rents and profits and the right to use and occupy the land aforesaid shall rest in my grandson David Gwin Kincaid.

Item: I give and bequeath to my son Robert Gwin and his present wife, Polly Gwin, and the longest liver of them the right during their natural lives to live on and enjoy the lands on Jackson's River allotted them for their son David by Adam Lightner and James Campbell and after the death of the longest liver of the said Robert and wife, I give and bequeath the said land to David Gwin, my Grandson (and son of Robt. and Polly Gwin) to him, his heirs and assigns forever.

Item: I give and bequeath to my son John Gwin and his present wife and the longest liver of them, the right to live on and enjoy the lands allotted them for their son David by Adam Lightner and James Campbell on Jackson's River and after the death of the longest liver of the said John and wife, I give and bequeath the said land to my grandson David Gwin (son of the said John) to him and his heirs and assigns forever.

Item: I give and bequeath to my said Grandsons David Gwin Kincaid, David Gwin (son of Robert) and David Gwin (son of John) all my lands in the Big and Little Valleys on the waters of Wilson's Mill Run in the County of Bath to be equally divided

98

between them, to them their heirs and assigns forever.

Item: I give and bequeath to my daughter Isabell and her heirs forever, one negro girl named Agnes and her future increase.

Item: I give and bequeath to my daughter Margaret and her heirs forever one negro girl named Betsy and her future increase.

Item: I give and bequeath to my daughter Rachel and her heirs forever one negro girl named Jane and her future increase.

Item: I give and bequeath to my daughter Susan and her heirs forever one negro girl named Violet and her future increase.

Item: I give and bequeath to my son-in-law Robert Lockridge and Polly his wife and their heirs forever Two dollars to be paid them by my executors in full for their portion of my estate.

Item: I give and bequeath to my son James Gwin, one hundred pounds in money to him and his heirs forever to be paid him by my Executors soon after my decease.

Item: To my sons Robert Gwin and John Gwin, I give and bequeath the sum of two dollars cash to them and their heirs forever. To Thos. Kincaid and Sally his wife the sum of two dollars. To Jas. Wiley and Nancy his wife two dollars. To John Cleek and Jane his wife the sum of two dollars and to Samuel Givens and Elizabeth his wife the sum of two dollars which said legacies I hereby direct my Executors to pay as soon as may be after my decease, it is my will and desire that my Executors herein after named soon after my decease take into possession of the slaves Isaac and Fown which I loaned to Robt. Gwin, a negro named Ned I loaned to Thos. Kincaid and a negro woman named Daffney I loaned to John Cleek which said several slaves were loaned to be returned whenever demanded.

Item: I give and bequeath to my daughter Rachel one feather bed and furniture also sum of sixty pounds in money to her and her heirs forever.

Item: I give and bequeath to my daughter Susan one feather bed and furniture also the sum of sixty pounds in money to her and her heirs forever.

Item: It is my will and desire that my Executors as soon as they shall have paid my funeral expenses and just debts and satisfy all the legacies hereinbefore named do proceed to ascertain the amount of all the residue of my estate of every kind whatsoever including my slaves not hereinbefore devised, my debts, money, stock, etc., which residue when so ascertained I desire shall be divided into seven equal parts. One-seventh thereof I give and bequeath to my daughter Isabella her heirs and assigns forever. I give and bequeath one-seventh part thereof to my daughter Margaret her heirs and assigns forever. Same to my daughter Rachel her heirs and assigns forever. Same to my daughter Susan her heirs and assigns forever. One-seventh part to be equally divided among the children of my daughter Elizabeth Givens and to be paid over to them by my executors as they come of age resp. but it is my wish and meaning that out of this seventh part shall be deducted the amount of Bonds due and owing to me from Samuel Givens the husband of my said daughter Elizabeth. I give and bequeath one-seventh part thereof to be equally divided among the children of my daughter Jane Cleek and to be paid over to them by my Executors as they come of age resp. and the remaining one-seventh of said residue I give and bequeath to the children of my daughter Nancy Wiley by her husband Jas. Wiley to be equally divided between them, to them and their heirs forever and to be paid over to them by my executors as they respectively become of age.

Item: It is my will and desire that if any of my sons or daughters, sons-in-law or daughters-in-law, or any of my grandchildren shall be dissatisfied with the disposition I have made herein of my property and shall attempt to set aside this writing as my true last will and testament, they shall be excluded from all benefit of any portion of my estate whatever and every devise herein made to such person in such case shall be null and void.

Lastly, I appoint Wm. Hogshead, my son-in-law, my son Jas. Gwin and my friend, Otho Wade Executors of this my last will and testament, hereby repeating the same to be such and renouncing and revoking all former wills by me made.

In testimony whereof I have hereunto subscribed my name and affixed my seal this 18th day of April 1820 and have caused the same to be witnessed in my presence.

His
David   T Gwin (SEAL)
mark

The above writing was signed, sealed, and declared to be the last will and testament of David Gwin in our presence by him and at his request and in his presence we subscribed the same as witnesses.

John Steuart
James Hicklin
John Carlile
Martin Coyner

Children: 9 - first marriage

20. i.   John Gwin (3), born April 13, 1769; died in infancy.
+ 21. ii.   Nancy Gwin (3), born August 18, 1770.
+ 22. iii. James Gwin (3), born June 27, 1774.
+ 23. iv.   Mary Gwin (3), born March 8, 1776.
+ 24. v.   Elizabeth Gwin (3), born April 8, 1778.
  25. vi.   Jane Gwin (3), born July 1, 1780 in Bath County, (now Highland County), Virginia; died October 16, 1856 at Cleek's Mill, Bath County, Virginia; married in 1800 in Bath County, Virginia, John Cleek, born 1777 in Rockbridge County, Virginia; died April 16, 1848 at Cleek's Mill, Bath County, Virginia, son of Jacob Cleek and Christina Croddy. (See Cleek Family).
+ 26. vii. Sarah Gwin (3), born July 10, 1782.
+ 27. viii. Robert Gwin (3), born March 10, 1785.
+ 28. ix.   John Gwin (3), born 1787.

Children: 5 - second marriage

+ 29. x.   Isabella Gwin (3).
+ 30. xi.   Margaret (Peggy) Gwin (3), born 1800.

+ 31. xii. Susan Henderson Gwin (3), born March 11, 1806.
+ 32. xiii. Rachel Viola Gwin (3), born December 21, 1802.
+ 33. xiv. David Sitlington Gwin (3), born 1809.

7. James Gwin (2), son of Robert Gwin (1) and Jean (or Jane) Kincaid, married Marca Estill, born November 4, 1749 in Augusta County, Virginia, daughter of Captain Wallace Estill (1702-1792) and his second wife, Marca Boude. They settled in Greenbrier County, Virginia (now West Virginia) near the present site of Lewisburg in 1770. (A Centennial History of Alleghany County, Virginia, Oren F. Morton, page 200; and A History of Monroe County, West Virginia, Oren F. Morton, pages 348-349).

Children: 4

  34. i. Robert Gwin (3).
  35. ii. James Gwin (3), said to be the first white child born in Monroe County, West Virginia (then Virginia) after the Clendennin Massacre.
  36. iii. Joseph Gwin (3), married in 1805, Polly Taylor.
  37. iv. Samuel Gwin (3).

8. Samuel Gwin (2), son of Robert Gwin (1) and Jean (or Jane) Kincaid, married Elizabeth (Lockridge) Graham, daughter of James Lockridge and Isabella Kincaid (a sister of Jean (or Jane) Kincaid who married Robert Gwin). Elizabeth (Lockridge) Graham was the widow of Robert Graham, who she married June 24, 1763. (See Graham and Lockridge Families). In 1776 they settled on Muddy Creek, now in Summers County, West Virginia. Samuel Gwin, although living in a frontier community, divided $12,000 in specie among his sons before his death. (Abstracts from the Records of Augusta County, Virginia, Lyman Chalkley, Vol. I, page 185; A History of Monroe County, West Virginia, Oren F. Morton, pages 348 and 349).

Children: 16

  38. i. Samuel Gwin, Jr. (3), married in 1803, Elizabeth Taylor.
  39. ii. Moses Gwin (3), married Mary Sergent.
  40. iii. Andrew Gwin (3), married Mary Newsome.
  41. iv. John Gwin (3), married Sarah George, daughter of Thomas George.
  42. v. Ephraim Gwin (3), married Rachel Keller, daughter of Conrad Keller. Conrad Keller was a soldier in the Revolution, and was the father-in-law of Peter Boyer of the Shenandoah County, Virginia.
  43. vi. Ruth Gwin (3), married in 1803, James Jarrett, son of James Jarrett. (History of Greenbrier County, J. R. Cole, page 179).
  44. vii. Elizabeth Gwin (3), married Robert Newsome.
  45. viii. Ivy Gwin (3), married Thomas Busby.
  46. ix. Jane Gwin (3), married David Withrow.
  47. x. Alexander Gwin (3), married Mary Givens.

48.   xi.   Salathiel Gwin (3), married Margaret Black,
daughter of Samuel Black and a sister-in-law of William Feamster.
49.   xii.   Robert Gwin (3), married Nancy Ellison.
50.   xiii.   Thompson Gwin (3), married in 1841, Rachel Harra.
51.   xiv.   Margaret Gwin (3), married Nathan Viney.
52.   xv.   James Gwin (3), married Jane Pyne.
53.   xvi.   Mary E. Gwin (3), married in 1845, William C.
Riner, born 1820, son of Simeon Riner and Mary Thompson.

13.   Moses Gwin (3), son of Joseph Gwin (2) and Mary Jane
Kincaid, died in 1867; married _____ Kincaid.

Children: 3

+   54.   i.   William B. Gwin (4).
+   55.   ii.   Joseph Corbett Gwin (4), born September 1802.
    56.   iii.   Margaret Gwin (4), married William R. Stuart.

14.   Mary Elizabeth Gwin (3), daughter of Joseph Gwin (2) and
Mary Jane Kincaid, married January 1, 1799 in Bath County, Virginia
Robert Lockridge, son of James Lockridge and Isabella Kincaid. (See
Lockridge Family).

Children: 1

57.   i.   Anne Lockridge (4), married (as his second wife)
James Lockridge, son of Andrew Lockridge and Jean Graham. (See
Lockridge Family).

15.   William Kinkead Gwin (3), son of Joseph Gwin (2) and
Mary Jane Kincaid, married in 1823, Jane Kincaid.

58.   i.   Rachel Gwin (4), married William B. Gwin (4), son
of Moses Gwin and _____ Kincaid.
+   59.   ii.   James Henderson Gwin (4), born November 7, 1851.

21.   Nancy Gwin (3), daughter of David Gwin (2) and Jane
Carlile, was born August 18, 1770; married (1) January 1794,
Hugh McGlaughlin, died 1807; married (2) in 1810, James Wiley,
son of Robert Wiley (died 1812) and Hester _____.

Children: 1 - first marriage

+   60.   i.   Jane McGlaughlin (4), born November 1794.

Children: 2 - second marriage

+   61.   ii.   Sarah Alexander Wiley (4), born November 14,1811.
    62.   iii.   Esther (Acie) Wiley (4), died young.

22.   James Gwin (3), son of David Gwin (2) and Jane Carlile,
was born June 27, 1774; died in 1844; married in 1799, Rachel
Stephenson, daughter of James Stephenson and Rachel Davis. He
was a soldier in the Virginia Militia in the War of 1812.

His will was dated July 19, 1844 and recorded in August 1844 in Will Book 5, page 67, Bath County, Virginia. It mentions sons, Matthew, James, John, Samuel, and David Gwin; daughters, Eliza, Anna, and Alcinda Gwin; children of deceased daughter Jane Hamilton; Davis Hamilton; and daughter Rachel Hiner. Executors were Adam Stephenson, Jr. and James B. Campbell. Witnesses were R(euben) Slaven, William Townsend, and Adam Stephenson.

Children: 10

```
     63.  i.    Matthew Gwin (4), died unmarried.
+    64.  ii.   James Gwin (4).
     65.  iii.  David Gwin (4), married in 1842, Martha E. Pray.
+    66.  iv.   Samuel Gwin (4).
+    67.  v.    John Gwin (4).
     68.  vi.   Eliza Gwin (4), died unmarried.
+    69.  vii.  Rachel Gwin (4).
     70.  viii. Anna Gwin (4), died unmarried.
     71.  ix.   Alcinda Gwin (4), married George W. Hollar of
Rockingham County, Virginia.
     72.  x.    Jane Gwin (4), married October 4, 1827 in Bath
County, Virginia, Davis Hamilton, born 1808, son of John Hamilton
and Mary McGuffin.
```

23. Mary Gwin (3), daughter of David Gwin (2) and Jane Carlile, was born March 8, 1776; married in 1798, Robert Lockridge, born 1777, died 1856, son of Andrew Lockridge and Jean Graham. (See Lockridge Family).

Children: 9

```
+    73.  i.    David Gwin Lockridge (4), born 1799.
+    74.  ii.   Andrew Lockridge (4), born September 23, 1801.
     75.  iii.  George Lockridge (4), migrated to Kentucky where
he married.
     76.  iv.   Jane Lockridge (4), married January 27, 1841 in
Bath County, Virginia (as his first wife) David Gwin (4), born
1809; died 1863 while a prisoner of war at Camp Chase, Ohio, son
of Robert Gwin and Mary Stephenson.
     77.  v.    John Lockridge (4), died unmarried in Kentucky.
+    78.  vi.   Robert Lockridge (4), born September 14, 1809.
+    79.  vii.  William Lockridge (4), born 1811.
+    80.  viii. Mary (Polly) Graham Lockridge (4), born 1816.
     81.  ix.   Elizabeth (Betsy) Lockridge (4), died unmarried
at an advanced age.
```

24. Elizabeth Gwin (3), daughter of David Gwin (2) and Jane Carlile, was born April 8, 1778; died October 31, 1864 near Moberly, Randolph County, Missouri; married in 1801 at Warm Springs, Bath County, Virginia, Samuel Givens, born October 3, 1776 at Warm Springs, Virginia; died June 10, 1851 at Middle Grove, Monroe County, Missouri, son of William Givens and Agnes Bratton. (See Givens Family).

103

Children: 6

82.	i.	William Givens (4), born 1803; married Susan
83.	ii.	Robert Givens (4), married Mary Blaker.
84.	iii.	David Gwin Givens (4).
85.	iv.	Polly Givens (4), married John Irons from

Scotland.

86.	v.	Martha Givens (4), died at age 18.
+ 87.	vi.	Nancy Elizabeth Givens (4), born December 2,

1818.

26. Sarah Gwin (3), daughter of David Gwin (2) and Jane Carlile, was born July 10, 1782; married Thomas Kincaid, son of Thomas Kincaid and Isabell (nee) Kincaid.

Children: 4

88.	i.	Mary (Polly) Kincaid (4), married Alexander Terry.
89.	ii.	Margaret Kincaid (4), died unmarried.
90.	iii.	Nancy Kincaid (4), died unmarried.
+ 91.	iv.	David Gwin Kincaid (4).

27. Robert Gwin (3), son of David Gwin (2) and Jane Carlile, was born March 10, 1785; died in 1869; married in 1805, Mary Stephenson, born 1787, daughter of James Stephenson and Rachel Davis. He served as Corporal in Jones' Company, 59th Virginia Militia in the War of 1812.

Children: 12

+ 92.	i.	Jane Gwin (4).
+ 93.	ii.	David Gwin (4), born 1809.
+ 94.	iii.	Cynthia Gwin (4).
+ 95.	iv.	James Stephenson Gwin (4).
+ 96.	v.	Esther R. (Hettie) Gwin (4).
97.	vi.	Emmeline M. Gwin (4), born February 14, 1818;

died April 1, 1900; married October 24, 1839 in Bath County, Virginia (as his second wife) Robert Lockridge (4), born September 14, 1809; died March 28, 1891, son of Robert Lockridge and Mary Gwin.

+ 98.	vii.	Amanda Gwin (4).
99.	viii.	Robert S. Gwin (4), born 1829; died August 11,

1859.

100.	ix.	Caroline Gwin (4), died with diphtheria.
101.	x.	Mary A. Gwin (4), died with diphtheria.
+ 102.	xi.	Houston F. Gwin (4).
+ 103.	xii.	Moses Gwin (4), born 1832.

28. John Gwin (3), son of David Gwin (2) and Jane Carlile, was born in 1787; died in 1873; married in 1809 (1) Margaret Bradshaw, born November 20, 1785; died April 1, 1838, daughter of John Bradshaw (born 1758; died January 6, 1835) and Isabella

McKamie; married (2) Lydia Gum, daughter of Isaac Gum (born 1802; died 1891) and Mary Ruckman (married in 1825).

Children: 6 - first marriage

+ 104. i.   John Wesley Gwin (4), born July 22, 1816.
+ 105. ii.   David Gwin (4), born November 23, 1818.
  106. iii. Jane Gwin (4), married George Starr, son of Jere Starr, and they migrated to Illinois.
  107. iv.   Elizabeth A. Gwin (4), married September 4, 1834 in Bath County, Virginia, Mustoe Bratton Givens, born December 10, 1814, son of Henry Givens and Nancy McGuffin Mustoe. They migrated to Illinois. (See Givens Family).
+ 108. v.   Nancy Gwin (4).
  109. vi.   Luella Susan Gwin (4), married in 1871, William Kincaid, son of William Kincaid and Rebecca Lockridge. (See Lockridge Family).

Children: 3 - second marriage

  110. vii. James K. Polk Gwin (4), died in a prairie fire in Illinois.
  111. viii. Caleb Gwin (4), died in a prairie fire in Illinois.
  112. ix.   Eleanor (Nellie) Gwin (4), married (1) _____ Blume; married (2) _____ Coleman of Chicago, Illinois. No children.

29. Isabella Gwin (3), daughter of David Gwin (2) and Viola Crawford, married Captain William Hogshead. She was named for a girl Captain David Gwin took from the Indians on the Muskinghum River, and who afterward married a McDowell of Kentucky and lived in Nashville, Tennessee. Her granddaughter married Hon. John S. Wise of Virginia and New York City.

Children: 10

  113. i.   David Gwin Hogshead (4), died unmarried.
  114. ii.   Robert Hogshead (4), migrated to Missouri.
  115. iii. James Hogshead (4), married _____ Price and lived in New Market, Virginia.
  116. iv.   Henry Hogshead (4), married _____ Blackburn and lived in Staunton, Virginia.
  117. v.   William Hogshead (4), died in California; married _____. He was a physician. No children.
  118. vi.   Sarah Hogshead (4), married _____ Blakemore.
  119. vii. Susan Hogshead (4), married _____ Ruebush.
  120. viii. Mary Jane Hogshead (4), married James Davis.
  121. ix.   Walter Hogshead (4), drowned in the South Branch of the Potomac River; married _____ Dudley.
  122. x.   Martha Hogshead (4), married Henry Sieg and lived in Churchville, Virginia.

30. Margaret (Peggy) Gwin (3), daughter of David Gwin (2) and Viola Crawford, was born in 1800; died in 1847 in Ross County, Ohio; married August 1818 in Bath County, Virginia (as his first wife) Robert Coyner, born in 1794 in Augusta County, Virginia; died July 1874, son of Martin Luther Coyner and Elizabeth Rhea. They moved about 1836 from Augusta County, Virginia to Ross County, Ohio, and settled in Buckskin Township, near the village of Lyndon, South Salem. The farm first purchased was near Waugh's, a small country church, and in 1848 he moved to the farm he purchased just out of the village of Lyndon, spending the remainder of his life there. Robert Coyner, popularly known as "Judge" or "Squire" was a judge in Ross County. He was buried in the Presbyterian Churchyard at South Salem, and his three wives were buried there too. After the death of his first wife, he married (2) in 1849, Martha Edmiston; and married (3) Frances Wallace. He was a staunch member of the Presbyterian Church at Pisgah and later South Salem, and he held offices in both churches. (A Historical Sketch of Michael Keinadt and Margaret Diller, - Koiner-Kyner-Coiner-Coyner, Michael Koiner Memorial Association, 1893 with 1941 supplement, pages 113-115).

Children: 6 - first marriage

123.	i.	Sarah Coyner (4), died young.
124.	ii.	(Infant) Coyner (4), died young.
+ 125.	iii.	Elizabeth Susan Coyner (4), born August 1, 1822.
+ 126.	iv.	David Silas Coyner (4), born 1825.
+ 127.	v.	John McCutcheon Coyner (4), born 1826.
+ 128.	vi.	Robert Crawford Coyner (4), born July 18, 1838.

31. Susan Henderson Gwin (3), daughter of David Gwin (2) and Viola Crawford, was born March 11, 1806; died February 17, 1853; married October 24, 1824, Captain Silas Hinton, born September 16, 1792; died April 21, 1852, son of Benjamin Hinton and Sarah Hopkins. They lived at Mt. Meridan, Virginia. They are buried at Augusta Stone Church, Fort Defiance, Virginia, as are all their children except Robert. Silas Hinton served in Captain Daniel Mathews' Company, 116th Regiment, Virginia Volunteers, in the War of 1812. (A History of Rockingham County, Virginia, John W. Wayland, page 450).

Children: 9

129. i.   Sarah M. Hinton (4), born September 18, 1825; died December 26, 1850, unmarried.
+   130. ii.   Rachel Adelaide Hinton (4), born February 17, 1827.
131. iii.   Susan J. Hinton (4), born October 1, 1828; died March 4, 1849, unmarried.
132. iv.   D. Benjamin Hinton (4), born November 23, 1830 at Mt. Meridan, Virginia; died April 25, 1902; married January 1860, Elizabeth Lewis Wilson, daughter of Thomas P. Wilson and Hannah Miller.

133. v. William S. Hinton (4), born November 26, 1832; died May 26, 1856, unmarried.
134. vi. Robert Alexander Hinton (4), born December 24, 1834; died March 22, 1894; married July 25, 1860, Martha Hannah McCulloch, daughter of Dr. George McCulloch and Nancy Crawford Miller.
135. vii. Hannah F. Hinton (4), born June 16, 1837; died June 2, 1853.
136. viii. Elizabeth V. Hinton (4), born September 26, 1841; died February 9, 1866; married William Davis, M.D. No children.

32. Rachel Viola Gwin (3), daughter of David Gwin (2) and Viola Crawford, was born December 21, 1802; died February 15, 1847; married in 1821, William McClung, born April 17, 1793; died November 8, 1865, son of John (Bath John) McClung and Sarah McCutcheon. William McClung bought the Peoples Farm at Clover Creek, Virginia from his brother-in-law, David Sitlington Gwin. (The McClung Genealogy, Rev. William McClung, 1904, pages 189-192).

Children: 12

+ 137. i. John Henderson McClung (4), born June 12, 1822.
+ 138. ii. David Gwin McClung (4), born February 16, 1824.
  139. iii. William Alexander McClung (4), born 1826; died 1847, unmarried.
  140. iv. Sarah Susan McClung (4), born 1828; died 1842, unmarried.
  141. v. Andrew Crawford McClung (4), born 1830; died 1847, unmarried.
+ 142. vi. Silas Brown McClung (4), born October 5, 1832.
  143. vii. Robert T. McClung (4), born 1834; died 1840.
+ 144. viii. Frances Violet McClung (4), born March 13, 1836.
+ 145. ix. Mary Margaret McClung (4), born January 28,1838.
  146. x. Susan Agnes McClung (4), born 1840.
  147. xi. Samuel A. McClung (4), died young.
+ 148. xii. Louis Martin McClung (4), born June 1, 1846.

33. David Sitlington Gwin (3), son of David Gwin (2) and Viola Crawford, was born in 1809; died in Baltimore, Maryland and was buried at Alexandria, Virginia. He was the only child born on the Peoples Farm on the Bullpasture River. He married Frances T. Beckham of Clover Farms on the Rapidan River, Culpepper County, Virginia. Her brother, Fountaine Beckham, was mayor of Harper's Ferry, and was killed by John Brown in 1859. David Sitlington Gwin sold the Peoples Farm to his brother-in-law, William McClung, and became a merchant at Bridgewater, Virginia.

Children: 7

  150. i. Thomas Gwin (4), married Maggie Moler.
+ 151. ii. William David Gwin (4), born December 6, 1838.
  152. iii. Frances Viola Gwin (4), married Dr. Duke Powers

of Kentucky.
153. iv. George B. Gwin (4), married _____.
They lived in Baltimore, Maryland.
154. v. Mary (Molly) Gwin (4), married Rev. _____
Chambliss of South Carolina, a Baptist minister. They lived in
Kansas City, Missouri.
155. vi. Louise Gwin (4), married _____ Chambliss.
She died in Baltimore, Maryland.
156. vii. Ella Gwin (4), died unmarried.

54. William B. Gwin (4), son of Moses Gwin (3) and _____
Kincaid, married Rachel Gwin (4), daughter of William Kinkead
Gwin and Jane Kincaid.

Children: 1

157. i. Nelson Gwin (5).

55. Joseph Corbett Gwin (4), son of Moses Gwin (3) and
_____ Kincaid, was born September 15, 1802; died November 20,
1875; married November 12, 1829 in Bath County, Virginia, Mary
Jane Benson, born January 6, 1812, daughter of Hamilton Benson
and Elizabeth Hodge, a sister of Renick Hodge.

Children: 8

158. i. Amanda Ellen Gwin (5), born September 7, 1834;
married James N. Kincaid, son of Willis Kincaid and Margaret T.
Rhea.
+ 159. ii. George Hamilton Guinn (5), born November 12,
1836. This family spelled their surname GUINN.
160. iii. Robert A. Gwin (5), born May 3, 1839; married
Harriet Esom. They lived in Illinois.
161. iv. Martha Ann Gwin (5), born December 12, 1844;
married Robert Grant.
162. v. Rebecca Jane Gwin (5), born May 17, 1848; died
unmarried.
163. vi. Mary Celestine Gwin (5), born October 12, 1849;
married William Lange.
164. vii. James W. B. Gwin (5), born March 12, 1853; died
unmarried.
165. viii. Joseph Gwin (5), migrated to the west.

59. James Henderson Gwin (4), son of William Kinkead Gwin
(3) and Jane Kincaid, was born November 7, 1851; married in 1880,
Mary Frances Ervine, daughter of William E. Ervine and Elizabeth
Edmond.

Children: 9

166. i. Rennick Gwin (5).
167. ii. Lloyd Gwin (5).
168. iii. Jesse Gwin (5).

```
169.  iv.    Ervin Gwin (5).
170.  v.     Warren Gwin (5).
171.  vi.    Charles Gwin (5).
172.  vii.   Clarence Gwin (5).
173.  viii.  Russell Gwin (5).
174.  ix.    Virgil Gwin (5).
```

60. Jane McGlaughlin (4), daughter of Hugh McGlaughlin and Nancy Gwin (3), was born November 1794; married February 1811, Samuel Kirkpatrick and settled in West Branch, Iowa.

Children: 4

175. i. Nancy (Agnes) Kirkpatrick (5), born December 1811; died July 6, 1891; married David Gwin Lockridge (4), born in 1799; died December 20, 1880, son of Robert Lockridge and Mary Gwin.
176. ii. William Kirkpatrick (5), married C. Kirkpatrick in Illinois.
177. iii. Robert Kirkpatrick (5), married in the west.
178. iv. Hugh Kirkpatrick (5), married in the west.

61. Sarah Alexander Wiley (4), daughter of James Wiley and Nancy Gwin (3), was born November 14, 1811; died January 20, 1897; married (1) Mustoe Hamilton, born February 14, 1806; died May 18, 1841, son of John Hamilton and Mary McGuffin; married (2) John McGlaughlin, Jr., son of John McGlaughlin.

Children: 4 - first marriage

+   179. i.   John Gwin Hamilton (5), born June 23, 1837.
+   180. ii.   Esther Alice Hamilton (5), born July 13, 1839.
+   181. iii. Mary Jane Hamilton (5), born March 16, 1841.
    182. iv.   James W. Hamiton (5), born April 15, 1836; died
January 31, 1862. He served in the CSA.

Children: 5.- second marriage

    183. v.   Sarah F. McGlaughlin (5), died young.
+   184. vi.   Ewing A. McGlaughlin (5), born 1847.
    185. vii. Maria L. V. McGlaughlin (5), died at age 12.
    186. viii. John Letcher McGlaughlin (5), died February 10,
1924. He was blind from early childhood due to an accident.
    187. ix.   Henry H. McGlaughlin (5), died at age 19.

64. James Gwin (4), son of James Gwin (3) and Rachel Stephenson, married Mahala Pray.

Children: 3

188. i. John Pray Gwin (5), died July 17, 1934; married (as her second husband) Mary C. (Bradshaw) Oliver, daughter of Franklin Bradshaw and Esteline Kiser. She was a school teacher.

189. ii.   Armenia A. Gwin (5), married in 1867, John W.
Jordan.
190. iii.   Savannah Gwin (5), died unmarried.

66. Samuel Gwin (4), son of James Gwin (3) and Rachel Stephenson, married in 1854, Ellen Dever, daughter of John Dever and
Eliza Gilmore.

    191. i.   Walter Gwin (5), married _____.
+   192. ii.   Ruhama Gwin (5).
    193. iii.   Signora Gwin (5), married Robert Warwick, son of
William Fechtig Warwick and Phoebe Anthea Pray. They lived in
Alva, Oklahoma. (See Warwick Family).

67. John Gwin (4), son of James Gwin (3) and Rachel Stephenson, married Nancy McGlaughlin.

Children: 1

194. i.   John McGlaughlin Gwin (5), married Mamie Marshall
He was a physician at Williamsville, Virginia.

69. Rachel Gwin (4), daughter of James Gwin (3) and Rachel
Stephenson, married October 14, 1841 in Bath County, Virginia
(as his first wife), John Hiner, born 1810; died 1890, son of
Alexander B. Hiner and Jemima McCoy.

Children: 4

+   195. i.   Almira Hiner (5), born 1842.
+   196. ii.   James Polk Hiner (5), born 1844.
    197. iii.   Hardin A. Hiner (5), died in 1866, unmarried.
+   198. iv.   Benjamin Franklin Hiner (5), born 1848.

73. David Gwin Lockridge (4), son of Robert Lockridge and
Mary Gwin (3), was born in 1799; died December 20, 1880; married
Nancy (Agnes) Kirkpatrick (5), born 1811; died July 6, 1891,
daughter of Samuel Kirkpatrick and Jane McGlaughlin.

Children: 2

199. i.   David Gwin Lockridge, Jr. (5), born 1840; died
of diphtheria during the War Between the States; married February
25, 1862, Elizabeth Susan Bratton, born 1825; died 1908, daughter
of Robert Bratton and Susannah Feamster. There is a government
marker at his grave. No children.
+   200. ii.   Sarah Lockridge (5), born 1843.

74. Andrew Lockridge (4), son of Robert Lockridge and Mary
Gwin (3), was born September 23, 1801; died April 19, 1872 at
Rocky Ridge, Bath County, Virginia; married January 14, 1823
in Bath County, Virginia (1) Elizabeth Carlile, born November 16,
1801; died February 19, 1861 in Bath County, Virginia, daughter

of Robert Carlile and Margaret Hamilton; married (2) Mrs. Nancy (Hudson) Seybert, daughter of John Hudson and widow of Richard Seybert.

Children: 11 - first marriage

201. i. Mary Jane Davis Lockridge (5), born May 7, 1824 in Bath County, Virginia; died August 25, 1878; married August 20, 1850 in Bath County, Virginia, Rev. Stuart Slaven Ryder, died January 1903, Presiding Elder of Lewisburg District (now District Superintendent), M. E. Church. No children.
202. ii. Elizabeth R. Lockridge (5), married March 30, 1848 in Bath County, Virginia,(as his second wife) Edgar Campbell, son of Alexander Campbell and Margaret Brown. (See Campbell Family).
+ 203. iii. Robert Carlile Lockridge (5), born 1826.
204. iv. Agnes M. Lockridge (5), born September 19, 1828; died December 27, 1903, unmarried.
205. v. Andrew Jackson Lockridge (5), born August 8, 1831; died October 14, 1902, unmarried. He was a soldier in the CSA.
206. vi. John Wiley Lockridge (5), born May 30, 1833; died January 22, 1909; married Harriet Elizabeth Baldwin, born 1853. He was a soldier in the CSA. No children.
207. vii. Cooper Lockridge (5), drowned in the Cowpasture River, unmarried.
208. viii. Charles Carlile Lockridge (5), born July 13, 1837; died November 30, 1860.
209. ix. Lewis Collins Lockridge (5), born August 4, 1840; died November 18, 1904, unmarried.
210. x. William Lockridge (5), married Mollie Fletcher and lived in Colorado.
211. xi. Lancelot Lockridge (5), lived in Colorado.

78. Robert Lockridge (4), son of Robert Lockridge and Mary Gwin (3), was born September 14, 1809; died March 28, 1891; married (1) Rachel Jane Carlile, daughter of Robert Carlile and Margaret Hamilton; married (2) October 24, 1839 in Bath County, Virginia, Emmeline M. Gwin (4), born February 14, 1818; died April 11, 1900, daughter of Robert Gwin and Mary Stephenson. There were two children by the first marriage, but both died young.

Children: 10 - second marriage

+ 212. i. Susan R. Lockridge (5), born March 17, 1842.
+ 213. ii. Stephen A. Lockridge (5), born November 9,1843.
214. iii. William Henry Lockridge (5), born November 29, 1845; died June 28, 1885.
+ 215. iv. Mary Ann (Polly) Lockridge (5), born October 29, 1847.
+ 216. v. Ruhama Lockridge (5).
+ 217. vi. David E. Lockridge (5), born 1856.
+ 218. vii. George Henderson Lockridge (5), born 1859.

111

+   219. viii.   Robert Pierce Lockridge (5).
+   220. ix.   Frances Emily Lockridge (5), born 1861.
+   221. x.   John J. Lockridge (5).

   79. William Lockridge (4), son of Robert Lockridge and Mary Gwin (3), was born March 13, 1811; died January 26, 1892; married (1) Nancy Susan Burns, born May 8, 1834; died June 5, 1876; married (2) December 1891, Mrs. Eliza (Huffer) Poole.

Children: 6 - first marriage

+   222. i.   Aquilla Reese Lockridge (5), born November 30, 1852.
+   223. ii.   Elizabeth Jane Lockridge (5), born April 20, 1854.
+   224. iii.   William Peter Buchanan Lockridge (5), born December 24, 1857.
   225. iv.   Mary Lockridge (5), married _____ Linnard of Belle Aire, Ohio.
+   226. v.   Emma R. Lockridge (5).
+   227. vi.   George M. Lockridge (5).

   80. Mary (Polly) Graham Lockridge (4), daughter of Robert Lockridge and Mary Gwin (3), was born in 1816; died in 1896; married in 1836, Jacob P. Keister, born 1817; died 1895 in Mason County, West Virginia, son of George Keister and Susannah Peck. They lived for a time near Williamsville near Blue Springs in the shadow of the Devil's Race Path, a peculiar rock formation on the Bullpasture Mountain. Later they migrated to Mason County, West Virginia.

Children: 8

+   228. i.   Mary S. G. Keister (5).
+   229. ii.   George R. Keister (5), born in 1839.
+   230. iii.   William J. Keister (5).
   231. iv.   Jacob Keister (5), died at age 15.
+   232. v.   John D. Keister (5), born April 7, 1845.
   233. vi.   Anthony W. Keister (5), died at age 21.
+   234. vii.   Margaret Elizabeth Keister (5), born September 11, 1849.
+   235. viii.   Samuel Keister (5), born February 14, 1854.

   87. Nancy Elizabeth Givens (4), daughter of Samuel Givens and Elizabeth Gwin (3), was born December 2, 1818 in Bath County, Virginia; died January 19, 1885 near Moberly, Randolph County, Missouri; married in 1839 in Bath County, Virginia, Thomas Irons, born December 22, 1808 at Edinburg, Scotland; died April 14, 1876 in Randolph County, Missouri.

Children: 10

   236, i.   Robert Irons (5), born July 12, 1840; died January 7, 1899; married February 8, 1871, Frances M. Matthews.

237. ii.   Elizabeth Irons (5), born April 23, 1842; married
John McKinsey.
238. iii.   William Irons (5), born October 1843; married
Mary Oliver.
239. iv.   Mary Anne Irons (5), born 1845; married
Mathew Neal.
240. v.   Susan Irons (5), born 1847; married James Genolia.
241. vi.   Thomas Irons (5), born 1849; married Mary Dent.
242. vii.   Dazarine Irons (5), born 1850; married Sanford
Anderson.
243. viii.   John Irons (5), born 1852; married Mary Ellen
Crinmons.
244. ix.   Presley Irons (5), born 1854; married Fannie
C. Galbrath.
245. x.   Nasley Irons (5), born 1854, twin to Presley;
married Margaret Ragsdale.

91. David Gwin Kincaid (4), son of Thomas Kincaid and Sarah
Gwin (3), married (1) Mary Buzzard; married (2) Lucinda (Mullenax)
Wagoner, widow of Solomon Wagoner.

Children: 7 - first marriage

246. i.   Mary Kincaid (5), died.
247. ii.   John Kincaid (5), married Luemma Mills.
248. iii.   Wesley Kincaid (5), married Lizzie Griffen.
249. iv.   Susan Kincaid (5), married Thomas Luther Shrader.
250. v.   Ella Kincaid (5), married _____ Sharp.
251. vi.   Sarah Kincaid (5), died.
252. vii.   Isabel Kincaid (5), married Jacob Shrader.

Children: 3 - second marriage

253. viii.   Arminta J. Kincaid (5), married (1) Leslie
Bussard; married (2) Charles Gibbs.
254. ix.   George Thomas Kincaid (5), married (1) Matilda
Turner; married (2) Siggie Loury Carpenter.
255. x.   Edward Kincaid (5), married Martha Gutshall.

92. Jane Gwin (4), daughter of Robert Gwin (3) and Mary
Stephenson, married March 7, 1833 in Bath County, Virginia, Thomas
Blundell.

Children: 1

+ 256. i.   Americus R. Blundell (5), born Mary 2, 1834.

93. David Gwin (4), son of Robert Gwin (3) and Mary Stephen-
son, was born in 1809; died in 1863; married January 27, 1841 in
Bath County, Virginia (1) Jane Lockridge (4), daughter of Robert
Lockridge and Mary Gwin; married (2) Hannah Folks. He was captured
by the Yankees at his brother-in-law's, Henry Folks, near Hightown,
Highland County, Virginia, and was taken to Camp Chase, Ohio, where

113

he died and was buried. He had a rifle of John Cleek, Sr. which was broken by the Yankees. This rifle is now in the possession of Geo. W. Cleek of Staunton, Virginia, a grandson of John Cleek, Sr.

Children: 2 - first marriage

+ 257. i. Catherine Gwin (5).
  258. ii. Sarah A. Gwin (5), married John Eldridge C. Pullins, son of John S. Pullins and Nancy Pray. He served in Company E, 31st Virginia Infantry, CSA.

Children: 4 - second marriage

+ 259. iii. David W. Gwin (5), born October 15, 1858.
  260. iv. Emma Virginia Gwin (5), born April 25, 1859; died 1949; married in 1874, Henry Rodgers (5), son of Nelson Rodgers and Amanda Gwin.
  261. v. Margaret R. Gwin (5), died young.
+ 262. vi. Moses B. Gwin (5), born 1864.

94. Cynthia Gwin (4), daughter of Robert Gwin (3) and Mary Stephenson, married Thomas Brown. He served in the War of 1812.

Children: 6

  263. i. Elizabeth Brown (5), born 1832; died unmarried.
  264. ii. James Brown (5), died young.
  265. iii. William Brown (5), died young.
  266. iv. Martha Brown (5), died with diphtheria.
  267. v. Irene Brown (5), died with diphtheria.
  268. vi. Georgiana Zoe Brown (5), died July 7, 1933; married Joseph Hamilton Burns, died June 7, 1937.

95. James Stephenson Gwin (4), son of Robert Gwin (3) and Mary Stephenson, married Margaret (Peggy) Bodkin. She is buried at Elkins, West Virginia. He is buried at the Jacob Cleek Cemetery in Bath County, Virginia. There is a government marker at his grave for his service in the Confederate Army.

Children: 10

  269. i. William E. Gwin (5), born 1837; died January 12, 1862 with diphtheria.
+ 270. ii. Mary Emily Gwin (5), born 1841.
+ 271. iii. James Robert Gwin (5), born February 10, 1842.
  272. iv. Malinda Frances Gwin (5), born 1845; died November 21, 1862 with diphtheria.
  273. v. Moses F. Gwin (5), born 1850; died December 1, 1862 with diphtheria.
  274. vi. Cynthia Agnes Gwin (5), born January 20, 1856; died December 17, 1862 with diphtheria.
+ 275. vii. David Gwin (5).

114

+   276.   viii.   Martha Jane Gwin (5).
+   277.   ix.   Laura Gwin (5), born 1859.
    278.   x.   Hiram Gwin (5), died young.

96. Esther R. (Hettie) Gwin (4), daughter of Robert Gwin (3) and Mary Stephenson, married November 1, 1842 in Bath County, Virginia, David Stephenson, son of John Stephenson and Margaret J. Green.

Children: 6

    279.   i.   Roxanna F. Stephenson (5), born 1843; married in 1875 (as his second wife) Professor Stephen C. Lindsay. No children. She was a teacher in public schools.
+   280.   ii.   Mahala P. Stephenson (5), born December 26, 1845.
    281.   iii. Mary D. Stephenson (5), married Rev. Frank Davis. No children.
+   282.   iv.   Anderson F. Stephenson (5), born February 22, 1850.
+   283.   v.   John Bolar Stephenson (5), born 1853.
+   284.   vi.   Charles Crawford Stephenson (5), born 1856.

98. Amanda Gwin (4), daughter of Robert Gwin (3) and Mary Stephenson, married Nelson Rodgers.

Children: 5

+   285.   i.   Mary Anne Rodgers (5), born 1851.
+   286.   ii.   Henry Rodgers (5), born 1852.
    287.   iii. Robert Moses Rodgers (5), married Harriet F. Cobb. They lived in Augusta County, Virginia.
    288.   iv.   Americus Rodgers (5), married Mariah Pullin. They lived in Rockingham County, Virginia.
    289.   v.   Nancy Rodgers (5), married in 1881, Adam S. Hicklin.

102. Houston F. Gwin (4), son of Robert Gwin (3) and Mary Stephenson, married Jane Seybert. They migrated to Arkansas.

Children: 5

    290.   i.   Clarence Gwin (5), died young.
    291.   ii.   Elizabeth Gwin (5).
    292.   iii. William Gwin (5).
    293.   iv.   Robert Gwin (5).
    294.   v.   Hiram Gwin (5), lived in Conway, Arkansas.

103. Moses Gwin (4), son of Robert Gwin (3) and Mary Stephenson, was born in 1832; married Elizabeth Cobb, born 1854, a sister of Samuel Augustus Cobb who married Martha Jane Gwin.

Children: 3

+   295. i.   William Tell Gwin (5), born July 16, 1875, a
twin to Frances Belle.
     296. ii.   Frances Belle Gwin (5), born July 16, 1875, a
twin to William Tell; died young.
     297. iii. Mary A. Gwin (5), died young.

104. John Wesley Gwin (4), son of John Gwin (3) and Margaret
Bradshaw, was born July 22, 1816; died May 7, 1898; married May
30, 1844 in Bath County, Virginia, Emmeline Gillespie, born
February 3, 1824; died February 3, 1893, daughter of James
Gillespie and Margaret Wandless. James Gillespie served in the
War of 1812, and there is a government marker at his grave in
the John Wiley graveyard.

     Children: 10

+   298. i.   John Clayton Gwin (5), born 1845.
+   299. ii.   Roberta V. Gwin (5), born 1850.
     300. iii. Margaret Anne Gwin (5), born 1852; died January
1940; married (1) Caleb A. Moxley; married (2) Wyatt Holmes. No
children.
     301. iv.   Clara Belle Gwin (5), born September 12, 1854;
died February 16, 1899, unmarried.
+   302. v.   David Franklin Gwin (5), born January 24, 1857.
     303. vi.   Bolar Austin Gwin (5), born November 14, 1857;
died August 17, 1926, unmarried.
+   304. vii. Luella Robertine Gwin (5), born January 29,
1861, a twin to Rosella Josephine.
     305. viii. Rosella Josephine Gwin (5), born January 29,
1861, a twin to Luella Robertine; died April 27, 1936, unmarried.
+   306. ix.   Annie Lee Gwin (5), born May 6, 1862.
     307. x.   Georgia L. Gwin (5), born February 5, 1870;
died young.

105. David Gwin (4), son of John Gwin (3) and Margaret
Bradshaw, was born November 23, 1818; died February 25, 1885;
married Eliza Jane Stephenson, born September 6, 1815; died January
28, 1885, daughter of John Stephenson and Margaret J. Green.

     Children: 1

308. i.   Anna Eliza Gwin (5), born July 12, 1850; died
April 25, 1907; married October 18, 1873 in Bath County, Virginia
(1) Andrew Gawen Bonner, born March 31, 1840; died April 30, 1922,
son of Scipio Addison Bonner and Mary Jane Hamilton; married (2)
Ellsworth Wright, born April 17, 1866; died September 21, 1894;
married (3) Marion Taylor of Janesville, Illinois. No children.

108. Nancy Gwin (4), daughter of John Gwin (3) and Margaret
Bradshaw, married December 20, 1825 in Bath County, Virginia (as
his first wife) Hugh McGlaughlin, born February 24, 1801; died
May 19, 1870. They lived in Pocahontas County, West Virginia.
He married (2) Elizabeth (Lightner) Gum, widow of Otho Gum. (See
Lightner Family).

Children: 5

309. i.   Margaret McGlaughlin (5), died young.
310. ii. Elizabeth McGlaughlin (5), married George
Rowan and settled in Bath County, Virginia. He served in the
Confederate Army.
+ 311. iii. William Jacob McGlaughlin (5).
312. iv. John Calvin McGlaughlin (5), married Isabella M.
(Lightner) Bird, born 1840, daughter of Adam Lightner and Eleanor
Slaven, and widow of David Bird. (See Lightner Family).
+ 313. v.   George H. McGlaughlin (5).

125. Elizabeth Susan Coyner (4), daughter of Judge Robert
Coyner and Margaret Gwin (3), was born August 1, 1822; married
(1) John Edward Wilson; married (2) May 24, 1849, William Curran
Ghormley. They migrated to South Dakota.

Children: 1 - first marriage

+ 314. i.   John Edward Coyner Wilson (5), born April 30,
1845.

Children: 10 - second marriage

+ 315. ii. Robert Hugh Ghormley (5), born April 3, 1856.
+ 316. iii. William Fairfield Ghormley (5), born October
14, 1858.
317. iv. Moses Lincoln Ghormley (5), born September
8, 1861; died March 24, 1928; married Mrs. Collins.
+ 318. v.   Newton Baxter Ghormley (5), born January 18,
1868;
319. vi. Samuel C. Ghormley (5), died young.
320. vii. Martha Ghormley (5), died young.
321. viii. Judith Ghormley (5), died young.
322. ix. Margaret Ghormley (5), died young.
323. x.   Nancy Ghormley (5), died young.
324. xi. Isabel Ghormley (5), died young.

126. David Silas Coyner (4), son of Judge Robert Coyner and
Margaret Gwin (3), was born in 1025 in Augusta County, Virginia;
died in 1899 in Highland County, Ohio; married (1) in 1848,
Matilda Heizer, died 1875; married (2) in 1880, Elizabeth Lyle,
died 1890.

Children: 11 - first marriage

325. i.   Mary Coyner (5), died in infancy.
+ 326. ii. Samuel Robert Coyner (5).
+ 327. iii. Henry Martin Coyner (5).
+ 328. iv. David Gwin Coyner (5).
+ 329. v.   Daniel Moore Coyner (5).
+ 330. vi. Fred Ware Coyner (5).
331. vii. Margaret Elvine Coyner (5), born 1860; died in
1895 while doing mission work in Los Angeles, California.

117

332. viii. Silas Crawford Coyner (5), married in Nebraska and reared a large family.
+ 333. ix. John Edward Coyner (5).
+ 334. x. Fanny Carolina Coyner (5).
335. xi. Harriet Matilda Coyner (5), born 1870; married Rev. Edwin Ashcraft. Both were missionaries of the Methodist Church in China.

127. John McCutcheon Coyner (4), son of Judge Robert Coyner and Margaret Gwin (3), was born in 1826; died and was buried at Hopkinsville, Kentucky; married (1) Mary Wilson, sister of John Edward Wilson; married (2) Mrs. Anna D. Parrett. He was a Presbyterian minister and missionary. The first Presbyterian Church in Utah was organized and built by him in Salt Lake City.

Children: 2 - first marriage

336. i. William Coyner (5), died young.
337. ii. Emma Margaret Coyner (5), died August 31, 1876; married October 6, 1875, Rev. Josiah Fielch, pastor of the First Presbyterian Church, Salt Lake City, Utah.

128. Robert Crawford Coyner (4), son of Judge Robert Coyner and Margaret Gwin (3),was b.July 18, 1838 in Ross County, Ohio; died in 1902; married (1) in 1861 Anna Garrett, died 1861; married (2) Mary A. Dunkle, born August 26, 1842. He served in the War Between the States.

Children: 6 - second marriage

338. i. Jennie Edith Coyner (5), born November 1, 1870; married _____ Shuttleworth.
339. ii. William Robert Coyner (5), born April 1, 1873.
340. iii. Heber Wright Coyner (5), born December 2, 1875.
341. iv. Frederick Coyner (5), born November 28, 1877.
343. v. John Coyner (5), born November 28, 1877, a twin to Frederick.
344. vi. Ralph Coyner (5), born May 18, 1883.

130. Rachel Adelaide Hinton (4), daughter of Silas Hinton and Susan Henderson Gwin (3), was born February 17, 1827; died December 10, 1862; married Daniel Price Reamer, M. D. They lived in Augusta County, Virginia.

Children: 2

345. i. Sudie Elizabeth Reamer (5), born June 10, 1849 at Mt. Meridan, Virginia; died August 18, 1885; married November 19, 1873 (as his first wife) Louis Martin McClung (4), born June 1, 1846; died October 16, 1926, son of William McClung and Rachel Viola Gwin.
346. ii. Fanny Reamer (5), died unmarried.

118

137. John Henderson McClung (4), son of William McClung and Rachel Viola Gwin (3), was born June 12, 1822; died in 1898 in Montezuma, Georgia; married (1) in 1850, Martha Frances Booton; married (2) Bettie Lipscomb, died May 2, 1904.

Children: 2 - first marriage

347. i. Irving McClung (5).
348. ii. Mary Bassie McClung (5), married E. O. Buff. She was a school teacher.

Children: 4 - second marriage

349. iii. Nellie H. McClung (5), died June 2, 1901; married A. J. Tilson.
350. iv. Rosa Rena McClung (5), died 1919; married August 19, 1900, William T. Lockett, Albany, Georgia.
351. v. Eva Lynnette McClung (5), married November 26, 1901, J. N. Wynne, Cochrane, Georgia.
353. vi. Richard Henry McClung (5), born c. 1880, Montezuma, Georgia.

138. David Gwin McClung (4), son of William McClung and Rachel Viola Gwin (3), was born February 16, 1824; died March 3, 1901; married in 1852, Sarah Ann Cornelia Maupin, died March 11, 1904 at Franklin, West Virginia. He served a Sheriff of Pendleton County, West Virginia. He engaged in merchandizing for more than 40 years. At the beginning of the War Between the States he went to Richmond, Virginia and conducted a mercantile house which supplied the Confederate Army with uniforms. After the war he returned to Franklin, West Virginia and organized the Farmers' Bank of Pendleton, and served as president and director until his death.

Children: 5

+ 354. i. Tyree Maupin McClung (5), born August 18, 1856.
+ 355. ii. William Wallace McClung (5), born September 26, 1858.
+ 356. iii. Marshall Gwin McClung (5), born May 8, 1864.
357. iv. John Louis McClung (5), born December 25, 1867. He was a Presbyterian minister.
+ 358. v. Maude Budles McClung (5), born November 12, 1869.

142. Silas Brown McClung (4), son of William McClung and Rachel Viola Gwin (3), was born October 5, 1832; died November 8, 1925; married in 1868, Nancy Jane Lemon, daughter of Jonathan Juliet Lemon. He served in Company C, 14th Virginia Cavalry, CSA. They lived in Pendleton County, West Virginia.

Children: 6

359. i.   Rachel Virginia McClung (5), born January 20,
1869; married P. A. Switzer.
    360. ii.   Warren Crawford McClung (5), born May 7, 1872;
died unmarried.
    361. iii.   Clarence Reamer McClung (5), born November 25,
1875, unmarried.
    362. iv.   Josie Lemon McClung (5), born September 12,
1878; married Rev. W. M. Compton of the Methodist Church.
    363. v.   Henry Preston McClung (5), born August 20,
1881; married December 25, 1903, Sarah Jane Bond, born June 9,
1883.
    364. vi.   Edgar Neal McClung (5), born July 27, 1884.

    144. Frances Violet McClung (4), daughter of William McClung
and Rachel Viola Gwin (3), was born March 13, 1836; died in 1908;
married in 1859, Judge James M. Sieg, born May 5, 1827; died
December 21, 1875 in Richmond, Virginia.

    Children: 3

    365. i.   Sully Sieg (5), born February 5, 1868; died in
Chicago, Illinois; married Mattie Craig. He was an attorney -
A.B., LL.B.
    366. ii.   James McClung Sieg (5), born July 18, 1873;
died October 2, 1953. He was a Missionary of the Presbyterian
Church in Africa.
    367. iii.   Boude Sieg (5), died young.

    145. Mary Margaret McClung (4), daughter of William McClung
and Rachel Viola Gwin (3), was born January 28, 1838; died June
5, 1901; married December 26, 1865, John S. McNulty, born in
1833, son of John McNulty and Margaret Stephenson.

    Children: 6

    368. i.   William M. McNulty (5), a lawyer, unmarried.
    369. ii.   Edwin Alexander McNulty (5), married October
24, 1906, Mrs. Cornelia Adams Pearsall.
    370. iii.   Louis Dudley McNulty (5), born November 1,
1870; died May 28, 1954; married (1) Nettie Wallace, died June
11, 1901; married (2)in 1917,Mary Lesley Condon.
    371. iv.   Annie J. McNulty (5), married in 1908,
Benjamin Hiner, son of John J. Hiner.
    372. v.   Harriett C. McNulty (5), married in 1897,
Rev. Charles H. Dobbs. They lived in Texas.
    373. vi.   Mamie McNulty (5), died unmarried.

    146. Susan Agnes McClung (4), daughter of William McClung
and Rachel Viola Gwin (3), was born in 1840; married William M.
Sommers. He served as Sheriff of Highland County, Virginia.
He also served as Sergeant in Company E, 31st Virginia Infantry,
CSA.

Children: 5

+ 374. i. Rachel Violet Sommers (5), born 1868.
  375. ii. Sadie Sommers (5), married September 18, 1901
Charles M. McClintic. They lived at Lost Creek, West Virginia.
No children.
+ 376. iii. Lena Sommers (5).
  377. iv. Samuel Sommers (5), married Dora Myers. No
children.
  378. v. William Sommers (5), married Iona Bowsby. They
live in West Virginia. No children.

148. Louis Martin McClung (4), son of William McClung and
Rachel Viola Gwin (3), was born June 1, 1846; died October 16,
1926; married (1) November 19, 1873, Sudie Elizabeth Reamer, (5)
born June 10, 1849 at Mt. Meridan, Virginia; died August 18, 1885,
daughter of Daniel Price Reamer and Rachel Adelaide Hinton;
married (2) September 1, 1887, Lucy D. Blair, born 1846; died
January 30, 1925, daughter of Dr. William R. Blair and Nettie
Wallace. He served in Company C, 14th Virginia Cavalry, CSA
and was wounded at the Battle of Winchester on September 19,
1864.

Children: 7 - first marriage

  379. i.   Addie McClung (5), died young.
  380. ii. Frances Sieg McClung (5), born January 2, 1878;
married September 18, 1906 (as his second wife) George Washington
Wallace, born June 17, 1869; died December 31, 1931, son of
Thomas Brown Wallace and Nancy Givens Cleek. (See Cleek Family).
  381. iii. Joseph B. McClung (5), died young.
  382. iv. Frank W. McClung (5), died young.
  383. v.   Reamer McClung (5), died young.
  384. vi. Harry Seabrooke McClung (5), born August 21,
1881, unmarried.
+ 385. v.   Louis Edwin McClung (5), born April 21, 1883.

151. William David Gwin (4), son of David Sitlington Gwin
(3) and Frances T. Beckham, was born December 6, 1838 at Bridgewater, Virginia; married Lucy Howell. They lived in Nashville,
Tennessee and Columbia, South Carolina. He was a prominent
clergyman, educator, editor and author.

Children: 1

  386. i. Howell Gwin (5), a physician of Nashville,
Tennessee.

159. George Hamilton Guinn (5), son of Joseph Corbett
Gwin (4) and Mary Jane Benson, was born November 12, 1836; died
February 16, 1929; married December 21, 1865, Margaret Ellen
Kincaid, born 1835, daughter of Willis Kincaid (born March 10,
1811; died June 6, 1887) and Margaret T. Rhea (born March 18,
1813; married October 1, 1832 in Bath County, Virginia; died
July 28, 1888). (See Lockridge Family).

Children: 9

+ 387. i.   Joseph Willis Guinn (6).
+ 388. ii. Margaret Ann Guinn (6).
+ 389. iii. James F. Guinn (6).
+ 390. iv. Mary Dudley Guinn (6), born January 2, 1870.
  391. v.   Theodora Gertrude Guinn (6), born August 31,
1871; died September 30, 1918; married June 1, 1897, James
Cameron Lightner, born May 21, 1867; died June 17, 1924, son
of Jacob Lightner and Nancy Jane Warwick. (See Lightner Family).
  392. vi. Lilly Florence Guinn (6), unmarried.
+ 393. vii. Emmett Vasco Guinn (6).
  394. viii. Sidney Brown Guinn (6), married B. C. Perkins.
They have one child.
  395. ix. George Rennick Guinn (6), unmarried.

179. John Gwin Hamilton (5), son of Mustoe Hamilton and
Sarah Alexander Wiley (4), was born June 23, 1837; died June
24, 1919; married September 6, 1866, Mary Caroline Townsend,
born September 8, 1844. He was a member of Hutton's Mounted
Infantry, CSA.

Children: 4

+ 396. i.   John Mustoe Hamilton (6), born November 26,
1867.
  397. ii. Sarah A. Hamilton (6), born May 15, 1869; died
unmarried.
+ 398. iii. Elizabeth J. Hamilton (6), born June 23, 1870.
  399. iv. David Gwin Hamilton (6), born April 17, 1872;
died July 2, 1911. He was married twice.

180. Esther Alice Hamilton (5), daughter of Mustoe Hamilton
and Sarah Alexander Wiley (4), was born July 13, 1839; died May
17, 1917; married July 13, 1860, John M. Armstrong, born in 1835;
died in 1912, son of George Armstrong and Sarah Hiner. He served
in the CSA.

Children: 9

  400. i.   Sallie Armstrong (6), died.
+ 401. ii. John Morgan Armstrong (6), born 1863.
  402. iii. Lucy Armstrong (6), married Robert J. Carpenter.
  403. iv. Della Armstrong (6), married Joseph Carpenter.
  404. v.   James H. Armstrong (6), married Ella Hicks, who
died October 5, 1924.
  405. vi. George W. Armstrong (6), married in 1895 (1)
Viola McNett; married (2) Mrs. M. L. Dickson.
  406. vii. Charles Reese Armstrong (6), married in 1900,
Cecil C. Farrote.
  407. viii. Rena J. Armstrong (6), married in 1889, Andrew
J. Terry, son of Alexander Terry and Mary Kincaid.
  408. ix. Harmon M. Armstrong (6), married Myrtle Jack.

181. Mary Jane Hamilton (5), daughter of Mustoe Hamilton and Sarah Alexander Wiley (4), was born March 16, 1841; died June 16, 1918; married October 1, 1857, (as his second wife) William Trimble, born December 19, 1818; died March 9, 1880, son of James Trimble and Catherine Susanna Shinnaberger.

Children: 5

409. i.   Mary Esther Trimble (6), born October 2, 1858.
410. ii.   Martha Ann Trimble (6), born September 13, 1861; died January 16, 1892.
+ 411. iii. William Mustoe Trimble (6), born September 3, 1864.
412. iv. Washington Lafayette Trimble (6), born March 6, 1867; died unmarried.
+ 413. v.   Alice Virginia Trimble (6), born August 26, 1871.

184. Ewing A. McGlaughlin (5), son of John McGlaughlin, Jr. and Sarah Alexander Wiley (4), was born in 1847; died in 1911; married February 5, 1874, Sarah Elizabeth Hite, born April 10, 1849; died February 9, 1928, daughter of George W. Hite and Cecelia Matheny.

Children: 9

+ 414. i.   Ada Ethel McGlaughlin (6), born November 1875.
+ 415. ii.   Minnie S. McGlaughlin (6), born 1877.
+ 416. iii. Sarah E. McGlaughlin (6).
+ 417. iv. Harriet E. McGlaughlin (6).
+ 418. v.   J. Boyd McGlaughlin (6), born July 10, 1884.
419. vi.   (Infant son) McGlaughlin (6), born July 10, 1884, twin to J. Boyd, died young.
+ 420. vii. William Odie McGlaughlin (6).
421. viii. Kenton McGlaughlin (6), died young.
+ 422. ix. Emma McGlaughlin (6).

192. Ruhama Gwin (5), daughter of Samuel Gwin (4) and Ellen Dever, married Job Eckard, born 1845; died 1910.

Children: 7

423. i.   Charles Pinckney Eckard (6).
424. ii.   Isaac Eckard (6), married Emma Erma.Hull, daughter of Jacob N. Hull and Eliza Rexrode. (See Hull Family).
425. iii. William Eckard (6), married Rose Halterman.
+ 426. iv. Kenton Eckard (6), born 1888.
427. v.   Oliver Eckard (6), born January 28, 1894; died September 22, 1954.
428. vi.   Samuel Eckard (6), died young.
429. vii. Lucy Eckard (6), married Samuel Lee Lindsay, son of Robert Lee Lindsay and Victoria Samuel Cleek. (See Cleek Family).

195. Almira Hiner (5), daughter of John Hiner and Rachel Gwin (4), was born in 1842; married in 1867, John C. Pruitt, born in 1837 in Worcester County, Maryland.

Children: 7

430. i.   Harriet A. Pruitt (6), married in 1896, John Morgan Armstrong (6), born in 1863, son of John M. Armstrong and Esther Alice Hamilton.
431. ii.   Rachel Ann Pruitt (6), born 1869; died June 25, 1947; married (as his second wife) Hugh A. Jordan.
432. iii. John H. Pruitt (6), married Lillie M. Crawley.
433. iv.   Charlotte Pruitt (6), died young.
434. v.   Bishop Pruitt (6), died young.
435. vi.   Martha B. Pruitt (6), died January 1937; married (as his second wife) John M. Corbett.
436. vii. Mary V. Pruitt (6), married (as his first wife) Charles P. Hollihan.

196. James Polk Hiner (5), son of John Hiner and Rachel Gwin (4), was born in 1844; married Berdicia J. Mick from West Virginia.

Children: 12

437. i.   Asbury W. Hiner (6), married Linnie McGlaughlin.
438. ii.   M. Rosa Hiner (6), died young.
439. iii. Georgiana Hiner (6), a minister, died unmarried.
440. iv.   Susan A. Hiner (6), married Peter Kincaid Kramer.
441. v.   Edward Hiner (6), died young.
442. vi.   Joseph Hiner (6), married Edith Ruckman, Hunterville, West Virginia.
443. vii. Patrick R. Hiner (6), married in 1906, Bertha L. Gutshall.
444. viii. John B. Hiner (6), died young.
445. ix.   Minnie E. Hiner (6), married (as his first wife, Joseph Hamilton Burns, Pocahontas County, West Virginia.
446. x.   William C. Hiner (6), married _____ Sheets, Mountain Grove, Virginia.
447. xi.   James E. Hiner (6), married Hattie Acord.
448. xii. Lloyd W. Hiner (6), married Susie Chestnut, Mountain Grove, Virginia.

198. Benjamin Franklin Hiner (5), son of John Hiner and Rachel Gwin (4), was born in 1848; married in 1871, Mary E. Townsend, born 1854.

Children: 7

     449. i.   Sarah E. Hiner (6), died unmarried.
+   450. ii.   Jerusha A. Hiner (6).
     451. iii. David H. A. Hiner (6), died unmarried.
     452. iv.   Charles W. Hiner (6), died at age 19.

453. v.   Laverna J. Hiner (6), died young.
454. vi.   Stella J. Hiner (6), married Adam McAllister.
No children.
455. vii. Henry Tucker Hiner (6), born 1889; married
Mary Harris.

200.   Sarah Lockridge (5), daughter of David Gwin Lockridge
(4) and Nancy (Agnes) Kirkpatrick, was born in 1843; died April
27, 1889; married April 4, 1861 in Bath County, Virginia (as his
first wife) George Washington Bratton, born 1834, son of Robert
Bratton and Susannah Feamster. He married (2) Frances Emily
Lockridge (5). (See Bratton Family).

Children: 3

+   456. i.   Lillie R. Bratton (6).
    457. ii.   Susan Agnes Bratton (6), died in young woman-
hood. She was a school teacher.
+   458. iii.   David Washington Bratton (6).

203.   Robert Carlile Lockridge (5), son of Andrew Lockridge
(4) and Elizabeth Carlile, was born in 1826 in Bath County,
Virginia; died June 22, 1894 and was buried in Columbus, Ohio;
married in 1855, Lydia M. Kutz, born August 24, 1829 in Somerset
County, Pennsylvania; died December 7, 1906 in Bath County,
Virginia. He was a soldier in the CSA.

Children: 8

459. i.   Minnie Herman Lockridge (6), born January 3,
1859 in Highland County, Virginia; died May 10, 1932 at Mitchelltown, Virginia; married David Franklin Gwin (5), born January 24,
1857; died July 16, 1937, son of John Wesley Gwin and Emmeline
Gillespie.
460. ii.   Andrew Lockridge (6), married Virginia Pickett.
461. iii.   Charles Lockridge (6), married Effie Peters.
462. iv.   Robert Lockridge (6), married Cora Corell.
463. v.   Lillie Lockridge (6), died February 1953,
unmarried.
464. vi.   Hampton Lockridge (6), married Ada Shumaker.
+   465. vii.   Ollie Gertrude Lockridge (6), born June 4, 1870.
466. viii. William Lockridge (6), died.

212.   Susan R. Lockridge (5), daughter of Robert Lockridge
(4) and Emmeline M. Gwin (4), was born in 1842; died June 5,
1898; married in 1857, John R. Revercomb, born May 6, 1836; died
March 24, 1892.

Children: 11

+   467. i.   George Robert Revercomb (6), born 1860.
    468. ii.   Anna Revercomb (6), married John Campbell
Marshall. No children.

+   469. iii.   Mary E. Revercomb (6).
+   470. iv.   Archibald Jacob Revercomb (6), born February
4, 1869.
+   471. v.   Ruhama B. Revercomb (6), born January 5, 1872.
+   472. vi.   John Henderson Revercomb (6).
    473. vii.   William Griffith Revercomb (6), married Mabel
Sutton.
    474. viii. Susie Revercomb (6), born June 3, 1877; died
January 1, 1881.
+   475. ix.   Wreathie Susan Revercomb (6), born January 4,
1882.
    476. x.   Rebecca E. Revercomb (6), born 1844; died 1913;
married November 29, 1911 (as his first wife) Holmes Stephenson.
    477. xi.   William Revercomb (6), died in infancy.

213. Stephen A. Lockridge (5), son of Robert Lockridge (4)
and Emmeline M. Gwin (4), was born November 9, 1843; died July
21, 1896; married (1) Laura Ervine, born 1843; died 1887, daughter
of James Addison Ervine and Elizabeth Bruffey; married (2) Mrs.
Julia(Nottingham) Sutton. (See Warwick Family).

Children: 8 - first marriage

+   478. i.   Bertie Hull Lockridge (6), born February 22,
1867.
    479. ii.   William Robert Lockridge (6), born December 3,
1871; died in 1943; married April 12, 1900, Jeanie Orbison
Bratton, born September 17, 1875, daughter of John Feamster
Bratton and Cornelia Goul. (See Bratton Family).
+   480. iii.   Henderson Marshall Lockridge (6), born 1878.
    481. iv.   Stella Pearl Lockridge (6), born December 8,
1880; married March 9, 1904, Wade Hampton Cleek, born July 24,
1880 in Bath County, Virginia; died October 26, 1951 in Bath
County, Virginia, son of George Washington Cleek and Malcena
Catherine Lightner. (See Cleek Family).
    482. v.   George Lockridge (6), died in early manhood.
    483. vi.   David Mackey Lockridge (6), died in early 1940's.
    484. vii.   Calvin Lockridge (6), married _____
in the west.
    485. viii. Hattie Lockridge (6), died in young womanhood.

Children: 2 - second marriage

+   486. ix.   Lollie Gray Lockridge (6), born 1889.
    487. x.   Rema A. Lockridge (6), born 1894; died April
3, 1896.

215. Mary Ann (Polly) Lockridge (5), daughter of Robert
Lockridge (4) and Emmeline M. Gwin (4), was born October 29,
1847; died February 5, 1923; married Jeremiah Strother Helms,
son of James M. Helms and Jane Carlile (married April 4, 1835 in
Bath County, Virginia).

```
Children:  7

+   488.  i.    Emma Virginia Helms (6).
+   489.  ii.   William Strother Helms (6), born September 14,
1875.
+   490.  iii.  Frances Josephine Helms (6).
    491.  iv.   Elizabeth Bratton Helms (6), married Herbert
Bradshaw.  He is treasurer of Highland County, Virginia.  No
children.
+   492.  v.    Jeremiah Graham Helms (6), born 1887.
+   493.  vi.   Leota S. Helms (6).
+   494.  vii.  Robert Quidore Helms (6), born January 5,1884.
```

216. Ruhama Lockridge (5), daughter of Robert Lockridge (4) and Emmeline M. Gwin (4), married John S. Hamilton. They settled in Missouri.

```
Children:  4

    495.  i.    Walter Hamilton (6).  Missouri.
    496.  ii.   Mackey Hamilton (6).  Missouri.
    497.  iii.  Annie Hamilton (6), married B. W. Crum, Staunton,
Virginia.  No children.
    498.  iv.   Sadie Hamilton (6).
```

217. David E. Lockridge (5), son of Robert Lockridge (4) and Emmeline M. Gwin (4), was born in 1856; married in 1883, Susan V. Vance.

```
Children:  2

+   499.  i.    Russell Vance Lockridge (6), born May 7, 1890.
+   500.  ii.   Frank Lockridge (6).
```

218. George Henderson Lockridge (5), son of Robert Lockridge (4) and Emmeline M. Gwin (4), was born in 1859; married in 1895, Adaline H. Kincaid, born September 13, 1870; died March 3, 1938, daughter of Floyd Kincaid and Elizabeth Steuart.

```
Children:  1

    501.  i.    John Robson Lockridge (6), born 1897, unmarried.
```

219. Robert Pierce Lockridge (5), son of Robert Lockridge (4) and Emmeline M. Gwin (4), married Ella Josephine Folks.

```
Children:  5

+   502.  i.    David Marvin Lockridge (6).
+   503.  ii.   Steward Ryder Lockridge (6).
+   504.  iii.  Robert Lockridge (6).
+   505.  iv.   Howard Luther Lockridge (6).
+   506.  v.    Maysie Lockridge (6).
```

220. Frances Emily Lockridge (5), daughter of Robert

Lockridge (4) and Emmeline M. Gwin (4), was born in 1861; married in 1893 (as his second wife) George Washington Bratton, born 1834; son of Robert Bratton and Susannah Feamster. (See Bratton Family).

Children: 2

507. i.   Nannie Virginia Bratton (6), born September 2, 1895; married December 29, 1920, Willard Lindsay Stephenson (6), born August 14, 1889, son of Charles Crawford Stephenson and Mary Lindsay.
508. ii.   George Robert Bratton (6), born January 4, 1899; married Sudie Gibbs.

221. John J. Lockridge (5), son of Robert Lockridge (4) and Emmeline M. Gwin (4), died February 7, 1931; married Frances Colaw.

Children: 5

+   509. i.   Clifton Hylie Lockridge (6), born February 27, 1892.
+   510. ii.   Merle G. Lockridge (6),
+   511. iii.   James C. Lockridge (6).
    512. iv.   Julian Lockridge (6), married Ruth Carpenter. No children.
    513. v.   Granite Lockridge (6).

222. Aquilla Reese Lockridge (5), son of William Lockridge (4) and Nancy Susan Burns, was born November 30, 1852; died February 6, 1916; married August 1877, Amanda Huffer, born December 4, 1851 in Augusta County, Virginia; died October 14, 1935, a sister to Jane Huffer and Eliza (Huffer) Poole.

Children: 10

+   514. i.   John W. Ernest Lockridge (6).
+   515. ii.   Kenny C. Lockridge (6).
    516. iii.   James Kemper Lockridge (6), married Lottie M. Hamilton. They live at Waynesboro, Virginia. No children.
    517. iv.   Edward R. Lockridge (6), married Mary Lyle Marshall, daughter of James Henry Marshall and Hattie Lawrence.
    518. v.   Abraham Isaac Jacob Lockridge (6), died July 9, 1952; married Lula Belle Curtis.
    519. vi.   Pinckney S. Lockridge (6), married Hazel (Carpenter) Robertson, daughter of Joseph Carpenter and Della Armstrong. They have two children.
+   520. vii.   Andrew Lee Lockridge (6).
    521. viii.   Grover Cooper Lockridge (6), born October 10, 1893; died September 5, 1894.
+   522. ix.   Annie F. Lockridge (6).
    523. x.   Casper Bryant Lockridge (6), born October 22, 1880; died February 23, 1908.

128

223. Elizabeth Jane Lockridge (5), daughter of William Lockridge (4) and Nancy Susan Burns, was born April 20, 1854; died March 2, 1908; married (1) George W. Shaffier, died March 10, 1889; married (2) Harvey Bell Shaver, born March 12, 1863; died April 6, 1934.

Children: 8 - first marriage

524. i.   Rachel Susan Shaffier (6), born July 26, 1870; died December 11, 1913; married Lee Walmsley. They lived at Huttonsville, West Virginia.
525. ii.   John Henry Shaffier (6), born July 20, 1873; died March 29, 1919; married Dora Petts. They lived in Ohio.
526. iii.   Jeanette George Shaffier (6), born February 27, 1876; married Charles Chowling. They lived in Georgia.
527. iv.   Sarah Amanda Shaffier (6), born May 16, 1877; married John Walmsley. They lived at Huttonsville, West Virginia.
528. v.   Jane Shaffier (6), born February 3, 1879; married H. Minor Boyers. They live at Harrisonburg, Virginia.
529. vi.   William Lockridge Shaffier (6), born April 5, 1880; married Rachel Belle Rodgers (6), born February 24, 1885, daughter of Henry Rodgers and Emma Virginia Gwin. No children.
530. vii.   Rosella Shaffier (6), born 1882; married Stuart Pinckley, Elkins, West Virginia.
531. viii.   Ida Louise Shaffier (6), born October 19, 1884; married Adam Ernest Buchanan.

Children: 5 - second marriage

532. ix.   Oscar Shaver (6), married _____ Hise.
533. x.   David Shaver (6).
534. xi.   Lanie Shaver (6), married James Hodge.
535. xii.   Mary Siron Shaver (6), married Henry Wise Gum, son of Gilbert Gum and Virginia Hull.
536. xiii.   Annie Shaver (6), married William J. Carpenter.

224. William Peter Buchanan Lockridge (5), son of William Lockridge (4) and Nancy Susan Burns, was born December 24, 1857; died April 8, 1935; married October 2, 1883, Hannah Jane Huffer of Augusta County, Virginia.

Children: 9

537. i.   Lula Blanche E. Lockridge (6), born August 30, 1884; married Charles Graham.
538. ii.   Hannah Emma M. Lockridge (6), born November 17, 1885; married April 1, 1908, Daniel D. Atkinson of California.
+ 539. iii.   Leona May Lockridge (6), born May 7, 1887.
+ 540. iv.   Lucius Homer Lockridge (6), born September 3, 1888.
541. v.   Nellie S. V. Lockridge (6), born May 5, 1892; married Summers Middleton.

542. vi.   Emory M. Lockridge (6), born December 4, 1893;
married January 25, 1918, Emma Terry, daughter of Andrew J. Terry
and Irene Armstrong.
+   543. vii.   Mary Treacy M. Lockridge (6), born October
18, 1895.
+   544. viii.   William Peter Buchanan Lockridge, Jr. (6),
born September 28, 1897.
545. ix.   Mildred F. S. Lockridge (6), born January 24,
1900; married July 25, 1917, John Curry of Augusta County,
Virginia.

226. Emma R. Lockridge (5), daughter of William Lockridge
(4) and Nancy Susan Burns, married (1) Wesley Beverage, died
November 30, 1904; married (2) Samuel Hevener; married (3)
Cornelius Wimer. No children by the second and third marriages.

Children: 2 - first marriage

546. i.   George Beverage (6), died in young manhood.
547. ii.   Mary Beverage (6), died in young womanhood.

227. George M. Lockridge (5), son of William Lockridge (4)
and Nancy Susan Burns, died December 20, 1954; married December
1895, Mary E. Gillett, born June 2, 1871, daughter of Andrew
Gillett and Margaret Bradshaw.

Children: 5

548. i.   Grace Lockridge (6), died young.
549. ii.   Virginia Lockridge (6), died young.
550. iii.   Margaret Lockridge (6), married Alonzo Hiser
of Pendleton County, West Virginia.
551. iv.   (Infant son) Lockridge (6), twin to Margaret,
died in infancy.
+   552. v.   Ransom Hill Lockridge (6).

228. Mary S. G. Keister (5), daughter of Jacob P. Keister
and Mary (Polly) Graham Lockridge (4), married in 1853 in Bath
County, Virginia, William A. Tuning. They resided in Mason
County, West Virginia.

Children: 5

553. i.   John Tuning (6), married _____ Roadcap.
554. ii.   Jefferson Tuning (6), married _____.
555. iii.   Frank Tuning (6), lives in Ohio.
556. iv.   Ida Tuning (6), married William Runnels.
557. v.   Helen Tuning (6), married _____.

229. George R. Keister (5), son of Jacob P. Keister and
Mary (Polly) Graham Lockridge (4), was born in 1839; married in
1865, Byrd Roberts of Tennessee. They migrated west.

Children: 1

558. i.   Ida Keister (6), married _____.

230. William J. Keister (5), son of Jacob P. Keister and
Mary (Polly) Graham Lockridge (4), married Lavina Cobb. They
lived in Ashton, West Virginia.

Children: 9

559. i.   Stephen Keister (6), migrated to Oklahoma.
560. ii.   Lillie Keister (6), married _____ McNeel.
561. iii. Wreathie Keister (6), married _____ O'Bryan.
They lived in Cincinnati, Ohio.
562. iv.   Rose Keister (6), married George Eakle. They
lived in West Virginia.
563. v.   Elizabeth Keister (6), married _____
Martindale.
564. vi.   Worthy Keister (6), married Hearford.
565. vii. Byrd Keister (6), married _____ Rockwell.
566. viii. Leona Keister (6), married Clyde Scott, a
lawyer in Beckley, West Virginia.
567. ix.   Jay Keister (6), married Nora Harrison. They
live in Ashton, West Virginia. He is a R.F.D. Mailcarrier.

232. John D. Keister (5), son of Jacob P. Keister and Mary
(Polly) Graham Lockridge (4), was born April 7, 1845 in Bath
County, Virginia; died October 1929; married (1) in 1865, Ella
Bennett of Kentucky; married (2) in 1891, Marvelina Welling.

Children: 2 - first marriage

568. i.   Clay Keister (6), married Myrtle McCoy.
569. ii.   Rella Keister (6), married Nile King.

Children: 6 - second marriage

570. iii. Alta Ola Keister (6), born May 26, 1892, a twin
to Iva Osa; married Irma Camp.
571. iv.   Iva Osa Keister (6),born May 26, 1892, a twin
to Alta Ola; married December 26, 1910, James Warren Young, born
May 10, 1884. He is a druggist in Huntington, West Virginia.
572. v.   Clyde Seymour Keister (6), born January 19,
1895; married March 26, 1928, Rose Brooks Moore, born January
19, 1907.
573. vi.   Chancey Erwin Keister (6), born August 18,
1898; married in 1917, Anna Wise.
574. vii. Walter Eugene Keister (6), born February 26,
1900; married (1) Nora Belle Cornwell, died January 1943; married
(2) Geneva McCoy. He is a Rural Mailcarrier, Glenwood, West
Virginia.
575. viii. John Rudolph Keister (6), born November 21,
1910; married (1) Ruby Hamilton, born 1917; married (2) October
9, 1949, Mary Schurman.

131

234. Margaret Elizabeth Keister (5), daughter of Jacob P.
Keister and Mary (Polly) Graham Lockridge (4), was born September
11, 1849; died January 20, 1944; married (1) in 1870 Andrew
Jackson McFann; married (2) Captain Jack Ward.

Children: 6 - first marriage

576. i.   Grace McFann (6), born August 29, 1871 in
Kentucky; died February 24, 1933; married Jeff Riggs.
577. ii.   LeGrande McFann (6), born March 12, 1874; was
killed in an accident in 1892 at Dubuque, Iowa.
578. iii. Wells A. McFann (6), born March 18, 1876, a
twin to Oscar F.; married Artie Roe, Bladen, Ohio, died March 2,
1957.
579. iv.   Oscar F. McFann (6), born March 18, 1876, a
twin to Wells A.; married Zelda Thevenir, died June 8, 1944.
580. v.   William Wilson McFann (6), born August 23,
1882; died February 20, 1952; married February 7, 1904, Maggie
M. Crawford.
581. vi.   Helena McFann (6), married (1) in 1911, Floyd
Kinder; married (2) in 1926, Werner Roesch, killed in an accident;
married (3) in 1948, Robert Smeltz.

235. Samuel Keister (5), son of Jacob P. Keister and Mary
(Polly) Graham Lockridge (4), was born February 14, 1854; died
March 18, 1916; married in 1879, Mary Beale Jordan, born January
26, 1861; died April 1, 1947.

Children: 2

+   582. i.   Hattie Augusta Keister (6).
+   583. ii.   Willa Evelyn Keister (6).

256. Americus R. Blundell (5), son of Thomas Blundell and
Jane Gwin (4), was born May 2, 1834; died March 26, 1920; married
Margaret G. Pence, born September 1, 1837; died August 23, 1915,
of Mt. Crawford, Virginia. He served in Company E, 31st Virginia
Regiment, CSA. Both are buried at Mt. Crawford, Virginia.

Children: 2

584. i.   Lera J. Blundell, died October 26, 1887, aged
26 years and 8 days.
585. ii.   William Blundell.

257. Catherine Gwin (5), daughter of David Gwin (4) and Jane
Lockridge (4), married (as his first wife) in 1866, Francis Marion
Trimble, born 1844, son of William Trimble and his first wife,
Sarah Harper. He served in Company H, Barbour Grays, 31st Virginia
Regiment, CSA.

Children: 1

586. i.   Cornelia Trimble (6), married Ashby Cason.

259. David W. Gwin (5), son of David Gwin (4) and Hannah Folks, was born October 15, 1858; married Elizabeth J. Carpenter, died April 22, 1937, daughter of Morgan Carptenter and Martha Robinson.

Children: 4

587. i.   Lula Gray Gwin (6), married James B. Terry.
588. ii.   Lacy May Gwin (6), twin to Lula Gray, married Steward Ryder Ginger.
+ 589. iii.   Grace Gwin (6).
590. iv.   Cecil B. Gwin (6), married Alice Ryder.

262. Moses B. Gwin (5), son of David Gwin (4) and Hannah Folks, was born in 1864 after his father's death; married June 9, 1887 in Bath County, Virginia, Martha Ann Burns, died May 10, 1950, daughter of Joseph Burns and Martha Carpenter.

Children: 6

+ 591. i.   Carmen E. E. Gwin (6).
592. ii.   Mervin E. Gwin (6), died October 3, 1906 at age 17.
593. iii.   Fred W. Gwin (6), married Hettie P. Stephenson, (6), daughter of Charles Crawford Stephenson and Mary M. Lindsay.
594. iv.   Margaret L. Gwin (6).
595. v.   Layton E. Gwin (6), married Gertrude Coursey. They have one child.
596. vi.   Annie Lois Gwin (6), married _____ Watson.

270. Mary Emily Gwin (5), daughter of James Stephenson Gwin (4) and Margaret (Peggy) Bodkin, was born in 1841; died November 16, 1896; married January 24, 1877, Charles T. Kirkpatrick, son of Benjamin Kirkpatrick and Jane Gaylor. He served in Company K, 52nd Infantry, CSA.

Children: 2

597. i.   Margaret Jane Kirkpatrick (6), married George L. Eakle.
598. ii.   James Benjamin Kirkpatrick (6), died in infancy.

271. James Robert Gwin (5), son of James Stephenson Gwin (4) and Margaret (Peggy) Bodkin, was born February 10, 1842; died October 3, 1923; married December 7, 1865 by Rev. John W. Canter, Rebecca Sutton Gillett, born March 19, 1844; died April 5, 1927, daughter of George Gillett and Alban Starr. He served in Company F, 11th Virginia Cavalry, CSA.

Children: 2

599. i.   William Oscar Gwin (6), born December 1869; died July 27, 1914; married October 4, 1899, Emma May Bond.

133

600. ii.   Mary (Molly) Susan Gwin (6), born December 3, 1873; married September 17, 1905, Nixon Howard Cobb (6), son of Samuel Augustus Cobb and Martha Jane Gwin.

275. David Gwin (5), son of James Stephenson Gwin (4) and Margaret (Peggy) Bodkin, married (as her first husband) Alice Rowan, daughter of George W. Rowan and a sister of Amelia Rowan who married James Cleek. She married (2) Alexander Robertson.

Children: 2

601. i.   Fred Gwin (6).
602. ii.   Gertrude Gwin (6), married Harlow Waugh.

276. Martha Jane Gwin (5), daughter of James Stephenson Gwin (4) and Margaret (Peggy) Bodkin, married in 1873, Samuel Augustus Cobb, born in 1851.

Children: 9

603. i.   William Stricker Cobb (6), born July 16, 1874; died February 2, 1955; married in 1900, Effie Harriet Blagg.
604. ii.   David Gwin Cobb (6), married Ada Davis. No children.
+ 605. iii.   John Blaine Cobb (6), born in 1884.
606. iv.   Nixon Howard Cobb (6), married September 17, 1905, Mary (Molly) Susan Gwin (6), born December 3, 1873, daughter of James Robert Gwin and Rebecca Sutton Gillett.
+ 607. v.   Ella R. Cobb (6).
608. vi.   Henderson Cobb (6), born in 1887; married Eugenia Florence Ryder.
609. vii. Gray Cobb (6), married Ethel Alsop. They live in Ohio.
610. viii. Kenton Cobb (6), married Rowinda _____.
611. ix.   Charles S. F. Cobb (6), married (1) Alice Stinebuch; married (2) Margaret Drowers. He is a teacher.

277. Laura Gwin (5), daughter of James Stephenson Gwin (4) and Margaret (Peggy) Bodkin, was born in 1859; married December 21, 1882 in Bath County, Virginia, James William Kirkpatrick, son of John Kirkpatrick and Nancy _____.

Children: 1

612. i.   French Kirkpatrick (6), married Anna Richards. He served in World War I. He died March 23, 1950, aged 56 years.

280. Mahala P. Stephenson (5), daughter of David Stephenson and Esther R. (Hettie) Gwin (4), was born December 26, 1845; died August 25, 1931; married John W. Reed of Spring Hill, Augusta County, Virginia.

Children: 1

+   613. i.   Clara J. Reed (6).

282. Anderson F. Stephenson (5), son of David Stephenson and Esther R. (Hettie) Gwin (4), was born February 22, 1850; died September 1925; married (1) December 18, 1883, Lina Virginia Hanna, born in 1858 at Mt. Solon, Augusta County, Virginia; died December 17, 1902, daughter of Franklin Hanna; married (3) October 4, 1906, Lillie Jane Cleek, born May 6, 1868; died March 2, 1935, daughter of Jacob Crawford Cleek and Margaret Thompson. (See Cleek Family).

Children: 3 - first marriage

614. i.   John Anderson Stephenson (6), born December 12, 1888; died October 11, 1918 in the flu epidemic in Philadelphia; married Jemima Goodlad of Scotland. She returned to Scotland in 1923. No children.
615. ii.   David Campbell Stephenson (6), married Meda Underwood.
+   616. iii. Bayard Suddarth Stephenson (6).

283. John Bolar Stephenson (5), son of David Stephenson and Esther R. (Hettie) Gwin (4), was born in 1853; married in 1876, Minnie B. Alexander, born 1863. She married (2) Samuel K. McClung and married (3) Prof. J. G. Dunsmore.

Children: 1

+   617. i.   Louis Bolar Stephenson (6).

284. Charles Crawford Stephenson (5), son of David Stephenson and Esther R. (Hettie) Gwin (4), was born in 1856; married Mary M. Lindsay, daughter of Professor Stephen C. Lindsay and his first wife, Anne Morgan.

Children: 8

+   618. i.   Charles O. Stephenson (6).
+   619. ii.   Hubert Layton Stephenson (6), born 1887.
+   620. iii. Annie Morgan Stephenson (6).
+   621. iv.   Willard Lindsay Stephenson (6), born August 14, 1889.
+   622. v.   Hettie P. Stephenson (6).
+   623. vi.   Meade White Stephenson (6), born May 21, 1894.
     624. vii. Harry A. Stephenson (6), married _____.
     625. viii. Marion M. Stephenson (6), born November 19, 1900; died August 8, 1935; married Bessie Bennett. No children.

285. Mary Anne Rodgers (5), daughter of Nelson Rodgers and Amanda Gwin (4), was born in 1851; married September 4, 1869 in Bath County, Virginia, Hughart M. Pullin, born in 1839, son of Samuel and Sarah Pullin.

Children: 12

135

626. i. Edward L. Pullin (6), married Maude Rodgers
(6), daughter of Henry Rodgers and Emma Virginia Gwin.
627. ii. William M. Pullin (6), died young.
628. iii. Charles Pullin (6), married Mrs. Ava (Marshall)
Brown, daughter of James Henry Marshall and Hattie Lawrence.
629. iv. Harriett F. Pullin (6), married John W.
Ernest Lockridge (6), son of Aquilla Reece Lockridge and Amanda
Huffer.
630. v. Sarah Virginia Pullin (6), married May 25,
1904, William Strother Helms (6), born September 14, 1875, died
May 11, 1954, son of Jeremiah Strother Helms and Mary Ann
Lockridge.
+ 631. vi. Amanda E. Pullin (6).
632. vii. Isaac Pullin (6), died young.
633. viii. James Pullin (6), died.
634. ix. Henry Pullin (6), died young.
635. x. Elizabeth (Bess) Pullin (6), born August 21,
1882; died December 12, 1954; married Louis Edwin McClung (5),
born April 21, 1883; died November 25, 1929, son of Louis Martin
McClung and Sudie Elizabeth Reamer.
636. xi. Sue Pullin (6), married John Rodgers (6), son
of Henry Rodgers and Emma Virginia Gwin.
637. xii. John Pullin (6), married Eunice Hume of Orange
County, Virginia.

286. Henry Rodgers (5), son of Nelson Rodgers and Amanda
Gwin (4), was born in 1852; died December 1939; married July 2,
1874, Emma Virginia Gwin (5), born April 25, 1858; died 1949,
daughter of David Gwin (4) and Hannah Folks.

Children: 5

+ 638. i. David Rodgers (6).
+ 639. ii. John Rodgers (6).
640. iii. Rachel Belle Rodgers (6), born February 24,
1885; married William Lockridge Shaffier (6), born April 5, 1880,
son of George W. Shaffier and Elizabeth Jane Lockridge. No
children.
+ 641. iv. Ida Rodgers (6).
+ 642. v. Maude Rodgers (6).

295. William Tell Gwin (5),son of Moses Gwin (4) and Elizabeth Cobb, was born July 16, 1875; died May 25, 1945; married
December 20, 1911, Maude Elern Roberts, born 1886, daughter of
Frank Roberts and Henrietta Burns. His father, Moses Gwin, served
in the CSA, Company E, 26th Virginia Cavalry. There is a government marker at his grave.
Children: 6

+ 643. i. Ruth Ailene Gwin (6), born March 21, 1913.
+ 644. ii. Amelia Tell Gwin (6), born October 27, 1914.
+ 645. iii. Milford Collins Gwin (6), born December 11,1915.
+ 646. iv. Randall Fletcher Gwin (6), born June 10, 1917.

    647. v.   Reba Clementine Gwin (6), born September 24,1918.
+   648. vi.   Thelma Frances Gwin (6), born October 1, 1925.

    298.   John Clayton Gwin (5), son of John Wesley Gwin (4)
and Emmeline Gillespie, was born in 1845; married March 21,
1878 in Bath County, Virginia, America Gillespie, born in 1853,
daughter of John Gillespie and Margaret _____.

    Children: 5

+   649. i.   Leola Gwin (6).
    650. ii.   Clayton Gwin (6), married _____.
    651. iii.   Herman Gwin (6), married Lula Lucas.
    652. iv.   Maggie Gwin (6), married William Lucas.
    653. v.   Howard Gwin (6), died young.

    299.   Roberta V. Gwin (5), daughter of John Wesley Gwin (4)
and Emmeline Gillespie, was born in 1850; married March 26, 1874
in Bath County, Virginia, Charles A. Robinson, born 1850, son of
William Robinson.

    Children: 4

    654. i.   Austin Robinson (6), married Hortense Henderson.
He served in the Virginia Legislature in 1920.
    655. ii.   John Robinson (6), unmarried.
    656. iii.   Callie Robinson (6), married (1) Henry Jackson;
married (2) William Clement.
    657. iv.   Maude Robinson (6), unmarried.

    302.   David Franklin Gwin (5), son of John Wesley Gwin (4)
and Emmeline Gillespie, was born January 24, 1857 in Bath County,
Virginia; died July 16, 1937 at Warm Springs, Virginia; married
Minnie Herman Lockridge (6), born January 3, 1859 in Highland
County, Virginia; died May 10, 1932 at Mitchelltown, near Hot
Springs, Virginia, daughter of Robert Carlile Lockridge and
Lydia M. Kutz.

    Children: 6

    658. i.   Elizabeth Agnes Gwin (6), born March 28, 1886,
at Chauncey, Ohio; married February 8, 1906 at Washington, D. C.
by Justice O'Neil, John (Jack) Cleek, born March 7, 1881 in
Bath County, Virginia; died April 18, 1933 in Highland County,
Virginia, son of John Cleek, Jr. and Rachel McNiel Myers. (See
Cleek Family).
+   659. ii.   Charles Harrison (Harry) Gwin (6), born June
1889.
+   660. iii.   Andrew Earl Gwin (6), born 1891.
    661. iv.   Robert Gwin (6), died young.
+   662. v.   Ralph Rose Gwin (6), born April 27, 1895.
+   663. vi.   Austin Dow Gwin (6).

304. Luella Robertine Gwin (5), daughter of John Wesley Gwin (4) and Emmeline Gillespie, was born January 29, 1861; married October 5, 1887 in Bath County, Virginia, Dallas D. Dollins, born in 1862, son of John Dollins and Sallie _____.

Children: 3

664. i.   Hubert Dollins (6).
665. ii.   Carl Dollins (6).
666. iii. _____ Dollins (6).

306. Annie Lee Gwin (5), daughter of John Wesley Gwin (4) and Emmeline Gillespie, was born May 6, 1862; married May 18, 1881 in Bath County, Virginia, James O. Wood, born in 1859, son of F. M. Wood and Rebecca Burger.

Children: 7

    667. i.   David Isadore Wood (6), married Myrtle Adams.
+   668. ii.   Edna Blanche Wood (6).
    669. iii. Una Wood (6), married Russell White. They have two children.
    670. iv.   Georgia Wood (6), married (1) Edward Douglas; married (2) Charles W. Goodwin.
    671. v.   Merritt Wood (6), married Ruth Simmons.
    672. vi.   Darius Wood (6), married Corlie Callahan.
    673. vii. Bernard Wood (6), married (1) Mabel Clark; married (2) Edna _____; married (3) Mrs. Effie Roberts Dulaney.

311. William Jacob McGlaughlin (5), son of Hugh McGlaughlin and Nancy Gwin (4), married (1) Sarah Gum, daughter of Otho Gum and Elizabeth Lightner; married (2) September 19, 1854 in Pocahontas County, West Virginia, Susan Bible, daughter of Jacob Bible and Sallie Lightner. His wives were first cousins. (See Lightner Family).

Children: 1 - first marriage

674. i.   Nancy Jane McGlaughlin (6), died young.

Children: 4 - second marriage

675. ii.   Sarah Elizabeth McGlaughlin (6), married May 14, 1872 in Pocahontas County, West Virginia, John M. Lightner, son of Jacob Lightner and Elizabeth Moore.
676. iii. Alcinda McGlaughlin (6), married Dennis W. Dever, Knapps Creek, West Virginia.
677. iv.   Mitchell D. McGlaughlin (6), born 1858; died 1935; married December 8, 1880 in Bath County, Virginia, Emma K. Greaver, daughter of Jacob Y. Greaver and Lizzie Withrow. They lived in Greenbrier County, West Virginia.
678. v.   Jacob Andrew McGlaughlin (6), married Sallie Gibson. They lived at Broomfield, Indiana.

138

313. George H. McGlaughlin (5), son of Hugh McGlaughlin
and Nancy Gwin (4), married (1) Ruhama Wiley, daughter of John
Wiley and Elizabeth Gillespie; married (2) Mrs. Lula (Gabbert)
Matheny. He served in the CSA. (See Crawford Family).

Children: 9 - first marriage

679. i.   John McGlaughlin (6), born 1866; died February
15, 1950; married Mary McClung of Bath County, Virginia, died
1946. He served in the State Legislature. No children.
+ 680. ii.   Edward F. McGlaughlin (6).
   681. iii.   William McGlaughlin (6), married Laura Middie
Kee, born 1879; died September 16, 1952.
   682. iv.   Clarence McGlaughlin (6), died unmarried.
   683. v.   Fred McGlaughlin (6), married Nelle Yeager,
daughter of Charles Andrew Yeager and Allie Arbogast. (See
Lightner Family).
   684. vi.   Fannie McGlaughlin (6), married Solon H. Moore.
No children.
+ 685. vii.   Mary McGlaughlin (6).
   686. viii. Edith McGlaughlin (6), married Lucius Homer
Stephenson, Jr., as his second wife. No children. He was a
son of Lucius Homer Stephenson and Mary L. Campbell. (See
Campbell Family).
   687. ix.   Annie McGlaughlin (6), died.

314. John Edward Coyner Wilson (5), son of John Edward
Wilson and Elizabeth Susan Coyner (4), was born April 30, 1845;
died April 26, 1926; married (1) Sarah Ann Pyle; married (2)
Mary M. Brazelton; married (3) Nancy McCartney. He served in
the War Between the States, and moved to Los Angeles, California.

Children: 4 (by which marriage unknown)

   688. i.   Elizabeth Wilson (6), married March 16, 1880,
_____ Lawson.
   689. ii.   May Wilson (6).
   690. iii. Edna Wilson (6).
   691. iv.   Alta Wilson (6), died March 1895, unmarried.

315. Robert Hugh Ghormley (5), son of William Curran
Ghormley and Elizabeth Susan Coyner (4), was born April 3, 1856;
died June 29, 1908; married March 6, 1877, Sarah Margaret Brazelton.

Children: 4

+ 692. i.   Pearl Ghormley (6), born April 11, 1878.
+ 693. ii.   Delma Ghormley (6), born July 31, 1879.
+ 694. iii. Nelson B. Ghormley (6), born December 3, 1880.
+ 695. iv.   Gladys Roberta Ghormley (6), born December 25,
1889. She spelled her surname Gormley.

139

316. William Fairfield Ghormley (5), son of William Curran Ghormley and Elizabeth Susan Coyner (4), was born October 14, 1858; married December 28, 1880 (1) Martha A. Froso; married (2) December 25, 1900, Nellie E. Gardner.

Children: 3 - first marriage

696. i. Bertha May Ghormley (6), married Glenn Tidrick.
697. ii. Eleanor Madelaine Ghormley (6), married
Charles Housch.
698. iii. Grace Belle Ghormley (6), married Leland Parr.

Children: 1 - second marriage

699. iv. Hugh William Ghormley (6), married Mary Hall.

318. Newton Baxter Ghormley (5), son of William Curran Ghormley and Elizabeth Susan Coyner (4), was born January 18, 1868; married Rachel Baird.

Children: 3

700. i. Glenn Ghormley (6).
701. ii. Dale Ghormley (6).
702. iii. Vern Ghormley (6).

326. Samuel Robert Coyner (5), son of David Silas Coyner (4) and Matilda Heizer, married Celia Cozzens. They lived in New Mexico.

Children: 5

703. i. David Coyner (6).
704. ii. Mac Coyner (6).
705. iii. Earle Coyner (6).
706. iv. Harvey Coyner (6).
707. v. Charles Coyner (6), died young.

327. Henry Martin Coyner (5), son of David Silas Coyner (4) and Matilda Heizer, died in 1908; married Emma Larrimer.

Children: 13.

708. i. Matilda Coyner (6).
709. ii. Margaret Coyner (6).
710. iii. Jean Coyner (6).
711. iv. Fred Coyner (6).
712. v. Paul Coyner (6), served in World War I.
713. vi. Ruth Coyner (6).
714. vii. Wallace Coyner (6).
715. viii. Raymond Coyner (6).
716. ix. Florence Coyner (6).
717. x. Mary Coyner (6), died young.

718. xi. Harry Coyner (6), died young.
719. xii. Fanny Coyner (6), died young.
720. xiii. Neil Coyner (6), died young.

328. David Gwin Coyner (5), son of David Silas Coyner (4)
and Matilda Heizer, died in 1918; married in 1880, Sarah Stinson.

Children: 3

721. i.   Clara Coyner (6).
722. ii. Robert Coyner (6).
723. iii. James Coyner (6), married Ruth Smalley.

329. Daniel Moore Coyner (5), son of David Silas Coyner (4)
and Matilda Heizer, married Flora James.

Children: 2

724. i. Fay Coyner (6).
725. ii. Annie Coyner (6), married _____ Ford.

330. Fred Ware Coyner (5), son of David Silas Coyner (4)
and Matilda Heizer, married in 1881, Clara Pommert.

Children: 2

726. i. Pearle Coyner (6), married Charles T. Hiser.
727. ii. Mabel Elizabeth Coyner (6), married F. H.
Broyles.

333. John Edward Coyner (5), son of David Silas Coyner (4)
and Matilda Heizer, married Mary Manara in Los Angeles, California.

Children: 1

728. i. Helen Coyner (6).

334. Fanny Carolina Coyner (5), daughter of David Silas
Coyner (4) and Matilda Heizer, was born in 1868; died in 1893;
married James Jenson. She was a missionary in Utah.

Children: 1

729. i. Frances Jenson (6), died young.

354. Tyree Maupin McClung (5), son of David Gwin McClung
(4) and Sarah Ann Cornelia Maupin, was born August 18, 1856;
married December 25, 1879, Roberta Maupin, born December 8, 1853.
He was a Methodist minister.

Children: 4

141

730. i. Alvin Junius McClung (6), born July 20, 1885.
731. ii. Lois Minerva McClung (6), born September 2, 1887.
732. iii. Eunice Roberta McClung (6), born June 29, 1891.
733. iv. Arla Ruth McClung (6), born September 16, 1894.

355. William Wallace McClung (5), son of David Gwin McClung (4) and Sarah Ann Cornelia Maupin, was born September 26, 1858; married March 23, 1881, Emma Elizabeth Littell. Editor of the Salem Sentinel, Salem, Virginia.

Children: 5

734. i. Littell Gwin McClung (6), born February 10, 1882.
735. ii. William Lyle McClung (6), born October 2, 1885.
736. iii. Marshall Wainsborough McClung (6), born December 7, 1888.
737. iv. Edith Randolph McClung (6), born November 12, 1893.
738. v. Christine Randolph McClung (6), born July 28, 1897.

356. Marshall Gwin McClung (5), son of David Gwin McClung (4) and Sarah Ann Cornelia Maupin, was born May 8, 1864; married June 5, 1895, Mrs. Lizzie (Simmons) Koiner, born November 17, 1864, widow of Dr. A. Z. Koiner and daughter of Captain S. F. Simmons of Salem, Virginia.

Children: 1

739. i. David Simmons McClung (6), born March 20, 18'

358. Maude Budles McClung (5), daughter of David Gwin McClung (4) and Sarah Ann Cornelia Maupin, was born November 12, 1869; married August 14, 1894, Benjamin H. Hiner, an atto of Franklin, West Virginia.

Children: 2

740. i. Ralph McClung Hiner (6), born December 25, 1896; died at Charleston, West Virginia. He was Assistant Attorney General of West Virginia.
741. ii. Helen Hiner (6), married _____ Osborne.

374. Rachel Violet Sommers (5), daughter of William M Sommers and Susan Agnes McClung (4), was born in 1868; died June 9, 1916; married in 1886, William W. Stephenson, born 1856; died in 1915.

Children: 8

742. i. Amelia Wilson Stephenson (6), born Octo!

142

18, 1887., a teacher.
    743. ii.   Susan Agnes Stephenson (6), born May 5, 1889.
    744. iii.   Charlotte Frances (Rose) Stephenson (6), born
November 6, 1890.
+ 745. iv.   Harriett Sommers Stephenson (6), born May 12,
1892.
    746. v.   Eliza Warwick Stephenson (6), born February 4,
1894; died June 20, 1929, unmarried. She was a R.N.
    747. vi.   Frank Stephenson (6), born September 26,
1895, unmarried.
    748. vii.   Robert Alexander Stephenson (6), born March
13, 1897; died June 3, 1906.
    749. viii. Wallace Woodworth Stephenson (6), born
November 22, 1900; died June 3, 1906.

    376. Lena Sommers (5), daughter of William M. Sommers
and Susan Agnes McClung (4), married in 1903, Andrew Wallace
Revercomb. They lived at Lost Creek, West Virginia.

    Children: 1

    750. i.   Sommers Revercomb (6), married Paul Stoneking.

    385. Louis Edwin McClung (5), son of Louis Martin McClung
(4) and Sudie Elizabeth Reamer (5), was born April 21, 1883;
died November 25, 1929; married Elizabeth (Bess) Pullin (6),
born August 21, 1882; died December 12, 1954, daughter of
Hughart Montgomery Pullin and Mary Anne Rodgers.

    Children: 3

+ 751. i.   Montgomery Reamer McClung (6), born July 17,
1916.
+ 752. ii.   Mary Vaiden McClung (6), born October 10, 1918.
    753. iii.   Frances Louis McClung (6), born February 23,
1921; married Charles Buchanan. They live in Arlington, Virginia.

    387. Joseph Willis Guinn (6), son of George Hamilton Guinn(5)
and Margaret Ellen Kincaid, married Margaret Agnor.

    Children: 5

    754. i.   Julia Guinn (7), married Thomas Robertson.
They live in Georgia.
    755. ii.   Marylyn Josephine Guinn (7), married Robert
Gardner. They live in Alabama.
    756. iii.   William Guinn (7), married Helen Thompson.
    757. iv.   Warfield (Bud) Guinn (7), married Jessie
Saunders.
    758. v.   Joseph Willis Guinn, Jr. (7), died young.

    388. Margaret Ann Guinn (6), daughter of George Hamilton
Guinn (5) and Margaret Ellen Kincaid, married E. L. Jones.

Children: 5

759. i.   Audrey Jones (7), married Earl Thomas.
760. ii.   Irene Jones (7), married Edward Bell.
761. iii.   Margaret Jones (7), married Wayland Kerns.
762. iv.   Leland Madison Jones (7), married Mollie Ford.
763. v.   Elizabeth Jones (7), died young.

389. James F. Guinn (6), son of George Hamilton Guinn (5) and Margaret Ellen Kincaid, married Elsie Alpha Bayliss.

Children: 2

764. i.   Marian Guinn (7), married June Miller. They live in California.
765. ii.   Dorothy Guinn (7), married Lieutenant Colonel Stanton F. Blaine. He is a professor at VMI, Lexington, Virginia.

390. Mary Dudley Guinn (6), daughter of George Hamilton Guinn (5), was born January 2, 1870; died July 4, 1953; married May 16, 1900, Perry Arthur Tankersley, born 1866; died 1929. Both are buried at Woodland Cemetery, Bath County, Virginia.

Children: 2

766. i.   Samuel Arthur Tankersley (7), married Evelyn Marshall, died October 3, 1956, daughter of Thomas Marshall and Minnie Butler.
+ 767. ii.   Isabell Tankersley (7).

393. Emmett Vasco Guinn (6), son of George Hamilton Guinn (5) and Margaret Ellen Kincaid, married (1) Bessie Watson; married (2) Mrs. Elizabeth (Durham) Lyle.

Children: 3 - first marriage

768. i.   Vasco Guinn (7), married Mary Stombock.
769. ii.   Naomi Guinn (7), married Thomas R. Trigg, Radford, Virginia. She is a teacher.
770. iii.   Mildred Guinn (7), married Jack Craig.

396. John Mustoe Hamilton (6), son of John Gwin Hamilton (5) and Mary Caroline Townsend, was born November 26, 1867; married in 1897, Sarah B. Carpenter.

Children: 7

771. i.   Carrie L. Hamilton (7), married September 5, 1923, Boyd L. Bussard, son of H. Sheffey Bussard and Fannie Stephenson.
772. ii.   Kenton Hamilton (7), married Emma McGlaughlin.
773. iii.   John Hamilton (7), unmarried.

774. iv.   Willis Hamilton (7), twin to Willie; married
Ruby Gum.
    775. v.   Willie Hamilton (7), twin to Willis; married
_____ Bird.
    776. vi.   Elva Hamilton (7), married Jacob Gutshall.
    777. vii.   Annie Hamilton (7), died.

398. Elizabeth J. Hamilton (6), daughter of John Gwin
Hamilton (5) and Mary Caroline Townsend, was born June 23, 1870;
married in 1892, John Robert Woods, died April 18, 1924, son of
James M. Woods and Sarah D. Wiley.

Children: 3

+   778. i.   Lottie Woods (7).
    779. ii.   Jennings Woods (7), married Sylva Leary.
    780. iii. Elmer Woods (7), married Virginia Plecker.

401. John Morgan Armstrong (6), son of John M. Armstrong
and Esther Alice Hamilton (5), was born in 1863; died June 20,
1953; married in 1896, Harriet A. Pruitt (6), daughter of John
C. Pruitt and Almira Hiner.

Children: 5

    781. i.   Clyde Armstrong (7), Keswick, Virginia.
    782. ii.   Ward Armstrong (7), Charlottesville, Virginia.
    783. iii. Virginia Armstrong (7), married May 7, 1924,
Guy E. Crawford, Lynchburg, Virginia.
    784. iv.   _____ Armstrong (7), married E. M. Gutshall,
Norton, West Virginia.
    785. v.   _____ Armstrong (7), married H. R. Goad,
Charlottesville, Virginia.

411. William Mustoe Trimble (6), son of William Trimble
and Mary Jane Hamilton (5), was born September 3, 1864; married
November 8, 1892, Mary Mildred Patterson, born August 15, 1867,
daughter of J. H. Patterson and Margaret Slaven.

Children: 1

    786. i.   Lillian Lee Trimble (7), born September 7, 1893;
married October 16, 1916, Arnet P. Gum, son of Robert Lee Gum
and Ruby Williams.

413. Alice Virginia Trimble (6), daughter of William Trimble
and Mary Jane Hamilton (5), was born August 26, 1871; married
March 18, 1897, William Allen Bussard, born June 4, 1872, son of
Jesse Allen Bussard and Annie Pence Swadley. They live at Lake
Wales, Florida.

Children: 10

    787. i.   Elsie Bussard (7), born 1898.

145

788. ii.   Arlie Williams Bussard (7), born September 22,
1899.
789. iii.   Hubert Bussard (7), born June 12, 1901.
790. iv.   Robert Bussard (7).
791. v.   Mabel Gladys Bussard (7), born October 17,1903.
792. vi.   Eula Lillian Bussard (7), born June 2, 1906.
793. vii.   Edgar Lee Bussard (7).
794. viii. Margie Mildred Bussard (7), born March 4, 1909.
795. ix.   Hazel Audray Bussard (7), born September 24,
1910; died May 1, 1915.
796. x.   Geneva May Bussard (7), born March 1, 1913.

414. Ada Ethel McGlaughlin (6), daughter of Ewing A. (5)
McGlaughlin and Sarah Elizabeth Hite, was born November 1875;
died February 6, 1952; married (1) in 1893, William A. G.
McGlaughlin, son of Hugh McGlaughlin and Nancy Ratcliff; married
(2) in 1928, John Cleek Vance, born April 16, 1875, son of
Charles Vance and Sarah Jane Cleek. (See Cleek and Crawford
Families).

Children: 2 - first marriage

797. i.   Edith McGlaughlin (7), married (1) Forrest
Pritt; married (2) Wayland Ratcliff.
798. ii.   Elva McGlaughlin (7), married Howard Ratcliff.

415. Minnie S. McGlaughlin (6), daughter of Ewing A.
McGlaughlin (5) and Sarah Elizabeth Hite, was born in 1877; died
May 2, 1952; married in 1897, Brown Letcher McGlaughlin, son of
Hugh McGlaughlin and Nancy Ratcliff. (See Crawford Family).

Children: 7

799. i.   Lyle McGlaughlin (7).
800. ii.   Nealie McGlaughlin (7).
801. iii.   Leta McGlaughlin (7).
802. iv.   Marvin McGlaughlin (7).
803. v.   Mollie McGlaughlin (7).
804. vi.   Gladys McGlaughlin (7).
805. vii.   Dorothy McGlaughlin (7).

416. Sarah E. McGlaughlin (6), daughter of Ewing A.
McGlaughlin (5) and Sarah Elizabeth Hite, married Ira D. Gutshall.

Children: 13

806. i.   Ray Gutshall (7), married Florence Corbett.
807. ii.   Harper Gutshall (7), married Rebecca Terry.
808. iii.   Woodrow Gutshall (7), married Janet Newman.
809. iv.   Andrew Gutshall (7), married Leona Hammer.
810. v.   Ira D. Gutshall, Jr. (7), born in 1926, single.
811. vi.   Janet Gutshall (7), married Glenn Corbett.
812. vii.   Icie Gutshall (7), married Otis Chestnut.

146

813. viii. Ruth Gutshall (7), married (as his first wife) Sewell Warner.
814. ix. Delia Gutshall (7), married H. C. (Buzz) Rodgers.
815. x. Josephine Gutshall (7), married Charles B. Fox, Jr.
816. xi. Lucy Gutshall (7), married A. W. Long.
817. xii. (Infant) Gutshall (7), died young.
818. xiii. (Infant) Gutshall (7), died young.

417. Harriet E. McGlaughlin (6), daughter of Ewing A. McGlaughlin (5) and Sarah Elizabeth Hite, married P. Berlin Gutshall.

Children: 6

819. i. Mack Gutshall (7), died.
820. ii. Grant Gutshall (7).
821. iii. Paul Gutshall (7).
822. iv. Clara Gutshall (7).
823. v. Maude Gutshall (7).
824. vi. Kyle Gutshall (7), married Pauline Gardner.

418. J. Boyd McGlaughlin (6), son of Ewing A. McGlaughlin (5) and Sarah Elizabeth Hite, was born July 10, 1884; died August 20, 1935; married October 19, 1910, J. May Corbett.

Children: 9

825. i. Clem McGlaughlin (7), married Agnes Terry, daughter of Andrew Terry and Irene Armstrong.
826. ii. Opal McGlaughlin (7).
827. iii. Iva McGlaughlin (7), married Clement Waggy.
828. iv. Glenna McGlaughlin (7), married _____ Cauley, son of Raymond Cauley and Edna Robertson.
829. v. Ralph McGlaughlin (7).
830. vi. Amy McGlaughlin (7).
831. vii. Gale McGlaughlin (7).
832. viii. Effic McGlaughlin (7).
833. ix. Delmar McGlaughlin (7).

420. William Odie McGlaughlin (6), son of Ewing A. McGlaughlin (5) and Sarah Elizabeth Hite, married Dora Varner.

Children: 7

834. i. Esther McGlaughlin (7), married Everett Terry.
835. ii. Clarence McGlaughlin (7), married Edna Hamilton.
836. iii. Charles McGlaughlin (7).
837. iv. June McGlaughlin (7).
838. v. Lillian McGlaughlin (7).
839. vi. Grant McGlaughlin (7).
840. vii. Audrey McGlaughlin (7).

422. Emma McGlaughlin (6), daughter of Ewing A. McGlaughlin
(5) and Sarah Elizabeth Hite, married Kenton Hamilton (7), son
of John Mustoe Hamilton and Sarah B. Carpenter.

Children: 6

```
841.  i.    Blanche Hamilton (7), married Lee Folks.
842.  ii.   Margaret Hamilton (7), unmarried.
843.  iii.  Annie Hamilton (7), married Lantz Baldwin.
844.  iv.   Norma Hamilton (7), married Burgess Hunt.
845.  v.    Lloyd Hamilton (7), unmarried.
846.  vi.   Carlin Hamilton (7), married Dorothy Staid.
```

426. Kenton Eckard (6), son of Job Eckard and Ruhama Gwin
(5), was born in 1888; died October 24, 1956; married June 29,
1933, Lula R. Williams.

Children: 1

847. i.   Robert Kenton Eckard (7), married September
23, 1955, Mary Louise Hiner.

450. Jerusha A. Hiner (6), daughter of Benjamin Franklin
Hiner (5) and Mary E. Townsend, married in 1897, David M.
Gutshall.

Children: 2

```
848.  i.    Sadie Gutshall (7), married Clarence Gardner.
849.  ii.   Edna Gutshall (7), married Robert Moyers.
```

456. Lillie R. Bratton (6), daughter of George Washington
Bratton and Sarah Lockridge (5), married L. P. Blackwell. She
was buried near Rustburg, Virginia.

Children: 2

```
850.  i.    Faye Blackwell (7), born 1894.
851.  ii.   Ethel Blackwell (7), married _____ McCabe.
```
They live at Buena Vista, Virginia.

458. David Washington Bratton (6), son of George Washington
Bratton and Sarah Lockridge (5), died December 20, 1934; married
July 5, 1894, Myrtie S. Shuey, born March 2, 1872; died May 10,
1952, daughter of Adam H. Shuey and Eliza Arbogast.

Children: 3

```
      852.  i.    (Infant son) Bratton (7), died in infancy.
+     853.  ii.   Janet Shuey Bratton (7).
+     854.  iii.  Helen Bratton (7).
```

465. Ollie Gertrude Lockridge (6), daughter of Robert

Carlile Lockridge (5) and Lydia M. Kutz, was born June 4, 1870; married in 1895, Peter Lightner Hickman, born February 23, 1858, son of Roger Hickman and Margaret Campbell. (See Campbell Family).

Children: 7

+   855. i.   Roger Hickman (7), born July 4, 1896.
     856. ii.   Forrest Hickman (7), died unmarried.
     857. iii.   Virginia Hickman (7), married Warren Campbell, son of Oscar J. Campbell and Annie L. Slaven. (See Campbell Family). No children.
+   858. iv.   Ruth Hickman (7).
     859. v.   Clare Brown Hickman (7), married Juanita Rohr.
     860. vi.   Julian K. Hickman (7), married Neva Martin. He is a lawyer.
ᵗ+   861. vii.   Harry H. Hickman (7).

467. George Robert Revercomb (6), son of John R. Revercomb and Susan R. Lockridge (5), was born in 1860; died April 19, 1945; married Lucretia Burns.

Children: 4

+   862. i.   Ressie Revercomb (7).
+   863. ii.   Hugh W. Revercomb (7), born November 20,1886.
     864. iii.   Dyle Revercomb (7), married Henderson Marshall Lockridge (6), son of Stephen A. Lockridge and Laura Ervine.
+   865. iv.   Layton Gray Revercomb (7).

469. Mary E. Revercomb (6), daughter of John R. Revercomb and Susan R. Lockridge (5), married in 1894, Floyd Wamsley of Randolph County, West Virginia.

Children: 3

     866. i.   Susan Wamsley (7), married Robert Dartnell.
     867. ii.   Janet Wamsley (7), married Hershell Straight.
     868. iii.   William Wamsley (7).

470. Archibald Jacob Revercomb (6), son of John R. Revercomb and Susan R. Lockridge (5), was born February 4, 1869; died July 10, 1945; married May 30, 1906, Jane Armstrong.

Children: 2

     869. i.   Mary Susan Revercomb (7), unmarried, a teacher.
     870. ii.   Harriet Ann (Roonie) Revercomb (7), married Hugh Coursey.

471. Ruhama B. Revercomb (6), daughter of John R. Revercomb and Susan R. Lockridge (5), was born January 5, 1872; died June 1944; married in 1896, William Bratton McGuffin, born May 30, 1867; died May 2, 1940, son of James McGuffin and Nannie Bratton. (See Bratton Family).

Children: 1

871. i.　William Holmes McGuffin (7), born July 30,
1903; married June 1, 1928, Refa Belle Hoover. No children.

472.　John Henderson Revercomb (6), son of John R. Revercomb and Susan R. Lockridge (5), married Emma Lyle.

Children: 5

   872. i.　　Archie B. Revercomb (7), died in infancy.
+ 873. ii.　　Frances Revercomb (7).
   874. iii.　Lina Revercomb (7), married Al Whitson. No
children.
+ 875. iv.　John Henderson Revercomb,Jr. (7).
+ 876. v.　　Ruth Revercomb (7).

475.　Wreathie Susan Revercomb (6), daughter of John R.
Revercomb and Susan R. Lockridge (5), was born January 4, 1882;
died February 10, 1940; married October 15, 1914, William
Hampton Bratton, born July 21, 1877, son of John Feamster
Bratton and Cornelia Goul. (See Bratton Family). They have
two adopted children: Marie Bratton; and Leonard Bratton,
married December 25, 1937, Evelyn Elizabeth Moore.

Children: 1

877. i.　John Revercomb Bratton (7), died in infancy.

478.　Bertie Hull Lockridge (6), daughter of Stephen A.
Lockridge (5) and Laura Ervine, was born February 22, 1867;
died March 26, 1901; married May 27, 1890, Robert E. Lee
Nottingham, born 1864; died March 25, 1948. She was a teacher.

Children: 5

878. i.　　Vera Lee Nottingham (7), married Melvin George
Haverfield, deceased.
879. ii.　Arta Lockridge Nottingham (7), married Maurice
Kistler Chappins.
880. iii.　Henrietta Ruth Nottingham (7), married (1)
William Dearth, deceased; married (2) Herbert Hutson, deceased.
881. iv.　Alma Laura Nottingham (7), married Paul H.Jones.
882. v.　　Robert Paul Nottingham (7), married Violet Hill,
deceased.

480.　Henderson Marshall Lockridge (6), son of Stephen A.
Lockridge (5) and Laura Ervine, was born in 1878; married Dyle
Revercomb (7), daughter of George Robert Revercomb and Lucretia
Burns.

Children: 2

883. i. Margaret Lockridge (7).
884. ii. Katherine Lockridge (7), married John Youel.

486. Lollie Gray Lockridge (6), daughter of Stephen A. Lockridge (5) and Mrs. Julia (Nottingham) Sutton, was born in 1889; died March 13, 1956; married Gadas K. Cavenah.

Children: 2

885. i. Gadas K. Cavenah,Jr. (7), Portland, Oregon.
886. ii. Julian Cavenah (7), Portland, Oregon.

488. Emma Virginia Helms (6), daughter of Jeremiah Strother Helms and Mary Ann (Polly) Lockridge (5), married David C. Graham. She was a teacher. He was Sheriff of Highland County, Virginia.

Children: 2

+ 887. i. Virginia Graham (7).
888. ii. Dennis Graham (7), unmarried.

489. William Strother Helms (6), son of Jeremiah Strother Helms and Mary Ann (Polly) Lockridge (5), was born September 14, 1875; died May 11, 1954; married May 25, 1905, Sarah Virginia Pullin (6), daughter of Hughart M. Pullin and Mary Anne Rodgers.

Children: 1

+ 889. i. Charles Carlile Helms (7).

490. Frances Josephine Helms (6), daughter of Jeremiah Strother Helms and Mary Ann (Polly) Lockridge (5), married in 1909, Charles W. Samples. She was a teacher.

Children: 6

890. i. Herbert Hyler Samples (7), married Grace Todd, R.N.
891. ii. Carlile Samples (7), married Elwood Beck, R.N.
892. iii. Ruth Samples (7), married Raleigh Clem. She is a R. N.
893. iv. Josephine Samples (7), married William Long. She is a R. N.
894. v. Charles Samples (7), married Sarah Carner. He is a school teacher.
895. vi. Diana Samples (7), married Albert Jones.

492. Jeremiah Graham Helms (6), son of Jeremiah Strother Helms and Mary Ann (Polly) Lockridge (5), was born in 1887; married Mary Bradshaw, sister of Herbert Bradshaw.

Children: 1

896. i. James Helms (7), unmarried. M.A., University of Virginia, Charlottesville, Virginia.

493. Leota S. Helms (6), daughter of Jeremiah Strother Helms and Mary Ann (Polly) Lockridge (5), married in 1896 (as his first wife) William T. (Bud) Hamilton, born March 22, 1857; died August 11, 1935, son of Daniel C. Hamilton and Margaret Wright.

Children: 4

897. i. Elsie Hamilton (7), married Martin M. Folks, Clerk of the Court, Highland County, Virginia.
898. ii. Mary Bess Hamilton (7), married H. L. (Jack) Marshall.
899. iii. Willie Hamilton (7), married William S. Ross. No children.
900. iv. R. Mason Hamilton (7), married Viola Southers.

494. Robert Quidore Helms (6), son of Jeremiah Strother Helms and Mary Ann (Polly) Lockridge (5), was born January 5, 1884; married in 1907, Richie Edith Burns, born 1888.

Children: 6

901. i. Robert McAvoy Helms (7), born 1908.
902. ii. Rupert Burns Helms (7), born 1910.
903. iii. Rembert Helms (7).
904. iv. Rowena Helms (7), born 1916; married _____ Bell, M. D.
905. v. Ritchie Lorena Helms (7), born April 6, 1921; married _____ Allers.
906. vi. Raymond Helms (7), married Delores Gutshall.

499. Russell Vance Lockridge (6), son of David E. Lockridge (5) and Susan V. Vance, was born May 7, 1890; died June 20, 1943; married September 1, 1917, Alice Dandridge Lemmon, born February 13, 1893; died January 9, 1932.

Children: 4

+ 907. i. Robert Spottswood Lockridge (7), born January 22, 1919.
+ 908. ii. Russell Vance Lockridge (7), born November 1, 1920.
909. iii. Flora Susan Lockridge (7), born December 20,1922. She served in the Women's Army Corps from January 3, 1945 to July 17, 1948 and was in Vienna, Austria for 21 months. She lives at 1016 University Drive, Alexandria, Virginia.
910. iv. Elizabeth Dandridge Lockridge (7), born October 5, 1929; married August 17, 1956, David Tannenbaum, born August 11, 1932. They live in Brooklyn, New York.

500. Frank Lockridge (6), son of David E. Lockridge (5) and Susan V. Vance, died October 4, 1955; married Kate J. Shumate, died November 25, 1955.

Children: 1

+ 911. i. Mary Susan Lockridge (7).

502. David Marvin Lockridge (6), son of Robert Pierce Lockridge (5) and Ella Josephine Folks, married Nellie Mackey.

Children: 6

912. i. David M. Lockridge, Jr. (7), died young.
913. ii. Steward Lockridge (7), married Louise Baldwin.
914. iii. Inez Lockridge (7), married _____ Layman.
915. iv. Wallace Lockridge (7), died young.
916. v. Luella Lockridge (7), married (1) _____ Cauley; married (2) William McFadden. They live at Ellerson, Virginia.
917. vi. Thelma Lockridge (7), married _____.

503. Steward Ryder Lockridge (6), son of Robert Pierce Lockridge (5) and Ella Josephine Folks, died in 1937; married Lenna Vines, died January 1929.

Children: 6

+ 918. i. Josephine Lockridge (7), born March 3, 1915.
919. ii. Clementine Lockridge (7), married (1) Frank Harlow; married (2) James Henry.
920. iii. Estelle Lockridge (7), married _____.
921. iv. Robert Carson Lockridge (7).
922. v. Stuart Walker Lockridge (7).
923. vi. McKey Lockridge (7), married _____.

504. Robert Lockridge (6), son of Robert Pierce Lockridge (5) and Ella Josephine Folks, married (1) Katie Bell Coursey; married (2) Mrs. Flora Belle (Chrisman) Dudley.

Children: 4 - first marriage

+ 924. i. Mason Lockridge (7).
925. ii. Roberta Lockridge (7), married Fred T. Carter.
+ 926. iii. Max Lockridge (7).
927. iv. Doris Lockridge (7), born May 30, 1928; died in 1953; married W. C. Asbell.

505. Howard Luther Lockridge (6), son of Robert Pierce Lockridge (5) and Ella Josephine Folks, married August 18, 1924, Adele Key. He served in World War I.

Children: 6

153

928. i. Bobbie Kay Lockridge (7), married in 1952, Mary Ellen Caldwell. He served from January 1945 to February 1946 as a PFC in the Infantry and received a medical discharge. He was overseas with the Japanese Occupation Forces. He is a deacon in Tinkling Springs Presbyterian Church, Augusta County, Virginia.
929. ii. George William Lockridge (7), married May 14, 1955, Goldie Snyder. He served as a PFC in the Army Medical Corps from November 1950 to July 1952 in the Korean Police action.
930. iii. Nancy Jane Lockridge (7), married June 30, 1956 William L. Henderson.
931. iv. Margaret Ella Lockridge (7), married June 18, 1949, Hugh C. Ewing, Jr. They live in Newport News, Virginia.
932. v. Betty Lee Lockridge (7), married April 25, 1949, James R. Witt. They live in Richmond, Virginia.
933. vi. Ronnie Lee Lockridge (7).

506. Maysie Lockridge (6), daughter of Robert Pierce Lockridge (5) and Ella Josephine Folks, married Alton Brumfield.

Children: 2

934. i. Nancy Wonder Brumfield (7).
935. ii. Mickie Brumfield (7).

509. Clifton Hylie Lockridge (6), son of John J. Lockridge (5) and Frances Colaw, was born February 27, 1892; married June 16, 1915, Wreathie Loving.

Children: 6

+ 936. i. Clifton Hylie Lockridge, Jr. (7).
+ 937. ii. Clarence Lockridge (7).
+ 938. iii. Warren Lockridge (7).
+ 939. iv. Helen Lockridge (7).
+ 940. v. Hilda Lockridge (7).
+ 941. vi. Nancy Lockridge (7).

510. Merle G. Lockridge (6), son of John J. Lockridge (5) and Frances Colaw, married in 1931, Eula Wagoner.

Children: 1

942. i. Janet Lockridge (7), married Dennis Crutchfield.

511. James C. Lockridge (6), son of John J. Lockridge (5) and Frances Colaw, married Grace Bishop.

Children: 3

+ 943. i. Gerald Collin Lockridge (7).
+ 944. ii. Maxine Lockridge (7).
945. iii. James Harry Lockridge (7), married Louise Pullin (7), daughter of John Pullin and Eunice Hume.

514. John W. Ernest Lockridge (6), son of Aquilla Reese Lockridge (5) and Amanda Huffer, married Harriett F. Pullin (6), daughter of Hughart Montgomery Pullin and Mary Anne Rodgers.

Children: 2

946. i.   Charles Lockridge (7), married Dorothy Lipscomb.
947. ii. Ruth Lockridge (7), married Roy Grant.

515. Kenny C. Lockridge (6), son of Aquilla Reese Lockridge (5) and Amanda Huffer, married Etta E. Marshall.

Children: 1

948. i.   Leo Lockridge (7), married Anne McClintic, born March 3, 1916, daughter of Robert G. McClintic and Janie Bell Dickenson. He is Sheriff of Bath County,Virginia.

520. Andrew Lee Lockridge (6), son of Aquilla Reese Lockridge (5) and Amanda Huffer, married Hazel Butler, daughter of George W. Butler and Della Ray Harouff.

Children: 1

949. i.   Audrey Lockridge (7).

522. Annie F. Lockridge (6), daughter of Aquilla Reese Lockridge (5) and Amanda Huffer, died April 22, 1935; married (as his second wife) William T. (Bud) Hamilton, son of Daniel C. Hamilton and Margaret Wright.

Children: 1

950. i.   Florence Hamilton (7), married David Michael.

539. Leona May Lockridge (6), daughter of William Peter Buchanan Lockridge (5) and Hannah Jane Huffer, was born May 7, 1887; married November 6, 1907, Arlie A. Carpenter, born October 26, 1886; died January 23, 1936, son of John W. Carpenter and Christina Burns.

Children: 4

951. i.   Chalmers Carpenter (7), married Geneva Burnette. He is Trust Officer, Augusta National Bank, Staunton, Virginia.
952. ii. Anderson William Carpenter (7), married Lucille Rimel.
953. iii. Ernestine Carpenter (7), married Robert S. Givler, Jr., Richmond, Virginia.
954. iv. Josephine Carpenter (7), married Guy A. Kerby.

540. Lucius Homer Lockridge (6), son of William Peter Buchanan Lockridge (5) and Hannah Jane Huffer, was born September 3, 1888; married May 21, 1912, Minnie Terry, daughter of Andrew

155

Terry and Irene Armstrong.

Children: 5

955.	i.	Andrew Lockridge (7), born 1915.
956.	ii.	Eula Mae Lockridge (7), born 1913.
957.	iii.	Ora Lockridge (7), born 1917.
958.	iv.	Elmer Lockridge (7), born 1920.
959.	v.	Lucy Lockridge (7), born 1929.

543. Mary Treacy M. Lockridge (6), daughter of William Peter Buchanan Lockridge (5) and Hannah Jane Huffer, was born October 18, 1895; married October 11, 1916, Arthur B. Neal, Staunton, Virginia.

Children: 1

960. i. Arthur B. Neal, Jr. (7).

544. William Peter Buchanan Lockridge (6), son of William Peter Buchanan Lockridge (5) and Hannah Jane Huffer, was born September 28, 1877; married January 18, 1922, Elizabeth Terry, daughter of Andrew J. Terry and Irene Armstrong.

Children: 3

961.	i.	Dale Lockridge (6), married _____ Bussard.
962.	ii.	_____ Lockridge (6).
963.	iii.	_____ Lockridge (6).

552. Ransom Hill Lockridge (6), son of George M. Lockridge (5) and Mary E. Gillett, married Opal Barlow.

Children: 2

964.	i.	Ann Barlow Lockridge (7).
965.	ii.	Ray Edward Lockridge (7).

582. Hattie Augusta Keister (6), daughter of Samuel Keister (5) and Mary Beale Jordan, married March 3, 1910, Wallace Nathan Rardin, born October 26, 1884; died December 27, 1943.

Children: 1

966. i. Thomas Keister Rardin (7), born April 9, 1911; died January 31, 1957; married March 18, 1933, Mildred Nell Mahone.

583. Willa Evelyn Keister (6), daughter of Samuel Keister (5) and Mary Beale Jordan, was born March 18, 1886; married (1) November 9, 1907, Walter Jacob Withers, M.D., born March 26, 1879; died February 26, 1930; married (2) September 18, 1947, Rollo D. Atchinson, born August 20, 1875.

Children: 2 - first marriage

967. i.   Mary Margaret Withers (7), born October 25,
1909; died November 8, 1909.
968. ii.   Frances Emogene Withers (7), born December 14,
1910; married March 26, 1928, Rowan Glenn Atchinson.

589. Grace Gwin (6), daughter of David W. Gwin (5) and
Elizabeth J. Carpenter, married David Kincaid.

Children: 1

969. i.   Lennie Kincaid (7).

591. Carmen E. E. Gwin (6), daughter of Moses B. Gwin (5)
and Martha Ann Burns, married in 1906, Hollie Gutshall.

Children: 8

970. i.   _____ Gutshall (7), married H. N. Haskins.
971. ii.   _____ Gutshall (7), married J. M. Farmer.
972. iii.   _____ Gutshall (7), married W. W. Kemp.
973. iv.   _____ Gutshall (7), married Joseph Proiette.
974. v.   _____ Gutshall (7), married W. V. Chappell.
975. vi.   Vancel V. Gutshall (7).
976. vii.   Clyde B. Gutshall (7).
977. viii. Edward G. Gutshall (7).

605. John Blaine Cobb (6), son of Samuel Augustus Cobb and
Martha Jane Gwin (5), was born in 1884; married in 1909, Zella
Eakle.

Children: 5

978. i.   Ralph Bonner Cobb (7), married Jessie Porter.
979. ii.   Marie Agnes Cobb (7), married William Reavis.
980. iii. Lucille Lillian Cobb (7), married James Swartz.
981. iv.   George Elmo Cobb (7), married Dorothy Porter.
982. v.   Laura Frances Cobb (7), married Monroe Barnes.

607. Ella R. Cobb (6), daughter of Samuel Augustus Cobb and
Martha Jane Gwin (5), married in 1906, Arthur Hevener.

Children: 2

983. i.   Clarence Hevener (7), married Lena Thornton.
984. ii.   Arnett Hevener (7), married Ocie Simmons.

613. Clara J. Reed (6), daughter of John W. Reed and
Mahala P. Stephenson (5), died October 1, 1904; married in 1904,
Robert G. McGuffin.

Children: 1

985. i.   Clara McGuffin (7), married Fred Corbett.

157

616. Bayard Suddarth Stephenson (6), son of Anderson F. Stephenson (5) and Lina Virginia Hanna, married (1) Annie ____; married (2) ____; married (3) ____.

Children: 1 - first marriage

986. i. B. Stuart Stephenson (7), an Instructor at Washington and Lee University, Lexington, Virginia.

617. Louis Bolar Stephenson (6), son of John Bolar Stephenson (5) and Minnie B. Alexander, married Nannie Sutton.

Children: 2

987. i. Louis Bolar Stephenson, Jr. (7), married Edna Moles.
988. ii. Hubert Stephenson (7), married Edith Supinger.

618. Charles O. Stephenson (6), son of Charles Crawford Stephenson (5) and Mary M. Lindsay, died May 1936; married January 12, 1922, Mary Kate Campbell, born April 5, 1891; died in 1949, daughter of Filmore T. Campbell and Mary Ada Sively. (See Campbell Family).

Children: 3

989. i. Charles Filmore Stephenson (7), died young.
+   990. ii. Dorothy Stephenson (7).
991. iii. Edward L. Stephenson (7).

619. Hubert Layton Stephenson (6), son of Charles Crawford Stephenson (5) and Mary M. Lindsay, was born in 1887; married ____. He served in World War I.

Children: 1

992. i. Virginia Dare Stephenson (7).

620. Annie Morgan Stephenson (6), daughter of Charles Crawford Stephenson (5) and Mary M. Lindsay, married William Maxey.

Children: 1

993. i. William Maxey, Jr. (7), killed in World War II.

621. Willard Lindsay Stephenson (6), son of Charles Crawford Stephenson (5) and Mary M. Lindsay, was born August 14, 1889; married December 29, 1920, Nannie Virginia Bratton (6), born September 2, 1895, daughter of George Washington Bratton and Frances Emily Lockridge.

Children: 1

994.   i.   Mary Frances Stephenson (7), married William
Thomas Johnson.

622.   Hettie P. Stephenson (6), daughter of Charles Crawford
Stephenson (5) and Mary M. Lindsay, married Fred W. Gwin (6), son
of Moses B. Gwin and Martha Ann Burns.

Children: 1

995.   i.   Evelyn Gwin (7).

623.   Meade White Stephenson (6), son of Charles Crawford
Stephenson (5) and Mary M. Lindsay, was born May 21, 1894;
married Bonnie Maloy, daughter of E. J. Maloy and Georgiana B.
Vance.

Children: 2

996.   i.   Ellen Stephenson (7), married Roy Johnson.
997.   ii.   William Emmett Stephenson (7), married Elizabeth Crittenberger.

631.   Amanda E. Pullin (6), daughter of Hughart Montgomery
Pullin and Mary Anne Rodgers (5), married in 1910, James E.
Carwell.

Children: 1

998.   i.   Charles Carwell (7).

638.   David Rodgers (6), son of Henry Rodgers (5) and Emma
Virginia Gwin (5), married Priscilla Stephenson.

Children: 3

999.   i.   Lina Rodgers (7), married Leroy Giles.
1000. ii.   Charles Rodgers (7).
1001. iii.   Robert Rodgers (7).

639.   John Rodgers (6), son of Henry Rodgers (5) and Emma
Virginia Gwin (5), married Sue Pullin (6), daughter of Hughart
Montgomery Pullin and Mary Anne Rodgers.

Children: 4

1002. i.   Donald Rodgers (7), married Elva Poindexter.
1003. ii.   Edward Rodgers (7), married Thelma Baldwin.
1004. iii.   Woodrow Rodgers (7), married Clarice Carpenter.
1005. iv.   Chloe Rodgers (7), married Rev. Lee Chattin,
a Methodist minister.

641.   Ida Rodgers (6), daughter of Henry Rodgers (5) and
Emma Virginia Gwin (5), married John Godlove McAllister.

159

Children: 2

1006. i.   Hertha McAllister (7), twin to Bertha; married
Cecil Marshall.
1007. ii.   Bertha McAllister (7), twin to Hertha, died young.

642. Maude Rodgers (6), daughter of Henry Rodgers (5) and
Emma Virginia Gwin (5), married Edward L. Pullin (6), son of
Hughart Montgomery Pullin and Mary Anne Rodgers.

Children: 4

1008. i.   Herman Pullin (7), married Ruth Phillips.
1009. ii.   Fred Pullin (7), married Ruth Huffer.
1010. iii.   Ralph M. Pullin (7), born May 16, 1905; married
Charlotte Ruth Simpson, born October 26, 1909, daughter of Andrew
Milton Simpson and Lula Feaster. (See Cleek Family).
1011. iv.   Virginia Pullin (7), married Clarence Roberts,
son of George W. Roberts and Fannie Woodzell.

643. Ruth Ailene Gwin (6), daughter of William Tell Gwin
(5) and Maude Elern Roberts, was born March 21, 1913 at Bolar,
Bath County, Virginia; married May 2, 1953 at Williamsburg,
Virginia, James Boyle Brennen.

Children: 1

1012. i.   James Gwin Brennen (7), born January 10, 1956
at Washington, D. C.

644. Amelia Tell Gwin (6), daughter of William Tell Gwin
(5) and Maude Elern Roberts, was born October 27, 1914 at Bolar,
Bath County, Virginia; married September 23, 1950 at Salem
Lutheran Church, Mt. Sidney, Virginia, John Paul Link, born
August 17, 1914. John Paul Link is a descendant of the same Link
Family as President Dwight D. Eisenhower. (See The Link Family,
Paxson Link, 1951).

Children: 2

1013. i.   John Daniel Link (7), born March 15, 1953 at
Harrisonburg, Virginia.
1014. ii.   Suzanne Gwin Link (7), born March 28, 1955 at
Harrisonburg, Virginia.

645. Milford Collins Gwin (6), son of William Tell Gwin (5)
and Maude Elern Roberts, was born December 11, 1915 at Bolar,
Bath County, Virginia; married March 5, 1943 at Staunton, Virginia,
Helen Meredith Paxton, daughter of Lloyd Wilson Paxton and Gladys
Hanger. He served in the Navy in World War II.

Children: 4

1015. i.   Carolyn Virginia Gwin (7), born November 18,
1944 in Staunton, Virginia.

160

1016. ii.   William Lloyd Gwin (7), born January 27, 1948 in Staunton, Virginia.
1017. iii. Elizabeth Ann Gwin (7), born April 13, 1950 in Waynesboro, Virginia.
1018. iv.   Stephen Paxton Gwin (7), born August 21, 1954 in Waynesboro, Virginia.

646. Randall Fletcher Gwin (6), son of William Tell Gwin (5) and Maude Elern Roberts, was born June 10, 1917 at Bolar, Bath County, Virginia; married July 17, 1943, Lois Virginia Sheets. Mrs. Gwin is also a descendant of the Link Family. (See The Link Family, Paxson Link, 1951). He served in the Army in World War II, and is now stationed at Langeley Field, Virginia.

Children: 5

1019. i.   Joan Patricia Gwin (7), born May 17, 1944.
1020. ii.   Carlyle Evans Gwin (7), born August 2, 1945.
1021. iii. Alvin Lloyd Gwin (7), born September 16, 1946.
1022. iv.   Leslie Wayne Gwin (7), born August 25, 1947.
1023. v.   Clyde David Gwin (7), born June 25, 1955.

648. Thelma Frances Gwin (6), daughter of William Tell Gwin (5) and Maude Elern Roberts, was born October 1, 1925 at Bolar, Bath County, Virginia; married June 3, 1951 at Salt Lake City, Utah, Jack Welch.

Children: 2

1024. i.   Jack Gwin Welch (7), born July 17, 1953.
1025. ii.   Mark Evans Welch (7), born January 28, 1956.

649. Leola Gwin (6), daughter of John Clayton Gwin (5) and America Gillespie, married Carl Clemmer.

Children: 2

1026. i.   Iva Clemmer (7), married Fred Trimble.
1027. ii.   Clayton Clemmer (7).

659. Charles Harrison (Harry) Gwin (6), son of David Franklin Gwin (5) and Minnie Herman Lockridge (6), was born June 1889; married Grace Price, born June 3, 1892, daughter of Samuel Davies Price and Margaret Caroline McClure.

Children: 3

1028. i.   Curtis Holmes Gwin (7), born April 1, 1917. He served in World War II.
1029. ii.   Herman Price Gwin (7), born June 9, 1921.
1030. iii. Herbert Lewis Gwin (7), born April 26, 1930.

660. Andrew Earl Gwin (6), son of David Franklin Gwin (5) and Minnie Herman Lockridge (6), was born in 1891; married July 5, 1919 at Warm Springs, Virginia by Rev. Charles W. Reed, Agatha Lois Matheney, born in 1894, daughter of Ervin Perry Matheney and Alice H. Simmons. He served in the 80th Infantry Division and the 29th Regiment, 33rd Infantry Division overseas in World War I. Mrs. Agatha Lois Matheney Gwin is a descendant of Robert and Agnes Young who came from Ireland to Virginia with three of their seven children in 1740 and lived at Beverley Manor near Staunton, Virginia. Robert Young died intestate in 1761. Robert Young's son, John Young, married Agnes Elizabeth Davis and had four children. Their second child was Susanna Young who married June 13, 1768, James Gilliland and they had thirteen children, one of whom was Nancy Gilliland. Nancy Gilliland married April 13, 1801, Conrad Lemon and had twelve children, one of whom was Elizabeth Lemon. Elizabeth Lemon married December 15, 1825 in Alleghany County, Virginia, William Brown, and had six children, one of whom was Catherine J. Brown. Catherine J. Brown married August 26, 1856 in Alleghany County, Virginia, Oliver Perry Matheney, and had three children, one of whom was Ervin Perry Matheney. Ervin Perry Matheney married December 31, 1885 in Covington, Virginia, Alice H. Simmons. They had four children: Edward C. Matheney, married Bettie Armentrout and had two children; Emmett L. Matheney, died without issue; Guy H. Matheney, married Isabel West and had four children; and Agatha Lois Matheney.

Children: 5

    1031. i.   Edward Earl Gwin (7), born June 9, 1920.
+ 1032. ii.   Robert Pearl Gwin (7), born August 10, 1921.
    1033. iii.   Frank Ervin Gwin (7), born March 16, 1923; married December 15, 1946 at Hot Springs, Virginia, Frances Steinbock.
    1034. iv.   Hugh Sterling Gwin (7), born March 10, 1929.
    1035. v.   Claudia Beatrice Gwin (7), born April 28, 1937.

662. Ralph Rose Gwin (6), son of David Franklin Gwin (5) and Minnie Herman Lockridge (6), was born April 27, 1895; died May 7, 1951; married Maude Clarkson. He served in the Blue Ridge Division, 317th Infantry in World War I. He is buried at Arlington National Cemetery.

Children: 2

    1036. i.   Kathleen Lois Gwin (7), married Dante P. Ridolfi. They live at Santa Rosa, California. No children.
+ 1037. ii.   Jean Gwin (7).

663. Austin Dow Gwin (6), son of David Franklin Gwin (5) and Minnie Herman Lockridge (6), married Eunice Christian, R.N.

Children: 2

+ 1038. i.   June Gwin (7).
  1039. ii.   Betty Lou Gwin (7), married N. P. Roland. No
children.

668. Edna Blanche Wood (6), daughter of James O. Wood and
Annie Lee Gwin (5), married Homer Lucas.

Children: 2

1040. i.   Donald Lucas (7).
1041. ii.   Hugh Lucas (7).

680. Edward F. McGlaughlin (6), son of George H. McGlaughlin
(5) and Ruhama Wiley, married Margaret Mann.

Children: 5

1042. i.   Claude McGlaughlin (7), married Pearl Sydenstricker. They live in Lewisburg, West Virginia.
1043. ii.   Frank McGlaughlin (7), married Irene Logan.
They live in Marlinton, West Virginia.
1044. iii. Gray McGlaughlin (7), married Elizabeth
Blackhurst. They live in Romney, West Virginia.
1045. iv.   Glenna McGlaughlin (7), married _____.
1046. v.   Margaret McGlaughlin (7).

685. Mary McGlaughlin (6), daughter of George H. McGlaughlin
(5) and Ruhama Wiley, married James Smith.

Children: 2

1047. i.   Helen Smith (7), unmarried. She is a school
teacher.
1048. ii.   Louise Smith (7), married Charles Miles,
Birmingham, Michigan.

692. Pearl Ghormley (6), daughter of Robert Hugh Ghormley
(5) and Sarah Margaret Brazelton, was born April 11, 1878;
married March 3, 1898, Marcus Lafayette Ingle.

Children: 7

+ 1049. i.   Esther Margaret Ingle (7), born March 17, 1900.
  1050. ii.   Florence Bertha Ingle (7), born December 4,
1902; married Arthur Lee McIntosh.
  1051. iii. Gladys Lillian Ingle (7), born December 7,
1904; married Francis Burns.
  1052. iv.   Robert Thomas Ingle (7), born December 27,1905.
  1053. v.   Marcus Ghormley Ingle (7), born October 7,1908.
  1054. vi.   Miriam Ruth Ingle (7), born March 25, 1911.
  1055. vii. Frances Pearl Ingle (7), born May 20, 1912.

693. Delma Ghormley (6), daughter of Robert Hugh Ghormley

(5) and Sarah Margaret Brazelton, was born July 31, 1879; married November 12, 1904, Fred Caryl Robey.

Children: 1

1056. i. Ralph Robey (7), born August 6, 1910.

694. Nelson B. Ghormley (6), son of Robert Hugh Ghormley (5) and Sarah Margaret Brazelton, was born December 3, 1880; married February 26, 1908, Florence L. Davis. This family spelled their surname Gormley.

Children: 4

1057. i. Dorothy Alice Gormley (7), born February 12, 1910.
1058. ii. Mildred Gormley (7), born March 23, 1911.
1059. iii. Robert James Gormley (7), born May 17, 1913.
1060. iv. Nelson Addison Gormley (7), born August 19, 1920.

695. Gladys Roberta Ghormley (6), daughter of Robert Hugh Ghormley (5) and Sarah Margaret Brazelton, was born December 25, 1889; died November 12, 1921; married October 7, 1908, Lester Bence. She spelled her surname Gormley.

Children: 4

1061. i. Burris Gormley Bence (7), born January 1, 1911.
1062. ii. Mary Margaret Bence (7), born February 5, 1913; died April 8, 1928.
1063. iii. Joy Maxine Bence (7), born June 6, 1919.
1064. iv. Robert Lester Bence (7), born November 5, 1921; died January 5, 1922.

745. Harriett Sommers Stephenson (6), daughter of William W. Stephenson and Rachel Violet Sommers (5), was born May 12, 1892; married October 30, 1918 (as his second wife) Boyd Stephenson, born January 23, 1879, son of Lucius H. Stephenson and Mary L. Campbell. (See Campbell Family). He served as Commonwealth Attorney of Highland County, Virginia for several terms.

Children: 2

1065. i. Lucius Stephenson (7), an attorney at Richmond, Virginia. He served in World War II.
1066. ii. Boyd Wilson Stephenson (7), married Dorothy Colaw.

751. Montgomery Reamer McClung (6), daughter of Louis Edwin McClung (5) and Elizabeth (Bess) Pullin (6), was born July 17, 1916; married July 19, 1938 (1) William F. Hunter; married (2) Kenneth Terrell Linkous.

Children: 1 - first marriage

1067. i.   William Snowden Hunter (7), born November 21,
1939.

Children: 1 - second marriage

1068. ii.   Marylin Terrell Linkous (7).

752. Mary Vaiden McClung (6), daughter of Louis Edwin
McClung (5) and Elizabeth (Bess) Pullin (6), was born October
10, 1918; married September 1942, Cornell Leake. They live in
Ottawa, Canada.

Children: 3

1069. i.   Monty Kaye Leake (7), born June 22, 1944.
1070. ii.   Vickey Frances Leake (7).
1071. iii.   Charles McClung Leake (7).

767. Isabell Tankersley (7), daughter of Perry Arthur
Tankersley and Mary Dudled Guinn (6), married Samuel Hatch
McLaughlin.

Children: 2

1072. i.   Hugh Arthur McLaughlin (8).
1073. ii.   Elizabeth Allen McLaughlin (8), married William
Edwin Link, a Presbyterian minister.

778. Lottie Woods (7), daughter of John Robert Woods and
Elizabeth J. Hamilton (6), married John Slaven.

Children: 1

1074. i.   Mae Slaven (8).

853. Janet Shuey Bratton (7), daughter of David Washington
Bratton (6) and Myrtie S. Shuey, married Roy Moffitt, Greensboro,
North Carolina.

Children: 1

1075. i.   Roy Bratton Moffitt (8).

854. Helen Bratton (7), daughter of David Washington
Bratton (6) and Myrtie S. Shuey, married (1) Frank M. Merriken;
married (2) Clinton Stevens.

Children: 1 - first marriage

1076. i.   Frank M. Merriken, Jr. (8).

855. Roger Hickman (7), son of Peter Lightner Hickman and
Ollie Gertrude Lockridge (6), was born July 4, 1896; married

165

Nellie Shaw. He is a physician. They live in Arkansas.

Children: 1

1077. i.   Ann Maudine Hickman (8).

858.   Ruth Hickman (7), daughter of Peter Lightner Hickman
and Ollie Gertrude Lockridge (6), married Hermann William
Gabriel, II.

Children: 2

1078. i.   Hermann William Gabriel, III (8).
1079. ii.   Hemmar Ruskin Gabriel (8).

861.   Harry H. Hickman (7), son of Peter Lightner Hickman
and Ollie Gertrude Lockridge (6), married (1) Zella Carpenter;
married (2) Virginia Jefferson.

Children: 1 - first marriage

1080. i.   Dianne C. Hickman (8).

Children: 1 - second marriage

1081. ii.   Ralph Herman Hickman (8).

862.   Ressie Revercomb (7), daughter of George Robert Revercomb (6) and Lucretia Burns, married Henry Swadley.

Children: 2

1082. i.   Leona Swadley (8), married Patrick Maloy.
1083. ii.   Virginia Swadley (8), married E. C. Rexroad.

863.   Hugh W. Revercomb (7), son of George Robert Revercomb
(6) and Lucretia Burns, was born November 20, 1886; married
Loretta Baylor.

Children: 9

   1084. i.   Paul Revercomb (8), married Alene Sorrels.
No children.
+ 1085. ii.   Hugh W. Revercomb, Jr. (8).
   1086. iii.   Waldin Revercomb (8).
+ 1087. iv.   Thomas Eugene Revercomb (8).
+ 1088. v.   Mary Lucretia Revercomb (8).
+ 1089. vi.   Edith Revercomb (8).
+ 1090. vii.   Virginia Revercomb (8).
   1091. viii. Frances Revercomb (8).
   1092. ix.   Myrtha Jane Revercomb (8).

865.   Layton Gray Revercomb (7), daughter of George Robert

Revercomb (6) and Lucretia Burns, married Robert James Erwin.

Children: 3

1093. i.   James Gray Erwin (8), born July 12, 1915;
married in Germany, Bettie _____.
+   1094. ii.   Samuel Revercomb Erwin (8), born August 11, 1918.
+   1095. iii.   Robert McAllister Erwin (8), born May 24, 1923.

873. Frances Revercomb (7), daughter of John Henderson
Revercomb (6) and Emma Lyle, married Alpheus Hoover.

Children: 2

1096. i.   Susan Hoover (8).
1097. ii.   _____ Hoover (8), a son.

875. John Henderson Revercomb, Jr. (7), son of John
Henderson Revercomb (6) and Emma Lyle, married Dorothy Phillips.
She is a teacher.

Children: 1

1098. i.   John Revercomb (8).

876. Ruth Revercomb (7), daughter of John Henderson Revercomb (6) and Emma Lyle, married Lawrence Hoy.

Children: 2

1099. i.   John Hoy (8).
1100. ii.   Rebecca Hoy (8).

887. Virginia Graham (7), daughter of David C. Graham and
Emma Virginia Helms (6), married Harry Webb.

Children: 1

1101. i.   Harry Webb, Jr. (8), married Sara Wiley,
daughter of Oscar Wiley and Amy Samples. (See Crawford Family).

889. Charles Carlile Helms (7), son of William Strother
Helms (6) and Sarah Virginia Pullin (6), married (1) Helen Gum;
married (2) Mary Louise Morrison.

Children: 1 - first marriage

1102. i.   Helen Helms (8), married _____ Morris.

Children: 1 - second marriage

1103. ii.   Diane Carlile Helms (8).

167

907. Robert Spottswood Lockridge (7), son of Russell Vance Lockridge (6) and Alice Dandridge Lemmon, was born January 22, 1919; married February 21, 1942, Mary Henrietta Bryan, born August 22, 1917. They live on Route 34, Lynchburg, Virginia.

Children: 3

1104. i.   Judith Ann Lockridge (8), born March 13, 1944.
1105. ii.   Robert Spottswood Lockridge (8), born December 13, 1948.
1106. iii. Susan Patricia Lockridge (8), born October 31, 1952.

908. Russell Vance Lockridge (7), son of Russell Vance Lockridge (6) and Alice Dandridge Lemmon, was born November 1, 1920; married August 31, 1944, Lillian Elvie Coakley, born February 24, 1918. He served in the Army from January 16, 1941 to July 31, 1945, and was in Panama for 34 months and in the Phillipines for nine months. They live at 2112 Manley Avenue, Granite City, Illinois.

Children: 1

1107. i.   Russell Vance Lockridge (8), born May 28, 1946.

911. Mary Susan Lockridge (7), daughter of Frank Lockridge (6) and Kate J. Shumate, married W. M. Mayo, Jr.

Children: 2

1108. i.   Mary Jane Mayo (8).
1109. ii.   William M. Mayo (8).

918. Josephine Lockridge (7), daughter of Steward Ryder Lockridge (6) and Lenna Vines, was born March 3, 1915; married (1) Bruce Smith; married (2) William Palmer.

Children: 1 - first marriage

1110. i.   Bruce Smith, Jr. (8), died in the Navy.

924. Mason Lockridge (7), son of Robert Lockridge (6) and Katie Bell Coursey, married (1) Pauline Putman; married (2) Helen Burroughs.

Children: 1 - first marriage

1111. i.   Mason Lockridge, Jr. (8), now serving in the Navy.

926. Max Lockridge (7), son of Robert Lockridge (6) and Katie Bell Coursey, married May 30, 1928, Eleanor Kincaid.

Children: 1

1112. i.   Katrinka Lockridge (8).

936. Clifton Hylie Lockridge, Jr. (7), son of Clifton
Hylie Lockridge (6) and Wreathie Loving, married Helen Hundley.
They live at Covington, Virginia.

Children: 1

1113. i.   Clifton Hylie Lockridge, III (8).

937. Clarence Lockridge (7), son of Clifton Hylie Lockridge
(6) and Wreathie Loving, married Grace Mann in Texas.

Children: 2

1114. i.   Nina Loving Lockridge (8).
1115. ii.   Betty Paige Lockridge (8).

938. Warren Lockridge (7), son of Clifton Hylie Lockridge
(6) and Wreathie Loving, married Josephine Kessinger. They
live in Covington, Virginia.

Children: 3

1116. i.   Warren Lockridge, Jr. (8).
1117. ii.   John Hylie Lockridge (8).
1118. iii. Robin Lockridge (8), a daughter.

939. Helen Lockridge (7), daughter of Clifton Hylie Lockridge (6) and Wreathie Loving, married George Leitch. They live
in Covington, Virginia.

Children: 1

1119. i.   Becky Leitch (8).

940. Hilda Lockridge (7), daughter of Clifton Hylie Lockridge (6) and Wreathie Loving, married George Hodges. They live
in Portsmouth, Virginia.

Children: 2

1120. i.   George Hodges, Jr. (8).
1121. ii.   Robert Stevens Hodges (8).

941. Nancy Lockridge (7), daughter of Clifton Hylie Lockridge (6) and Wreathie Loving, married James W. Alvey, Jr.

Children: 3

1122. i.   Gayle Alvey (8).

1123. ii.   Jeanette Alvey (8).
1124. iii.   James W. Alvey, III (8).

943. Gerald Collin Lockridge (7), son of James C. Lockridge (6) and Grace Bishop, married Margaret Kennedy.

Children: 1

1125. i.   Jerry Lockridge (8).

944. Maxine Lockridge (7), daughter of James C. Lockridge (6) and Grace Bishop, married Grover Yancey.

Children: 1

1126. i.   Kathy Sue Yancey (8).

990. Dorothy Stephenson (7), daughter of Charles O. Stephenson (6) and Mary Kate Campbell, married Jennings Killian.

Children: 2

1127. i.   Wayne Killian (8).
1128. ii.   Walker Jay Killian (8).

1032. Robert Pearl Gwin (7), son of Andrew Earl Gwin (6) and Agatha Lois Matheney, was born August 10, 1921; married February 23, 1946 at Glendale, Long Island, New York, Arlene Merkel.

Children: 2

1129. i.   Robert Herman Gwin (8), born December 22, 1949.
1130. ii.   James Earl Gwin (8), born November 4, 1954.

1037. Jean Gwin (7), daughter of Ralph Rose Gwin (6) and Maude Clarkson, married Phil DeLozier.

Children: 2

1131. i.   Donna DeLozier (8).
1132. ii.   Joann DeLozier (8).

1038. June Gwin (7), daughter of Austin Dow Gwin (6) and Eunice Christian, married C. P. Humke.

Children: 2

1133. i.   Dana Humke (8).
1134. ii.   David Humke (8).

1049. Esther Margaret Ingle (7), daughter of Marcus Lafayette Ingle and Pearl Ghormley (6), was born March 17, 1900; married

Garrett Van Ginkell.

Children: 8

1135. i.   Mary Van Ginkell (8), born January 1, 1919.
1136. ii.   John Van Ginkell (8), born February 18, 1920.
1137. iii.   Esther Van Ginkell (8), born September 11, 1923.
1138. iv.   Garrett Van Ginkell (8), born August 1, 1924.
1139. v.   Marcus Van Ginkell (8), born August 17, 1925;
died September 28, 1925.
1140. vi.   Florence Van Ginkell (8), born July 20, 1926.
1141. vii.   Joe Van Ginkell (8), born August 14, 1927.
1142. viii. Elizabeth Ann Van Ginkell (8), born September
15, 1928.

1085. Hugh W. Revercomb, Jr. (8), son of Hugh W. Revercomb
(7) and Loretta Baylor, married Doris Hildebrand.

Children: 2

1143. i.   James Walker Revercomb (9).
1144. ii.   Brenda Gayle Revercomb (9).

1087. Thomas Eugene Revercomb (8), son of Hugh W. Revercomb
(7) and Loretta Baylor, married Myrtle Necessary.

Children: 1
1145. i.   Judy Lynn Revercomb (9).

1088. Mary Lucretia Revercomb (8), daughter of Hugh W.
Revercomb (7) and Loretta Baylor, married Kenneth Law.

Children: 1

1146. i.   Allen Wayne Law (9).

1089. Edith Revercomb (8), daughter of Hugh W. Revercomb
(7) and Loretta Baylor, married Arthur Miller.

Children: 1

1147. i.   Don Eugene Miller (9).

1090. Virginia Revercomb (8), daughter of Hugh W. Revercomb
(7) and Loretta Baylor, married Wallace Sprouse.

Children: 2

1148. i.   Wallace Sprouse, Jr. (9).
1149. ii.   Hugh Franklin Sprouse (9).

1094. Samuel Revercomb Erwin (8), son of Robert James
Erwin and Layton Gray Revercomb (7), was born August 11, 1918;

married Beulah Virginia Cales, August 5, 1937. They live in Arlington, Virginia.

Children: 3

1150. i. Laten Gray Erwin (9), born August 15, 1938.
1151. ii. Jerry Allen Erwin (9), born September 4, 1939.
1152. iii. Alice Gail Erwin (9), born October 25, 1944.

1095. Robert McAllister Erwin (8), son of Robert James Erwin and Layton Gray Revercomb (7), was born May 24, 1923; married Frances _____. They live RFD, Cincinnatus, New York.

Children: 2

1153. i. Jerry Robert Erwin (9).
1154. ii. Shirley Jean Erwin (9).

PART III

LIGHTNER FAMILY

The Lightner Family is of German origin. The name is found in records as Lochtner, Leitner, and Lightner.

Thirty Thousand Names of Immigrants by Prof. I. Daniel Rupp shows the following:

Page 75 - Sept. 19, 1732. Palatines imported in the ship Johnson, of London, David Crocket, Master, from Rotterdam, last from Deal.

John Michel Lochtner.

1. John Michel Lochtner (Lightner) (1), emigrated from Leipsic, Germany in 1732 with his wife. The far flung Lightner lines of Pennsylvania descend from his two sons.

    2.   i.   Joseph Lightner (2).
+ 3.   ii.   William Lightner (2), born c. 1730.

3. William Lightner (2), the progenitor of the Virginia branch of the Lightner Family, was born c. 1730 in Germany; died in 1811 in Bath County, Virginia; married (1) Elizabeth Ann (nicknamed Sally) Robey, died before 1809, daughter of Patrick Robey; married (2) in 1809, Mrs. Katie Sharat. William Lightner served as a soldier in Captain Skile's Company, 1st Battalion, Lancaster County Militia, Pennsylvania. (Vol. 7, page 61, 5th Series, Pennsylvania Archives.) He also served earlier in other companies whose muster rolls have been destroyed. There is a government marker over his grave in Highland County, Virginia, near the Bath County line. The following is a copy of a letter from the Historical Society of York County, Pennsylvania, regarding his services:

York, Penna., Aug. 18, 1923

Registrar General, D. A. R.
    Washington, D. C.

I hereby certify that William Lightner was a soldier in Captain Skiles' Company, 1st Battalion, Lancaster County Militia in 1782, and in the same company in 1784. See Page 61, Vol 7, 5th Series, Pennsylvania Archives. He is then supposed to have been more than fifty years old, and served before that time in other military companies of which records are not in existence, because some of the muster rolls of Lancaster County was destroyed in early days.

Respectfully submitted,

/s/ Geo. R. Prowell

173

He signed the Oath of Allegiance and Fidelity as required by the Act of the General Assembly of Pennsylvania passed on June 13, 1777. His certificate, now in the possession of Mrs. G. Jesse Hiner of Highland County, Virginia, reads as follows:

York County,
    In Pennsylvania, S.S.

        I do hereby certify that William Lightner hath voluntarily subscribed the oath of Allegiance and Fidelity, as directed by an ACT of GENERAL ASSEMBLY of Pennsylvania, passed the 13 day of June A. D. 1777.

        Witness my hand and Seal, the 25 day of July A.D.
                                                            1778.
        Henry Hagle (L.S.)
No. 453
(A History of Highland County, Virginia, Oren F. Morton, page 408.)

        The following certified statement was made by the great grandson of William Lightner:

        This is to certify that this is a true copy of the Attest of Loyalty of William Lightner, now in my possession, given me by my Father, Jacob Lightner who was born Sept. 11, 1821, and died Nov. 8th, 1904. This paper was given to him by his father Adam Lightner, who was born Sept. 10th, 1760, and died January 3rd 1843. Adam Lightner was the son of William Lightner.

                            J. Brown Lightner
                            Son of Jacob Lightner

                I was born 30 of Jany 1859

        Subscribed and sworn to before me this 7 day of Aug. 1923.

                        A.P. Gum   Highland
                        Notary Public   County

                        My commission expires
                        Feb. 4, 1925.

        William Lightner came to Virginia from York County, Pennsylvania with his sons and daughters about 1790, and settled in Bath County, Virginia near the Highland County line. Before leaving Pennsylvania, William Lightner and his wife, Elizabeth A. Lightner, deeded their land in Spring Garden Township, York County, Pennsylvania, to Peter Wilt. (Ibid., page 313).

        Children: 9 - first marriage

+   4.   i.   Peter Lightner (3).

+   5.   ii.   William Lightner (3).
+   6.   iii. Adam Lightner (3), born September 10, 1760.
+   7.   iv.   Samuel Lightner (3).
+   8.   v.   Christopher Lightner (3).
    9.   vi.   John Michael Lightner (3), married Elizabeth
Reeder (later Ryder) and remained in Lancaster County, Pennsylvania, where his descendants are living.
    10. vii. Elizabeth Lightner (3), died in 1876 aged 96
years; married in 1799, Henry Harper, died in 1859 aged 70 years,
son of Lieutenant Nicholas Harper and Elizabeth Peninger. (See
Harper Family).
    11. viii. Mary Lightner (3), married September 7, 1813
in Bath County, Virginia, Adam Matheny. They migrated to
Missouri.
    12. ix.   Andrew Lightner (3), died in childhood.

    4. Peter Lightner (3), son of William Lightner (2) and
Elizabeth Ann Robey, died in 1853; married in 1796, Annis E.
Harper, daughter of Lieutenant Nicholas Harper and Elizabeth
Peninger. (See Harper Family). They lived on Knapps Creek,
Pocahontas County, West Virginia. His will was dated March 10,
1849 and recorded in March 1853 in Will Book 3, page 10, Poca-
hontas County, West Virginia. It mentions daughter, Phebe Cleek
and husband and Peter son of Phebe; Peter, Henry, and Abraham
Sharp, sons of daughter Elizabeth Sharp; daughters, Elizabeth,
Polly, Susan, and Phebe; and son, Jacob, deceased. Executors
were George Gay and Sheldon Clark. Witnesses were Peter Lightner
and Andrew V. Bird.

        Children: 6

+   13. i.   Mary (Polly) Lightner (4).
+   14. ii.   Elizabeth (Betsy) Lightner (4).
    15. iii. Phoebe Ann Lightner (4), born February 26, 1813;
died September 26, 1885; married March 11, 1834 in Pocahontas
County, West Virginia, John Cleek, born July 19, 1809; died June
27, 1859, son of Michael Cleek and Margaret Henderson Crawford.
(See Cleek Family).
    16. iv.   Peter Lightner (4), died unmarried.
+   17. v.   Jacob Lightner (4).
    18. vi.   Susan Lightner (4), married October 31, 1826
in Pocahontas County, West Virginia, George M. Gay.

    5. William Lightner (3), son of William Lightner (2) and
Elizabeth Ann Robey, married in 1796 Elizabeth Harper, daughter
of Lieutenant Nicholas Harper and Elizabeth Peninger, and a sister of Annis E. Harper who married Peter Lightner. After the
death of William Lightner, Elizabeth married (2) Nicholas Harper,
son of Adam Harper and Christina _____. (See Harper Family).
The descendants of William Lightner lived near Buckeye, Pocahontas
County, West Virginia. Some of them migrated to Lewis County,
West Virginia. One of their children was:

175

19. i. Arista Lightner (4), married Amos Hevener, born in 1817. They lived in Randolph County, West Virginia.

6. Adam Lightner (3), son of William Lightner (2) and Elizabeth Ann Robey, was born September 30, 1760 in Lancaster County, Pennsylvania; died January 3, 1843 at Back Creek, Bath County, Virginia; married in 1798 in Pendleton County, Virginia (now West Virginia), Susannah Harper, born in 1777 in Pendleton County, Virginia (now West Virginia); died March 25, 1868 on Back Creek, Bath County, Virginia and was buried on the Thomas Campbell farm near the Bath-Highland County lines, daughter of Lieutenant Nicholas Harper and Elizabeth Peninger. Adam Lightner served as a prison guard in 1778, being one of a company of young men guarding British prisoners at York, Pennsylvania. (Vol, 2, page 710, Pennsylvania Archives, Sixth Series). He came with his father, William Lightner, from Pennsylvania to Virginia about 1790. His will is recorded in Will Book 4, page 594, Bath County, Virginia. It reads as follows:

I Adam Lightner of the county of Bath and State of Virginia being weak in body but of sound disposing mind and memory do make and ordain this my last will and testament -- 1st I direct that all my debts be paid as soon as may be after my death.

2nd I give to my oldest Daughter Sally Bible wife of Jacob Bible all the property she took away with her when she was married and the land that the said Jacob Bible sold to Jacob Hefner (?) on the head of Jacksons River.

3rd I will and bequeath to my second daughter Elizabeth wife of Otho Gum all the property she took with her when she was married and also a Bond of about ninety Dollars and two horse beasts I let them have to pay a part for the land they bought of Collins and further that she shall have one thousand dollars more; five hundred Dollars of which shall be paid out of my personal property and the other five hundred Dollars to be paid out of the land that I now live on.

4th I give to my eldest Son John and my second Son Adam all the property they took with them when they left me and also the plantation that I bought for them on the head of Jacksons River of Joshua Wood.

5th I give to my third Son William all the land that I bought of Jacob Gum in Pocahontas County.

6th I give to my fourth Son Peter and my fifth Son Jacob the plantation that I now live on with its appurtenances to them and their heirs forever upon the following conditions (to Wit) that they pay the above named sum of five hundred Dollars to Elizabeth wife of Otho Gum within four or five years after my decease; or sooner if they can; and that they furnish my Wife Susan with everything necessary for her comfortable support so long as she lives and keep for her all the property that I give her that is herein after mentioned.

7th I give to my wife Susan one negro Slave named Hannah and her increase (if any) during her life time and at her death the said negro woman and her increase shall be sold and the price

be equally divided amongst all my heirs I also give her one horse
beast and one cow the choice of any that I have.
    8th I give also to my fifth Son Jacob one horse beast six
head of cows and heifers, one Bed and bedding two plows (a Shovel
and McCormic) one mattock and chopping axe, one hoe and one log
chain and eight or nine Sheep and one Iron wedge.
    9th I will that my negro man Thornton and negro Boy Jordan
and all the residue of my personal Estate be sold at public
Sale and the price equally divided amongst all my heirs.
    Lastly I do appoint my Son John Lightner my sole Executor
of this my last Will and Testament, In Witness whereof I have
hereunto set my hand and affixed my seal this 12th day of
February 1839.

Attest   Adam Lightner (SEAL)
Thos. Campbell
Jas. Hickman
Charles Hamilton

    Schedule, I direct that a division line between the land
that I have willed to my Sons Peter and Jacob shall commence
at a Sugar tree and Sycamore at the edge of the Creek thence to
run with the Middle fence across to near a Muddy Spring below
the milk house leaving said muddy Spring in the upper (or Jacob's)
part and to extend across in a straight line from one out side
line to the other and Jacob to have the upper part and Peter the
lower - I further direct that my part of a tract of land lying
in the Alleghany mountain being one third of a tract of 6800
acres which was purchased by me and others from John Berry, be
divided between my two Sons Peter and Jacob giving to each one
equal quantity the line to commence opposite the mouth of the
dry run and then extend across the mountain the upper tract of
which I give to Jacob and lower to Peter, I do further give to
my two sons Jacob and Peter all my right title and interest in
an undivided tract of land in the Alleghany Mountain of about
twenty thousand Acres. In witness whereof I have hereunto set
my hand and seal this 2nd day of January 1843.

Witness   Adam Lightner (SEAL)
Thos. Campbell
Charles Hamilton

Recorded January Term 1843.

        Children: 7

+   20. i.   Sallie Lightner (4).
+   21. ii.   Elizabeth Lightner (4), born October 8, 1800.
+   22. iii. John Lightner (4), born October 3, 1803.
+   23. iv.   Adam Lightner (4), born 1808.
+   24. v.   William Lightner (4), born December 5, 1812.
+   25. vi.   Peter Lightner (4), born 1816.
+   26. vii. Jacob Lightner (4), born September 11, 1821.

7. Samuel Lightner (3), son of William Lightner (2) and Elizabeth Ann Robey, married Elizabeth Sensabaugh. He moved from Bath County to Augusta County, Virginia and settled near Greenville.

Children: 9

+	27.	i.	Eliza Lightner (4).
	28.	ii.	Sarah Lightner (4), died unmarried.
	29.	iii.	William Lightner (4), migrated to California.
	30.	iv.	John Lightner (4), migrated to California.
+	31.	v.	Jacob Lightner (4).
+	32.	vi.	James Lightner (4).
+	33.	vii.	Samuel Lightner (4).
+	34.	viii.	Thomas Lightner (4).
+	35.	ix.	Alexander Brownlee Lightner (4), born 1804.

8. Christopher Lightner (3), son of William Lightner (2) and Elizabeth Ann Robey, married Catherine Zickafoose and migrated to Kentucky.

Children: 1

   36. i. William Lightner (4).

13. Mary (Polly) Lightner (4), daughter of Peter Lightner (3) and Annis E. Harper, married Sheldon Clark. They settled in Little Levels, Greenbrier County, West Virginia. Sheldon Clark came from Connecticut.

Children: 5

+	37.	i.	Sherman H. Clark (5).
+	38.	ii.	Alvin Clark (5), born 1832.
+	39.	iii.	Henry N. Clark (5).
+	40.	iv.	Preston S. Clark (5).
	41.	v.	Peter Clark (5), married Martha Blair.

She married (2) Abram Beard, son of William Ryneck Beard and Margaret McNeel.

14. Elizabeth (Betsy) Lightner (4), daughter of Peter Lightner (3) and Annis E. Harper, married November 12, 1818 in Bath County, Virginia, Joseph Sharp, son of John Sharp and Elizabeth Curry.

Children: 8

   42. i. Peter Sharp (5), married Mary Ann Herron. He served in the CSA.
   43. ii. Henry Sharp (5), married Caroline Curry, daughter of J. Harvey Curry.
   44. iii. Abraham Sharp (5), married Martha Ellen Sharp, daughter of John Sharp and Elizabeth Slaven Wade. He was a Union soldier.

+   45.   iv.   Anne Sharp (5), born November 11, 1821.
     46.   v.   Polly Sharp (5), married John Hannah, son of
Joseph Hannah and Elizabeth Burnsides.
     47.   vi.   Rachel Sharp (5), died unmarried.
     48.   vii.   Phoebe Sharp (5), married (1) Henry Harper, Jr.,
son of Henry Harper and Elizabeth Lightner; married (2) Abraham
Rankin. (See Harper Family).
     49.   viii. Susan Sharp (5), married William Burr.

     17. Jacob Lightner (4), son of Peter Lightner (3) and Annis
E. Harper, died in 1842; married June 19, 1823 in Pocahontas County,
West Virginia, Elizabeth Moore, died in 1850, daughter of John
Moore and Elizabeth McClung. (See Moore Family). His will was
dated October 22, 1842 and recorded December 1842 in Will Book 2,
page 42, Pocahontas County, West Virginia. It mentions wife,
Elizabeth; eldest son, Peter; second son, John; son, Samuel; and
youngest son, Henry; daughters, Alcinda, Mary, and Alice; Mrs.
Elizabeth Moore, mother-in-law. Executors were friend, Ralph
Wanless and wife, Elizabeth. Witnesses were J. B. Campbell and
George Rider. The will of Elizabeth Moore Lightner was dated
August 24, 1850 and recorded November 1850 in Will Book 2, page
472, Pocahontas County, West Virginia. It mentions daughters,
Mary C. and Alice P. Executor, son, Peter Lightner. Witnesses
were Joseph Moore, Wm. Skeen, and S. Lightner.

     Children: 7

+   50.   i.   John M. Lightner (5).
+   51.   ii.   Samuel M. Lightner (5).
     52.   iii.   Mary C. Lightner (5), married Rev. John W.
Hedges.
     53.   iv.   Alcinda C. Lightner (5), married June 26,
1845 in Pocahontas County, West Virginia, James B. Campbell,
son of Alexander Campbell and Margaret Brown. (See Campbell
Family). No children.
     54.   v.   Alice P. Lightner (5), died.
     55.   vi.   Peter Lightner (5), died.
     56.   vii.   Henry Lightner (5).

     20. Sallie Lightner (4), daughter of Adam Lightner (3) and
Susannah Harper, married December 18, 1832 in Bath County,
Virginia, Jacob Bible.

     Children: 5

     57.   i.   Susan Bible (5), married September 19, 1854 in
Pocahontas County, West Virginia (as his second wife) William
Jacob McGlaughlin, son of Hugh McGlaughlin and Nancy Gwin. (See
Gwin Family).
+   58.   ii.   Mary Margaret Bible (5), born March 3, 1836.
     59.   iii.   Rachel Bible (5), married (1) Morgan Bird;
married (2) _____ McCutchan.
     60.   iv.   John Bible (5), was wounded and died during
the War Between the States. He died at Adam Lightner's at

Valley Center, Virginia.
    61. v.   William Bible (5), taken prisoner by the Yankees
and never heard of again.

    21. Elizabeth (4), daughter of Adam Lightner (3) and
Susannah Harper, was born October 8, 1800; died July 8, 1885;
married (1) October 21, 1819 in Bath County, Virginia, Otho
Gum, son of Abraham Gum and Priscilla Wade; married (2) (as
his second wife), Hugh McGlaughlin, born February 24, 1801;
died May 19, 1870. He married first, Nancy Gwin, daughter of
John Gwin and Margaret Bradshaw. (See Gwin Family).

        Children: 9 - first marriage

    62. i.   Adam Lightner Gum (5), married Sarah Ryder,
daughter of William J. Ryder and Rosanna Sharp. They lived
at Meadow Dale, Virginia. No children.
  + 63. ii. Abraham W. Gum (5).
    64. iii. William Gum (5), died young.
  + 65. iv. Susan Gum (5).
    66. v.   Sarah Gum (5), married (as his first wife)
William Jacob McGlaughlin. He married second, Susan Bible (5),
daughter of Jacob Bible and Sallie Lightner. (See Gwin Family).
    67. vi. Priscilla Gum (5), married Jacob Cackley.
    68. vii. Mary G. Gum (5), married Wellington Daniels
of Randolph County, West Virginia.
  + 69. viii. Peter Lightner Gum (5), born 1836.
  + 70. ix. Otho Gum (5), born after his father's death.

        Children: 2 - second marriage

  + 71. x.   Andrew Matthews McGlaughlin (5), born December
1, 1844.
  + 72. xi. Harper McGlaughlin (5).

    22. John Lightner (4), son of Adam Lightner (3) and Susannah
Harper, was born October 3, 1803; died July 7, 1863; married
September 28, 1826 in Pocahontas County, West Virginia, Jane Moore,
born December 25, 1807; died May 23, 1886, daughter of John Moore
and Elizabeth McClung. (See Moore Family).

        Children: 4

  + 73. i.   Susan Harper Lightner (5), born September 2,
1827.
  + 74. ii. Elizabeth Lightner (5).
    75. iii. Paul Moore Lightner (5), died in 1888, unmarried.
He was educated at Dickinson College in Pennsylvania and at Princeton University. He practiced law in Alton, Illinois and served
in the Virginia Legislature.
  + 76. iv. Rachel Lightner (5).

    23. Adam Lightner (4), son of Adam Lightner (3) and

                              180

Susannah Harper, was born in 1808; died in 1882; married November 1830, Eleanor Slaven, born 1808, daughter of Stewart Slaven and Isabella Johnson.

Children: 5

77.   i.   Samuel Lightner (5), born September 30, 1831; died November 30, 1900; married c. 1880, Katherine Bird, died November 22, 1900, daughter of Peter H. Bird and Sophia Wade. No children.
+   78.   ii.   William Stuart Lightner (5), born 1832.
    79.   iii.   John H. Lightner (5), born 1834; died 1862 at Middletown, Virginia, as a result of service in the CSA, Company E. 31st Virginia Regiment. Never married.
+   80.   iv.   Anthony Lightner (5), born October 18, 1836.
+   81.   v.   Isabelle M. Lightner (5), born 1840.

24.   William Lightner (4), son of Adam Lightner (3) and Susannah Harper, was born December 5, 1812; died November 15, 1887; married (1) November 27, 1834 in Bath County, Virginia, Mary Davis Hamilton, born December 10, 1812; died October 11, 1858, daughter of Charles Hamilton and Alice Erwin; married (2) April 13, 1871 in Pocahontas County, West Virginia, Elizabeth Wooddell, born July 8, 1830; died April 1, 1922. They first lived near Green Bank, now in West Virginia, and in 1852 moved to Back Creek, Highland County, Virginia. After the War Between the States he returned to West Virginia. His will was dated September 15, 1885 and recorded in Will Book 4, page 408, Pocahontas County, West Virginia. It mentions wife, Elizabeth; son, Charles A. Lightner; and daughters, Alice S. Gibson and Medora M. Lightner. Executor - son, Charles A. Lightner. Witnesses were Wm. H. Hull, James H. Bluny, Jr. and Henry A. Yeager.

Children: 3 - first marriage

+   82.   i.   Alice Susan Davis Lightner (5), born November 25, 1841.
    83.   ii.   Madora Mildred Lightner (5), born September 26, 1847; died May 10, 1909; married in 1868, William Thomas Lightner (5), born January 17, 1846; died September 5, 1925, son of Alexander Brownlee Lightner and Sarah Gardner.
+   84.   iii.   Charles Adam Lightner (5), born January 20, 1852.

25.   Peter Lightner (4), son of Adam Lightner (3) and Susannah Harper, was born in 1816; died in 1871 in Shelby County, Missouri; married November 25, 1838 in Bath County, Virginia, Rachel Berry Hamilton, born October 25, 1821; died in 1894, daughter of Charles Hamilton and Alice Erwin. They first lived in Bath County, Virginia, on the Andrew Sharp farm and then on the Sively farm, and in 1858 migrated to Shelby County, Missouri.

Children: 11

181

85.   i.   Mary Susan Lightner (5), died in 1904; married
Dr. Hanger.
86.   ii.   Elizabeth Lightner (5), died young.
87.   iii. William Lightner (5), died in Virginia.
+   88.   iv.   Sabina Alice Lightner (5), born January 23,
1846.
89.   v.   Newton Brown Lightner (5), born 1849; died
1916.
+   90.   vi.   Adam Henry Lightner (5), born 1851.
91.   vii. John Jacob Lightner (5), born March 31, 1857;
died 1910.
92.   viii. Charles Eldredge Lightner (5), born 1859; died
1910.
93.   ix.   (Son) Lightner (5), died young.
94.   x.   (Son) Lightner (5), died young.
95.   xi.   Ida Lightner (5), married _____ Wood. She
died and left an infant son.

26. Jacob Lightner (4), son of Adam Lightner (3) and
Susannah Harper, was born September 11, 1821 on Back Creek, Bath
County, Virginia; died November 8, 1904 on Back Creek, Bath
County, Virginia; married April 6, 1843 in Pocahontas County,
West Virginia, Nancy Jane Warwick, born February 7, 1826 at
Green Bank, Pocahontas County, Virginia (now West Virginia);
died May 28, 1900 at a hospital in Staunton, Virginia, daughter
of Robert Craig Warwick and Esthur Hull. (See Warwick and Hull
Families). His will was recorded in Will Book 7, page 515, Bath
County, Virginia. It reads as follows:

I, Jacob Lightner of the County of Bath in the State of
Virginia, do make and publish this my last Will and Testament
as follows:
1st. I direct that all my just debts and funeral expenses
be paid by my executor hereinafter named.
2nd. I bequeath to my three daughters, Malcena C. Cleek,
Virginia R. Wallace and Marietta Gum, all my household and kitchen
furniture of every kind and description except the clock to be
equally divided between them; Brown to have the clock.
3rd. I bequeath to my daughter Malcena C. Cleek the sum of
$500.00 and to my son John A. Lightner the sum of $500.00 to be
paid to them respectively, with interest from one year after my
death, out of the proceeds of the sale of my lands hereinafter
directed to be made.
4th. To my sons Robert W., Peter H., and James C. Lightner,
I give nothing, as they have already received all of my estate
to which they are entitled.
5th. After my death, I direct my executor hereinafter named,
to sell all the lands of which I may die seized and possessed,
either publicly or privately, and in such parcels, and on such
terms, as will in his best judgment tend to secure the best price,
and pay out the proceeds as hereinbefore and hereinafter directed.
6th. All the rest and residue of my estate both real and
personal, I give and bequeath to my children Malcena C. Cleek,

Virginia R. Wallace, and Marietta Gum and John A. Lightner, in equal parts.

    7th. I appoint my son J. Brown Lightner, executor of this will, and request the Court in which he shall qualify to take his personal bond as such without security.

    Given under my hand and seal this 4th day of October, 1901.

                        Jacob Lightner (SEAL)

    In witness whereof we have in the presence of the testator, and at his request, and in the presence of each other hereunto subscribed our names as witnesses.

                    W. V. Watson
                    G. W. Carroll

Codicil

    I, Jacob Lightner, do hereby make this codicil to my will above written.

    I give and bequeath to Miss Mary Carroll my bay riding mare, Fanny, to her and her heirs forever.

    Given under my hand and seal this 20th day of February 1903.

                        Jacob Lightner (SEAL)

Witnesses:
W. V. Watson
R. Lee Gum

His will was recorded November 25, 1904.

    The following was copied from the Family Bible of Jacob Lightner. This Family Bible was published in 1847 and is now in the possession of Geo. W. Cleek, Staunton, Virginia.

FAMILY RECORD

Marriages	Marriages
Adam Lightner and Susannah Harper daughter of Nicholas Harper were married in 1798	Robert W. Lightner and Augusta Bird were married Nov. 22d 1877
Jacob Lightner and Nancy Jane Warwick were married the 6th day of April 1843	Peter H. Lightner and Carrie E. Siple were married Nov. 25th 1885
George W. Cleek and Malcena C. Lightner were married the 26th day of Nov. 1867	Jacob B. Lightner and Mary E. Curry were married 22d September 1891
John S. Wallace and Virginia R. Lightner were married the 11th day of September 1873.	Marietta E. Lightner and Peter Gum were married Sept 9th 1896
John A. Lightner and Myrtle M. Gum were married Feb 26th /91	James C. Lightner and Theodora G. Guinn were married June 1, 1897

Births

Adam Lightner, son of Wm. Lightner and Elizabeth Ann (Sallie) Robey Lightner was born in Pennsylvania Sept 10, 1760. Susannah Harper was born on the South Branch in 1777.

Jacob Lightner was born the 11th day of September 1821

Nancy J. Lightner was born the 7th day of February 1826

Malcena C. Lightner was born February the 22nd 1844

Virginia R. Lightner was born January the 6th 1846

John A. Lightner was born January the 7th 1848

Births

Robert W. Lightner was born July the 20th 1850

William C. Lightner was born the 7th day of January 1854

Mary E. Lightner was born the 4th day of June 1856

Jacob Brown Lightner was born the 30th day of January 1859

Peter H. Lightner was born January 30th 1861

George W. Lightner was born August 13th 1865

James C. Lightner was born May 21st 1867

Deaths

George W. Lightner, son of Jacob and Nancy Lightner departed this February 14th 1866

William C. Lightner son of Jacob and Nancy Lightner departed this life Sept 29, 1887

Nancy J. Lightner wife of Jacob Lightner departed this Life May the Twenty eighth Nineteen hundred.

Jacob Lightner departed this life November 8, 1904

Dora Guinn Lightner died Sept 30, 1918

John S. Wallace died Oct 5th 1923

Carrie E. Lightner died Feb 21 1916

Mary Etta Gum died May 11th 1935

Deaths

Adam Lightner departed this life Jany 3rd 1843

Susan Lightner wife of Adam Lightner departed this life March 25th 1868 In the 91st year of her age

Peter H. Lightner died March 16, 1912 in the fifty-first year of his age

Virginia Rachel Lightner died May 21st 1922

James C. Lightner died June 17, 1924

Geo. W. Cleek died Jan. 1, 1910.

Malcena C. Cleek died Dec. 15, 1937

Robert W. Lightner died Feb. 27, 1930

184

Deaths

Deaths

Augusta Bird Lightner died May 7,
1933 Sunday

John A. Lightner died June
16, 1925

Jacob Brown Lightner died Dec.
3rd, 1935

The following was taken from the Family Bible of Mrs. John
Sitlington Wallace, nee Virginia Rachel Lightner. This Family
Bible was published in 1880 and is now in the possession of Geo.
W. Cleek, Staunton, Virginia.

This certifies that the rite of Holy Matrimony was celebrated
between John S. Wallace of Bath Co., Va. and Virginia R. Lightner
of Bath Co., Va. on Thursday, Sept. 11th 1873 at Brides Residence
by The Rev. George L. Brown, pastor of Warm Springs Presbyterian
Church.
Witness: Geo Mustoe   Witness: J. R. Warwick

Marriages

Jacob Lightner of Bath County, Va. and Nancy J. Warwick of Pocahontas County, Va. was married on the 6th of April 1843.

George W. Cleek and Malcena Lightner was married November 26,1867.

Robert W. Lightner and Augusta Bird was married November 22nd,
1877.

Peter H. Lightner and Carrie E. Siple was married November 25th
1885.

Jacob B. Lightner and Mary E. Curry was married September 22nd
1891.

Births

John Sitlington Wallace was born near Williamsville, Bath Co.,
Virginia on the 28th day of October A.D. 1844.

Virginia Rachel Wallace was born near Sun Rise, Bath Co., Virginia,
on the 6th day of January A. D. 1846.

Jacob Lightner was born Sept 11 1821.

Nancy J. Lightner was born Feb 7th 1826.

Malcena Lightner was born Feb 22nd 1844.
John A. Lightner was born Jan 7th 1848.
Robert W. Lightner was born July 20th 1850.
Wm. C. Lightner was born Jan 7, 1854.
Mary E. Lightner was born June 4th 1856.
Jacob B. Lightner was born Jan 30 1859.

185

Births

Peter H. Lightner was born Jan 30 1861.
George W. Lightner was born Aug 13th 1865.
James C. Lightner was born May 21st 1867.
Harry H. Robison was born 25 of March 1894.

Deaths

Adam Lightner departed this life January 3rd, 1843.
Susan Lightner wife of Adam Lightner, nee Harper, departed this life March 25th 1868.
George W. Lightner departed this life February 14th 1866.
William C. Lightner born of Jacob and Nancy J. Lightner departed this life September 29th 1887.
Nancy J. Lightner wife of Jacob Lightner departed this life May 28th 1900 74 yr 3 mo 21 days.
Jacob Lightner departed this life November 8th 1904 aged 83 years 1 month and 27 days.
Peter H. Lightner departed this life March 16th 1912 aged 51 years one month and 15 days.
Virginia Rachel Wallace departed this life May 21, 1922.

A Record of Important Events

Christopher C. R. Wallace born April 8, 1838, and died Dec. 18, 1915.
Sarah Elizabeth Wallace born August 19, 1839.
Mathew W. Wallace born Dec. 11, 1840.
William Henry Wallace born Sept. 11, 1842.
John Sitlington Wallace born Oct. 28, 1844.
Susan Martha Wallace born Jan. 9, 1848.
Stephen Robert Wallace born Jan. 10, 1850.
Matilda Ann Wallace born Dec. 8, 1852.
Ann Roadcap Wallace born Jan 9, 1808.
Robert Wallace born Aug. 22, 1804 and died Aug. 17, 1875.

Robert C. Warwick was born the 8th of September 1801.
Robert C. Warwick died the 8th of March 1845.

Esther Warwick was born September the 14th 1804.
Esther Warwick died the 17th of March 1853.

The following tombstone inscriptions were copied at the Wallace Cemetery in Bath County, Virginia:

Sarah Ann Wallace
Born Feb. 25, 1827
Died Jan. 12, 1913

Christopher Roadcap Wallace
Died Dec. 18, 1916
Aged 78 years

Margaret Hull Wallace
Died April 30, 1915
Aged 78 years

Lucy A. Wallace
May 9, 1875
April 19, 1901

186

Edward M. Wallace
Born Oct. 14, 1872
Died May 27, 1901

Thomas Brown Wallace
Born June 10, 1812
Died July 28, 1898

Agnes McMath Wallace
Born May 15, 1818
Died Oct. 17, 1855

Matthew Wallace
Born Feb. 5, 1772
Died Oct. 5, 1848

Sarah Brown Wallace
Born Nov. 8, 1775
Died March 30, 1851

Mary E. Wallace
Born Nov. 3, 1840
Died Dec. 2, 1863

Frank B. Wallace
Born Dec. 8, 1895
Died Oct. 15, 1940

George Wallace
Born June 17, 1869
Died December 31, 1931

William J. Weldon
Born Aug. 20, 1796
Died June 24, 1864

Ann Roadcap Wallace
Born Jan. 19, 1808
Died Jan. 30, 1893

Robert Sitlington Wallace
Born August 22, 1804
Died August 17, 1875

Mathew M. Morrison
Born October 29, 1811
Died April 5, 1902

Cynthia Ann Wallace
Wife of M. M. Morrison
Born July 2, 1817
Died Aug. 2, 1870

Prestley F. Burns
Died Oct. 29, 1895
Aged 59 yrs 11 mo 25 days

Virginia Bragg Wallace
Born Dec. 17, 1869
Died April 1, 1904

The following are additional Wallace Family notes collected by the compiler:

Christopher C. Roadcap Wallace, married Margaret Hull, daughter of John Hull and Margaret Warwick. He served in Company F, 11th Virginia Cavalry, CSA.

Sarah Elizabeth Wallace married Prestley F. Burns. He served in Company F, 11th Virginia Cavalry, CSA.

Mathew W. Wallace was captured at Darksville and died at Camp Chase, Ohio in 1862. He served in the CSA.

William Henry Wallace married Anna Stewart. He served in the CSA.

Susan Martha Wallace married (as his second wife) Rev. John Taylor, Staunton, Virginia.

Stephen Robert Wallace married in 1876, Ella Steuart.

Matilda Ann Wallace married Robert Ramsey.

Children: 10

96. i.   Malcena Catherine Lightner (5), born February
22, 1844 on Back Creek, Bath County, Virginia; died December 15,
1937 at Cleek's Mill, Bath County, Virginia; married November 26,
at her father's home, George Washington Cleek, born June 3, 1835
at Cleek's Mill, Bath County, Virginia; died January 1, 1910 at
Cleek's Mill, Bath County, Virginia, son of John Cleek II and
Sarah Kimes-Givens. (See Cleek Family).

97. ii.   Virginia Rachel Lightner (5), born January 6,
1846 on Back Creek, Bath County, Virginia; died May 21, 1922 in
Bath County, Virginia; married September 11, 1873 in Bath County,
Virginia, John Sitlington Wallace, born October 28, 1844; died
October 5, 1923, son of Robert Sitlington Wallace (born August
22, 1804; died August 17, 1875) and Ann Roadcap (born January
19, 1808; died January 30, 1893). He served in Company G, 18th
Virginia Cavalry, CSA, and was wounded at Darksville. No
children.

+   98.   iii.   John Adam Lightner (5), born January 7, 1848.
+   99.   iv.   Robert Warwick Lightner (5), born July 20, 1850.
     100. v.   William Craig Lightner (5), born January 7,
1854; died September 29, 1887, unmarried.
     101. vi.   Marietta Ellen Lightner (5), born June 4, 1856;
died May 11, 1935; married September 9, 1896 (as his second wife),
Peter Lightner Gum (5), born 1836; died 1916, son of Otho Gum and
Elizabeth Lightner. No children.
+   102. vii.   Jacob Brown Lightner (5), born January 30, 1859.
+   103. viii. Peter Hull Lightner (5), born January 30, 1861.
     104. ix.   George Washington Lightner (5), born August
13, 1865; died February 14, 1866.
+   105. x.   James Cameron Lightner (5), born May 21, 1867.

27. Eliza Lightner (4), daughter of Samuel Lightner (3) and
Elizabeth Sensabaugh, married John T. Hawpe.

Children: 6

106. i.   Henry Hawpe (5).
107. ii.   James Hawpe (5).
108. iii.   John Hawpe (5).
109. iv.   Samuel Hawpe (5).
110. v.   Charlotte Hawpe (5).
111. vi.   Esteline Hawpe (5).

31. Jacob Lightner (4), son of Samuel Lightner (3) and
Elizabeth Sensabaugh, married Mary Pilson, daughter of George
Pilson (born 1765; died 1833) and Elizabeth Thompson (married
January 4, 1796, born 1764; died December 17, 1861).

Children: 3

112. i.   George P. Lightner (5), died January 1925,
unmarried.

113. ii. John Lightner (5), died young.
+ 114. iii. Samuel A. Lightner (5), born 1841.

32. James Lightner (4), son of Samuel Lightner (3) and Elizabeth Sensabaugh, married Adaline Martin and moved to St. Louis, Missouri.

Children: 2

115. i. Flora Lightner (5).
116. ii. James Lightner (5).

33. Samuel Lightner (4), son of Samuel Lightner (3) and Elizabeth Sensabaugh, married Lucy Ann Darst.

Children: 9

117. i. John Samuel Lightner (5), born February 15, 1840; died January 1916; married 1875, Anna Eliza Armentrout. He served in Company E, 5th Virginia Infantry, Stonewall Brigade, CSA. They had one child that died in infancy.
118. ii. Thomas Ray Lightner (5), died in prison in New York during the War Between the States.
119. iii. Mary Charlotte Tate Lightner (5), born April 24, 1844; married in 1867, Anthony Lightner (5), born October 18, 1836; died June 12, 1916, son of Adam Lightner and Eleanor Slaven.
+ 120. iv. Elizabeth Jane Lightner (5).
+ 121. v. Signora Frances Lightner (5).
122. vi. Lucy Jane Lightner (5), died unmarried.
123. vii. Estelle Virginia Alice Lightner (5), born March 24, 1855; married May 6, 1873, Charles Adam Lightner (5), born January 20, 1852; died March 9, 1908, son of William Lightner and Mary Davis Hamilton.
+ 124. viii. Milton Hitt Lightner (5).
125. ix. Eliza Catherine Lightner (5), died young.

32. Thomas Lightner (4), son of Samuel Lightner (3) and Elizabeth Sensabaugh, married Elizabeth Brubeck.

Children: 2

126. i. James T. Lightner (5), married Mabel Tinsley, daughter of J. E. Tinsley.
+ 127. ii. Lula Lightner (5).

35. Alexander Brownlee Lightner (4), son of Samuel Lightner (3) and Elizabeth Sensabaugh, was born in 1804; died in 1891; married (1) Sarah Gardner; married (2) July 22, 1848, Sarah Ellen Wayland, born November 18, 1830; died January 31, 1905, daughter of Albert Gallitin Wayland and Jane Ledgerwood Moffitt. He served in the Virginia Legislature for a number of years. He also served as Sheriff of Augusta County, Virginia.

189

Children: 2 - first marriage

+   128. i.   William Thomas Lightner (5), born January 17,
1846.
     129. ii.   (Daughter) Lightner (5), died young.

Children: 7 - second marriage

     130. iii. Ella Virginia Lightner (5), married November
3, 1874, David O'Rorke, born May 14, 1848; died in 1935, son of
James T. O'Rorke and Isabella Manor.
+   131. iv.   James Shields Lightner (5), born 1867.
     132. v.   George Samuel Lightner (5), died 1933; married
(1) _____Stump; married (2) _____Stump, twin sisters of
Maryland. He was a Methodist minister.
+   133. vi.   John A. Lightner (5), born 1858.
     134. vii. Clarence Lightner (5), married _____Smiley.
     135. viii. Florence Lightner (5), married Milton Bucher.
+   136. ix.   Charles A. W. Lightner (5), born 1850.

     37. Sherman H. Clark (5), son of Sheldon Clark and Mary
(Polly) Lightner (4), married Mary Frances Hill, born May 31,
1834; died 1914, daughter of Joel Hill and Rebecca Levisay.
They were the parents of eight children, two of whom were:

     137. i.   Emma Clark (6), born June 19, 1865; married
November 18, 1885, Mathew Lee Beard, son of William Thomas Beard
and Mary G. McNeel.
     138. ii.   Sherman H. Clark, Jr. (6), died in young manhood.

     38. Alvin Clark (5), son of Sheldon Clark and Mary (Polly)
Lightner (4), was born in 1832; died August 23, 1906; married
Mary Agnes Beard, daughter of Josiah Beard and Rachel Cameron
Poage.

     Children: 7

     139. i.   Samuel Clark (6), died young.
     140. ii.   Hubert Clark (6), died young.
     141. iii. Cameron L. Clark (6), married Florence Smith.
     142. iv.   Mary Blanche Clark (6), married Thomas A.
Sydenstricker.
     143. v.   Rachel Clark (6), died young.
     144. vi.   Grace Leigh Clark (6), married in 1897, Andrew
Price, born in 1871; died March 26, 1930.
     145. vii. Robert Clark (6), died young.

     39. Henry N. Clark (5), son of Sheldon Clark and Mary (Polly)
Lightner (4), died in 1902; married Mary Serene Loveridge, died
October 20, 1920.

     Children: 9

146. i.   Remus H. Clark (6), a Methodist minister.
147. ii. R. C. Clark (6).
148. iii. Peter Clark (6).
149. iv. Ryce Clark (6).
150. v.   Sheldon Clark (6), died young.
151. vi. (Infant son)Clark (6), died young
152. vii. (Infant daughter) Clark (6), died young.
153. viii.(Infant daughter) Clark (6), died young.
154. ix. (Infant daughter) Clark (6), died young.

40. Preston S. Clark (5), son of Sheldon Clark and Mary
(Polly) Lightner (4), died in 1921; married December 9, 1868,
Josephine Levisay, born September 29, 1844; died January 28,
1931, daughter of Joseph Levisay and Rachel Bright.

Children: 7

+   155. i.   Lula Clark (6).
    156. ii. Minnie Clark (6), died August 28, 1955; married
L. Guy Bell.
+   157. iii. Annie Clark (6).
    158. iv. Myrtle Clark (6), died June 20, 1941, unmarried.
    159. v.   Norvel Clark (6).
    160. vi. Lee Clark (6).
    161. vii. Rachel Clark (6), married Forrest Lee Beard,
son of Edwin L. Beard and Mollie Hevener.

45. Anne Sharp (5),•daughter of Joseph Sharp and Elizabeth
(Betsy) Lightner (4), was born November 11, 1821; died December
20, 1903; married Andrew Sharp, born August 5, 1810; died October
17, 1901. They lived on Back Creek.

Children: 2

162. i.   Mark Sharp (6), born October 7, 1844; died
March 25, 1925; married Nancy Jane McGlaughlin, daughter of
Samuel McGlaughlin and Elizabeth Wright.
163. ii. Matilda Lena Sharp (6), born May 7, 1854;
married (as his second wife), George W. Carroll.

50. John M. Lightner (5), son of Jacob Lightner (4) and
Elizabeth Moore, died near Abilene, Texas; married May 14, 1872
in Pocahontas County, West Virginia, Sarah Elizabeth McGlaughlin
(5), daughter of William Jacob McGlaughlin and Susan Bible.
He was a lawyer. He served in the CSA.

Children: 4

+   164. i.   John Emmett Lightner (6), born August 17,1879.
    165. ii. Daisy Lightner (6).
    166. iii. Carlotta Lightner (6).
    167. iv. William Lightner (6).

51. Samuel M. Lightner (5), son of Jacob Lightner (4) and Elizabeth Moore, married Sally Mildred Poage. He was educated at Washington College (now Washington and Lee University), Lexington, Virginia for the Presbyterian ministry. He was a member of the "Liberty Hall Volunteers," CSA and his name is inscribed on the memorial table at Washington and Lee University. He only lived a few months after his marriage and his widow married (2) Rev. Edward Lane.

Children: 1

168. i.   James Lightner (6).

58. Mary Margaret Bible (5), daughter of Jacob Bible and Sallie Lightner (4), was born March 3, 1836; died August 2, 1900; married December 17, 1857 in Pocahontas County, West Virginia, Peter Dilley Yeager, born June 22, 1830; died December 6, 1906, son of Andrew Yeager and Elizabeth Dilley. He was a Confederate soldier, became a prisoner and spent a long time at Camp Chase, Ohio. He was not released until July 1865. (See Hull Family).

Children: 6

+ 169. i.   Charles Andrew Yeager (6).
+ 170. ii.   William Jacob Yeager (6).
   171. iii. Etta Jane Yeager (6), married March 22, 1881 in Pocahontas County, West Virginia (as his second wife), Harper McGlaughlin (5), son of Hugh McGlaughlin and Elizabeth (Lightner) Gum.
+ 172. iv.   Malcena Elizabeth Yeager (6).
   173. v.   Alice Yeager (6), born April 1, 1866; died September 20,1903; married Henry Flenner, born May 10, 1849; died February 22, 1907.
+ 174. vi.   Gertrude Yeager (6).

63. Abraham W. Gum (5), son of Otho Gum and Elizabeth Lightner (4), married in 1854, Margaret A. Ryder, daughter of William J. Ryder and Rosanna Sharp. They migrated to Kansas.

Children: 6

175. i.   William H. P. Gum (6), died young.
176. ii.   Hortense Gum (6), born 1858; married A. G.Wolf.
177. iii. Alfaretta Gum (6), married Jesse L. Allen.
178. iv.   Lorenzo D. Gum (6), died young.
179. v.   Charles D. Gum (6), married Mary Burdett.
180. vi.   Rosanna Gum (6).

65. Susan Gum (5), daughter of Otho Gum and Elizabeth Lightner (4), married (1) in 1845, Stewart S. Wade, born 1823; 1904, son of John Wade and Matilda Slaven; married (2) (as his third wife), Thomas Campbell, born January 1, 1800; died January 22, 1876, son of Alexander Campbell and Margaret Brown. (See Campbell Family).

Children: 1 - second marriage

+ 181. i. Mary Susan Campbell (6), born November 4, 1868.

69. Peter Lightner Gum (5), son of Otho Gum and Elizabeth
Lightner, was born in 1836; died in 1916; married (1) May 6,
1861, Nancy Jane Dever, born 1838; died August 8, 1895, daughter
of John Dever and Eliza Gilmer; married (2) September 9, 1896,
Marietta Ellen Lightner (5), born June 4, 1856; died May 11, 1935;
daughter of Jacob Lightner and Nancy Jane Warwick. He served in
Company F, 25th Virginia Regiment, CSA, and lost a leg at the
battle of Cedar Mountain. No children by second marriage.

Children: 10 - first marriage

182. i. Robert Lee Gum (6), born November 11, 1863;
died August 28, 1949; married (1) in 1883, Ruby Williams;
married (2) in 1927, Fleeta Coakley.
183. ii. Harry S. Gum (6).
184. iii. Cameron O. Gum (6), died unmarried.
185. iv. Agnes Gum (6), died in childhood.
186. v. Clara V. Gum (6), died 1899, unmarried.
+ 187. vi. Paul L. Gum (6).
188. vii. Otho Clay Gum (6), died April 1, 1906, unmarried.
189. viii. Homer Gum (6), died April 1908, unmarried.
+ 190. ix. Dennis Hamilton Gum (6).
191. x. John Harper Gum (6), died March 31, 1908,
unmarried.

70. Otho Gum (5), son of Otho Gum and Elizabeth Lightner
(4), was born after his father's death; died December 30, 1904;
married in 1865, Virginia Wade, born 1844; died 1918, daughter
of James Wade.

Children: 6

+ 192. i. Allie Gum (6).
+ 193. ii. H. Albert (Bert) Gum (6).
+ 194. iii. James Lightner Gum (6), born July 1877.
+ 195. iv. Mary Gum (6).
+ 196. v. Ruby Gum (6).
+ 197. vi. Maude Gum (6).

71. Andrew Matthews McGlaughlin (5), son of Hugh McGlaughlin and Elizabeth Lightner (4), was born December 1, 1844 near
Huntersville, West Virginia; died March 8, 1913; married May 14,
1867 in Pocahontas County, West Virginia, Mary Margaret Price,
daughter of James Atlee Price and Margaret Davies Poage. He
served in Company I, 19th Virginia Cavalry, CSA, and was a
Colonel on the staff of General Bennet H. Young.

Children: 6

193

+   198. i.   Henry Woods McGlaughlin (6), born June 13, 1869.
+   199. ii.   Margaret Anna McGlaughlin (6), born July 29,
1874.
+   200. iii.   Lee Pruyn McGlaughlin (6), born May 1, 1878.
+   201. iv.   Mary Elizabeth McGlaughlin (6), born April 17,
1880.
+   202. v.   Edgar Hugh McGlaughlin (6), born July 18, 1882.
+   203. vi.   Grace Davies McGlaughlin (6), born June 21, 1887.

72. Harper McGlaughlin (5), son of Hugh McGlaughlin and
Elizabeth Lightner (4), died March 1, 1924; married (1) April
8, 1867 in Pocahontas County, West Virginia, Caroline Y. Cackley,
daughter of Valentine Cackley and Mary Moore; married (2) March
22, 1881 in Pocahontas County, West Virginia, Etta Jane Yeager
(5), daughter of Peter Dilley Yeager and Mary Margaret Bible.
He served in Company I, 19th Virginia Cavalry, CSA.

     Children: 2 - first marriage

     204. i.   Alice McGlaughlin (6), born 1870; married
October 19, 1892 in Bath County, Virginia, William A. Greaver,
born 1862, son of Jacob Y. Greaver and Lizzie Withrow.
+   205. ii.   Calvin McGlaughlin (6).

     Children: 6 - second marriage

+   206. iii.   Archie Yeager McGlaughlin (6).
     207. iv.   Charles H. McGlaughlin (6), died September 19,195
+   208. v.   Vernon Pole McGlaughlin (6).
+   209. vi.   Mamie Iva McGlaughlin (6), born 1890.
     210. vii.   Austin McGlaughlin (6), died in 1919.
     211. viii. William Cameron McGlaughlin (6), married Wardie
Gum (7), daughter of H. Albert Gum and Virginia Wade.

73. Susan Harper Lightner (5), daughter of John Lightner
(4) and Jane Moore, was born September 2, 1827; died July 16,
1896; married June 24, 1848, James Gay, born September 24, 1813;
died May 25, 1872, son of Samuel Gay and Margaret Catherine
Mustoe. They lived and died at Gaymont, near Hightown, Highland
County, Virginia.

     Children: 9

     212. i.   Susan Jane Gay (6), born April 1, 1849; died
April 25, 1886; married Greenlee Meredith Kerr. Buried at
Shemariah Presbyterian Church, Augusta County, Virginia.
     213. ii.   James William Gay (6), born October 2, 1850;
died February 22, 1873.
     214. iii.   Margaret Ann Gay (6), born October 5, 1855;
died July 27, 1863.
+   215. iv.   Paul Lightner Gay (6), born March 4, 1858.
+   216. v.   Lelia Bell Gay (6), born April 26, 1860.
     217. vi.   Lucy Haywood Gay (6), born January 26, 1863;

died December 3, 1863.
   218. vii. John Samuel Gay (6), born April 23, 1865; died
February 23, 1866.
   219; viii. Helen Moore Gay (6), born April 14, 1867; died
September 15, 1955; married July 27, 1892, Richard Paul, born
October 3, 1865. No children.
   220. ix. John Lightner Gay (6), born March 30, 1870;
died May 8, 1871.

   74. Elizabeth Lightner (5), daughter of John Lightner (4)
and Jane Moore, married (1) _____ Rice; married (2) Dr. Mortimer
Williams. They lived at Olney, Illinois. After the death of Dr.
Williams, she resided in Monterey, Virginia.

   Children: 1 - first marriage

   221. i. Ella Rice (6), died in childhood.

   Children: 1 - second marriage

   222; ii. Ella Williams (6), married Amicy Paul, brother
of Richard Paul, who married Helen Moore Gay (6).

   76. Rachel Lightner (5), daughter of John Lightner (4) and
Jane Moore, married Rev. James Andrew McCauley, born October 7,
1822 in Cecil County, Maryland; died December 1896. He graduated
from Dickenson College, Carlisle, Pennsylvania and later became
President of Dickenson College. He entered the Methodist ministry in 1850.

   Children: 1

   223. i. Fannie M. McCauley (6).

   78. William Stuart Lightner (5), son of Adam Lightner (4)
and Eleanor Slaven, was born in 1832; married in 1867, Mary   ·
Jordan. He served four years in the CSA in Company E, 31st
Virginia Regiment.

   Children: 4

+ 224. i. Signora Isabel Lightner (6), born September 19,
1868.
+ 225. ii. Marietta Slaven Lightner (6), born June 11,
1873.
   226. iii. Lelia Lightner (6), married Joseph Monroe.
   227. iv. Samuel L. Lightner (6), married Mary Westerman.
No children.

   80. Anthony Lightner (5), son of Adam Lightner (4) and
Eleanor Slaven, was born October 18, 1836; died June 12, 1916;
married in 1867, Mary Charlotte Tate Lightner (5), daughter of
Samuel Lightner and Lucy Ann Darst. He served in Company E,
31st Virginia Regiment and in Company I, 19th Virginia Cavalry,
CSA.

Children: 3

+ 228. i.   Lucy Pearl Lightner (6), born December 5, 1879.
  229. ii.   Ada Stella Lightner (6), born August 13, 1882,
unmarried.
+ 230. iii. Adam Samuel Lightner (6), born August 13, 1882,
a twin to Ada Stella.

81. Isabelle M. Lightner (5), daughter of Adam Lightner (4)
and Eleanor Slaven, was born in 1840; married (1) David Bird who
died in the Confederate Army; married (2) John Calvin McGlaughlin,
son of Hugh McGlaughlin and Nancy Gwin.

Children: 8 - second marriage

+ 231. i.   Hugh Adam McGlaughlin (6).
  232. ii.   Harry Mathews McGlaughlin (6), born in 1867;
died in 1945; married Laura Sophia Ransberger, born in 1857;
died in 1931. They have an adopted daughter, Nelle McGlaughlin,
a R. N. in California.
  233. iii. John Samuel McGlaughlin (6), died young.
  234. iv.   James McGlaughlin (6), died in young manhood.
  235. v.   Nellie McGlaughlin (6), died in young womanhood.
+ 236. vi.   Elizabeth McGlaughlin (6), born May 6, 1875.
  237. vii. Willie Sue McGlaughlin (6), married Ben F.
Traxler. They lived in Ohio.
  238. viii. Minerva McGlaughlin (6), died in young womanhood.

82. Alice Susan Davis Lightner (5), daughter of William
Lightner (4) and Mary Davis Hamilton, was born November 25, 1841;
died December 1, 1904; married January 29, 1861, John Lynn Given
Gibson, born June 13, 1830; died November 6, 1896, son of Samuel
L. Gibson and Sarah Given. They lived at Vanderpool, Virginia.

Children: 9

+ 239. i.   Mary Emma Gibson (6), born December 25, 1861.
  240. ii.   Willis Gibson (6), born September 10, 1865,
unmarried. He served as Treasurer and Surveyor of Highland County,
Virginia.
+ 241. iii. Virginia Madora Gibson (6), born January 30,
1868.
  242. iv.   (Infant) Gibson (6), born May 5, 1871; died
May 19, 1871.
  243. v.   Charles Lightner Gibson (6), born February 22,
1873; died January 27, 1875.
  244. vi.   Buzzie Gibson (6), born June 29, 1875; died
January 2, 1877.
  245. vii. Althea Elizabeth Gibson (6), born June 5, 1877;
died April 21, 1935.
  246. viii. Lillie Ward Gibson (6), born July 26, 1879;
died January 10, 1882.
  247. ix.   Sallie Minnie Gibson (6), born February 7, 1882;

196

married March 18, 1914, Rylan M. Swope, son of John Henry Swope
and Nannie J. Williams. They live at Vanderpool, Highland County,
Virginia.

84. Charles Adam Lightner (5), son of William Lightner (4)
and Mary Davis Hamilton, was born January 20, 1852; died March
9, 1908; married May 6, 1873, Estelle Virginia Alice Lightner
(5), daughter of Samuel Lightner and Lucy Ann Darst. She was
born March 24, 1855. They lived at Green Bank, West Virginia.
His will was recorded in Will Book 6, page 332, Pocahontas
County, West Virginia.

Children: 3

248. i. Annie May Lightner (6), born March 6, 1874;
married (1) November 6, 1895 in Pocahontas County, West Virginia,
Joel Wade Hampton Siple, born August 17, 1866, son of George W.
Siple and Hannah Rebecca Hopkins Warwick; married (2) John
Robert Gum, born October 11, 1874. No children.
+ 249. ii. William Austin Lightner (6), born June 17,
1882.
250. iii. Minnie Lee Lightner (6), born January 16,
1885; died November 5, 1889.

88. Sabina Alice Lightner (5), daughter of Peter Lightner
(4) and Rachel Berry Hamilton, was born January 23, 1846; died
February 11, 1926; married May 3, 1869, Naylor Inskept Claggett,
born June 3, 1843 in Winchester, Virginia; died August 20, 1926
in Fullerton, Nebraska. He served in the CSA. They migrated to
Missouri and finally settled in Nebraska in 1903. They had
three sons who died in infancy.

Children: 4

251. i. Frances Louise Claggett (6), married Frank G.
Frame.

90. Adam Henry Lightner (5), son of Peter Lightner (4) and
Rachel Berry Hamilton, was born in 1851; married in 1873, Laura
A. Davis, daughter of Sawyers Davis and Nancy Hamilton of High-
land County, Virginia. They lived in Ossawaloma, Kansas.

Children: 3

252. i. Ora Lee Lightner (6), born 1873; married _____
Frost.
253. ii. Guy Davis Lightner (6), born 1875.
254. iii. Edgar Howard Lightner (6), born 1882.

98. John Adam Lightner (5), son of Jacob Lightner (4) and
Nancy Jane Warwick, was born January 7, 1848 on Back Creek, Bath
County, Virginia; died June 16, 1925 at Coldwater, Kansas; married
February 26, 1891 in McPherson, Kansas, Myrtle Gum, born January

197

23, 1870 in Highland County, Virginia; died June 3, 1956, daughter
of Giles Gum and Estaline Tomlinson. The Gums migrated to Kansas
from Highland County, Virginia, in the early 1880's.

Children: 1

255. i.   Virginia Wallace (Jean) Lightner (6).

99, Robert Warwick Lightner (5), son of Jacob Lightner (5)
and Nancy Jane Warwick, was born July 20, 1850 on Back Creek,
Bath County, Virginia; died February 27, 1930 and was buried at
Green Hill Church, Highland County, Virginia; married November
22, 1877, Augusta H. Bird, born April 5, 1853; died May 7, 1933,
daughter of George Hull Bird and Matilda M. Wade. (See Hull
Family).

Children: 7.

+   256. i,   Sadie Irene Lightner (6), born December 9,
1878.
+   257. ii.   Jacob Hull Lightner (6), born September 1880.
+   258. iii.   Margaret Lightner (6), born December 22, 1882.
    259. iv.   Rachel Cleveland Lightner (6), died in 1887.
+   260. v.   Georgia Lightner (6), born July 14, 1885.
+   261. vi.   Harry Robert Lightner (6), born September 24,
1890.
+   262. vii.   Delana Cameron Lightner (6), born July 23, 1893.

102, Jacob Brown Lightner (5), son of Jacob Lightner (4)
and Nancy Jane Warwick, was born January 30, 1859 on Back Creek,
Bath County, Virginia; died December 3, 1935 and was buried in
the Monterey Cemetery, Monterey, Highland County, Virginia;
married September 22, 1891, Mary Elizabeth Curry, born June 2,
1868, daughter of Andrew Curry and Elizabeth Wade Gum.

Children: 2

+   263, i.   Eunice Brown Lightner (6), born July 4, 1896.
    264. ii.   Lillian Marie Lightner (6), born August 6,
1898; married Bernard L. Karicofe. No children.

103. Peter Hull Lightner (5), son of Jacob Lightner (4)
and Nancy Jane Warwick, was born January 30, 1861 on Back Creek,
Bath County, Virginia; died March 16, 1912 and was buried at
Clifton Presbyterian Church, Maxwelton, West Virginia; married
November 25, 1885, Caroline Elizabeth Siple, born December 1,
1860; died February 21, 1916 and was buried at Clifton Presby-
terian Church, Maxwelton, West Virginia, daughter of James
Madison Siple and Isabelle Wilson, and granddaughter of Joel
Siple and Mary A. Hiner.

Children: 4

265. i.   Lillie Ethel Lightner (6), born November 3,

198

1886, unmarried.
+   266. ii.   Chesley Madison Lightner (6), born July 7, 1893.
+   267; iii.   Marvin Siple Lightner (6), born August 1, 1895.
    268. iv.   Jacob Paul Lightner (6), born March 1900; died
November 1900.

105. James Cameron Lightner (5), son of Jacob Lightner (4)
and Nancy Jane Warwick, was born May 21, 1867 on Back Creek, Bath
County, Virginia; died June 17, 1924 was was buried on the home
farm in Bath County, Virginia; married June 1, 1897, Theodora
Gertrude Guinn, born August 31, 1871; died September 30, 1918,
daughter of George Hamilton Guinn and Margaret Ellen Kincaid.
He attended Fishburn Military School at Waynesboro, Virginia
and graduated in law in 1891 from Washington and Lee University,
Lexington, Virginia, finishing a three year law course in 18
months. He practiced law in Bath and Highland Counties, Virginia.

Children: 3

    269; i.   James Cameron Lightner (6), born March 10,
1898.
    270. ii.   John King Lightner (6), born July 30, 1904;
died October 10, 1906.
    271. iii.   Fay McLarn Lightner (6), born 1907; died 1952
in Boston, Massachusetts; married (1) _____; married
(2) _____.

114. Samuel Adam Lightner (5), son of Jacob Lightner (4)
and Mary Pilson, was born in 1841; died in 1904; married (1)
_____Harris, daughter of John Harris; married (2) Jane Ann
McClure, born August 26, 1853, daughter of George W. McClure
(born January 1, 1822; died December 11, 1890 at his home near
Spottswood, Augusta County, Virginia) and Margaret Finley
Humphreys (born October 5, 1829; died March 27, 1870, daughter
of Aaron-Finley Humphreys, an elder in Bethel Church, Augusta
County, Virginia).

Children: 4 - second marriage

+   272. i.   Charles Thompson Lightner (6), born January 20,
1885.
    273. ii.   Frank Bell Lightner (6), born January 5; 1887,
unmarried.
    274; iii.   John Pilson Lightner (6), born September 20,
1882; died November 10, 1884.
    275. iv.   Finley Alexander Lightner (6), born January
20, 1893; died July 27, 1893.

120. Elizabeth Jane Lightner (5), daughter of Samuel
Lightner (4) and Lucy Ann Darst, married John Artemus Brownlee.

Children: 10

199

276.	i.	Annie Bet Brownlee (6).
277.	ii.	Dora Brownlee (6), a school teacher.
278.	iii.	Samuel Brownlee (6).
279.	iv.	William Brownlee (6).
280.	v.	Jerome Brownlee (6).
281.	vi.	John Brownlee (6).
282.	vii.	Albert Brownlee (6).
283.	viii.	Clarence Brownlee (6).
284.	ix.	Lettie Brownlee (6).
285.	x.	Lorene Brownlee (6).

121. Signora Frances Lightner (5), daughter of Samuel Lightner (4) and Lucy Ann Darst, married Robert Brownlee.

Children: 2

286.	i.	Harry Brownlee (6).
287.	ii.	Frank Brownlee (6).

124. Milton Hitt Lightner (5), son of Samuel Lightner (4) and Lucy Ann Darst, married Caladonia Rush Greene, died May 31, 1935.

Children: 9

288. i. Gordon Hitt Lightner (6), died August 10, 1954; married Amelia Benson Bain. He served as a Lieutenant in the Naval Medical Corps in World War I. No children.

+	289.	ii.	Louis Lightner (6).
+	290.	iii.	Wheatley Lightner (6).
+	291.	iv.	Nimrod Lightner (6).
+	292.	v.	Thomas Ashton Lynn (Jack) Lightner (6).
	293.	vi.	George Lightner (6), died young.
	294.	vii.	Virginia Lee Lightner (6), died young.
+	295.	viii.	Lillian Lightner (6).
+	296.	ix.	Jane Lightner (6).

127. Lula Lightner (5), daughter of Thomas Lightner (4) and Elizabeth Brubeck, married Charles C. Armstrong.

Children: 2

+	297.	i.	Frank Lightner Armstrong (6).
	298.	ii.	Elizabeth Armstrong (6), married Carl Freed.

128. William Thomas Lightner (5), son of Alexander Brownlee Lightner (4) and Sarah Gardner, was born January 17, 1846; died August 29, 1925; married in 1868, Madora Mildred Lightner (5), born September 26, 1847; died May 10, 1909, daughter of William Lightner and Mary Davis Hamilton.

Children: 11

+   299. i.   Clarence Alexander Lightner (6), born April 10, 1869.
      300. ii.   Annie Mary Lightner (6), born September 28, 1870; married July 8, 1915, William Thomas Whitesell, born November 30, 1846.
      301. iii.   Sallie Alice Lightner (6), born April 20,1872.
      302. iv.   Lizzie Virginia Lightner (6), born January 24, 1874.
      303. v.   William Walter Lightner (6), born December 6, 1875; died unmarried.
+   304. vi.   Melvin Hamilton Lightner (6), born July 9, 1878.
+   305. vii.   Florence Lee Lightner (6), born August 30, 1880.
+   306. viii. Charles Thomas Lightner (6), born February 13, 1882.
+   307. ix.   Edna Madora Lightner (6), born November 9,1883.
+   308. x.   Grover Cleveland Lightner (6), born November 26, 1884.
      309. xi.   George Ray Lightner (6), born April 25, 1886; died August 1, 1886.

131. James Shields Lightner (5), son of Alexander Brownlee Lightner (4) and Sarah Ellen Wayland, was born in 1867; died in 1896; married Lelia Clay Hayden, born 1874; died 1896.

Children: 3

      310. i.   Lelia James Lightner (6).
      311. ii.   Russy Lightner (6).
      312. iii.   Alene Lightner (6).

133. John A. Lightner (5), son of Alexander Brownlee Lightner (4) and Sarah Ellen Wayland, was born in 1858; died in 1896; married Mary Virginia Dinkle, born 1859; died 1953, daughter of Robert McGill Dinkle and Sarah Ann Hite.

Children: 5

+   313. i.   Mary V. Lightner (6).
      314. ii.   John Dewitt Lightner (6), married (1) _____
_____; married (2) _____. They live in Alaska.
+   315. iii.   Robert Archibald Lightner (6).
      316. iv.   Julian Lightner (6), died young.
      317. v.   Frank Lightner (6), died young.

136. Charles A. W. Lightner (5), son of Alexander Brownlee Lightner (4) and Sarah Ellen Wayland, was born in 1850; died in 1892; married Mollie Hanger, born 1851; died 1926.

Children: 4

      318. i.   Ivan Lightner (6).

```
        319.  ii.     Emmett Lightner (6), married Jeanette Johnson
of Pennsylvania.
        320.  iii.    Harry Lightner (6).
        321.  iv.     Lillian Lightner (6), married Millard Hamilton.

        155. Lula Clark (6), daughter of Preston S. Clark (5) and
Josephine Levisay, married (1) in 1899, Patrick Henry McNulty;
married (2) John Brock.

        Children:  5 - first marriage

 +      322.  i.      Frances McNulty (7), born 1903.
        323.  ii.     _____ McNulty (7), married M. D. Vaughan.
        324.  iii.    _____ McNulty (7), married L. A. Gladwell.
        325.  iv.     _____ McNulty (7), married F. C. Scalf.
        326.  v.      Patrick Henry McNulty, Jr. (7).

        156. Minnie Clark (6), daughter of Preston S. Clark (5) and
Josephine Levisay, died August 28, 1955; married L. Guy Bell.

        Children:  5

        327.  i.      Josephine Bell (7), married _____ Harmon.
        328.  ii.     Rebecca Bell (7), married _____ Marshall.
        329.  iii.    _____ Bell (7), married Luther Houchins.
        330.  iv.     Preston Clark Bell (7).
        331.  v.      Alexander Bell (7).

        157. Annie Clark (6), daughter of Preston S. Clark (5)
and Josephine Levisay, married Clarence Kelly.  Children not
known.

        164. John Emmett Lightner (6), son of John M. Lightner
(5) and Sarah Elizabeth McGlaughlin, was born August 17, 1879;
died April 5, 1930; married May 11, 1904 in Pocahontas County,
West Virginia, Etta Florence Moore, born November 13, 1880;
died December 6, 1947, daughter of William D. Moore and Hannah
E. Beverage.

        Children:  9

        332.  i.      Elizabeth Lightner (7), R.N., married H. Clayton
Woolwine.
 +      333.  ii.     John Gwin Lightner (7).
        334.  iii.    Josephine Lightner (7), married Dorsey McCarty.
        335.  iv.     Maude Lee Lightner (7).
        336.  v.      Brownie Lightner (7), married Clyde Varner.
        337.  vi.     Dock Lockridge Lightner (7), born March 4, 1919;
died June 29, 1948.
        338.  vii.    Susie Clay Lightner (7), a R.N. in Wisconsin.
        339.  viii.   Hazel Lightner (7), married Harry Tolley.
        340.  ix.     June Lightner (7), a son, died young.
```

169. Charles Andrew Yeager (6), son of Peter Dilley Yeager and Mary Margaret Bible (5), married Allie Arbogast. They lived at Marlinton, West Virginia.

Children: 3

+ 341. i.   Mary Yeager (7).
   342. ii.   Nelle Yeager (7), married Fred McGlaughlin, son of George H. McGlaughlin and Ruhama Wiley. (See Gwin Family).
+ 343. iii. Ralph A. Yeager (7).

170. William Jacob Yeager (6), son of Peter Dilley Yeager and Mary Margaret Bible (5), married Grace Josephine Hull, daughter of William Henry Hull and Rachel Curry.

Children: 4

   344. i.   Mary Yeager (7), married Dale Thompson. She is an instructor at Concord College, Athens, West Virginia.
+ 345. ii.   William Hull Yeager (7).
+ 346. iii. Henry Arnout Yeager (7).
+ 347. iv.   Winston Dilley Yeager (7).

172. Malcena Elizabeth Yeager (6), daughter of Peter Dilley Yeager and Mary Margaret Bible (5), married Charles Pritchard.

Children: 5

   348. i.   Jean Pritchard (7), married Richard McGlaughlin.
   349. ii.   Lucille Pritchard (7), married June McElwee, son of Bernard Francis McElwee and Mary Katherine Siple. (See Warwick Family).
   350. iii. John Pritchard (7), married Isabel Heathery.
   351. iv.   Forest Pritchard (7), married Mamie Moore.
   352. v.   Corlin Pritchard (7), married Sophia Monzley.

174. Gertrude Yeager (6), daughter of Peter Dilley Yeager and Mary Margaret Bible (5), married Dyer Gum. They lived near Leesburg, Virginia.

Children: 3

   353. i.   Yeager Gum (7), married Mary Brown.
   354. ii.   Marie Gum (7), married Nelson Titus.
   355. iii. Leroy Gum (7), unmarried.

181. Mary Susan Campbell (6), daughter of Thomas Campbell and Susan Gum (5), was born November 4, 1868; died December 23, 1940; married June 12, 1889, George Anson Bird, born May 27, 1863; died June 8, 1937, son of George Hull Bird and Matilda M. Wade.

Children: 1

+   356. i.   Lloyd Campbell Bird (7).

187. Paul L. Gum (6), son of Peter Lightner Gum (5) and·
Nancy Jane Dever, married Alice Townsend.

Children: 1

357. i.   Nancy Jane Gum (7).

190. Dennis Hamilton Gum (6), son of Peter Lightner Gum
(5) and Nancy Jane Dever, married January 22, 1912, Bessie
Bradshaw.

Children: 1

358. i.   Mary Jane Gum (7), married Whitfield Sellers.

192. Allie Gum (6), daughter of Otho Gum (5) and Virginia
Wade, married Henry Slaven.

Children: 6

359. i.   Roy Slaven (7), married _____ Wimer.
360. ii.   John R. Slaven (7), married Lottie Woods.
He served in World War I.
361. iii. Alma Slaven (7), unmarried.
362. iv.   Sallie Slaven (7).
363. v.   Beryl Slaven (7), married William White.
364. vi.   Blanche Slaven (7), married Paulser Pullin.

193. H. Albert (Bert) Gum (6), son of Otho Gum (5) and
Virginia Wade, died in 1911; married Adelaide Wiley, daughter
of Oscar T. Wiley and Priscilla Wade. (See Crawford Family).

Children: 1

365. i.   Wardie Gum (7), married William Cameron
McGlaughlin (6), son of Harper McGlaughlin and Etta Jane Yeager.

194. James Lightner Gum (6), son of Otho Gum (5) and
Virginia Wade, was born in 1877; married October 1909 (as her
second husband), Virginia Madora Gibson (6), born January 30,
1868; died June 6, 1934, daughter of John Lynn Given Gibson
and Alice Susan Davis Lightner.

Children: 1

+   366. i.   Alice Catherine Gum (7), born August 18, 1910.

195. Mary Gum (6), daughter of Otho Gum (5) and Virginia
Wade, married William H. Wilson.

Children: 3

204

+ 367. i.   Meade Wilson (7).
  368. ii.   Hale Wilson (7), married Doris Judy, teacher
at Warm Springs, Virginia.
  369. iii. Blake Wilson (7), died.

196. Ruby Gum (6), daughter of Otho Gum (5) and Virginia
Wade, married William N. Bird.

Children: 2 .

370. i.   Frank Bird (7), married Lavenia Vance. No
children.
371. ii.   Constance Bird (7), married George Graham.
No children.

197. Maude Gum (6), daughter of Otho Gum (5) and Virginia
Wade, married Lawrence Ralston.

Children: 1

372. i.   Doreen Ralston (7), born June 1917, unmarried.

198. Henry Woods McGlaughlin, D.D. (6), son of Andrew
Matthews McGlaughlin (5) and Mary Margaret Price, was born June
13, 1869 in Marlinton, West Virginia; married August 31, 1897,
Nellie Swann Brown, born June 1, 1876, daughter of Rev. John
Calvin Brown of Malden, West Virginia and Amanda Virginia
Tompkins. He was a Presbyterian minister. The old spelling
of this surname was McGlaughlin, however, it is usually spelled
now McLaughlin. In order to avoid confusion in this manuscript
it has been spelled McGlaughlin throughout, except in one or
two places.

Children: 9

373. i.   Virginia Tompkins McGlaughlin (7), born
September 12, 1898 in Hampton, Virginia.
374. ii.   Margaret Price McGlaughlin (7), born October
19, 1899 in Hampton, Virginia; died April 7, 1938; married
August 30, 1923, William Fulton Hogshead, born April 8, 1899,
son of Richard H. Hogshead and Ella Fulton.
375. iii. John Calvin Brown McGlaughlin (7), born
February 14, 1901 at Dunsmore, West Virginia; married July 6,
1927, Frances Dargan McCay, born August 1, 1900, daughter of
William Lowndes McCay and Adelaide Leona Noble. Her grandfather,
Samuel Noble came from Cornwall, England, and made cannons for
CSA and founded Anniston, Alabama.
376. iv.   Andrew Mathews McGlaughlin (7), born August
23, 1903 at Greenbank, West Virginia; married August 27, 1938,
Betty Watkins Martin, born October 7, 1916, daughter of Alex-
ander Lambert Martin and Grace Truman. He is a M.D. at
Waynesboro, Virginia.
377. v.   Henry Woods McGlaughlin, Jr. (7), born February

18, 1906 at Louisville, Kentucky; married June 26, 1934, Mary Garrett Watkins, born July 11, 1913, daughter of Tucker Carrington Watkins, Jr. and Louise Barksdale. He is a lawyer.

378. vi. James Moore McGlaughlin (7), born January 4, 1909 at Louisville, Kentucky; married September 1937, Bernice Cross. He served in World War II.

379. vii. Samuel Brown McGlaughlin (7), born July 10, 1911; married August 26, 1939, Nancy Harrison, born August 5, 1912, daughter of Richard Marcellus Harrison and Lillian Whitmore.

380. viii. Mary Moore McGlaughlin (7), born December 3, 1914; married October 5, 1940, Colonel Harry Downing Temple, U.S. Army, son of John Clarence Temple and Eloise Johnson.

381. ix. Lee Massey McGlaughlin (7), born February 28, 1917; married May 23, 1942, Rosa Batte Hodges, born February 1, 1919, daughter of Lt. Col. Leroy Hodges. He served in the Navy in World War II.

199. Margaret Anna McGlaughlin (6), daughter of Andrew Matthews McGlaughlin (5) and Mary Margaret Price, was born July 29, 1874 at Marlinton, West Virginia; married October 8, 1902, Julian Davis Arbuckle, M.D., son of John Davis Arbuckle and Elizabeth Van Lear.

Children: 7

382. i. Elizabeth Van Lear Arbuckle (7), born September 8, 1903; married June 15, 1940, Richard Renick Dickson, son of Clarence Frazier Dickson and Lyda Renick. He is an attorney.

383. ii. Mary Price Arbuckle (7), born December 5, 1904. She is a secretary.

384. iii. Janet Randolph Arbuckle (7), born August 27, 1906; married December 31, 1928, Frank Cyrus McCue, Jr., son of Frank Cyrus McCue and Mary Lysle Francisco.

385. iv. Margaret Davis Arbuckle (7), born July 23, 1908. She is a R.N.

386. v. Anna Laura Arbuckle (7), born August 11, 1910. She is a teacher.

387. vi. Emily Massey Arbuckle (7), born September 7, 1914. She is a secretary.

388. vii. Julian Davis Arbuckle, Jr. (7), born March 29, 1917. He is a farmer.

200. Lee Pruyn McGlaughlin (6), son of Andrew Matthews McGlaughlin (5) and Mary Margaret Price, was born May 1, 1878; died May 30, 1939; married June 6, 1901, Julia Bell Arbuckle, daughter of Alexander A. Arbuckle and Elizabeth Creigh.

Children: 5

389. i. Elizabeth Price McGlaughlin (7), born July 17, 1902. She is a teacher.

390. ii. Andrew Wayte McGlaughlin (7), born October

27, 1903; married April 29, 1939, Dorothy Field, daughter of
Irving Philip Field and Daisy Mary Verdier.
  391. iii. Alexander Arbuckle McGlaughlin (7), born May
27, 1907; married August 16, 1937, Virginia Wood, daughter of
John Wood and Vivian Jarret.
  392. iv. Lee Preston McGlaughlin (7), born November
9, 1910, a twin to Margaret Lynn; married November 29, 1939,
Cleatrice Smith, daughter of Arlen Elias Smith and Minnie Ellen
Smith.
  393. v. Margaret Lynn McGlaughlin (7), born November
9, 1910, a twin to Lee Preston; married November 18, 1939,
William H. Unger, son of Edwin W. Unger and Mary Zoe Sprigg.

  201. Mary Elizabeth McGlaughlin (6), daughter of Andrew
Matthews McGlaughlin (5) and Mary Margaret Price, was born
April 17, 1880; married August 31, 1905, Hale Houston Arbuckle,
son of John Davis Arbuckle and Elizabeth Van Lear.

Children: 6

  394. i. Anna Davies Arbuckle (7), born July 5, 1906.
She is a teacher.
  395. ii. Julia Bell Arbuckle (7), born November 19,
1908; married October 21, 1931, Woodson Legg. He is a farmer.
  396. iii. Mary Mathews Arbuckle (7), born October 16,
1911. She is a secretary.
  397. iv. John Davis Arbuckle (7), born November 19,
1912; married July 29, 1941, Mattie Winlock Harrison. He is
a Presbyterian minister.
  398. v. Millard Filmore Arbuckle (7), born September
19, 1917.
  399. vi. Hale Houston Arbuckle, Jr. (7), born January
16, 1927.

  202. Edgar Hugh McGlaughlin (6), son of Andrew Matthews
McGlaughlin (5) and Mary Margaret Price, was born July 18, 1882;
died July 3, 1955; married October 1905, Lillian May McElwee,
born August 14, 1886; died February 1, 1955, daughter of Bernard
Francis McElwee and Mary Katherine Siple. (See Warwick Family).

Children: 10

  400. i. Bernard Francis McGlaughlin (7), born July
19, 1906; married July 21, 1930, Helen Spain.
  401. ii. Mary Katherine McGlaughlin (7), born April
20, 1908; married July 5, 1934, Andrew Muncy Groseclose, M.D.
She is a R.N.
  402. iii. Edgar Hopkins McGlaughlin (7), born March 29,
1910; married August 31, 1935, Christine Robinson, daughter of
Robert Kitchen Robinson and Chloe Miller.
  403. iv. Lillian May McGlaughlin (7), born March 29,
1910, a twin to Edgar Hopkins; died June 6, 1910.
  404. v. Winifred Lee McGlaughlin (7), born October 9,

1911, a twin to Anna Bell; married May 7, 1939, James Clifford
Nipp, son of James Robert Nipp and Rose Everman. She is a R.N.
405. vi. Anna Bell McGlaughlin (7), born October 9,
1911; married David Hamlin, Silver Springs, Maryland.
406. vii. Andrew Mathews McGlaughlin (7), born 1913;
died in infancy.
407. viii. (Infant son) McGlaughlin (7), born dead, 1915.
408. ix. Hugh Price McGlaughlin (7), born September
10, 1916.
409. x. (Infant daughter) McGlaughlin (7), born and
died October 1918.

203. Grace Davies McGlaughlin (6), daughter of Andrew
Matthews McGlaughlin (5) and Mary Margaret Price, was born
June 21, 1887; married October 23, 1907, Rev. James Buckner
Massey, D.D. of North Carolina, born May 26, 1879, a Presby-
terian minister, son of Benjamin Henry Massey and Banna
Madora Cunningham.

Children: 5

410. i. Banna Price Massey (7), born October 3, 1908;
married September 7, 1938, Joseph T. Trotter.
411. ii. Eugenia Woods Massey (7), born October 19,1910.
412. iii. James Buckner Massey, Jr. (7), born March 1,
1913; married Helen Thomas Collings, daughter of Thomas James
Collings and Helen Thomas Luke. He served in the Navy in
World War II.
413. iv. Benjamin Henry Massey (7), born February 27,
1918; married February 20, 1943, Arabella Diehl, born c. 1919,
daughter of Rev. Samuel Reynolds Diehl and Florence Amanda
Myers.
414. v. Margaret Poague Massey (7), born July 1, 1924.

205. Calvin McGlaughlin (6), son of Harper McGlaughlin
(5) and Caroline Y. Cackley, married Alice Landes.

Children: 1

415. i. Callie McGlaughlin (7), married John Mitchell.

206. Archie Yeager McGlaughlin (6), son of Harper McGlaughlin (5) and Etta Jane Yeager, married (1) Myrtie Grose; married
(2) Eva Taylor.

Children: 2 - first marriage

416. i. Holmes McGlaughlin (7), married Clarice Ayers.
417. ii. Julian McGlaughlin (7), married Katherine
Patterson.

Children: 4 - second marriage

208

417.　iii.　Normand McGlaughlin (7), married Ilene Jamison.
418.　iv.　Maryetta McGlaughlin (7), married T. W. (Dick)
Ergenbright.
419.　v.　Edmund McGlaughlin (7), married Elsie Smith,
420.　vi.　Roland McGlaughlin (7), married Shirley Loan.

208.　Vernon Pole McGlaughlin (6), son of Harper McGlaughlin
(5) and Etta Jane Yeager (5), married in 1924, Grace Friel.

Children:　6

421.　i.　Nobel Grace McGlaughlin (7).
422.　ii.　Edith Price McGlaughlin (7).
423.　iii.　Vernon Tate McGlaughlin (7).
424.　iv.　Jack Dempsey McGlaughlin (7), married August
8, 1954,.Phyllis Schoolcraft.
425.　v.　Harper Junior McGlaughlin (7), married
Shirley Lee May.
426.　vi.　James Lee McGlaughlin (7), married Hattie Lee
Schoolcraft.

209.　Mamie Iva McGlaughlin (6), daughter of Harper McGlaughlin (5) and Etta Jane Yeager (5), was born in 1890; died January
1941; married (as his first wife), Charles N. Loving on April.
30, 1912.　He served as a member of the Board of Supervisors of
Bath County, Virginia; as a State Senator; and as a member of
the Virginia Legislature from Bath, Highland, and Rockbridge
Counties, Virginia.

Children:　4

427.　i.　Elizabeth Loving (7), married F. G. Thompson.
He served as Sheriff of Bath County, Virginia and is now County
Judge of Bath County, Virginia.
428.　ii.　Robert Harper Loving (7), D.D.S.; married
_____.
429.　iii.　William Loving (7), married Iona Purkey.
430.　iv.　(Infant daughter) Loving (7), died.

215.　Paul Lightner Gay (6), son of James Gay and Susan
Harper Lightner (5), was born March 4, 1858; died September 5,
1930; married Blanche L. Mann, sister of S. P. Mann. They are
buried in Thornrose Cemetery, Staunton, Virginia.

Children:　7

431.　i.　James Gay (7).
432.　ii.　Richard Gay (7).
433.　iii.　Mann Gay (7).
434.　iv.　Petus Gay (7).
435.　v.　Paul Lightner Gay, Jr. (7).
436.　vi.　_____ Gay (7), married William Sanders.
437.　vii.　_____ Gay (7), married _____ Webster.

216. Lelia Bell Gay (6), daughter of James Gay and Susan Harper Lightner (5), was born April 26, 1860; died December 23, 1908; married S. Allen Porter, died 1934. They are buried in Thornrose Cemetery, Staunton, Virginia.

Children: 6

+ 438. i. John Russell Porter (7).
439. ii. Ernest G. Porter (7), married Grace Hosford.
440. iii. Forest Porter (7).
441. iv. Charles Sidney Porter (7).
442. v. Howard Porter (7).
443. vi. Lucille Porter (7), died in early womanhood.

224. Signora Isabel Lightner (6), daughter of William Stuart Lightner (5) and Mary Jordan, was born September 19, 1868; married June 30, 1902, William Edgar Trout, born August 24, 1867, son of James Russell Trout and Amanda Arey.

Children: 1

+ 444. i. William Edgar Trout, Jr. (7), born July 30, 1903.

225. Marietta Slaven Lightner (6), daughter of William Stuart Lightner (5) and Mary Jordan, was born June 11, 1873; died January 4, 1938; married April 21, 1891, Robert Sylvester Lee Arey, born November 10, 1864; died June 30, 1944.

Children: 7

445. i. Russell Warren Arey (7), born March 9, 1893; died November 26, 1929 in North Carolina; married September 16, 1925, Mary Earnhardt. No children.
+ 446. ii. Muriel Virginia Arey (7), born June 26, 1895.
447. iii. Mary Lightner Arey (7), born March 4, 1897; died January 9, 1901.
448. iv. Elizabeth Hunter Arey (7), born November 27, 1900; died January 4, 1901.
449. v. William Laird Arey (7), born March 9, 1903; married (1) April 6, 1924, Mary Boteler; married (2) Frances
_____
450. vi. . Lula Mae Arey (7), born November 12, 1905; married June 7, 1934, Lawrence W. Wallace, born August 5, 1881 in Webberville, Texas. He graduated from A & M College in Texas in 1903 in Mechanical Engineering. He received a M.E. degree from Purdue University in 1912. In 1932 he received a honorary degree of Doctor of Engineering from Purdue University. He became Vice President of W. S. Lee Engineering Corporation, Washington, D. C. in 1934. He was selected as Director of equipment research of the Research Advisory Board of the Association of American Railroads.
451. vii. Edgar McWain Arey (7), born February 19, 1908;

married August 21, 1937, Lillie G. Massey.

228. Lucy Pearl Lightner (6), daughter of Anthony Lightner
(5) and Mary Charlotte Tate Lightner (5), was born December 5,
1879; married May 1, 1907, Rev. Lewis Lynch Lowance, born
February 8, 1875 near Lewisburg, West Virginia; died August
8, 1935 at Mill Gap, Highland County, Virginia and was buried
at Rosewood Cemetery, Lewisburg, West Virginia. He was a
Methodist minister.

Children: 3

452. i. Lewis Lynch Lowance, Jr. (7), married Mary
Clendennen (7), daughter of Gillian G. Clendennen and Elizabeth McGlaughlin.
453. ii. Alma Lowance (7), unmarried. She is a
teacher, Richmond, Virginia.
454. iii. Edna Lowance (7), died September 28, 1956;
married W. A. Judd, Arlington, Virginia.

230. Adam Samuel Lightner (6), son of Anthony Lightner
(5) and Mary Charlotte Tate Lightner (5), was born August 13,
1882; married April 6, 1905 in Pocahontas County, West Virginia,
Lucy Frances Poague, born May 23, 1878, daughter of John Robert
Poague and Elizabeth Sharp. He died in an accident in Ohio in
1923.

Children: 3

455. i. Tate Poage Lightner (7), born June 30, 1906;
killed in an automobile accident May 28, 1925.
+ 456. ii. John Anthony Lightner (7), born May 2, 1910.
+ 457. iii. Ralph Jewel Lightner (7), born June 21, 1915.

231. Hugh Adam McGlaughlin (6), son of John Calvin McGlaughlin and Isabelle M. Lightner (5), married Flora Steuart.

Children: 8

458. i. Charles Sheffey McGlaughlin (7), born October
2, 1880; died April 2, 1957 at Wilson, North Carolina; married
Noka Stephenson, daughter of Bernard C. Stephenson and Myrtle
Woodzell. He served in World War I.
459. ii. John Martin McGlaughlin (7), married Mabel
Kenny. He is Chairman of the Board of Supervisors of Bath
County, Virginia.
460. iii. Samuel Hatch McGlaughlin (7), married Isabell
Tankersley, daughter of Perry Arthur Tankersley and Mary Dudley
Guinn. He is a Supervisor on the Board of Supervisors of Augusta
County, Virginia. (See Gwin Family).
461. iv. Adam T. McGlaughlin (7), married (1) Esther
Dague; married (2) Thelma Garrett.
462. v. James McGlaughlin (7), unmarried.

211

463. vi.   Nina McGlaughlin (7), married Dr. V. L. Chambers, Huntington, West Virginia. She is a R. N.
464. vii.   Lucy McGlaughlin (7), unmarried, Plainfield, New Jersey.
465. viii.   Mary McGlaughlin (7), married A. L. Gregory, Huntington, West Virginia. She is a R. N.

236. Elizabeth McGlaughlin (6), daughter of John Calvin McGlaughlin and Isabelle M. Lightner (5), was born May 6, 1875; died in 1940; married September 22, 1897, Gillian G. Clendennen. They lived in Greenbrier County, West Virginia.

Children: 3

466. i.   Jacob Gillian Clendennen (7), born June 19, 1898; married Hallie Stewart Fleisher, born October 3, 1898.
467. ii.   Harry Clendennen (7).
468. iii.   Mary Clendennen (7), married Lewis Lynch Lowance, Jr. (7), son of Lewis Lynch Lowance and Lucy Pearl Lightner.

239. Mary Emma Gibson (6), daughter of John Lynn Given Gibson and Alice Susan Davis Lightner (5), was born December 25, 1861; died August 21, 1902; married January 29, 1879, Hugh A. Jordan, born July 8, 1853. They lived on Jackson River and later on Knapps Creek, Pocahontas County, West Virginia.

Children: 8

+   469. i.   Maude Elsie Jordan (7), born July 10, 1881.
+   470. ii.   Bertie Edith Jordan (7), born March 31, 1883.
+   471. iii.   Mary Etta (Nettie) Jordan (7), born June 23, 1885.
472. iv.   Lloyd Edward Jordan (7), born April 13, 1887; died July 1, 1914.
473. v.   Annie Alice Jordan (7), born August 23, 1889; died August 1, 1891.
474. vi.   Hubert Allen Jordan (7), born August 29,1891. He served in World War I.
475. vii.   Zula Agnes Jordan (7), born July 18, 1893; married (1) _____ Carrier; married (2) A. C. Henderson. She was a R.N.
476. viii.   (Infant) Jordan (7), born August 7, 1902; died August 8, 1902.

241. Virginia Madora Gibson (6), daughter of John Lynn Given Gibson and Alice Susan Davis Lightner (5), was born January 30, 1868; died June 6, 1934; married (1) October 1886, James Matthias Benson, born August 21, 1863; married (2) October 1909, James Lightner Gum (6), born 1877, son of Otho Gum and Virginia Wade. They lived at Vanderpool, Virginia.

Children: 2 - first marriage

+   477. i.   Ninnie Edith Benson (7), born February 24,
1887.
+   478. ii.   William Given Benson (7), born March 8, 1896.

256. Sadie Irene Lightner (6), daughter of Robert Warwick
Lightner (5) and Augusta H. Bird, was born December 9, 1878;
married November 18, 1896, Coe Beverage, died June 10, 1948.

Children: 6

+   479. i.   Hildreth Helena Beverage (7).
+   480. ii.   Hallie Beverage (7).
     481. iii.   Charlsy Beverage (7), married Harry Snyder.
     482. iv.   Hazel Beverage (7), married Richard Lovell.
     483. v.   Margie Beverage (7), married Byron Dickson.
     484. vi.   Roscoe Trimble Beverage (7), married Edith
Sharp. No children.

257. Jacob Hull Lightner (6), son of Robert Warwick
Lightner (5) and Augusta H. Bird, was born September 1880;
married (1) in 1904, Abigail Swadley, died December 28, 1905;
daughter of A. Frank Swadley and Phoebe Trimble; married (2)
October 1910, Florence Dever, daughter of Samuel Dever and
Virginia Shirley.

Children: 1 - first marriage

485. i.   Frank May Lightner (7), born December 10,
1905; died September 10, 1935, unmarried, and was buried by his
mother's grave at Hightown Methodist Church.

Children: 6 - second marriage

486. ii.   Julian Gilmer Lightner (7), married January
14, 1942 in Pocahontas County, West Virginia, Evelyn Dill.
     487. iii.   Rembert Lee Lightner (7), married _____.
     488. iv.   Wallace Gatewood Lightner (7), married
Kathlyn Newlen.
     489. v.   Charlotte Meredith Lightner (7).
     490. vi.   Helen Nadine Lightner (7), married Julian
Harper.
     491. vii.   Virginia Dare Lightner (7), married J. Neeson
Workman.

258. Margaret Lightner (6), daughter of Robert Warwick
Lightner (5) and Augusta H. Bird, was born December 22, 1882;
married October 4, 1899, Edward Beverage, born 1878; died
February 15, 1926.

Children: 12

+   492. i.   Edna Beverage (7).
+   493. ii.   Mary Nadine Beverage (7), born August 30, 1913.
+   494. iii.   Caleb Beverage (7).

495. iv. Robert Beverage (7), married Kay _____.
They live in California.
+ 496. v. Cameron Beverage (7).
497. vi. Harry Beverage (7), unmarried.
498. vii. Mabel (Betty) Beverage (7), married (1) ___
_____ Metzell; married (2) Carl E. Reid. They live in California.
They have two children.
+ 499. viii. Marguerite Beverage (7).
+ 500. ix. Mildred Beverage (7).
+ 501. x. Walker Beverage (7).
+ 502. xi. Eugene Beverage (7).
503. xii. Helen Beverage (7), married (1) Jake Webster;
married (2) Olin Fitzgerald.

260. Georgia Lightner (6), daughter of Robert Warwick
Lightner (5) and Augusta H. Bird, was born July 14, 1885; married October 18, 1904, Mack Plummer Wade, born February 28,
1883.

Children: 9

504. i. Warwick Plummer Wade (7), born August 27,
1905; married November 1, 1931, Mary K. Sadler.
505. ii. Ralph Wade (7), born November 4, 1906;
married August 8, 1931, Ida Spearlock.
+ 506. iii. Harry Wade (7), born May 15, 1908.
507. iv. Maxie Wade (7), born June 16, 1910; married
(1) Earl Spitzel who died; married (2) November 19, 1945, Robert
Lee Edwards.
508. v. Elizabeth Wade (7), born January 10, 1914.
509. vi. Lloyd Anson Wade (7), born April 25, 1916;
died April 6, 1936.
510. vii. (Infant daughter) Wade (7), born November 18,
1918, died young.
511. viii. (Infant son) Wade (7), born October 16, 1921;
died young.
512. ix. (Infant son) Wade (7), born November 17, 1923;
died young.

261. Harry Robert Lightner (6), son of Robert Warwick
Lightner (5) and Augusta H. Bird, was born September 24, 1890;
married January 22, 1922, Bessie Lee Cleek, born September 25,
1892, daughter of Bias Ashby Cleek and Allie Baldwin.

Children: 7

513. i. Swanny Lightner (7), died in infancy.
+ 514. ii. Irene Lee Lightner (7), born November 20, 1923.
515. iii. Harry Robert Lightner, Jr. (7), born July 12,
1925; married November 3, 1950, Jean Wimer, born March 26, 1932;
died March 10, 1952, daughter of Arvie Glenn Wimer and Elizabeth
Hull. He served as PFC with the 3186 Signal Service Battalion
in Japan. He entered service on June 15, 1946 and was discharged.
July 9, 1947. (See Hull Family).

+ 516. iv. Vernon Cleek Lightner (7), born February 9,
1927.
+ 517. v. Ernest Hartley Lightner (7), born December
20, 1928.
+ 518. vi. Robert Bias Lightner (7), born September 21,
1930.
+ 519. vii. Leta Brown Lightner (7), born December 21,
1932.

262. Delana Cameron Lightner (6), daughter of Robert
Warwick Lightner (5) and Augusta H. Bird, was born July 23,
1893; married January 9, 1915 in Pocahontas County, West
Virginia, Donald Spotwood Ryder.

Children: 6

+ 520. i. Alfred Brown Ryder (7), born April 23, 1916.
  521. ii. Abbie Grace Ryder (7), married September 7,
1939, Harvey Hull Warwick, born 1913, son of Forrest Warwick and
Bertie Nottingham. (See Warwick Family).
+ 522. iii. Robert Warren Ryder (7).
+ 523. iv. Helen Louise Ryder (7).
+ 524. v. Algernon Spotwood Ryder (7).
+ 525. vi. Jarrett Delford Ryder (7).

263. Eunice Brown Lightner (6), daughter of Jacob Brown
Lightner (5) and Mary Elizabeth Curry, was born July 4, 1896;
married G. Jesse Hiner.

Children: 3

+ 526. i. Joyce Marie Hiner (7).
+ 527. ii. Elsie Brown Hiner (7).
  528. iii. Elizabeth Frances Hiner (7). She graduated
from Strayer's Business College, Washington, D. C.

266. Chesley Madison Lightner (6), son of Peter Hull Lightner (5) and Caroline Elizabeth Siple, was born July 7, 1893 at
Valley Center, Highland County, Virginia; died October 24, 1949
and was buried at Clifton Presbyterian Church, Maxwelton, West
Virginia; married December 31, 1913, May L. Tilson, born March
8, 1892 in McDowell County, West Virginia. He served in World
War I.

Children: 11

  529. i. Brownie Lightner (7), born August 9, 1914 at
Maxwelton, West Virginia.
+ 530. ii. Mildred Lightner (7), born October 24, 1915.
+ 531. iii. Paul M. Lightner (7), born September 29, 1916.
+ 532. iv. Eugene H. Lightner (7), born November 19, 1917.
+ 533. v. Anna Mae Lightner (7), born January 14, 1920.
+ 534. vi. Ray Wilson Lightner (7), born August 11, 1922.

215

+   535.   vii.   Lillie Caroline Lightner (7), born October 13, 1924.

      536.   viii. Clara Marie Lightner (7), born February 8, 1926; died January 1928.

      537.   ix.   Chesley Madison Lightner, II (7), born December 18, 1929. He served in World War II and in the Army of Occupation of Japan.
+   538.   x.   Frank T. Lightner (7), born September 2, 1932.
+   539.   xi.   Kent Lightner (7), born March 25, 1935.

      267. Marvin Siple Lightner (6), son of Peter Hull Lightner (5) and Caroline Elizabeth Siple, was born August 1, 1895 at Sun Rise, Virginia; married (1) Blanche E. Yates, born April 22, 1887; died October 21, 1953; married (2) Mrs. Bird Henry Dietz.

      Children: 1 - first marriage

+   540.   i.   Thomas Hull Lightner (7), born April 30, 1917.

      272. Charles Thompson Lightner (6), son of Samuel Adam Lightner (5) and Jane Ann McClure, was born January 20, 1885; married February 23, 1910, Bessie Wilson Ruff, died August 15, 1951 of Bedford County, Virginia. She was a school teacher.

      Children: 1

      541.   i.   C. G. Lightner (7).

      289. Louis Lightner (6), son of Milton Hitt Lightner (5) and Caladonia Rush Greene, married Estelle Burgess.

      Children; 6

      542.   i.   Louis Field Lightner (7), married _____.
      543.   ii.   Louise Lightner (7).
      544.   iii.   Anne Lightner (7), married _____ Park.
      545.   iv.   Margaret Lightner (7), married _____ Seay.
      546.   v.   Helen Lightner (7), married _____ Ray.
      547.   vi.   Charlotte Lightner (7), married _____ Hall.

      290. Wheatley Lightner (6), son of Milton Hitt Lightner (5) and Caladonia Rush Greene, married Hazel Sturgil.

      Children: 1

      548.   i.   Wheatley Lightner (7).

      291. Nimrod Lightner (6), son of Milton Hitt Lightner (5) and Caladonia Rush Greene, married Bernice Thomas.

      Children: 4

      549.   i.   Katherine Lightner (7), married _____ Piercy.

550. ii.   Sarah Jane Lightner (7), married _____ Alvey.
551. iii. Thomas Gordon Lightner (7).
552. iv.   Linda Lightner (7).

292. Thomas Ashton Lynn (Jack) Lightner (6), son of Milton
Hitt Lightner (5) and Caladonia Rush Greene; married Mary Benson.
He is a Lieutenant Commander in the Navy.

Children: 2

553. i.   Mary Benson Lightner (7).
554. ii.   Ashton Lightner (7), died young.

295. Lillian Lightner (6), daughter of Milton Hitt Lightner
(5) and Caladonia Rush Greene, married Joseph Norman.

Children: 4

+ 555. i.   Mary Norman (7).
+ 556. ii.   Jean Norman (7).
+ 557. iii. Betty Norman (7).
   558. iv.   John Norman (7).

296. Jane Lightner (6), daughter of Milton Hitt Lightner
(5) and Caladonia Rush Greene, married (1) Grant Lyons; married
(2) Robert Walker.

Children: 2 - which marriage unknown

559. i.   Deanna _____ (7).
560. ii.   Robbie _____ (7).

297. Frank Lightner Armstrong (6), son of Charles C. Armstrong and Lula Lightner (5), married Doris Elsie Beard.

Children: 1

561. i.   Anne Beard (7), married Paterson Kerr.

299. Clarence Alexander Lightner (6), son of William Thomas
Lightner (5) and Madora Mildred Lightner (5), was born April 10,
1869; married May 12, 1891, Mattie Ellen Sellers.

Children: 8

+ 562. i.   Ralph Gibson Lightner (7), born April 27, 1892.
+ 563. ii.   Irby Clarence Lightner (7), born June 3, 1894.
   564. iii. Hugh Eyster Lightner (7), born November 5,
1895. He served in World War I.
   565. iv.   Mildred Madora Lightner (7), born September
27, 1897.
+ 566. v.   Margaret Sellers Lightner (7), born September
7, 1899.

217

567. vi. William Jerome Lightner (7), born July 25, 1901.
568. vii. Helen Josephine Lightner (7), born May 29, 1904.
569. viii. Fay Lois Lightner (7), born July 25, 1907.

304. Melvin Hamilton Lightner (6), son of William Thomas Lightner (5) and Madora Mildred Lightner (5), was born July 9, 1878; married October 26, 1905, Margaret May Rohrer, born April 5, 1881.

Children: 4

570. i. Dorothy Hazel Lightner (7), born August 1, 1907.
571. ii. Katherine Pauline Lightner (7), born April 21, 1910.
572. iii. Edith Melva Lightner (7), born September 11, 1917; married Clifton H. Curtis.
573. iv. David Phillo Lightner (7), born July 3, 1920; served in World War II.

305. Florence Lee Lightner (6), daughter of William Thomas Lightner (5) and Madora Mildred Lightner (5), was born August 30, 1880; died April 1933; buried at Woodland Cemetery, Bath County, Virginia; married Elmer Leonard Dannel, born May 12, 1883.

Children: 3

574. i. George William Dannel (7), born May 11, 1911.
575. ii. Virginia Ethel Dannel (7), born February 25, 1913.
576. iii. Elmer Lee Dannel (7), born December 3, 1919.

306. Charles Thomas Lightner (6), son of William Thomas Lightner (5) and Madora Mildred Lightner (5), was born February 13, 1882; died February 20, 1953; married December 22, 1909, Alice Elizabeth Baylor, born April 3, 1885; died 1954, daughter of George W. Baylor and Mrs. Mary Crosby.

Children: 3

577. i. Janett Ruth Lightner (7), born May 23, 1912; married Carl Caudill.
578. ii. Dorothy Neff Lightner (7), born August 13, 1914; died 1934, unmarried.
579. iii. George Thomas Lightner (7). He served in World War II.

307. Edna Madora Lightner (6), daughter of William Thomas Lightner (5) and Madora Mildred Lightner (5), was born November 9, 1883; married November 6, 1912 in Pocahontas County, West Virginia, Walter B. Cole, born October 10, 1866; died March 1934.

Children: 3

580, i. Friel Robert Cole (7), born February 16, 1915; married Margaret Virginia Lightner (7), daughter of William Austin Lightner and Icea May Wealthy.
581. ii. Frances Marie Cole (7), born March 5, 1917; married Grover Taylor.
582. iii. Paul Foster Cole (7), born October 18, 1919; died in young manhood.

308. Grover Cleveland Lightner (6), son of William Thomas Lightner (5) and Madora Mildred Lightner (5), was born November 26, 1884; married August 28, 1918, Lillie Ruth Jordan, born September 10, 1895.

Children: 2

583. i. Mary Jane Lightner (7), born February 26, 1920; married Homer Bast, Salem, Virginia.
584. ii. Nancy Jane Lightner (7), born January 14, 1924; married Robert D. Pugh, Roanoke, Virginia.

313. Mary V. Lightner (6), daughter of John A. Lightner (5) and Mary Virginia Dinkle, married W. W. Thompson.

Children: 3

585. i. Elnora Thompson (7), married Caldwell Daffin.
586. ii. Emma Jean Thompson (7), married Ralph Young.
587. iii. Julian McDonald Thompson (7).

315. Robert Archibald Lightner (6), son of John A. Lightner (5) and Mary Virginia Dinkle, married Ednora Hamilton. She married (2) H. G. P. McNeil.

Children: 6

588. i. Janet Lightner (7), married Harry Cook.
589. ii. Margaret Lightner (7), married Charles Swatts.
590. iii. Nora Lee Lightner (7), married Howard Rankin.
591. iv. Anna Belle Lightner (7), married Meriwether Jones.
592. v. Evelyn Lightner (7), married Richard Beard.
593. vi. Robert Archibald Lightner, Jr. (7), married Annabelle Bauserman.

322. Frances McNulty (7), daughter of Patrick Henry McNulty and Lula Clark (6), was born in 1903; died January 29, 1939; married November 23, 1925, Edward E. Walker.

Children: 5

594, i. Mildred Mae Walker (8).
595. ii. Dallas Ray Walker (8).
596, iii. Mary Walker (8),

219

597. iv.   Franklin Walker (8).
598. v.   Austin Walker (8).

333. John Gwin Lightner (7), son of John Emmett Lightner
(6) and Etta Florence Moore, married April 10, 1931, Roxie M.
Puffenbarger.

Children: 3

599. i.   John Gwin Lightner,Jr. (8), married _____
Rexrode, a R.N.
600. ii.   Susan Lightner (8).
601. iii.   James Lightner (8).

341. Mary Yeager (7), daughter of Charles Andrew Yeager
(6) and Allie Arbogast, married C. Moody Kincaid, died April 30,
1946, son of Joel B. Kincaid and Catherine Armentrout. He served
as Clerk of the Court, Pocahontas County, West Virginia. (See
Lockridge Family).

Children: 2

602. i.   Kathyrn Jane Kincaid (8).
603. ii.   Bettie Lee Kincaid (8).

343. Ralph A. Yeager (7), son of Charles Andrew Yeager (6)
and Allie Arbogast, married _____.

Children: 2

604. i.   Ralph A. Yeager,Jr. (8).
605. ii.   Charles B. Yeager (8).

345. William Hull Yeager (7), son of William Jacob Yeager
(6) and Grace Josephine Hull, married Bettie Matulias. They
live in Michigan.

Children: 4

606. i.   Bettie Louise Yeager (8).
607. ii.   William Hull Yeager (8), twin to Caroline.
608. iii.   Caroline Yeager (8), twin to William Hull.
609. iv.   David Yeager (8).

346. Henry Arnout Yeager (7), son of William Jacob Yeager
(6) and Grace Josephine Hull, married Helen Friel. He received
a B.S. degree from the University of West Virginia, Morgantown,
West Virginia, and he also attended Buckner Coaching School.
He is Principal of Marlinton High School, Marlinton, West Virginia.

Children: 5

610. i.   Anne Yeager (8), married Clarence Mulheren.

611. ii.   Nancy Auburn Yeager (8).
612. iii. Henry Arnout Yeager, Jr. (8).
613. iv.   James Andrew Yeager (8).
614. v.   Margaret Susan Yeager (8).

347. Winston Dilley Yeager (7), son of William Jacob
Yeager (6) and Grace Josephine Hull, married Artis Stoats.
He is Assistant Cashier, Kanawha Valley Bank, Charleston, West
Virginia.

Children: 2

615. i.   Robert William Yeager (8).
616. ii.   John Andrew Yeager (8).

356. Lloyd Campbell Bird (7), son of George Anson Bird
and Mary Susan Campbell (6), married Mrs. Lucille Crutchfield.
He is State Senator and a partner of Phelps and Bird, Richmond,
Virginia.

Children: 2

617. i.   George Campbell Bird (8).
618. ii.   Mary Susan Bird (8).

366. Alice Catherine Gum (7), daughter of James Lightner
Gum (6) and Virginia Madora Gibson (6), was born August 18, 1910;
married Emmett Crummett.

Children: 2

619. i.   Carol Alice Crummett (8), married Harry Harlow.
620. ii.   James Gibson Crummett (8).

367. Meade Wilson (7), son of William H. Wilson and Mary
Gum (6), married Sylvia Dunamay.

Children: 1

621. i.   Mary Wilson (8).

438. John Russell Porter (7), son of S. Allen Porter and
Lelia Bell Gay, died February 23, 1949, aged 69 in Atlanta,
Georgia; married Augusta Tinsley of Richmond, Virginia.

Children: 4

622. i.   John Russell Porter, Jr. (8).
623. ii.   James T. Porter (8).
624. iii. Augusta Porter (8), married Frederick Orr.
625. iv.   Pattie Porter (8), married John Holmes.

444. William Edgar Trout, Jr. (7), son of William Edgar

Trout and Signora Isabel Lightner (6), was born July 30, 1903
at Clifton Forge, Virginia; married June 21, 1934, Harriett
Creighton McCurley. He attended John Hopkins University, Balti-
more, Maryland, where he received an A.B. degree in 1925 and a
Ph.D. degree in 1935. He was Professor of Natural Science and
Mathematics, Maryland College for Women, 1927-1929; Assistant at
John Hopkins University, 1930-1932; Junior Instructor at John
Hopkins University, 1932-1935; Professor of Chemistry, Mary
Baldwin College, Staunton, Virginia, 1935-1946; Professor
of Chemistry, University of Richmond, Richmond, Virginia since
1946 and he has been Chairman of the Chemistry Department
since 1953. He is a member of: Fellow, A.A.A.S.; American
Institute of Chemists; Chemical Society (London); American
Chemical Society; Virginia Academy of Science; Sigma Xi;
Omicrom Delta Kappa; and Kappa Alpha. He is co-author of
Introductory College Chemistry, 1940.

Children: 2

626. i.   William Edgar Trout, III (8).
627. ii.   Stran Lippincott Trout (8).

446. Muriel Virginia Arey (7), daughter of Robert Sylvester
Lee Arey and Marietta Slaven Lightner (6), was born June 26, 1895;
married June 21, 1920, John William Ellis.

Children: 1

628. i.   Robert Gordon Ellis (8), born June 27, 1923;
killed in World War II on November 23, 1944.

456. John Anthony Lightner (7), son of Adam Samuel Lightner
(6) and Lucy Frances Poague, was born May 2, 1910; died March
10, 1953; married March 28, 1936, Susie Valhaltz. He served in
World War I. They lived in Trumbull County, Ohio.

Children: 5

629. i.   Frances Ann Lightner (8).
630. ii.   Shirley Marie Lightner (8).
631. iii. Bonnie Lightner (8).
632. iv.   John Anthony Lightner, Jr. (8).
633. v.   Ronald Lightner (8), born 1942.

457. Ralph Jewel Lightner (7), son of Adam Samuel Lightner
(6) and Lucy France Poague, was born June 21, 1915; married
January 30, 1937, Aileen Pajanen.

Children: 2

634. i.   Judy Ann Lightner (8).
635. ii.   Nancy Carol Lightner (8).

469. Maude Elsie Jordan (7), daughter of Hugh A. Jordan and Mary Emma Gibson (6), was born July 10, 1881; married June 25, 1903, William Peyton Moore, born October 1, 1880, son of Isaac Brown Moore and Kate Curry. They lived at Huntersville, West Virginia.

Children: 5

636. i. William Paris Moore (8), born July 5, 1904. He served in World War II.
637. ii. Reta Lee Moore (8), born May 5, 1906; married Harry Fenwick.
638. iii. Jack Carlton Moore (8), born May 14, 1909; married _____ Varner. He served in World War II.
639. iv. Hugh Brown Moore (8), born June 17, 1911; married Margaret Alice _____.
640. v. Lynn Milton Moore (8), born December 30, 1914; married Mrs. Dorothy _____. He served in World War II.

470. Bertie Edith Jordan (7), daughter of Hugh A. Jordan and Mary Emma Gibson (6), was born March 31, 1883; married November 28, 1914, Milton Dolly, born January 12, 1883 at Onego, Pendleton County, West Virginia; died January 24, 1951.

Children: 4

641. i. Hubert Milton Dolly (8), born December 27, 1916.
642. ii. John Richard Dolly (8), born December 12, 1917.
643. iii. Willis Lynn Dolly (8), born June 13, 1920; married McNeer Kerr.
644. iv. Read Dolly (8).

471. Mary Etta (Nettie) Jordan (7), daughter of Hugh A. Jordan and Mary Emma Gibson (6), was born June 23, 1885; married December 21, 1904, Cameron Preston McElwee, born April 20, 1880.

Children: 2

645. i. Helen Vivian McElwee (8), born August 27, 1905.
646. ii. Guy Cameron McElwee (8), born September 14, 1909.

477. Ninnie Edith Benson (7), daughter of James Matthias Benson and Virginia Madora Gibson (6), was born February 24, 1887; married October 9, 1907, Everette Willington Ruckman, born September 10, 1885. They lived on Knapps Creek, West Virginia.

Children: 7

647. i. Mary Virginia Ruckman (8), born August 27, 1908; married Lieutenant Max Workman.
648. ii. Leo Wellington Ruckman (8), born August 10, 1910; married Maude Beard.
649. iii. Sallie Lucille Ruckman (8), born January 26,

223

1912; married Keller _____.

650. iv. Margaret Althea Ruckman (8), born February 5, 1914; married (1) _____; married (2) _____Asher.

651. v. Guy Everett Ruckman (8), born December 15, 1915; married Pauline Miller. He served in World War II.

652. vi. Willis M. Ruckman (8), born August 10, 1917. He served in World War II.

653. vii. Earl Benson Ruckman (8), born April 25, 1921; married Jane Moore, daughter of Elmer Moore and Grace Jones. He served in World War II.

478. William Given Benson (7), son of James Matthias Benson and Virginia Madora Gibson (6), was born March 8, 1896; married Gretchen Williams. He served in World War I.

Children: 4

654. i. Clara Winifred Benson (8), married Lewis Russell.
655. ii. Betty Jean Benson (8), married Collin Emison.
656. iii. Barbara Given Benson (8), married Gene Winters.
657. iv. William George Benson (8).

479. Hildreth Helena Beverage (7), daughter of Coe Beverage and Sadie Irene Lightner (6), died in Ohio in the influenza epidemic in 1918; married Earl Dever.

Children: 1

658. i. Ruth Dever (8), married _____ Rohr.

480. Hallie Beverage (7), daughter of Coe Beverage and Sadie Irene Lightner (6), married Glen Barlow.

Children: 1

659. i. Nancy Barlow (8).

492. Edna Beverage (7), daughter of Edward Beverage and Margaret Lightner (6), married William A. Madison.

Children: 2

660. i. Ralph Madison (8), married Wanda Owens.
661. ii. Robert Madison (8).

493. Mary Nadine Beverage (7), daughter of Edward Beverage and Margaret Lightner (6), was born August 30, 1913; married November 22, 1930, Harry Samuel Hunter, born December 27, 1910. He served in the Navy in World War II in 1944 and 1945.

Children: 6

+ 662. i. William Samuel Hunter (8), born December 4, 1931.

+   663.   ii.   Margaret Lucinda Hunter (8), born March 3,
1934.
        664.   iii.   Harry Claybron Hunter (8), born September 2,
1935.   He is now serving overseas in the Air Force.
        665.   iv.   Jack Wayne Hunter (8), born May 7, 1937.
        666.   v.   Edward Hawkins Hunter (8), born July 18, 1940.
        667.   vi.   Susan Belle Hunter (8), born December 26, 1945.

    494. Caleb Beverage (7), son of Edward Beverage and Margaret
Lightner (6), married Golda Bailey.

    Children: 2

        668.   i.   Charles Beverage (8), married _____.
+   669.   ii.   Shirley Beverage (8).

    496. Cameron Beverage (7), son of Edward Beverage and
Margaret Lightner (6), married Golda Shrader.

    Children: 3

        670.   i.   Kenneth Beverage (8), married _____ Ervine.
        671.   ii.   Leanna Beverage (8), married Joe Friel.
        672.   iii.   Hertha Beverage (8).

    499. Marguerite Beverage (7), daughter of Edward Beverage
and Margaret Lightner (6), married Harry Bussard.

    Children: 2

        673.   i.   Gerald Bussard (8), died in infancy.
        674.   ii.   Karen Bussard (8).

    500. Mildred Beverage (7), daughter of Edward Beverage and
Margaret Lightner (6), married (1) James Taylor; married (2)
Arthur Mitchell.

    Children: 2 - first marriage

        675.   i.   Jimmy Taylor (8).
        676.   ii.   Richard Taylor (8).

    Children: 1 - second marriage

        677.   iii.   _____ Mitchell (8).

    501. Walker Beverage (7), son of Edward Beverage and
Margaret Lightner (6), married Lucille Wilfong McCune.

    Children: 1

        678.   i.   Peggy Beverage (8).

225

502. Eugene Beverage (7), son of Edward Beverage and Margaret Lightner (6), married Lorraine Jones.

Children: 3

679. i.   Marilyn Beverage (8).
680. ii. Marvin Beverage (8).
681. iii. Michael Beverage (8).

506. Harry Wade (7), son of Mack Plummer Wade and Georgia Lightner (6), was born May 15, 1908; married (1) July 22, 1933, Christine Green; married (2) July 30, 1940, Nona Pugh.

Children: - second marriage

682. i.   Robert Lloyd Wade (8).
683. ii. Barbara Wade (8).

514. Irene Lee Lightner (7), daughter of Harry Robert Lightner (6) and Bessie Lee Cleek, was born November 20, 1923; married December 26, 1940, Merle Bogan, born December 29, 1914, son of Warwick Cameron Bogan and Martha Shelton.

Children: 3

684. i.   Ellen Jean Bogan (8).
685. ii. Carolyn Lee Bogan (8).
687. iii. Brenda Irene Bogan (8).

516. Vernon Cleek Lightner (7), son of Harry Robert Lightner (6) and Bessie Lee Cleek, was born February 9, 1927; married August 26, 1950, Mary Ellen Lucas. He served as Seaman First Class in World War II in the 144 N.C.B. United States Navy Reserve. He served overseas. He entered the service March 3, 1945 and was discharged April 30, 1946.

Children: 4

688. i.   Nancy Campbell Lightner (8).
689. ii. Gary Wayne Lightner (8).
690. iii. Gene Cleek Lightner (8).
691. iv. Martha Lightner (8).

517. Ernest Hartley Lightner (7), son of Harry Robert Lightner (6) and Bessie Lee Cleek, was born December 20, 1928; married November 22, 1950, Rebecca Harold, daughter of Robert Harold and Beulah Hull.

Children: 2

692. i.   Ernest Hartley Lightner, Jr. (8).
693. ii. David Lightner (8).

518. Robert Bias Lightner (7), son of Harry Robert Lightner (6) and Bessie Lee Cleek, was born September 21, 1930; married November 22, 1952, Norma Fay Swartz. They live in Texas.

Children: 1

694.   i.   Linda Fay Lightner (8).

519. Leta Brown Lightner (7), daughter of Harry Robert Lightner (6) and Bessie Lee Cleek, was born December 21, 1932; married December 22, 1951, Arvie Glenn Wimer, Jr., son of Arvie Glenn Wimer and Elizabeth Hull. (See Hull Family).

Children: 1

695.   i.   Debra Sue Wimer (8).

520. Alfred Brown Ryder (7), son of Donald Spotwood Ryder and Delana Cameron Lightner (6), was born April 23, 1916; married June 5, 1940, Fannie Ruth Spencer, born January 30, 1921.

Children: 2

696.   i.   Roger Blair Ryder (8).
697.   ii. Beverley Anne Ryder (8).

522. Robert Warren Ryder (7), son of Donald Spotwood Ryder and Delana Cameron Lightner (6), married June 26, 1942, Ruth Worth.

Children: 1

698.   i.   Robert Warren Ryder, Jr. (8), born October 26, 1942.

523. Helen Louise Ryder (7), daughter of Donald Spotwood Ryder and Delana Cameron Lightner (6), married March 4, 1949, Paul Edward Craft.

Children: 2

699.   i.   Ann Louise Craft (8), born March 14, 1952.
700.   ii. Edward Arthur Craft (8), born March 8, 1954.

524. Algernon Spotwood Ryder (7), son of Donald Spotwood Ryder and Delana Cameron Lightner (6), married February 28, 1944, Norma Gene Bryant.

Children: 4

701.   i.   Vic Algene Ryder (8), born October 8, 1945.
702.   ii.   Judy Lyn Ryder (8), born April 19, 1952.
703.   iii. Martha Lee Ryder (8), born August 27, 1953.

227

704. iv. Dixie Gail Ryder (8), born September 26, 1956.

525. Jarrett Delford Ryder (7), son of Donald Spotwood Ryder and Delana Cameron Lightner (6), married September 4, 1954, Stella Lee Paula.

Children: 2

705. i.   Jarrett Delford Ryder, Jr., (8), born June 16, 1955.
706. ii. Patricia Lee Ryder (8), born August 23, 1956.

526. Joyce Marie Hiner (7), daughter of G. Jesse Hiner and Eunice Brown Lightner (6), married E. S. Solomon. He is an attorney at Hot Springs, Virginia. She graduated from Madison College, Harrisonburg, Virginia, and taught school.

Children: 2

707. i.   Michael Hiner Solomon (8).
708. ii. Deborah Solomon (8).

527. Elsie Brown Hiner (7), daughter of G. Jesse Hiner and Eunice Brown Lightner (6), married (1) Hal Herold; married (2) Curtis Terry.

Children: 1 - first marriage

709. i.   Douglas Herold (8).

530. Mildred Lightner (7), daughter of Chesley Madison Lightner (6) and May L. Tilson, was born October 24, 1915; married Floyd Fleshman. He served in World War II in the European Theatre.

Children: 2

710. i.   Robert Fleshman (8).
711. ii. Wanda Fleshman (8).

531. Paul M. Lightner (7), son of Chesley Madison Lightner (6) and May L. Tilson, was born September 29, 1916; married Loretta O'Brian. He served in World War II.

Children: 2

712. i.   Dennis Madison Lightner (8).
713. ii. Sandra Jean Lightner (8).

532. Eugene H. Lightner (7), son of Chesley Madison Lightner (6) and May L. Tilson, was born November 19, 1917; married (1) Polly White; married (2) _____. He served in World War II.

Children: 1 - first marriage

714. i.   Eugene H. Lightner, Jr. (8).

533. Anna Mae Lightner (7), daughter of Chesley Madison
Lightner (6) and May L. Tilson, was born January 14, 1920;
married James Fleshman.

Children: 2

715. i.   Sarah Fleshman (8).
716. ii.   Jack Fleshman (8).

534. Ray Wilson Lightner (7), son of Chesley Madison Lightner (6) and May L. Tilson, was born August 11, 1922; married
Vivian Freeman. He served in World War II.

Children: 3

717. i.   Bonnie Jean Lightner (8).
718. ii.. David Ray Lightner (8).
719. iii. Rebecka Ann Lightner (8).

535. Lillie Caroline Lightner (7), daughter of Chesley
Madison Lightner (6) and May L. Tilson, was born October 13,
1924; married Arthur Bostic.

Children: 4

720. i.   Patricia Bostic (8).
721. ii.   Lynda Bostic (8).
722. iii. Larry Bostic (8).
723. iv.   Joyce Marie Bostic (8).

538. Frank T. Lightner (7), daughter of Chesley Madison
Lightner (6) and May L. Tilson, was born September 2, 1932;
married Peggy Hern. He served in the Army after World War II.

Children: 2

724. i.   Carol Ann Lightner (8).
725. ii.   Sharon Lightner (8).

539. Kent Lightner (7), son of Chesley Madison Lightner (6)
and May L. Tilson, was born March 25, 1935; married Bertie Slaven.
He served in the Army after World War II.

Children: 1

726. i.   Michele Lightner (8).

540. Thomas Hull Lightner (7), son of Marvin Siple Lightner
(6) and Blanche E. Yates, was born April 30, 1917; married Jeanie

Dandrow. He received an A. B. degree from Hampden-Sydney College, Hampden-Sydney, Virginia and is a teacher and farmer. He served in the Navy during World War II.

Children: 4

727. i. Donna Lightner (8).
728. ii. Diana Lightner (8).
729. iii. Julia Lightner (8), died in infancy.
730. iv. Thomas Hull Lightner, Jr. (8).

555. Mary Norman (7), daughter of Joseph Norman and Lillian Lightner (6), married Tom Wiley.

Children: 2

731. i. James Wiley (8).
732. ii. Janet Wiley (8).

556. Jean Norman (7), daughter of Joseph Norman and Lillian Lightner (6), married Roger Lee Elgin, Jr.

Children: 3

733. i. Roger Lee Elgin, III (8).
734. ii. Rebecca Jane Elgin (8).
735. iii. Frank Gordon Elgin (8).

557. Betty Norman (7), daughter of Joseph Norman and Lillian Lightner (6), married Joseph Norris.

Children: 2

736. i. Joseph Norris, Jr. (8).
737. ii. William Norris (8).

562. Ralph Gibson Lightner (7), son of Clarence Alexander Lightner (6) and Mattie Ellen Sellers, was born April 27, 1892; married October 7, 1914, Annie Thomas, born September 17, 1888.

Children: 2

738. i. Rebecca Sellers Lightner (8), born January 31, 1916; died July 17, 1918.
739. ii. Ralph Gibson Lightner (8), born October 22, 1919.

563. Irby Clarence Lightner (7), son of Clarence Alexander Lightner (6) and Mattie Ellen Sellers, was born June 3, 1894; married September 2, 1915, Josephine White, born September 1896 of Lewisburg, West Virginia.

Children: 2

740. i.   Margaret Elizabeth Lightner (8), born August 3,
1916.
741. ii.   Irby Clarence Lightner, Jr..(8), born August 3,
1918.

566. Margaret Sellers Lightner (7), daughter of Clarence
Alexander Lightner (6) and Mattie Ellen Sellers, was born September 7, 1899; married October 16, 1918, John Thomas Hickman,
born July 23, 1869 of Mt. Jackson, Virginia.

Children: 1

742. i.   Margaret Adalen Hickman (8), born February
25, 1920.

662. William Samuel Hunter (8), son of Harry Samuel Hunter
and Mary Nadine Beverage (7), was born December 4, 1931; married
Shirley Darline Jackson of Las Vegas, Nevada. He has served four
years in the Air Force. They live in California.

Children: 3

743. i.   Pamela Jean Hunter (9), born January 2, 1953.
744. ii.   Judy Darline Hunter (9), born February 21, 1954.
745. iii.   Debra Sue Hunter (9), born July 20, 1955.

663. Margaret Lucinda Hunter (8), daughter of Harry Samuel
Hunter and Mary Nadine Beverage (7), was born March 3, 1934;
married June 16, 1955, Alexander Meeks. She is a R.N.

Children: 1

746. i..   Thimothy Creig Meeks (9), born March 26, 1956.

669. Shirley Beverage (8), daughter of Caleb Beverage (7)
and Golda Bailey, married Russell Durrett.

Children: 1

747. i.   Debbie Durrett (9).

231

PART IV

WARWICK FAMILY

This Warwick family is of English ancestry. The name is found in records as Warwick, Warick, Warrick, Worack, Worrack, Worick, Worrick, Warnock, Wirick and Wyrick.

The records relating to the Warwick family are confusing and this family has been very difficult to trace. The first mention of John Warwick is Augusta County, Virginia records is on August 20, 1748 when John Warnock makes oath he was not in the county on June 10, 1947. In 1748 there is a record of Jno. Warwick as being twice charged for taxes. A record dated November 25, 1755 shows that John Warnock has removed out of the county. However, on March 21, 1759, James Gay leases land on the Calf Pasture from Jno. Warrick. October 21, 1754 James Gay and Jenot Warrick are witnesses to the will of Robert Means. It is possible that this John Warwick was a brother to William Warwick, since William Warwick had obtained land on the Calf Pasture River before 1748. Surveys had been made for William Warwick prior to November 27, 1753. In reply to a bill filed April 23, 1798 regarding the estate of Carter Braxton filed by his widow, Elizabeth Braxton, William Warwick stated he purchased land from William and George Penn, Jr. This land was in Goochland (Amherst).

Family tradition states that four Warwick brothers came to America from England - James, John, Jacob and William Warwick. However, this has not been confirmed. Many historians state a Lieutenant Warwick (name given as John, William, and Jacob) came to Augusta County, Virginia from Williamsburg, James City County, Virginia as a surveyor about 1730. He is said to have come originally from England and was employed by the British Crown as a surveyor. However, no reference to a Warwick surveyor has been found in the Augusta County records.

The following history of the Warwick family is based on many years of research and study. Further research needs to be completed on the first two generations before all of the family connections are entirely unraveled.

1. William Warwick (1) came to Augusta County, Virginia about 1730-1740. He is said to have married Elizabeth Dunlap of Middlebrook, Augusta County, Virginia, a daughter of Alexander Dunlap and a sister of Captain Alexander Dunlap who married Anne McFarland. It is said that William Warwick returned to England for a visit. He was never heard from after his departure, and being given up for dead, his widow married in 1779 (as his second wife) Andrew Sitlington. Some records have William Warwick's death as 1764. Andrew Sitlington died April 15, 1804 in his 85th year in Bath County, Virginia. His widow, Elizabeth was still living December 3, 1805 when she testified regarding the will of

Andrew Sitlington. (Records in the Clerk's Office, Augusta County, Virginia). William Warwick served in the Colonial Wars. He is listed as a private in the roll of Captain George Wilson's Company, August 11, 1756. (A History of Highland County, Virginia, Oren F. Morton, page 192).

Children: 6

2. i.   Jean (or Jenot) Warwick (2), killed by the Indians in 1759; married James Gay, Sr, born 1729; died 1776.
3. ii.   Martha Warwick (2), killed by the Indians in 1759; married Major John Stevenson.
+ 4. iii. William Warwick (2).
+ 5. iv.   John Warwick (2), born 1745.
+ 6. v.   Jacob Warwick (2), born 1747.
7. vi.   James Warwick (2), married Martha Poague.
They lived for a time in Randolph County, West Virginia, finally locating in Ohio.

4. William Warwick (2), son of William Warwick (1) and Elizabeth Dunlap, was born _____; was living in 1796; married _____. He served in the Revolution for three years as a sergeant in the Virginia State Artillery for which he received Land Bounty Warrant No. 839 for 200 acres. On October 12, 1795, William Warwick, Sr. deeded to his three sons, Andrew, John, and William Warwick, Jr. land lying on Deer Creek (sometimes called Warwick's Creek). This land was then in Bath County, Virginia, but now in Pocahontas County, West Virginia. William Warwick received this land deeded to his sons in 1795 by patent (903 acres) dated May 13, 1783. His wife must have died before October 12, 1795 since she did not sign the deeds. The following deed is recorded in Deed Book 1, page 690, Pocahontas County, West Virginia:

This Indenture, made this 2nd day of December in the year of Christ, one thousand eight hundred and thirty one, between Henry M. Moffett of the County of Pocahontas and State of Virginia of the first part and William Slavens of the same County Samuel Ruckman and Margaret his wife (late Margaret Slavens) of the County of Bath and state of Virginia of the second part: Whereas, by a decree of the County Court of Pocahontas in Chancery pronounced on the 5th day of October 1830 in a cause then depending between the said William Slavens and Samuel Ruckman & Margaret his wife Plaintiffs and the heirs of William Warrick decd to wit William Warrick and Elizabeth Warrick widow of Andrew Warrick decd James Woodle and Jane his wife, Jacob Warrick, George Burner and Sarah his wife, Margaret Warrick, Nancy Warrick, Elizabeth Warrick, Polly Warrick and Ann Warrick Children of Andrew Warrick decd, John Slavens and Elizabeth his wife formerly Elizabeth Warrick, Andrew, Thomas, William, Anne and Clarenda Ingram Children of Anne Ingram formerly Anne Warrick, William, Hiram, & Polly Gregory children of Margaret Gregory, formerly Margaret Warrick, Thomas Blake husband of Jane Warrick, decd Thomas Woodle

233

and Polly formerly Polly Blake, Alexander Gillaspy and Jane his
wife formerly Jane Blake, Mary Cartmail, Polly Warrick widow,
and William, John, Margaret, George,Anne, Polly, Betsy, Andrew
and Davis Warrick children of John Warrick decd Defendants. It
was decreed and ordered that the said Henry M. Moffett (who was
appointed a Commissioner for that purpose) convey the land in
the bill mentioned to the said William Slavens and Samuel
Ruckman and Margaret his wife. This Indenture, therefore,
Witnesseth that the said Henry M. Moffett for and in consideration
of the premises aforesaid as also of one dollar, in hand paid the
receipt whereof is hereby acknowledged, hath granted bargained
and sold and by these presents doth grant bargain and sell unto
the said William Slaven and Samuel Ruckman and Margaret his wife,
their heirs and assigns the undivided moiety (or one half) of a
certain tract or parcel of land lying and being in the County
of Pocahontas on the Allegany mountain and on the west (sic -
this should be east) side of Greenbrier river at a place known
by the name of the big spring and extending towards Bomans
place and granted to William Warrick and George Poage by patent
bearing date on the 14th day of July 1796 and bounded as follows
(description of land given here). This deed was recorded
December 6, 1831.

Children: 8

+ 8.   i.   William Warwick (3).
+ 9.   ii.   Andrew Warwick (3).
+ 10. iii. Elizabeth Warwick (3).
+ 11. iv.   Anne Warwick (3).
+ 12. v.   Margaret Warwick (3).
+ 13. vi.   Jane Warwick (3).
  14. vii. Mary Warwick (3), married Thomas Cartmill.
+ 15. viii. John Warwick (3).

5.   John Warwick (2), son of William Warwick (1) and Elizabeth Dunlap, was born in 1745 in Augusta County, Virginia; died
1801; married March 19, 1771 in Augusta County, Virginia, Mary
Powell, born c. 1745; died 1786, daughter of Thomas Powell (died
1788) and Sally _____. After the death of Thomas Powell, his
widow married Colonel Thomas Moore. (Abstracts from the Records
of Augusta County, Virginia, Lyman Chalkley, Vol. II, page 131).
Thomas Powell served in the Revolution as a Lieutenant. (Historical Register of Virginians in the Revolution, John H. Gwathmey,
page 265). John Warwick married (2) c. 1787 Eleanor Crouch.
John Warwick served as overseer of roads, Indian Scout, and
in the Revolution in transport of supplies to Virginia Continental Lines. There is a government marker to him in the family
burying ground near Greenbank, West Virginia. He was in Kentucky
by August 1, 1796, when he deeds land to his brother, Jacob
Warwick of Bath County, Virginia. This land was granted to John
Warwick by patent dated September 1, 1782 and was on both sides
of Cloverlick Creek, a branch of the Greenbrier River. (Deed
Book 1, page 304, Bath County, Virginia). His home in Kentucky
was near North Elkhorn.

Children: 7 - first marriage

+   16.   i.   Jacob Warwick (3), born 1773.
    17.   ii.   Eleanor Warwick (3), born 1775; married James
Flanigan of Clark County, Kentucky.
    18.   iii.   Margaret Warwick (3), born 1777; married John
Flanigan.
    19.   iv.   Ruth Warwick (3), born 1779; married in 1798,
Peter Flanigan.
+   20.   v.   Elizabeth Warwick (3), born 1780.
    21.   vi.   Lucy Warwick (3), born 1782; married in 1800,
_____Montgomery (?).
    22.   vii.   Mary Warwick (3), born 1785 in Clark County,
Kentucky; died in Indianapolis, Indiana; married (1) _____
Hamilton; married (2) Basil Brown, son of James Brown. No
children.

Children: 2 - second marriage

+   23.   viii. Malinda Ann Warwick (3), born May 24, 1788.
    24.   ix.   John Warwick,Jr. (3).

6. Jacob Warwick (2), son of William Warwick (1) and
Elizabeth Dunlap, was born in 1747 in Augusta County, Virginia;
died January 11, 1826 in his 80th year in Bath County, Virginia
and is buried on the west bank of Jackson River, six miles from
Warm Springs, Virginia, near Fort Dinwiddie. There is a government marker over his grave. He married in 1765, Mary Vance, born
1750; died 1823 at Clover Lick, Virginia, daughter of Colonel
John P. Vance and Martha _____. For a number of years Jacob
Warwick lived at Dunmore, and there all his children were born.
Afterwards he moved to land he had acquired in what is now Bath
County, Virginia. He was of necessity an Indian fighter. He
served as a private in the expedition to Point Pleasant and is
given credit for the victory at the battle there, October 10,
1774. He and several other men were detailed to kill deer, etc.,
for the army and were mistaken by Cornstalk as reenforcements
arriving and hence were the cause of the defeat of Cornstalk.
(History of Pocahontas County, William T. Price, pages 237-250).
(Annals of Augusta County, Virginia, Jas. A. Waddell, pages 352-
354). He served as Lieutenant in Captain William Kincaid's
Company in lower Virginia in 1781. When Bath County, Virginia
was organized in 1791, he was one of the Justices of the Peace.
He also built a fort called Fort Warwick which was located on
the Greenbrier River. His will was dated March 26, 1818 and
recorded February 1826 in Will Book 1, page 74, Pocahontas
County, West Virginia. It mentions wife, Mary; daughter,
Margaret and her husband, Adam See; grandchildren, George,Jacob,
Charles, and Mary Jane See, children of Adam See; Jacob Warwick
Mathews; Andrew Gatewood Mathews, Sampson Mathews,Jr., and Betsy
Mathews, children of Sampson Mathews; Andrew Warwick Lewis Cameron,
son of Charles Cameron; Rachel, Mary, Woods, Margaret, Betsey,
children of William Poage, Jr.; Andrew Mathews Gatewood; Jacob

235

Warwick, James Woods Warwick and John Wood Warwick, sons of son Andrew S. Warwick; William Woods who married daughter Betsey; Warwick Gatewood, Mary Jane Gatewood, children of William Gatewood; granddaughter, Hannah, daughter of Andrew and Sally Gatewood; granddaughter, Mary Jane, daughter of Jacob W. Mathews; granddaughter, Mary Jane, daughter of daughter Jane Gatewood; Patsy Warwick, wife of son Andrew S. Warwick; grandson, Sampson L. Mathews; and Charles Cameron Francisco and Mary M. Francisco, children of Charles L. Francisco. Executors - Charles Cameron and Andrew S. Warwick. Witnesses were Nat. White, William Sharp, and John Sharp.

Children: 8

+ 25. i. Rachel P. Warwick (3).
+ 26. ii. Jane Warwick (3).
+ 27. iii. Mary Warwick (3).
+ 28. iv. Margaret Warwick (3), born 1773.
  29. v. Charles Cameron Warwick (3), died while at school in Essex County, Virginia, aged 14.
+ 30. vi. Andrew Sitlington Warwick (3), born 1782.
  31. vii. Elizabeth Warwick (3), married June 22, 1807 in Bath County, Virginia, Colonel William Woods. No children.
+ 32. viii. Nancy Warwick (3).

8. William Warwick (3), son of William Warwick (2) and _____, was born _____; died after 1834; married November 2, 1797 in Greenbrier County, West Virginia, Nancy (Agnes) Craig, daughter of Robert Craig, Jr. and Nancy (Agnes) Johnson. They lived on Deer Creek, near Greenbank, Pocahontas County, West Virginia. (See Craig Family History).

Children: 3

+ 33. i. Robert Craig Warwick (4), born September 8, 1801.
+ 34. ii. Elizabeth Warwick (4).
  35. iii. Margaret M. Warwick (4), married June 21, 1821 in Bath County, Virginia, John Hull, son of Adam Hull and Esther Keister. They lived in Highland County (Meadowdale), Virginia. (See Hull Family).

9. Andrew Warwick (3), son of William Warwick (2) and _____, died prior to September 5, 1826; married December 15, 1798 in Greenbrier County, West Virginia, Elizabeth Craig, died 1832, daughter of Robert Craig, Jr. and Nancy (Agnes) Johnson. (See Craig Family). George Burner was appointed guardian for Margaret and Nancy Warwick, children of Andrew Warwick, deceased, on September 5, 1826. (Will Book 1, page 106, Pocahontas County, West Virginia). Patrick Bruffey was appointed guardian for Elizabeth, Polly, and Anny Warwick, orphans of Andrew Warwick, deceased with George Burner as security in August 1829. (Order Book 2, page 105, Pocahontas County, West Virginia). The Estate of

Elizabeth Warwick was appraised and recorded in September 1832 - George Burner, administrator. (Will Book 1, page 334, Pocahontas County, West Virginia).

Children: 8

36. i. Jane Warwick (4), married James Wooddell of near Green Bank, West Virginia.
37. ii. Margaret Warwick (4), married August 30, 1837 in Pocahontas County, West Virginia (as his first wife) Samuel Sutton.
+ 38. iii. Nancy Warwick (4).
39. iv. Mary C. Warwick (4), married January 18, 1866 in Pocahontas County, West Virginia (as his second wife), Isaac Hartman.
40. v. Elizabeth Warwick (4), was injuried by a horse and died unmarried.
41. vi. Sarah Warwick (4), married June 21, 1821 in Bath County, Virginia, George Burner, son of Abram Burner and Mary Hull. (See Hull Family).
42. vii. Anna Warwick (4), married December 14, 1833 in Pocahontas County, West Virginia, Henry Arbogast, son of Benjamin Arbogast.
+ 43. viii. Jacob Warwick (4).

10. Elizabeth Warwick (3), daughter of William Warwick (2) and _____, married (as his second wife), John Slaven, Jr., born 1760, son of John Slaven and Elizabeth Stuart of Scotland. John Slaven, Jr. had married (1), Sarah Wade. He served in the Revolution.

Children: 7

44. i. Sallie Slaven (4), married in 1801, John Dinwiddie. They lived for a time at the head of Jackson River, Bath County, Virginia, and then moved to Hardin County, Ohio.
45. ii. Priscilla Slaven (4), married Joseph Wooddell of Green Bank, West Virginia. They migrated to Pike County, Ohio.
+ 46. iii. Anna Slaven (1).
47. iv. Mary Slaven (4), married John Wooddell. They lived near Green Bank, West Virginia.
48. v. Margaret Slaven (4), married (as his second wife), Samuel Ruckman, born November 17, 1783 in New Jersey, son of David Ruckman and Susannah Little. Samuel Ruckman married (1) on July 18, 1809, Nancy Hartman.
49. vi. William Slaven (4), born July 6, 1798; married (1) in 1819, Margaret Wooddell, born June 27, 1800, daughter of Joseph Wooddell of Green Bank, West Virginia; married (2) Nancy Cline of Lewis County, West Virginia.
50. vii. Jacob Gillespie Slaven (4), married Eleanor Lockridge, daughter of Lancelot Lockridge and Elizabeth Benson. (See Lockridge Family).

11. Anne Warwick (3), daughter of William Warwick (2) and
_____, married in 1795 in Bath County, Virginia, John
Ingram. They migrated to Ohio.

Children: 5

   51. i. Andrew Ingram (4).
   52. ii. Thomas Ingram (4).
   53. iii. William Ingram (4).
   54. iv. Anne Ingram (4).
   55. v. Clarenda Ingram (4).

12. Margaret Warwick (3), daughter of William Warwick (2)
and _____, married February 2, 1789 in Augusta County,
Virginia, David Gregory, son of Mary Gregory. (Mary Gregory
was the widow of Naphthalum Gregory).

Children: 3

   56. i. William Gregory (4).
   57. ii. Hiram Gregory (4).
   58. iii. Mary Gregory (4).

13. Jane Warwick (3), daughter of William Warwick (2) and
_____, married Thomas Blake.

Children: 2

   59. i.. Polly Blake (4), married Thomas Wooddell.
   60. ii.. Jane Blake (4), married Alexander Gillaspie.

15. John Warwick (3), son of William Warwick (2) and _____
_____, died March 1814 in Bethel Township, Champaign County,
Ohio; married in 1794 in Bath County, Virginia, Mary Poage, born
July 6, 1778; living in 1830, daughter of Colonel William Poage
and Margaret Davies. (Their descendants are given in Descendants
of Robert and John Poage arranged by Robert Bell Woodworth, page
291).

Children: 11

   61. i. William Warwick (4), lived awhile in Mt. Pleasant,
Iowa; died in 1876 in Newark, Ohio, unmarried.
   62. ii. George W. Warwick (4), said to have married and
to have had two sons, James Warwick (5) who lived in Texas; and
William Warwick (5) who lived in Cambridge, Massachusetts.
   63. iii. Margaret Warwick (4), married _____.
   64. iv. Ann Warwick (4), married _____ Pumphrey,
died December 12, 1887 and buried at New Carlisle, Ohio.
   65. v. Mary Ann Warwick (4), born January 21, 1804;
died shortly after 1880; married December 26, 1822, Jesse
Chancellor, born April 26, 1796; died May 17, 1853.
   66. vi. Andrew Sitlington Warwick (4), born February

21,1807 in Virginia; died March 21, 1865 in Mt. Pleasant, Iowa; married September 12, 1833, Elizabeth Stafford, died December 21, 1860, daughter of James Stafford and Sarah Huey.
    67. vii. Elizabeth Warwick (4), born 1806; died July 1, 1829 aged 23, buried at New Carlisle, Ohio; married _____ Arnett, and had one son, George Arnett (5).
    68. viii. John Warwick (4).
    69. ix. Davis L. Warwick (4), married Margaret Miller.
    70. x. Sarah Warwick (4).
    71. xi. Nancy G. Warwick (4), may have married _____ Funsten.

    16. Jacob Warwick (3), son of John Warwick (2) and Mary Powell, was born in 1773 in Augusta County, Virginia (now Pocahontas County, West Virginia); died November 7, 1811 at Tippecanoe, Indiana; married in 1795, Jane Montgomery, born 1774 in Virginia; died September 3, 1846 in Indiana, daughter of "Pretty Tom" Montgomery and Martha Crockett, and a sister of Isaac Montgomery who married Martha McClure, and also a sister of Judge Thomas Montgomery (twin to Isaac) who married Margaret Elizabeth Warwick (4). Mrs. Jane Montgomery Warwick married (2) in 1813, Dr. John Maddox of Kentucky and moved with him to Red River, Texas; then to Alexandria, Louisiana in 1824; returning to Indiana in 1825. She remained in Indiana while Dr. Maddox made a prospecting trip to Lincoln, Illinois. He died on this trip and was buried in Illinois. After his death she read and studied his medical books and became a midwife. The weather was never too bad for her to answer calls.

    The last village inhabited by Indians in Gibson County, Indiana was located two miles west of Owensville. This village was destroyed in 1807 by Jacob Warwick and others. No name was more familiar to the older citizens of the county than Captain Jacob Warwick. At the age of 11, or in 1784, he moved to Fayette County, Kentucky, with his father who settled about 7 seven miles from Lexington. At the age of 21, or in 1794, he enlisted under the command of General Anthony Wayne and took part in Indian Skirmishes. They marched to Fort Defiance in Ohio and on August 20, 1794 he took part in the battle of the "Rapids of Maumee River.". He came to Indiana in 1807 from Kentucky and settled about two miles west of Owensville. He was a man of considerable wealth and brought with him from Kentucky quite a number of fine horses, cattle and slaves. When the Indians became troublesome in 1807-1811, the citizens chose him as their leader in making preparations for their defense. He was a close friend of Henry Clay and often consulted him in regard to Indiana finally becoming a slave state. Mr. Clay, who at one time had $80,000 invested in slaves, always told him Indiana would not be a slave state.

    At the call for militia in 1811, he organized a company of 80 rangers, and with General Harrison, participated in the battle of Tippecanoe where he was killed while gallantly leading a charge. He was mortally wounded, but as soon as his wound was dressed he

insisted on going to the head of his company. He died two days
later and was buried where his company was located, near the
south end of the battlefield. A marker stands at the grave.
General Harrison commended in the highest terms his bravery and
"Major" Smith, the old school teacher and surveyor of Gibson
County, wrote Captain Warwick's will on the battlefield, where
he had fought for the preservation of the lives he held dear,
and for the safety of the homes of the settlers.

In 1813, the territorial legislature of Indiana passed a
law authorizing the organization of two counties to be called
Warrick and Gibson. At that time Warrick County included all
the territory which now comprises the counties of Posey, Vander-
burg, Warrick, Spencer, Perry and a portion of Crawford. It
was named Warrick in honor of Captain Jacob Warwick, who fell
in the battle of Tippecanoe in November 1811. In naming this
county Warrick they misspelled the name , but it has continued
to remain Warrick.

Children: 7

+ 72. i. Montgomery Warwick (4), born 1797.
+ 73. ii. Eleanor (Nelly) Warwick (4), born 1799.
+ 74. iii. Nancy Divena Warwick (4), born November 1,1800.
  75.. iv. John C. Warwick (4), born 1803 near Lexington,
Kentucky; died January 8, 1847; married _____ Prince. No
children.
  76. v. Henry Clay Warwick (4), born 1805; died in
1824, aged 19.
+ 77. vi. Jacob G. Warwick (4), born March 2, 1807.
+ 78. vii. Martha (Patsy) Crockett Warwick (4), born June
3, 1809.

20. Elizabeth Warwick (3), daughter of John Warwick (2) and
Mary Powell, was born in 1780; died in 1817; married October 25,
1797, Judge Thomas Montgomery, born 1776 in Virginia; died in 1846;
son of "Pretty Tom" Montgomery and Martha Crockett. He married
(2) in 1818, Mrs. Catherine Teel Williams, born in 1809; died 1860.
There were six children of the second marriage.

Children: 6 - first marriage

+ 79. i. Polly Montgomery (4), born 1806.
+ 80.. ii.. Nelly Montgomery (4), born 1808.
  81. iii. Moses Montgomery (4), born 1810, married _____.
+ 82.. iv. Nancy Montgomery (4), born 1812.
  83. v. Jacob Montgomery (4), born 1814, married _____.
  84. vi. Thomas Montgomery (4), born 1816; died 1870;
married (1) Milly Harris; married (2) Mrs. Nancy (Skelton) Malone;
married (3) Hannah Forbis; married (4) Christina McCleveland.
There was a child of the first marriage, Mary Ellen Montgomery
(5) that died young.

23. Malinda Ann Warwick (3), daughter of John Warwick (2)

and Eleanor Crouch, was born May 24, 1788; died January 13, 1850 in Gibson County, Indiana; married June 12, 1808, James McClure, born October 6, 1785 at Annapolis, Maryland; died February 7, 1855 in Princeton, Indiana, son of Joseph McClure and Jane Trimble. Joseph McClure served in the Revolution and was killed in 1785. James McClure served under Captain Hargrove in the battle of Tippecanoe, as a private from September 19, to November 19, 1811. His brother-in-law was the lieutenant, Lieutenant Isaac Montgomery. He ran the first grist mill in this part of Indiana. He became Judge of the Court of Common Pleas in 1813 and was Probate Judge 1830-32. He served in the State Senate 1818-1821 and again 1825-1829. He served in the House of Representatives in 1840.

Children: 11

+ 85. i.   Albert Pickle McClure (4), born March 29, 1809.
+ 86. ii. Edwin McClure (4), born April 7, 1811.
  87. iii. James Brown McClure (4), born November 14, 1812; died July 31, 1838, unmarried.
  88. iv. Ellen Jane McClure (4), born June 6, 1814; died August 9, 1814.
+ 89. v.   Joseph Perry McClure (4), born October 6, 1815.
  90. vi. William Grady McClure (4), born February 7, 1818 in Princeton, Indiana; died September 10, 1897 in St. Louis, Missouri; married Mrs. Lucinda Palmer. No children.
+ 91. vii. Henry Clay McClure (4), born May 9, 1820.
+ 92. viii. David Hart McClure (4), born May 2, 1822.
+ 93. ix. Robert McClure (4), born March 16, 1825.
  94. x.   George Washington McClure (4), born February 22, 1827 in Princeton, Indiana; died February 9, 1864 in St. Louis, Missouri, unmarried.
  95. xi. John Warwick McClure (4), born December 28, 1830 in Princeton, Indiana; went to California. No further information.

25. Rachel P. Warwick (3), daughter of Jacob Warwick (2) and Mary Vance, died in 1858; married May 3, 1792 in Bath County, Virginia, Colonel Charles Edward Cameron, born February 22, 1752; died in 1829. He was a soldier at Point Pleasant, where his only brother was killed. General Lafayette, who esteemed his as a personal friend, presented him with a gold-headed cane in 1781. He became a Colonel. About 1790 he settled at Fassifern, Bath County, Virginia, which he named after his ancestral home in the Scottish Highlands. He was the first Clerk of Bath County, Virginia. They had only one son to grow to maturity.

+ 96. i.   Andrew Warwick Lewis Cameron (4),

26. Jane Warwick (3), daughter of Jacob Warwick (2) and Mary Vance, married August 25, 1799 in Bath County, Virginia (as his second wife), William Gatewood of Essex County, Virginia and a relative of President Tyler. Their home was at Mountain Grove, Virginia.

Children: 4

+ 97. i. Warwick Gatewood (4).
+ 98. ii. Samuel Vance Gatewood (4).
  99. iii. Mary Jane Gatewood (4), married (as his first wife), Cisereo Bias, died in 1866.
+ 100. iv. Frances Gatewood (4).

27. Mary Warwick (3), daughter of Jacob Warwick (2) and Mary Vance, married in 1794 in Bath County, Virginia, Sampson Lockhart Mathews, son of Sampson Mathews and Mary Lockhart.

Children: 5

101. i. Jacob Warwick Mathews (4), married Nancy McCue, daughter of Rev. John McCue of Augusta County, Virginia.
102. ii. Andrew Gatewood Mathews (4), married Mary Jane See (4), daughter of Adam See and Margaret Warwick. They first lived at Dunmore and then moved to Pulaski County, Virginia.
103. iii. Sampson Lockhart Mathews, Jr. (4), born 1800; died September 23, 1854; married in 1825, Nancy Mathews Edgar, daughter of Thomas Edgar and Ann Mathews. He was the first surveyor of Pocahontas County, West Virginia, and a member of the court for a number of years.
104. iv. Elizabeth Mathews (4), married _____ Miller of Rockingham County, Virginia. They migrated to Missouri.
105. v. Jane Mathews (4), married Captain George Woods. They lived near Ivy Depot, Albemarle County, Virginia.

28. Margaret Warwick (3), daughter of Jacob Warwick (2) and Mary Vance, was born in 1773; died in 1850; married in 1795 in Bath County, Virginia, Adam See, LL.D., born November 29, 1764; died 1840, son of Michael See and Barbara Harness. He attended Dickinson College and was a member of the Virginia Legislature for 30 years. He settled at Huttonville, Randolph County, West Virginia.

Children: 10

106. i. George See (4), married _____.
107. ii. Jacob Warwick See (4), born 1798; died 1862; married in 1825, Mary Ann Baxter, born 1805; died 1874, daughter of Dr. George Addison Baxter and Anne Fleming.
108. iii. Charles Cameron See (4), married Harriet Bosworth, daughter of Dr. Squire Bosworth.
109. iv. Dolly See (4), married Hon. John Hutton, who was a member of the Randolph County, West Virginia court and a delegate to the West Virginia Legislature.
110. v. Eliza See (4), married Dr. Robert Gamble.
111. vi. Christina See (4), married Washington Ward.
112. vii. Mary Jane See (4), married Andrew Gatewood Mathews (4), son of Sampson Lockhart Mathews and Mary Warwick.
113. viii. Rachel Cameron See (4), born 1816; died 1887; married Hon. Paul McNeel, born 1803; died 1870, son of Isaac McNeel and Rachel McKeever. He was a Colonel in the CSA.

114. ix. Hannah See (4), married Henry Harper.
115. x.   Margaret See (4), married Hon. Washington Long.

30. Andrew Sitlington Warwick (3), son of Jacob Warwick (2)
and Mary Vance, was born in 1782; died in 1828; married (1) in
1812, Mary N. Woods of Nelson County, Virginia, born 1791; died
1822; married (2) April 22, 1823 in Bath County, Virginia, Martha
Dickinson of Millboro Springs, Bath County, Virginia. Mrs. Martha
Dickinson Warwick married (2) June 14, 1832 in Bath County, Virginia,
James R. Erwin. Andrew Sitlington Warwick's will was dated May
17, 1828 and recorded in June 1828 in Will Book 3, page 264, Bath
County, Virginia. It mentions wife, Martha; little daughters,
Rachel C. and Mary; sons, James W., Jacob, and John W. Warwick.
Executors - Robert Bratton and William D. Kinkead. Witnesses
were Wm. D. Kincaid, Thos. M. Kincaid and Jas. B. Dean.

Children: 3 - first marriage

+ 116. i.   James Woods Warwick (4), born April 22, 1813.
  117. ii. Jacob Warwick (4), married Ellen Massie.
+ 118. iii. John Wood Warwick (4).

Children: 2 - second marriage

119. iv.   Rachel Cameron Warwick (4), married June 8,
1852 in Bath County, Virginia, Dr. Francisco E. Luckett.
120. v.   Mary Warwick (4).

The children of James R. Erwin and Martha (Dickinson) Warwick
were: (not Warwick descendants)

i.   Margaret E. Erwin married William M. McAllister.
ii.   Samuel Erwin married Lina Glendye.
iii. William D. Erwin married Mary Hutton Long. She married
      (2) James William Harper of Rockbridge County, Virginia.
      They lived at Warm Springs, Virginia.

32. Nancy Warwick (3), daughter of Jacob Warwick (2) and
Mary Vance, died in 1845; married (1) February 9, 1800 in Bath
County, Virginia, Thomas Gatewood, died c. 1805, son of William
Gatewood and his first wife. William Gatewood married (2), Jane
Warwick (3), a sister to Nancy Warwick. Nancy Warwick married·
(2) January 1, 1806 in Bath County, Virginia, Major William
Thomas Poage, born February 8, 1783; died May 27, 1827, son of
Colonel William Poage and Margaret Davies. William Thomas Poage
served as a Major in the 127th Virginia Regiment in the War of
1812.

Children: 1 - first marriage

+ 121. i.   Andrew Gatewood (4).

Children: 5 - second marriage

243

122. ii. Rachel Cameron Poage (4), born November 6, 1807; died August 21, 1873; married 1821, Josiah Beard, born December 23, 1792; died January 4, 1878, son of John Beard and Janett Wallace. He was the first Clerk of Pocahontas County, West Virginia(then Virginia).
123. iii. Mary Vance Poage (4), born February 11, 1809; died 1848; married (1) Robert Beale, died 1832; married (2) Henry Miller Moffett, born 1802; died 1851, son of James McDowell Moffett and Hannah Miller. He served as second Clerk of Pocahontas County, West Virginia (then Virginia).
124. iv. Margaret Davies Poage (4), born March 5, 1811; died 1874; married in 1829, James Atlee Price, born 1806. Calvin Wells Price, Editor and publisher of The Pocahontas Times, Marlinton, West Virginia, married Mabel Milligan, is a descendant of this couple.
125. v. William Woods Poage (4), born October 15, 1815; died June 19, 1871; married Julia Callison, born 1826; died September 1, 1880. He was a Colonel in the CSA.
126. vi. Elizabeth Woods Poage (4), born August 31, 1818; died November 11, 1869; married October 6, 1830, Colonel Joel Mathews, born October 2, 1809 in Oglethorpe County, Georgia; died May 11, 1874, of Selma, Alabama.

33. Robert Craig Warwick (4), son of William Warwick (3) and Nancy (Agnes) Craig, was born September 8, 1801 in Bath County, Virginia (now Pocahontas County, West Virginia); died March 8, 1845 in Pocahontas County, West Virginia; married in 1821, Esther Hull, born September 14, 1804 in Pendleton County, Virginia (now Highland County); died March 17, 1853 in Pocahontas County, Virginia (now West Virginia), daughter of Adam Hull and Esther Keister. They lived on Deer Creek, Pocahontas County, now West Virginia.

Children: 9

+   127. i. William Fechtig Warwick (5), born August 11, 1822.
+   128. ii. Catherine Hidy Warwick (5), born July 16, 1824.
     129. iii. Nancy Jane Warwick (5), born February 7, 1826 in Pocahontas County, Virginia (now West Virginia); died May 28, 1900 at a hospital in Staunton, Virginia and was buried in Bath County, Virginia; married April 6, 1843 in Pocahontas County, Virginia (now West Virginia), Jacob Lightner, born September 11, 1821; died November 8, 1904, son of Adam Lightner and Susannah Harper. (See Lightner Family).
+   130. iv. Sarah Elizabeth Warwick (5), born August 1828.
+   131. v. Margaret Ann Warwick (5).
+   132. vi. Hannah Rebecca Hopkins Warwick (5), born February 1, 1833.
+   133. vii. Louisa Susan Warwick (5), born 1836.
+   134. viii. Peter Hull Warwick (5), born November 3, 1839.
+   135. ix. John Robert Warwick (5), born October 1843.

34. Elizabeth Warwick (4), daughter of William Warwick (3) and Nancy (Agnes) Craig, married July 14, 1814 in Bath County, Virginia, Benjamin Tallman, son of James Tallman and Nancy Crawford. (See Crawford Family). He was a Lieutenant Colonel in the 127th Regiment, a member of the court of Pocahontas County, and represented Pocahontas County in the Virginia House of Delegates. He was also a justice of the peace. They lived near Green Bank, West Virginia.

Children: 6

136. i.   William Tallman (5).
137. ii.   James Tallman (5).
138. iii. Robert Boone Tallman (5), born February 29, 1820; died November 5, 1861; married February 24, 1842, Nancy Conley Hamilton, born April 5, 1823; died June 10, 1880, daughter of James Hamilton and _____ Erwin. He served in Company E, 6th Regiment, West Virginia Cavalry.
139. iv.   John Tallman (5).
140. v.   Cyrus Tallman (5).
141. vi.   Nancy Tallman (5), married Benjamin Tallman, son of Boone Tallman, born December 29, 1809; died 1849, and Mary Poage. They lived in Illinois.

38. Nancy Warwick (4), daughter of Andrew Warwick (3) and Elizabeth Craig, married Jacob Hartman. They migrated west.

Children: 4

142. i.   Sarah Lucretia Hartman (5).
143. ii.   Virginia Hartman (5).
144. iii. William Hartman (5).
145. iv.   James Hartman (5).

43. Jacob Warwick (4), son of Andrew Warwick (3) and Elizabeth Craig, married Elizabeth Hull, daughter of Adam Hull and Esther Keister. They moved from Pocahontas County, West Virginia to Indiana and finally settled in Missouri.

Children: 6

146. i.   Mathew Patton Warwick (5).
147. ii.   Amos Warwick (5).
148. iii. Andrew Jackson Warwick (5).
149. iv.   William Craig Warwick (5).
150. v.   Carolina Warwick (5), married George Tallman.
151. vi.   Rachel Warwick (5).

46. Anna Slaven (4), daughter of John Slaven, Jr. and Elizabeth Warwick (3), married March 26, 1812 in Bath County, Virginia, Patrick Bruffey, died 1853 in Pocahontas County, West Virginia. They lived near Green Bank, West Virginia. His will was dated February 1, 1853 and recorded March 1853 in Will Book 3, page 11, Pocahontas County, West Virginia. It mentions wife, Ann;

245

grandson, James P. Bruffey; son, William S. Bruffey; four living
daughters, Nancy Ervin, Elizabeth Ervin, Pressilla W. Bruffey,
and Caroline Ruckman; granddaughter, Polly Ann Ruckman; and
daughter Sarah Ann Hamilton. Executors were David W. Kerr and
William S. Bruffey. Witnesses were Beverly P. Gillaspie and John
W. Orndorff.

Children: 7

    152. i.   William S. Bruffey (5).
    153. ii.   Nancy Bruffey (5), married _____ Ervin.
+ 154. iii. Elizabeth Bruffey (5).
    155. iv.   Caroline Bruffey (5), married James Watts
Ruckman, son of David Little Ruckman and Priscilla Wade. He
served in the CSA.
    156. v.   Priscilla W. Bruffey (5).
    157. vi.   Mary Bruffey (5), married November 7, 1833,
John H. Ruckman, born November 11, 1810, son of John H. Ruckman
and Nancy Hartman.
    158. vii. Sarah Ann Bruffey (5), married _____ Hamilton.

72. Montgomery Warwick (4), son of Jacob Warwick (3) and
Jane Montgomery, was born in 1797 near Lexington, Kentucky;
married in 1819, Martha (Patsy) Jones, daughter of Cadwallard
Jones and Martha Pitt.

Children: 6

+ 159. i.   Mary E. Warwick (5).
    160. ii.   Henry Clay Warwick (5), died at age 4.
    161. iii. (Infant) Warwick (5), died.
    162. iv.   Jacob Warwick (5), never married.
    163. v.   Martha J. Warwick (5), married Robert Skelton.
No children.
+ 164. vi.   Julia Warwick (5).

74. Eleanor (Nelly) Warwick (4), daughter of Jacob Warwick
(3) and Jane Montgomery, was born in 1799 near Lexington, Kentucky;
died 1870; married February 20, 1819, Colonel Charles Jones, born
1791; died February 1864, son of Cadwallard Jones and Martha Pitt.
He was a soldier in the War of 1812 and a Colonel in the Militia.
    Children: 12
+ 165. i.   Eliza Jones(5), born January 2, 1820.
    166. ii.   Jacob W. Jones (5), born January 25, 1821, never
married.
+ 167. iii. Franklin Jones (5), born December 4, 1823.
+ 168. iv.   John Jones (5), born March 13, 1825.
    169. v.   Robert Jones (5), born 1827; died 1830.
+ 170. vi.   Nancy Jones (5), born 1829.
+ 171. vii. William Jones (5), born September 22, 1832.
    172. viii. Charles Jones (5), born 1835; died 1865.
    173. ix.   Martha Jones (5), born 1837; died January 28,
1890.

174. x.   Thomas Jones (5), born 1839; married Mary
Kesterson. They had four children.
    175. xi.   Marshal Jones (5), born 1841; married _____
Eddington.
    176. xii. James Jones (5), born 1843;died young.

    74. Nancy Divena Warwick (4), daughter of Jacob Warwick
(3) and Jane Montgomery, was born November 1, 1800 near Lexington,
Virginia; died January 7, 1863 at Stouts Grove, Illinois; married
(1) December 24, 1818 in Posey County, Indiana, Colonel Robert
McClure, born January 24, 1792 at Hopkinsville, Kentucky; died
August 8, 1835 at Danvers, Illinois, son of Thomas McClure and
Susan Hinds. He was in the War of 1812 and was a Colonel in
the Black Hawk War. Nancy Divena Warwick married (2), Benjamin
Conger.

    Children: 6 - first marriage

    177. i.   Permelia McClure (5), born April 18, 1820 near
New Harmony, Indiana; died January 2, 1905 in Gibson City, Illinois;
married February 6, 1842, Henry Clay McClure (4), born May 9, 1820
in Princeton, Indiana; died March 16, 1900 in Gibson City, Illinois,
son of James McClure and Malinda Ann Warwick.
    + 178. ii.   Jacob Warwick McClure (5), born December 18,1822.
    + 179. iii. Charles Jones McClure (5), born February 9, 1824.
    + 180. iv.   Thomas Bassel McClure (5), born 1827.
    181. v.   Susan Jane McClure (5), born June 13, 1831 at
Stouts Grove, Illinois; died in 1896 at Lawrence, Kansas; married
Robert McClure (4), born March 16, 1825 in Princeton, Indiana; died
in 1914 in Whittier, California, son of James McClure and Malinda
Ann Warwick.
    182. vi.   John Willis McClure (5), born May 14, 1833; died
at age 14.

    Children: 3 - second marriage

    183. vii. Isaac Conger (5), a Union soldier. He was never
heard of after the battle of Shiloh, Tennessee.
    184. viii. Elizabeth Conger (5), married Jesse Benson.
They had three sons.
    185. ix.   Robert Conger (5), lived at Burlington, Kansas.

    77. Jacob G. Warwick (4), son of Jacob Warwick (3) and Jane
Montgomery , was born March 2, 1807; died March 16, 1858; married
May 15, 1827, Elizabeth Skelton, born September 26, 1809 in
Kentucky; died March 23, 1875. He was a soldier in the Black Hawk
War.

    Children: 12

    186. i.   Montgomery Warwick (5), born January 26, 1828;
died December 18, 1848; married in 1845, May Marvel. No children.
    187. ii.   Sarah Warwick (5), born June 14, 1829; died

April 1, 1861; married (1) October 10, 1850, James Music, died
January 1, 1853; married (2) January 29, 1856, John Thomas.
    188. iii. Robert Warwick (5), born January 24, 1831;
died May 21, 1856.
    189. iv. Emily Warwick (5), born March 14, 1833; died
September 12, 1833.
    190. v. John C. Warwick (5), born November 12, 1835;
married August 8, 1870, Maggie Lapper. No children.
    191. vi. William Warwick (5), born December 28, 1837;
died February 28, 1863. He served in Company C, 106th Illinois
Regiment.
    192. vii. Benjamin C. Warwick (5), born January 30, 1840;
married August 8, 1861, Bettie Rankin.
    193. viii. Nancy E. Warwick (5), born July 6, 1842; died
December 22, 1879; married August 1, 1861, Moses H. Fletcher.
    194. ix. Martha C. Warwick (5), born June 7, 1845;
married (1) September 15, 1870, William A. McCord; married (2)
December 14, 1881, James Cochran.
    195 and 196. x. and xi. (Infant twins) Warwick (5), born
and died in 1847.
+   197. xii. Louisa Warwick (5).

    78. Martha (Patsy) Crockett Warwick (4), daughter of Jacob
Warwick (3) and Jane Montgomery, was born June 3, 1809; died
September 22, 1868; married (1) Dr. Willis Jackman Smith, born
1800; married (2) Jacob Paden.

    Children: 4 - first marriage

+   198. i. Emily Smith (5), born November 24, 1827.
+   199. ii. Louisa Smith (5), born June 12, 1829.
+   200. iii. Warwick Smith (5), born September 23, 1831.
    201. iv. Elizabeth Smith (5), born February 12, 1834;
died June 12, 1887; married (1) January 1853, Morgan Williams,
died March 2, 1871; married (2) April 30, 1872, Alfred Martin.

    Children: 3 - second marriage

    202. v. Martha Paden (5), born March 1, 1837; never
married.
    203. vi. Jane Paden (5), born December 26, 1839; never
married.
    204. vii. Frank Paden (5), born June 1, 1846; died August
14, 1872. He served in an Illinois Regiment.

    79. Polly Montgomery (4), daughter of Judge Thomas Mont-
gomery and Elizabeth Warwick (3), was born in 1806; died in 1869;
married November 4, 1822, Major James Skelton, died 1866. He
was a Major of the State Militia. They lived near Princeton,
Indiana.

    Children: 10

+   205. i. Elizabeth Skelton (5), born 1826.

+ 206. ii. Amanda Skelton (5), born 1827.
+ 207. iii. Barnes Skelton (5), born 1829.
  208. iv. Thomas Skelton (5), born 1831; died 1852.
+ 209. v. Benjamin Franklin Skelton (5), born 1833.
+ 210. vi. Sarah Skelton (5), born 1835.
+ 211. vii. Newton O. Skelton (5), born 1837.
  212. viii. (Infant) Skelton (5), born 1839; died young.
+ 213. ix. Maria Skelton (5), born 1840.
+ 214. x. Emily Skelton (5), born 1842.

80. Nelly Montgomery (4), daughter of Judge Thomas Montgomery and Elizabeth Warwick (3), was born in 1808; married James Joseph Roberts.

Children: 3

  215. i. Joseph Roberts (5), married Eliza Waters. No children.
  216. ii. Thomas Roberts (5), died unmarried.
  217. iii. Dr. William Roberts (5), married Octavia Burner. They had three children.

82. Nancy Montgomery (4), daughter of Judge Thomas Montgomery and Elizabeth Warwick (3), was born in 1812; died March 8, 1884; married Joseph S. Skelton.

Children: 12

  218. i. Mary R. Skelton (5), born January 27, 1831; died September 18, 1850.
  219. ii. Ellen Skelton (5), born May 3, 1833.
  220. iii. Martha Skelton (5), born July 9, 1835.
  221. iv. Louisa Skelton (5), born March 22, 1839; died September 22, 1850.
+ 222. v. Elizabeth Skelton (5), born September 3, 1840.
+ 223. vi. Levi Skelton (5), born August 3, 1842.
+ 224. vii. Sarah Skelton (5), born June 25, 1845.
  225. viii. John R. Skelton (5), born April 10, 1847; died September 26, 1850.
  226. ix. Elisha E. Skelton (5), born November 4, 1849; died September 19, 1850.
  227. x. Thomas E. Skelton (5), born August 14, 1851; married August 20, 1878, Sarah E. Smiley. They had two children.
+ 228. xi. Harriet Skelton (5), born June 5, 1853.
  229. xii. James Skelton (5), died in 1856.

85. Albert Pickle McClure (4), son of James McClure and Malinda Ann Warwick (3), was born March 29, 1809 at Princeton, Indiana; died November 15, 1884 at Owensville, Indiana; married November 1, 1857, Mrs. Sivilla English Braselton.

Children: 2

249

230. i.   Lucius McClure (5), died November 14, 1884.
231. ii.   Wesley McClure (5).

86. Edwin McClure (4), son of James McClure and Malinda
Ann Warwick (3), was born April 7, 1811 at Princeton, Indiana;
died August 5, 1847 at New Orleans, Louisiana; married December
17, 1835 at Evansville, Indiana, Mary Ann Newman. She married
(2) _____ Dutton.

Children: 4

+   232. i.   James Newman McClure (5).
     233. ii.   Augusta McClure (5), married Finis McClure,
son of Ben and Frankie McClure. They had four children.
     234. iii. Maria McClure (5), died unmarried.
     235. iv.   Edward Orlando McClure (5), married Belle
McMillian, died March 1933. They had several children.

89. Joseph Perry McClure (4), son of James McClure and
Malinda Ann Warwick (3), was born October 6, 1815; died January
23, 1898 in Princeton, Indiana; married February 13, 1834,
Catherine Ann Devin, born July 8, 1812; died November 27, 1888.

Children: 12

+   236. i.   Eleanor Jane McClure (5), born January 7, 1835.
+   237. ii.   Mary Brown McClure (5), born June 9, 1836.
+   238. iii. Alexander Devin McClure (5), born December 22,
1837.
     239. iv.   Susan Ann McClure (5), born May 10, 1839; died
April 16, 1867, unmarried.
     240. v.   James McClure (5), born January 20,1841; died
March 14, 1913. He was a doctor and never married. He served
in Company H, 17th Indiana Mounted Infantry, Union Army.
+   241. vi.   Margaret Caroline Elizabeth McClure (5), born
November 6, 1842.
+   242. vii. Joseph David McClure (5), born July 9, 1844.
+   243. viii. Robert Moffit McClure (5), born September 16,
1846.
+   244. ix.   William McGrady McClure (5), born March 29,
1848.
+   245. x.   George Washington McClure (5), born July 17,
1850.
+   246. xi.   Nancy Virginia McClure (5), born December 15,
1852.
+   247. xii. Franklin Perry Prentice McClure (5), born May
9, 1855.

91. Henry Clay McClure (4), son of James McClure and Malinda
Ann Warwick (3), was born May 9, 1820 in Princeton, Indiana; died
March 16, 1900 in Gibson City, Illinois; married February 6, 1842,
Permelia McClure (5), born April 18, 1820 in New Harmony, Indiana;
died January 2, 1905 in Gibson City, Illinois, daughter of Robert

McClure and Nancy Divena Warwick. He was a school teacher in
Gibson County, Illinois when he married. In July 1843 they moved
near Princeton, Indiana and in 1885 they moved to Gibson City,
Illinois.

Children: 6

+   248. i.   Robert Augustus McClure (5), born January 3,
1843.
     249. ii.   Susan Augusta McClure (5), born June 5, 1850;
died September 15, 1851.
+   250. iii. Horace Adrian McClure (5), born September 26,
1852.
+   251. iv.   Herman Warwick McClure (5), born August 16,
1855.
+   252. v.   Frances Olivia McClure (5), born December 6,
1858.
+   253. vi.   George Lincoln McClure (5), born September
27, 1863.

92. David Hart McClure (4), son of James McClure and
Malinda Ann Warwick (3), was born May 2, 1822 in Princeton,
Indiana; died November 9, 1871 in Memphis, Tennessee; married
April 22, 1848, Mrs. Lidia Basset.

Children: 1

254. i.   David Hart McClure (5), died young.

93. Robert McClure (4), son of James McClure and Malinda
Ann Warwick (3), was born March 16, 1825 in Princeton, Indiana;
died in 1914 in Whittier, California; married Susan Jane McClure
(5), born June 13, 1831 at Stouts Grove, Illinois; died 1896 in
Lawrence, Kansas, daughter of Robert McClure and Nancy Divenna
Warwick.

Children: 6

255. i.   Katie B. McClure (5), died April 14, 1863 and
was buried at St. Louis, Missouri.
256. ii.   Frank T. McClure (5), died May 22, 1863 and
was buried at St. Louis, Missouri.
257. iii. Robert McClure (5), died in Whittier, California.
258. iv.   Laura McClure (5), died at San Francisco,
California.
259. v.   Nancy McClure (5), married Irwin Wilson of
Whittier, California.
260. vi.   Cora McClure (5), lived at Whittier, California.

96. Andrew Warwick Lewis Cameron (4), son of Colonel
Charles Edward Cameron and Rachel P. Warwick (3), married Ellen
McCue Hyde. He represented Bath County in the Virginia Legi-
slature.

Children: 1

+ 261. i.   Charles Jacob Cameron (5).

97. Warwick Gatewood (4), son of William Gatewood and Jane Warwick (3), married Margaret Beale of Botetourt County, Virginia and a relative of President Madison.

Children: 2

262. i.   Eliza Jane Gatewood (5), born August 2, 1823; died December 24, 1898; married January 28, 1844 in Bath County, Virginia (as his second wife), James Woods Warwick (4), born April 22, 1813; died July 18, 1897, son of Andrew Sitlington Warwick and Mary N. Woods.
+ 263. ii.   Mary Catherine Gatewood (5), born 1827.

98. Samuel Vance Gatewood (4), son of William Gatewood and Jane Warwick (3), married Eugenia Massie. They lived at Mountain Grove, Bath County, Virginia.

Children: 4

264. i.   Susan Gatewood (5), married William Taliaferro.
265. ii.   Mary Pleasants Gatewood (5), married Samuel Goode.
266. iii.   William Bias Gatewood (5).
+ 267. iv.   Andrew Cameron Lewis Gatewood (5), born 1843.

100. Frances Gatewood (4), daughter of William Gatewood and Jane Warwick (3), married (1) _____ Patton; married (2) _____ Dorman.

Children: 2 - first marriage

268. i.   _____ Patton (5), a daughter, married _____ ___ Crockett.
269. ii.   _____ Patton (5), a daughter, married _____ ___ Kent.

116. James Woods Warwick (4), son of Andrew Sitlington Warwick (3) and Mary N. Woods, was born April 22, 1813; died July 18, 1897 in Bath County, Virginia; married (1) Eliza Ann Hyde, born 1816; died 1842, of Rockbridge County, Virginia; married (2) January 18, 1844 in Bath County, Virginia, Eliza Jane Gatewood (5), born August 2, 1823; died December 24, 1898, daughter of Warwick Gatewood and Margaret Beale. He was Justice of Peace of Bath County, Judge of the County Courts of Bath and Highland Counties, and Chairman of the Board of Supervisors of Bath County, Virginia.

Children: 2 - first marriage

+ 270. i. John Andrew Warwick (5), born March 30, 1837.
271. ii. James Woods Warwick (5), married Mary Virginia Patterson. He was a teacher and superintendent of schools in Pocahontas County, West Virginia. He served in the CSA.

Children: 7 - second marriage

272. iii. Mary S. Warwick (5), born 1845; married December 1, 1869 in Bath County, Virginia, Andrew Cameron Lewis Gatewood (5), son of Samuel Vance Gatewood and Eugenia Massie.
273. iv. Lillie Gatewood Warwick (5), born 1847; married December 1, 1869 in Bath County, Virginia, James A. Frazier, born 1846, son of John W. and Bettie S. Frazier.
274. v. Eliza Gatewood Warwick (5), married Hon. John W. Stephenson.
275. vi. Ida Netherland Warwick (5), born July 3, 1856; died April 15, 1918; married October 24, 1877, Jacob Hunter McClintic, born June 25, 1852.
276. vii. Charles William Warwick (5), born March 20, 1860; died November 1894.
277. viii. Constance Frazier Warwick (5), married James Reid.
278. ix. Cellestine Beale Warwick (5), died unmarried.

118. John Wood Warwick (4), son of Andrew Sitlington Warwick (3) and Mary N. Woods, married (1) Hannah Moffett Gatewood (5), daughter of Andrew Gatewood and Sally Moffett. He married (2) September 10, 1848 in Pocahontas County, West Virginia, Caroline Elizabeth Craig, daughter of George E. Craig and Matilda Guthrie. (See Craig Family).

Children: 1 - first marriage

+ 279. i. Sally Gatewood Warwick (5).

Children: 5 - second marriage

280. ii. Emma Warwick (5). She was a teacher in the public schools of West Virginia.
281. iii. Mary Woodsie Warwick (5), married October 5, 1880 in Pocahontas County, West Virginia, Ernest N. Moore.
282. iv. Margaret E. Warwick (5), married September 28, 1886 in Pocahontas County, West Virginia, Dr. James Bedford Lockridge, son of Colonel James T. Lockridge and Lillie Moser. (See Lockridge Family).
283. v. John Warwick (5), died in 1896.
284. vi. George Warwick (5), died while a student at Washington and Lee University, Lexington, Virginia.

121. Andrew Gatewood (4), son of Thomas Gatewood and Nancy Warwick (3), married Sally Moffett.

Children: 2

285. i. Charles Gatewood (5).
286. ii. Hannah Moffett Gatewood (5), married (as his first wife), John Wood Warwick (4), son of Andrew Sitlington Warwick and Mary N. Woods.

127. William Fechtig Warwick (5), son of Robert Craig Warwick (4) and Esther Hull, was born August 11, 1822; died December 20, 1902; married Phoebe Anthea Pray, born August 11, 1833; died May 1, 1905. They lived near Mountain Grove, Bath County, Virginia.

Children: 11

+ 287. i. Paul McNeel Warwick (6).
+ 288. ii. Robert Warwick (6).
  289. iii. Peter Hull Warwick (6), married Minnie _____.
They lived in Kansas.
  290. iv. Nelson Pray Warwick (6), married _____.
They lived in Oklahoma.
+ 291. v. George Craig Warwick (6).
+ 292. vi. Charles Fechtig Warwick (6), born August 31, 1865.
+ 293. vii. James Warwick (6).
+ 294. viii. Amelia E. Warwick (6), born July 16, 1853.
+ 295. ix. Amanda Gabriella Warwick (6), born 1871.
  296. x. Sallie Warwick (6), died unmarried.
  297. xi. Louisa Catherine Warwick (6), died unmarried.
She was a teacher.

128. Catherine Hidy Warwick (5), daughter of Robert Craig Warwick (4) and Esther Hull, was born June 16, 1824; died August 29, 1911; married May 20, 1851 in Pocahontas County, West Virginia, William Wallace Byrd, born May 8, 1821; died May 6, 1901. He was a Major in command of Company K, 52d Virginia Regiment, CSA, in the battle of McDowell and was in charge of a regiment of reserves in the battle of New Hope. He was a school teacher.

Children: 5

+ 298. i. Elvira Louisa Byrd (6).
  299. ii. Robert Craig Byrd (6), married (1) Emma Brown; married (2) Mary Withrow, Bath County, Virginia.
+ 300. iii. John Henry Byrd (6), born May 12, 1859.
  301. iv. George Newton Byrd (6), married Mollie Bolton, Greenbrier County, West Virginia.
+ 302. v. William Lee Byrd (6).

130. Sarah Elizabeth Warwick (5), daughter of Robert Craig Warwick (4) and Esther Hull, was born August 1828; died October 12, 1908; married in 1852 in Pocahontas County, West Virginia Daniel Matheny, born 1827; died 1886, son of Abijah Matheny & Margaret Bird. They lived at Valley Center, Virginia.

Children: 4

303. i. Esther Ann Katherine Matheny (6), born June 11, 1853; died December 27, 1941, unmarried.
+ 304. ii. Melissa A. Matheny (6), born 1855.
305. iii. William M. Matheny (6), died young.
+ 306. iv. Robert Lee Matheny (6).

131. Margaret Ann Warwick (5), daughter of Robert Craig Warwick (4) and Esther Hull, married April 16, 1843 in Pocahontas County, West Virginia, John Nelson Pray.

Children: 5

307. i. Ruhama Pray (6), a twin to Regina; died in childhood.
308. ii. Regina Pray (6), a twin to Ruhama; died in childhood.
309. iii. Amanda Crawford Pray (6), died in childhood.
310. iv. Ella Pray (6), married John Mc. Riley and lived at Fairmont, West Virginia.
311. v. Libby Pray (6), married George Jamison and lived at Fishinghawk, Oklahoma.

132. Hannah Rebecca Hopkins Warwick (5), daughter of Robert Craig Warwick (4) and Esther Hull, was born February 1, 1833; died May 24, 1909; married January 2, 1855 in Pocahontas County, West Virginia, George Washington Siple, born 1829; died February 23, 1908, son of Joel Siple and Mary M. Hiner. He was a Captain in the 31st Virginia Infantry, CSA. He was a member of the West Virginia Legislature.

Children: 9

+ 312. i. Nancy Jane Siple (6).
+ 313. ii. Anna Siple (6).
+ 314. iii. Mary Katherine Siple (6), born August 17, 1866, a twin to Joel Wade Hampton.
+ 315. iv. Joel Wade Hampton Siple (6), born August 17, 1866, a twin to Mary Katherine.
+ 316. v. William Madison Siple (6), born April 11, 1864.
317. vi. Clara Belle Siple (6), born August 26, 1870 in Pocahontas County, West Virginia; died August 10, 1927; married October 18, 1899 in Pocahontas County, West Virginia, Andrew William Cleek, born May 10, 1871; died February 8, 1938, son of George Washington Cleek and Malcena Catherine Lightner. (See Cleek Family).
+ 318. vii. Lucy Siple (6).
319. viii. Ashbury Siple (6), died in infancy.
320. ix. Virgie Siple (6), died in infancy.

133. Louisa Susan Warwick (5), daughter of Robert Craig Warwick (4) and Esther Hull, was born in 1836; died August 11, 1923 at Lambert, Oklahoma; married October 31, 1854 in Pocahontas

County, West Virginia, Eli Seybert, son of Isaac Seybert and Ruth Wilson. They first lived near Mountain Grove, Bath County, Virginia and later moved to Oklahoma.

Children: 2

321. i.   Robert W. Seybert (6), born October 4, 1855; died July 31, 1858.
+ 322. ii.   Mary Amaret Seybert (6).

134. Peter Hull Warwick (5), son of Robert Craig Warwick (4) and Esther Hull, was born November 3, 1839; died January 16, 1925; married November 23, 1865, Sarah Caroline Matheny, born February 29, 1836; died March 26, 1896, daughter of Levi Matheny and Mary Hazlett. He enlisted in the CSA on April 19, 1861, becoming a member of Company G, 31st Virginia Infantry. He served through the entire war and was discharged April 9, 1865. He was wounded June 9, 1862 at the battle of Port Republic.

Children: 4

+ 323. i.   Otis D. Warwick (6).
+ 324. ii.   Forrest Warwick (6).
+ 325. iii.   Jessie Lee Warwick (6).
   326. iv.   Elbert Warwick (6), died in 1895, unmarried.

135. John Robert Warwick (5), son of Robert Craig Warwick (4) and Esther Hull, was born October 29, 1843; died May 30, 1915 in Pocahontas County, West Virginia; married October 14, 1873, Mary Jane Cleek, born October 11, 1839 in Bath County, Virginia; died October 22, 1919, daughter of John Cleek II and Sarah Kimes-Givens. (See Cleek Family). He served as a Lieutenant in the 31st Virginia Infantry, CSA. He served as Court Commissioner of Pocahontas County, West Virginia. He was a teacher in the public schools of Pocahontas County, West Virginia.

Children: 5

   327. i.   Harriet Warwick (6), died in infancy.
   328. ii.   Mary Rebecca Warwick (6), born September 6, 1875; married December 21, 1922 in Pocahontas County, West Virginia, Frank Smith Webb.
   329. iii.   Sallie Warwick (6), died in infancy.
+ 330. iv.   Nancy Esther Givens Warwick (6), born March 27, 1879.
   331. v.   Anne Warwick (6), died in infancy.

154. Elizabeth Bruffey (5), daughter of Patrick Bruffey and Anna Slaven (4), married James Addison Ervine, born 1818, son of Edward Ervine (born April 2, 1790) and Mary Curry (born June 20, 1794). James Addison Ervine was the grandson of Benjamin Ervine who served in the Revolution. They migrated to Missouri and located near St. Louis.

Children: 9

332. i.   William Ervine (6).
333. ii.   Calvin Ervine (6).
334. iii. James Patrick Ervine (6).
335. iv.   Laura Ervine (6), born 1843; died 1887; married
Stephen A. Lockridge, born November 9, 1843; died July 21, 1896;
son of Robert Lockridge and Emmeline M. Gwin. (See Gwin Family).
336. v.   Mary Ervine (6).
337. vi.   Harriet Ervine (6).
338. vii. Elizabeth Ervine (6).
339. viii. Caroline Ervine (6).
340. ix.   Rose Ervine (6).

159. Mary E. Warwick (5), daughter of Montgomery Warwick
(4) and Martha (Patsy) Jones, married (1) Herod Music; married
(2) _____ Jackson. There were five children of the second
marriage, names unknown. There were four children of the first
marriage, one of whom was:

+ 341. i.   Nancy Elizabeth Music (6).

164. Julia Warwick (5), daughter of Montgomery Warwick (4)
and Martha (Patsy) Jones, married Curt Turley.

Children: 1

342. i.   Georgia Ann Turley (6), married James Townsend.

165. Eliza Jones (5), daughter of Charles Jones and Eleanor
(Nelly) Warwick (4), was born January 2, 1820; died February 3,
1901; married March 22, 1838, Lieutenant William A. Waters, born
March 31, 1813; died August 5, 1886. He served in the 42d Indiana
Regiment.

Children: 11

343. i.   Charles C. Waters (6), born August 25,1839.
+ 344. ii.   Nancy J. Waters (6), born November 8, 1841.
345. iii. James B. Waters (6), born September 26, 1844.
346. iv.   Eleanor Waters (6), died young.
347. v.   Eliza A. Waters (6), died young.
348. vi.   (Infant) Waters (6), died.
349. vii. Elizabeth L. Waters (6), married Frank P. Yeager.
350. viii. Jacob J. Waters (6).
351. ix.   Mary Waters (6), died.
352. x.   John F. Waters (6), died May 1935.
353. xi.   Martha Waters (6), born June 12, 1862; died 1939.

167. Franklin Jones (5), son of Charles Jones and Eleanor
(Nelly) Warwick (4), was born December 4, 1823; died June 16,1908;
married December 16, 1847, Comfort Sharp, born April 28, 1828;
died August 29, 1907, daughter of John Wright Sharp and Temperance
(nee) Sharp.

257

Children: 8

354. i. Ellen W. Jones (6).
355. ii. Maria Jones (6).
356. iii. John Jones (6), married Dovie Kell.
357. iv. Mat Jones (6).
358. v. Eliza J. Jones (6).
+ 359. vi. Mary E. Jones (6), born May 22, 1861.
+ 360. vii. Sarah Alice Jones (6), born January 2, 1865.
361. viii. William F. Jones (6), married August 19, 1900,
Bertie G. Stephens.

168. John Jones (5), son of Charles Jones and Eleanor
(Nelly) Warwick (4), was born March 13, 1825; died September
23, 1902; married October 30, 1856, Permelia Montgomery, born
August 27, 1836, daughter of Hon. J. W. Montgomery and Jane
McFadin.

Children: 6

362. i. Ella J. Jones (6), married Thomas Marvel.
363. ii. Warwick Jones (6).
364. iii. Charles Jones (6), married Minnie Cross.
365. iv. Frank Jones (6).
367. v. Matt Jones (6), twin to Mary.
368. vi. Mary Jones (6), twin to Matt, married Guy A.
Randolph. They have one child.

170. Nancy Jones (5), daughter of Charles Jones and Eleanor
(Nelly) Warwick (4), was born in 1829; died March 12, 1861; married
July 20, 1848, Abraham Mauck, born February 7, 1821; died January
2, 1901.

Children: 2

368. i. William Mauck (6).
+ 369. ii. Eliza Mauck (6), born August 7, 1850.

171. William Jones (5), son of Charles Jones and Eleanor
(Nelly) Warwick (4), was born September 22, 1832; married in
1874, Martha Massey.

Children: 2

370. i. Florence Jones (6).
371. ii. Fanney Jones (6),

178. Jacob Warwick McClure (5), son of Robert McClure and
Nancy Divena Warwick (4), was born December 18, 1822; married
Alice Hall of Stouts Grove, Illinois. They moved to Huntsville,
Alabama.

Children: 2

372. i. Israel McClure (6), died young.
373. ii. Mary McClure (6), married _____ Harris of Memphis,.Tennessee.

179. Charles Jones McClure (5), son of Robert McClure and Nancy Divena Warwick (4), was born February 9, 1824; died 1908 at Fort Riley, Kansas; married Sereptia Vansickle.

Children: 4

374. i. Winfield McClure (6).
375. ii. Clara McClure (6).
376. iii. Harry McClure (6).
377. iv. John McClure (6).

180. Thomas Bassel McClure (5), son of Robert McClure and Nancy Divena Warwick (4), was born in 1827; died 1898 in Memphis, Tennessee; married Emma Clark.

Children: 1

378. i. Sarah McClure (6).

197. Louisa Warwick (5), daughter of Jacob G. Warwick (4) and Elizabeth Skelton, married (1) Joseph Mauck (6), son of Samuel Mauck, Sr. and Elizabeth Skelton; married (2) October 25, 1881, W. H. Turner.

Children: 2 - second marriage

379. i. Matilda E. Turner (6), born December 21, 1881.
380. ii. William E. Turner (6), born March 21, 1890.

198. Emily Smith (5), daughter of Dr. Willis Jackman Smith and Martha (Patsy) Crockett Warwick (4), was born November 24, 1827; died January 2, 1902; married in 1846, William S. Armstrong, born May 1, 1824; died July 24, 1877, son of Kirby Armstrong and Miranda Gambrel.

Children: 8

+ 381. i. Willis Armstrong (6), born May 23, 1847.
+ 382. ii. Warwick Armstrong (6), born February 6, 1849.
383. iii. (Infant) Armstrong (6), born April 17, 1851; died April 24, 1851.
384. iv. John F. Armstrong (6), born October 11, 1852; married September 6, 1874, Lucinda Mauck. They had four children.
+ 385. v. James H. Armstrong (6), born March 31, 1858.
386. vi. Morgan Armstrong (6), born March 31, 1858; died March 4, 1859.
387. vii. Mary L. Armstrong (6), born April 22, 1860; died June 6, 1888; married October 6, 1880, Joseph Knowles.
388. viii. Pinckney S. Armstrong (6), born November 24,

259

1866; married (1) December 1, 1887, Martha Roberts, born October 2, 1867; died June 14, 1909, daughter of John Roberts and Sarah Jane Montgomery;married (2) May 21, 1911, Nora Smith, daughter of Henry Smith and Matilda Mauck.

199. Louisa Smith (5), daughter of Dr. Willis Jackman Smith and Martha (Patsy) Crockett Warwick (4), was born June 12, 1829; married October 21, 1848, Levi Johnson, born December 25, 1824; died November 25, 1904, son of George W. Johnson and Anna Williams.

Children: 6

+ 389. i.   John Willis Johnson (6), born December 19, 1849.
+ 390. ii.   George Washington Johnson,jr. (6), born June 2, 1852.
  391. iii. Martha Johnson (6), born April 27, 1854; died July 10, 1934, unmarried.
+ 392. iv.   Emma A. Johnson (6), born October 14, 1858.
+ 393. v.   Warwick D. Johnson (6), born February 1, 1865.
  394. vi.   Laura E. Johnson (6), born August 1871; died November 16, 1876, aged 6 years.

200. Warwick Smith (5), son of Dr. Willis Jackman Smith and Martha (Patsy) Crockett Warwick (4), was born September 23, 1831; died June 26, 1902; married (1) February 1856, Margaret M. Simpson, born December 4, 1838; died January 24, 1895, daughter of John C. Simpson and Margaret Stewart; married (2) July 28, 1895, Serrelda Smith.

Children: 4 - first marriage

  395. i.   John Willis Smith (6), born January 1, 1857.
+ 396. ii.   George Washington Smith (6), born June 22, 1859.
  397. iii. Lillie Smith (6), married Charles Murnahan.
  398. iv.   (Infant) Smith (6), died.

205. Elizabeth Skelton (5), daughter of Major James Skelton and Polly Montgomery (4), was born in 1826; married Samuel Mauck, Sr., brother of Abraham Mauck.

Children: 4

+ 399. i.   Julius Mauck (6).
  400. ii.   James Mauck (6), died 1903; married Sarah Malone.
+ 401. iii. Joseph Mauck (6).
+ 402. iv.   Mary Mauck (6), born July 17, 1850.

206. Amanda Skelton (5), daughter of Major James Skelton and Polly Montgomery (4), was born in 1827; married Henry Mauck, Sr.

Children: 7

403. i.   Sarah Mauck, (6), born February 18, 1848; died
November 27, 1899; married October 19, 1865, William Forbis.
They had ten children.
+   404. ii.   Samuel Q. Mauck (6), born September 14, 1854.
    405. iii.   James F. Mauck (6), born February 5, 1856.
    406. iv.   Mary Mauck (6), born January 7, 1857; married
July 23, 1873, J. I. Moore, born March 17, 1852.
    407. v.   Charles Mauck (6), born 1859, moved west.
    408. vi.   Frank S. Mauck (6), born May 15, 1862; married
January 31, 1886, Corene Montgomery, born July 8, 1864, daughter
of Benjamin F. Montgomery and Hannah Sharp.
    409. vii.   Howard W. Mauck (6), born March 4, 1865; married
March 15, 1885, Levina J. Clark, born November 15, 1860. They
had ten children.

207. Barnes Skelton (5), son of Major James Skelton and
Polly Montgomery (4), was born in 1829; married Lucinda Mauck.

Children: 2

    410. i.   Nancy J. Skelton (6).
+   411. ii.   Elizabeth Skelton (6).

209. Benjamin Franklin Skelton (5), son of Major James
Skelton and Polly Montgomery (4), was born in 1833; died October
17, 1898; married Louisa Summers, born 1831, daughter of Richey
Summers, Sr. and Polly Montgomery.

Children: 10

    412. i.   Mary Skelton (6).
    413. ii.   Martha Skelton (6), married James Daugherty.
    414. iii.   Manerva Skelton (6).
    415. iv.   Amanda Skelton (6), married August 13, 1874,
Albert Lagrange.
    416. v.   (Infant) Skelton (6), died.
    417. vi.   Ollie Skelton (6), married David Cleveland.
    418. vii.   Ida Skelton (6), married August 4, 1881,
Marshall Stone, died July 1933. He married (2) Isabell Shanner.
    419. viii. Joseph Skelton (6).
    420. ix.   Ophelia Skelton (6), married June 11, 1891,
Edgar Lowe.
    421. x.   Nannie Skelton (6), married James Williams.

210. Sarah Skelton (5), daughter of Major James Skelton
and Polly Montgomery (4), was born in 1835; married John J.
Hollis. They reared William K. Knowles.

Children: 2

    422. i.   Mary E. Hollis (6), died young.
    423. ii.   Newton Hollis (6), died young.

211. Newton O. Skelton (5), son of Major James Skelton and
Polly Montgomery (4), was born in 1837; died January 28, 1880;
married December 5, 1860, Catherine Richards, born 1838; died
1928 of Owensville.

Children: 5

      424. i.   William R. Skelton (6).
      425. ii.   Mattie Skelton (6), died at age 12.
      426. iii. Jessie Skelton (6), died April 30, 1908; mar-
ried _____ Butler. They had two children.
  +   427. iv.   Mary Skelton (6).
      428. v.   Nelly Skelton (6), died young.

213. Maria Skelton (5), daughter of Major James Skelton
and Polly Montgomery (4), was born in 1840; died 1900; married
John Thomas Ervin.

Children: 3

  +   429. i.   Lily Ervin (6).
  +   430. ii.   Emma Ervin (6).
      431, iii. (Infant) Ervin (6), died.

214. Emily Skelton (5), daughter of Major James Skelton
and Polly Montgomery (4), was born in 1842; married Samuel Reavis.
They had ten children and all died young except:

  +   432. i.   John H. Reavis (6).
      433. ii.   Fred Reavis (6), died at age 19.

222. Elizabeth Skelton (5), daughter of Joseph S. Skelton
and Nancy Montgomery (4), was born September 3, 1840; died August
31, 1873; married N. Wood Martin.

Children: 2

      434. i.   Lee Martin (6).
      435. ii.   Ed Martin (6).

223. Levi Skelton (5), son of Joseph S. Skelton and Nancy
Montgomery (4), was born August 3, 1842; married Elizabeth J.
Humphrey.

Children: 4

  +   436. i.   Etta Skelton (6), born January 1867.
  +   437. ii.   Mary Skelton (6).
  +   438. iii. Nannie Skelton (6).
      439. iv.   Arthur Skelton (6); married 1902, Pearl Sharp.

224. Sarah Skelton (5), daughter of Joseph S. Skelton and
Nancy Montgomery (4), was born June 25, 1845; married Columbus

Emmerson. He married (2) Mollie Daugherty DePriest, and married
(3) Hannah DePriest Baldwin.

Children: 5

+ 440. i. Florence Emmerson (6), born December 21, 1867.
+ 441. ii. Joseph L. Emmerson (6), born September 29, 1870.
442. iii. Dr. Jesse D. Emmerson (6), born September 22,
1872; married April 26, 1894, Ada Bixler, died April 17, 1902.
He is a dentist.
443. iv. Otis Emmerson (6), born August 19, 1875; married
Anna Cushman.
+ 444. v. Gussie Emmerson (6), born April 15, 1878.

228. Harriet Skelton (5), daughter of Joseph S. Skelton
and Nancy Montgomery (4), was born June 5, 1853; died June 25,
1890; married August 1876 (as his second wife), Benjamin F.
Montgomery, born December 1838, son of Samuel Montgomery.

Children: 1

+ 445. i. Lawrence O. Montgomery (6), born September 23,
1880.

232. James Newman McClure (5), son of Edwin McClure (4) and
Mary Ann Newman, married Mrs. Medora Privit.

Children: 4

446. i. Lulu McClure (6).
447. ii. Will McClure (6).
448. iii. Ed McClure (6).
449. iv. Lavina McClure (6).

236. Eleanor Jane McClure (5), daughter of Joseph Perry
McClure (4) and Catherine Ann Devin, was born January 7, 1835;
died September 4, 1924; married September 28, 1858, James Wesley
Key, born March 10, 1832; died February 10, 1919, son of William
Key and Sarah Druner.

Children: 10

450. i. James Alexander Key (6), born July 23, 1859;
died July 20, 1860.
+ 451. ii. Joseph Perry Key (6), born July 13, 1861.
452. iii. Louella Key (6), born May 30, 1863.
453. iv. Ada Jane Key (6), born December 18, 1864; died
June 20, 1915.
+ 454. v. William Finis Key (6), born July 18, 1866.
455. vi. Sarah Frances Key (6), born February 23, 1868;
died September 3, 1944; married August 2, 1927 (as his second
wife), Charles Homer Hudelson, born March 17, 1889; died May 1943.
456. vii. Catherine Ann Key (6), born January 17, 1870.

+   457. viii. Margaret Elizabeth Key (6), born September 3,
1871.
+   458. ix.   Robert Sherman Key (6), born May 22, 1873.
      459. x.   Charles Fletcher Key (6), born January 21, 1877.

      237. Mary Brown McClure (5), daughter of Joseph Perry McClure
(4) and Catherine Ann Devin, was born June 9, 1836; died January
31, 1914; married April 18, 1860, Henry Gibson Wheeler, born
April 26, 1839, son of William Henry Wheeler and Sarah Ann Neill.

      Children: 2

      460. i.   Alma Wheeler (6), born June 17, 1861; died
August 14, 1879.
+   461. ii.   Lawrence Wheeler (6), born October 9, 1863.

      238. Alexander Devin McClure (5), son of Joseph Perry McClure
(4) and Catherine Ann Devin, was born December 22, 1837; died
March 6, 1907; married (1) October 19, 1865, Sarah Green, born
July 6, 1845; died August 28, 1871; married (2) November 18, 1877,
Maria Weber, born June 5, 1854 in Germany, daughter of Henry
Weber. He served in Company H, 17th Indiana Mounted Infantry,
Union Army. Maria Weber died December 10, 1927.

      Children: 2 - first marriage

      462. i.   Catherine Louisa McClure (6), born December 6,
1866; died October 16, 1907.
+   463. ii.   Mary Ellen McClure (6), born November 9, 1868.

      Children: 5 - second marriage

      464. iii. Nora Charlotte McClure (6), born September 12,
1878; died July 12, 1879.
+   465. iv.   Clara McClure (6), born November 6, 1879.
      466. v.   Ella D. McClure (6), born September 28, 1881;
died young.
+   467. vi.   Alle McClure (6), born September 28, 1881, a
twin to Ella.
+   468. vii. Ada Ann McClure (6), born November 26, 1886.

      241. Margaret Caroline Elizabeth McClure (5), daughter of
Joseph Perry McClure (4) and Catherine Ann Devin, was born November
6, 1842; died January 14, 1908; married September 2, 1869, William
Barnett Whitsitt, born September 3, 1844, son of Samuel Whitsitt
and Jane Finney.

      Children: 4

      469. i.   Samuel Whitsitt (6), born March 28, 1871; died
June 1895.
      470. ii.   Joseph Perry Whitsitt (6), died young.
      471. iii. Anna Belle Whitsitt (6), born October 3, 1874;
died September 13, 1891.

+   472. iv.   William Arthur Whitsitt (6), born July 15, 1880.

424.   Joseph David McClure (5), son of Joseph Perry McClure
(4) and Catherine Ann Devin, was born July 9, 1844; died January
5, 1919; married (1) October 1867, Sarah Frances McIntosh, daughter of Rosswell'McIntosh and Jane McMillan; married (2) May 25,
1883, Isabelle Seamon. He served in Company F, 33rd Indiana
Regiment, Union Army.

Children: 4 - first marriage

473. i.   James McClure (6), born July 24, 1870; died
June 3, 1878.
474. ii.   Eva McClure (6), born April 25, 1871; died
April 15, 1874.
475. iii. Rosswell P. McClure (6), born January 14, 1875;
died January 6, 1896.
476. iv.   Anna Steele McClure (6), born November 6, 1879;
died May 18, 1898; married Norman Thornburg.

Children: 2 - second marriage

+   477. v.   Maude McClure (6), born April 1, 1884.
+   478. vi.   Earle McClure (6), born December 19, 1889.

243.   Robert Moffit McClure (5), son of Joseph Perry McClure
(4) and Catherine Ann Devin, was born September 16, 1846; died
December 26, 1926 at Mound City, Kansas; married September 16,
1874, Isabelle Wheeler, born August 11, 1855; died January 29,
1910. He served in Company H, 17th Indiana Mounted Infantry,
Union Army.

Children: 8

479. i.   Catherine Ann McClure (6), born 1875; died 1906;
married _____ Smith.
480. ii.   Joseph Perry McClure (6), born 1875.
481. iii. Quincy D. McClure (6).
482. iv.   Claude O. McClure(6), married _____.
They had a son, Robert McClure (7).
483. v.   Pearl McClure (6), died in infancy.
484. vi.   Montague Moffit McClure (6).
485. vii. Edith McClure (6), married Courtland Klopfenstein,
Mound City, Kansas.
486. viii. James C. McClure (6).

244.   William McGrady McClure (5), son of Joseph Perry
McClure (4) and Catherine Ann Devin, was born March 29, 1848; died
February 29, 1920 at Princeton, Indiana; married October 23, 1878,
Martha Ellen Lathom, born July 5, 1858; died March 13, 1933, dau-
ghter of James C. Lathom and Julia Ann Davis. He served in Com-
pany H, 17th Indiana Mounted Infantry, Union Army.

Children: 9

+ 487. i. Amy Alice McClure (6), born March 30, 1881.
+ 488. ii. Julia Ann McClure (6), born December 2, 1882.
+ 489. iii. Lester Latham McClure (6), born July 19, 1884.
+ 490. iv. James Devin McClure (6), born July 23, 1887.
  491. v. Von Raymond McClure (6), born April 8, 1891;
married Pearl Latham, died October 13, 1955.
+ 492. vi. Percy William McClure (6), born October 5,1894.
  493. vii. Joseph Perry McClure (6), born July 17, 1897;
married August 21, 1920, Mildred Myers.
  494. viii. Harry Hop McClure (6), born December 27, 1899;
died June 7, 1922.
  495. ix. Cloyd Latham McClure (6), born January 12, 1903;
married April 7, 1927, Minnie Hazen.

245. George Washington McClure (5), son of Joseph Perry
McClure (4) and Catherine Ann Devin, was born July 17, 1850; died
November 1, 1922; married March 21, 1871, Catherine Decker, born
November 25, 1848; died December 28, 1919, daughter of Abe Decker
and Susan Spain.

Children: 8

  496. i. Clarence Loren McClure (6), born May 7, 1872;
died July 16, 1873.
  497. ii. Ida Ann McClure (6), born December 1, 1873;
died January 11, 1925.
  498. iii. Daniel Prentice McClure (6), born November 12,
1875.
  499. iv. Alma M. McClure (6), born December 29, 1878;
died July 13, 1879.
  500. v. Mary Melitta McClure (6), born November 6,
1883; died July 12, 1884.
  501. vi. Ethel Adelaide McClure (6), born February 5,
1886; died December 16, 1932.
+ 502. vii. Minnie Eva McClure (6), born March 26, 1889.
  503. viii. Artimesa McClure (6), born June 23, 1890;
died January 16, 1943.

246. Nancy Virginia McClure (5), daughter of Joseph Perry
McClure (4) and Catherine Ann Devin, was born December 15, 1852
near Princeton, Indiana; died January 14, 1946 near Princeton,
Indiana and was buried in Maple Cemetery; married May 28, 1885
by Rev. William Clark of the General Baptist Church (as his
second wife), William Crawford Hudelson, born December 4, 1844
near Princeton, Indiana; died June 4, 1921 near Princeton, Indiana
and was buried at Maple Cemetery, son of Alexander Hudelson and
Julia Ann Kellog. He had married (1) Joanna Tucker, born April
24, 1847; died April 2, 1871 and was buried in the Warnock Cemetery
daughter of Owen Tucker and Winnifred _____. William Crawford
Hudelson was a farmer, school teacher, bank director. He served
in Company H, 17th Indiana Regiment and saw action at Elizabeth-
town, Kentucky; Chattanooga, Tennessee, Chickmaugua; Rome, Georgia;
and Selma, Alabama. He was a student of D. Eckley Hunter and

attended.the Normal at Merom, Indiana.

Children: 3

504. i. Anna Hudelson (6), born October 3, 1886 near
Princeton, Indiana. Miss Hudelson furnished much of the information relating to the descendants Of John Warwick (2) and Mary
Powell. She lives at Route 2, Princeton, Indiana.
+ 505. ii. Earl Hudelson (6), born October 16, 1888.
+ 506. iii. Laura Hudelson (6), born October 28, 1893.

247. Franklin Perry Prentice McClure (5), son of Joseph
Perry McClure (4) and Catherine Ann Devin, was born May 9, 1855;
died March 5, 1934 in Princeton, Indiana; married May 23, 1889,
Martha Arbuthnot, born October 28, 1858; died January 2,1908,
daughter of Ulyses Arbuthnot and Loraine Davis.

Children: 3

507. i. Nellie McClure (6), born August 8, 1893; died
August 19,1953; married March 1922, Sidney Williams, died March
1923 of Anniston, Alabama. No children.
508. ii. Naomi McClure (6), born June 9, 1896; married
June 2, 1927, Raymond Dill, son of Willard and Rhoda Dill.
+ 509. iii. Olive McClure (6), born September 6, 1899.

248. Robert Augustus McClure (5), son of Henry Clay McClure
(4) and Permelia McClure (5), was born January 3, 1843 in Princeton, Indiana; died 1905 in Gibson City, Illinois, married Ann
McLaughlin.

Children: 5

510. i. Elizabeth McClure (6), married J. P. Lowry.
They have two children.
+ 511. ii. Mary McClure (6).
512. iii. Katherine McClure (6).
+ 513. iv. John Clay McClure (6).
514. v. Edyth Lyle McClure (6), married (1) _____
Nagel; married (2) _____. She has two children.

250. Horace Adrian McClure (5), son of Henry Clay McClure
(4) and Permelia McClure (5), was born September 26, 1852; died
February 19, 1934 in Gibson City, Illinois; married Ella Martin.

Children: 2

515. i. Ethel A. McClure (6), born November 23, 1881;
married _____ McCall.
516. ii. Lewis M. McClure (6), born February 11, 1885.

251. Herman Warwick McClure (5), son of Henry Clay McClure
(4) and Permelia McClure (5), was born August 16, 1855; died 1923

in Atlanta, Illinois; married (1) March 16, 1881, Ella May Vance, died July 30, 1894; married (2) October 22, 1895, Harriet Montgomery, died 1953, daughter of Henry Montgomery and Luna Ann Beardsley.

Children: 5 - first marriage

517. i.   Mabel L. McClure (6), born March 16, 1892; married _____ Fisher.
518. ii. Vance E. McClure (6), born January 5, 1884.
519. iii. Julia McClure (6), born December 31, 1885; married _____ McKown.
520. iv. Cora McClure (6), born March 6, 1889; married _____ McCord.
521. v.   Adelle McClure (6), born April 15, 1891.

252. Frances Olivia McClure (5), daughter of Henry Clay McClure (4) and Permelia McClure (5), was born December 6, 1858; died March 15, 1897; married John Jones.

Children: 2

522. i.   Marshall Jones (6), born 1885.
523. ii. Ruth Jones (6), born 1892.

253. George Lincoln McClure (5), son of Henry Clay McClure (4) and Permelia McClure (5), was born September 27, 1863; died March 6, 1950; married (1) Alice Kirkpatrick; married (2) Lucile Revin, died 1955 at Normal, Illinois.

Children: 5 - second marriage

524. i.   Henry McClure (6).
525. ii.   Robin McClure (6).
526. iii. Louis McClure (6).
527. iv.   Josephine McClure (6), married _____ Lafferty.
They have a daughter, Barbara Lafferty (7).
528. v.   Stephen McClure (6), married _____.

261. Charles Jacob Cameron (5), son of Andrew Warwick Lewis Cameron (4) and Ellen McCue Hyde, died in 1877; married November 9, 1864, Isabella E. Tate, born September 6, 1843; died January 27, 1909, daughter of William Poage Tate and Margaret Keyser. He served in the CSA in the 14th Virginia Regiment under General J.E.B. Stuart.

Children: 4

529. i.   William Tate Cameron (6), M.D., born October 2, 1866 in Bath County, Virginia; died April 12, 1940 in Randolph County, West Virginia; married June 19, 1890, Mamie Preston Gatewood (6), died 1912, daughter of Andrew Cameron Lewis Gatewood and Mary S. Warwick.

530. ii.   Ellen Warwick Cameron (6), born November 27, 1868; married (1) Robert Alexander Palmer; married (2) Rear Admiral H. O. Dunn. No children.
531. iii.   Margaret Keyser Cameron (6), born December 25, 1873; married June 24, 1894, John Newton Opie, Jr.
531. iv.   Charlye Cameron (6), born June 6, 1877; married February 21, 1900, John James Crews, son of Archibald Aaron Crews and Eliza Jane Loudermilk.

263.   Mary Catherine Gatewood (5), daughter of Warwick Gatewood (4) and Margaret Beale, was born in 1827; died in 1874; married June 9, 1852 in Bath County, Virginia, (as his second wife), Cisereo Bias, who was brought to the United States by his brother from Venice; died in Richmond, Virginia in 1866 and was buried at Warm Springs, Virginia. Two of their children were:

532. i.   James W. W. Bias (6), a Presbyterian minister; died in North Carolina.
533. ii.   Kate Bias (6), a missionary in Brazil; married in Brazil in 1894, Rev. Frank A. Cowan.

267.   Andrew Cameron Lewis Gatewood (5), son of Samuel Vance Gatewood (4) and Eugenia Massie, was born in 1843; married December 1, 1869 in Bath County, Virginia, Mary S. Warwick (5), born 1845, daughter of James Woods Warwick and Eliza Jane Gatewood. He was a Colonel in the 11th Virginia (Bath) Cavalry, CSA.

Children: 6

534. i.   William Beale Gatewood (6), died August 5, 1943; aged 65; married (1) Goldie Yeager; married (2) Eva Mayo Gardner.
535. ii.   Eugene Samuel Gatewood (6), died April 23, 1954; married Minnie Rhea.
536, iii.   Massie Cameron Gatewood (6), married Kathyrn Hall. No children.
537, iv.   Andrew Warwick Gatewood (6), married Brownie Yeager. No children.
538, v.   Mamie Preston Gatewood (6), died 1912; married June 19, 1890, William Tate Cameron (6), M.D., born October 2, 1866 in Bath County, Virginia; died April 12, 1940 in Randolph County, West Virginia, son of Charles Jacob Cameron and Isabella E. Tate.
539. vi.   Eliza Pleasant Gatewood (6), married John Mackee Dunlap, born 1874; died 1934, son of Robert Kerr Dunlap and Elisabeth Moore.

270.   John Andrew Warwick (5), son of James Woods Warwick (4) and Eliza Ann Hyde, was born March 30, 1837; died May 29, 1900; married October 13, 1869 in Bath County, Virginia, Martha Cochran Lewis, born July 26, 1844; died May 24, 1929, daughter of Samuel Lewis and Elizabeth R. Crawford. He served as a Lieutenant in the CSA.

Children: 1

540. i. Harry Warwick (6), married Jane Tate Van Lear.
No children.

279. Sally Gatewood Warwick (5), daughter of John Wood
Warwick (4) and Hannah Moffett Gatewood, married Dr. John Ligon.

Children: 9

541. i. Belle Ligon (6), married C. P. Dorr, an
attorney, Webster Springs, West Virginia.
542. ii. Elizabeth Ligon (6), married Dr. Frank F.
McClintic, son of James McClintic and Marietta Mann.
543. iii. Lou Ligon (6), married J. Jackson Coyner of
Augusta County, Virginia. They lived at Clover Lick, West
Virginia.
544. iv. Annette Ligon (6), married Luther Coyner, a
brother of J. Jackson Coyner. They lived at Clover Lick, West
Virginia.
545. v. Rosa Ligon (6), married Charles Arbuckle.
They migrated to Missouri.
546. vi. Eva Ligon (6), married Henry McNeel, Hillsboro,
West Virginia. He was killed instantly when thrown from a horse.
547. vii. Mabel Ligon (6), married Major Hankins, Richmond,
Virginia.
548. viii. Georgia Ligon (6), married _____ King. They
lived at the Ligon home.
549. ix. Yancey Ligon (6), married in Kentucky. He was
a superintendent of a construction company in Kentucky and was
killed by a dissatisfied laborer.

287. Paul McNeel Warwick (6), son of William Fechtig Warwick
(5) and Phoebe Anthea Pray, was born in 1856; married November 29,
1888 in Bath County, Virginia, Susan F. Simpson, born in 1857,
daughter of Preston R. Simpson

+ 550. i. Cornelia Ruth Warwick (7).
551. ii. William Warwick (7), married Edna Hiner. They
had one child that died in infancy.

288. Robert Warwick (6), son of William Fechtig Warwick
(5) and Phoebe Anthea Pray, married Signora Gwin, daughter of
Samuel Gwin and Ellen Dever. (See Gwin Family). They lived
in Alva, Oklahoma.

Children: 2

+ 552. i. Constance Warwick (7).
553. ii. William Warwick (7), died young.

291. George Craig Warwick (6), son of William Fechtig
Warwick (5) and Phoebe Anthea Pray, married in 1896, Annie Weldom

Cleek, born December 26, 1878; died January 25, 1955, daughter
of David Gwin Cleek and Annie Maria Louisa Weldon. (See Cleek
Family).

Children: 7

554.	i.	George W. Warwick (7).
+ 555.	ii.	James Woods Warwick (7).
+ 556.	iii.	David Warwick (7).
+ 557.	iv.	Harry Lee Warwick (7), born November 12, 1904.
+ 558.	v.	Edward Gathright Warwick (7).
559.	vi.	Grace Warwick (7).
+ 560.	vii.	Lucy Warwick (7).

292. Charles Fechtig Warwick (6), son of William Fechtig
Warwick (5) and Phoebe Anthea Pray, was born August 31, 1865;
died October 31, 1938; married January 20, 1909, Mary Constance
Kellison, born September 9, 1889.

Children: 9

+ 561. i. Robert Nelson Warwick (7), born December 12,
1909.
562. ii. Hazel Lockridge Warwick (7), born August 19,
1911; married in 1951, Luther Thompson.
563. iii. Lilliam Charlsy Warwick (7), born September
8, 1913; married June 13, 1934, David Blaine Roberts.
564. iv. Mary Anthea Warwick (7), born February 18,
1916; married June 11, 1934, Albert Peary Robinson.
565. v. Bessie Pauline Warwick (7), born January 30,
1918; married June 13, 1956, Marvin Fisher.
566. vi. Gertrude Bradford Warwick (7), born April 29,
1920; married September 16, 1948, Finnan Woods. She is a R.N.
567. vii. Winston Frazier Warwick (7), born August 19,
1923; married April 16, 1950, Delphia Sue Childs.
568. viii. Geraldine Frances Warwick (7), born February
25, 1925; married June 27, 1950, John C. Knick. She is a R.N.
569. ix. Vincent Gray Warwick (7), born February 8,
1927. He is now serving in the Navy.

293. James Warwick (6), son of William Fechtig Warwick (5)
and Phoebe Anthea Pray, married Eva Price.

Children: 3

570. i. Gladys Warwick (7), married Clayton Smith.
571. ii. May Warwick (7), married Robert Patterson.
572. iii. Calvin Warwick (7), married Alice Gunn.

294. Amelia E. Warwick (6), daughter of William Fechtig
Warwick (5) and Phoebe Anthea Pray, was born July 16, 1853; died
October 22, 1922; married (1) January 18, 1872 in Pocahontas
County, West Virginia, George M. Dilley, son of John Dilley and

271

Naomi McNeil; married (2), March 29, 1889, Stephen Hopkins Wandless.

Children: 3 - first marriage

+ 573. i. Prime S. Dilley (7), married Bertha Burns.
+ 574. ii. Emma Dilley (7).
575. iii. Bessie Dilley (7), married Frank Hughes.

295. Amanda Gabriella Warwick (6), daughter of William Fechtig Warwick (5) and Phoebe Anthea Pray, was born in 1871; married May 16, 1894, John L. Landes, born 1871, son of John Landes and Catherine _____.

Children: 5

576. i. Warwick Landes (7), married _____ Ryder.
577. ii. Enid Landes (7), unmarried. She is a teacher.
578. iii. Mabel Landes (7), married Glenn Roudasill.
She is a R.N.
579. iv. John Landes (7).
580. v. James Landes (7).

298. Elvira Louisa Byrd (6), daughter of William Wallace Byrd and Catherine Hidy Warwick (5), married William McClune.

Children: 3

+ 581. i. Minnie McClune (7).
582. ii. Emma McClune (7), married George Carlisle.
583. iii. Lee McClune (7).

300. John Henry Byrd (6), son of William Wallace Byrd and Catherine Hidy Warwick (5), was born May 12, 1859; died March 3, 1946; married (1) Ida Criser; married (2) Rosa Venable.

Children: 2 - first marriage

584. i. Ida Byrd (7), married Rev. F. M. Lucas.
585. ii. Ernest Byrd (7), married Blanche Davenport.

Children: 1 - second marriage

586. iii. Bernice Byrd (7), married (1) _____ Rhea; married (2) Arch Snead.

302. William Lee Byrd (6), son of William Wallace Byrd and Catherine Hidy Warwick (5), married Laura Wright.

Children: 2

587. i. Robert Byrd (7), Greensboro, North Carolina.
588. ii. Ruth Byrd (7), married _____ Hillman, Norfolk, Virginia.

304. Melissa A. Matheny (6), daughter of Daniel Matheny and Sarah Elizabeth Warwick (5), was born in 1855; died March 3, 1935; married in 1877, Charles T. Bird.

Children: 7

589. i. Sallie Bird (7), married Rev. S. Roger Snead, born 1867; died 1930.
590. ii. Cecil Bird (7), married (1) _____; married (2) Bessie Scruggs.
591. iii. Clarence Bird (7), married Wilda Helen Rexrode.
592. iv. David Given Bird (7), married Gladys White.
593. v. Clinton Bird (7), died unmarried.
594. vi. Kenneth Bird (7).
595. vii. Mabel Bird (7), married A. Clyde Herold.

306. Robert Lee Matheny (6), son of Daniel Matheny and Sarah Elizabeth Warwick (5), died in 1906; married Lula Gabbart.

Children: 3

596. i. Wallace Matheny (7).
597. ii. Brown Matheny (7), died in infancy.
598. iii. Edith Matheny (7), died in infancy.

312. Nancy Jane Siple (6), daughter of George Washington Siple and Hannah Rebecca Hopkins Warwick (5), married Pierce Wooddell.

Children: 6

599. i. Joe Wooddell (7), married Mamie Curry.
600. ii. William Wooddell (7), married Jessie Gladwell.
601. iii. Harry Wooddell (7), married Rachel Wooddell.
602. iv. Cordelia Wooddell (7), married Irby Beard.
603. v. Eva Wooddell (7), married Carl McCoy.
604. vi. Fay Wooddell (7), married _____ Cooper.

313. Anna Siple (6), daughter of George Washington Siple and Hannah Rebecca Hopkins Warwick (5), married William Jackson.

Children: 7

605. i. Hattie Jackson (7), married Connell Gillespie.
606. ii. Ruth Jackson (7), married _____ Furman.
607. iii. Lucy May Jackson (7), married Harland Brown.
608. iv. Mary Jackson (7), married William Lowry.
609. v. Maude Jackson (7), married John Arbogast.
610. vi. Frank Jackson (7).
611. vii. Paul Jackson (7).

314. Mary Katherine Siple (6), daughter of George Washington Siple and Hannah Rebecca Hopkins Warwick (5), born August 17, 1866,

a twin to Joel Wade Hampton; died January 26, 1903; married Bernard Francis McElwee.

Children: 6

612. i. Lillian May McElwee (7), born August 14, 1886; died February 1, 1955; married October 1905, Edgar Hugh McGlaughlin, born July 18, 1882; died July 3, 1955, son of Andrew Matthews McGlaughlin and Mary Margaret Price. (See Lightner Family).
+ 613. ii. June McElwee (7).
+ 614. iii. Winfred McElwee (7).
615. iv. Callie McElwee (7`, died in infancy.
616. v. (Infant) McElwee (7), a twin, died in infancy.
617. vi. (Infant) McElwee (7), a twin to 616, died in infancy.

315. Joel Wade Hampton Siple (6), son of George Washington Siple and Hannah Rebecca Hopkins (5), was born August 17, 1866; married (1) Annie May Lightner, born March 6, 1874, daughter of Charles Adam Lightner and Mary Davis Hamilton; married (2) September 18, 1901, Brassie Gibson.

Children: 7 - second marriage

618. i. Janet Siple (7), married _____ Uttinger.
619. ii. Nelle Parker Siple (7), married (1) Henry McNeel; married (2) Collett Gay.
620. iii. Hallie Siple (7), married (1) _____; married (2) _____ Tabor.
621. iv. Nancy Siple (7), married Sterling McNeel.
622. v. Robert Siple (7), died young.
623. vi. Hunter Siple (7).
624. vii. Rodney Siple (7).

316. William Madison Siple (6), son of George Washington Siple and Hannah Rebecca Hopkins Warwick (5), was born April 11, 1864; died April 12, 1936; married March 16, 1921, Alice Rayburn.

Children: 6

625. i. Roy Siple (7).
626. ii. Oden Siple (7).
627. iii. Basil Siple (7).
628. iv. Colleen Siple (7), married Lake Oliver.
629. v. Verna Siple (7), died in an automobile accident March 2, 1937. She was a R. N.
630. vi. Alma Siple (7), R.N.

318. Lucy Siple (6), daughter of George Washington Siple and Hannah Rebecca Hopkins Warwick (5), married November 6, 1901, Samuel Sheets.

Children: 1

631. i.   ,June Sheets (7), died in the influenza epidemic.

322. Mary Amaret Seybert (6), daughter of Eli Seybert and
Louisa Susan Warwick (5), married Morgan Matheny.

Children: 6

632. i.   Annie Matheny (7), married _____Grant,
Lambert, Oklahoma.
    633. ii.   Ira Matheny (7), married Grace Marshall.
    634. iii.   Leslie Matheny (7).
    635. iv.   Henry Matheny (7).
    636. v.   Lee Matheny (7).
    637. vi.   Wesley Matheny (7), died in infancy.

323. Otis D. Warwick (6), son of Peter Hull Warwick (5) and
Sarah Caroline Matheny, died March 30, 1926; married June 28,1893
in Pocahontas County, West Virginia, Annie M. Carter, born October 19, 1873; died June 6, 1945, daughter of A. Burton Carter and
Susan Jane Aulridge.

Children: 3

638. i.   Gladys M. Warwick (7), married October 12,
1915 in Pocahontas County, West Virginia, Edward M. Baker.
    639. ii.   Marjorie L. Warwick (7), married June 19, 1919
in Pocahontas County, West Virginia, Robert W. Howard.
    640. iii.   Jewel Dent Warwick (7), married December 22,
1930 in Pocahontas County, West Virginia, Dewey T. Mullins.

324. Forrest Warwick (6), son of Peter Hull Warwick (5)
and Sarah Caroline Matheny, married Bertie Nottingham.

Children: 3

+   641. i.   Eula Hill Warwick (7).
    642. ii.   James Berlin Warwick (7), died in young manhood.
+   643. iii.   Harvey Hull Warwick (7), born 1913.

325. Jessie Lee Warwick (6), son of Peter Hull Warwick (5)
and Sarah Caroline Matheny, died July 21, 1939; married in 1898,
Nancy Carolina Cleek, born in 1871; died November 20, 1918,
daughter of David Gwin Cleek and Annie Maria Louisa Weldon. (See
Cleek Family).

Children: 5

+   644. i.   Ruth Lee Warwick (7), born 1899.
+   645. ii.   Sallie Weldon Warwick (7).
+   646. iii.   Ralph Neil Warwick (7).
+   647. iv.   Mabel Claire Warwick (7).
    648. v.   Mary Cordelia Warwick (7), married Fred Richards.

330. Nancy Esther Givens Warwick (6), daughter of John Robert Warwick (5) and Mary Jane Cleek, was born March 27, 1879; died July 12, 1941 in Delta, York County, Pennsylvania; married October 4, 1905 in Pocahontas County, West Virginia, Henry Abbott Wickes, born July 19, 1867 in Wayne County, Pennsylvania; died February 4, 1916, son of Benjamin Franklin Wickes and Carolina L. Abbott.

Children: 5

+ 649. i.   Theordore J. Wickes (7), born June 14, 1906.
  650. ii.   Virginia Warwick Wickes (7), born February 9, 1909 at Clarksburg, West Virginia, a R.N., lives at Norristown, Pennsylvania.
+ 651. iii. Mildred Eleanor Wickes (7), born October 25, 1912.
+ 652. iv.   Robert Henry Wickes (7), born May 1, 1914.
+ 653. v.   Frank Abbott Cleek Wickes (7), born December 1, 1915.

341. Nancy Elizabeth Music (6), daughter of Herod Music and Mary E. Warwick (5), married (as his second wife), John Wesley Harmon, born January 18, 1840, son of Laxton Harmon and Elizabeth Ann Simpson.

Children: 1

+ 654. i. - Grace Harmon (7).

344. Nancy J. Waters (6), daughter of William A. Waters and Eliza Jones (5), was born November 8, 1841; died April 9, 1879; married February 25, 1864, Thomas J. Johnson, died May 1, 1890.

Children: 6

  655. i.   George W. Johnson (7).
  656. ii.   James A. Johnson (7).
  657. iii. Elmer Johnson (7).
  658. iv.   Mary Johnson (7).
  659. v.   Ella Johnson (7).
  660. vi.   (Infant) Johnson (7).

359. Mary E. Jones (6), daughter of Franklin Jones (5) and Comfort Sharp, was born May 22, 1861; died 1932; married October 16, 1884, Theodore W. Crawford.

Children: 6

  661. i.   Eva M. Crawford (7), born October 19, 1885.
  662. ii.   Franklin L. Crawford (7), born March 29, 1887; died October 1933.
  663. iii. Opha T. Crawford (7), born July 31, 1889; married Lowell Mauck. They have two children.

664. iv. Minnie J. Crawford (7), born February 5, 1892.
665. v.   Delia A. Crawford (7), born July 5, 1894.
666. vi. Mary Mabel Crawford (7), born December 19, 1900;
died July 1901.

360. Sarah Alice Jones (6), daughter of Franklin Jones (5)
and Comfort Sharp, was born January 2, 1865; married September
3, 1885, W. Oscar Jones.

Children: 6

667. i.   Effie E. Jones (7).
668. ii.   Elsie C. Jones (7).
669. iii. Fannie F. Jones (7).
670. iv.   Albert T. Jones (7).
671. v.   Roxia A. Jones (7), a twin to Ruth M.
672. vi.   Ruth M. Jones (7), a twin to Roxia A., died.

369. Eliza Mauck (6), daughter of Abraham Mauck and Nancy
Jones (5), was born August 7, 1850; married James Albert Tichenor,
born September 22, 1851; died May 23, 1900.

Children: 2

    673. i.   Mabel Elizabeth Tichenor (7).
+   674. ii. Maud Tichenor (7).

381. Willis Armstrong (6), son of William S. Armstrong and
Emily Smith (5), was born May 23, 1847; married August 16, 1868,
Naomi Clark.

Children: 8

+   675. i.   Elmer Armstrong (7), born May 28, 1869.
    676. ii.   W. C. Armstrong (7).
    677. iii. George Armstrong (7).
    678. iv.   Emily F. Armstrong (7), married John G. Benson.
They have three children.
    679. v.   Eliza G. Armstrong (7).
+   680. vi.   Arthur P. Armstrong (7), born February 8, 1883.
    681. vii. Ora K. Armstrong (7).
    682. viii. Stella B. Armstrong (7), married W. F. Rainey.

382. Warwick Armstrong (6), son of William S. Armstrong and
Emily Smith (5), was born February 6, 1849; married Nancy Mauck.

Children: 12

    683. i.   Clara Armstrong (7), born November 29, 1872;
married Oscar Mounts.
    684. ii.   Arthur Armstrong (7).
    685. iii. Clarence Armstrong (7).
    686. iv.   Henry Armstrong (7).

277

687. v.   Mary Armstrong (7).
688. vi.   Florence Armstrong (7), married Oscar Bruce.
689. vii.   Ada Armstrong (7), married _____ McCarty.
690. viii. Luther Armstrong (7).
691. ix.   Clemma Armstrong (7).
692. x.   Williard Armstrong (7).
693. xi.   Chester Armstrong (7).
694. xii.   Ensel Armstrong (7).

385. James H. Armstrong (6), son of William S. Armstrong
and Emily Smith (5), was born March 31, 1858; married July 6,
1879, Lilia Grace Bingham, born April 8, 1860; daughter of Garner
Bingham and Jane Roberts.

    Children: 11

695. i.   Charles Armstrong (7), died at age 13 months.
696. ii.   Mary L. Armstrong (7), born July 22, 1882;
married John S. Cushman.
697. iii.   Harvey Armstrong (7), married Florence Brumfield.
698. iv.   Lemuel Armstrong (7), twin to William Edgar,
married Nettie Spore.
699. v.   William Edgar Armstrong (7), twin to Lemuel.
700. vi.   Elva F. Armstrong (7), died August 12, 1913;
married Orville Spore.
701. vii.   John B. Armstrong (7), died in 1955; married
Edith Woods.
702. viii. Flora L. Armstrong (7).
703. ix.   Ruth Armstrong (7).
704. x.   Hershel Armstrong (7), died at age 6 months.
705. xi.   James H. Armstrong (7).

389. John Willis Johnson (6), son of Levi Johnson and Louisa
Smith (5), was born December 19, 1849; died September 29, 1901;
married November 22, 1876, Lucinda Jane Thompson, born February
12, 1857; died May 31, 1934, daughter of Anderson Thompson and
Eliza Mauck.

    Children: 3

706. i.   Louella Johnson (7), born September 28, 1878;
died 1940.
+   707. ii.   Elsie Johnson (7), born February 1, 1887.
708. iii.   John Willis Johnson, Jr. (7), born March 11,
1890.

390. George Washington Johnson, Jr. (6), son of Levi
Johnson and Louisa Smith (5), was born June 2, 1852; died
February 23, 1936; married January 21, 1877, Marovia Johnson,
daughter of George Buckley Johnson and Lizzie Martin.

    Children: 2

+   709. i.   Laura Louella Johnson (7), born September 9,
1877.
     710. ii. (Infant son) Johnson(7), died in infancy.

     392. Emma A. Johnson (6), daughter of Levi Johnson and
Louisa Smith (5), was born October 14, 1858; married September
5, 1878, J. D. Thompson, born November 20, 1858, son of Anderson
Thompson and Eliza Mauck.

     Children: 3

     711. i.   Archie Thompson (7).
     712. ii.   Will S. Thompson (7).
     713. iii. Albert Thompson (7).

     393. Warwick D. Johnson (6), son of Levi Johnson and Louisa
Smith (5), was born February 1, 1865; married May 12, 1887, Phena
A. Boren, daughter of Samuel Boren and Seralda Marvel.

     Children: 5

     714. i.   Mattie F. Johnson (7), born November 21, 1888;
married Harvey Witherspoon.
+   715. ii. Warren Boren Johnson (7), born February 13, 1890.
     716. iii. Warner Lee Johnson (7), born January 25, 1895.
     717. iv. George Washington Johnson (7), born December 18,
1897.
     718. v.   Ella Marie Johnson (7), born November 25, 1899.

     396. George Washington Smith (6), son of Warwick Smith (5)
and Margaret M. Simpson, was born June 22, 1859; died October 31,
1931; married March 27, 1890, Wilmina Montgomery, daughter of
Benjamin F. Montgomery and Hannah Sharp.

     Children: 8

     719. i.   Lyle Warwick Smith (7), born October 31, 1892.
     720. ii.   Chauncy M. Smith (7), born May 6, 1894.
     721. iii. Willis F. Smith (7), born February 29, 1896.
     722. iv.   Heber W. Smith (7), born February 9, 1898.
     723. v.   Margaret Smith (7), born April 10, 1900;
married _____ Wade.
     724. vi.   Madeline Smith (7), born February 18, 1902;
died February 24, 1902.
     725. vii. Mona A. Smith (7), born July 5, 1906; married
_____ McFetridge.
     726. viii. Norman Smith (7), born May 25, 1908.

     399. Julius Mauck (6), son of Samuel Mauck, Sr. and Eliza-
beth Skelton (5), married (1) Cordelia McNeeley of Princeton,
Indiana; married (2) in 1870, Sarah Ellen Wasson, born January
22, 1852. They moved to Missouri.

     Children: 4 - second marriage
279

727. i.   Corwin Mauck (7).
728. ii.   Mary Mauck (7).
729. iii.   Mattie Mauck (7).
730. iv.   Clay Mauck (7).

401. Joseph Mauck (6), son of Samuel Mauck, Sr. and Elizabeth Skelton (5), married Louisa Warwick (5), daughter of Jacob
G. Warwick and Elizabeth Skelton.

Children: 2

731. i.   Charles Mauck (7), born December 5, 1875.
732. ii.   Richard Mauck (7), born September 29, 1877.

402. Mary Mauck (6), daughter of Samuel Mauck, Sr. and
Elizabeth Skelton (5), was born July 17, 1850; died February 4,
1939; married (1) in 1867, Luther Abner; married (2) Louis H.
Wheeler, died December 1906.

Children: 1 - first marriage

733. i.   Hattie Abner (7), died.

Children: 1 = second marriage

734. ii.   Joseph Walter Wheeler (7), married Maude _____.

404. Samuel Q. Mauck (6), son of Henry Mauck, Sr. and
Amanda Skelton (5), was born September 14, 1854; married
February 5, 1875, Julia E. Stewart, born March 1, 1855.

Children: 6

735. i.   Amanda E. Mauck (7).
736. ii.   C. Henry Mauck (7).
737. iii.   J. Frank Mauck (7).
738. iv.   Nora Mauck (7).
739. v.   S. Noble Mauck (7).
740. vi.   Mary M. Mauck (7).

411. Elizabeth Skelton (6), daughter of Barnes Skelton (5)
and Lucinda Mauck, married (1) in 1875, Joseph Thompson; married
(2) December 28, 1878, A. N. Bennett. There were six children
of the second marriage, names unknown.

Children: 1 - first marriage

741. i.   Maria Thompson (7).

427. Mary Skelton (6), daughter of Newton O. Skelton (5)
and Catherine Richards, married Jerald Welborn.

Children: 1

742. i. Mary Catherin Welborn (7).

429. Lily Ervin (6), daughter of John Thomas Ervin and
Maria Skelton (5), married Joseph French.

743. i.   Anna French (7).
744. ii.   Lucius French (7).
745. iii. Sylvester J. French (7).

430. Emma Ervin (6), daughter of John Thomas Ervin and
Maria Skelton (5), married Stanley Crawford.

Children: 2

746. i.   Gertrude Crawford (7).
747. ii. Edith Crawford (7).

432. John H. Reavis (6), son of Samuel Reavis and Emily
Skelton (5), married _____ Milburn.

Children: 2

748. i.   Margaret Reavis (7).
749. ii. Samuel Reavis (7).

436. Etta Skelton (6), daughter of Levi Skelton (5) and
Elizabeth J. Humphrey, was born January 1867; married November
1, 1885, Millard Lucas.

Children: 1

750. i.   Arthur Lucas (7).

437. Mary Skelton (6), daughter of Levi Skelton (5) and
Elizabeth J. Humphrey, married September 7, 1887, John P. Moore.

Children: 3

751. i.   Willis Moore (7), born 1889.
752. ii.   Prentice Moore (7), born July 1895.
753. iii. John L. Moore (7), born October 1897.

438. Nannie Skelton (6), daughter of Levi Skelton (5) and
Elizabeth J. Humphrey, married Greenbury McCarty.

Children: 1

754. i.   Adolph McCarty (7).

440. Florence Emmerson (6), daughter of Columbus Emmerson
and Sarah Skelton (5), was born December 21, 1867; died 1956;
married Morton Woods.

281

755. i. Edith Woods (7).

441. Joseph L. Emmerson (6), son of Columbus Emmerson and Sarah Skelton (5), was born September 29, 1870; married May 12, 1897, Agnes Pegram.

Children: 2

756. i. Herman L. Emmerson (7), born April 26, 1898.
757. ii. Hildred Emmerson (7), born May 4, 1901.

444. Gussie Emmerson (6), daughter of Columbus Emmerson and Sarah Skelton (5), was born April 51, 1878; married in 1900, Oscar Daugherty, died 1933.

Children: 1

758. i. Doris E. Daugherty (7), born May 5, 1901; died May 1950.

445. Lawrence O. Montgomery (6), son of Benjamin F. Montgomery and Harriet Skelton (5), was born September 23, 1880; married March 8, 1899, Sarah E. Fisher.

Children: 1

759. i. Franklin Montgomery (7), born 1900.

451. Joseph Perry Key (6), son of James Wesley Key and Eleanor Jane McClure (5), was born July 13, 1861; died June 4, 1907; married September 28, 1898, Phoebe Boyd, born April 5, 1867 in Enniskillen, Ireland; died March 28, 1907 in Princeton, Indiana, daughter of Edward Boyd and his second wife, Catherine Cairns.

Children: 3

+   760. i. Catherine Ellen Key (7), born February 18, 1900.
    761. ii. Margaret Elizabeth Key (7), born February 12, 1903; died June 25, 1905.
    762. iii. Leonora Helen Key (7), born March 26, 1905; married in 1952, Chester Langston.

454. William Finis Key (6), son of James Wesley Key and Eleanor Jane McClure (5), was born July 18, 1866; died April 3, 1948; married November 21, 1900, Eva M. Goff, born September 29, 1870; died April 17, 1924, daughter of Julius and Isophena Goff.

Children: 4

763. i. William Franklin Key (7), born January 3, 1902; married March 26, 1932, Mrs. Ruth Moore.
+   764. ii. Mary Ellen Key (7), born March 18, 1903.

282

765, iii.   Helen Lucile Key (7), born March 24, 1905; died
November 6, 1925.
+   766; iv.   Charles Wesley Key (7), born January 8, 1916.

457.   Margaret Elizabeth Key (6), daughter of James Wesley
Key and Eleanor Jane McClure (5), was born September 3, 1871;
married October 14, 1891, John Howard Stewart, born February 1,
1871; died March 25, 1916, son of Thomas Stewart and Susan
Laura Hudelson.

Children: 4

     767. i.   Eleanor Stewart (7), born February 16, 1892.
+   768. ii.   Ruth Stewart (7), born June 21, 1893.
+   769; iii. Margaret Stewart (7), born November 21, 1901.
     770; iv.   John Howard Stewart (7), born December 19,
1905; married April 1935, Beulah Kolb, daughter of Joseph and
Margaret May Kolb;

458.   Robert Sherman Key (6), son of James Wesley Key and
Eleanor Jane McClure (5), was born May 22, 1873; died December
27, 1952; married August 16, 1905, Geneva Harvey, born January
24, 1877, daughter of Thomas and Sarah Frances Harvey.

Children: 3

+   771. i.   Thomas Wesley Key (7), born January 24, 1909.
     772. ii.   Ethel Key (7), born March 17, 1911; died
October 17, 1943.
+   773. iii. Jennie Key (7), born February 3, 1913.

461.   Lawrence Wheeler (6), son of Henry Gibson Wheeler
and Mary Brown McClure (5), was born October 9, 1863; died
December 6, 1906; married November 11, 1897, Flora Massey,
daughter of John Massey and Julia Kirkpatrick.

Children: 2

+   774; i.   Lawrence Wheeler, Jr. (7), born November 25,
1898.
     775; ii.   Maurice Wheeler, (7), born January 21, 1901;
April 19, 1902..

463.   Mary Ellen McClure (6), daughter of Alexander Devin
McClure (5) and Sarah Green, was born November 9, 1868; died
September 4, 1943; married (1) December 23, 1889, Christropher
Opperman; married (2), October 30, 1912, Leonard Askins.

Children: 2 - first marriage

     776; i.   Marie Henrietta Opperman (7), born December
21, 1893; married March 11, 1915, Roy F. Moore, died 1940.
     777; ii.   Margaret Elizabeth Opperman (7), born September

283

20, 1905; married (1) March 11, 1915, Charles B. Jarratt; married
(2) Paul Johnson.

465. Clara McClure (6), daughter of Alexander Devin McClure
(5) and Maria Webber, was born November 6, 1879; married November
6, 1898, John Julian Palmer.

Children: 7

   778. i. Dorothy Inez Palmer (7), born September 25,
1899; married Millard Brown.
+   779, ii. Janice Ada Palmer (7), born October 25, 1902.
   780. iii. Weber Palmer (7), born August 14, 1906; married
(1) Margaret E. Bell; married (2) _____.
+   781. iv. Charlotte Palmer (7), born December 24, 1907.
   782. v. Martha A. Palmer (7), born June 23, 1911;
married Charles Albright. They have two children.
   783, vi. Eugenia Palmer (7), born October 30, 1918;
married Carroll Gould. They have three children.
   784. vii. Iris Palmer (7), born July 4, 1924.

467. Alle McClure (6), daughter of Alexander Devin McClure
(5) and Maria Webber, was born September 28, 1881; died August 10,
1954; married (1) Clarence Barker, died August 18, 1913; married
(2), Robert Bullivant, died _____.

Children: 2 - first marriage

+   785. i. John Alexander Barker (7), born May 1905.
   786. ii. Alma Fay Barker (7), born September 18, 1908;
married in 1931, _____ Turpin.

468. Ada Ann McClure (6), daughter of Alexander Devin
McClure (5) and Maria Webber, was born November 26, 1886; married
February 6, 1907, Gordon Byron Bingham, born April 6, 1866; died
February 10, 1942, son of Gordon Byron Bingham and Minerva Stock-
well.

Children: 1

+   787. i. Mary Agnes Bingham (7), born June 23, 1908;663,

472. William Arthur Whitsitt (6), son of William B. Whitsitt and Margaret Elizabeth McClure (5), was born July 15, 1880;
married January 29, 1903, Leafie Myers, born June 28, 1883, daughter of Aaron Myers and Hannah Cole.

Children: 6

+   788. i. Helen Flo Whitsitt (7), born August 6, 1905.
+   789, ii. William Edward Whitsitt (7), born March 6,
1907.
+   790. iii. Robert Franklin Whitsitt (7), born March 15,
1909.

+   791. iv.   Wayne Arthur Whitsitt (7), born February 11,
1912.
+   792. v.   Samuel Joseph Whitsitt (7), born April 12,1915.
+   793. vi.   Don Ted Whitsitt (7), born July 19, 1921.

477. Maude McClure (6), daughter of Joseph David McClure
(5) and Isabelle Seamon, was born April 1, 1884; died April 16,
1938, married Hiram Nelson.

Children: 1

794. i.   Cecil Nelson (7), born March 18, 1917; married
_____.

478. Earle McClure (6), son of Joseph David McClure (5)
and Isabelle Seamon, was born December 19, 1889; died February
18, 1918; married Dollie _____.

Children: 2 .

795. i.   Earle McClure, Jr. (7).
796. ii.   Violet McClure (7).

487. Amy Alice McClure (6), daughter of William McGrady
McClure (5) and Martha Ellen Lathom, was born March 30, 1881;
died 1943; married March 12, 1903, Jesse B. French.

Children: 10

797. i.   Darwin French (7), born February 25, 1904;
married _____ Adkins.
798. ii.   William Glen French (7), born October 3, 1905;
married December 25, 1943, Gertrude Violet.
+   799. iii. Marjorie Louise French (7), born October 31,
1907.
800. iv.   Roy J. French (7), born January 23, 1910;
married Chloe _____.
+   801. v.   Dorothy Marie French (7), born March 6, 1912.
802. vi.   Doyle French (7), born June 29, 1914; married
September 28, 1940, Irene Taylor.
803. vii. George Simon French (7), born January 1, 1918.
804. viii. Martha Julia French (7), born December 23, 1920;
married Harry Smith.
805. ix.   Jesse French (7), born May 23, 1922.
806. x.   Charles Edward French (7), born September 13,
1926; married November 17, 1950, Dorothy Farrow.

488. Julia Ann McClure (6), daughter of William McGrady
McClure (5) and Martha Ellen Lathom, was born December 2, 1882;
died December 21, 1955; married April 26, 1902, Purnell W. Kell,
died November 29, 1909.

Children: 4

+   807. i.   Lester Lathom Kell (7), born September 21, 1903.
    808. ii.   Edna Kell (7), married Steve Chinaurd. They
have six children.
    809. iii. Martha Theresa Kell (7), died aged 13.
    810. iv.   George B. Kell (7), died aged 9.

489. Lester Latham McClure (6), son of William McGrady
McClure (5) and Martha Ellen Lathom, was born July 19, 1884;
married June 5, 1906, Mary Ethel Arburn.

Children: 3

+   811. i.   Elizabeth McClure (7).
    812. ii.   William McClure (7).
    813. iii. _____ (son) McClure (7).

490. James Devin McClure (6), son of William McGrady McClure
(5) and Martha Ellen Lathom, was born July 23, 1887; died January
28, 1945; married (1) September 6, 1908, Bertha Glazier; married
(2) _____ Bruce; married (3) in 1932, Amelia Duncan; married
(4) _____.

Children: 2 - first marriage

    814. i.   Von Raymond McClure (7), died March 17, 1925.
    815. ii.   James Arthur McClure (7).

Children: 3 - second marriage

    816. iii. William McClure (7), married _____ Cargil.
    817. iv.   Betty McClure (7).
    818. v.   Ellen McClure (7).

492. Percy William McClure (6), son of William McGrady
McClure (5) and Martha Ellen Lathom, was born October 5, 1894;
died October 13, 1955; married Glenora Ott.

Children: 1

    819. i.   Billy Lou McClure (7), married December 25,
1942, Rodney Anderson. They have two children.

502. Minnie Eva McClure (6), daughter of George Washington
McClure (5) and Catherine Decker, was born March 26, 1889; married
October 20, 1910, James Walker, died November 12, 1955.

Children: 2

    820. i.   Gordon McClure Walker (7), married _____.
    821. ii.   James Walker, Jr. (7), married _____.

505. Earl Hudelson (6), son of William Crawford Hudelson
and Nancy Virginia McClure (5), was born October 16, 1888; mar-

286

ried February 24, 1915, Helena H. Houf, born January 31, 1891, daughter of Henry Houf and Louisa Bishop. He received B.A. and B.M. degrees from Indiana University, and a Ph.D. degree from Columbia University, New York City. He taught in Tome School for Boys, Bloomington, Indiana and at the University of Minnesota, Michigan and West Virginia, where he is at the present. He saw educational service in Germany in 1945-1946.

Children: 2

    822. i.   Virginia Louisa Hudelson (7), born January 6, 1916. She lives in Phoenix, Arizona.
+   823. ii. William Henry Hudelson (7), born June 14,1917.

506. Laura Hudelson (6), daughter of William Crawford Hudelson and Nancy Virginia McClure (5), was born October 28, 1893; married August 12, 1924, Robert Allison Henry, born April 25, 1896, son of Hugh Renwick Henry and Mary Gertrude Allison. She received an A.B. degree from Indiana University and did graduate work at Columbia University, New York City. She taught school in Indiana and Minnesota.

Children: 1

    824. i.   Mary Ann Henry (7), born February 12, 1932; married July 9, 1955, James Nelson Wetherbee, born May 28, 1931, son of Solon Wetherbee and Alice Nelson of Marshall, Minnesota. She attended Hamline University and graduated from the University of Minnesota in 1955. He served in the military forces after World War II.

509. Olive McClure (6), daughter of Franklin Perry Prentice McClure (5) and Martha Arbuthnot, was born September 6, 1899; married September 10, 1918, Ralph M. Carithers.

Children: 7

+   025. i.   Joseph Prentice Carithers (7), born October 5, 1920.
+   826. ii. Samuel Warren Carithers (7), born November 13, 1921.
+   827. iii. James Ralph Carithers (7), born October 3, 1922.
+   828. iv. Mary Martha Carithers (7).
    829. v.   Florence Marie Carithers (7).
+   830. vi. Olive Jean Carithers (7), born March 16, 1925.
    831. vii. William Robert Carithers (7), born August 11, 1930.

511. Mary McClure (6), daughter of Robert Augustus McClure (5) and Ann McLaughlin, married William Strathers.

Children: 2

```
832,  i.     Hazel Strathers (7).
833.  ii.    Helen Strathers (7).
```

513, John Clay McClure (6), son of Robert Augustus McClure
(5) and Ann McLaughlin, married October 10, 1900, Bertha Beardsley.

Children: 2

```
834,  i.     Frederick Paul McClure (7).
835.  ii.    Robert McClure (7).
```

550. Cornelia Ruth Warwick (7), daughter of Paul McNeel
Warwick (6) and Susan Simpson, married Horace Franklin Hicks,
born 1878; died September 5, 1954, son of Ewing Hicks and Mary
Jane Chestnut.

Children: 6

```
836,  i.     Ralph Hicks (8), married Lucille Bonner. He
was killed in World War II.
837.  ii.    Harrison Merle Hicks (8), married Claudia
Stephenson.
838.  iii.   Clyde Hicks (8), died young in childhood.
+  839.  iv.    Gladys Hicks (8).
+  840,  v.     Willard Hicks (8).
+  841,  vi.    Lucille Hicks (8).
```

552. Constance Warwick (7), daughter of Robert Warwick (6)
and Signora Gwin, married William John McGill.

Children: 2

```
842,  i.     Merl McGill (8). He received an A.B. degree
from the University of Kentucky.
843.  ii.    Robert McGill (8), died.
```

555. James Woods Warwick (7), son of George Craig Warwick
(6) and Annie Weldon Cleek, married Thelma Elizabeth Snyder.

Children: 3

```
844,  i.     Norma Lorraine Warwick (8), born August 23, 1936.
845,  ii.    Brenda Carol Warwick (8), born March 6, 1946.
846,  iii.   Mary Ann Warwick (8), born May 4, 1949.
```

556. David Warwick (7), son of George Craig Warwick (6)
and Annie Weldon Cleek, married (1) Ina Bacon; married (2) Evelyn
Smith.

Children: 1 - first marriage

```
847,  i.     _____ (son) Warwick (8).
```

Children: 2 - second marriage

848.   ii.   Arlie Clarice Warwick (8), born July 19, 1940.
849.   iii. Betty Lou Warwick (8), born April 7, 1942.

557. Harry Lee Warwick (7), son of George Craig Warwick (6)
and Annie Weldon Cleek, was born November 12, 1904; died November
19, 1949 and was buried at Glen Haven Memorial Gardens, Spring-
field, Ohio; married July 24, 1924 at Minnehaha, West Virginia,
Elsie Davis Jones.

Children: 5

+ 850.   i.   Lee Roosevelt Warwick (8), born July 10, 1925.
+ 851,   ii.   Roy Robert Warwick (8), a twin to Ruth Weldon,
was born April 26, 1930.
   852.   iii. Ruth Weldon Warwick (8), a twin to Roy Robert,
was born April 26, 1930.
   853.   iv.   Daisy Adeline Warwick (8), born April 2, 1933;
died December 25, 1941.
   854.   v.   James Daniel Warwick (8), born September 19,
1934.

558. Edward Gathright Warwick (7), son of George Craig
Warwick (6) and Annie Weldon Cleek, married Juanita Smith.

Children: 5

855.   i.   Nancy Sue Warwick (8), born August 21, 1940.
856.   ii.   Elnora Mae Warwick (8), born September 29, 1942.
857,   iii. Paul Edward Warwick (8), born June 4, 1949.
858,   iv.   Charles Craig Warwick (8), born August 9, 1950.
859.   v.   Michael Berkley Warwick (8), born December 31,
1952.

560. Lucy Warwick (7), daughter of George Craig Warwick (6)
and Annie Weldon Cleek, married James Young.

Children: 4

860.   i.   James Lee Young (8), born November 29, 1936.
861,   ii.   Robert Weldon Young (8), born December 20, 1939.
862.   iii. Shirley Ann Young (8), born March 5, 1941.
863,   iv.   Doris Ellen Young (8), born August 13, 1943.

561, Robert Nelson Warwick (7), son of Charles Fechtig
Warwick (6) and Mary Constance Kellison, was born December 12,
1909; married May 2, 1931, Pauline Head.

Children: 9

864,   i.   Robert Nelson Warwick (8), born July 20, 1932.
865.   ii.   Charlotte Hazel Warwick (8), born April 20,
1934; married Charles Martin.

289

866. iii. Janet Corrine Warwick (8), born May 1, 1936.
867. iv. Elizabeth Lucille Warwick (8), born September 1937; married John Henry Plauger.
868. v. Eleanor Frances Warwick (8), born October 28, 1940.
869. vi. Mary Loretta Warwick (8), born January 29, 1942.
870. vii. Mildred Tschudy Warwick (8), born March 5, 1944.
871. viii. Roberta Nell Warwick (8), born March 29, 1948.
872. ix. Sharon Pansy Warwick (8), born June 9, 1954.

574. Emma Dilley (7), daughter of George M. Dilley and Amelia E. Warwick (6), married Otho E. Gum.

Children: 4

873. i. Lelia Gum (8).
874. ii. Ruth Gum (8).
875. iii. Mabel Gum (8).
876. iv. George Gum (8).

581. Minnie McClune (7), daughter of William McClune and Elvira Louisa Byrd (6), married (1) Robert LaRue; married (2) _____ Cochran; married (3) John Bear.

Children: 1 - first marriage

877. i. Wilfred LaRue (8), married _____ Graham.

613. June McElwee (7), son of Bernard Francis McElwee and Mary Katherine Siple (6), married Lucille Pritchard, daughter of Charles Pritchard and Malcena Elizabeth Yeager. (See Lightner Family).

Children: 3

878. i. Francis McElwee (8), received a B.A. degree from Hampden Sydney College, Hampden Sydney, Virginia and a M.A. degree from the University of West Virginia. He is an instructor at Marlinton High School, Marlinton, West Virginia.
879. ii. Alfred McElwee (8), married Margaret Williams. He is a Chemist with Dupont Company.
880. iii. Charles E. McElwee (8), married Lois Brill.

614. Winfred McElwee (7), son of Bernard Francis McElwee and Mary Katherine Siple (6), married Merl Moore, daughter of Harry Moore and Cora Jones.

Children: 2

881. i. Charles Richard McElwee (8), married February 5, 1955, Barbara Ellen Clark. He graduated in law at the University of West Virginia, and is now Assistant Attorney General of West Virginia.
882. ii. Cora Sue McElwee (8).

641. Eula Hill Warwick (7), daughter of Forrest Warwick (6) and Bertie Nottingham, married September 26, 1927 in Pocahontas County, West Virginia, Claude Leon Gaujot.

Children: 7

883. i. Muriel Gaujot (8), married November 15, 1955, Richard Fowler.
884. ii. Constance Gaujot (8), married October 4, 1953, Kenneth M. Walmsley.
885. iii. Phyllis Ann Gaujot (8), married April 10, 1956, Edgar F. Rogers.
886. iv. Jane Caroline Gaujot (8).
887. v. Claude E. Gaujot (8).
888. vi. Philip D. Gaujot (8).
889. vii. Diane Sue Gaujot (8).

643. Harvey Hull Warwick (7), son of Forrest Warwick (6) and Bertie Nottingham, was born in 1913; married September 7, 1939, Abbie Grace Ryder, daughter of Donald Spotwood Ryder and Delana Cameron Lightner. (See Lightner Family).

Children: 4

890. i. Barbara Kay Warwick (8), born January 1, 1943.
891. ii. Douglas Harvey Warwick (8), born April 6, 1945.
892. iii. Charlotte Delana Warwick (8), born April 19, 1946.
893. iv. Jack Kingsley Warwick (8), born March 25, 1951.

644. Ruth Lee Warwick (7), daughter of Jessie Lee Warwick (6) and Nancy Carolina Cleek, was born in 1899; married April 10, 1924 in Pocahontas County, West Virginia, Bert McNeer Kerr.

Children: 2

894. i. Roberta Lee Kerr (8).
895. ii. Carolyn Claire Kerr (8).

645. Sallie Weldon Warwick (7), daughter of Jessie Lee Warwick (6) and Nancy Carolina Cleek, married June 4, 1924 in Pocahontas County, West Virginia, Andrew Thomas Beale.

Children: 4

+ 896. i. Kenneth Warwick Beale (8), born May 30, 1926.
+ 897. ii. Gene Allen Beale (8), born July 11, 1929.
   898. iii. Thomas Jennings Beale (8), born October 19, 1938.
   899. iv. Gary Douglas Beale (8), born June 18, 1944.

646. Ralph Neil Warwick (7), son of Jessie Lee Warwick (6) and Nancy Carolina Cleek, married October 6, 1927 in Pocahontas

County, West Virginia, Golda Leona Smith.

Children: 2

+ 900. i. Claire Frances Warwick (8), born November 22, 1930.

901. ii. Thomas Lee Warwick (8), born December 19, 1932; married June 30, 1956, Jean Smith.

647. Mabel Claire Warwick (7), daughter of Jessie Lee Warwick (6) and Nancy Carolina Cleek, married July 6, 1933, Guy Nottingham.

Children: 2

902. i. Linda Lee Nottingham (8), born October 2, 1947.
903. ii. Lawrence Darrell Nottingham (8), born April 15, 1949.

649. Theordore J. Wickes (7), son of Henry Abbott Wickes and Nancy Esther Givens Warwick (6), was born June 14, 1906 at Green Bank, West Virginia; married November 1934, Helen Carter of Clarksburg, West Virginia. They live in Baltimore, Maryland.

Children: 1

904. i. Theordore E. Wickes (8), born November 13, 1942.

651. Mildred Eleanor Wickes (7), daughter of Henry Abbott Wickes and Nancy Esther Givens Warwick (6), was born October 25, 1912 at Clarksburg, West Virginia; married June 29, 1935 at Fleetwood, Berks County, Pennsylvania, Russell L. Campman, Jr. of Norristown, Pennsylvania. She is a R.N.

Children: 2

905. i. Russell L. Campman, III (8), born June 19, 1936 at Norristown, Pennsylvania.
906. ii. Jonathan Wickes Campman (8), born March 14, 1949 at Norristown, Pennsylvania.

652. Robert Henry Wickes (7), son of Henry Abbott Wickes and Nancy Esther Givens Warwick (6), was born May 1, 1914 at Clarksburg, West Virginia; married Helen Roberts of Delta, Pennsylvania. They live at China Lake, California.

Children: 2

907. i. Sue Pamela Wickes (8), born October 11, 1941 at Montgomery County, Maryland.
908. ii. Robin Sandra Wickes (8), born June 14, 1946 at Washington, D. C.

653. Frank Abbott Cleek Wickes (7), son of Henry Abbott

Wickes and Nancy Esther Givens Warwick (6), was born December 1, 1915 at Clarksburg, West Virginia; married January 31, 1941 at Bel Air, Maryland, Frances Menges of Gettysburg, Pennsylvania. They live at York, Pennsylvania.

Children: 1

909. i. Frank Abbott Cleek Wickes, Jr. (8), born July 3, 1942.

654. Grace Harmon (7), daughter of John Wesley Harmon and Nancy Elizabeth Music (6), married Rufus Barnett.

Children: 3

910. i. Robert Barnett (8).
911. ii. Warren Barnett (8).
912. iii. Marriam Barnett (8).

674. Maud Tichenor (7), daughter of James Albert Tichenor and Eliza Mauck (6), married James P. Witherspoon.

Children: 2

913. i. Louise Witherspoon (8), born October 15, 1915; married _____ Anadel.
914. ii. Ruth Witherspoon (8), born December 31, 1922; married _____.

675. Elmer Armstrong (7), son of Willis Armstrong (6) and Naomi Clark, was born May 28, 1869; died 1890; married February 26, 1896, Dora Hopkins.

Children: 4

915. i. Essie Armstrong (8).
916. ii. Hershell Armstrong (8).
917. iii. Darwin Armstrong (8), twin to Dorothy.
918. iv. Dorothy Armstrong (8), twin to Darwin.

680. Arthur P. Armstrong (7), son of Willis Armstrong (6) and Naomi Clark, was born February 8, 1883; died 1956; married Edna McClurkin.

Children: 4

919. i. Nancy Armstrong (8).
920. ii. Joe Armstrong (8).
921. iii. Harold Armstrong (8).
922. iv. Mary Eleanor Armstrong (8).

707. Elsie Johnson (7), daughter of John Willis Johnson (6) and Lucinda Jane Thompson, was born February 1, 1887; died

February 25, 1951; married Marsh Lewis.

Children: 1

923. i. Eloise Jane Lewis (8).

709. Laura Louella Johnson (7), daughter of George Washington Johnson, Jr. (6) and Marovia Johnson, was born September 9, 1877; married August 28, 1898, Dr. Ralph W. Emmerson, born October 23, 1869.

Children: 5

924. i. Wash Johnson Emmerson (8), born September 8, 1901.
925. ii. Ralph Waldo Emmerson (8).
926. iii. Louisa E. Emmerson (8).
927. iv. John Warwick Emmerson (8), twin to Myron Titus.
928. v. Myron Titus Emmerson (8), twin to John Warwick.

715. Warren Boren Johnson (7), son of Warwick D. Johnson (6) and Phena A. Boren, was born February 13, 1890; married February 3, 1914, Violet Benson.

Children: 1

929. i. Virginia Johnson (8), married Charles Langford. They have one child.

760. Catherine Ellen Key (7), daughter of Joseph Perry Key (6) and Phoebe Boyd, was born February 18, 1900; married July 30, 1922, Glen V. Ford, born June 24, 1900, son of Samuel Ford and Julia Minnear.

Children: 4

930. i. William Robert Ford (8), born April 17, 1924; married July 11, 1953, Lucille Holland.
+ 931. ii. Wesley Glen Ford (8), born December 3, 1925.
+ 932. iii. Luphoebe Ford (8), born April 25, 1928.
933. iv. Doyne Franklin Ford (8), born December 10, 1932.

764. Mary Ellen Key (7), daughter of William Finis Key (6) and Eva Goff, was born March 18, 1903; married John Ballard, Jr.

Children: 2

934. i. Joseph Thomas Ballard (8).
935. ii. Laurence Ballard (8), died.

766. Charles Wesley Key (7), son of William Finis Key (6) and Eva M. Goff, was born January 8, 1916; married Helen Pauley.

Children: 2

936. i.   Eva May Key (8), born June 20, 1941.
937. ii.   Cynthia Key (8).

768. Ruth Stewart (7), daughter of John Howard Stewart
and Margaret Elizabeth Key (6), was born June 21, 1893; married
June 18, 1924, William Arthur Kelly of Seattle, Washington, son
of Thomas Kelly of Neilsville, Wisconsin.

Children: 2

938. i.   William Robb Kelly (8), born January 20, 1927;
married _____. Seattle, Washington.
939. ii.   John Stewart Kelly (8), born August 27, 1930;
married ·_____. Seattle, Washington.

769. Margaret Stewart (7), daughter of John Howard Stewart
and Margaret Elizabeth Key (6), was born November 21, 1901; married March 9, 1921, Leotis Kolb, son of Joseph Kolb and Margaret
May Phillips.

Children: 6

+ 940. i.   Anna Lou Kolb (8), born September 4, 1923.
  941. ii.   Helen Louise Kolb (8), born June 24, 1925.
  942. iii.   Joe Howard Kolb (8), born November 26, 1929;
married _____.
  943. iv.   Susan Stewart Kolb (8), born June 10, 1935.
  944. v.   Eleanor Jane Kolb (8), born May 17, 1936.
  945. vi.   John Leotis Kolb (8), born February 8, 1938.

771. Thomas Wesley Key (7), son of Robert Sherman Key (6)
and Geneva Harvey, was born January 24, 1909; married November
26, 1950, Mrs. Mildred Hasselbrink.

Children: 2

946. i.   Thomas Key (8).
947. ii.   Sandra Key (8).

773. Jennie Key (7), daughter of Robert Sherman Key (6) and
Geneva Harvey, was born February 3, 1913; married September 4,
1934, Loren Purcell, born 1910; died August 3, 1955. ·

Children: 3

948. i.   Betty Joe Purcell (8), born March 10, 1936.
949. ii.   Phylis Ann Purcell (8), born February 17, 1939.

774. Lawrence Wheeler, Jr. (7), son of Lawrence Wheeler (6)
and Flora Massey, was born November 25, 1898; married June 17,
1922, Ruth White, born March 25, 1897, daughter of Rev. Thomas
White.

Children: 2

295

+   950.   i.   Lawrence Wheeler, III (8), born April 4, 1923.
+   951.   ii.   Jane Wheeler (8), born May 3, 1928.

779. Janice Ada Palmer (7), daughter of John Julian Palmer and Clara McClure (6), was born October 25, 1902; married September 8, 1921, Clarence Kolb, born January 4, 1901.

Children: 4

952.   i.   Nancy Lee Kolb (8), married September 5, 1942, Harold O. Wilson.
953.   ii.   Antionette Kolb (8), married _____ Meeks.
954.   iii.   Williard Julian Kolb (8), married February 4, 1951, Carol Ingle.
955.   iv.   Robert Kolb (8), married _____.

781. Charlotte Palmer (7), daughter of John Julian Palmer and Clara McClure (6), was born December 24, 1907; married (1) November 1, 1926, Glen Austin; married (2) Haskell Thompson.

Children: 2 - first marriage

956.   i.   Joe Ann Austin (8), married January 18, 1949, Jack Sanders.
957.   ii.   _____ Austin (8).

785. John Alexander Barker (7), son of Clarence Barker and Alle McClure (6), was born May 1905; married Elizabeth McClure.

Children: 1

956.   i.   James Barker (8).

787. Mary Agnes Bingham (7), daughter of Gordon Byron Bingham and Ada Ann McClure (6), was born June 23, 1908; married March 1938, French Witherspoon, son of W. W. Witherspoon and Cornelia French.

Children: 4

957.   i.   Laura Ann Witherspoon (8), born February 19, 1939.
958.   ii.   Jane Ellen Witherspoon (8), born February 15, 1942.
959.   iii.   Bonnie Bingham Witherspoon (8), born February 4, 1943.
960.   iv.   Margarretta Witherspoon (8), born 1945.

788. Helen Flo Whitsitt (7), daughter of William Arthur Whitsitt (6) and Leafie Myers, was born August 6, 1905; married May 14, 1932, Kermit White, born October 15, 1902; died November 12, 1953, son of Cassius White and Ida Key.

Children: 3

961.   i.   Ann White (8), born February 22, 1935;
died February 23, 1935.
962.   ii.   Joe Brian White (8), born June 2, 1936.
963.   iii.   Judith Jane White (8), born April 9, 1938;
died October 26, 1953.

789.   William Edward Whitsitt (7), son of William Arthur
Whitsitt (6) and Leafie Myers, was born March 6, 1907; married
February 10, 1944, Hazel Whiteacre.

Children: 2

964.   i.   Ellen Whitsitt (8)
965.   ii.   _____(son) Whitsitt (8), died October 1956.

790.   Robert Franklin Whitsitt (7), son of William Arthur
Whitsitt (6) and Leafie Myers, was born March 15, 1909; married
December 31, 1937, Grace _____.

Children: 2

966.   i.   Lynn Shirley Whitsitt (8).
967.   ii.   Karen Sue Whitsitt (8), born 1943.

791.   Wayne Arthur Whitsitt (7), son of William Arthur
Whitsitt (6) and Leafie Myers, was born February 11, 1912; mar-
ried August 9, 1942, Nancy Ann Daugherty, daughter of Paul and
Tot Daugherty.

Children: 4

968.   i.   Ann D. Whitsitt (8), born March 20, 1944.
969.   ii.   Debra Whitsitt (8).
970.   iii.   Michael Wayne Whitsitt (8).
971.   iv.   Mary Beth Whitsitt (8), born 1955

792.   Samuel Joseph Whitsitt (7), son of William Arthur
Whitsitt (6) and Leafie Myers, was born April 12, 1915; married
1945, Mary Elizabeth Owen, born May 16, 1920 in Virginia.

Children: 3

972.   i.   Stephen Whitsitt (8),born 1945.
973.   ii.   Brenda Lee Whitsitt (8), born September 14,
1947.
974.   iii.   Linda B. Whitsitt (8), born 1948.

793.   Don Ted Whitsitt (7), son of William Arthur Whitsitt
(6) and Leafie Myers, was born July 19, 1921; married 1943,
Barbara Baldwin, daughter of Russell Baldwin.

Children: 3

975. i.   Terry Whitsitt (8).
976. ii. Susan Whitsitt (8).
977. iii. Don Whitsitt (8).

799. Marjorie Louise French (7), daughter of Jesse B. French and Amy Alice McClure (6), was born October 31, 1907; married October 24, 1927, Louis King.

Children: 3

978. i.   Joan Marie King (8), born February 17, 1931.
979. ii. Jerry King (8), born April 26, 1936, a twin to Larry.
980. iii. Larry King (8), born April 26, 1936, a twin to Jerry.

801. Dorothy Marie French (7), daughter of Jesse B. French and Amy Alice McClure (6), was born March 6, 1912; married Raymond Sherrill.

Children: 1

981. i. Raymond French Sherrill (8), born August 1,1948.

807. Lester Lathom Kell (7), son of Purnell W. Kell and Julia Ann McClure (6), was born September 21, 1903; married July 15, 1926; Jennie Lambert, born February 23, 1900.

Children: 1

982. i.   Joy Kell (8), born April 27, 1927.

811. Elizabeth McClure (7), daughter of Lester Latham McClure (6) and Mary Ethel Arburn; married John Barker.

Children: 1

983. i.   James Barker (8).

823. William Henry Hudelson (7), son of Earl Hudelson (6) and Helena H. Houf, was born June 14, 1917; married January 3, 1942; Wilma O'Dell Fuller, born August 11, 1920, daughter of Hallie Edwin Fuller and Ozie Ethel Lawhon.

Children: 3

984. i.   William Henry Hudelson, Jr. (8), born October 11, 7, 1942.
985. ii. John Edwin Hudelson (8), born November 1, 1946.
986. iii. Kathleen Ann Hudelson (8), born October 5, 1949.

825. Joseph Prentice Carithers (7), son of Ralph M. Carithers and Olive McClure (6), was born October 5, 1920; married April 6,

1947, Martha A. Smith.

Children: 1

    987. i.   Robert Prentice Carithers (8), born June 30, 1950.

    826. Samuel Warren Carithers (7), son of Ralph M. Carithers and Olive McClure (6), was born November 13, 1921; married August 1, 1942, Melba E. Kolb.

Children: 2

    988. i.   Sammy Jane Carithers (8), born 1944.
    989. ii.   Christopher William Carithers (8), born July 9, 1950.

    827. James Ralph Carithers (7), born of Ralph M. Carithers and Olive McClure (6), was born October 3, 1922; married _____ _____.

Children: 1

    990. i.   Rebin Carithers (8).

    828. Mary Martha Carithers (7), daughter of Ralph M. Carithers and Olive McClure (6), was born February 28, 1923; married August 1, 1945, Milton J. Harrel.

Children: 3

    991. i.   Ann B. Harrel (8), born May 4, 1946.
    992. ii.   Mary Sue Harrel (8), born January 8, 1949.
    993. iii. Malinda Jane Harrel (8), born June 9, 1950.

    830. Olive Jean Carithers (7), daughter of Ralph M. Carithers and Olive McClure (6), was born March 16, 1925; married February 23, 1947, James Shoulders.

Children: 4

    994. i.   Carol Jean Shoulders (8), born December 16, 1947.
    995. ii.   Joyce Marie Shoulders (8),
    996. iii. William James Shoulderer (8), born July 19, 1951.
    997. iv. James Lee Shoulders (8), born September 24, 1955.

    839. Gladys Hicks (8), daughter of Horace Franklin Hicks and Cornelia Ruth Warwick (7), married Roy Gutshall.

Children: 2

    998. i.   Jane Gutshall (9).
    999. ii.   Roy Gutshall, Jr. (9).

840. Willard Hicks (8), son of Horace Franklin Hicks and
Cornelia.Ruth.Warwick (7), married Helen Gray Cleek, daughter of
Roy Moffett Cleek and Carey Knopp. (See Cleek Family).

Children: 3

1000. i.   Gray Lee Hicks (9).
1001. ii.   Ann Hicks (9).
1002. iii. Lynn Hicks (9).

841. Lucille Hicks (8), daughter of Horace Franklin Hicks
and Cornelia Ruth Warwick (7), married Anthony J. Miano.

Children: 1

1003. i.   Rodney Miano (9).

850. Lee Roosevelt Warwick (8), son of Harry Lee Warwick
(7) and Elsie Davis Jones, was born July 10, 1925; married March
30, 1946, Ruby Irons.

Children: 2

1004. i.   Joy Elaine Warwick (9), born June 11, 1950.
1005. ii.   Sandra Lee Warwick (9), born October 28, 1955.

851. Roy Robert Warwick (8), son of Harry Lee Warwick (7)
and Elsie Davis Jones, was born April 26, 1930; married November
22, 1951, Mary Shaw.

Children: 2

1006. i.   Sherry Lee Warwick (9), born October 19, 1952.
1007. ii.   David Carl Warwick (9), born May 10, 1955.

896. Kenneth Warwick Beale (8), son of Andrew Thomas Beale
and Sallie Weldon Warwick (7), was born May 30, 1926; married
Mary June Morrison of Chicago, Illinois.

Children: 1

1008. i.   James Andrew Beale (9), born June 15, 1947.

897. Gene Allen Beale (8), son of Andrew Thomas Beale
and Sallie Weldon Warwick (7), was born July 11, 1939; married
September 3, 1948, Mary Frances Plyler.

Children: 2

1009. i.   Geraldine Kay Beale (9), born July 30, 1949.
1010. ii.   Sally Faye Beale (9).

900. Claire Frances Warwick (8), daughter of Ralph Neil

Warwick (7) and Golda Leona Smith, was born November 22, 1930; married January 9, 1951, William Nasser.

Children: 1

1011. i. David Lee Nasser (9), born November 6, 1953.

931. Wesley Glen Ford (8), son of Glen V. Ford and Catherine Ellen Key (7), was born December 3, 1925; married 1948, Barbara McEowen.

Children: 2

1012. i. Debby Ford (9).
1013. ii. Mac Ford (9).

932. Luphoebe Ford (8), daughter of Glen V. Ford and Catherine Ellen Key (7), was born April 25, 1928; married July 1, 1950, John Newman.

Children: 2

1014. i. Janette Newman (9).
1015. ii. Cheryl Ann Newman (9).

940. Anna Lou Kolb (8), daughter of Leotis Kolb and Margaret Stewart (7), was born September 4, 1923; married Roy Haufman.

Children: 3

1016. i. Philip Haufman (9).
1017. ii. Rebecca Haufman (9).
1018. iii. Cinthia Haufman (9).

950. Lawrence Wheeler, III (8), son of Lawrence Wheeler, Jr. (7) and Ruth White, was born April 4, 1923; married June 29, 1946, Elizabeth Ann Smith, daughter of Alan Gerald Smith.

Children: 2

1019. i. Lawrence Wheeler, IV (9).
1020. ii. Susan Wheeler (9).

951. Jane Wheeler (8), daughter of Lawrence Wheeler, Jr. (7) and Ruth White, was born May 3, 1928; married (1) December 31, 1947, Lyle Warrick of Bloomington, Indiana, died May 5, 1951; married (2) January 29, 1955, Charles Noel Boling.

Children: 1 - first marriage

1021. i. Malinda Ann Warrick (9), born October 11, 1948.
Children: 1 - second marriage
1022. ii. Elizabeth Boling (9), born 1956 in Germany.

301

PART V

BRATTON FAMILY

Four brothers came to America from Ireland in 1733. This family is one of the so-called Scotch-Irish families.

+   1.   Robert Bratton (1), born 1712.

    2.   James Bratton (1), one of the four brothers, married Dorothy Fleming and settled near Christiansburg, Montgomery County, Virginia. His children were Anne C. Bratton, Melvina Bratton, and Cary Bratton. Descendants are still living in Montgomery County.

    3.   Samuel Bratton (1), remained in Mufflin County, Pennsylvania.

    4.   William Bratton (1), migrated to York County, South Carolina. His will was dated December 27, 1813 and probated February 13, 1815 in York County, South Carolina, Will Book D, page 51. It mentions wife, Martha Bratton; daughter, Mary Bratton, son, John S. Bratton; daughter, Jean Simpson; daughter, Martha Poster; daughter, Elsey Sadler; daughter, Agnes McCaw; daughter, Elizabeth Erwin; son, William Bratton. Executors = Wife, Martha Bratton, Dr. William Bratton, and Dr. James Simpson.

    1.   Robert Bratton (1), the immigrant, was born in Northern Ireland, May 20, 1712; died 1785; married in 1745 in Augusta County, Virginia, Ann (McFarland) Dunlap, born 1718 in Scotland; still living in 1785, daughter of Robert McFarland and Esther Houston, and widow of Captain Alexander Dunlap. Robert Bratton came to Orange County, Virginia (now Augusta) in 1733. He was a Captain in the French and Indian War 1756-58; a member of the council of war for protection of the Virginia frontier, 1756; owner of 2,284 acres in Augusta County, Virginia and other lands in the western territories. His will was dated May 10, 1783 and recorded in Will Book 6, page 492, Augusta County, Virginia. (Abstracts from the Records of Augusta County, Virginia, Lyman Chalkley, Vol. III, page 173). (See McFarland Family).

    Children: 6

+   5. . i.   James Bratton (2), born 1746.
    6.   ii.   John Bratton (2), married Sarah Anderson and settled in Pennsylvania.
    7.   iii.   George Bratton (2), settled in Madison County, Kentucky.
+   8.   iv.   Adam Bratton (2), born 1750.
    9. . v.   Agnes Bratton (2), born 1747; died 1827; married in 1764, William Givens, born 1746; died 1793, son of John Givens and Mary Margaret Sitlington. (See Givens Family).
    10. . vi.   Mary Bratton (2), died single.

5. James Bratton (2), son of Robert Bratton (1) and Ann
(McFarland) Dunlap, was born in 1746; died 1828; married 1774,
Rebecca Hogshead. He lived at "Rock Rest," Bath County, Virginia,
which he built in 1806. He owned 2,650 acres of land. He was a
Captain at the battle of Guilford Courthouse, North Carolina, and
was a pensioner of the American Revolution.

Children: 10

11. i. Robert Bratton (3), born 1776; died 1833 in
Clark County, Kentucky; married in 1800, Ann Dunlap, born 1768;
died 1850, daughter of John Dunlap and Anne Clark.
12. ii. Mary Bratton (3), born 1779; died 1834; married
Edward Erwin.
13. iii. William Bratton (3), born 1782; married Mary G.
Berry, born 1789. He was one of the picked men of the Lewis and
Clark Expedition of 1803. A monument stands over his grave in
Indiana which gives his service in the Expedition.
14. iv. John Bratton (3), born 1793; married Elizabeth
Graham, daughter of John Graham and Martha Patton. (See Graham
Family).
15. v. David Bratton (3), married Agnes Kirkpatrick.
They migrated to Kentucky.
16. vi. Margaret Bratton (3), married William Crawford.
17. vii. Rebecca Bratton (3), married John McClung.
18. viii. Elizabeth Bratton (3), born 1787; died 1824;
married 1787, John Porter.
+ 19. ix. Andrew Sitlington Bratton (3), born 1799.
+ 20. x. Lewis Bratton (3).

8. Adam Bratton (2), son of Robert Bratton (1) and Ann
(McFarland) Dunlap, was born in 1750; his will was proved in 1800;
married (1) Agnes Givens, daughter of John Givens and Mary Margaret
Sitlington; married (2) July 9, 1788, Elizabeth Feamster, daughter
of Thomas Feamster and Elizabeth Bratton. (See Givens Family).

Children: 2 - first marriage

21. i. Susan F. Bratton (3), married William Feamster.
22. ii. Margaret A. Bratton (3), married (1) Thomas
Feamster, Jr.; married (2) Andrew Sitlington.

Children: 6 - second marriage

+ 23. iii. Robert Bratton (3).
24. iv. Elizabeth Bratton (3), born 1789; married Samuel
Craig, born 1780; died July 18, 1843, son of James Craig and Jean
Stuart. (See Craig Family).
25. v. Nancy Bratton (3), married George Feamster.
26. vi. Martha W. Bratton (3), died young.
27. vii. Sallie Bratton (3), married William Sitlington
in his older years and they settled in Missouri.
28. viii. Jane Sitlington Bratton (3), married James M.
Montague, a school teacher.

303

19. Andrew Sitlington Bratton (3), son of James Bratton (2) and Rebecca Hogshead, was born in 1799; died 1881; married in 1829, Mary Jane Tilford McKee, daughter of James McKee, a soldier and pensioner of the American Revolution, and a granddaughter of Jane Logan McKee who was killed in the Massacre of Kerr's Creek in 1763. He was an elder of the Windy Cove Presbyterian Church for 38 years. They lived at "Rock Rest" in Bath County, Virginia.

Children: 4

+ 29. i. James L. Bratton (4), born 1831.
  30. ii. Robert Bratton (4), died in young manhood.
  31. iii. Rebecca A. Bratton (4), born 1836, married May 15, 1856 in Bath County, Virginia, George W. McDanald, born 1823, son of John F. McDanald and H. B. _____.
+ 32. iv. Andrew Sitlington Bratton (4), born 1842.

20. Lewis Bratton (3), son of James Bratton (2) and Rebecca Hogshead, married Martha Dunlap.

Children: 2

+ 33. i. John Mitchell Bratton (4), born 1837.
+ 34. ii. Martha Bratton (4).

23. Robert Bratton (3), son of Adam Bratton (2) and Elizabeth Feamster, married his first cousin, Susannah Feamster, daughter of William Feamster and Mary Fulton.

Children: 8

  35. i. Elizabeth Susan Bratton (4), born 1825; died 1908; married February 25, 1862, David Gwin Lockridge, Jr., born 1840; died of diphtheria during the War Between the States, son of David Gwin Lockridge and Nancy (Agnes) Kirkpatrick. (See Gwin Family).
+ 36. ii. John Feamster Bratton (4), born 1827.
  37. iii. William Bratton (4), served in the CSA and was killed in the battle of the Wilderness.
  38. iv. Robert Bratton, Jr. (4), died young.
  39. v. George Washington Bratton (4), born 1834; married (1) April 6, 1861, in Bath County, Virginia, Sarah Lockridge, born 1843; died April 27, 1889, daughter of David Gwin Lockridge and Nancy (Agnes) Kirkpatrick; married (2) in 1893, Frances Emily Lockridge, born 1861, daughter of Robert Lockridge and Emmeline M. Gwin. (See Gwin Family).
  40. vi. Margaret Bratton (4), died young.
+ 41. vii. Nannie Bratton (4), born 1838.
  42. viii. Martha Bratton (4), married Griffith Revercomb. They migrated to Missouri.

29. James L. Bratton (4), son of Andrew Sitlington Bratton (3) and Mary Jane Tilford McKee, was born in 1831; married May 5,

304

1859, Mary Moore Brown, born 1835 in Rockbridge County, Virginia;
daughter of Sam and Ellen R. Brown.

Children: 9

43.   i.   Samuel Brown Bratton (5), died young.
44.   ii.   Andrew Lewis Bratton (5), died young.
45.   iii. Mary Ella Bratton (5), died March 21, 1951,
unmarried.
46.   iv.   Margaret Bratton (5), R.N., lived in Philadelphia, Pennsylvania.
47.   v.   Martha Elizabeth Bratton (5). She was a teacher.
48.   vi.   John M. Bratton (5), died young.
49.   vii. James L. Bratton (5), died young.
50.   viii. Edith Bratton (5), died young.
51.   ix.   William A. Bratton (5), died young.

32.   Andrew Sitlington Bratton (4), son of Andrew Sitlington
Bratton (3) and Mary Jane Tilford McKee, was born in 1842; died in
1914; married (1) in 1867, Mary Moore Guy, born 1839; died 1875;
married (2) in 1883, Sue (Guy) McDannald; married (3) in 1898,
Elizabeth Handley. He was a member of the Bath Squadron, CSA. He
was an elder in the Windy Cove Presbyterian Church, Bath County,
Virginia for 35 years.

Children: 3 - first marriage

+   52.   i.   William Andrew Bratton (5), born December 24,
1869.
53.   ii.   Robert James Glendye Bratton (5), born 1873;
died 1891.
54.   iii. Susan Rebecca Bratton (5), born 1875; died 1891.

33.   John Mitchell Bratton (4), son of Lewis Bratton (3) and
Martha Dunlap, was born in 1837; married July 13, 1870 in Bath
County, Virginia, Mary Jane Grove, born 1852, daughter of John
and Ellen Grove. He served in Company B, 11th Virginia Cavalry,
CSA.

Children: 12

55.   i.   John Bratton (5), married (1) Bessie Gross;
married (2) Joyce Gross. Nashville, Tennessee.
56.   ii.   Charles Bratton (5), died unmarried.
57.   iii, Lewis Bratton (5), died in young manhood.
58.   iv,   Dewitt T. Bratton (5), married Rosa Barksdale.
Craigsville, Virginia.
+   59.   v.   Jesse M. Bratton (5).
60.   vi.   Albert Bratton (5), died in 1937 near Lexington,
Virginia; married Gertrude Blagg. No children.
61.   vii. Mary Bratton (5), died unmarried.
62.   viii. Lora Belle Bratton (5), married Elmer R. Flippo.
63.   ix.   Martha (Patsy) Bratton (5), married Seldon Turner.
She is a Home Missionary in Kentucky.

64. x. Annie Bratton (5), married Charles C. Lewis,
Point Pleasant, West Virginia.
+ 65. xi. Edith Bratton (5).
66. xii. Clyde Bratton (5), married Lillian Eastman,
California.

34. Martha Bratton (4), daughter of Lewis Bratton (3) and
Martha Dunlap, married Townley B. Cauthorn.

Children: 9

67. i. Ashley Cauthorn (5), died unmarried.
68. ii. Mason Cauthorn (5), married Eva Hartsook.
69. iii. Robert Cauthorn (5), married Hilda Curry.
70. iv. Martha Cauthorn (5), married _____ Davis.
71. v. Margaret Cauthorn (5), married Dr. A. F. Kerr.
72. vi. Sallie Cauthorn (5), married William McCormick.
73. vii. Rose Cauthorn (5), married Walter McCormick.
74. viii. Callie Cauthorn (5), married Chess Miller.
75. ix. Charles Cauthorn (5), married (1) Mary F. Taylor;
married (2) Mrs. Julia Hamilton.

36. John Feamster Bratton (4), son of Robert Bratton (3) and
Susannah Feamster, was born in 1827; died in 1919; married January
26, 1862, Cornelia Goul, born October 10, 1837; died January 16,
1892; daughter of Christian Goul and Nancy Ella Kinnear McCown.
John McCown was born in 1755; died in 1817; married in 1780, Nancy
Kinnear. They had three children:

i. John McCown, born 1784; died 1850; married in
1810, Mary Culton.
ii. Moses McCown, died 1854; married in 1823,
Isabella Moore.
iii. Nancy Ella Kinnear McCown, married (1) in 1811,
David Orbison; married (2) Christian Goul who
died in 1841; married (3) as his second wife,
James Wilson.
John Feamster Bratton served in Company F, 11th Virginia Cavalry,
CSA.

Children: 10

76. i. Ella Susan Bratton (5), born March 15, 1863;
died January 31, 1914; married in 1887, Charles Byrd. She was
a school teacher.
+ 77. ii. Margaret Kinnear Bratton (5), born August 20,
1865.
78. iii. John Samuel Bratton (5), born October 6, 1867;
died June 8, 1929; married Maizy Kinnear.
+ 79. iv. Bettie Moore Bratton (5), born October 10, 1869.
80. v. Robert Christian Bratton (5), born January 29,
1871; died June 10, 1871.
+ 81. vi. Frank Harris Bratton (5), born September 16,
1872.

82. vii. Clarence Bratton (5), born September 8, 1874; died October 30, 1874.
+ 83. viii. Jeanie Orbison Bratton (5), born September 17, 1875.
84. ix. William Hampton Bratton (5), born July 21, 1877; married October 14, 1914, Wreathie Susan Revercomb, born January 4, 1882; died February 10, 1940, daughter of John R. Revercomb and Susan R. Lockridge. (See Gwin Family).
85. x. Georgia Lee Goul Bratton (5), born May 27, 1879; died May 6, 1955; married May 26, 1912, Bias Ashby Cleek, born February 19, 1866; died March 16, 1942, son of Jacob Crawford Cleek and Margaret Thompson. (See Cleek Family).

41. Nannie Bratton (4), daughter of Robert Bratton (3) and Susannah Feamster, was born in 1838; married April 12, 1866 in Bath County, Virginia, James McGuffin, born 1839, son of Adam Given McGuffin and Eliza Orbison. He served as Second Lieutenant in Company F, 11th Virginia Cavalry, CSA.

Children: 4

86. i. William Bratton McGuffin (5), born May 30, 1867; died May 2, 1940; married in 1896, Ruhama B. Revercomb, born January 5, 1872; died June 1944, daughter of John R. Revercomb and Susan R. Lockridge. (See Gwin Family).
87. ii. George Lloyd McGuffin (5), married in 1894, Mabel Gould of Vermont. They have one son, Harry McGuffin (6), who lives in Vermont.
88. iii. Susan McGuffin (5), married April 29, 1896, Jesse Gilmore. They have one son, Lloyd Gilmore (6).
89. iv. Harry McGuffin (5), married (1) Ida Shelton; married (2) Nellie Anderson. He had one daughter by his first wife, Hattie McGuffin (6).

52. William Andrew Bratton (5), son of Andrew Sitlington Bratton (4) and Mary Moore Guy, was born December 24, 1869; married September 9, 1896, Fanny Berry Cologne, born October 10, 1874 at Marshall, Virginia; died April 25, 1951, daughter of J. C. Cologne and Fanny Gray Maddux. He was educated at Washington and Lee University, Lexington, Virginia and graduated in law in 1890. He was Prosecuting Attorney of Pocahontas County, West Virginia, 1906-1915. He served as Assistant Counsel to the U.S. Food Administrator, Washington, D. C. in World War I.

Children: 4

+ 90. i. Mary Frances Bratton (6), born January 22, 1898.
+ 91. ii. Virginia Guy Bratton (6), born August 16, 1900.
+ 92. iii. Sue McKee Bratton (6), born December 30, 1905.
+ 93. iv. Robert Andrew Bratton (6), born December 20, 1914.

59. Jesse M. Bratton (5), son of John Mitchell Bratton (4) and Mary Jane Grove, married Pearl Hanger. She is a R.N. in Staunton, Virginia, where they live.

307

Children: 2

94. i. Jesse Melville Bratton, Jr. (6), married Mary
Jo Jackson of Bluefield, West Virginia. He is a Presbyterian
minister.
95. ii. Paul Hanger Bratton (6), married Marian Crewe
Jones, daughter of Ben C. Jones.

65. Edith Bratton (5), daughter of John Mitchell Bratton (4)
and Mary Jane Grove, married H. H. Jolly of Millboro, Virginia.

Children: 12

96. i. Mary Frances Jolly (6), married Dr. Webb. They
live in North Carolina.
97. ii. Harry H. Jolly, Jr. (6), married Dorothy Swanson.
98. iii. Robert Lewis Jolly (6), married Betty Lou Carter.
99. iv. Ralph Bratton Jolly (6), married Ruth Rutledge.
100. v. Edith Marie Jolly (6).
101. vi. Anna Virginia Jolly (6), married Francis Grallaha
102. vii. Charles William Jolly (6), married Shirley Corbin
103. viii. Betty Lou Jolly (6), married Wesley Manning.
104. ix. Ruth Elizabeth Jolly (6), married Al Woolgar.
105. x. Frank Moore Jolly (6).
106. xi. Donald Lee Jolly (6).
107. xii. Martha Jane Jolly (6).

77. Margaret Kinnear Bratton (5), daughter of John Feamster
Bratton (4) and Cornelia Goul, was born August 20, 1865; died April
30, 1946; married October 18, 1905, Isaac Sharp. She was educated
at Ann Smith Academy, Lexington, Virginia and Farmville State
Teachers College. She was a school teacher.

Children: 1

108. i. John Isaac Sharp (6), born 1906; married Elizabeth Gay. They have two children, John Isaac Sharp, Jr. (7) and
Betty Sharp (7).

79. Bettie Moore Bratton (5), daughter of John Feamster
Bratton (4) and Cornelia Goul, was born October 10, 1869; died
April 1939; married April 15, 1902, Samuel Feamster Littlepage.
She was educated at Valley Seminary, Waynesboro, Virginia. She
was a school teacher.

Children: 2

109. i. Cornelia Littlepage (6), unmarried, a R.N. in
Philadelphia, Pennsylvania.
110. ii. Virginia Littlepage (6), married _____
Black. She is a school teacher.

81. Frank Harris Bratton (5), son of John Feamster Bratton
(4) and Cornelia Goul, was born September 16, 1872; died August 8,

1948; married (1) October 1902, Johnnie Berry who died December 28, 1916; married (2) December 7, 1926, Bessie Gum.

Children: 2 - first marriage

   111. i.   Charles Bratton (6), born 1903; married (1) Pearl Barlow; married (2) Agnes Price.
+ 112. ii.   Cornelia Fulton Bratton (6), born April 6, 1909.

   83. Jeanie Orbison Bratton (5), daughter of John Feamster Bratton (4) and Cornelia Goul, was born September 17, 1875; married April 12, 1900, William Robert Lockridge, born December 3, 1871; died 1943, son of Stephen A. Lockridge and Laura Ervine. (See Gwin Family). She was educated at Wildwood School for Girls, Millboro, Virginia, and was a school teacher.

Children: 13

   113. i.   Ervine Goul Lockridge (6), married Louise Styer.
   114. ii.   William Lockridge (6), died in young manhood in Ohio.
   115. iii. Vivian Lockridge (6), born in 1904, a twin to Marion, married Sidney Bear.
   116. iv.   Marion Lockridge (6), born in 1904, a twin to Vivian, died in infancy.
   117. v.   Ara Beatrice Lockridge (6), died in 1906, an infant.
   118. vi.   Robert Lee Lockridge (6), born January 19, 1907; married December 24, 1924, Evelyn Christian Bell, born February 22, 1901.
   119. vii. Stephen A. Lockridge (6), married Virginia Cox.
   120. viii. Eleanor Lockridge (6), married Robert Wilson. She is a R.N.
   121. ix.   Louise Lockridge (6), married John Gardner.
   122. x.   John Lockridge (6), married Sadie Hall.
   123. xi.   Jean Lockridge (6), married Alex Valz.
   124. xii. Delbert Earl Lockridge (6), died in infancy.
   125. xiii. (Son) Lockridge (6), died in infancy.

   90. Mary Frances Bratton (6), daughter of William Andrew Bratton (5) and Fanny Berry Cologne, was born January 22, 1898 at Marshall, Virginia; married April 12, 1929, French Harden Moore, born August 7, 1898 at Huntersville, West Virginia; died May 30, 1938 at Mt. Alto Hospital, Washington, D. C. and was buried at Marlinton, West Virginia.

Children: 3

   126. i.   James McLaughlin Moore (7), born July 8, 1931. at Marlinton, West Virginia.
   127. ii.   Guy Bratton Moore (7), born August 22, 1933 at Marlinton, West Virginia.
   128. iii. French Harden Moore, Jr. (7), born November 19, 1934 at Huntersville, West Virginia.

91. Virginia Guy Bratton (6), daughter of William Andrew Bratton (5) and Fanny Berry Cologne, was born August 16, 1900 at Marlinton, West Virginia; died April 1951 and was buried at Marlinton, West Virginia; married March 30, 1926, Ray I. Frame, M.D.

Children: 2

129. i.   William Ray Frame (7).
130. ii.   Fanny Gray Frame (7).

92. Sue McKee Bratton (6), daughter of William Andrew Bratton (5) and Fanny Berry Cologne, was born December 30, 1905 at Marlinton, West Virginia; died April 1941 and was buried at Marlinton, West Virginia; married Lambert Duncan Dorworth of Pittsburg, Pennsylvania.

Children: 1

131. i.   Fanny Berry Dorworth (7).

93. Robert Andrew Bratton (6), son of William Andrew Bratton (5) and Fanny Berry Cologne, was born December 20, 1914; died January 1951 in Korea while serving with the Armed Forces and was buried at Mt. View Cemetery, Marlinton, West Virginia; married Hazel Boxley from Tuscaloosa, Alabama.

Children: 2

132. i.   Mallory Sue Bratton (7).
133. ii.   Roberta Ann Bratton (7).

112. Cornelia Fulton Bratton (6), daughter of Frank Harris Bratton (5) and Johnnie Berry, was born April 6, 1909; married in 1931, William Brock, died October 7, 1952, son of George H. Brock and Lucy A. Hull. (See Hull Family).

Children: 3

134. i.   Charles Brock (7).
135. ii.   William Brock (7).
136. iii. Joanne Brock (7).

PART VI

CAMPBELL FAMILY

The Campbell family is of the Scottish Clan Campbell. One of the Clan Campbell, was a companion of Robert the Bruce. He killed the largest boar in the county, by cutting off his head with one stroke. Hence the boar's head on the crest of the Campbell Coat of Arms.

The first Earl of Argyll was Colin Campbell, nephew of Sir Colin Campbell who married a daughter of the Lord Lorn. The Clan Campbell claims Constantine of France, A.D. 104, as an ancestor, taking in Ambrose, the forty-third King of Scots, and also King Arthur of the Round Table.

1. John Campbell (1), was born in Scotland; died before 1741; married Grace Hay. John Campbell emigrated from Ireland to America with his large family. He came to Virginia in 1733 from Lancaster County, Pennsylvania, settling in part of Orange County, Virginia which in 1738 became Augusta County. Four of his sons came with him to Augusta County, Virginia. Family tradition says that he came to New Jersey in 1684 and migrated to Pennsylvania and then to Virginia.

2. i. Patrick Campbell (2). He was the grandfather of General William Campbell, son of Charles Campbell. General William Campbell was born in 1744. He was appointed Captain of Militia in 1774 and the following year he commanded a company in Patrick Henry's regiment. At the battle of King's Mountain, North Carolina, he greatly distinguished himself and was commended by Washington. In 1781 he was with General Greene at the battle of Guilford Court House. He married Elizabeth Henry, sister of Patrick Henry, and daughter of Colonel John Henry and Sarah (Winston) Symes. He died in 1781, and his widow married General William Russell, another soldier of the Revolution.

3. ii. David Campbell (2), married Mary Hamilton in Augusta County, Virginia, and they were the parents of a large family of which several migrated to the Holston River settlement. Two sons of David Campbell were soldiers in the Revolution -- Arthur and John Campbell.

4. iii. Robert Campbell (2), migrated to Tennessee.

+ 5. iv. William Campbell (2).

5. William Campbell (2), son of John Campbell (1) and Grace Hay, died in 1759 in Augusta County, Virginia; married Sarah _____. His will was recorded November 22, 1759 in Will Book 2, page 343, Augusta County, Virginia. On November 22, 1759, Samuel Campbell gave bond as administrator of the estate of William Campbell, deceased, with James Carlile, Jr. and George Wilson as sureties. The appraisement of William Campbell's estate was made by Andrew Hamilton, James Carlile, Jr., and Daniel O'Hara on March 18, 1760. The will of William Campbell reads as follows:

In the name of God Amen, I William Campbell of the county of Augusta & Colony of Virginia considering the uncertainty of this mortal life and being of sound and perfect mind & memory blessed be almighty God for the Same but being now indisposed do make and publish this my last will and testament in manner and form following That is to say first of all I leave & bequeath unto my sons James Campbell & John Campbell one shilling each. I also give & bequeath unto my daughters Mary Clements, Margaret Gillham, Elizabeth Price, Mary Ann Ashton, and Rachel Carlile one shilling each and it is also my will that the above mentioned Legacies be paid or tendered the day of my Burial and it is also my will that one hundred acres of land that my son-in-law Thomas Gillham now lives on it being part of that tract of land where my dwelling house now stands be equally divided amongst my daughter Margaret Gillhams children equally at her decease and I also leave and bequeath unto my son Samuel work horses and the pough & Irons and my plantation at my wife's decease that is to say my wife having the one third of said plantation during her life and I also leave & bequeath unto my well beloved wife Sarah Campbell all the residue of my estate whatsoever & to have it in her power to dispose of it as she shall think proper at her decease and I do hereby appoint my well beloved wife Sarah Campbell my sole Executrix & Executor of this my last will & testament hereby revoking all former wills by me made & witness whereof I have hereunto set my hand & Seal this fifth day of October one Thousand Seven hundred and fifty four 1754.

Signed Sealed and delivered   William Campbell (SEAL)
In the presence of
Jacob Clements
Chas. Gillham

        Children: 8

        6.   i.   James Campbell (3), married Lettice _____.
        7.   ii.   John Campbell (3), married Mary Ann _____.
    +   8.   iii. Samuel Campbell (3).
        9.   iv.   Mary Campbell (3), married Jacob Clements, whose
will was proved November 21, 1759 in Augusta County, Virginia.
        10.   v.   Margaret Campbell (3), married Thomas Gillham.
        11.   vi.   Elizabeth Campbell (3), married Augustine Price.
        12.   vii. Mary Ann Campbell (3), married Wallace Ashton.
        13.   viii. Nancy Rachel Campbell (3), still living in 1802;
married in 1746, James Carlile, Jr., born in 1725 in Augusta County,
Virginia; died in 1802 in Bath County (now Highland County), Virgini
son of James Carlile and Elizabeth _____. (See Carlile Family).

        8.   Samuel Campbell (3), son of William Campbell (2) and Sarah
_____, married Eleanor _____.

        Children: 1 (others?)

    +   9.   .i.   Alexander Campbell (4).

        9.   Alexander Campbell (4), son of Samuel Campbell (3) and
Eleanor _____, married (1) Margaret Brown; married (2) Mary
                              312

(Wandless) Moore, widow of Presley Moore; married (3) Rachel (Grimes) Bussard. They settled in what is now Highland County, Virginia. No children of the second marriage.

Children: 9 - first marriage

+ 14. i. Thomas Campbell (5), born January 1, 1800.
+ 15. ii. Benjamin Brown Campbell (5), born November 1, 1808.
+ 16. iii. John Campbell (5).
  17. iv. (Son) Campbell (5), died.
+ 18. v. Samuel B. Campbell (5).
  19. vi. James B. Campbell (5), married June 26, 1845 in Pocahontas County, West Virginia, Alcinda C. Lightner, daughter of Jacob Lightner and Elizabeth Moore. No children. (See Lightner Family).
+ 20. vii. William Campbell (5).
+ 21. viii. A. Hanson Campbell (5).
+ 22. ix. Edgar Campbell (5).

Children: 3 - third marriage

  23. x. Azariah Campbell (5), died young with diphtheria.
  24. xi. Milton Campbell (5), died young with diphtheria.
  25. xii. Laura Campbell (5), died young with diphtheria.

14. Thomas Campbell (5), son of Alexander Campbell (4) and Margaret Brown, was born January 1, 1800; died January 22, 1876; married (1) Elizabeth Slaven; married (2) Jane (Hamilton) Bonner; married (3) Susan (Gum) Wade, daughter of Otho Gum and Elizabeth Lightner and widow of Stewart S. Wade. (See Lightner Family).

Children: 10 - first marriage

+ 26. i. Margaret Campbell (6).
+ 27. ii. Isabella Campbell (6), twin to Matilda.
  28. iii. Matilda Campbell (6), twin to Isabella, died.
+ 29. iv. Adella Campbell (6).
+ 30. v. Austin Campbell (6).
+ 31. vi. Amos Campbell (6).
+ 32. vii. Newton Campbell (6).
  33. viii. Rebecca (1) Campbell (6), died from effects of scalds.
  34. ix. Albert Campbell (6), died.
  35. x. Rebecca (2) Campbell (6), died.

15. Benjamin Brown Campbell (5), son of Alexander Campbell (4) and Margaret Brown, was born November 1, 1808; died March 13, 1884; married (1) Margaret Slaven; married (2) Laura Russell.

Children: 6 - first marriage

  36. i. Martha A. Campbell (6), born July 26, 1835; died

313

April 12, 1925.
+   37.   ii.   J. Brown Campbell (6).
    38.   iii. Mary E. Campbell (6), died.
+   39.   iv.   Elizabeth Campbell (6).
    40.   v.   Stewart Campbell (6), married (1) Agnes Slaven;
married (2) Emma Lowry.
+   41.   vi.   Luther Campbell (6).

16. John Campbell (5), son of Alexander Campbell (4) and
Margaret Brown, married Sarah Johnston.

Children: 5

    42.   i. Emily Campbell (6), married Dr. Henry Patterson.
+   43.   ii.   Morgan B. Campbell (6).
    44.   iii. Catherine Campbell (6), married William H. M.
Smith.
+   45.   iv.   Oscar J. Campbell (6).
    46.   v.   Amos Campbell (6), died.

18. Samuel B. Campbell (5), son of Alexander Campbell (4)
and Margaret Brown, married (1) Jane Woods; married (2) Isabella
Woods.

Children: 8 - first marriage ?

    47.   i.   Mary S. Campbell (6), unmarried.
    48.   ii.   Alexander Campbell (6), married (1) Susan E.
Matheny; married (2) Margaret Hoover.
    49.   iii. Rollin Campbell (6), married Louise Rodgers.
+   50.   iv.   Rachel R. Campbell (6).
    51.   v.   Ananias Campbell (6), died.
    52.   vi.   Caleb Campbell (6), married Phoebe Sullenberger.
    53.   vii. Margaret Campbell (6), married Gideon Burns.
They lived in Tennessee.
    54.   viii. Vernon Campbell (6), married in 1860, Elizabeth
A. Bird. They lived in Oklahoma.

20. William Campbell (5), son of Alexander Campbell (4) and
Margaret Brown, married Mary Jane Warwick McGuffin, daughter of
James McGuffin and Elizabeth Ervin.

Children: 9

+   55.   i.   Louisa Campbell (6).
+   56.   ii.   David H. Campbell (6).
+   57.   iii. J. Kenny Campbell (6).
+   58.   iv.   Almira Campbell (6).
    59.   v.   Laura Campbell (6), died September 29, 1895.
    60.   vi.   Clara Campbell (6), died at Churchville, Virginia.
+   61.   vii. William Price Campbell (6).
    62.   viii. Robert Campbell (6), died of diphtheria.
+   63.   ix.   Filmore T. Campbell (6).

314

21. A. Hanson Campbell (5), son of Alexander Campbell (4)
and Margaret Brown, married Isabelle Lewis.

Children: 3

```
    64.   i.    Charles L. Campbell (6), married in California.
+   65.   ii.   Mary L. Campbell (6).
+   66.   iii.  William A. Campbell (6).
```

22. Edgar Campbell (5), son of Alexander Campbell (4) and
Margaret Brown, married (1) Susan Boone; married (2) March 30,
1848 in Bath County, Virginia, Elizabeth R. Lockridge, daughter
of Andrew Lockridge and Elizabeth Carlile. (See Gwin Family).

Children: 3 - first marriage

```
    67.   i.    Mary K. Campbell (6), married John M. Burns.
They lived at Burnsville, West Virginia.
    68.   ii.   Calvin Campbell (6), died.
    69.   iii.  Caroline Campbell (6), died.
```

Children: 4 - second marriage

```
+   70.   iv.   Alice Campbell (6).
    71.   v.    Thomas Campbell (6), married in the west.
    72.   vi.   Horace Campbell (6), married in the west.
    73.   vii.  James Campbell (6), died.
```

26. Margaret Campbell (6), daughter of Thomas Campbell (5)
and Elizabeth Slaven, married (as his second wife), Roger Hickman,
son of William Hickman and Mary Elliot.

Children: 9

```
+   74.   i.    Thomas Brown Hickman (7).
    75.   ii.   James Hickman (7), died.
    76.   iii.  Peter Lightner Hickman (7), born February 23,
1858; married 1895, Ollie Gertrude Lockridge, born June 4, 1870,
daughter of Robert Carlile Lockridge and Lydia M. Kutz. (See
Gwin Family).
    77.   iv.   Andrew Johnston Hickman (7), died.
    78.   v.    Ellen Hickman (7), died.
    79.   vi.   Emma Hickman (7), married James Bulger. They
lived in Bath County, Virginia. No children.
    80.   vii.  Virginia Hickman (7), married Joseph Hamilton.
No children.
+   81.   viii. Matilda Hickman (7).
    82.   ix.   Laura Hickman (7), died.
```

27. Isabella Campbell (6), daughter of Thomas Campbell (5)
and Elizabeth Slaven, married Moses Moore.

Children: 2

83.   i.   Isaac Brown Moore (7), married (1) Kate Curry; married (2) Addie Watts; married (3) Sadie Hamilton.
84.   ii.   Alice Moore (7), married Horace M. Lockridge (as his first wife), son of James T. Lockridge and Lillie Moser. (See Lockridge Family).

29. Adella Campbell (6), daughter of Thomas Campbell (5) and Elizabeth Slaven, married Anson Wade.

Children: 3

85.   i.   Florence Wade (7), married (as his second wife) James Fleisher.
+   86.   ii.   Edward Amos Wade (7), born August 13, 1864.
+   87.   iii,   Harry A. G. Wade (7), born 1868.

30. Austin Campbell (6), son of Thomas Campbell (5) and Elizabeth Slaven, married Susan Hamilton.

Children: 4

+   88.   i.   Walter Price Campbell (7), born May 7, 1854.
89.   ii.   Jennie Campbell (7), married W. O. Robinson, Hinton, West Virginia.
90.   iii.   Maude Campbell (7), married Charles Brown, Hinton, West Virginia.
91.   iv.   Lillie Campbell (7), married R. P. Boyd, Ronceverte, West Virginia.

31. Amos Campbell (6), son of Thomas Campbell (5) and Elizabeth Slaven, married Martha Gammon. She married (2) Rev. John Canter.

Children: 2

+   92.   i.   Leonidas Campbell (7).
93.   ii.   John Campbell (7), settled in the west.

32. Newton Campbell (6), son of Thomas Campbell (5) and Elizabeth Slaven, married Margaret J. Bonner.

Children: 2

94.   i.   Clarence Campbell (7), died.
95.   ii.   Ella Campbell (7), died.

37. J. Brown Campbell (6), son of Benjamin Brown Campbell (5) and Margaret Slaven, married Amanda Fleisher.

Children: 1

+   96.   i.   Robert Campbell (7).

316

39. Elizabeth Campbell (6), daughter of Benjamin Brown Campbell (5) and Margaret Slaven, married Dr. S. Pruyne Patterson.

Children: 3

97.   i.   Margaret Patterson (7), married J. W. Baxter.
98.   ii.   Anna Mary Patterson (7), married W. H. Barlow.
99.   iii. Harry P. Patterson (7), married Mary Barlow.
Pennsylvania.

41. Luther Campbell (6), son of Benjamin Brown Campbell (5) and Margaret Slaven, married Mary E. Benson.

Children: 10

+ 100. i.   Benjamin B. Campbell (7).
+ 101. ii.   O. James Campbell (7), born April 6, 1889.
+ 102. iii. Russell Campbell (7).
+ 103. iv.   Gay Campbell (7), a twin to Guy.
+ 104. v.   Guy Campbell (7), a twin to Gay.
+ 105. vi.   Ernest Campbell (7)
  106. vii. Alexander Campbell (7), married Alice _____.
+ 107. viii. Mary Campbell (7).
+ 108. ix.   Ruth Campbell (7).
+ 109. x.   Margaret Katherine Campbell (7).

43. Morgan B. Campbell (6), son of John Campbell (5) and Sarah Johnston, married (1) Annie Lupton; married (2) Lillie Woodzell. He was a physician in Highland County, Virginia.

Children: 4 - second marriage

110. i.   Annie Lupton Campbell (7), married Wallace G. Hoover. She is a teacher in Bath County, Virginia.
111. ii.   Stanley Campbell (7), married Emily Rector.
112. iii. Winifrey W. Campbell (7), married India Brown.
113. iv.   Mildred Campbell (7), married Dr. Ramon Garcin, Jr. She is a R. N.

45. Oscar J. Campbell (6), son of John Campbell (5) and Sarah Johnston, died February 8, 1935; married Annie L. Slaven. He was a dentist at Monterey, Virginia.

Children: 9

+ 114. i.   Helen Campbell (7).
+ 115. ii.   Eva Campbell (7).
+ 116. iii. Sallie Campbell (7).
+ 117. iv.   Jessie Campbell (7).
  118. v.   Katherine Campbell (7), unmarried.
  119. vi.   Warren Campbell (7), married Virginia Hickman, daughter of Peter Lightner Hickman and Ollie Gertrude Lockridge. No children. (See Gwin Family).

```
120.   vii.    Cornelia Campbell (7), died.
121.   viii.   John (1) Campbell (7), died.
122.   ix.     John (2) Campbell (7), died.
```

    50. Rachel R. Campbell (6), daughter of Samuel B. Campbell
(5) and Jane Woods (or Isabella Woods?), married William Kring
Rodgers.

    Children: 6

```
      123.  i.     Minnie Rodgers (7).  She was a teacher.
  +   124.  ii.    Maggie Rodgers (7).
  +   125.  iii.   Annie Rebecca Rodgers (7).
  +   126.  iv.    Charles W. Rodgers (7).
  +   127.  v.     George R. Rodgers (7).
  +   128.  vi.    Eugene K. Rodgers (7).
```

    55. Louisa Campbell (6), daughter of William Campbell (5)
and Mary Jane Warwick McGuffin, married William H. Shumate.

    Children: 4

```
  +   129.  i.     Lillie Shumate (7).
  +   130.  ii.    Lucy Shumate (7).
  +   131.  iii.   Dick Shumate (7).
      132.  iv.    Clara Shumate (7), died young.
```

    56. David H. Campbell (6), son of William Campbell (5) and
Mary Jane Warwick McGuffin, married Eliza J. Dever. He lived in
Kansas.

    Children: 4

```
      133.  i.     James Campbell (7), born July 9, 1871; died
August 8, 1953; married January 13, 1903, Georgia Harouff.
      134.  ii.    Mack Campbell (7), married _____.
      135.  iii.   Frank Campbell (7).
      136.  iv.    Quilligan Campbell (7).
```

    57. J. Kenny Campbell (6), son of William Campbell (5) and
Mary Jane Warwick McGuffin, married July 9, 1873, Georgia Ball.
He was an attorney in Covington, Virginia. He served as Superintendent of Schools in Highland County, Virginia in the early
1870's.

    Children: 1

```
      137.  i.     Bruce Campbell (7), a daughter, died unmarried.
```

    58. Almira Campbell (6), daughter of William Campbell (5)
and Mary Jane Warwick McGuffin, married Sidney Ruckman. They
lived in Oklahoma.

Children: 2

138. i.   William Ruckman (7).
139. ii.   Charles Ruckman (7).

61. William Price Campbell (6), son of William Campbell (5)
and Mary Jane Warwick McGuffin, married in 1889, Annie L. Ruckman,
daughter of David V. Ruckman and Anna Herring. He was an elder
in the Presbyterian Church.

Children: 10

+ 140. i.   Boyd L. Campbell (7).
+ 141. ii.   Glenn Campbell (7).
  142. iii. Roy Campbell (7), married Pleas Richardson,
daughter of Charles J. Richardson and Annie Thomas. (See Cleek
Family).
  143. iv.   Arthur Campbell (7), married (1) in 1927,
Louise Williams; died March 1952; married (2) Mrs. Elizabeth
McCauley Hunter.
  144. v.   Robert Campbell (7), married Mary Harris.
  145. vi.   Edna Campbell (7), married Rev. L. M. Moffett.
+ 146. vii. Lena May Campbell (7).
  147. viii. Lucille Campbell (7), married William M. Goodall.
  148. ix.   Margaret Campbell (7), married Harold Barrett.
  149. x.   Lillian Campbell (7), married Orval Karicofe.

63. Filmore T. Campbell (6), son of William Campbell (5) and
Mary Jane Warwick McGuffin, died January 1920; married Mary Ada
Sively, died February 19, 1940, Warm Springs, Virginia. He served
as Post Master at Warm Springs, Virginia.

Children: 8

  150. i.   George William Campbell (7), born June 1889;
died June 14, 1949; married Della Page, daughter of Lewis Page and
Malcena Thomas. No children. (See Cleek Family).
  151. ii.   Mary Kate Campbell (7), born April 5, 1891; died
in 1949; married January 12, 1922, Charles O. Stephenson, died May
1936, son of Charles Crawford Stephenson and Mary M. Lindsay. (See
Gwin Family).
  152. iii. Howard Campbell (7), married Ellen Turner, South
Carolina.
  153. iv.   Alberta Campbell (7), died July 1952.
  154. v.   Edward Campbell (7), died March 1944; married
Lucille Carey. No children.
  155. vi.   Almira Campbell (7), married H. Morton Hull.
No children.
  156. vii. Scott McKinley Campbell (7), married (1) Rose
Hepler; married (2) Geneva Hodge Burns, died April 3, 1957. No
children.
  157. viii. Lillian Campbell (7), married John D. Ghent.

65. Mary L. Campbell (6), daughter of A. Hanson Campbell (5) and Isabelle Lewis, married Lucius Homer Stephenson.

Children: 4

158. i. Josephine Stephenson (7), married Joseph W. Boyer, Woodstock, Virginia.
159. ii. Boyd Stephenson (7), born January 23, 1879; married (1) Louise Haile; married (2) October 30, 1918, Harriett Sommers Stephenson, born May 12, 1892, daughter of William W. Stephenson and Rachel Violet Sommers. He served as Commonwealth Attorney of Highland County, Virginia for several terms. (See Gwin Family).
160. iii. Lucius Homer Stephenson, Jr. (7), married (1) Elsie Hiner; married (2) Edith McGlaughlin, daughter of George H. McGlaughlin and Ruhama Wiley. No children of the second marriage. (See Gwin Family).
161. iv. Janet Stephenson (7), married Colonel Charles S. Roller, Fort Defiance, Virginia.

66. William A. Campbell (6), son of A. Hanson Campbell (5) and Isabelle Lewis, married Mary McCoy, Franklin, West Virginia.

Children: 2

162. i. Roy L. Campbell (7), married Kate Priest, Franklin, West Virginia.
163. ii. Carrie Campbell (7), married M. S. Hodges, an attorney, Franklin, West Virginia.

70. Alice Campbell (6), daughter of Edgar Campbell (5) and Elizabeth R. Lockridge, married John Flanagan.

Children: 3

164. i. Dr. T. O. Flanagan (7), Hinton, West Virginia.
165. ii. _____ Flanagan (7), married E. N. Faulconer, Hinton, West Virginia.
166. iii. _____ Flanagan (7), married Robert Murrell, Hinton, West Virginia.

74. Thomas Brown Hickman (7), son of Roger Hickman and Margaret Campbell (6), married (1) Mary Payne; married (2) Kate Whitmer.

Children: 4 - first marriage

167. i. Carrie Hickman (8).
168. ii. Leona Hickman (8).
169. iii. Brownie Hickman (8).
170. iv. Sallie Hickman (8).

Children: 2 - second marriage

171. v.   Margaret Hickman (8).
172. vi.   Hanson Hickman (8).

81. Matilda Hickman (7), daughter of Roger Hickman and Margaret Campbell (6), married Charles I. Hepler, Bath County, Virginia.

Children: 4

+   173. i.   William B. Hepler (8).
+   174. ii.   Forest F. Hepler (8).
    175. iii.   Minnie Hepler (8), married W. Valentine Wade.
They have two children.
    176. iv.   Eugene Hepler (8), died unmarried.

86. Edward Amos Wade (7), son of Anson Wade and Adella Campbell (6), was born August 13, 1864; died December 12, 1950; married September 1, 1886, Lucy Ruckman, died June 16, 1941. They lived at Mill Gay, Highland County, Virginia.

Children: 9

    177. i.   Evelyn Wade (8), unmarried.
    178. ii.   Annie Della Wade (8), unmarried.
    179. iii.   Sarah Wade (8), married (1) William Hevener; married (2) Charles H. Judy.
    180. iv.   Cornelia Wade (8), married Travis Fauver.
    181. v.   Virginia Wade (8), married Mack Briscoe.
    182. vi.   Edythe Wade (8), married Kenny C. Judy.
    183. vii.   Wilbur Wade (8), married Edmonia Ogilvie.
    184. viii. Anson Wade (8), unmarried.
    185. ix.   Charles Wade (8), married Ruth Maloy. She is a teacher.

87. Harry A. G. Wade (7), son of Anson Wade and Adella Campbell (6), was born in 1868; died in 1946; married in 1899, Lillie Curry, daughter of William Curry and Lucy Hill. They lived at Mill Gay, Highland County, Virginia.

Children: 3

    186. i.   May Wade (8), married _____ Hesley.
    187. ii.   Lorinne Wade (8), married Rex Loury.
    188. iii.   Hollis Wade (8), married Virgil Fox.

88. Walter Price Campbell (7), son of Austin Campbell (6) and Susan Hamilton, was born May 7, 1854; married (1) Gertrude Ball, born August 5, 1855; died March 22, 1900; married (2) Emma McClintic.

Children: 2 - first marriage

    189. i.   Raleigh Campbell (8), unmarried.
    190. ii.   Walter Prentiss Campbell (8), died September 24, 1954; married February 22, 1921, Lucy Thacker.

Children: 3 - second marriage

191. iii. Mary McClintic Campbell (8), twin to Margaret
Price, born June 9, 1906; died October 3, 1953.
192. iv. Margaret Price Campbell (8), twin to Mary
McClintic, born June 9, 1906; married Lewis Whites Carver.
193. v. Andrew Byrd Campbell (8), born August 30, 1908.

92. Leonidas Campbell (7), son of Amos Campbell (6) and
Martha Gammon, married Virginia Kincaid, daughter of Willis Kincaid
and Margaret T. Rhea. (See Lockridge Family).

Children: 4

194. i. Benton Kincaid (8), died February 1, 1957;
married Cleo Snider.
195. ii. Leonidas Preston Kincaid (8).
196. iii. Mabel Kincaid (8), married Ernest Doyle.
197. iv. Clementine Kincaid (8), married A. B. Saddler.

96. Robert Campbell (7), son of J. Brown Campbell (6) and
Amanda Fleisher, married Mary Boggs.

Children: 1

+ 198. i. J. Brown Campbell (8).

100. Benjamin B. Campbell (7), son of Luther Campbell (6)
and Mary E. Benson, died June 25, 1935; married (1) Bessie Moore,
daughter of I.Brown Moore and Kate Curry; married (2) Mrs. Dora
Cougar Moomau.

Children: 1 - first marriage

199. i. Luther Brown Campbell (8).

101. O. James Campbell (7), son of Luther Campbell (6) and
Mary E. Benson, was born April 6, 1880; died July 6, 1953; married
Louise Moore, daughter of Harry Moore and Cora Jones.

Children: 4

200. i. Katherine Campbell (8), Dunmore, West Virginia.
201. ii. Virginia Campbell (8), married _____ Garber
of S. Charleston, West Virginia.
202. iii. Dorothy Campbell (8), Washington, D. C.
203. iv. Martha Jean Campbell (8), married _____
Lovelace, of Dunmore, West Virginia.

102. Russell Campbell (7), son of Luther Campbell (6) and
Mary E. Benson, married Onie Thompson.

Children: 2

204. i. Eldon Campbell (8).
205. ii. Marilee Campbell (8).

103. Gay Campbell (7), son of Luther Campbell (6) and Mary
E. Benson, married Stella Dilley.

Children: 3

206. i. Ruth Campbell (8).
207. ii. Thelka Campbell (8).
208. iii. Feem Campbell (8).

104. Guy Campbell (7), son of Luther Campbell (6) and Mary
E. Benson, married (1) Florence Austin; married (2) Ercel Wheeler.

Children: 4 - first marriage

209. i. Austin Campbell (8).
210. ii. Mary Frances Campbell (8).
211. iii. Harriet Campbell (8).
212. iv. Jean Campbell (8).

105. Ernest Campbell (7), son of Luther Campbell (6) and
Mary E. Benson, was born September 24, 1893; died January 29, 1956;
married Elizabeth Hiner.

Children: 6

213. i. Evelyn Campbell (8), married _____ McQuain of
Baltimore, Maryland.
214. ii. Pauline Campbell (8), married _____ Hite.
They live in Richmond, Virginia.
215. iii. Eolyn ' Campbell (8).
216. iv. Wanda Campbell (8), married _____ James.
217. v. Lee Campbell (8).
218. vi. William Campbell (8).

107. Mary Campbell (7), daughter of Luther Campbell (6) and
Mary E. Benson, married E. Herbert Taylor. They live at Richmond,
Virginia.

Children: 2

219. i. Charles Taylor (8).
220. ii. Edward Taylor (8).

108. Ruth Campbell (7), daughter of Luther Campbell (6) and
Mary E. Benson, married (1) Herbert Noel; married (2) Charles
Hagey. They live in Los Angeles, California.

Children: 2 - first marriage

221. i. Jaunita Noel (8).
222. ii. Helen Noel (8).

323

109. Margaret Katherine Campbell (7), daughter of Luther Campbell (6) and Mary E. Benson, married Rev. Kemp D. Swecker.

Children: 2

223. i. Virginia Swecker (8), married W. L. Johnston.
224. ii. Nancy Swecker (8), married Clifford Watkins.

114. Helen Campbell (7), daughter of Oscar J. Campbell (6) and Annie L. Slaven; married W. H. Lumsford.

Children: 3

225. i. Kathleen Lumsford (8), married Herbert Mackey. No children.
226. ii. Mary Lumsford (8), married Dr. Hunter Wiltshire. No children. They live at Richmond, Virginia.
227. iii. Harry William Lumsford (8), unmarried, Washington, D. C.

115. Eva Campbell (7), daughter of Oscar J. Campbell (6) and Annie L. Slaven, married Adam Stephenson.

Children: 1

228. i. Anna Margaret Stephenson (8).

116. Sallie Campbell (7), daughter of Oscar J. Campbell (6) and Annie L. Slaven, married William R. Stephenson.

Children: 1

229. i. William R. Stephenson, Jr. (8), married Sarah Hope.

117. Jessie Campbell (7), daughter of Oscar J. Campbell (6) and Annie L. Slaven, married Harry Bird (8), son of D. O. Bird and Lillie Shumate.

Children: 2

230. i. Warren Bird (8), married Ruth Henderson.
231. ii. Eugene Bird (8), married Ramona Duncan.

124. Maggie Rodgers (7), daughter of William Kring Rodgers and Rachel R. Campbell (6), married J. M. Plowden, a Presbyterian minister.

Children: 5

232. i. J. McCollam Plowden (8).
233. ii. Eldridge R. Plowden (8).
234. iii. Josephine Plowden (8), married G. T. Lemmon.

235. iv. Marie Plowden (8).
236. v. Reba Plowden (8).

125. Annie Rebecca Rodgers (7), daughter of William Kring
Rodgers and Rachel R. Campbell (6), married Hughart Irvine of
Staunton, Virginia.

Children: 1

237. i. Rachel Irvine (8), married _____ Pritchard.

126. Charles W. Rodgers (7), son of William Kring Rodgers
and Rachel R. Campbell (6), married Margaret Van Lear. He was
a physician.

Children: 3

238. i. Charles W. Rodgers (8), a physician.
239. ii. William Kring Rodgers (8).
240. iii. Rachel Rodgers (8).

127. George R. Rodgers (7), son of William Kring Rodgers
and Rachel R. Campbell (6), married Sadie McCune. He was a
physician.

Children: 2

241. i. Elizabeth Rodgers (8).
242. ii. George R. Rodgers, Jr. (8).

128. Eugene K. Rodgers (7), son of William Kring Rodgers
and Rachel R. Campbell (6), married Edna Slaven.

Children: 1

243. i. Kring Rodgers (8), a daughter, married O. L.
Denton.

129. Lillie Shumate (7), daughter of William H. Shumate
and Louise Campbell (6), married D. O. Bird.

Children: 6

244. i. Harry Bird (8), married Jessie Campbell (7),
daughter of Oscar J. Campbell and Annie L. Slaven.
+ 245. ii. Arthur Bird (8).
+ 246. iii. D. Russell Bird (8).
247. iv. Forrest Bird (8), married Rebecca Hiner. No
children.
+ 248. v. Lucy G. Bird (8).
250. vi. Ernest Bird (8), married Naomi Adam. They have
a daughter, Sandra Bird (8).

130. Lucy Shumate (7), daughter of William H. Shumate and Louise Campbell (6), married Newman McClung of Greenbrier County, West Virginia.

Children: 3

250. i. Janie McClung (8), unmarried.
251. ii. Andrew McClung (8), married Lola Hanna.
252. iii. Lillis McClung (8), married Kathlenn Burgess.

131. Dick Shumate (7), son of William H. Shumate and Louise Campbell (6), died in Waynesboro, Virginia; married Lelia McClung.

Children: 4

253. i. Mary Campbell Shumate (8), a R.N.
254. ii. John Shumate (8), married Iva Patterson.
255. iii. Warwick Shumate (8), married Janet Knopp.
256. iv. Anna Guy Shumate (8), married Clyde Smith.

140. Boyd L. Campbell (7), son of William Price Campbell (6) and Annie L. Ruckman, married October 1, 1913, Maude Lockridge, daughter of Dr. James Bedford Lockridge and Margaret Warwick. She died November 23, 1951. (See Lockridge Family).

Children: 6
257. i. Bedford Campbell (8), married Elizabeth Thompson.
258. ii. Lacy Campbell (8), died in infancy.
259. iii. Newton Wood Campbell (8), married Cookie Campbell.
260. iv. Charlotte Campbell (8), married Elmer G. Walker.
261. v. Janet Campbell (8), married Arthur Frey.
262. vi. Craig Campbell (8), married Lena Allen.

141. Glenn Campbell (7), son of William Price Campbell (6) and Annie L. Ruckman, married Mary Katherine Pierce. He is a physician in Staunton, Virginia. She is a R.N.

Children: 4

263. i. Glenn Campbell,Jr. (8), married Jean Rolen of Peterstown, West Virginia.
264. ii. Louise Campbell (8), married Dr. David Christian, III. He.was killed at Appomattox, Virginia.
265. iii. William Campbell (8), married Rosalie Shirkey.
266. iv. Alice Campbell (8), married Claude Shifflet.

146. Lena May Campbell (7), daughter of William Price Campbell (6) and Annie L. Ruckman, married Rev. B. L. Wood. He was a Presbyterian minister.

Children: 4

267. i. B. L. Wood, Jr. (8).
268. ii. Virginia Campbell Wood (8), married Earl S. King,

326

Jr., a Missionary in Africa.-
269. iii. William Wood (8).
270. iv. James Wood (8).

173. William B. Hepler (8), son of Charles I. Hepler and
Matilda Hickman (7), married _____ Goddin. He was Commissioner
of Revenue of Eastern District of Bath County, Virginia.
Children: 13
271. i.   Merlin Hepler (9), married Belle Vines.
272. ii.   Vina Hepler (9), married Ralph Shaver.
273. iii. Emma Hepler (9), married William Snyder.
274. iv.   _____ Hepler (9), married W. L. Maust.
275. v.   _____ Hepler (9), married Ted Zoff.
276. vi.   _____ Hepler (9), married Ray Congleton.
277. vii. _____ Hepler (9), married Howard Wilt.
278. viii. Charles William Hepler (9).
279. ix.   Hunter Hepler (9).
280. x.   Eloise Hepler (9).
281. xi.   Kathleen Hepler (9).
282. xii. _____ Hepler (9), married Jack Terry.
283. xiii. Mary Florence Hepler (9).

174. Forest F. Hepler (8), son of Charles I. Hepler and
Matilda Hickman (7), married Lula McClung.

Children: 4

284. i.   Bryan F. Hepler (9), married (1) Love Lantz;
married (2) Reba Chaplin.
285. ii.   Murray Hepler (9), married Lillian Corbett.
286. iii. James Hepler (9).
287. iv.   Louise Hepler (9), married George Brown
Venable, Jr.

198. J. Brown Campbell (8), son of Robert Campbell (7) and
Mary Boggs, married Lorena Terry.

Children: 2

288. i.   J. Brown Campbell, Jr. (9), married Kring Woods.
289. ii.   Harl Campbell (9), married Anna Lee Hoover.

245. Arthur Bird (8), son of D. O. Bird and Lillie Shumate
(7), married Maude Patrick.

Children: 2

290. i.   W. Arthur Bird (9).
291. ii.   Dorothy Bird (9).

246. D. Russell Bird (8), son of D. O. Bird and Lillie
Shumate (7), married Thelma Dever.

327

Children: 2

292. i. Mary Idena Bird (9), married Brooks Rexrode.
293. ii. James Bird (9).

248. Lucy G. Bird (8), daughter of D. O. Bird and Lillie Shumate (7), married Thomas J. Diamond.

Children: 2

294. i. Thomas J. Diamond, Jr. (9), married Helga Runkle.
295. ii. David Diamond (9), unmarried.

PART VII

CARLILE FAMILY

The name Carlile is also found as Carlisle, Corolile, and
Carlyle. The original spelling was Carlisle. In this family
history the spelling Carlile has been used throughout. This
family is one of the so-called "Scotch-Irish" families.

1. James Carlile (1), born 1670 in County Down, Ireland;
died 1752 in Augusta County, Virginia; married 1695 in Ireland,
Elizabeth _____. James Carlile and his wife, Elizabeth, came
to America from Ireland and were of staunch Scotch-Irish descent.
They settled in Augusta County, Virginia, on the Calfpasture
River. On March 21, 1753, Elizabeth Carlile and James Carlile, Jr.
qualified as administrators of the estate of James Carlile, Sr.,
deceased, with sureties William Smith and Robert Bratton. (Abstracts from the Records of Augusta County, Virginia, Lyman
Chalkley, Vol. III, page 33.) Elizabeth Carlile sold land on the
Calfpasture River to William Hamilton for $87.50, and the Carlile
family moved to Newfound Creek, Clover Creek, or what is now known
as Bullpasture River in Highland County, Virginia.

Children: 3

+ 2. i. Robert Carlile (2).
+ 3. ii. John Carlile (2).
+ 4. iii. James Carlile, Jr. (2), born 1725.

2. Robert Carlile (2), son of James Carlile (1) and Elizabeth
_____, died c. 1800; married (1) in 1747, Nancy _____; married
(2) Mary Wandless. He served in the Revolution and was at the Battle of Guilford Court House, North Carolina.

Children: 7 - first marriage

5. i. George Carlile (3).
6. ii. Elizabeth Carlile (3), married _____ Ham.
7. iii. John Carlile (3), married Nancy _____. They
moved to Kentucky. John Griffin Carlile, a descendant, was Senator of Kentucky and a member of President Cleveland's cabinet.
8. iv. Jean Carlile (3), born 1750; died 1838; married Christopher Graham, born July 9, 1755; died 1840, and was
buried at Clover Creek, Highland County, Virginia, son of Robert
Graham and Jean Hicklin. (See Graham Family). (Abstracts from
the Records of Augusta County, Virginia, Lyman Chalkley, Vol. I,
page 161).
9. v. Rachel Esther Carlile (3), died 1823; married
Robert ("the Big") Carlile (3), son of John Carlile (2) and Mary
Elizabeth _____.
10. vi. Robert ("the Little") Carlile (3), died in 1821;
married Elizabeth Jenkins.
11. vii. Nancy Carlile (3), married _____ Glenn.

3. John Carlile (2), son of James Carlile (1) and Elizabeth
_____; died in 1796; married (1) Mary Elizabeth _____; mar-
ried (2) Margaret Wandless. He served in the Revolution and was
at the Battle of Guilford Court House, North Carolina.

Children: 9 - first marriage

12. i. Samuel Carlile (3), married Margaret (Peggy)
Hamilton.
13. ii. George Carlile (3), married _____ Malcolm.
No children.
+ 14. iii. Robert ("the Big") Carlile (3).
15. iv. Rachel Carlile (3), married Jonathan Moore.
16. v. Joseph Carlile (3). In 1782 Joseph Carlile
and David Carlile had military claims on Indian Creek, Monroe
County, Virginia.
17. vi. David Carlile (3). His property in Monroe County,
Virginia was appraised in 1786 by Hutchinson, Hugh Caperton, Roger
Kilpatrick, and Valentine Cook.
18. vii. James Carlile (3).
19. viii. Mary Carlile (3), married _____ Mims.
20. ix. Margaret Carlile (3), married _____ Alford.

4. James Carlile, Jr. (2), son of James Carlile (1) and
Elizabeth _____, was born in 1725 in Augusta County, Virginia;
died in 1802 in Bath County (now Highland County), Virginia; mar-
ried in 1746, Nancy Rachel Campbell, still living in 1802, dau-
ghter of William Campbell and Sarah _____. (See Campbell Family)
James Carlile, Jr. was severely wounded at the Battle of Guilford
Court House, North Carolina and was taken home by his brothers,
John and Robert Carlile and his son-in-law, Captain David Gwin.
(A Hand Book of Highland County, O. F. Morton, page 193). (Also
Virginians in the Revolution, John H. Gwathmey, page 130). His
will is recorded in Bath County, Virginia in Will Book 1, page 212,
and was dated January 16, 1802 and probated June 1802. It mentions:
Wife, Nancy Carlile; sons, John, James, Robert, William, Samuel,
and Alexander Carlile; and daughters, Jinny Carlile, Elizabeth
Hicklin, and Nancy Carlile. Witnesses were John Erwin, Robert
Carlile, and Thos Peebles. Executors were sons, John and James
Carlile.

Children: 9

21. i. Jane Carlile (3), born November 26, 1746 in
Augusta County, Virginia; died 1787 and was buried on Jackson
River, Bath County (now Highland County), Virginia; married 1768,
David Gwin, born 1742 in Orange County Wales; died 1822 at Clover
Creek, Bath County (now Highland County), Virginia, son of Robert
Gwin and Jean Kincaid. (See Gwin Family).
22. ii. Robert Carlile (3), born 1748; married _____.
Griffen of Connecticut.
23. iii. William Carlile (3), born 1747; married (1)
_____ McClure; married (2) _____ Thompson.
24. iv. Nancy Rachel Carlile (3), born 1750; married
Robert Peoples.

<pre>
+   25.   v.   John Carlile (3), born 1752.
    26.   vi. Elizabeth Carlile (3), born 1754; married George
Hicklin, son of John Hicklin and Jane _____.
    27.   vii. Samuel Carlile (3), born 1756.
    28.   viii. George Alexander Carlile (3), born 1757.
    29,   ix. James Carlile (3), born 1759, died young.
</pre>

14.   Robert ("the Big") Carlile (3), son of John Carlile (3)
and Mary Elizabeth _____, married Rachel Esther Carlile (3), died
in 1823, daughter of Robert Carlile and Nancy _____.

Children: 7

<pre>
+   30.   i.   Robert Carlile (4).
+   31.   ii. Nancy Carlile (4).
    32.   iii. Elizabeth Carlile (4), born November 16, 1801;
</pre>
died February 19, 1861; married January 14, 1823 in Bath County,
Virginia (as his first wife), Andrew Lockridge, born September
23, 1801; died April 19, 1872, son of Robert Lockridge and Mary
Gwin. (See Gwin Family).
<pre>
    33.   iv. Jane Carlile (4), married April 14, 1835 in
</pre>
Bath County, Virginia, James M. Helms. (See Gwin Family).
<pre>
    34.   v.   Rachel Jane Carlile (4), married (as his first
</pre>
wife), Robert Lockridge, born September 14, 1809; died March 28,
1891, son of Robert Lockridge and Mary Gwin. They had two children, but both died young. (See Gwin Family).
<pre>
    35.   vi. George Carlile (4), died unmarried.
    36.   vii. Margaret Carlile (4), died unmarried.
</pre>

25.   John Carlile (3), son of James Carlile, Jr. (2) and
Nancy Rachel Campbell, was born in 1752; married Rachel Feamster,
daughter of Thomas Feamster. They migrated to Missouri.

Children: 3

<pre>
+   37.   i.   Mary Rachel Carlile (4).
    38.   ii. Christopher Carlile (4), married _____. They
</pre>
migrated to Shelby County, Missouri. Two letters written by
Christopher Carlile to John Cleek read as follows:

                              Oak Dale, Shelby Co., Mo.,
                              Oct. 3th (sic), 1858
John Cleek, Esq.:
    Dear Sir: After my best respects to you and family I will
just (say) to you that we are well except myself and Mougot the
black woman. We have got up and about again. There is very little
sickness in this neighborhood but along Salt and all the other small
streams they have the chills and fevers badly and from newspapers
rumors along the Mississippi and Missouri Bottoms that were over-
so long there is not well ones enough to help the sick. I would be
very glad if you could send me the exact amount of Sallie Doughlas
claim as quick as you can. I want to send her Rest on and let the
commissioner finish his settlement. I intend to go down to Bird's

in a few days and settle your note as requested. He was up here
some time ago buying hogs to fatten and I lent him $100 to go to
Va. but I understand he give it out upon account of Corn cutting an
seedtime being too close at hand. You wished to know when I was
coming to Va. That is a question I cannot answer at present. It
may be the month of December before I start. I want you to let me
know if I can get anything that is coming to me first before I
start.
     I was up at Bethel a few days ago and I rode out to A.S.C.
Cleek's an hour or two. They are all well and his wife was more
than pleased when she found her daughter was on the way home.
     Corn crops is pretty fair, wheat tolerable. R. Doughlas
has 50 bushels. Davis upwards of 100 and a great many none a
tall. There is a good bit sowed but not doing well in consequence of the drouth. Davis has sowed some for Lightner on his
farm. As directed there is a great reduction in the value of lands
since you were here. There is farms here that could not be bought
for less than $15 per acre now they would be glad to get $10 and
don't pretend to ask any more.
     I will close by requesting you to let me know what prospect
there will be to get what little is coming to me as soon as you can
find it convenient to do so.
     Give my respects to all enquiring and except the same yourself

John Cleek   /s/ Christopher Carlisle

     I forgot to say to you that the Texas cattle was driven in
on the prairie here about harvest in lots of 500 and a 1000 in a
drove. They herded them here until they sold. One of the firms
went to New York and brought a butcher here and sold him 150 head
and some drove to Chicago to have butchered and pact.

                         Oak Dale, P.O., Shelby Co., Mo.
                         Sept. 18th--60

Dear Friend:
     Your letter of 7th Inst. was received on yesterday. We are al
well except R. W. Doughlas' children. Some of them is complaining
but still running about. The health is better in this country
this year than any year since I came here. We are sorry to hear
of Mrs. Cleek (this is Mrs. Jane Gwin Cleek) lingering so long.
I am busy how cutting up my corn. It is ripe and very heavy. We
have had some cold nights and a little frost that bit the vines a
little but not enough to hurt buckwheat. Pork Cutters at Palmyra
are running about trying to make engagements at $6.00 per lb. to
be delivered at killing time.
     S. Moyers is filing his bill of injunction against Davis has
made Jane and me parties in it. It was received here since I wrote
to you last by D. Fultz for us to answer which was done instantly.
He has made some of the gravest charges I ever heard. I hope his
bill will be dissolved at the sitting of the Court.
     I have written to Fultz and given him a proposition to make to
Moyers' counsel in case the bill is not rejected that I think will

settle all difficulties. I don't want you to say anything about it until after the Circuit Court. Whenever Moyers pays you any money send it without delay. I have got nothing more to write to you at present. I bid you an affectionate farewell for the present and hope these few lines may find you and family enjoying better health than you have had.

John Cleek   /s/ Christopher Carlisle

P.S. P, Davis daughter Phebe was married on yesterday to Thomas B. Broughton.

39. iii. Jane Carlile (4), moved to Missouri.

30. Robert Carlile (4), son of Robert ("the Big") Carlile (3) and Rachel Esther Carlile (3), married Margaret Hamilton. They migrated to Iowa in 1850.

Children: 4

40. i.   Rachel Carlile (5).
41. ii.   Elizabeth Carlile (5).
42. iii. Charles Carlile (5).
43. iv.   James Carlile (5).

31. Nancy Carlile (4), daughter of Robert ("the Big") Carlile (3) and Rachel Esther Carlile (3), married April 8, 1818 in Bath County, Virginia, Andrew Sitlington, son of John Sitlington and his second wife, Elizabeth McDonald.

Children: 5

44. i.   Charles Sitlington (5), died unmarried.
45. ii.   William Sitlington (5), married _____ Walker.
46. iii. Margaret Ann Sitlington (5), married (1) Joseph B. Dickenson; married (2) _____ Stoakley.
47. iv.   Martha Sitlington (5), married John Porter.
48. v.   George Sitlington (5).

37. Mary Rachel Carlile (4), daughter of John Carlile (3) and Rachel Feamster, married June 29, 1830 in Bath County, Virginia, Paschal Davis. They lived in Missouri.

Children: 1 (and others?)

49. i.   Phoebe Davis (5), married September 17, 1860 in Missouri, Thomas B. Broughton.

PART VIII

CRAIG FAMILY

The Craig Family belongs to the so-called Scotch-Irish group. They came to America from the north of Ireland about 1721. It is believed that Rev. John Craig, who arrived in America on August 17, 1734, and who was the first Presbyterian minister regularly settled in the Colony of Virginia, was the brother or William Craig. John Craig was born in the parish of Dunager, County of Antrim, Ireland on August 17, 1709; married June 11, 1744 in Pennsylvania, Isabella Helena Russell. He died April 22, 1774 and was buried at the Old Stone Church in Augusta County, Virginia. He served as an early minister to both the Old Stone Church and the Tinkling Spring Church in Augusta County, Virginia. (The Tinkling Spring by Howard McKnight Wilson).

1. William Craig (1), born in Ireland c. 1685; died 1759 in Augusta County, Virginia; married in Ireland, Janet _____. William Craig and Janet, his wife, landed in America from the north of Ireland in 1721-22 with three sons, Robert, James, and John. He settled first in Pennsylvania (Lancaster or Chester County) and moved to Augusta County, Virginia with his family by 1744. Little is known of William Craig beyond the fact that he was an adherent to the Scotch-Irish Covenanter Presbyterian. The Craig family aided in building the Old Stone Church in Augusta County, Virginia. His wife, Janet, was still living in 1759 but nothing is known of her further history nor the date of her death. The will of William Craig was recorded in Will Book 2, Page 348, Augusta County, Virgini and reads as follows:

In the name of God Amen the twenty first Day of Febry anno Dom 1756. I William Craig in the Collony of Virginia & County of Augusta ye man being very sick and weak in body but of perfect mind and memory thanks be given unto God therefore calling unto mind the mortality of my body and knowing that it is appointed for all men once to die Do make & ordain this my last Will and Testament. That is to say principally and first of all I give and recommend my Soul into the hand of God that gave it and for my body I recommend it to the earth to be buried in a Christian like & decent manner at the direction of my Executors nothing doubting but at the general resurrection I shall receive the same again by the mighty power of God and as touching such worldly Estate where with it hath pleased God to bless me in this Life I give devise & dispose of the same in the following manner and form. Imprimis I give & bequeath to Janet my dearly beloved wife the whole of my estate, Lands, chattels and household goods except one mare branded with DL and another branded this pc which I give to my Eldest Son Robbert Craig, and further I order that what remains of sd Estate at my wife's decease shall be divided betwixt my three sons Robbert James & John Craig and 2 shares shall be given to whom my said wife shall think fit. Further I likewise construct and ordain Robert Craig and James Craig my only & sol Executors of this my last Will and Testament

and I do hereby utterly disallow revoke & disanul all and every
other former Testaments Wills & Legacies bequests and Executed by
me in any wise before this Time & bequeathed Ratifying and confirming this and no other to be my last will and Testament in witness
whereof I have here Set my hand and Seal the day and year above
written.

His
William (CC) Craig (SEAL)
Mark

Witnesses were George Crawford and James Leard. The will was
recorded November 26, 1759 in Augusta County, Virginia.

Children: 3

+   2   i.   Robert Craig (2).
+   3.   ii.   James Craig (2), born c. 1715.
    4.   iii.   John Craig (2), born c. 1717; died in Lincoln
County, Kentucky. He left a number of descendants.

2. Robert Craig (2), son of William Craig (1) and Janet
_____, was born in Ireland; died June 1788 in Augusta County,
Virginia; married _____. His will was recorded in
Augusta County, Virginia in Will Book 7, page 90, and reads as
follows:

In the name of God Amen I Robert Craig of the County of
Augusta in the middle river Farmer being sick and diseased in body
but of perfect mind and memory thanks be given to God Calling to
mind the mortality of the body and knowing that it is appointed
for all men once to die Do make and ordain this my last will and
testament that is to say principally and first of all I give and
recommend my soul to the hands of Almighty God that gave it and
I recommend my body to the earth to be buried in decent and
Christian burial at the discretion of my executors nothing doubting
but that at the general resurrection I shall receive the same by
the Almighty power of God and as touching such worldly estate wherewith it has pleased God to bless me in this Life I give and devise
and dispose of the same in the following manner and form.
Item, I give and bequeath unto my son John Craig the two
tracts of land one whereon I now live containing 192 acres and the
other adjoining thereto containing 200 acres Except as is hereafter
excepted to wit that the said tracts of land shall not be his so or
in any such manner as he may have power or right to dispose of or
Sell the same whilst either of my daughters Anne or Rebecca Craig
remain unmarried and also if my son John Craig Should die without
Leaving any Living Legitimate Issue behind him the said two tracts
of Land is to descend to my son Robert Craig and to my two daughters
Anne and Rebecca Craig to them and their heirs and assigns in three
equal divisions forever and to be sold or otherwise conducted so
that each may have their Due share and that the said son Robert and
daughters Anne and Rebecca if the Land above mentioned decends to
them they are to pay the sum of ten pounds in Gold or Silver arising from the value or Sale of Land to each of my other two sons

and each of my other four daughters But if my Son John Craig is
blessed with Living Legitimate children at death the Land is to
be his and his heirs and assigns forever but not to be sold wilst
Either of my daughters Anne and Rebecca Craig remain unmarried
without consent.

Item, I also give and bequeath to my daughters Anne and Rebecca Craig the sum of twenty pounds each current money of Virginia
to be paid by my son John Craig also a negro woman named Sall with
her increase I give and Bequeath to my daughters Anne and Rebecca
Craig (equally proportioned) to them their heirs and assigns. Likewise I give to my daughter Anne Craig a negro boy named Jacob and
a green rug. I also give to my daughter Rebecca a Negro child
(female) named Amy and a large pot I likewise give and bequeath
to my daughters Anne and Rebecca Craig all my household goods and
all my household furniture Equally valued or Divided Except the
bed where I dye Blankets Sheets etc. Them I give to my son Robert
Craig Likewise I confirm to my daughters Anne and Rebecca the horse
_____ I had heretofore given them. Likewise all the Cattle I
had heretofore given them Likewise all the cattle I now possess I
divide equally Betwixt my daughters Anne and Rebecca Craig except
two cows and two calves which I give to my son John Craig Likewise
I give to my daughters Anne and Rebecca Craig all my sheep Except
the third herd I give to my son John Craig Likewise I give to my
daughters Anne and Rebecca Craig or either of them whilst they remain unmarried my dwelling house kitchen smoke house and one convenient Stable freely to possess and enjoy. Likewise I constitute
and ordain that after my Dissase my son John Craig shall provide
and deliver to my two daughters Anne and Rebecca Craig yearly to
each of them whilst they remain unmarried (or to her that will be
single) one hundred weight of hemp clear and good for Spining,
twenty bushels of corn ten bushels of wheat and five bushels of
rye and two hundred weight of meal and a bushel of salt and necessary Root or Sallet also a half acre of flax sowed on good ground
and a small garden spot also the free use of water Springs water
and so forth and the one sixth of my fruit trees and fruit also
necessary firewood cut and haled also my son John Craig to provide
necessary forage Pasturage and keep one mare or horse for each
whilst unmarried as also to provide sufficient forage and keep two
calves for each while unmarried and that the calves of said cows
shall be provided by him till they are one year and a half old
Likewise he shall if they require it grant the Liberty and find
sufficient forage to raise any of said calves to take the place of
their Dame when old or Dead Lastly I give and bequeath to my son
John Craig a negro fellow named Will and also implements of hus-
bandry – Horses and Hogs that are mine on the premises As for the
other of my children that I left nothing certain to above I give
them ten shillings each to be paid by son John Craig whom with my
son Robert Craig I constitute executors of this my last will and
testament and do utterly disallow revoke and disannul all and every
other testament wills _____ by me in anywise before named willed
or bequeathed, Ratifying and confirming this and no other to be my
last will and testament in witness whereof I have hereunto Set my

hand and seal this fifth day of October in the year of our Lord
one thousand seven hundred and eighty seven.

Robert Craig (SEAL)

Witnesses were Jas. Henderson, Andrew Henderson and Alexander
Henderson. His will was proved on September 16, 1788 in Augusta
County, Virginia by John and Robert Craig, executors.

A Record of Baptisms, 1740-1749, by Rev. John Craig, D.D.,
while pastor in Augusta County, Virginia, gives the following as
children of Robert Craig (apparently there was more than one
Robert Craig):

John Craig	March 15, 1741
Elenor Craig	July 19, 1741
Elisabeth Craig	May 2, 1742
Jennet Craig	September 4, 1743
Margaret Craig	April 7, 1745
John Craig	April 6, 1746
William Craig	December 13, 1747
Frances Craig	June 12, 1748

Children: 10 (as given in will)

5.	i.	John Craig (3).
+ 6.	ii.	Robert Craig (3).
7.	iii.	Anne Craig (3).
8.	iv.	Rebecca Craig (3).
9.	v.	(Son) Craig (3).
10.	vi.	(Son) Craig (3).
11.	vii.	(Daughter) Craig (3).
12.	viii.	(Daughter) Craig (3).
13.	ix.	(Daughter) Craig (3).
14.	x.	(Daughter) Craig (3).

3. James Craig (2), son of William Craig (1) and Janet _____
____, was born c. 1715 in the north of Ireland; died February 7,
1791 in his 76th year; married Mary Laird, died February 20, 1785.
They lived near Mount Meridian, Virginia in Augusta County. His
will was dated February 2, 1791 and recorded February 15, 1791 in
Will Book 7, page 335, Augusta County, Virginia. It mentions sons,
James, William, George, Samuel; daughters, Sarah Ely or Thorp;
heirs of daughter Mary Craig, deceased; daughter Agnes Anderson
and her husband James Anderson; to each grandson named of testator,
viz: James Craig's son, James; William Craig's son, James; Samuel
Craig's son, James (if he have one); James Ely's son, James; James
Anderson's son, James. Executors - James, George, and William
Craig.

Children: 8

15. i. Sarah Craig (3), born February 1, 1743; married

337

(1) _____ Thorpe; married (2) James Ely. She moved to Lincoln
County, Kentucky shortly after her second marriage.
+ 16.   ii.   James Craig (3), born July 23, 1745.
   17.   iii. Samuel Craig (3), born June 26, 1746; died September 25, 1795; married _____. They migrated to Lincoln
County, Kentucky.
   18.   iv.   John Craig (3), born November 21, 1747; died
November 21, 1772, unmarried.
+ 19.   v.   George Craig (3), born January 4, 1749.
   20.   vi.   William Craig (3), born January 8, 1750; died
September 8, 1829; married in 1778, Jean Anderson, born 1744; died
June 9, 1811, daughter of John Anderson, and widow of Lieutenant
Hugh Allen who was killed in the battle of Point Pleasant in 1774.
William Craig served during the Revolution as a private from 1778
to 1781 in the company of Captain John Givens.
   21.   vii. Mary Craig (3), born May 10, 1752; died January
16, 1778; married William Anderson. William Anderson was a captain
in the Revolution. He moved to Kentucky in 1784.
   22.   viii. Agnes Craig (3), born April 10, 1754; married
James Anderson. James Anderson served as a captain in the Revoluti
They migrated to South Carolina.

6. Robert Craig (3), son of Robert Craig (2) and _____
___, died in 1804 in Greenbrier County, now in West Virginia; married Nancy (Agnes) Johnson, daughter of James Johnson and Susanna
_____. James Johnson and Susanna _____ first lived in August
County, Virginia and then moved to Greenbrier County, now in West
Virginia. They were married prior to 1768. (Abstracts from the
Records of Augusta County, Virginia, Lyman Chalkley, Vol. III, page
479). They had at least three children:

            i.   James Johnson, married Isabella Jenkins.
            ii. Elenor Johnson, married Hugh Hannah.
            iii. Nancy (Agnes) Johnson, married Robert Craig.

James Johnson served as a Lieutenant in the Augusta Militia. He
served in Captain Baskins Company. He took his oath March 21, 1782
(Historical Register of Virginias in the Revolution, John H. Gwathmey, pages 421 and 424; Virginia Militia in the Revolutionary War,
J. T. McAllister, pages 182 and 207).
   Robert Craig served in Captain John Given's Company of militia
in Augusta County, Virginia from October 1777 to March 1782 with
two uncles and three cousins. (Gleanings of Virginia History,
William Fletcher Boogher, page 223; Register of Virginians in the
Revolution, John H. Gwathmey, page 187). Robert Craig and his wife
lived above Sinking Creek near the Richlands in Greenbrier County,
now West Virginia. His will was recorded in Will Book 1, page 190,
Greenbrier County, now in West Virginia. It reads as follows:

   In the name of God Amen. I Robert Craig of the County of
Greenbrier and the State of Virginia being at present in a doubtful state of Health & well aware of my mortality & the uncertainty
of life do in duty to my Family make ordain and declare This Instru
ment of writing to be my last Will & Testament Revoking all other

338

wills by me before made. 1st Item to my well beloved wife Nancy I give and bequeath the plantation I now live on with all the household furniture & plantation utensils my negro boy Humphrey During her natural Life Except such of the furniture as I shall otherwise dispose of.

2d Item to my son Robert Craig I give and bequeath the plantation I now live on after his Mothers Death to go to him & his heirs forever also my negro Boy Humphrey I give to my said son Robert in Like manner I also allow my said Son Robert to take the plantation & the plantation utensils in possession at my death & to keep them until his Mothers Death provided he keep his Mother in a decent & plentiful manner but if he does not provide for his mother as I have denoted he must give up the plantation & etc until his mothers Death.

3d Item to my daughter Jane I give & bequeath in addition to the horse creature bed & that she has got forty dollars.

4th Item to my Daughter Betsy I give & bequeath one horse creature in addition to what she has got to be worth Eighty Dollars.

5th Item to my Daughter Rebecca I give & bequeath one young mare rising three years old Known by the name of the Bachus filly & Saddle one bed & furniture & two cows and calfs.

6th Item to my three Eldest Daughters to witt Mary, Nancy & Margaret I give & bequeath each of them one dollar & no more as they have recd their full share long since.

7th Item After my just debts paid if any there be I give & bequeath to my beloved wife Nancy all the balance of my estate trusting to her it be worth while that she will make an Equitable Deviation (sic) among our children at her death.

And this I do declare to be my last will & for the due execution of the Same, I do hereby appoint my well beloved son Robert Executor. In testimony whereof I have hereunto Set my hand & seal & Subscribed my name this 20th day of September in the year of our Lord one thousand eight hundred & four.

Robert Craig (SEAL)

Witnesses were Joseph Hannah, John Brown, John Clutter, and Wm. Renick. The will was recorded October 30, 1804.

Children: 7

23. i. Robert Craig (4), married December 9, 1810 in Greenbrier County, now West Virginia, Frances (Fanny) Pinnel.
24. ii. Mary Craig (4), married Robert Stephens.
25. iii. Nancy (Agnes) Craig (4), married November 2, 1797 in Greenbrier County, now West Virginia, William Warwick, son of William Warwick and _____. (See Warwick Family).
26. iv. Margaret Craig (4), married April 18, 1816 in Greenbrier County, now in West Virginia, Joseph Westlake.
27. v. Sarah Jane Craig (4), married February 7, 1810 in Greenbrier County, West Virginia, Thomas Westlake.
28. vi. Elizabeth (Betsy) Craig (4), married December 15, 1798 in Greenbrier County, now in West Virginia, Andrew Warwick, son of William Warwick and _____. (See Warwick Family.'

339

29. vii. Rebecca Craig (4), married July 28, 1803 in Greenbrier County, now in West Virginia, William Benson.

16. James Craig (3), son of James Craig (2) and Mary Laird, was born July 23, 1745; died in 1807; married Jane Stuart. He served during the Revolution in the company of Captain John Givens. His will was dated April 19, 1807 and recorded June 22, 1807 in Will Book X, page 132, Augusta County, Virginia. It mentions wife, Jane; sons, John, James, Samuel, George, William, Elijah, and Robert; daughters, Sarah, Betsy, Agness, Jane, and Mary McGill. Executors were son-in-law Robert McGill and son, John Craig.

Children: 12

30. i. John Craig (4), died in 1840 in Augusta County, Virginia.
31. ii. James Craig (4).
32. iii. Samuel Craig (4), born 1780; died July 18, 1843; married Elizabeth Bratton, born 1789, daughter of Adam Bratton and Elizabeth Feamster. (See Bratton Family).
33. iv. George Craig (4).
34. v. William Craig (4), migrated to Kentucky.
35. vi. Elijah Craig (4), born 1789; died 1862. Moved to Richmond, Virginia.
36. vii. Sarah Craig (4), married John C. Hamilton.
37. viii. Elizabeth Craig (4).
38. ix. Agnes (Nancy) Craig (4), married Andrew Hamilton.
39. x. Jane Craig (4).
40. xi. Robert Craig (4).
41. xii. Mary Craig (4), married Robert McGill.

19. George Craig (3), son of James Craig (2) and Mary Laird, was born January 4, 1749; died November 26, 1801; married December 16, 1790, Elizabeth Evans, died April 29, 1801. He served during the Revolution in the company of Captain John Givens. His wife died at age 32.

Children: 4

42. i. James Craig (4), married _____ Crawford. They migrated to Missouri.
43. ii. Mary Craig (4), married John A. Patterson.
44. iii. Margaret Craig (4), married Samuel Patterson.
+ 45. iv. George E. Craig (4), born April 29, 1801.

45. George E. Craig (4), son of George Craig (3) and Elizabeth Evans, was born April 29, 1801; died in Pocahontas County, West Virginia; married in 1824, Matilda Guthrie.

Children: 4

46. i. Margaret Ann Craig (5), died March 19, 1892; married Robert I. Crawford.

47. ii. Caroline Elizabeth Craig (5), married September 10, 1848 in Pocahontas County, West Virginia, John Wood Warwick, son of Andrew Sitlington Warwick and Mary N. Woods. (See Warwick Family).
48. iii. John Newton Craig (5), died October 1900; married Lydia Brevard Harris of Cabarrus County, North Carolina. John Newton Craig,D.D., was a Presbyterian minister. He served as Chaplain in the CSA. For many years he was Secretary of the Home Mission Work of the Southern Presbyterian Church.
49. iv. Hugh Brown Craig (5), was born in 1837. He graduated from Washington College in 1858. He served as Adjutant of Edgar's 26th Virginia Battalion in the CSA. He was killed at the battle of Cold Harbor on June 3, 1864.

PART IX

CRAWFORD FAMILY

The Crawford Family is of Scottish ancestry. They were among the earliest settlers of Augusta County, Virginia. The Crawfords first arrived in Pennsylvania and came from Pennsylvania to Orange and Augusta Counties, Virginia about 1740.

Two brothers, said to be sons of Colonel William Crawford and Mary Douglas who were married in Scotland and migrated to the north of Ireland, were:

+ 1.   Alexander Crawford (1).
+ 2.   Patrick Crawford (1).

1. Alexander Crawford (1), married Mary McPheeters. He and his wife were killed by the Indians about October 1764. The administrator of his estate qualified during the November Court,1764, Augusta County, Virginia.

Children: 12

+ 3.   i.   William Crawford (2).
  4.   ii.   Edward Crawford (2), a Presbyterian minister of Tennessee.
  5.   iii. John Crawford (2), married (1) Peggy Crawford, daughter of Patrick Crawford; married (2) Mary Craig; married (3) Sally Newman.
  6.   iv.   James Crawford (2), died in 1803; married Catherine _____. He was a Presbyterian minister and migrated to Kentucky.
+ 7.   v.   Alexander Crawford (2).
  8.   vi.   Rebecca Crawford (2), born 1752; married John Sawyers.

341

```
9.      vii.    Bettie Crawford (2), married William Stainer.
10.     viii.   Margaret Crawford (2), married John Houston.
11.     ix.     Samuel Crawford (2), born 1759.
12:     x.      Robert Crawford (2), married Martha Paxton, who
was born 1753.
13.     xi.     Martha Crawford (2), married Alexander Craig.
14.     xii.    Mary Crawford (2), married in 1797, Gilbert
Campbell.
```

2. Patrick Crawford (1), died in 1787; married Sally Wilson.
He came to Orange County, Virginia and proved his importation on
July 24, 1740, bringing with him Ann, James, George, Margaret
and Mary Crawford. (Order Book II, page 211, Orange County,
Virginia). His will was dated December 4, 1786 and recorded
December 18, 1787 in Will Book VII, page 31, Augusta County,
Virginia: It mentions sons, George, John, James and William
(twins); daughters Martha and Mary; grandson George McChensey;
and "other children have received their part." Executors - sons,
George and John.

3. William Crawford (2), son of Alexander Crawford (1) and
Mary McPheeters, died in 1792; married Rachel Sawyers. After the
death of William Crawford, she married William Bell, bond dated
September 17, 1799. (Abstracts from the Records of Augusta County,
Virginia, Lyman Chalkley, Vol. II, page 331). William Crawford's
will was dated October 2, 1792 and recorded December 1792 in Will
Book VIII, page 23, Augusta County, Virginia. It mentions wife,
Rachel; sons, Alexander, James, John, William, and George; daughters
Polly Armstrong, Nancy Tallman, Jenny, and Rachel. Executors were
wife, Rachel, John Crawford, Samuel Crawford, Alexander Craig, and
son Alexander. Witnesses were Joseph Thompson, Hannah Sawyers,
Rachel Crawford, and Rebecca Sawyers.

Children: 9

```
15.     i.      Alexander Crawford (3).
16.     ii.     James Crawford (3).
17.     iii.    John Crawford (3).
18.     iv.     William Crawford (3).
19:     v.      George Crawford (3).
20.     vi.     Polly Crawford (3), married December 4, 1790,
John Armstrong.
+   21:     vii.    Nancy Crawford (3).
22:     viii.   Jane Crawford (3), born 1781; married c. 1800,
Thomas Paxton, born 1769.
23:     ix.     Rachel Crawford (3), married Thomas Mitchell.
```

7. Alexander Crawford (2), son of Alexander Crawford (1)
and Mary McPheeters, died in 1830; married (1) _____ Hopkins;
married (2) in 1796, Mrs. Elizabeth McClure, widow of Malcom
McClure. He served at the battle of Point Pleasant. He also
served as Ensign in the Revolution - sworn in office November 11,
1780 under J. Cartmill. (Virginia Militia in the Revolution,
J. T. McAllister, page 181).

Children: 4 - first marriage

24. i.   Polly Crawford (3), married John Poague.
25. ii.   Betsy Crawford (3), married William Logan.
26. iii.   Catherine Crawford (Kitty) (3).
27. iv.   Sallie Crawford (3), married John Walker.

Children: 5 - second marriage

28. v.   James E. Crawford (3), married Phoebe McClung.
+   29. vi.   William Crawford (3).
30. vii.   George Crawford (3).
31. viii. Samuel Crawford (3).
32. ix.   Robert Crawford (3).

21. Nancy Crawford (3), daughter of William Crawford (2) and Rachel Sawyers, married January 13, 1789 (as his first wife), James Tallman. They lived in Pocahontas County, now West Virginia. James Tallman married (2) Jemima Gillespie.

Children: 5

33. i.   Rachel Tallman (4), married (as his first wife), Peter Adam Hull, born 1794; died 1838, son of Adam Hull and Esther Keister. (See Hull Family).
34. ii.   Rebecca Tallman (4), married Reuben Slaven.
35. iii.   Benjamin Tallman (4), married July 14, 1814 in Bath County, Virginia, Elizabeth Warwick, daughter of William Warwick and Nancy (Agnes) Craig. (See Warwick Family).
36. iv.   William Tallman (4), married (as her first husband), Jane Bradshaw, daughter of John Bradshaw and Nancy McKamie.
37. v.   Boone Tallman (4), married Mary Poage, daughter of George W. Poage.

29. William Crawford (3), son of Alexander Crawford (2) and Mrs. Elizabeth McClure, married Margaret Henderson, daughter of William Henderson and Susannah Gillespie. (See Henderson Family). He died in 1802. William Crawford served in the Revolution. Both are buried on Dry Branch, Highland County, Virginia. Their graves are unmarked.

Children: 8

38. i.   Robert Crawford (4), married Sarah Stephenson. They migrated to Randolph County, West Virginia.
+   39. ii.   Mary Crawford (4).
40. iii.   James Crawford (4), married in 1786, Mary Bridger. They migrated west.
41. iv.   Viola (or Violet) Crawford (4), married November 11, 1790, in Augusta County, Virginia, Captain David Gwin. (See Gwin Family).
+   42. v.   Andrew Crawford (4).

343

43.   vi.—   Margaret Henderson Crawford (4), married Michael
Cleek, died in 1834, son of Jacob Cleek and Christina Croddy. (See
Cleek Family).
44.   vii.   William Crawford, Jr. (4), married in 1786,
Martha Cooper. They migrated west.
+   45.   viii.   Agnes Crawford (4).

39.   Mary Crawford (4), daughter of William Crawford (3) and
Margaret Henderson, married John Armstrong.

Children: 12

46.   i.   Elizabeth Armstrong (5).
47.   ii.   William Armstrong (5).
48.   iii.   Jared Armstrong (5), married Agnes Hiner.
49.   iv.   Jane Armstrong (5), married Joseph Hiner.
50.   v.   John Armstrong (5), married Margaret Jones.
51.   vi.   Margaret Armstrong (5), married George Crummett.
52.   vii.   Mary Armstrong (5), twin to Margaret, married
John Bodkin.
53.   viii.   James Armstrong (5), married (1) Elizabeth Hiner;
married (2) _____ Smith.
54.   ix.   George Armstrong (5), married Sarah Hiner.
55.   x.   Thomas Armstrong (5), married Sarah Pullin.
56.   xi.   Nancy Armstrong (5), married John Nicely.
57.   xii.   Samuel Armstrong (5), married Mary Taylor.

42.   Andrew Crawford (4), son of William Crawford and Margaret
Henderson, married (1) Elizabeth Stephenson, died in 1829; married
(2) _____ Hyre of Upshur County, West Virginia. He migrated to
Randolph County, West Virginia c. 1800. He was one of the organize
of the Presbyterian Church in Randolph County. (A History of Randolph County, Dr. A. A. Bosworth, page 327.)

Children: 10 - first marriage

58.   i.   James S. Crawford (5), settled in Clermont County
Ohio.
59.   ii.   William H. Crawford (5), migrated to Tuscaroras
County, Ohio.
60.   iii.   Absalom Crawford (5), married Emily Hart,
daughter of Joseph Hart.
61.   iv.   Adam Crawford (5), married Mary Bosworth, daughter of Dr. Squire Bosworth.
62.   v.   John W. Crawford (5), married Edith Buckey,
daughter of Peter Buckey.
63.   vi.   Eliza Crawford (5), married Elias Wilmoth.
64.   vii.   Robert Crawford (5), moved to Lewis County, West
Virginia, near Walkersville.
65.   viii.   Jennie Crawford (5), died in childhood.
66.   ix.   Andrew Crawford (5).
67.   x.   Bushrod W. Crawford (5), born 1818; died 1893;
married (1) _____ Wilson; married (2) in 1850, Anzina Early,
daughter of Archibald Early.

45. Agnes Crawford (4), daughter of William Crawford (3) and Margaret Henderson, married James Wiley.

Children: 4

68. i. Elizabeth Wiley (5), married March 5, 1822 in Bath County, Virginia, Jacob Cleek Potts, son of Benjamin Potts, Jr. and Margaret Cleek. (See Cleek Family).
+ 69. ii. Nancy Wiley (5).
+ 70. iii. John Wiley (5).
+ 71. iv. Robert Wiley (5).

69. Nancy Wiley (5), daughter of James Wiley and Agnes Crawford (4), married William McGlaughlin.

Children: 6

+ 72. i. Hugh McGlaughlin(6).
73. ii. Jacob C. McGlaughlin (6), was killed at the battle of Cedar Creek on October 19, 1864. He served in the CSA.
74. iii. Robert McGlaughlin (6), married (1) Menta Rusmisel; married (2) Lydia Rusmisel.
75. iv. Jane McGlaughlin (6), married John Hiner.
76. v. Rachel McGlaughlin (6), married Jacob Beverage.
77. vi. Bettie McGlaughlin (6), married James Townsend.

70. John Wiley (5), son of James Wiley and Agnes Crawford (4), married Elizabeth Gillespie, daughter of James Gillespie who served in the War of 1812. After the death of John Wiley, his widow married Francis Sheridan.

Children: 5

+ 78. i. Mary Wiley (6).
79. ii. Ruhama Wiley (6), married George H. McGlaughlin.
+ 80. iii. Marcellus Franklin Wiley (6), born March 14, 1847.
81. iv. John Treville Wiley (6), died.
82. v. Eliza Wiley (6), died.

71. Robert Wiley (5), son of James Wiley and Agnes Crawford (4), married Susan Douglas. After the death of Robert Wiley, his widow married James Terry.

Children: 6

+ 83. i. Sarah Wiley (6).
+ 84. ii. Mary Anne Wiley (6).
+ 85. iii. James C. Wiley (6).
+ 86. iv. Oscar T. Wiley (6).
87. v. Robert C. Wiley (6), died.
+ 88. vi. Nancy J. Wiley (6).

72. Hugh McGlaughlin (6), son of William McGlaughlin and

Nancy Wiley (5), married Nancy Ratcliff.

Children: 10

    89. i. Mary Alice McGlaughlin (7), married _____
Brooks.
    90. ii. Lena McGlaughlin (7), married _____ Deputy.
    91. iii. William A. G. McGlaughlin (7), married Ada Ethel
McGlaughlin, daughter of Ewing A. McGlaughlin and Sarah Elizabeth
Hite. (See Gwin Family).
    92. iv. Jacob R. C. McGlaughlin (7), married Grace Scruggs
    93. v. Brown Letcher McGlaughlin (7), born 1877; died
May 2, 1952, married in 1897, Minnie McGlaughlin, daughter of
Ewing A. McGlaughlin and Sarah Elizabeth Hite. (See Gwin Family).
    94. vi. Mustoe Hamilton McGlaughlin (7).
    95. vii. Minnie Belle McGlaughlin (7).
    96. viii. Annie McGlaughlin (7), married Omer Corbett.
    97. ix. Charles McGlaughlin (7).
    98. x. Lola McGlaughlin (7).

    78. Mary Wiley (6), daughter of John Wiley (5) and Elizabeth
Gillespie, married Lancelot Hickman.

Children: 8

    99. i. Elizabeth Hickman (7), married James Folks.
    100. ii. Ida Hickman (7), married Thomas Cummings.
    101. iii. Eva Hickman (7), married Fred Kime.
    102. iv. John R. Hickman (7), married Viola Williams.
    103. v. Fannie May Hickman (7), married Frank Blackhart.
    104. vi. Harry McGlaughlin Hickman (7), married Pearl (
Craver.
    105. vii. Cecil William Hickman (7), married Myrtle Boggs.
    106. viii. Martha Lockridge Hickman (7), married Frank Mower.

    80. Marcellus Franklin Wiley (6), son of John Wiley (5) and
Elizabeth Gillespie, was born March 14, 1847; died February 13,
1936; married in 1914, Pearl K. Burns, died February 13, 1957,
daughter of Charles Joseph Burns and Minnie Trainor. He served
in Company I, 19th Virginia Cavalry, CSA.

Children: 2

+ 107. i. John Franklin Wiley (7).
+ 108. ii. Robert Vaiden Wiley (7), born October 1919.

    83. Sarah Wiley (6), daughter of Robert Wiley (5) and Susan
Douglas, married James Woods.

Children: 8

    109. i. Mary S. Woods (7), died.
    110. ii. Howard Woods (7), married _____ Armstrong.
They settled in Arizona.

111. iii. J. Robert Woods (7), married Elizabeth J.
Hamilton.
+   112. iv. Melissa Woods (7).
    113. v. David O. Woods (7), married Arminta Gum.
    114. vi. Edward C. Woods (7), married (1) Julia Gum;
married (2) Nellie Hicks.
    115. vii. Anne L. Woods (7), married William H. Hiner.
No children.
    116. viii. Myrtle Woods (7), married Nathan Bussard. They
have four children, one of whom is Guy Bussard (8). He served
as Supervisor of Monterey District, Highland County, Virginia
1952 - 1956.

84. Mary Anne Wiley (6), daughter of Robert Wiley (5) and
Susan Douglas, married Howard Wade.

Children: 10

    117. i. James Oscar Wade (7),died unmarried.
    118. ii. Otho E. Wade (7), married Lucy Gum.
    119. iii. Eva S. Wade (7), married Joseph C. Chestnut(7),
son of John Anderson Chestnut and Nancy J. Wiley.
    120. iv. Nancy E. Wade (7), married J. Harmon Woods.
    121. v. Mary L. Wade (7), married F. Clark Hiner.
    122. vi. Robert H. Wade (7), married Lillie B. Wiley,
(7), daughter of Oscar T. Wiley and Priscilla Wade.
    123. vii. Catherine A. Wade (7), married James Wade.
    124. viii. Cora Wade (7), married Henry Hiner.
    125. ix. Grace Wade (7), married William Hiner.
    126. x. Edith Wade (7), married James A. Chestnut,(7),
son of John Anderson Chestnut and Nancy J. Wiley.

85. James C. Wiley (6), son of Robert Wiley (5) and Susan
Douglas, married Mary E. Kramer.

Children: 9

    127. i. Cordelia Wiley (7), died in youth.
    128. ii. Lucy Wiley (7), married (1) Robert Whitelaw;
married (2) William Dever.
    129. iii. Margie Wiley (7), married Arlie Ervin.
    130. iv. Robert Wiley (7), married Blanche Redding.
    131. v. Howard Wiley (7), was killed accidentally.
    132. vi. Mary Wiley (7), married Charles Monroe.
    133. vii. Ella Wiley (7), unmarried.
    134. viii. Guy Wiley (7), married Ruth Matta.
    135. ix. Dale Wiley (7), married Dale Aves.

86. Oscar T. Wiley (6), son of Robert Wiley (5) and Susan
Douglas; married (1) Priscilla Wade; married (2) Nancy Reed.

Children: 6 - first marriage

347

+   136. i.   Emma P. Wiley (7).
+   137. ii.   Adelaide Wiley (7).
+   138. iii.   Florence Wiley (7).
     139. iv.   Lillie B. Wiley (7), married Robert H. Wade (7),
son of Howard Wade and Mary Anne Wiley.
     140. v.   Susan Wiley (7), married William H. Fertig.
They lived in Bath County, Virginia.
+   141. vi.   Robert Wiley (7).

    88. Nancy J. Wiley (6), daughter of Robert Wiley (5) and
Susan Douglas, married John Anderson Chestnut.

Children: 9

    142. i.   Joseph C. Chestnut (7), married Eva S. Wade (7),
daughter of Howard Wade and Mary Anne Wiley.
    143. ii.   Robert Chestnut (7), a twin to Joseph.
    144. iii.   Sarah Chestnut (7), married William Smith of
Grant County, West Virginia.
    145. iv.   James A. Chestnut (7), married Edith Wade (7),
daughter of Howard Wade and Mary Anne Wiley.
    146. v.   Gertrude Chestnut (7), married Oscar Sarcen of
North Carolina.
    147. vi.   David N. Chestnut (7), was killed in November
1936 in a hunting accident.
    148. vii.   Russell Chestnut (7).
    149. viii.   Elizabeth Chestnut (7), married Thomas Chestnut.
    150. ix.   Kenton Chestnut (7), married _____ Bussard.

    107. John Franklin Wiley (7), son of Marcellus Franklin Wiley
(6) and Pearl K. Burns, married Betty Ann Brown. They live at
Morristown, Tennessee.

Children: 2

    151. i.   John Franklin Wiley, Jr. (8).
    152. ii.   James Marcellus Wiley (8).

    108. Robert Vaiden Wiley (7), son of Marcellus Franklin
Wiley (6) and Pearl K. Burns, was born October 1919; married April
10, 1948, Doreene Naomi Huffman. They live at Bridgeport, Pennsylvania.

Children: 4

    153. i.   Barbara Wiley (8).
    154. ii.   Jane Wiley (8).
    155. iii.   Robert Vaiden Wiley, Jr. (8).
    156. iv.   Linda Wiley (8).

    112. Melissa Woods (7), daughter of James Woods and Sarah
Wiley (6), married John Mackey.

Children: 5

157. i.   William Mackey (8), married Juanita Gum.
158. ii.   Herbert Mackey (8), married Kathleen Lunsford.
159. iii. Harper Mackey (8), married Lillian Grose.
160. iv.   Genevieve Mackey (8), married Cabel Bowls.
161. v.   Annie Mackey (8), married William Dickenson.

136. Emma P. Wiley (7), daughter of Oscar T. Wiley (6) and
Priscilla Wade, married in 1889, Kirby Hull, son of Crawford Adam
Hull and Mary Crist. They live in Texas. (See Hull Family).

Children: 2

162. i.   K. S. Hull (8).
163. ii.   _____ Hull (8).

137. Adelaide Wiley (7), daughter of Oscar T. Wiley (6) and
Priscilla Wade, married H. Albert Gum, son of Otho Gum and Virginia
Wade. (See Lightner Family).

Children: 1

164. i.   Wardie Gum (8), married William Cameron McGlaughlin, son of Harper McGlaughlin and Etta Jane Yeager. They had one
daughter, Addie Jane McGlaughlin (9), who married Walter Gentry.

138. Florence Wiley (7), daughter of Oscar T. Wiley (6) and
Priscilla Wade, married Harry Herman of Bath County, Virginia.

Children: 4

165. i.   Bonnie Herman (8), married George Taylor.
166. ii.   Berlin Herman (8), married Nora Farnsworth.
167. iii. Harriet Herman (8), married Thomas Carpenter.
168. iv.   Morris Herman (8), married Martha Cauthorn.

141. Robert Wiley (7), son of Oscar T. Wiley (6) and Priscilla
Wade, married Elizabeth Woods.

Children: 5

169. i.   Manilla Wiley (8), married Walter Hiner.
170. ii.   John Wiley (8), married Elizabeth Cale.
+ 171. iii. Oscar Wiley (8).
172. iv.   Harper Wiley (8), married Emma Colaw.
173. v.   Mary Wiley (8), married George Simpson, son of
Alfred Simpson and Rachel Price Cleek. (See Cleek Family).

171. Oscar Wiley (8), son of Robert Wiley (7) and Elizabeth
Woods, married Amy Samples.

Children: 1

174. i.   Sara Wiley (9), married Harry Webb, Jr. (See
Gwin Family).

349

PART X

DYER FAMILY

The progenitor of this family was of Scotch descent. There is some ground for thinking this family belonged to the Quakers.

1. Roger Dyer (1) came to Virginia from Pennsylvania and first located near Moorefield, but finding the damp bottom land to be malarious, moved higher up the valley in what is now Pendleton County, West Virginia. His wife's name was Hannah Britton (or Bratton). Roger Dyer was middle aged when he settled in Pendleton County and he bought land on November 5, 1747 from Robert Green. Roger Dyer was killed by the Indians in 1758 at the massacre at Fort Seybert on April 28, 1758. His son, William Dyer, was also killed in the same massacre. The complete story of the attack on Fort Seybert is given in A History of Pendleton County, West Virginia, Oren F. Morton, pages 39 to 51. The will of Roger Dyer was recorded in Will Book 2, page 301, Augusta County, Virginia. It reads as follows:

In the name of God Amen the twenty fourth Day of February in the year of our Lord 1757. I Roger Dyer of Augusta County being weak in body but of perfect mind and memory thanks be given to God thereto calling to mind the mortality of my Body and knowing that it is appointed for all men once to dye do make and Ordain this to be my Last will and Testament that is to say -- principly and first of all I give and Recommend my Soul in the hands of God that gave it and my body I recommend it to the Earth to be buried in a christian manner Executors Nothing Doubting but at the Resurrection I shall receive the same again by the Mighty power of God and as Touching such Wordly Estate wherewith it pleased God to bless me in this Life I give Devise and Dispose of them in the following
Item I give and Bequeath unto my well beloved wife Hanna Dyer after Debts and charges be paid the full third part of all my movabels Estaid of Goods and Credits within this Colloney or any Other and one good bed and one horse or mear which she shall use out of my stock over and above the third part and the Plantation I now live on until my son James comes of age of twenty one years Unless my wife be married again then the Plantation to be Rented out for the use of my son James Dyer I likewise constitute make and Ordain my well Beloved wife my only and Sole Executor of this my last will and Testament.
Item, I give and Bequeath to my well beloved Son William Dyer two Shears to be Equaly to be divided between him and my three Daughters after the Rest is nomyrated (?) in this will.
Item I give & bequeath unto my well beloved Son James dyer the plantation I now live on with all the Improvements there on to belonging and fifty acres Survaried by it self joining the same plantation I now live on pattoned as yet Messuages (?) and all profits there unto belonging in anywise and fifty pounds current money with the lands to His heirs and assigns forever.
Item I give and bequeath unto my well beloved Daughter Hanna

Gester a certain tract of land lying in Hampshire County containing 427 acres of Land more or less to her Heirs & Assigns forever. Item I give and bequeath unto my Grandson Roger Dyer Son of William Dyer Twenty pounds Current Money of Virginia N 3. Now after all the above legacies are paid the Remainder of My Moveables is to be Divided into five parts and my Beloved Son William Dyer is to have two parts and my beloved daughters as Hester Patton and Sarah Hase & Hanna Gester each of them one part and I do hereby disalow revoke and Disanull all and Every other Testament Ratifying and confirming this and no Other to be my last will and Testament in witness whereof I have hereunto set my hand and Seal the day and year first above written.

Signed Sealed in the   Roger (his mark) Dyer (SEAL)
Presence of us
William Miller
Adam Hider
William Gibson.

At a Court held for Augusta County, March 21, 1759, the last will and testament of Roger Dyer was proved by the oath of William Gibson, one of the witnesses thereto and ordered to be in the office for further proof. On May 16, 1759, Adam Hider further proved the will and it was probated.

Children: 6

2. i.   William Dyer (2), killed at the massacre at Fort Seybert on April 28, 1758; married Margaret Dunkle.
3. ii.   Hannah Dyer (2), married Frederick Keister. (See Keister Family).
4. iii. Hester Dyer (2), born 1739; married Matthew Patton. Matthew Patton was one of the very first members of the Dyer Settlement, and after the murder of Roger Dyer he became a leading citizen of the Pendleton territory. He was commissioned a justice of the peace on August 19, 1761, and for a number of years he took the lists of tithables for this portion of Augusta County.
5. iv. Sarah Dyer (2), married (1) Peter Hawes who died in 1760; married (2) c. 1764, Robert Davis. She was taken captive by the Indians April 28, 1758 and held in capitivity for three and one half years. Her brother, James Dyer, is said to have been instrumental in effecting her release. Robert Davis was a Major in the Continental Army and saw active service, especially among the Indians, west of the Alleghanies. In 1779 he was commissioned Captain of Militia for Rockingham County, and he resigned in 1781. (A History of Pendleton County, West Virginia, Oren F. Morton, page 89.)
6. v.   James Dyer (2), born 1744; died 1807; married (1) Anne _____; married (2) October 13, 1780, Jane Ralston. (A History of Rockingham County, Virginia, John W. Wayland, page 444). He was taken captive by the Indians at the massacre at Fort Seybert on April 28, 1758 and held for about two years when he managed to escape. He became a prominent citizen of Pendleton County.

7. vi. Roger Dyer, Jr. (2), married Margaret Dinwiddie.

PART XI

GAY FAMILY

The name Gay is English and can be traced by a long and
continuous line of ancestry to very prominent families for centuries in England. This name is also found in records as Guy.
The first one of the name in America was William Gay, who came
to America in 1634.

1. Samuel Gay (1), born 1699; died 1781; married Margaret
_____. He was the first of the name to locate west of the Blue
Ridge Mountains. He came to Orange County, Virginia (now Augusta
County) and purchased 324 acres of land from William Berkley on
June 5, 1738. He was one of the twelve captains appointed in
1742 for military purposes. He was appointed a member of the
first court of Augusta County which was organized July 19, 1746.
About 1747, he purchased a farm on the Calfpasture River in the
Borden Grant (now in Rockbridge County). He had a son:

2. Robert Gay (2), born about 1729; died 1816; married in
1750, Sarah Johnson. They lived on the farm which had been purchased by his father in 1747. He was a Justice of the Peace in
1812. They had a son:

3. Samuel Gay (3), born about 1774; died about 1851; married September 12, 1799 in Bath County, Virginia, Margaret Catherine Mustoe, born January 16, 1782; died May 10, 1840, daughter of
Anthony Mustoe and Dorothy Silor. Anthony Mustoe was a Sergeant
in the Revolution in the 12th Regiment commanded by Colonel James
Wood. He also served in the 5th Virginia Regiment, commanded by
Colonel William Russell during 1777-1778. He served a Postmaster
at Warm Springs, Virginia, then known as Bath Court House, from
January 1, 1796 to October 1, 1802.

Anthony Mustoe was a descendant of Anthony Mustoe, born about
1677 and Margaret _____. They lived in their ancestral home near
White Chapple Church, London, England. Their son, George Mustoe,
born c. 1723; died 1767; married 1744. George Mustoe's son was
Anthony Mustoe, born September 23, 1748 in Tongue Yard, near White
Chapple Church, London, England; died June 18, 1807 in Bath County,
Virginia; married March 13, 1780 in Staunton, Virginia, Dorothy
Silor, born February 6, 1760 in Frederick County, Maryland; died
July 25, 1831 in Bath County, Virginia, daughter of Jacob Silor
(died 1785) and Dorothy _____, who came from Elsaw, Germany
to Maryland. Anthony Mustoe and Dorothy Silor had the following
children:

i. Sarah Mustoe, born February 28, 1781; died March 6, 1781.
ii. Margaret Catherine Mustoe, born January 16, 1782; died May 10, 1840; married September 12, 1799, Samuel Gay.
iii. Anthony Mustoe, Jr., born May 26, 1784; married January 31, 1804, Anna Givens.
iv. Elizabeth Mustoe, born May 6, 1787; married February 13, 1808, William G. Littlepage.
v. Nancy Mustoe, born February 2, 1790; died March 28, 1834; married November 11, 1813, Henry Givens.
vi. Catherine Chambers Mustoe, born July 8, 1793; married November 17, 1825, Samuel McGuffin.
vii. Chambers Mustoe, born November 26, 1797; died March 3, 1801.

Samuel Gay and Margaret Catherine Mustoe lived and died near Warm Springs, Bath County, Virginia.

Children: 6

+ 4. i. Mustoe Gay (4), born July 11, 1800.
+ 5. ii. Jane Gay (4), born November 18, 1803.
+ 6. iii. Andrew Warwick Gay (4), born January 29, 1806.
7. iv. Nancy M. Gay (4), born June 3, 1808; died March 2, 1867; married August 1, 1833, Robert Johnson, born February 18, 1807; died August 5, 1879. They lived at Warm Springs, Virginia. His home is now called "The Chimneys."
+ 8. v. Margaret Gay (4), born September 27, 1810.
9. vi. James Gay (4), born September 24, 1813; died May 25, 1872; married June 24, 1848, Susan Harper Lightner, born September 2, 1827; died July 16, 1896, daughter of John Lightner and Jane Moore. They lived and died at Gaymont, near Hightown, Highland County, Virginia. (See Lightner and Moore Families).

4. Mustoe Gay (4), son of Samuel Gay (3) and Margaret Catherine Mustoe, was born June 11, 1800; died March 1853; married March 13, 1834, Judith Hamilton, born c. 1812; died February 1853, daughter of James Hamilton.

Children: 2

10. i. Mary E. Gay (5), born November 29, 1838; died January 20, 1912; married June 29, 1870, James B. Andrews, died April 23, 1904.
11. ii. Margaret Alice Gay (5), born in 1845; married October 23, 1866, Marshall P. Haymond, born 1837, son of Wilson M. Haymond and Sarah _____. He enlisted February 12, 1862 in the 25th Virginia Regiment, CSA. He served as a Lieutenant.

5. Jane Gay (4), daughter of Samuel Gay (3) and Margaret Catherine Mustoe, was born November 18, 1803; died April 16, 1879; married August 15, 1825, Richard Snead, Jr.

Children: 1

12.   i.   Samuel Snead (5), born June 26, 1826.

   6. Andrew Warwick Gay (4), son of Samuel Gay (3) and Margaret
Catherine Mustoe, was born January 29, 1806; married March 15, 1831,
Martha Nolen.

Children: 2

13.   i.   James Gay (5), born November 25, 1834.
14.   ii.   Margaret Gay (5), born 1837.

   8. Margaret Gay (4), daughter of Samuel Gay (3) and Margaret
Catherine Mustoe, was born September 27, 1810; died January 19,
1875; married June 30, 1836, Joseph D. Wilkinson, born 1807; died
December 27, 1891.

Children: 7

15.   i.   Nannie Wilkinson (5), born 1838; married 1859,
J. D. Lowman, died 1912.
16.   ii.   Robert S. Wilkinson (5), born July 26, 1841;
married December 17, 1874, Sue Criser, born April 8, 1854; died
March 7, 1922. They had one son, Robert C. Wilkinson(6), born
March 29, 1879; died June 1942.
17.   iii.   James S. Wilkinson (5), born November 11, 1838;
drowned in Jackson River, Bath County, Virginia, March 16, 1885.
18.   iv.   David Wilkinson (5), born November 1846; died
October 9, 1847.
19.   v.   Maggie Wilkinson (5), married William Law.
20.   vi.   Alexander Wilkinson (5), married Maggie Donovan.
21.   vii.   Fannie Wilkinson (5), married Thomas B.
McCollister.

PART XII

GIVENS FAMILY

   The Givens Family is of Scottish origin. The name is found
in old records as Givins, Given, Givens, and is sometimes spelled
Gibbons. It has often been confused with the name Gwin in the old
records since when written in longhand the names Given and Gwin
look almost identical.

   1. Samuel Givens (1), settled in Orange County, Virginia
(now Augusta County) in 1738. He was one of the early justices.
His will was recorded May 28, 1741 in Will Book 1, page 147,
Orange County, Virginia. It was dated October 2, 1740. It mentions

354

wife, Sarah Givens; oldest son, John Givens; second son, Samuel Givens; youngest son, William Givens; son, James Givens; "my young children"; and an unborn child. Witnesses were James Cathey and Robert Turk. John and Samuel Givens were appointed executors. After the death of Samuel Givens, his widow, Sarah Givens, married Robert Allen of Frederick County, Virginia. (Abstracts from the Records of Augusta County, Virginia, Lyman Chalkley, Vol. I, page 316).

Children: 10 (Order Book II, page 109, Orange County, Virginia).
+ 2. i. John Givens (2), born 1719.
 3. ii. Samuel Givens, Jr. (2), married Martha Deane. (Ibid, Vol. I, pages 89 and 91).
 4. iii. James Givens (2), married Jane _____. (Ibid, Vol. I, page 293).
 5. iv. Martha Givens (2).
 6. v. William Givens (2), married Jean McClure, daughter of James McClure. (Ibid., Vol. III, pages 64 and 345). William Givens lived in South Carolina for a time, but returned to Augusta County, Virginia. He was killed by the Indians in 1764. (Ibid., Vol. I, pages 91 and 330).
+ 7. vi. Elizabeth Givens (2).
 8. vii. Margaret Givens (2).
 9. viii. Sarah Givens (2), married John Stuart. (Ibid., Vol. I, page 316).
 10. ix. Jane Givens (2).
+ 11. x. George Givens (2), born in 1740 after the date of his father's will. He was baptized March 11, 1741.

2. John Givens (2), son of Samuel Givens (1) and Sarah _____, was born in 1719 in Ireland; died in 1790; married in 1745, Mary Margaret Sitlington, born 1729, daughter of Robert Sitlington and Mary Feamster. His will was recorded in Will Book VII, page 220 of Augusta County, Virginia. It was dated January 14, 1790 and proved April 20, 1790. It mentions wife, Margaret; son, Thomas Givens; son, James; daughter, Mary; daughter, Sarah Lofftis; daughter, Ann Henderson; son, John; son, George; son, Samuel; son, William; and daughter, Elizabeth Lamme. He commanded a company of militia from Augusta County, Virginia from October 16, 1777 to March 15, 1782, inclusive. (Gleanings of Virginia History, William Fletcher Boogher, page 223).

Children: 13

+ 12. i. William Givens (3), born 1746.
 13. ii. Agnes Givens (3), married Adam Bratton, born 1750; died 1800, son of Robert Bratton and Ann (McFarland) Dunlap. (See Bratton Family).
 14. iii. Thomas Givens (3), married Elizabeth Kerr, daughter of James Kerr.
 15. iv. James Givens (3), married Elizabeth Graham, daughter of Robert Graham and Jean Hicklin. She married (2) _____ McDonald. James Givens served as a soldier in the Virginia Regiment and was dead by December 1775.

355

16. v. Mary Givens (3), married June 6, 1798, James Allison, (Abstracts from the Records of Augusta County, Lyman Chalkley, Vol. II, page 323).
17. vi. Sarah Givens (3), married _____ Lofftis.
18. vii. Anne Givens (3), married John Henderson, died 1787. (See Henderson Family).
19. viii. John Givens, Jr. (3), died in 1812; married Jane (or Jean) Robertson, died in 1812, daughter of William Robertson. John Givens, Jr. left a will, as did his wife, and her father. (Ibid., Vol. III, pages 238 and 239).
20. ix. George Givens (3), married Isabel Robertson, daughter of William Robertson. They migrated to Kentucky. (Ibid., Vol. III, page 239).
21. x. Samuel Givens (3), married March 19, 1785, Elizabeth Robertson. (Ibid., Vol. II, page 281).
22. xi. Elizabeth Givens (3), married _____ Lamme.
23. xii. Margaret Givens (3), married April 21, 1788, James Agnew. (Ibid., Vol. II, page 303).
24. xiii. Robert Givens (3), born May 22, 1759; died October 26, 1833; married July 4, 1782, Margaret Robertson, born July 31, 1761, daughter of William Robertson. (Ibid., Vol. II, page 281). He served in the Revolution in Captain John Given's Company. (Gleanings of Virginia History, William Fletcher Boogher, page 224). They migrated to Lincoln County, Kentucky.

7. Elizabeth Givens(2), daughter of Samuel Givens (1) and Sarah _____, married in 1749, General Andrew Lewis, born 1720 in Ireland; died September 26, 1781 in Bedford County, Virginia, son of John Lewis and Margaret Lynn. Andrew Lewis settled at the base of Bent Mountain on the upper Roanoke River, in what became Botetourt County, Virginia. He was long engaged in the Indian Wars and served as a Brigadier General in the Revolution. He was in command at the Battle of Point Pleasant which took place October 10, 1774. He was appointed Brigadier General on March 1, 1776. His will was dated January 23, 1780 and proved February 14, 1782 and recorded in Botetourt County, Virginia.

Children: 6

25. i. John Lewis (3), married Patsy Love of Alexandria, Virginia.
26. ii. Thomas Lewis (3), married _____ Evans of Point Pleasant, West Virginia.
27. iii. Samuel Lewis (3), died unmarried in Greenbrier County, West Virginia.
28. iv. Andrew Lewis (3), married (1) Eliza Madison, daughter of Thomas Madison; married (2) _____ Bryan. He served as a Colonel in the Army and in the Revolution. He died c. 1844 aged c. 84.
29. v. Anne Lewis (3), married Roland Madison. They lived in Kentucky.
30. vi. William Lewis (3), born 1764; married (1) Lucy Madison; married (2) Nancy McClenahan.

11. George Givens (2), son of Samuel Givens (1) and Sarah
_____, was born in 1740 after the date of his father's will
and was baptized March 11, 1741; died in 1822 in Kentucky; married Rachel Black, an older sister of Susan Black, wife of
William Feamster. He was a Captain in the Botetourt County,
Virginia Militia in 1776. He received land in Kentucky for his
services. (Historical Register of Virginians in the Revolution,
John H. Gwathmey, page 310).

Children: 8

31. i.   John Givens (3), married Catherine Wallace.
32. ii.   George Givens, Jr. (3).
33. iii. Samuel Givens (3).
34. iv.   James Givens (3).
35. v.   William Givens (3).
36. vi.   (Daughter) Givens (3), married Alexander Givens,
son of John Givens, Jr. and Jane (or Jean) Robertson.
37. vii. Sally Givens (3), married December 2, 1794,
Abraham Miller.
38. viii. (Daughter) Givens (3), married Robert Walker.
Some descendants of George Givens (2) remained in Craig County,
Virginia. Others migrated to Fayette County, Kentucky. Dr. H.
C. Givens, former State Veterinarian,was a descendant of George
Givens.

12. William Givens (3), son of John Givens (2) and Mary
Margaret Sitlington, was born in 1746; died in 1793; married in
1764, Agnes Bratton, born 1747; died 1827, daughter of Robert
Bratton and Ann (McFarland) Dunlap. (See Bratton Family). He
served as a Lieutenant in the Virginia Militia. His will was
dated November 24, 1792 with a codicil added on September 29,
1793. It was recorded in December 1793 in Will Book 1, page
27, Bath County, Virginia. It mentions wife, Nancy (Agnes);
sons, Samuel, Adam, James, John, George, and Henry; two youngest
daughters, Ann and Peggy; son, William; four youngest daughters,
Mary, Isabel, Ann, and Peggy; eldest sons, Robert and William;
daughters, Sally and Jenny (Janet); and son-in-law, John Berry.
Executors were son, Robert and wife, Nancy. Witnesses were Robert
Given, John Berry, and John Wilson.

Children: 15

+ 39. i.   Robert Givens (4), born February 20, 1765.
   40. ii.   Sarah Givens (4), born August 18, 1766; married
in 1790, Isaac Gregory.
   41. iii. Janet Givens (4), born March 27, 1770; married
in 1790, John Berry.
   42. iv.   Mary Givens (4), born 1771; married in 1798,
William Dinwiddie.
   43. v.   William Givens (4), born 1773; married December
16, 1792, Nancy Jane Frame.
   44. vi.   Isabella Givens (4), born 1775; married in 1795,
Isaac Duffield.

45. vii. Samuel Givens (4), born October 3, 1776; died June 10, 1851; married in 1801, Elizabeth Gwin, born April 8, 1778; died October 31, 1864, daughter of David Gwin and Jane Carlile. (See Gwin Family).

46. viii. Adam Givens (4), born 1778; died 1856; married in 1797, Nancy McGuffin, daughter of Robert McGuffin. He served as a member of the State Legislature. This couple adopted Sarah Kimes who married John Cleek, II, and Harriett Kimes who married Robert Solomon Carner Bradley. They also adopted Adam Givens McGuffin, son of James McGuffin and Elizabeth Ervin.

47. ix. James Givens (4), born 1781; married July 31, 1806, Elizabeth Graham, born 1788, daughter of Christopher Graham and Jane Carlile. (See Graham Family).

48. x. John Givens (4), born 1783; married Rachel Pickens.

49. xi. George Givens (4), born 1784; married Margaret McGuffin.

+ 50. xii. Henry Givens (4), born June 22, 1786.

+ 51. xiii. Anne Givens (4), born 1788.

52. xiv. Margaret Givens (4), born 1792; married April 20, 1813, John Gibson.

53. xv. Agnes Givens (4), born 1793; married George McGuffin.

39. Robert Givens (4), son of William Givens (3) and Agnes Bratton, was born February 20, 1765; married in 1785, Margaret Elliot, born January 26, 1764, daughter of William Elliott. He served as a young boy in the Revolution. He represented Bath County in the Virginia Legislature from 1791 to 1811 and also served as constable of Bath County, Virginia.

Children: 5

54. i. Sarah Givens (5), born in 1789; died 1864; married April 9, 1812, Samuel Lynn Gibson, born 1774; died 1841, son of David Gibson, born at Kilraine, Ireland in 1743; died 1833 and Jane Lynn, daughter of John and Jean Lynn. David Gibson came to Augusta County, Virginia c. 1745-46.

55. ii. Mary Givens (5), married in 1807, James McAvoy.

56. iii. Samuel Givens (5), born December 15, 1793 in Bath County, Virginia; died July 9, 1862; married March 18, 1823, Mary Gibson, born October 28, 1800; died May 3, 1862.

57. iv. William Givens (5), married Rebecca Kenny.

58. v. Adam Givens (5), married Granville Rose of Braxton County, West Virginia.

50. Henry Givens (4), son of William Givens (3) and Agnes Bratton, was born June 22, 1786; died February 3, 1853; married (1) November 11, 1813, Nancy Mustoe, born February 2, 1790; died March 21, 1834, daughter of Anthony Mustoe and Dorothy Silor; (See Gay Family) married (2) June 25, 1835, Elizabeth(Gibson) Slaven, born July 26, 1807; died February 15, 1840, widow of William Slaven; married (3) September 13, 1842, Margaret Jane (Patton) Wickline,

died October 5, 1846; married (4) August 9, 1848, Susan (Benson) Gibson, widow of David W. Gibson. Mrs. Susan (Benson) Gibson Givens married as her third husband, William Botkin, a teacher and merchant of Braxton County, West Virginia.

Children: 7 - first marriage

59. i. Mustoe Bratton Givens (5), born December 10, 1814; married September 4, 1834 in Bath County, Virginia, Elizabeth A. Gwin, daughter of John Gwin and Margaret Bradshaw. They migrated to Illinois. (See Gwin Family). They lived in in McHenry County, Illinois.
60. ii. William Dinwiddie Givens (5), born January 10, 1817; married May 31, 1838, Rachel B. Slaven.
61. iii. Jane Catherine Givens (5), born September 1, 1820; married July 1840, George Grose. They migrated to Illinois.
62. iv. Charles Francisco Givens (5), born July 29, 1823; married January 25, 1844, Mary C. Rider. They migrated to Illinois.
63. v. Nancy McGuffin Givens (5), born October 11, 1825; died October 17, 1828.
64. vi. Henry Kile Givens (5), born September 20, 1826; married June 3, 1847, Julia Ann Hamilton. They migrated west.
+ 65. vii. Adam Givens (5), born October 15, 1829.

Children: 2 - second marriage

66. viii. James Montague Givens (5), born April 8, 1836. He migrated west.
67. ix. George Givens (5), born December 27, 1837. He migrated west.

Children: 3 - third marriage

68. x. Elizabeth Susan Givens (5), born June 20, 1843, married _____ Frame. They migrated to Illinois.
+ 69. xi. John Crawford Givens (5), born March 21, 1845.
70. xii. Henry Austin Givens (5), died in childhood.

Children: 2 - fourth marriage

71. xiii. Caroline Benson Givens (5), born September 20, 1850; died February 3, 1853.
72. xiv. Margaret Ann Givens (5), born March 22, 1852; died in childhood.

51. Anna Givens (4), daughter of William Givens (3) and Agnes Bratton, was born in 1788; married January 3, 1800, Anthony Mustoe, Jr., born May 26, 1784; son of Anthony Mustoe and Dorothy Silor. (See Gay Family).

Children: 9

73. i. Elizabeth Mustoe (5), born 1805; died 1808.

359

74. ii. Chambers Mustoe (5), born 1807; married in 1831,
Margaret Gibson.
75. iii. James Mustoe (5), born 1809; married in 1832,
Rachel Hill.
76. iv. Henry Mustoe (5), born 1812; married in 1841,
Margaret Wilson.
77. v. William Kile Mustoe (5), born 1814; married in
1837, Nancy J. Cash.
78. vi. Nancy Bratton Mustoe (5), born 1816; married in
1836, Erasmus Williams.
79. vii. Anthony Mustoe (5), born 1819; married in 1841,
Nancy McElwee.
80. viii. Adam Givens Mustoe (5), born 1821; married in
1846, Nancy Wilson.
81. ix. Catherine Mustoe (5), born 1823; died 1826.

65. Adam Givens (5), son of Henry Givens (4) and Nancy Mustoe,
was born October 15, 1829; married Caroline Benson. Caroline Benson
was a sister of Mrs. Susan (Benson) Gibson who became the fourth
wife of Henry Givens, father of Adam Givens. Caroline Benson and
Susan (Benson) Gibson were daughter of Mathias Benson and Susan
Trimble. Adam Givens and his wife lived in Louisville, Kentucky,
where he practiced medicine.

Children: 2

82. i. Mustoe Bratton Givens (6), born April 25, 1854.
He lived in Florida.
83. ii. Elmer Benson Givens (6), born October 9, 1855.
He was a M.D. and lived in Florida.

69. John Crawford Givens (5), son of Henry Givens (4) and
Mary Jane (Patton) Wickline, was born March 21, 1845 in Bath County,
Virginia near Cleek's Mill; married (1) May 18, 1866, Mollie Ryder,
daughter of Peter H. Ryder and Sarah Green; married (2) March 4,
1892, Savilla (House) Cochran, born 1855 in Ohio; died January 20,
1924 in Kansas City, Missouri, a widow of a Baptist minister.
John Crawford Givens, D.D., was a minister of the Methodist Church.
He was Chaplain of the Missouri Penitentiary, Jefferson City,
Missouri. He served as Chaplian in the Spanish American War.

Children: 1 - first marriage

+ 84. i. Kate Givens (6), born May 13, 1869.

Children: 1 - second marriage

85. ii. Ione Givens (6), born April 29, 1894; married
(1) Harold Stroude, who died during the influenza epidemic in
1918; married (2) Richard Blume. She has one son.

84. Kate Givens (6), daughter of John Crawford Givens (5)
and Mollie Ryder, was born May 13, 1869; married November 26,
1896, George Johnson of Missouri. He was Clerk of the Court of
Cass County, Missouri.

Children: 4

86. i. Cowan Wilson Johnson (7), born May 9, 1898;
married October 8, 1918, _____. They have one son,
Jack Barkley Johnson (8), born October 23, 1919.
87. ii. Mary Katherine Johnson (7), born February 11,
1901; married _____ Zumwalt. They have one son, George Walter
Zumwalt (8), born August 12, 1919.
88. iii. Dixie Lee Johnson (7), born November 23, 1904;
married November 22, 1921, _____ Patterson.
89. iv. John Givens Johnson (7), born May 12, 1907;
died May 20, 1907.

PART XIII

GRAHAM FAMILY

This Graham Family descends from the ancient Clan Graemme.
As was true of many other families during the time of King James,
the Grahams living on the border of England fled from Scotland to
Ireland. Soon they, or their descendants, came to the American
Colonies. The Grahams were Presbyterians.

1. Christopher Graham (1) was born c. 1670 in Scotland or
Ireland; died c. 1745 in Augusta County, Virginia; married Margaret
Risk (some say Florence _____). When he first came to America
he first settled in Paxton Township, Lancaster County, Pennsylvania
where some of his children were born. His son, Robert Graham, was
appointed as administrator of his father's estate on February 19,
1746. (Abstracts from the Records of Augusta County, Virginia,
Lyman Chalkley, pages 6 and 10, Vol. III). Christopher Graham
came to America before 1700.

Children: 5 (perhaps others)

+ 2. i. John Graham (2), born c. 1700.
+ 3. ii. Robert Graham (2), born c. 1712.
   4. iii. William Graham (2), died 1748; married Jane May.
   5. iv. Archibald Graham (2), died 1748; married Margaret
Shed.
   6. v. Jane Graham (2), married Thomas Feamster, Jr.

2. John Graham (2), son of Christopher Graham (1) and
Margaret Risk, was born c. 1700; died in 1771 in Augusta County,
Virginia; married in 1722, Elizabeth Elliott, daughter of William
Elliott. His will was recorded in Will Book 4, page 452, Augusta
County, Virginia, on November 19, 1771. It reads as follows:

In the name of God Amen. The 29 of July A.D. 1771, I John
Graham being sick in body but of sound mind and memory thanks be

361

to God Almight and calling remembrance the uncertainty of this
transitory life and that all flesh must yield to death when it
pleaseth God to call, I do make constitut and ordain and declare
this to be my last will and testament, in manner and form following revoking and annulling by these presents all former wills and
testaments either written or by word of mouth, this to be my last
and none other, I first recommend my Soul to God my Savior and Re-
deemer, and my body to the dust to be decently buried at the discretion of my executors here after named and appointed, And as to
my worldly goods which God hath granted me I leave and bequeath
in the following manner Viz, To my oldest son Lanty I devise and
leave my plantation where on I dwell to him and his heirs forever,
upon his allowing my beloved wife her living off it with what stock
she pleases to keep, also the said Lanty is to give six pounds to
James Graham's son John, and six pounds to his brothers John's son
also. To my daughter Anne I leave thirty pounds besides my roan
horse and chest drawers. To my beloved wife Elizabeth Elliott
Graham, I leave twenty pounds my bay mare, two cows her choice of
the flock and all the house hold furnishing. To Jane Lockridge
I leave 15 pounds, to Rebeca my buckles and to her son John one
cow, also. To Robert Graham half of the mill that belongs to me,
to my two daughters Florence and Betty ten pounds each, to my
sons Robert and John ten pounds each, to Rebeca Lanty's daughter
I leave ten pounds, and all the rest of the estate remaining to be
enjoyed by my wife whilst unmarried but if married to be divided
equally between my daughters Flory, Jane, Betty, and Ann, but,
if she never marries to be left by said wife to her four daughters
here named at her death, also I appoint my beloved wife and my son
Lanty Graham to be my executors. I here by revoke all other wills
and testaments, appointing and making this my last. In the 11th yr
of our sovereign Lord George King of Great Britton & in the year of
our Lord God 1771. Signed Sealed published and prounounced in the
presence of

                              John Graham (SEAL)
Joseph Romson
John Kinkead
John Armstrong

        Children: 10

        7.   i.   Lancelot Graham (3), born 1724; died 1780; mar-
ried Elizabeth _____. His will was dated December 29, 1779 and
recorded February 15, 1780 in Will Book VI, page 116, Augusta
County, Virginia. It mentions wife, Elizabeth; daughter, Rebecca;
brother John Graham's sons, John, James, and Lanty; brother, Robert
Graham's daughter Sarah Graham; and mother. Executors were wife an
brother, John Graham.
        8.   ii.   John Graham (3), born 1726; died in 1815; married
Martha Patton, daughter of Colonel John Patton. His will was dated
April 4, 1813 and recorded September 25, 1815 in Will Book XII, pag
72, Augusta County, Virginia. It mentions daughters, Margaret,
Elizabeth Bratton, and Martha Dunlap; sons, James, Robert, William,
Lanty, and John Graham.

9.   iii.   James Graham (3).
10.   iv.   Robert Graham (3), died in 1774; married June 24, 1763, Elizabeth Lockridge, daughter of James Lockridge and Isabella Kincaid. (See Lockridge Family). His will was dated August 19, 1773 and recorded March 16, 1774 in Will Book V, page 217, Augusta County, Virginia. It mentions wife; daughters, Sarah, Rebecca, and Jane Graham.
    11.   v.   Anne Graham (3), married John Kincaid.
    12.   vi.   Jane Graham (3), born 1742; married April 17, 1761, Andrew Lockridge, born 1730; died 1791 in Augusta County, Virginia, son of James Lockridge and Isabella Kincaid. (See Lockridge Family).
    13.   vii.   Rebecca Graham (3), married January 1, 1787, John Bell.
    14.   viii.   Florence Graham (3), born 1744; married in 1763, James Graham, son of William Graham who died in 1748 and Jane May.
    15.   ix.   Elizabeth Graham (3), born 1741; married in 1750, Robert Armstrong.
    16.   x.   William Graham (3), died in 1751; married Jane Walkup, daughter of Joseph Walkup.

    3.   Robert Graham (2), son of Christopher Graham (1) and Margaret Risk, was born c. 1712; died in 1763 in Augusta County, Virginia; married c. 1734, Jean Hicklin, daughter of Thomas Hicklin, Sr. After the death of Robert Graham, Jean Hicklin Graham married Ralph Laverty and they had a child, Rebecca Laverty who married John Hamilton. The will of Robert Graham was dated February 26, 1763 and recorded September 21, 1763 in Will Book 3, page 286, Augusta County, Virginia. It mentions wife, Jean; sons, Thomas and Christopher Graham; daughters, Elizabeth, Margaret, Rebecca and Jean; and brother, John Graham.

        Children: 6

    17.   i.   Thomas Graham (3), died in 1798 in Augusta County, Virginia; married _____. His will was dated November 18, 1794; and recorded June 19, 1798 in Will Book VIII, page 306, Augusta County, Virginia. It mentions sons, Robert, John, Thomas, James, Joseph, and Alexander; and daughters, Catcron and Mary.
    18.   ii.   Elizabeth Graham (3), born 1743; married in 1763, James Givens, son of John Givens and Mary Margaret Sitlington. She married (2) _____ McDanald. (See Givens Family).
    19.   iii.   Margaret Graham (3), married in 1785, John Wallace.
    20.   iv.   Rebecca Graham (3), married Joseph Walkup.
    21.   v.   Jean Graham (3), married John McClenahan.
+   22.   vi.   Christopher Graham (3), born July 9, 1755.

    22.   Christopher Graham (3), son of Robert Graham (2) and Jean Hicklin, was born July 9, 1755; died in 1840; married Jean Carlile, born 1750; died 1838, daughter of Robert Carlile and Nancy _____. (See Carlile Family).

        Children: 11

23.   i.   Robert Graham (4), born 1776.
24.   ii.   George W. Graham (4), born 1778; killed in 1837; married Sarah Devericks.
25.   iii.   John Graham (4), born 1780; died 1857, unmarried.
26.   iv.   Nancy Graham (4), unmarried.
27.   v.   Rachel Graham (4), born 1784; died 1855; married John Carlile.
28.   vi.   Thomas Graham (4), born 1786; died 1869; married Elizabeth Koontz, born 1829; died 1909 of Rockingham County, Virgin:
29.   vii.   Elizabeth Graham (4), born 1788; married July 31, 1806, James Givens, born 1781, son of William Givens and Agnes Bratton. (See Givens Family).
30.   viii.   Susan Graham (4), born 1790; died 1858; married Robert Wright.
31.   ix.   Virginia Graham (4), born 1792; died 1865, unmarried.
32.   x.   Rebecca Graham (4), born 1794; died 1874; married in 1825, Alexander Hamilton.
33.   xi.   Margaret Graham (4), born 1796; died 1817; married in 1816, John Hannah.

PART XIV

HARPER FAMILY

This Family is of German descent. The Harpers came from Germany about 1750 and settled in Augusta County, Virginia in what is now Pendleton County, West Virginia.

1.   Michael Harper (1), died in 1767; married Isabel _____. Administration of his estate was granted to Mathew Harper on May 20, 1767. (Abstracts from the Records of Augusta County, Virginia, Lyman Chalkley, Vol. III, page 99). Michael Harper bought land on Newfoundland Creek from John Justice in May 1754. On January 27, 1760, Michael Harper and Isabel Harper sold land on Newfoundland Creek to William Shannon. On November 24, 1760, Michael Harper, very aged, was exempted from levy. (Ibid, Vol. I, page 88). In November 1767, Mathew Harper as administrator of Michael Harper, took steps to collect Michael's bounty and pay as a soldier from Captain William Christian. Michael Harper furnished 16 pounds of butter to Captain Patrick Martin and company on duty in his Majesty's service October 22, 1756. (Ibid., Vol. I, pages 344, 351, and 519; List of Colonial Soldiers of Virginia, H. J. Eckenrode, page 46).. Mathew Harper and Hans Harper may have been brothers of Michael Harper, although the compiler believes that they were sons of Michael Harper. Mathew Harper and Hans Harper were added to the list of tithables September 1, 1750. Mathew Harper married Margaret _____, and Hans Harper married Elizabeth _____. (Abstracts from the Records of Augusta County, Virginia, Lyman Chalkley, Vol. I, page 42, and Vol. III, pages 323, 376, 411, 418, 470, and 473.)

Children: 5 (others?)

2. i. Jacob Harper (2), was a soldier in the Indian Wars. He was naturalized October 16, 1765. (Abstracts from the Records of Augusta County, Virginia, Lyman Chalkley, Vol. I, page 124; A History of Pendleton County, West Virginia, Oren F. Morton, page 214).

3. ii. Phillip Harper (2), was added to the list of tithables on August 22, 1760. (Abstracts from the Records of Augusta County, Virginia, Lyman Chalkley, Vol. I, page 87). He was naturalized on May 17, 1774. (Ibid., Vol. I, page 179).

4. iii. Eve C. Harper (2), married Matthew Dice.
+ 5. iv. Nicholas Harper (2), born in 1738.
+ 6. v. Adam Harper (2), born in 1741.

5. Nicholas Harper (2), son of Michael Harper (1) and Isabel _____, was born in 1738 on the Rhine River, Germany; died 1829 in South Branch Valley, Pendleton County, Virginia (now West Virginia); married in 1769, Elizabeth Peninger, born 1753 in Germany; died 1818 in South Branch Valley, Pendleton County, Virginia (now West Virginia); daughter of Henry Peninger and _____. Henry Peninger (this name is also found as Baninger, Penninger, Banniger, Bennigar, and Benninger) received his certificate of naturalization on May 18, 1762. (Ibid., Vol. I, page 97). He served as constable in 1773 and 1774. (Ibid., Vol. I, pages 175 and 179). He is listed as serving in the Augusta County, Virginia Militia in the Colonial Wars. (List of Colonial Soldiers of Virginia, H. J. Eckenrode, page 20 'and 69). He also furnished provisions. (Gleanings of Virginia History, William Fletcher Boogher, page 34). He was exempted from military service in 1794 by reason of physical infirmity. (A History of Pendleton County, West Virginia, Oren F. Morton, page 395). He died in 1815 and the name of his wife is not known. He had nine children:

i. William Peninger.
ii. John Peninger, married Barbara Propst in 1787.
iii. Henry Peninger.
iv. Elizabeth Peninger, married Nicholas Harper.
v. Catherine Peninger, married George Swadley.
vi. Mary Peninger.
vii. Barbara Peninger, married Peter Hull.
viii. Anna E. Peninger.
ix. Susannah Peninger, married in 1798, Henry Paulsel.

Nicholas Harper served in the 2d Battalion, Augusta County, Virginia, Militia, under Captain Peter Hull. In 1778 he served as First Lieutenant in Captain John McCoy's Company of Augusta County Militia. Augusta County records show that he furnished supplied for the Revolutionary Army and provisions for the soldiers. (Abstracts from the Records of Augusta County, Virginia, Lyman Chalkley, Vol. I, page 202; Virginia Militia in the Revolution, J. T. McAllister, pages 148 and 182; and Virginians in the Revolution, John H. Gwathmey, page 351.) There is a government marker over his grave, which is located 15 miles north of Monterey, Highland

County, Virginia on the Marion Moyers Farm.

Children: 11

7. i.   Barbara Harper (3), married in 1793, William
Michael of Bath County, Virginia.
+ 8. ii.   Henry Harper (3).
9. iii.   Annis E. Harper (3), married in 1796, Peter
Lightner, son of William Lightner and Elizabeth Ann Robey. They
lived on Knapps Creek, Pocahontas County, now in West Virginia.
(See Lightner Family).
10. iv.   Peter Harper (3), married Susannah Simmons.
11. v.   Elizabeth Harper (3), married in 1796, William
Lightner, son of William Lightner and Elizabeth Ann Robey. After
the death of William Lightner, she married (2) Nicholas Harper,
son of Adam Harper and Christina _____. (See Lightner Family).
12. vi.   Susannah Harper (3), born 1777 in Pendleton
County, now in West Virginia; died March 25, 1868 on Back Creek,
Bath County, Virginia and was buried on the Thomas Campbell farm
near the Bath-Highland County lines; married in 1798 in Pendleton
County, now in West Virginia, Adam Lightner, born September 10,
1760 in Lancaster County, Pennsylvania; died January 3, 1843 on
Back Creek, Bath County, Virginia, son of William Lightner and
Elizabeth Ann Robey. (See Lightner Family).
13. vii.   Catherine Harper (3), born 1780; married Conrad
Rexroad.
+ 14. viii. Mary Harper (3).
+ 15. ix.   Leonard Harper (3), born November 6, 1797.
16. x.   George Harper (3), born 1799; died 1868; married
in 1820, Margaret Wimer.
17. xi.   Sarah Harper (3), married Henry Hevener.

6. Adam Harper (2), son of Michael Harper (1) and Isabel
_____, was born in 1741; died in 1820; married Christina ____
____.

Children: 10

18. i.   Susannah Harper (3), married in 1792, Charles
Briggs.
19. ii.   Catharine Harper (3), married in 1794, Joseph
Briggs.
20. iii.   Nicholas Harper (3), married (as her second
husband), Elizabeth Harper (3), daughter of Nicholas Harper and
Elizabeth Peninger, and widow of William Lightner.
21. iv.   Jacob Harper (3), married Margaret Harman.
22. v.   Mary Harper (3), married Henry Simmons.
23. vi.   (Daughter) Harper (3), married Adam Mouse.
24. vii.   Christina Harper (3), married Jacob Judy.
25. viii. Sarah Harper (3), married Philip Wimer.
26. ix.   Philip Harper (3), born 1778; died 1860; married
Susannah Fultz.
27. x.   Daniel Harper (3), married in 1803, Rosanna Wise.

8. Henry Harper (3), son of Nicholas Harper (2) and Elizabeth Peninger, died in 1859, aged 70 years; married in 1799, Elizabeth Lightner, died 1876, aged 96 years, daughter of William Lightner and Elizabeth Ann Robey. About 1812 Nicholas Harper bought 200 acres from Abram Duffield and Colonel John Baxter located on Knapps Creek, Pocahontas County, now in West Virginia, and Henry Harper settled on this land. (See Lightner Family).

Children: 9

28.   i.   Elizabeth Harper (4), married James R. Poage.
29.   ii.   Sally Harper (4), married James Malcolm.
30.   iii. Anna Harper (4), married (as his first wife),
A. Washington Moore. He married (2), Margaret Dever, daughter of John Dever.
31.   iv.   Susan Harper (4), married John D. McCarty.
32.   v.   Jacob Harper (4), married Lydia Civey. They settled in Monroe County, now in West Virginia.
33.   vi.   William Harper (4), married Elizabeth Civey. They lived on Knapps Creek, now in Pocahontas County, West Virginia.
+ 34.   vii. Henry Harper, Jr. (4).
35.   viii. Samuel Harper (4), married (1) Malinda Moore; married (2) Mary Jane Gum, daughter of Isaac Gum and Mary Ruckman of what is now Highland County, Virginia.
36.   ix.   Nicholas Harper (4), died young.

14. Mary Harper (3), daughter of Nicholas Harper (2) and Elizabeth Peninger, married Henry Swadley.

Children: 5

37.   i.   George Swadley (4), married (1) Mary Peninger; married (2) Barbara Propst.
38.   ii.   Catherine Swadley (4), married Jacob Hevener.
39.   iii.   Anne Swadley (4), married _____ Gillespie. They migrated west.
40.   iv.   Henry Swadley, Jr. (4), married Mary Benson.
41.   v.   Maria Swadley (4).

15. Leonard Harper (3), son of Nicholas Harper (2) and Elizabeth Peninger, was born November 6, 1797; died May 17, 1870; married Phoebe Dice.

Children: 9

42.   i.   Mary Harper (4), born 1818; married George Hammer.
43.   ii.   Isaac Harper (4), married Sidney Wimer.
44.   iii.   Margaret Harper (4), married George W. Rymer.
45.   iv.   Hannah Harper (4), born 1824; died 1905; married John Trimble.
46.   v.   Jacob Harper (4), married Catharine McClure.
47.   vi.   Sarah Harper (4), married William Trimble, born 1823; died 1857.

48.   vii.   Phoebe Harper (4), married Samuel Sullenbarger.
49.   viii. Leonard Harper (4), died young.
50.   ix.   Catharine Harper (4), born 1836; married James
Trimble.

34. Henry Harper, Jr. (4), son of Henry Harper (3) and
Elizabeth Lightner, married Phoebe Sharp, daughter of Joseph
Sharp and Elizabeth (Betsy) Lightner.

Children: 2

51.   i.   Peter Harper (5).
52.   ii.   Rachel Ann Harper (5), married William Herold.

PART XV

HENDERSON FAMILY

The Henderson name is an old name of Scotland. The Hender-
sons lived there since the fifteenth century. Their chief seat
was at Fordell, County Fife, Scotland. A celebrated name in Scotland was that of Alexander Henderson, who next to John Knox, was
considered by many as the most famous Scottish Protestant Theolog-
ian. Alexander Henderson died in Edinburg in 1646 and his death
was the occasion of national mourning in Scotland.

The compiler of the Henderson Chronicles is of the opinion
that the progenitor of the Virginia branch of the Henderson Family
was Alexander Henderson, who was a son of John Henderson. It is
believed that John Henderson was a lineal descendant of Sir James
Henderson (1450-1513), first knight of Fordell and Lord Chief
Justice to King James IV of Scotland. Sons of Alexander Henderson
of Fordell Fifeshire, Scotland, settled on Owl Creek near Alexandria, Virginia, prior to 1740.

1. John Henderson (1), said to be a son of Alexander Henderson above; died in 1787; married Anne Givens, daughter of John
Givens and Mary Margaret Sitlington. John Henderson was a justice
of Greenbrier County, now in West Virginia. The military records
of Lieutenant Colonel John Henderson cites the fact that he served
throughout the Revolutionary War. At the battle of Point Pleasant
in 1774, he had the rank of Lieutenant of Militia. (History of
the Battle of Point Pleasant, Virgil A. Lewis, page 114). (See
Givens Family).

Children: 5

+ 2.   i.   William Henderson (2).
   3.   ii.   John Henderson, Jr. (2), married Elizabeth Harvey

4. iii. James Henderson (2), married in 1786, Prudence
Campbell.
5. iv. Samuel Henderson (2),
6. v. George Henderson (2), married Isabella Houston.

2. William Henderson (2), son of John Henderson (1) and
Anne Givens, married Susannah Gillespie.

Children: 10

7. i. David Henderson (3), settled in Randolph County,
now in West Virginia.
8. ii. Susan Henderson (3), married January 9, 1793,
James McComb.
9. iii. Sarah Henderson (3), married John Risk.
10. iv. Margaret Henderson (3), married William Crawford,
son of Alexander Crawford and Mrs. Elizabeth McClure. (See Crawford
Family).
11. v. John Henderson (3), married January 3, 1792,
Sarah Lessley, daughter of James Lessley.
12. vi. Robert Henderson (3), settled in Randolph County,
now in West Virginia, and married there.
13. vii. Alexander Henderson (3), married Rebecca Wilson.
14. viii. George Henderson (3), married Margaret Lockridge,
daughter of Andrew Lockridge and Jane Graham. (See Lockridge Family).
15. ix. Nancy Henderson (3), married _____ Mitchell.
16. x. Joseph Henderson (3), died 1791; married Sarah
Miller, daughter of John Miller.

PART XVI

HULL FAMILY

The Hull Family is of German ancestry. The name is found in
records as Hole, Hool, Hohl, Holle, and Hull.

1. Peter Thomas Hull (1), the progenitor of this branch of
the Hull Family was born c. 1706 in the Palatinate; died in 1776
in Augusta County, Virginia; married (1) in Germany, _____
_____; married (2) November 25th, 1750 in Lancaster County, Penn-
sylvania, Susannah Margaretha Dieffenbach (sometimes spelled as
Fieffenbach). Peter Thomas Hull came to Philadelphia from Rotterdam on the Ship Frances and Ann, Thomas Coatan, Master, arriving
in Philadelphia on May 30, 1741. (Thirty Thousand Names of German,
Swiss, Dutch and French Immigrants, Prof. I. Daniel Rupp, page 145).
He located in Lancaster County, Pennsylvania, and the records of
Trinity Lutheran Church show that "Peter Thomas Hohl, a widower
and a miller, on the Susquehanna River, and Susannah Margaretha
Dieffenbach, a single person, have been published several Sundays,
and are joined, in wedlock, 25th of November 1750." Peter Thomas

Hull, his bride, and his two sons by his former marriage, Peter and Francis Hull, took the trail towards the Valley of Virginia. They settled on land bought from Christopher Francisco, on Cub's Run, Rockingham County, Virginia on July 2, 1752. This land was a part of the Jacob Stover tracts. Jacob Stover was an ancestor of President Dwight D. Eisenhower. In 1765, they acquired land in Crab Apple Bottom, the garden spot of what is now Highland County, Virginia. The will of Peter Thomas Hull was recorded March 19, 1776 in Will Book 5, page 407, Augusta County, Virginia. It reads as follows:

In the name of God Amen:
The twenty-eighth day of November, one Thousand seven hundred, and seventy-five.

I, Peter Hohl, of Augusta County and Colony of Virginia, being sick in body but sound of mind and Memory, thanks be to Almighty God for the same, do make and declare this my last will and Testament, in manner and form following, first to my dearly beloved wife, Susannah Margaret, I give and bequeath the third part of the estate, after all my just debts are paid any my Eldest son Peter shall according to my will and desire after my decease give unto his (step) Mother the third part or share of the increase of Grain to the land produces and shall bring the same into the Barn and Thresh it for her. I likewise bequeath further unto my wife to have choice of two milk cows and the Pennsylvania Mare also a horse for her to ride and to work, which horse is to remain upon the plantation and not to be disposed of, likewise the choice of two sheep; the division of my land shall be in the following manner;
(1st) the land be surveyed from the lower end on the line up to the Dry Run. (2nd) from the Dry Run up to the corner tree. (3rd) from the corner tree on up to the Middle Corner tree on the upper land. (4th) from the Middle Corner Tree on up to the upper Corner Tree. (5th) The three of my eldest daughters shall be made equal. I bequeath unto them after my decease the sum of Twenty Pounds Current money each, and my youngest daughters shall also receive, each of them the sum of Twenty pounds Current Money, as soon as they shall attain their age.
(6th) I also desire that the three different pieces or parcels of land, viz., the first at the upper trace, the second in the (Vanderpool) Gap, third on Jackson's River, besides an entering, shall be sold at Public Vendue, and put to the estate. I empower hereby my Eldest son Peter to sell and dispose of the same as my Executor to this my last will and Testament and desire that Susannah Margaret, my wife and my son Peter shall educate my younger Children, in a Christian-like manner, as long as they behave dutiful; otherwise they shall have power to bind them out with this proviso to pay them interest on their money from the day they are bound out.

		His	
Witness present	Peter	(X) Hohl	(L.S)
Bernard Lantz		Mark	
Leonard Simon			
Peter Flesher			

Certify hereby the above is an Exact Copy Translated from the German Tongue into English this Nineteenth day of March, One Thousand Seven Hundred and Seventy Six.

John William Lee.

Children: 2 - first marriage

+ 2. i.   Peter Hull (2), born 1730.
+ 3. ii.   Francis Hull (2).

Children: 12 - second marriage

+ 4.   iii. Henry Hull (2).
+ 5.   iv.   George Hull (2), born 1757.
  6.   v.   William Hull (2), married Rebecca Bradford.
+ 7.   vi.   Mary Hull (2).
  8.   vii. Robert Hull (2).
  9.   viii. Catherine Hull (2), married Peter Zickafoose.
  10. ix.   David Hull (2).
  11. x.   John Hull (2).
+ 12. xi.   Phoebe Annis Hull (2).
  13. xii. Elizabeth Hull (2), married James Patterson.
+ 14. xiii. Margaret Hull (2).
  15. xiv. Eva Hull (2), married George Yeager.

2. Peter Hull (2), son of Peter Thomas Hull (1) and _____
_____, was born in 1730 in Germany; died January 1818 and was buried on the original Hull estate in Crab (Apple) Bottom; married in 1750, Barbara Keith, daughter of Alexander Keith and Lisey McAlpin. Alexander Keith was a soldier in the American Revolution. (Historical Register of Virginias in the Revolution, John H. Gwathmey, pages 434 and 435). On the formation of Pendleton County in 1788, Peter Hull was one of the first justices. Peter Hull served as a Captain in the American Revolution. (A History of Highland County, Oren F. Morton, page 194; Virginia Militia in the Revolutionary War, J. T. McAllister, Sections 72, 180, 253, and 256; and Historical Register of Virginias in the Revolution, John H. Gwathmey, page 402.) A government marker has been obtained for his grave. His will was dated April 16, 1817 and recorded in Pendleton County, Virginia. It mentions wife, Barbara; eldest son, Henry; son, Peter; daughter, Susannah Kinkead, wife of Thomas; daughter, Barbara Sitlington, wife of John; son, Adam; son, Jacob; son, William; son-in-law, William Harvey; and grandson, Mathew Harvey. (Abstracts from the Records of Augusta County, Virginia, Lyman Chalkley, Vol. II, page 240).

Children: 9

+ 16. i.   Adam Hull (3), born 1751.
  17. ii.   Henry Hull (3), born 1754; married Hannah Harness. They lived at Fort Seybert, Pendleton County, now in West Virginia.
  18. iii. Peter Hull (3), married Barbara Peninger, daughter of Henry Peninger and _____.

+ 19.   iv.   Susannah Hull (3).
+ 20.   v.   Barbara Hull (3).
   21.   vi.   Jacob Hull (3), married Jane Arbogast.
   22.   vii. William Hull (3), married Rachel Renick.
   23.   viii. Joseph Hull (3), migrated in young manhood to
Missouri.
   24.   ix.   Elizabeth Hull (3), married William Harvey.

   3. Francis Hull (2), son of Peter Thomas Hull (1) and _____
_____, married _____Linkenfelter. His will was dated Februar
1, 1806 and recorded March 28, 1808 in Will Book X, page 190, Augusta County, Virginia. It mentions sons, Henry, Daniel, Frederick,
and John Hull; daughters, Elizabeth Fulwider, Molly Hanger, Barbara Cook, Catherine Wiseman, and Susanna. Executors were Daniel
Hull and James Harris. Witnesses were John and Hugh Daugherty
and David Byers. (Abstracts from the Records of Augusta County,
Virginia, Lyman Chalkley, Vol. III, page 232).

   Children: 11

   25.   i.   Barbara Hull (3), married December 29, 1795,
Jacob Cook. (Ibid., Vol. II, page 316).
   26.   ii.   Catherine Hull (3), married January 8, 1799,
(as his second wife), Lewis Wiseman. (Ibid., Vol. II, page 336).
   27.   iii. Daniel Hull (3), married February 15, 1796 (1)
Barbara Summers, daughter of John Summers and Elizabeth _____;
married (2) Sarah Winegar. (Ibid., Vol. II, page 137).
   28.   iv.   Mary Hull (3), married May 4, 1785, Frederick
Hanger. (Ibid., Vol. II, page 281).
   29.   v.   John Hull (3), married in 1811, Amy Strickland.
They migrated to Highland County, Ohio. Their son, Dr. Albert Y.
Hull (4), was prominent in Iowa as an editor and abolitionist.
As a member of the Legislature, he was a leader in the movement to
move the state capital to Des Moines, where he and his father
owned land. J. A. T. Hull (5), son of Dr. Albert Y. Hull, was a
congressman from Iowa and for nearly twenty years was chairman of
the committee on military affairs. His son, Colonel John A. Hull
(6), was awarded the Distinguished Service Medal in World War I.
He served with the Judge Advocate General's Office.
   30.   vi.   Peter Hull (3), married Jennie Dickey.
   31.   vii. Philip Hull (3), married Elizabeth Newcomer.
   32.   viii. Frederick Hull (3), married Polly Cunningham.
   33.   ix.   Elizabeth Hull (3), married _____ Fulwider.
   34.   x.   Susannah Hull (3).
   35.   xi.   Henry Hull (3).

   4. Henry Hull (2), son of Peter Thomas Hull (1) and Susannah
Margaret Dieffenbach, married Elizabeth Keister, daughter of
Frederick Keister and Hannah Dyer. (See Keister Family).

   Children: 4

   36.   i.   John Hull (4), married Sophia Derieux. They
lived near Centennial, Monroe County, West Virginia.

37. ii. Elizabeth Hull (3), married Lewis A. Holmes.
38. iii. Polly Hull (3), married Jacob Baker.
39. iv. Henry Hull, Jr. (3), married Abigail Massey.

5. George Hull (2), son of Peter Thomas Hull and Susannah
Margaret Dieffenbach, was born in 1757; married Hannah Keister,
daughter of Frederick Keister and Hannah Dyer. (See Keister
Family). He served as a soldier in the American Revolution.

Children: 7

+ 41. i. Elizabeth Hull (3).
+ 42. ii. George Hull (3), born 1796.
   43. iii. Jesse Hull (3), born 1801; died 1875; married
in 1827, Elizabeth Cleek, born 1807; died 1879, daughter of
Michael Cleek and Margaret Henderson Crawford. (See Cleek Family).
   44. iv. Peter Hull (3), married _____.
+ 45. v. William Hull (3).
   46. vi, Mary Hull (3), died unmarried.
   47. vii. James Hull (3).

7. Mary Hull (2), daughter of Peter Thomas Hull (1) and
Susannah Margaret Dieffenbach, married Abram Burner from Shenandoah County, Virginia. They settled in Upper Tract.

Children: 7

   48. i. Mary Burner (3), married James Grimes, son of
Felix Grimes and Catherine _____.
   49. ii. Elizabeth Burner (3), married Hon. John Grimes,
son of Felix Grimes and Catherine _____. He represented Pocahontas County in the House of Delegates, 1841-42.
+ 50. iii. George Burner (3).
   51. iv. Jacob Burner (3), married Keziah Stump.
   52. v. Adam Burner (3), married Margaret Gillespie,
daughter of Jacob Gillespie.
   53. vi. Henry Burner (3), drowned in the east fork of
the Greenbrier River.
   54. vii. Daniel Burner (3), married Jennie Gillespie,
daughter of Jacob Gillespie. He was drowned and left one son,
Joshua Burner (4).

12. Phoebe Annis Hull (2), daughter of Peter Thomas Hull (1)
and Susannah Margaret Dieffenbach, married John Yeager, Sr.

Children: 3

   55. i. John Yeager, Jr. (3), migrated to Illinois.
   56, ii. Jacob Yeager (3), married Sarah Hidy.
+ 57, iii. Andrew Yeager (3).

14. Margaret Hull (2), daughter of Peter Thomas Hull (1)
and Susannah Margaret Dieffenbach, married Adam Arbogast, Sr.,
born 1760; died 1861, son of Michael Arbogast. He served in the

373

American Revolution. (Virginia Militia in the Revolutionary War, J. T. McAllister, Sections 4 and 180).

Children: 9

+ 58. i.   Benjamin Arbogast (3).
  59. ii.   William Arbogast (3), married Jane Tallman.
  60. iii.   Adam Arbogast (3), married Rachel Gregg, daughter of Zebulon Gregg.
  61. iv.   Jacob Hull Arbogast (3), married Elizabeth Wilson Bright.
  62. v.   Susan Arbogast (3), married in 1804, John Lunsford.
  63. vi.   Elizabeth Arbogast (3).
  64. vii.   Mary Arbogast (3), married William Nottingham, Jr.
  65. viii. Barbara Arbogast (3), died young.
  66. ix.   Catherine Arbogast (3), died young.

16. Adam Hull (3), son of Peter Hull (2) and Barbara Keith, was born in 1751; died in 1825; married Esther Keister, daughter of Frederick Keister and Hannah Dyer. (See Keister Family). Adam Hull served as a private in his father's company in the American Revolution. (Virginia Militia in the Revolutionary War, J. T. McAllister, page 149; and Historical Register of Virginians in the Revolution, John H. Gwathmey, page 401).

Children: 10

+ 67. i.   Sarah Hull (4), born 1792.
+ 68. ii.   Peter Adam Hull (4), born 1794.
+ 69. iii.   Frederick Keister Hull (4).
+ 70. iv.   John Hull (4).
  71. v.   Esther Hull (4), born September 14, 1804 in Pendleton County, now Highland County, Virginia; died March 17, 1853 in Pocahontas County, now in West Virginia; married in 1821, Robert Craig Warwick, born September 8, 1801 in Bath County, Virginia (now Pocahontas County, West Virginia); died March 8, 1845 in Pocahontas County, now West Virginia, son of William Warwick and Nancy (Agnes) Craig. (See Warwick Family).
  72. vi.   Jacob Hull (4), born 1806; died 1861; married Mahala Hoover. No children.
  73. vii.   Catherine Hull (4), married Jacob Hidy.
  74. viii. Susan Hull (4), married John Long of Randolph County, West Virginia.
  75. ix.   Hannah Hull (4), married in 1814, Adonijah Ward.
  76. x.   Elizabeth Hull (4), married Jacob Warwick, son of Andrew Warwick and Elizabeth Craig. They moved from Pocahontas County, Virginia to Indiana and finally settled in Missouri. (See Warwick Family).

19. Susannah Hull (3), daughter of Peter Hull (2) and Barbara Keith, married Thomas Kincaid.

374

Children: 5

| 77. | i. | Ann Kincaid (4), married Benjamin Pendleton. |
| 78. | ii. | Margaret Kincaid (4), married John Watson. |
+ | 79. | iii. | Peter Hull Kincaid (4), born 1802. |
| 80. | iv. | John J. Kincaid (4), died 1853. |
+ | 81. | v. | William P. Kincaid (4), born 1818. |

20. Barbara Hull (3), daughter of Peter Hull (2) and Barbara Keith, married in 1806 (as his first wife), John Sitlington, born 1781; died 1869. John Sitlington married (2) in 1842, Elizabeth Wallace, daughter of Matthew Wallace (born February 5, 1772; died October 5, 1848) and Sarah Brown (born November 8, 1775; died March 30, 1853). He was the great grandfather of John Robert Sitlington Sterret, noted archeologist.

Children: 10

82. i. Robert Sitlington (4), married (1) Nancy Snyder; married (2) Henrietta Ewing.
83. ii. Peter Hull Sitlington (4), died young.
84. iii. Mary A. Sitlington (4), married William Guy.
85. iv. Andrew Kincaid Sitlington (4), married Mary Hodge. They settled in Missouri.
86. v. Susan K. Sitlington (4), married John W. Frazier.
87. vi. Thomas O. Sitlington (4), married (1) Sarah J. Hunter; married (2) Margaret Stinnett.
88. vii. Margaret Sitlington (4), married William Rice.
89. viii. Elizabeth Sitlington (4), married George W. Kinney.
90. ix. John W. Sitlington (4), married Amanda Mann.
91. x. Barbara Hall Sitlington (4), died young, single.

41. Elizabeth Hull (3), daughter of George Hull (2) and Hannah Keister, married in 1806, David Bird, born 1781.

Children: 9

92. i. George Hull Bird (4), married (1) Eliza Ryder; married (2) in 1852 Mary Wiley; married (3) Matilda M. Wade.
93. ii. John J. Bird (4), married (1) Jane Chestnut; married (2) Margaret Callahan Matheny. They settled in Illinois.
+ 94. iii. Hannah Bird (4).
95. iv. David Bird (4), married Martha Ryder. They settled in Illinois.
96. v. Rachel Bird (4), married (as his first wife), Abraham Wade.
97. vi. Eliza Bird (4), married Benjamin Bird.
98. vii. Mary J. Bird (4), died unmarried.
99. viii. Margaret Bird (4), born 1813; died 1901; married (1) Abraham Mullenax; married (2) John Cook.
100. ix. Eleanor Bird (4), died unmarried.

42. George Hull (3), son of George Hull (2) and Hannah Keister, was born in 1796; married Rachel Smith, daughter of William Smith.

Children: 1

+ 101. i. James Wright Hull (4).

45. William Hull (3), son of George Hull (2) and Hannah Keister, married Sarah Keister, daughter of George Keister and Susannah Peck.

Children: 4 (and others)

    102. i. William Smith Hull (4), married Julia Ann Whiten.
+ 103. ii. George Hull (4).
    104. iii. Rachel Hull (4), married Joseph Smith.
    105. iv. Hannah Hull (4), married in 1821, George Perkins.

50. George Burner (3), son of Abram Burner and Mary Hull (2), married June 21, 1821 in Bath County, Virginia, Sarah Warwick, daughter of Andrew Warwick and Elizabeth Craig. (See Warwick Family). He married (2) Margaret Elizabeth Poage, daughter of George W. Poage.

Children: 8 - first marriage

    106. i. Andrew Burner (4).
    107. ii. Enoch Burner (4), married Rachel Ann Tallman. They settled in Missouri.
    108. iii. Allen Burner (4), married (1) Elizabeth Price, daughter of James Atlee Price and Margaret Davies Poage; married (2) Virginia Clark.
    109. iv. Lafayette Burner (4), married (1) Nannie Wooddell; married (2) Caroline Gum, daughter of William M. Gum and Sallie Tallman.
    110. v. Lee Burner (4), married Rebecca Gum, daughter of William M. Gum and Sallie Tallman.
    111. vi. Charles Burner (4), married Elizabeth Beard.
    112. vii. Nancy Burner (4), married William Wooddell.
    113. viii. Isabella Burner (4), married Lancelot Lockridge Slaven, son of Jacob Gillespie Slaven and Eleanor Lockridge.

57. Andrew Yeager (3), son of John Yeager, Sr. and Phoebe Annis Hull (2), died at Valley Center, Virginia; married Elizabeth Dilley, daughter of Martin Dilley and Hannah Moore.

Children: 3

    114. i. Peter Dilley Yeager (4), born June 22, 1830; died December 6, 1906;married December 17, 1857 in Pocahontas County, West Virginia, Mary Margaret Bible, born March 3, 1836;

376

died August 2, 1900, daughter of Jacob Bible and Sallie Lightner. (See Lightner Family). He was a Confederate soldier, and became a prisoner and spent a long time at Camp Chase, Ohio. He was not released until July 1865.
115. ii.. Martin Yeager (4), died c. 1861.
116. iii. Ella Yeager (4), died at age 15 of diphtheria.

58. Benjamin Arbogast (3), son of Adam Arbogast and Margaret Hull (4), married _____.

Children: 11

117. i. Henry Arbogast (4), married December 14, 1833 in Pocahontas County, West Virginia, Anna Warwick, daughter of Andrew Warwick and Elizabeth Craig. (See Warwick Family).
118. ii. Solomon Arbogast (4), married Nancy Nottingham.
119. iii. John Arbogast (4), married Margaret Yeager, daughter of Jacob Yeager and Sarah Hidy.
120. iv. Benjamin Arbogast, Jr. (4), married _____ Gibbons (or Givens).
121. v. Adam Arbogast (4), married Clarissa Sutton.
122. vi.. Carlotta Arbogast (4), married Jonathan Potts, son of Benjamin Potts, Jr. and Margaret Cleek. (See Cleek Family).
123. vii. Sally Arbogast (4), married (as his second wife), Ralph Wanless.
124. viii. Delilah Arbogast (4), married (1) Joseph Wooddell; married (2) Frederick Pugh.
125. ix.. Margaret Arbogast (4), married John Yeager, son of Jacob Yeager and Sarah Hidy.
126. x. Mary Arbogast (4), married Hamilton Stalnaker.
127. xi. Frances Arbogast (4), married Henry Wade.

67. Sarah Hull (4), daughter of Adam Hull (3) and Esther Keister, was born in 1792; married in 1812, Benjamin Fleisher, son of Henry Fleisher and Catherine Peninger.

Children: 7

128. i. Henry Fleisher (5), married Nancy Hiner. No children.
129. ii. Adam Hull Fleisher (5), born 1818; died 1889; married (1) Rachel Slaven; died 1859, daughter of Reuben Slaven and Rebecca A. Tallman; married (2) in 1860, Hannah P. Steuart.
130. iii. Narcissa Fleisher (5), died young.
131. iv. Catherine Fleisher (5), married in 1837, Jacob Seybert, Sr., son of Jacob Seybert and Mary Gum.
132. v. Elizabeth Fleisher (5), married Samuel Hiner, son of Jacob Hiner and Sarah McCoy.
133. vi.. Margaret Fleisher (5), married Jacob Seybert, Jr., son of Isaac Seybert and Ruth Wilson.
134. vii. Susan Fleisher (5), married Andrew Seybert, son of Isaac Seybert and Ruth Wilson.

68. Peter Adam Hull (4), son of Adam Hull (3) and Esther
Keister, was born in 1794; died in 1838; married (1) Rachel Tall-
man; daughter of James Tallman and Nancy Crawford; married (2)
Rachel Crawford.

Children: 6 - first marriage

135. i.   James Hull (5), married Mahala Armstrong. They
lived in Upshur County, West Virginia.
136. ii.   John P. Hull (5), married Elizabeth Hevener.
They lived in Lewis County, West Virginia.
137. iii. Rebecca Hull (5), married James Tallman.
138. iv.   Martha I. Hull (5), married in 1855, Thomas J.
Glenn.
139. v.   William Boone Hull (5), married Mary Hoover.
+ 140. vi.   Matthew Harvey Hull (5), born 1825.

Children: 4 - second marriage

+ 141. vii. Crawford Adam Hull (5), born June 9, 1829.
142. viii. Nancy E. Hull (5), married Cyrus Tallman.
They migrated to Kansas.
143. ix.   Mary A. Hull (5), born 1833; married John E.
Sipe.
144. x.   Adam L. Hull (5), married Susan Davis. They
migrated to Indiana.

69. Frederick Keister Hull (4), son of Adam Hull (3) and
Esther Keister, married (1) Amelia Wilson, daughter of William
Wilson; married (2) Julia Whitelaw.

Children: 3 - first marriage

+ 145. i.   John Wilson Hull (5), born 1838.
+ 146. ii.   Joseph Hull (5), born 1839.
147. iii. Morgan Hull (5), died young.

Children: 1 - second marriage

148. iv.   Luella N. Hull (5), born 1859; married Edward
Dudley.

70. John Hull (4), son of Adam Hull (3) and Esther Keister,
married June 21, 1821, Margaret M. Warwick, daughter of William
Warwick and Nancy (Agnes) Craig. (See Warwick Family).

Children: 6

149. i.   Warwick Hull (5).
150. ii.   Sarah Hull (5), born 1828; died January 12, 1913.
151. iii. Nancy Jane Hull (5), married Peter Hull Kincaid,
born 1802; died 1880; married in 1855, son of Thomas Kincaid and
Susannah Hull.

+   152. iv.   Margaret Hull (5), born 1837.
+   153. v.   Robert Hull (5).
     154. vi.   Irene E. Hull (5), born 1844; died 1892; married
in 1868, James A. Fleisher, son of Adam Hull Fleisher and Rachel
Slaven.

     79. Peter Hull Kincaid (4), son of Thomas Kincaid and
Susannah Hull (3), was born in 1802; died in 1880; married in
1855, Nancy Jane Hull (5), daughter of John Hull and Margaret M.
Warwick.

     Children: 2

     155. i.   Felix Kincaid (5), born 1859; died 1881 unmar-
ried.
+   156. ii.   Ida May Kincaid (5), born May 5, 1862.

     81. William P. Kincaid (4), son of Thomas Kincaid and
Susannah Hull (3), was born in 1818; married (1) in 1839 Hannah
B. Wilson; married (2) in 1862, Grace Mauzy; married (3) Eliza-
beth C. Swadley.

     Children: 3 - first marriage

     157. i.   Elizabeth Kincaid (5),died in childhood.
     158. ii.   Susan J. Kincaid (5), born 1840; married Adam
F. Gum.
     159. iii.   Louisa Kincaid (5), married James Newman, born
1841.
     Children: 3 - second marriage

     160. iv.   Mary Kincaid (5), married (1) in 1881, William
G. Arbogast; married (2) Warwick J. Collins.
     161. v.   John J. Kincaid (5), born 1866; married in 1890,
Carrie F. Rexrode.
     162. vi.   Grace Kincaid (5), married William Mullenax.

     94. Hannah Bird (4), daughter of David Bird and Elizabeth
Hull (3), married James Hamilton.

     Children: 2

     163. i.   Esther Hamilton (5), died in childhood.
     164. ii.   James D. Hamilton (5), married Rebecca Simpson.
No children.

     101. James Wright Hull (4), son of George Hull (3) and
Rachel Smith, married Jane Whitman.

+   165. i.   William Henry Hull (5).

     103. George Hull (4), son of William Hull (3)and Sarah
Keister, married Mary Ann Smith.

Children: 11

166. i.   Silas Hull (5), married Lina McClure.
167. ii.   George Hull (5), died.
168. iii.   Mary Hull (5), married Harvey Sydenstricker.
169. iv.   Phoebe Hull (5), married Ezra Waide.
170. v.   Wise Hull (5), married Annie McCoy.
171. vi.   Virginia Hull (5), married Gilbert Gum. They
lived at Mountain Grove, Virginia.
172. vii.   Annie Hull (5), married Kenton Simmons. They
lived at Bolar, Virginia.
173. viii.   Jackson Hull (5), married Jemima Dotson.
174. ix.   Margaret Hull (5), married Columbus McCarly.
175. x.   Robert Hull (5).
176. xi.   Thomas Hull (5).

140. Matthew Harvey Hull (5), son of Peter Adam Hull (4) and
Rachel Tallman, was born in 1825; died in 1911; married Annie
Rexrode, daughter of Samuel Rexrode and Susan Waybright.

Children: 5

+   177. i.   Jacob N. Hull (6), born 1846.
+   178. ii.   William C. Hull (6), born 1847, twin to Charles.
+   179. iii.   Charles C. Hull (6), born 1847, twin to William.
+   180. iv.   Cyrus S. Hull (6), born 1850.
    181. v.   John A. Hull (6), died in childhood.

141. Crawford Adam Hull (5), son of Peter Adam Hull (4) and
Rachel Crawford, was born June 9, 1829; died June 2, 1896; married
(1) Elizabeth Phillips; married (2) Mary Crist. They migrated to
Texas.

Children: 2 - first marriage

182. i.   Mary E. Hull (6), married in 1879, Andrew W.
Beverage.
183. ii.   George A. Hull (6), born 1860; died September
2, 1891 at Coperas Cove, Texas; married Mary Nottingham, died 1933.

Children: 2 - second marriage

184. iii.   Kirby Hull (6), married 1889, Emma P. Wiley,
daughter of Oscar T. Wiley and Priscilla Wade. (See Crawford
Family).
185. iv.   Archie Hull (6), married Bertie Golden.

145. John Wilson Hull (5), son of Frederick Keister Hull
(4) and Amelia Wilson, was born in 1838; married in 1866, Sarah
Seybert.

Children: 1

186. i.   Mary Hull (6), married Harris C. Fleisher in
Kansas.

146. Joseph Hull (5), son of Frederick Keister Hull (4) and Amelia Wilson, was born in 1839; married in 1868, Amanda J. Beverage.

Children: 10

187. i.   Edward R. Hull (6), born 1871; married in 1896, Harriet Rexrode, daughter of William C. Rexrode and Mary Waybright.
+ 188. ii.   Luther C. Hull (6), born April 19, 1872.
189. iii.   William F. Hull (6), married Maude Mullenax.
190. iv.   James W. Hull (6), married Lottie Rexrode, daughter of William C. Rexrode and Mary Waybright.
+ 191. v.   George Forest Hull (6).
+ 192. vi.   Lucy A. Hull (6).
+ 193. vii.   Allie Porter Hull (6), born November 26, 1885.
194. viii. Ernest B. Hull (6), married Theodosia Morrison of Upshur County, West Virginia.
+ 195. ix.   Thomas R. Hull (6).
196. x.   Kenton J. Hull (6), married in 1910, Mattie J. Hevener.

152. Margaret Hull (5), daughter of John Hull (4) and Margaret M. Warwick, was born in 1837; died April 30, 1915, aged 78 years; married Christopher C. Roadcap Wallace, born April 8, 1838; died December 18, 1916, son of Robert Sitlington Wallace and Ann Roadcap. He served in Company F, 11th Virginia Cavalry, CSA.

Children: 4

197. i.   Edward M. Wallace (6), born October 14, 1872; died May 27, 1901.
198. ii.   Lucy A. Wallace (6), born May 9, 1875; died April 19, 1901.
199. iii.   Madie Wallace (6), unmarried, migrated west.
200. iv.   Charlie Wallace (6), migrated west.

156. Ida May Kincaid (5), daughter of Peter Hull Kincaid (4) and Nancy Jane Hull (5), was born May 5, 1862; died November 17, 1930; married in 1878, Samuel Wilson Sterrett, born 1848; died 1910. He served several terms in the State Legislature, representing Bath, Highland, and Rockbridge Counties, Virginia. He served in Company H, 14th Virginia Cavalry, CSA.

Children: 4

201. i.   Nancy Kincaid Sterrett (6) of Staunton, Virginia.
202. ii.   Robert Sterrett (6); died in 1938; married Martha Jones.
203. iii.   Felix F. Sterrett (6), died in the early 1940's; married Mrs. Alice Price. He was Treasurer of Buena Vista, Virginia.
204. iv.   Samuel Tate Sterrett (6), died in the early 1940's; married (1) Jeanette Wilson; married (2) Lelia Echols.

381

153. Robert Hull (5), son of John Hull (4) and Margaret M. Warwick, married Ellen McCann.

Children: 2

205. i. Alice Gertrude Hull (6), born 1865; died in the early 1940's.
206. ii. Frank Hull (6) of Mt. Savage, Maryland.

165. William Henry Hull (5), son of James Wright Hull (4) and Jane Whitman, married Rachel Curry.

Children: 2

207. i. Lelia Hull (6), married Wardell H. Arbogast.
208. ii. Grace Josephine Hull (6), married William Jacob Yeager, son of Peter Dilley Yeager and Mary Margaret Bible. (See Lightner Family).

177. Jacob N. Hull (6), son of Matthew Harvey Hull (5) and Annie Rexrode, was born in 1846; married Eliza Rexrode, daughter of John N. Rexrode and Catherine Cooke.

Children: 13.

209. i. Minnie A. Hull (7), died unmarried.
210. ii. Ida J. Hull (7), born 1871; married in 1902, Samuel Berry of Rockingham County, Virginia.
211. iii. John H. Hull (7), married Camilla Auvil. They live in Tucker County, West Virginia.
212. iv. Harriet M. Hull (7), married Wallace D. Faurote.
213. v. James Hull (7), married in 1909, Frances Dickson.
214. vi. William F. Hull (7).
215. vii. Elzada B. Hull (7), married in 1901, Alva G. Wine.
216. viii. Annis K. Hull (7), married Benford Soule of Rockingham County, Virginia.
217. ix. Homer T. Hull (7), died January 17, 1916.
218. x. Harrison Morton Hull (7), married Almira Campbell. He served in World War I. No children.
219. xi. Hubert H. Hull (7).
220. xii. Emma Erma Hull (7), married Isaac Eckard, son of Job Eckard and Ruhama Gwin. (See Gwin Family).
221. xiii. Ethel W. Hull (7).

178. William C. Hull (6), son of Matthew Harvey Hull (5) and Annie Rexrode, was born in 1847; married (1) Minnie Amanda Rexrode, daughter of Solomon Rexrode and Eleanor Rymer; married (2) Sarah Keplinger of Grant County, West Virginia.

Children: 1 - first marriage

222. i. Charles A. Hull (7), born in 1877;married in 1896, Kate Whitelaw.

Children: 5 - second marriage

223. ii.   Nora Hull (7), died young.
224. iii. Wilbur Hull (7), died young.
225. iv.   Myrtle Hull (7), married Frank Strother.
226. v.   Frances Hull (7).
227. vi.   Albert Hull (7).

179. Charles C. Hull (6), son of Matthew Harvey Hull (5) and
Annie Rexrode, was born in 1847; married Sarah Layman of Grant County,
West Virginia.

Children: 9

228. i.   Cornelia Hull (7), died young.
229. ii.   Stella Hull (7), married Charles Rexrode, son of
William C. Rexrode and Mary Waybright.
230. iii. Emma Hull (7), married Charles Nine, Grant County,
West Virginia.
231. iv.   Rosa Hull (7), married Joe Reel, Grant County,
West Virginia.
232. v.   William Hull (7).
233. vi.   Lucy Hull (7), married Roy Nordeck, Monongalia
County, West Virginia.
234. vii. Arley Hull (7).
235. viii. Elsie Hull (7).
236. ix.   (Son) Hull (7), died as an infant.

180. Cyrus S. Hull (6), son of Matthew Harvey Hull (5) and
Annie Rexrode, was born in 1850; married Eunice Eleanor Rexrode,
daughter of Solomon Rexrode and Eleanor Rymer.

Children: 7

237. i.   Nettie Hull (7), died young.
+   238. ii.   William G. Hull (7).
239. iii. Elza P. Hull (7), married (1) Jessie K. Wimer,
daughter of Amby Wimer and Susan Palmer; married (2) Gladys Hevener.
240. iv.   Daisy Hull (7), died young.
241. v.   Robert L. Hull (7), married Cora Hevener.
242. vi.   Eva P. Hull (7), married George Gum.
243. vii. Edward H. Hull (7).

188. Luther C. Hull (6), son of Joseph Hull (5) and Amanda
J. Beverage, was born April 19, 1872; married in 1895, Artie Rexrode,
daughter of William C. Rexrode and Mary Waybright.

Children: 4

244. i.   Max Hull (7).
245. ii.   Fred Hull (7).
246. iii. Clyde Hull (7).
247. iv.   Lillian Hull (7), married Dr. Berlie Swecker.

191. George Forest Hull (6), M.D., son of Joseph Hull (5) and Amanda J. Beverage, married (1) Mary D. Sale; married (2) Mona Catheryne Heltzel.

Children: 2

248. i.   Virginia Hull (7), married _____ Pascover.
249. ii. George H. Hull (7), M.D.

192. Lucy A. Hull (6), daughter of Joseph Hull (5) and Amanda J. Beverage, married George H. Brock.

Children: 5

250. i.   Adam Brock (7), married Alta Crummett.
251. ii. William Brock (7), married Cornelia Fulton Bratton, born April 6, 1909, daughter of Frank Harris Bratton and Johnnie Berry. William Brock died October 7, 1952. (See Bratton Family).
252. iii. Grace Brock (7), married _____ York.
253. iv. Virginia Brock (7), married Cyrus Hammer.
254. v.   Mary Brock (7), married Merrill Wimer.

193. Allie Porter Hull (6), son of Joseph Hull (5) and Amanda J. Beverage, was born November 26, 1885; died January 31, 1955; married in 1909, Annie F. Eye.

Children: 5

+   255. i.   Elizabeth Hull (7).
    256. ii. Kermit Hull (7), married Kathleen Patterson.
    257. iii. Richard Hull (7), married Dorothy Hiner.
    258. iv. Roscoe Hull (7), married Evelyn Keith.
+   259. v.   Allie Ray Hull (7).

195. Thomas R. Hull (6), son of Joseph Hull (5) and Amanda J. Beverage, married Ethel Chew.

Children: 1

260. i.   Margaret Hull (7), married Edward Simmons.

238. William G. Hull (7), son of Cyrus S. Hull (6) and Eunice Eleanor Rexrode, married (1) Stella Stover; married (2) Hazel Page, daughter of Robert Lee Page and Minerva Wade.

Children: 1 - first marriage

261. i.   William Moffett Hull (8), married in 1931, Alma Margaret Gutshall.

255. Elizabeth Hull (7), daughter of Allie Porter Hull (6) and Annie F. Eye, married Arvie Glenn Wimer.

Children: 2

262. i.   Arvie Glenn Wimer, Jr. (8), married December 22,
1951, Leta Brown Lightner, born December 21, 1932, daughter of
Harry Robert Lightner and Bessie Lee Cleek. (See Lightner Family).
263. ii.   Jean Wimer (8), born March 26, 1932; died March
10, 1952; married November 3, 1950, Harry Robert Lightner, Jr.,
born July 12, 1925, son of Harry Robert Lightner and Bessie Lee
Cleek. No children.

259. Allie Ray Hull (7), son of Allie Porter Hull (6) and
Annie F. Eye, married Virginia Vaiden Burns, daughter of Guy
Burns and Annie Kincaid, and granddaughter of Charles Joseph
Burns and Minnie Trainor and George Thomas Kincaid and Matilda
Turner. (See Gwin Family). She is a R.N.

Children: 2

264. i.   Tiffany Hull (8).
265. ii.   Lucinda Allie Hull (8).

PART XVII

KEISTER FAMILY

This branch of the Keister Family came from Germany to Pennsylvania c. 1750. The name is found in records as Keister, Gester,
Kiester, Kister, Kester, Eister, and Keester.

1. Frederick Keister (1), born 1730; died 1814 and was buried
in Pendleton County, West Virginia; came from Pennsylvania to the
South Fork of the Potomac in Rockingham County, Virginia (now
Pendleton County, West Virginia). He married in 1755, Hannah Dyer,
daughter of Roger Dyer and Hannah Britton. Frederick Keister received his certificate of naturalization May 18, 1762. (Abstracts
from the Records of Augusta County, Virginia, Lyman Chalkley, Vol.
I, page 97). He served in the Revolution and qualified as Lieutenant on September 28, 1778. (Virginia Militia in the Revolution,
J. T. McAllister, page 230; Abstracts from the Records of Augusta
County, Virginia, Lyman Chalkley, Vol. II, page 364). His is listed
as furnishing supplies in an account dated May 29, 1782. (A History
of Rockingham County, Virginia, John W. Wayland, page 101). There
is a government marker over his grave. He also served as a soldier
in the Colonial Wars in the Augusta Militia. (Gleanings of Virginia
History, William Fletcher Boogher, page 41; List of Colonial Soldiers in Virginia, H. J. Eckenrode, page 37 - listed as Frederick
Eister).

Children: 7

385

2.　i.　James Keister (2), born 1756; died June 12, 1824; married Malinda Grim.
3.　ii.　Frederick Keister, Jr. (2), born 1774; married in 1791, Anne E. Propst. He was a great hunter. When he had obtained a substantial lot of game, he would build a signal fire on a high point on the Shenandoah Mountain. The smoke was a signal from him for help to pack the kill to his home.
4.　iii.　Esther Keister (2), married Adam Hull, born 1751; died 1825, son of Peter Hull and ·Barbara Keith. (See Hull Family).
+ 5.　iv.　George Keister (2), born February 13, 1777.
6.　v.　Elizabeth Keister (2), married Henry Hull, son of Peter Thomas Hull and Susannah Margaret Dieffenbach. (See Hull Family).
7.　vi.　Hannah Keister (2), married George Hull, son of Peter Thomas Hull and Susannah Margaret Dieffenbach. (See Hull Family).
8.　vii.　Mary Keister (2), married Gabriel Kile.

5.　George Keister (2), son of Frederick Keister (1) and Hannah Dyer, was born February 13, 1777; died July 18, 1854; married (1) in 1799, Susannah Peck; married (2) Mary Ann Jordan.

Children: 12 - first marriage

9.　i.　William Keister (3), married Elizabeth Bowman. They migrated to Iowa.
10.　ii.　George Keister (3), married in 1824, Sarah Propst.
11.　iii.　Jacob P. Keister (3), born in 1817; died in 1895; married in 1836, Mary (Polly) Graham Lockridge, daughter of Robert Lockridge and Mary Gwin. (See Gwin Family).
+ 12.　iv.　John D. Keister (3), born 1815.
13.　v.　Polly A. Keister(3), born 1821; died.1896; married Jess Cowger.
14.　vi.　Susan Keister (3), married George Hoover.
15.　vii.　Margaret Keister (3), married George Dean.
16.　viii.　Sarah Keister (3), married William Hull, son of George Hull and Hannah Keister. (See Hull Family).
17.　ix.　Elizabeth Keister (3), married Jacob Bowman.
18.　x.　Hannah Keister (3), married Captain Silas Hinton as his first wife. He married (2) Susan Henderson Gwin. (See Gwin Family). He served in the War of 1812. No children.
19.　xi.　Hester Keister (3), married Jeremiah Jordan of Highland County, Virginia.
20.　xii.　(Infant) Keister (3), died young.

Children: 6 - second marriage

21.　xiii.　James K. P. Keister (3), died young.
22.　xiv.　Jesse Keister (3), died young.
23.　xv.　Martin Keister (3), married Louisa Evick.
24.　xvi.　Mary A. Keister (3), married (1) Samuel A. Nelson; married (2) Hopkins Teter.

25. xvii. Benjamin Keister (3), died young.
26. xviii. Solomon Keister (3), married Sarah Lough. They migrated to Washington.

12. John D. Keister (3), son of George Keister (2) and Susannah Peck, was born in 1815; married Elizabeth Botkin.

Children: 6

+ 27. i. Andrew J. Keister (4), born 1840, a twin to John D.
+ 28. ii. John D. Keister (4), born 1840, a twin to Andrew J.
29. iii. Susannah Keister (4), died young.
30. iv. Sarah Keister (4), died young.
31. v. William Keister (4), married (1) Elizabeth Simmons; married (2) _____ Smith.
32. vi. Hannah Keister (4), married Arthur A. Hahn.

27. Andrew J. Keister (4), son of John D. Keister (3) and Elizabeth Botkin, was born in 1840; married (1) Sarah A. Hively; married (2) Hulda Armstrong.

Children: 4 - which marriage unknown.

33. i. Cora Keister (5), married Joseph Simmons.
34. ii. Harry Keister (5).
35. iii. Mary Keister (5), married Melvin Guyer.
36. iv. Mattie Keister (5), married Clay Shiflett.

28. John D. Keister (4), son of John D. Keister (3) and Elizabeth Botkin, was born in 1840; married Mary S. Trumbo.

Children: 5

37. i. Walter Keister (5), married Lena Weaver. They lived at Huntington, West Virginia.
38. ii. Emma Keister (5), married Jared Smith.
39. iii. Bowman Keister (5), married Mattie Nicholson.
40. iv. Myra Keister (5).
41. v. Elmer Keister (5), married Mary Hoover.

PART XVIII

LOCKRIDGE FAMILY

The Lockridge Family is of Scottish ancestry. The name is found in records as Lockridge, Louchridge, Lockbridge, Louchrage and Loughridge. Two brothers came to Augusta County, Virginia about 1730. These two brothers were:

+   1.   James Lockridge (1).
+   2.   William Lockridge (1).

1. James Lockridge (1), born c. 1690; married Isabella Kincaid, daughter of David Kincaid and Winnifred _____. He sold his land in Augusta County and moved to Granville County, South Carolina by 1767. (Abstracts from the Records of Augusta County, Virginia, Lyman Chalkley, Vol. III, pages 453 and 587). He was levy free in 1748.

Children: 4

+   3.   i.   Andrew Lockridge (2), born 1730.
    4.   ii.   Sarah Lockridge (2), married John Gay, son of James Gay. They migrated to Kentucky.
    5.   iii.   Elizabeth Lockridge (2), married June 24, 1763 (1) Robert Graham, son of John Graham and Elizabeth Elliott; married (2) Samuel Gwin, son of Robert Gwin and Jean Kincaid. (See Graham and Gwin Families).
    6.   iv.   Robert Lockridge (2), married Mary Elizabeth Gwin, daughter of Joseph Gwin and Mary Jane Kincaid. (See Gwin Family).

2. William Lockridge (1), died 1795 in Augusta County, Virginia; married Agnes Gwin, daughter of Robert Gwin and Jean Kincaid. (Abstracts from the Records of Augusta County, Virginia, Lyman Chalkley, Vol. III, pages 393 and 440). His will was dated March 12, 1793 and recorded September 1795 in Will Book VIII, page 181, Augusta County, Virginia. (Ibid., Vol. III, page 207). It mentions wife, Agness; son-in-law, John Eakin; daughter Elizabeth Eakin; sons, William, John, and Samuel; daughter Eleanor Cunningham; William Lockridge, son of John Lockridge. Witnesses were John Montgomery, Wm. Youel, James Guy, and Samuel Neil.

Children: 5

    7.   i.   Elizabeth Lockridge (2), married John Eakin.
    8.   ii.   Eleanor Lockridge (2), married _____ Cunningham.
+   9.   iii.   Samuel Lockridge (2).
    10.   iv.   William Lockridge (2).
    11.   v.   John Lockridge (2).

3. Andrew Lockridge (2), son of James Lockridge (1) and Isabella Kincaid, was born in 1730; died in 1791 in Augusta County, Virginia; married April 7, 1761, Jane Graham, born 1742, daughter of John Graham and Elizabeth Elliott. (See Graham Family). Andrew Lockridge was appointed Captain of the Militia of Augusta County, Virginia on March 16, 1768 and was in command of a company at the Battle of Point Pleasant. His will was dated January 7, 1791 and recorded April 19, 1791 in Will Book VII, page 353, Augusta County, Virginia. (Ibid, Vol. III, page 194). It mentions sons, John, Andrew, James, William, Robert and Lanty;

daughters, Margaret Henderson, Elizabeth Gwin, Elenor Dinwiddy, Sarah, Rebecca, Jean and Anne; and wife, Jean. Executors were sons, Andrew and William.

Children: 13

+ 12. i. John Lockridge (3), born 1762.
13. ii. Elizabeth Lockridge (3), born 1763; married (1) November 20, 1788, Robert Gay; married (2) Simon Gwin, son of Robert Gwin and Jean Kincaid. (Abstracts from the Records of Augusta County, Virginia, Lyman Chalkley, Vol. II, page 348). (See Gwin Family).
+ 14. iii. Eleanor Lockridge (3).
15. iv. Margaret Lockridge (3), married George Henderson, son of William Henderson and Susannah Gillespie. (See Henderson Family).
+ 16. v. Andrew Lockridge (3), born 1769.
17. vi. James Lockridge (3), married (1) April 5, 1791, Jane Guy (Ibid., Vol. II, pages 297 and 351); married (2) August 22, 1800, Ann Lockridge, daughter of Robert Lockridge and Mary Elizabeth Gwin. (Ibid., Vol. II, page 305). (See Gwin Family).
+ 18. vii. William Lockridge (3).
19. viii. Robert Lockridge (3), born 1777; died 1856; married 1798, Mary Gwin, born March 8, 1776, daughter of David Gwin and Jane Carlile. (See Gwin Family).
+ 20. ix. Lancelot Lockridge (3).
21. x. Sarah J. Lockridge (3), married in 1800, David Kincaid.
22. xi. Rebecca Lockridge (3), married November 18, 1788, Robert Gay. (Ibid., Vol. II, page 303).
23. xii. Jean Lockridge (3).
24. xiii. Anne Lockridge (3).

9. Samuel Lockridge (2), son of William Lockridge (1) and Agnes Gwin, died December 1812; married Elizabeth _____. (Ibid., Vol. I, pages 535 and 536).

Children: 14

25. i. Eleanor Lockridge (3).
26. ii. Polly Lockridge (3).
27. iii. Catherine Lockridge (3).
28. iv. Samuel Lockridge (3).
29. v. Savannah Lockridge (3).
30. vi. Alice Lockridge (3), married Andrew Guyto.
31. vii. Nancy Lockridge (3), married David Kincaid, son of Thomas Kincaid and Isabell (nee) Kincaid.
32. viii. Jane Lockrdidge(3), married William Fulton.
33. ix. Andrew Lockridge (3), married Anna Daggy, daughter of Jacob Daggy. (Ibid., Vol. II, page 182).
34. x. Betsy Lockridge (3), married April 8, 1800, Thomas Gwin, son of Robert Gwin and Jean Kincaid. (Ibid., Vol. II, page 339). (See Gwin Family).

35.   xi.   Sallie Lockridge (3), married Robert Gwin, Jr.,
son of Robert Gwin and Jean Kincaid. (See Gwin Family).
+   36.   xii.   Rebecca Lockridge (3).
37.   xiii.   Peggy Lockridge (3), married Robert Kincaid,
son of Thomas Kincaid and Isabell (nee) Kincaid. They had a son,
Guy Hamilton Kincaid. She was dead by December 1812.
38.   xiv.   Allen Lockridge (3).

12.   John Lockridge (3), son of Andrew Lockridge (2) and
Jane Graham, was born in 1762; died in 1799; married Anna Rhea,
daughter of William Rhea. (Abstracts from the Records of Augusta
County, Virginia, Vol. II, page 85). His will was dated December
4, 1798 and recorded June 24, 1799 in Will Book IX, page 8, Augusta County, Virginia. (Ibid., Vol. III, page 215). It mentions
wife, Anna and children; son, James (his schooling); three oldest
sons, Andrew, William, and John; daughters, Betsy, Sarah and
Anna.   Executors were brother, Andrew Lockridge, and James Berry.

Children: 7

39.   i.   Andrew Lockridge (4), married Easter Torbett.
(Ibid., Vol. II, page 88).
40.   ii.   William Lockridge (4).
41.   iii.   John Lockridge (4), married Eliza Ervine.
42.   iv.   James Lockridge (4).
43.   v.   Betsy Lockridge (4).
44.   vi.   Sarah Lockridge (4).
45.   vii.   Anna Lockridge (4).

14.   Eleanor Lockridge (3), daughter of Andrew Lockridge
(2) and Jane Graham, married August 16, 1785, James Dinwiddie.
(Ibid., Vol. II, page 280).

Children: 2

46.   i.   Robert Dinwiddie (4), married in Kentucky.
47.   ii.   Mary Dinwiddie (4), married John Kincaid, son
of Thomas Kincaid and Isabell (nee) Kincaid.

16.   Andrew Lockridge (3), son of Andrew Lockridge (2) and
Jane Graham, was born in 1769; married March 23, 1797, Christina
Youell. (Ibid., Vol. II, page 356).

Children: 2

48.   i.   Andrew Lockridge (4), a Presbyterian missionary
to the Cherokee Indians.
49.   ii.   Elizabeth Lockridge (4), married Robert Dunlap
McCutchan.

18.   William Lockridge (3), son of Andrew Lockridge (2) and
Jane Graham, died in 1798; married Elizabeth Benson, daughter of
Mathias Benson. After his death, his widow married his brother,
Lancelot Lockridge.

Children: 2

+ 50.   i.   Jane Lockridge (4).
  51.   ii. William Lockridge (4), married _____.

20.   Lancelot Lockridge (3), son of Andrew Lockridge (2) and
Jane Graham, married in 1802, Elizabeth (Benson) Lockridge, daughter of Mathias Benson and widow of William Lockridge.

Children: 9

  52.   i.   Andrew Lockridge (4), married Elizabeth
Gilliland, daughter of John Gilliland. They lived in Missouri.
  53.   ii. Mathias Lockridge (4), married _____ Crow.
They lived in Missouri.
  54.   iii. Lancelot Lockridge (4), married December 26,
1854 in Pocahontas County, West Virginia, Carolina Elizabeth
Cleek, daughter of John Cleek and Phoebe Ann Lightner. (See
Cleek Family).
+ 55.   iv. James T. Lockridge (4).
+ 56.   v.   Elizabeth Lockridge (4).
+ 57.   vi. Eleanor Lockridge (4).
+ 58.   vii. Harriet Lockridge (4).
+ 59.   viii. Rebecca Lockridge (4).
+ 60.   ix. Martha Lockridge (4).

36.   Rebecca Lockridge (3), daughter of Samuel Lockridge (2)
and Elizabeth _____; married William Kincaid, son of Thomas
Kincaid and Isabell (nee) Kincaid.

Children: 8

  61.   i.   John Kincaid (4), migrated to Missouri.
  62.   ii. Jordan Kincaid (4).
  63.   iii. William Kincaid (4), married in 1871, Luella
Susan Gwin, daughter of John Gwin and Margaret Bradshaw. (See Gwin
Family).
  64.   iv. Calvin Kincaid (4).
+ 65.   v.   Willis Kincaid (4), born March 10, 1811.
  66.   vi. Ellen Kincaid (4), born March 10, 1811, twin to
Willis, married _____ in Illinois.
  67.   vii. Malinda Kincaid (4), married David Brinkley.
  68.   viii. Charles Kincaid (4), married _____.

50.   Jane Lockridge (4), daughter of William Lockridge (3)
and Elizabeth Benson, married September 14, 1815 in Bath County,
Virginia, Edward S. Callahan, III.

Children: 8

  69.   i.   William Lockridge Callahan (5), born 1816.
  70.   ii. Mary J. Callahan (5), married William Briscoe.
  71.   iii. Elizabeth Callahan (5), married Thomas Ryder.

391

72. iv. Rebecca Callahan (5), married Thomas Townsend.
73. v. Otho W. Callahan (5), a dentist.
74. vi. Lancelot S. Callahan (5).
75. vii. Margaret Callahan (5), married (1) John Matheny; married (2) Dyer Bird.
76. viii. Charlotte Callahan (5), married Peter Bird. No children.

55. James T. Lockridge (4), son of Lancelot Lockridge (3) and Elizabeth Benson, married Lillie Moser of South Carolina. He was a Colonel in the 127th Virginia Militia. He was also a member of the Virginia House of Delegates.

Children: 4

+ 77. i. Horace M. Lockridge (5).
+ 78. ii. Florence Lockridge (5).
+ 79. iii. Dr. James Bedford Lockridge (5).
  80. iv. Laura Lockridge (5).

56. Elizabeth Lockridge (4), daughter of Lancelot Lockridge (3) and Elizabeth Benson, married Henry Herold, son of Christopher Herold and Elizabeth Cook. They migrated to Nicholas County, West Virginia.

Children: 7

81. i. Anderson Herold (5), married Annie _____.
82. ii. A. Washington Herold (5), married (1) Anna Harper, daughter of Samuel Harper and Malinda Moore; married (2) Margaret Dever, daughter of John Dever. (See Harper Family).
83. iii. William Herold (5), married Rachel Anne Harper, daughter of Henry Harper and Phoebe Sharp. (See Harper Family).
84. iv. Benjamin Herold (5).
85. v. Lancelot Herold (5).
86. vi. Elizabeth Herold (5), married _____ McClung, Nicholas County, West Virginia.
87. vii. Maria Herold (5), married John McClintic, Frankford, West Virginia.

57. Eleanor Lockridge (4), daughter of Lancelot Lockridge (3) and Elizabeth Benson, married Jacob Gillespie Slaven, son of John Slaven,Jr. and Elizabeth Warwick. (See Warwick Family).

Children: 12

88. i. Harriet Slaven (5), married Patrick Gallaher.
89. ii. Elizabeth Slaven (5), married William T. Gammon.
90. iii. Adelaide Eleanor Slaven (5), twin to Eveline Margaret, married (1) Washington Arbogast, died 1864 of wounds received at the battle of Spottsylvania Courthouse; married (2) William L. Brown. She died July 7, 1934.
91. iv. Eveline Margaret Slaven (5), twin to Adelaide Eleanor, married J. H. Patterson. He served in the CSA.

92. v. Mary P. Slaven (5), married Jesse B. Slaven.
93. vi. Martha Slaven (5), married J. T. Hogsett.
94. vii. Sarah Mildred Slaven (5), twin to Alice, married
(1) Peter H. Slaven; married (2) Arista Hartman.
95. viii. Alice Slaven (5), twin to Sarah Mildred, died
young.
96. ix. John Randolph Slaven (5),married Margaret P.
Wooddell.
97. x. Lancelot Lockridge Slaven (5), married Isabella
Burner, daughter of George Burner and Sarah Warwick. (See Hull
Family).
98. xi. Warwick Slaven (5), married Mary Riley.
99. xii. Wingfield T. Slaven (5), married Nancy
Priscilla Ruckman, daughter of James W. Ruckman and Carolina
Arbogast.

58. Harriet Lockridge (4), daughter of Lancelot Lockridge
(3) and Elizabeth Benson, married John McNeel.

Children: 5

+ 100. i. Isaac McNeel. (5).
101. ii. John Mathew McNeel (5), married _____.
102. iii. Evelina McNeel (5), born August 13, 1832 in
Pocahontas County, West Virginia; died September 11, 1902 in
Pocahontas County, West Virginia; married October 27, 1852,
Andrew Dyer Amiss, born July 28, 1827 in Pendleton County, Virginia;
died December 27, 1888 in Pocahontas County, West Virginia.
103. iv. Rachel A. McNeel (5), died July 12, 1890; married
Dr. Mathew Wallace, son of Benjamin Wallace and Hannah McNeel.
104. v. Elizabeth McNeel (5), married Abraham Crouch,
born 1832; died 1901, son of Andrew Crouch and Elizabeth Hutton.
Their descendants are given in A History of Randolph County, Dr.
A.S. Bosworth, page 318.

59. Rebecca Lockridge (4), daughter of Lancelot Lockridge
(3) and Elizabeth Benson, married Joseph Seybert.

Children: 4

105. i. Lancelot Seybert (5), died as a prisoner of
war at Elmira, New York.
106. ii. Jacob Seybert (5), married Mary Jones, Rockbridge County, Virginia.
107. iii. Maria Seybert (5), married Andrew Herold, son
of Christopher Herold and Elizabeth Cook.
+ 108. iv. Elizabeth Seybert (5).

60. Martha Lockridge (4), daughter of Lancelot Lockridge
(3) and Elizabeth Benson, married (as his first wife), Roger
Hickman, son of William Hickman and Mary Elliot.

Children: 3

393

109. i. Lancelot Hickman (5), married Mary Wiley.
110. ii. Ellen Hickman (5), died in infancy.
111. iii. Elizabeth Hickman (5), married (as his second wife), Rev. Stuart Ryder. No children.

65. Willis Kincaid (4), son of William Kincaid and Rebecca Lockridge (3), was born March 10, 1811; died June 6, 1887; married October 1, 1832 in Bath County, Virginia, Margaret T. Rhea, born March 18, 1813; died July 28,1888. Both are buried at Woodland Union Church, Bath County, Virginia.

Children: 9

+ 112. i. James N. Kincaid (5).
113. ii. Margaret Ellen Kincaid (5), born 1835; married December 21, 1865 in Bath County, Virginia, George Hamilton Guinn, born November 12, 1836; died February 16, 1929, son of Joseph Corbett Gwin and Mary Jane Benson. (See Gwin Family).
114. iii. Elizabeth H. Kincaid (5), born 1842; died March 6, 1890; married November 17, 1864 (as his first wife), Eli Cleek, born January 28, 1840; died October 17, 1902. Both are buried at Woodland Union Church, Bath County, Virginia. (See Cleek Family).
115. iv. Floyd Kincaid (5), born July 21, 1833; died August 23, 1914; married Elizabeth L. Steuart, born May 5, 1841; died January 18, 1913. Both are buried at Woodland Union Church, Bath County, Virginia.
+ 116. v. Joel B. Kincaid (5).
117. vi. John Kincaid (5), married _____. They lived in Baltimore, Maryland.
118. vii. Martha A. Kincaid (5), born May 3, 1838; died July 9, 1903 and was buried at Woodland Union Church, Bath County, Virginia; married James M. Dill.
119. viii. Virginia Kincaid (5), married Leonidas Campbell, son of Amos Campbell and Martha Gammon. (See Campbell Family).
120. ix. Charles Kincaid (5).

77. Horace M. Lockridge (5), son of James T. Lockridge (4) and Lillie Moser, married (1) Alice Moore; married (2) Elizabeth Milligan. Alice Moore was a daughter of Moses Moore and Isabella Campbell. (See Campbell Family).

Children: 1 - first marriage

121. i. Edith Lockridge (6), died young.

Children: 1 - second marriage

122. ii. Mary Margaret Lockridge (6), married Dr. Everett Herold.

78. Florence Lockridge (5), daughter of James T. Lockridge (4) and Lillie Moser, married Whit Milligan.

Children: 3

123. i. Lillie Milligan (6).
+ 124. ii. Mabel Milligan (6).
125. iii. (Son) Milligan (6), died.

79. Dr. James Bedford Lockridge (5), son of James T. Lockridge (4) and Lillie Moser; married September 28, 1886 in Pocahontas County, West Virginia, Margaret E. Warwick, daughter of
John Wood Warwick and Caroline Elizabeth Craig. (See Warwick
Family).

Children: 7

126. i. Dr. Raymond Lockridge (6), died in Tennessee;
married Sarah Ruckman.
127. ii. Maude Lockridge (6), died November 23, 1951;
married October 1, 1913, Boyd L. Campbell, son of William Price
Campbell and Annie L. Ruckman. (See Campbell Family).
128. iii. Georgia Lockridge (6), married Hurl Neel of
Blue Sulphur Springs, West Virginia.
129. iv. Newton Lockridge (6), married Dolly McGlaughlin.
130. v. Hal Lockridge (6), married _____.
131. vi. Horace Lockridge (6), married _____.
132. vii. Julian Lockridge (6), married Jean Dever, daughter of Dennis Dever and Alice McGlaughlin.

100. Isaac McNeel (5), son of John McNeel and Harriet Lockridge (4), married Miriam Nancy Beard.

Children: 4

133. i. T. Summers McNeel (6), married Mary McNulty.
He was a twin to Winters. He is a lawyer.
134. ii. Winters McNeel (6), twin to T. Summers, married
Elizabeth See Edgar, daughter of Captain A. M. Edgar. He is a
physician.
135. iii. J. Lancelot McNeel (6), married Nora Wilson.
136. iv. Mary Cold McNool (6), married William A.
Browning.

108. Elizabeth Seybert (5), daughter of Joseph Seybert and
Rebecca Lockridge (4), married in 1859, William D. Gibson, born
1824; died 1889.

Children: 8

137. i. Joseph Seybert Gibson (6), born 1868; married
Theresa Wicker.
138. ii. William A. Gibson (6).
139. iii. Kemper Gibson (6), died 1909..
140. iv. Eva Rebecca Gibson (6), died April 5, 1945;
married in 1881, David M. Kyle of Staunton, Virginia.

395

141. v.   Elizabeth Gibson (6), married in 1895, John M.
Colaw, as his second wife.
142. vi.   Clara Gibson (6), died.
143. vii.   Mary Kate Gibson (6), died.

112.   James N. Kincaid (5), son of Willis Kincaid (4) and
Margaret T. Rhea, married Amanda Ellen Gwin,, born September 7,
1834, daughter of Joseph Corbett Gwin and Mary Jane Benson.

Children: 10

144. i.   Margaret J. Kincaid (6), married Thomas Jackson.
145. ii.   Julia Kincaid (6), married John Hodge, son of
James Hodge and Sallie Benson.
146. iii.   Ella Kincaid (6), married Given Hodge, son of
James Hodge and Sallie Benson.
147. iv.   Nannie Kincaid (6), married Howard Mackey.
148. v.   Burton Kincaid (6), died in young womanhood.
149. vi.   Virginia Kincaid (6), married Jasper Kincaid.
150. vii.   Cora Kincaid (6), married Gordon Shuey.
151. viii.   George Bell Kincaid (6), married Mollie Jordan.
152. ix.   Robert Nelson Kincaid (6), married Bertie Carroll
153. x.   John Arthur Kincaid (6), married Blanch Grove.

116.   Joel B. Kincaid (5), son of Willis Kincaid (4) and
Margaret T. Rhea, married Catherine Armentrout, born August 17,
1849; died December 17, 1908 and was buried at Woodland Union
Church, Bath County, Virginia.

Children: 9

154. i.   Forrest Kincaid (6), married Hattie Patterson.
155. ii.   Mary Kincaid (6), born January 27, 1870; died
February 16, 1903 and was buried at Woodland Union Church, Bath
County, Virginia.
156. iii.   Rosa Kincaid (6), died February 14, 1957 and
was buried at Woodland Union Church, Bath County, Virginia.
157. iv.   Joel P. Kincaid (6), born February 27, 1874;
died December 25, 1946 and was buried at Woodland Union Church,
Bath County, Virginia; married Vesta Simpson, born October 24,
1875. They had two children: Emory Kincaid (7),and Marion
Kincaid (7), died in young manhood.
158. v.   John Kincaid (6), married Edith Hood.
159. vi.   Tim Kincaid (6), married (1) Brownie Pugh;
married (1) Lula Hickman.
160. vii.   C. Moody Kincaid (6), died April 30, 1946;
married Mary Yeager, daughter of Charles Andrew Yeager and Allie
Arbogast. He was Clerk of the County Court, Pocahontas County,
West Virginia. (See Lightner Family).
161. viii.   Fred Kincaid (6), married Eva Roberts.
162. ix.   Virginia Kincaid (6), married Orion Burns.

124.   Mabel Milligan (6), daughter of Whit Milligan and
Florence Lockridge (5), married May 22, 1906, Calvin Wells

Price, born November 22, 1880 at Mt. Clinton, Virginia, son of Rev. William Thomas Price and Anna Louise Randolph. He is editor and publisher of The Pocahontas Times, Marlinton, West Virginia.

Children: 4

 163. i. Elizabeth Price (7), born March 17, 1907; married March 25, 1933, John Branch Green.
 164. ii. Florence Randolph Price (7), born January 9, 1909; married November 28, 1935, Isaac McNeel, son of Dr. Winters McNeel and Elizabeth See Edgar.
 165. iii. Ann Lockridge Price (7), born September 1, 1914; married June 15, 1933, James Douglas Hubard.
 166. iv. Jane Stobo Price (7), born October 15, 1918; married 1934, Basil Sharp.

PART XIX

MCFARLAND FAMILY

 The Macfarlane Clan was one of the Highland Clans in Scotland. They moved from Argyleshire, Scotland to Ireland about 1601, where the name changed from Macfarlane to McFarland. There have been no fewer than 23 Lairds of Macfarlane, the last of whom came to America early in the 18th century.

 1. Duncan McFarland (1), died in Bath County, Virginia; married Anne Porter, daughter of a sea captain. Duncan McFarland was a weaver and was in Augusta County before 1750. He settled on Jackson River in what is now Bath County, Virginia. Both are buried near the George Cleek Cemetery in Bath County, Virginia in unmarked graves. The McFarland family abandoned their cabin home during an Indian raid in 1763 and took refuge in a nearby cave on the east side of Jackson River just opposite their cabin. From the cave they saw their home and personal belongings destroyed and their livestock tortured and killed. After several years of discouragement by being continually harassed by the cunning Indians, descendants of Duncan McFarland sold their real estate to Jacob Cleek in February 1792 and settled in that part of North Carolina which is now included in the state of Tennessee.

Children: 4 (others?)

 2. i. Robert McFarland (2), died in 1798; married Esther Houston, daughter of John Houston (1669-1755) and Margaret Crawford. He qualified a Lieutenant on November 16, 1752. (Abstracts from the Records of Augusta County, Virginia, Lyman Chalkley, Vol. II, page 55). Their daughter, Anne McFarland (3), born 1723; married (1) in 1738, Captain Alexander

Dunlap, born 1716; died 1744; married (2) in 1745, Robert Bratton, born May 20, 1712; died in 1785. (See Bratton Family).

3. ii. John McFarland (2), called "Old Scotland John", married Mary Montgomery. He was one of the first Elders in the Old Stone Church in Augusta County, Virginia. Two of his grandsons were active in the early settlement of the Tennessee border territory. They were Colonel Robert McFarland (son of Robert McFarland) and Colonel John McFarland (son of Benjamin McFarland). Colonel John McFarland represented Jefferson County, Tennessee in the Legislature at Nashville in 1824. John McFarland (2) qualified as Ensign on November 16, 1752. (Abstracts from the Records of Augusta County, Virginia, Lyman Chalkley, Vol. II, page 55).

4. iii. William McFarland (2), married (_____ Gibson, daughter of Alexander Gibson and Mary _____. William McFarland served in the Revolution.

5. iv. Alexander McFarland (2). He was wounded in the Battle of Point Pleasant, October 10, 1774. (Ibid, Vol. I, page 254.)

PART XX

MOORE FAMILY

1. Moses Moore (1), born c. 1686; died in November 1758. (Abstracts from the Records of Augusta County, Virginia, Lyman Chalkley, Vol. I, page 82). He left at least one son, Moses Moore (2).

2. Moses Moore (2), son of Moses Moore (1) was born in 1737; died in 1812; married c. 1760, Hannah Risk, born 1740; died 1810, daughter of John Risk of Timber Ridge in what is now Rockbridge County, Virginia. (Ibid., Vol. I, pages 355, 357, and 459 and Vol. III, page 147). Moses Moore moved from Timber Ridge to what is now Pocahontas County, West Virginia about 1770. Moses Moore was taken prisoner by the Indians in May 1758. (Ibid., Vol. II, page 512 and Annals of Augusta County, Virginia, Joseph A. Waddell, page 158). For full particulars of his capture and escape from the Indians see Historical Sketches of Pochontas County, West Virginia, William T. Price, pages 108 to 116. Moses Moore furnished beef for public use in 1785. (Abstracts from the Records of Augusta County, Virginia, Lyman Chalkley, Vol. I, page 24). He served as Scout in the expeditions against the Indians and as private in Captain Robert Doack's Company of Militia in Dunmore's War. (List of Colonial Soldiers, H. J. Eckenrode, page 64; and Virginia Colonial Militia, W. A. Crozier, page 80). The will of Moses Moore was dated June 9, 1812 and recorded September 1812 in Will Book 1, page 510, Bath County, Virginia. It mentions David Kayles; daughter Phoebe McNeel; granddaughters Hannah Dilley and Jean Moore; daughter Margaret Moore; son Isaac Moore; son

Robert Moore; son John Moore; Hannah Duffield; son William Moore; daughter Jean McNeel; Aaron Moore; son Moses Moore. Executors were Levi and Robert Moore. Witnesses were Alex. S. Waugh, Charles Grimes and Samuel Waugh.

Children: 13

+ 3. i. John Moore (3), born January 29, 1762.
  4. ii. James Moore (3), born October 5, 1763; died in 1791; married Jinet _____. His will is recorded in Augusta County, Virginia and was dated March 31, 1785, recorded September 1, 1791 in Will Book 1, page 8. It mentions wife, Jinet; sons, John and James; son, Joseph; daughters, Mary, Rachel and Jean; son, John and Hugh Kelso to be executors.
  5. iii. Margaret Moore (3), born March 29, 1765; married March 29, 1788, John Moore of Pennsylvania. (Sketches of Pocahontas County, West Virginia, William T. Price, page 289, and Abstracts from the Records of Augusta County, Virginia, Lyman Chalkley, Vol. II, page 305).
  6. iv. Moses Moore, Jr. (3), born February 8, 1767; married March 22, 1786, Jane Ewing, daughter of James Ewing. (Abstracts from the Records of Augusta County, Virginia, Lyman Chalkley, Vol. II, page 282).
  7. v. Nancy Moore (3), born 1769; married 1794, James Stuart.
  8. vi. Hannah Moore (3), born June 6, 1771; married Abraham Duffield. (Historical Sketches of Pocahontas County, West Virginia, William T. Price, page 452).
  9. vii. Robert Moore (3), born May 27, 1772; married Rebecca McCollam. (Ibid., page 464).
  10. viii. Phoebe Moore (3), born February 13, 1774; married Jonathan McNeil, son of Thomas McNeil and Mary Ireson. (Ibid., page 381).
  11. ix. Jane (Jennie) Moore (3), born 1776; married _____ McNeel.
  12. x. Rebecca Moore (3), born 1778; married _____ Cole and lived in Rockbridge County, Virginia.
  13. xi. Isaac Moore (3), born 1782, twin to Aaron, married Margaret McCutcheon. (Abstracts from the Records of Augusta County, Virginia, Lyman Chalkley, Vol. III, page 219).
  14. xii. Aaron Moore (3), born 1782, twin to Isaac, married Catherine Johnson, daughter of John Johnson. (Historical Sketches of Pocahontas County, West Virginia, William T. Price, page 114).
  15. xiii. William Moore (3), born September 18, 1784; married in 1812, Catherine Dods. (Ibid., page 114).

3. John Moore (3), son of Moses Moore (2) and Hannah Risk, was born January 29, 1762; died 1822; married April 20, 1793, Elizabeth McClung, born 1771; died March 9, 1852, daughter of Joseph McClung and Margaret Bell. Margaret Bell was the daughter of Joseph B. Bell. Joseph McClung (whose youngest brother, Charles McClung, was the first Clerk of Mason County, Virginia) was killed October 10, 1774 in the battle of Point Pleasant, and

was the son of John McClung, born in Ireland in 1704; died 1788 and was buried in the Stonewall Jackson Cemetery, Lexington, Virginia. This John McClung came to America in 1742 and married Janetta Stuart from Staunton, Virginia, a relative of Hon. Alexander Hugh Holmes Stuart of Staunton, Virginia, who was Secretary of State in President Franklin Pierce's cabinet from 1850 to 1853, and also U. S. Senator from Virginia 1857 - 1861.

Children: 8

16. i. Margaret Moore (4), born 1794; married in 1821, Adam Stephenson.
17. ii. Jane Moore (4), born December 25, 1807; died May 23, 1886; married September 20, 1826, John Lightner, born October 3, 1803; died July 7, 1863, son of Adam Lightner and Susannah Harper. (See Lightner Family).
18. iii. Elizabeth Moore (4), died 1850; married June 19, 1823 in Pocahontas County, West Virginia, Jacob Lightner, died 1842, son of Peter Lightner and Annis E. Harper. (See Lightner Family).
19. iv. John Moore (4), died aged 18 years.
20. v. Rachel Moore (4), married Miles Parsons late in life.' They lived near Moorfield, West Virginia.
21. vi. Mary Pheamster Moore (4), died October 6, 1897; unmarried, and was buried in the George Cleek Cemetery in Bath County, Virginia.
22. vii. Rebecca Moore (4), married David Garvin.
23. viii. Abigail Moore (4), born 1810; died 1846; married in 1830, _____ Myers. (See Cleek Family).

SOLDIERS OF THE VARIOUS EARLY WARS

Colonial, Indian and Frontier Wars

Revolutionary War

War of 1812

War Between the States

BIBLIOGRAPHY

Books and Pamphlets

A partial list of the books and pamphlets consulted by the compiler during the past fifty years are listed below. Almost all of these publications are in the compiler's personal library.

1. Abstracts from the Records of Augusta County, Virginia, 3 Vols., Lyman Chalkley, The Commonwealth Printing Company, Rosslyn, Virginia, 1912.
2. Albemarle County in Virginia, Rev. Edgar Woods, The Michie Company, Charlottesville, Virginia, 1901.
3. Augusta County, Virginia, Historical Atlas of, Jed Hotchkiss & J. A. Waddell, Waterman, Watkins & Co., Chicago, Illinois, 1885.
4. Abb's Valley, Captives of, Robert Bell Woodworth, The McClure Co., Inc., Staunton, Virginia, 1942.
5. Alleghany County, Virginia, A Centenial History of, Oren F. Morton, J. K. Ruebush Co., Dayton, Virginia, 1923.
6. Augusta Church, History of the, Rev. J. N. Van Devanter, The Ross Printing Company, Staunton, Virginia, 1900.
7. Augusta County, Virginia, Annals of, Joseph A. Waddell, C. Russel Caldwell, Staunton, Virginia, 1902.
8. Augusta County, Virginia, History of, J. Lewis Peyton, Samuel M. Yost & Son, Staunton, Virginia, 1882.
9. Bath County, Virginia, Annals of, Oren F. Morton, The McClure Co., Inc., Staunton, Virginia, 1917.
10. Berk and Lebanon, History of the Counties of, I. Daniel Rupp.
11. Berks County, Pa., The Story of, A. E. Wagner, Reading Eagle Co.
12. Border Settlers of Northwestern Virginia from 1768 to 1795, The, Lucullus Virgil McWhorter, The Republican Publishing Co., Hamilton, Ohio, 1915.
13. Border Warfare, Chronicles of, Alexander Scott Withers, Stewart and Kidd Co., Cincinnati, Ohio, 1895.
14. Boyers, American, Rev. Charles C. Boyer, Kutztown Publishing Co., Kutztown, Pa., 1915.
15. Boyers, American, Melville James Boyer, The Association of American Boyers, Inc., Allentown, Pa., 1940.
16. Braxton County and Central West Virginia, History of, John Davison Sutton, Sutton, West Virginia, 1919.
17. Casper, Henry, Baltzer, and George Spengler, The Annals of the Families of, E. W. Spangler, York, Pa., 1896.
18. Church on the Western Waters, The, Rev. Lloyd McF. Courtney, Whittet & Shepperson, Richmond, Va., 1940.
19. DAR Lineage Books.
20. Dunmore's War, 1774, R. G. Thwaite, Wisconsin Historical Society, Madison, Wisconsin, 1905.
21. Eisenhower - Man and Soldier, Francis Trevelyan Miller, John C. Winston Co., Philadelphia, Pa., 1944.
22. Emigrants in the Eighteenth Century to the American Colonies, Lists of Swiss, Albert B. Faust, 1920-1925.

23. Emigrants to America, Original Lists of, Hotten, New York, N.Y., 1874.
24. Emigrants to Virginia, Some, W. G. Stanard, 1911.
25. Encyclopedia Britannica.
26. Filson Club History Quarterly, The, Louisville, Ky.
27. Henry Funck and other Funk Pioneers, A Brief History of Bishop, A. J. Fretz, Mennonite Publishing Co., Elkart, Ind., 1889.
28. Genealogies and Sketches of Some Old Families, Benjamin F. Van Meter, John P. Morton & Co., Louisville, Ky., 1901.
29. German Baptist Brethren in Europe and America, A History of the, M. G. Brumbaugh, Brethren Pub. House, Mt. Morris, Ill, 1899.
30. German Colonization in America, Vol. V., pages 13 - 29, G. C. Heckman, Pennsylvania - German Society Publications, Philadelphia, Pa.
31. German Element of the Shenandoah Valley of Virginia, The, John Walter Wayland, The Michie Co., Charlottesville, Va., 1907.
32. German Element in Virginia, History of the, Hermann Schuricht, Theodore Kroh & Sons, Baltimore, Md., 1900.
33. German Immigration into Pennsylvania through the Port of Philadelphia and "The Redemptioners", The, F. R. Diffenderffer, Pennsylvania - German Society, Philadelphia, Pa., 1900.
34. Germans, The Maryland, Dieter Cunz, Princeton University Press.
35. Germans, The Pennsylvania, Ralph Wood, Princeton University Press.
36. German Sectarians of Pennsylvania, The (1708-1800), J. F. Sachse, Philadelphia, Pa., 1895.
37. Greenbrier County, History of, J. R. Cole, Lewisburg, West Va., 1919.
38. Harman-Harmon Genealogy and Biography, John William Harman, Parsons, West Virginia, 1928.
39. Heads of Families - First Census, 1790.
40. Highland County, Virginia, A History of, Oren F. Morton, Monterey, Va., 1911.
41. Highland County, A Hand Book of, Oren F. Morton, The Highland Recorder, Monterey, Va., 1922.
42. Historical and Geographical Encyclopedia - Hardesty's, R. A. Brock, H. H. Hardesty & Co., New York, N.Y., 1884.
43. History and Genealogies, W. H. Miller, Press of Transylvania Printing Co., Lexington, Ky, 1907.
43. Immigrants in Pennsylvania from 1727 to 1776, A Collection of Thirty Thousand Names of, Prof. I. Daniel Rupp, Leary, Stuart Co., Philadelphia, Pa., 1856, 1875, 1927.
44. Michael Keinadt and Margaret Diller, A Historical Sketch of, by a Committee of the Michael Koiner Memorial Assn., Stoneburner & Prufer, Staunton, Va., 1893.
45. King's Mountain Men, The, Kathrine Keogh White, Joseph K. Ruebush Co., Dayton, Va., 1924.
50. Lancaster County, Pa., History of, I. Daniel Rupp, Lancaster, Pa., 1844.

51. Land of Saddle-bags, The, James Watt Raine, Presbyterian Committee of Publication, Richmond, Va.,1924.
52. General Robert E. Lee, Recollections and Letters of, Capt. Robert E. Lee, Doubleday, Page & Co., New York, N. Y., 1905.
53. Link Family, The, Paxson Link, Paris, Illinois, 1951.
54. Lost Links, Elizabeth Wheeler Francis and Ethel Sively Moore, McQuiddy Printing Co., Nashville, Tenn., 1945.
55. Lutheran Church in Virginia, The, D. M. Gilbert, Henkel & Co., New Market, Va., 1876.
56. Marriages, Old Tenth Legion, Harry M. Strickler, Joseph K. Ruebush Co., Dayton, Va., 1928.
57. Marriages, Early Virginia, William Armstrong Crozier, Southern Book Co., Baltimore, Md., 1953.
58. Marshall County, West Virginia, History of, Scott Powell, Moundsville, W. Va., 1925.
59. Martinsburg and Berkeley County, West Va., History of, F. Vernon Aler, The Mail Publishing Co., Hagerstown, Md., 1888.
60. Middle New River Settlements, A History of, David E. Johnston, Standard Ptg & Pub Co., Huntington, W. Va., 1906.
61. Monroe County, West Virginia, A History of, Oren F. Morton, The McClure Co., Inc., Staunton, Va., 1916.
62. McClung Genealogy, Rev. William McClung, McClung Printing Co., Pittsburgh, Pa., 1904.
63. Page County, Virginia, A Short History of, Harry M. Strickler, The Dietz Press, Inc., Richmond, Va., 1952.
64. Pendleton County, West Virginia, A History of, Oren F. Morton, Ruebush Elkins Co., Dayton, Va., 1910.
65. Pioneers, Trans-Allegheny, John P. Hale, S. C. Cox & Co., Cincinnati, Ohio, 1886.
66. Robert and John Poage, The Descendants of, Robert Bell Woodworth, The McClure Printing Co., Staunton, Va., 1954.
67. Pocahontas County, West Virginia, Historical Sketches of, Rev. William T. Price, Price Brothers, Marlinton, W. Va., 1901.
68. Point Pleasant, History of the Battle of, Virgil A. Lewis, The Tribune Printing Co., Charleston, W. Va., 1909.
69. Preston County, West Virginia, A History of, J. R. Cole, The Journal Publishing Co., Kingwood, W.Va., 1914.
70. Protestant Dissenters for Religious Toleration in Virginia, Struggle of, H. R. McIlwaine, John Hopkins Press, Baltimore, Md., 1894.
71. Randolph County, West Virginia, A History of, Dr. A. S. Bosworth, Elkins, W. Va., 1916.
72. Records of the Revolutionary War, W. T. R. Saffell, Charles C. Saffell, Baltimore, Md., 1894.
73. Renicks of Greenbrier, The, B. F. Harlow, Jr., Lexington, Va., 1951.
74. Rockbridge County, Virginia, A History of, Oren F. Morton, The McClure Co., Inc., Staunton, Va., 1920.
75. Rockingham County, Virginia, A History of, John W. Wayland, Ruebush - Elkins Co., Dayton, Va., 1912.
76. Scotch Highlanders in America, An Historical Account of the Settlements, J. P. MacLean, The Helman-Taylor Co., Cleveland, Ohio, 1900.

77. Scotch-Irish of the Valley of Virginia, J. A. Waddell, Staunton, Virginia.
78. Shenandoah County, Virginia, A History of, John W. Wayland, Shenandoah Publishing House, Strasburg, Va., 1927.
79. Shenandoah Valley, In the Picturesque, Armistead C. Gordon, Garrett & Massie, Inc., Richmond, Va., 1930.
80. Soldier of Democracy, Kenneth S. Davis, Doubleday, Doran & Co., Inc., Garden City, N. Y., 1945.
81. Soldiers, List of Colonial, Ethenrode Barton.
82. Tinkling Spring - Headwater of Freedom, The, Howard McKnight Wilson, Garrett & Massie, Inc., Richmond, Va., 1954.
83. Tucker County, West Virginia, History of, Hu Maxwell, Preston Pub. Co., Kingwood, W.Va., 1884.
84. Veach and Stover Families, The American Lineages of the, Robert Spangler Veach, 1913.
85. Virginia, A History of the Valley of, Samuel Kercheval, 1833, 1850, 1902, 1925, Shenandoah Publishing House, Strasburg, Va.
86. Virginia and Maryland, Some Old Historic Landmarks of, W. H. Snowden, J. B. Lippincott Co., Philadelphia, Pa., 1894.
87. Virginia and Virginians, R. A. Brock, H. H. Hardesty, Richmond, Va., 1888.
88. Virginia Families, Some, H. M. McIlhany, Jr., Stoneburner & Prufer, Staunton, Va., 1903.
89. Virginia Colonial Militia, 1651-1776, William Armstrong Crozier, The Genealogical Association, New York, N. Y., 1905.
90. Virginia History, Gleanings of, William Fletcher Boogher, Washington, D. C. 1903.
91. Virginia, History of, 6 Vols., Philip Alexander Bruce, The American Historical Society, Chicago, Ill., 1924.
92. Virginia, History of, Charles Cambell, Philadelphia, Pa., 1860.
93. Virginia, History of, Henry Howe, 1845.
94. Virginians in the Revolution, Historical Register of, John H. Gwathmey, The Dietz Press, Richmond, Va., 1938.
95. Virginia History, Makers of, J. A. C. Chandler, Silver, Burdett & Co., New York, N. Y., 1904.
96. Virginia, Journals of the House of Burgesses of, J. P. Kennedy, Richmond, Va., 1905.
97. Virginia Land Patent Books, Richmond, Va.
98. Virginia Magazine of History and Biography, W. G. Stanard, Virginia Historical Society, Richmond, Va.
99. Virginia Militia in the Revolutionary War, J. T. McAllister, McAllister Publishing Co., Hot Springs, Va., 1913.
100. Virginia, Old Churches, Ministers and Families of, Rt. Rev. William Meade, J. B. Lippincott & Co., Philadelphia, Pa., 1857, 1872.
101. Virginia Revolutionary Land Bounty Warrants, Samuel M. Wilson, Southern Book Co., Baltimore, Md., 1953.
102. Virginia, Sketches of, Rev. William Henry Foote, William S. Martien, Philadelphia, Pa., 1850.
103. Virginia Soldiers in the Revolution, Index of Saffell's List of, J. T. McAllister, McAllister Pub. Co., Hot Springs, Va., 1913.

104. Virginia State Library List of the Colonial Soldiers of Virginia, H. J. Eckenrode, Richmond, Va., 1917.
105. Virginia State Papers and Other Manuscripts, Calendar of, Dr. W. P. Palmer, Sherwin McRae, H. W. Flournoy, 1875-1893, Richmond, Va.
106. Virginia Statutes at Large, W. W. Hening, 1812, Richmond, Va.
107. Statutes at Large - Being a Collection of all the Laws of Virginia, The, W. W. Hening, 1792, Richmond, Va.
108. Virginia Tax Payers 1782-1787, Augusta B. Fothergill and John Mark Naugle, 1940.
109. Virginia Valley Records, John W. Wayland, Shenandoah Pub. House, Inc., Strasburg, Va., 1930.
110. Virginia Wills Before 1799, William Montgomery Clemens, The Bilbio Co., Inc., Pompton Lakes, N. J., 1924.
111. Wallace Genealogical Data, George Selden Wallace, The Michie Co., Charlottesville, Va., 1927.
112. West Virginia, History and Government of, The, R. E. Fast and Hu Maxwell, The Acme Pub. Co., Morgantown, W.Va., 1901.
113. Windy Cove Presbyterian Church, A History of, Rev. A. J. Ponton, The McClure Co., Staunton, Va., 1929.
114. Who's Who in America, The A. N. Marquis Company.
115. William & Mary College Quarterly, Lyon G. Tyler, Editor.
116. Wood County, West Virginia, Sketches of, S. C. Shaw, Parkersburg, W. Va., 1878.

Archives and Libraries

1.   The Pennsylvania State Historical Society, Philadelphia, Pa.
2.   The Library of Congress, Washington, D. C.
3.   The Virginia State Historical Society, Richmond, Va.
4.   The New York Public Library, New York, N. Y.
5.   The New York Historical and Biographical Society, New York, N.Y.
6.   Pennsylvania Archives, Harrisburg, Pa.
7.   Virginia Archives, Richmond, Va.
8.   National Archives and Records, Washington, D.C.
9.   DAR Library, Washington, D. C.
10. Staunton Public Library, Staunton, Va.

Court Records

The Court Records of the following counties have been examined. If all reference to the families included herein had been copied, I would venture as a guess, that at least six volumes this size would be required to contain the extracted data.

1.   Albemarle County, Va. Court Records.
2.   Alleghany County, Va. Court Records.
3.   Amherst County, Va., Court Records.
4.   Augusta County, Va. Court Records.
5.   Bath County, Va. Court Records.
6.   Bedford County, Va. Court Records.

7. Berkeley County, Md. Court Records.
8. Botetourt Co., Va. Court Records.
9. Clark County Co., Va. Court Records.
10. Frederick County, Va. Court Records.
11. Green County, Va., Court Records.
12. Greenbrier County, W.Va. Court Records.
13. Hampshire County, W.Va. Court Records.
14. Hardy County, W.Va. Court Records.
15. Highland County, Va. Court Records.
16. Jefferson County, Md. Court Records.
17. Loudoun County, Va. Court Records.
18. Madison County, Va. Court Records.
19. Nelson County, Va. Court Records.
20. Orange County, Va. Court Records.
21. Page County, Va. Court Records.
22. Pendleton County, W.Va. Court Records.
23. Pocahontas County, W.Va. Court Records.
24. Rappahannock County, Va. Court Records.
25. Roanoke County, Va. Court Records.
26. Rockbridge County, Va. Court Records.
27. Rockingham County, Va. Court Records.
28. Shenandoah County, Va. Court Records.
29. Warren County, Va. Court Records

Church Records

Records of churches have been searched only to the extent
that they have been published in memorial books and pamphlets
from time to time. I have examined perhaps fifty such publications for the Shenandoah Valley area during the past fifty years.

National Government and State Records

1. Records of the War Department, Washington, D. C.
2. Records of the Adjutant General's Office, State of Pennsylvania, Harrisburg, Pennsylvania.
3. Records of the Adjutant General's Office, State of Virginia,
Richmond, Virginia.
4. U.S. Census Records for Pennsylvania.
5. Maryland and Virginia Census Records for the years 1790,
1800, 1810, 1820, 1830, 1840, and 1850.
6. Bureau of Pensions, U.S. Department of the Interior,
Washington, D. C.

Cemetery Records

The compiler has visited over a hundred family and public
cemeteries in the counties of Alleghany, Augusta, Bath, Highland, Page, Rockbridge, Rockingham, and Shenandoah in Virginia
and Greenbrier, Mason, Pocahontas, and Pendleton in West Virginia.

Family Records

Innumerable records have been obtained from Family Bibles
and personal records. The compiler has talked to perhaps a
thousand of the older residents of the Valley in his travels
over the area (most of whom are now dead).

409

410

411

415

416

Carlile, Jinny, 330
  John, 100, 329, 330, 331, 364
  John Griffin, 329
  Joseph, 330
  Margaret, 330, 331
  Mary, 330
  Mary Elizabeth, 329, 330
  Mary Rachel, 331, 333
  Nancy, 329, 330, 331, 333, 363
  Nancy Rachel, 330
  Rachel, 312, 330, 333
  Rachel Esther, 329, 331
  Rachel Jane, 111, 331
  Robert, 111, 329, 330, 331,
    333, 363
  Robert (the Big), 329, 330,331
  Robert (the Little), 329
  Samuel, 330, 331
  William, 330
Carlisle, George, 272
Carlock, Mary Elizabeth Susan,33
Carner, Sarah, 151
Carpenter, Anderson William, 155
  Arlie A., 155
  Chalmers, 155
  Clarice, 159
  Eleanor Ann, 92
  Elizabeth J., 133
  Ernestine, 155
  John W., 155
  Joseph, 122, 128
  Josephine, 155
  Lillie, 79
  Martha, 40, 133
  Mary, 27
  Morgan, 133
  Nelson Blair, 80, 92
  Nelson Blair, Jr., 92
  Robert J., 122
  Russell, 80
  Ruth, 128
  Samuel, 40
  Sarah B., 144, 148
  Siggie Loury, 113
  Thomas, 349
  Virginia, 80
  William J., 129
  Zella, 166
Carrier, _____, 212
Carroll, Bertie, 396
  G. W., 183
  George W., 191
  Mary, 183
Carter, A. Burton, 275
  Annie M., 275
  Betty Lou, 308

Carter, Fred, 153
  Helen, 292
Cartmail, Mary, 234
Cartmill, J., 342
  Thomas, 234
Carves, Lewis Whites, 322
Carwell, Charles, 159
  James E., 159
Cash, Nancy J., 360
Cason, _____, Mrs., 42
  Ashby, 132
Cathey, James, 355
Caudill, Carl, 218
Cauley, _____, 147, 153
  Blanche A., 64
  Helen Louise, 81
  James A., 64, 81
  James A., Jr., 64, 81
  Jane, 48
  Laura Ann, 93
  Mary E., 64
  Paul Curtis, 81
  Raymond, 147
  Restie Nickell, 64, 81
  Restie Nickell, Jr. 81, 93
  Ruth Cleek, 81, 93
  Susan Belle, 81
Cauthorn, Ashley, 306
  Callie, 306
  Charles, 306
  Margaret, 306
  Martha, 306, 349
  Mason, 306
  Robert, 306
  Rose, 306
  Sallie, 306
  Townley B., 306
Cavenah, Gadas K., 151
  Gadas K., Jr., 151
  Julian, 151
Chambers, V. L., Dr., 212
Chambliss, _____, 108
  _____, Rev., 108
Chancellor, Jesse, 238
Chaney, Roy, 74
Chaplin, Reba, 327
Chappell, W. V., 157
Chappins, Maurice Kistler,150
Chattin, Lee, Rev., 159
Chedester, Avery, 74
  Julia Ruth, 74, 89
Chestnut, David N., 348
  Elizabeth, 348
  Gertrude, 348
  James A., 347, 348
  Jane, 375

420

421

Cleek, John, Jr., 37, 39, 49,
  147
John, Sr., 38, 39, 114
John Andrew, 41, 52, 69.
John Crawford, 26
John David, 50
John Dudley, 28
John Henry Wise, 41, 49, 62
John J., 29
John Jacobs, 24, 28
John Jacobs, Jr., 28
John Leslie, 44, 55
John Lewis, 42, 49, 53
John Robert, 51, 67
John Robert, Jr., 67
John Vincent, 55, 73
John William 30
John (Jack) Wilson, 65
Judy, 89
Julia, 24
June, 82
Katherine, 64
Kenneth Allen, 75
Lamira Jane, 28
Laura Ellen, 31
Leila, 45, 58
Leola Merle, 45
Leonard, 45
Leslie, 63
Lillah Bell, 49, 63, 80, 81
Lillie Grace, 62, 78
Lillie Jane, 32, 135
Linda Ann, 85
Louisa Benjamin, 32, 46
Lucille, 54
Lyndon Crawford, 59
Mabel Gray, 47, 58
Mabel Lillian, 41
Malcena C., 184
Malcena Cathrine, 68
Margaret, 20, 21, 24, 27,
  345, 377
Margaret Eveline, 30, 42
Margaret J., 43, 54
Margaret Jane (Fleshman), 48
Margaret Julia, 28
Maria, 42
Martha, 26
Martha A., 43
Martha Elisabeth, 38, 39
Martha Elizabeth, 31
Martha Mildred, 28
Mary, 49, 54
Mary Ann, 24, 30, 40
Mary Anne, 31, 32, 44
Mary B., 32

Cleek, Mary E., 42
Mary Elizabeth Virginia, 49,
  62, 79
Mary Ethel, 50, 66, 83
Mary Jane, 26, 32, 37, 38, 39,
  42, 52, 70, 256
Mary Kay, 58
Mary Lou, 82
Mary Lydia, 64
Mary Susan, 41, 82
Mary Virginia, 51
Mathias, 20, 23, 24, 26
Mattie, 29
Micah, 23
Michael, 20, 24, 25, 39,
  175, 344, 373
Michael Given, 62
Mildred, 54
Moses, 25
Myrtle, 53, 70
Nancy, 30, 83
Nancy Carolina, 50, 275
Nancy G., 37, 38
Nancy Givens, 39, 49, 121
Norris, 55, 72
Otis Aubrey, 47
Palser, 20
Patty Lynn, 76
Paul, 73
Peter, 24, 25, 175
Peter L., 25
Peter Lightner, 30, 41
Petter, 23
Phebe, 175
Phyllis, 83
Phyllis Audrey, 47
Pinckney Lightner, 41
Rachel Price, 32, 55, 349
Ralph, 45
Ralph Allen, 65, 82
Raymond Gray, 47
Rebeccah Elizabeth (Hetty),
  24, 27
Rhuhamy A., 38
Richard, 55
Richard Stevens, 73
Robert, 55
Robert Austin, 65
Robert Charles, 57, 75
Robert Edward, 50, 66
Robert Finnell, 28
Robert Suddarth Bias, 58, 76
Robert Turner, 66
Romona, 89
Ronald Lloyd, 59
Ronald Paul, 90

432

434

436

437

444

446

448

453

McCormick, Charles David, 87
  Charles Hunter, 69
  Charles Revercomb, 69, 86
  Marie, 85
  Sallie Elizabeth, 69
  Walter, 306
  William, 306
McCown, John, 306
  Moses, 306
  Nancy Ella Kinnear, 306
McCoy, Annie, 380
  Carl, 273
  Geneva, 131
  Jemima, 110
  Mary, 320
  Myrtle, 131
  Sarah, 377
McCue, Frank Cyrus, 206
  Frank Cyrus, Jr., 206
  John, Rev., 242
  Nancy, 242
McCulloch, George, Dr., 107
  Martha Hannah, 107
McCune, Lucille Wilfong, 225
  Sadie, 325
McCurley, Harriett Creighton, 222
McCutchan, _____, 179
  Robert Dunlap, 390
McCutcheon, Margaret, 399
  Sarah, 107
McDanald, _____, 363
  George W., 304
  H. B., 304
  John F., 304
McDaniels, John A., 41
McDannald, Sue (Guy), 305
McDermott, _____, 29
  Margaret H., 25
McDonald, _____, 355
  Elizabeth, 333
McDowell, _____, 105
McElwee, _____, 274
  Alfred, 290
  Bernard Francis, 203, 207, 274
  Callie, 274
  Cameron Preston, 223
  Charles E., 290
  Charles Richard, 290
  Cora Sue, 290
  Elizabeth, 70
  Francis, 290
  Guy Cameron, 223
  Helen, 91
  Helen Vivian, 223
  June, 203, 274, 290
  Lillian May, 207, 274

McElwee, Nancy, 360
  Sue Ann, 94
  Winfred, 274, 290
McEowen, Barbara, 301
McFadden, William, 153
McFadin, Jane, 258
McFann, Andrew Jackson, 132
  Grace, 132
  Helena, 132
  LeGrande, 132
  Oscar, 132
  Wells A., 132
  William Nelson, 132
McFarland Family, 397
McFarland, Alexander, 22, 398
  Anne, 232, 397
  Benjamin, 398
  Duncan, 22, 397
  John, 398
  Robert, 302, 397, 398
  William, 398
McFetridge, _____, 279
McGill, Mary, 340
  Merl, 288
  Robert, 288, 340
  William John, 288
McGlaughlin, _____, 208'
  Abigail, 28
  Ada Ethel, 62, 123, 146, 346
  Adam T., 211
  Addie Jane, 349
  Alcinda, 138
  Alexander Arbuckle, 207
  Alice, 194, 395
  Amy, 147
  Andrew Matthews, 180, 193,
    205, 208, 274
  Andrew Wayte, 206
  Ann, 27
  Anna Bell, 208
  Annie, 139, 346
  Archie Yeager, 194, 208
  Audrey, 147
  Austin, 194
  Bernard Francis, 207
  Bettie, 345
  Brown Letcher, 146, 346
  Callie, 208
  Calvin, 194, 208
  Catherine, 27
  Charles, 147, 346
  Charles H., 194
  Charles Sheffey, 211
  Clarence, 139, 147
  Claude, 163
  Clem, 147

461

McGlaughlin, Sarah Elizabeth, 1?
   138, 191
   Vernon Pole, 194, 209
   Vernon Tate, 209
   Virginia Tompkins, 205
   William, 139, 345
   William A. G., 62, 146, 346
   William Cameron, 194, 204, 349
   William Jacob, 117,138,179,180,
   191
   William Odie, 123, 147
   Willie Sue, 196
   Winifred Lee, 207
McGuffin, Adam Given, 307, 358
   Clara, 157
   Elizabeth, 25
   Elizabeth Lee, 65
   George, 358
   George Lloyd, 307
   Harry, 307
   Hattie, 307
   James, 34,149,307,314,358
   John Crawford, 65
   Margaret, 358
   Mary, 103, 109
   Mary Jane Warwick, 314
   Nancy, 34, 105, 358
   Robert, 358
   Robert G., 157
   Samuel, 353
   Susan, 307
   William Bratton, 149, 307
   William Holmes, 150
McGuire, Louise, 82
McHone, Albert, 84
   Ginger, 93
   James Clayton, 84
   Nolan Wilson, 84
   Owen Heywood, 84, 93
McIntosh, Arthur Lee, 163
   Rosswell, 265
   Sarah Frances, 265
McIntyre, Jane, 36
McKamie, Isabella, 105
   Nancy, 343
McKee, James, 304
   Jane Logan, 304
   Mary Jane, 304
McKeever, Rachel, 242
McKinsey, John, 113
McKnight, Cordelia, 45
McKown, _____, 268
McLaughlin (see McGlaughlin)
McLaughlin, Ann, 267
   Elizabeth Allen, 165 .
   Hugh Arthur, 165

McMillan, Jane, 265
McMillian, Belle, 250
McNamara, Agnes, 83
McNeel, _____, 131, 399
   Elizabeth, 393
   Hannah, 393
   Henry, 270,274
   Evelina, 41, 393
   Isaac, 242,393,395,397
   J. Lancelot, 395
   Jean, 399
   John, 393
   John Mathew, 393
   Margaret, 178
   Mary G., 190
   Mary Gold, 395
   Mary Magdaline, 47, 48
   Paul, Hon., 242
   Phoebe, 398
   Rachel A., 393
   Sterling, 274
   T. Summers, 395
   Winters, 395, 397
McNeeley, Cordelia, 279
McNeil, H. G. P., 219
   Jonathan, 399
   Naomi, 272
   Thomas, 399
McNett, Viola, 122
McNulty, _____, 202
   Annie J. 120
   Edwin Alexander, 120
   Frances, 202, 219
   Harriett, 120
   John, 120
   John S., 120
   Louis Dudley, 120
   Mamie, 120
   Mary, 395
   Patrick Henry, 202
   Patrick Henry, Jr., 202
   William M., 120
McPheeters, Mary, 341
McQuain, _____, 323
McRiley, John, 255
Means, Robert, 232
Meeks, _____, 296
   Alexander, 231
   Thimothy Creig, 231
   Melvin, Beulah Mae, 86
Menges, Frances, 293
Merican, Alma, 90
Merkel, Arlene, 170
Merriken, Frank M., 165
   Frank M., Jr., 165
Merrill, Randolph, 70

464

475

487

488

ADDITIONS AND ERRATA

Additions

Hull Family. Page 371.

18. Peter Hull (3), son of Peter Hull (2) and Barbara Keith, married Barbara Peninger, daughter of Henry Peninger and _____.

Children: 4

a. George Washington Hull (4), died 1862; married Sarah A. Swope. They lived at McDowell, Virginia, in a brick house later owned by James Bradshaw and known as the "Mansion House."
    Children: 2
    (1) George Washington Swope Hull (5), married Mary Dever. They settled in California.
        Children: 5
        (a) Clarence Hull,(6).
        (b) Georgia Hull,(6).
        (c) Fayette Hull,(6).
        (d) Howard Hull,(6).
        (e) Bonnie Hull,(6).
    (2) William Renick Hull (5), married Virginia Wilson.
        Children: 2
        (a) Lena T. Hull (6), married William T. Green.
        (b) Renick Ward Hull (6), married Lola Ralston, daughter of James M. Ralston and Mary J. Hook. They migrated to Illinois.

b. Felix Hull (4), died 1862; married Elizabeth Mathews, daughter of Jacob Warwick Mathews and Nancy McCue. They lived at McDowell, Virginia, in a brick house now owned by Frank S. Hiner. Felix Hull led a company of 200 men into Grafton, West Virginia in May 1861. After the death of Felix Hull, his widow married R. S. Turk of Staunton, Virginia.
    Children: 4
    (1) Renick Hull (5), migrated west.
    (2) Felix Hull, Jr. (5), migrated west.
    (3) Edgar Hull (5), migrated west.
    (4) Lillie Hull (5), married _____ Huff. They lived at Waynesboro, Virginia.

c. Peter Kinkead Hull (4), married _____ Houston. He was a physician in Ohio.

d. Margaret A. Hull (4), married James Brown of Albemarle County, Virginia. They migrated to Illinois.

Hull Family. Page 372.

21. Jacob Hull (3), son of Peter Hull (2) and Barbara Keith, married Jane Arbogast.

Children: 3

a. Henry Hull (4), migrated west.
b. Mary Jane Hull (4), migrated west.
c. Welton Hull (4), migrated west.

Errata

Page 54. No. 214. Emma V. McFadden Trimble, born October 14, 1884, instead of 1844.
Page 62. No. 292. Nannie Mayse, daughter of Anderson Mayse and Rebecca McDanald, instead of Rebecca _____.
Page 81. No. 534. Floyd Lee LaRue (7) married in 1921, instead of 1931.
Pages 110 and 213. No. 35. Elizabeth Susan Bratton, born 1824, instead of 1825.
Page 113. No. 256. Americus R. Blundell (5) born May 2, 1834, instead of Mary 2, 1834.
Pages 114 and 133. No. 259. David W. Gwin (5) born October 15, 1859, instead of 1858.
Page 114. No. 260. Emma Virginia Gwin (5) born April 25, 1858, instead of 1859.
Page 116. No. 303. Bolar Austin Gwin (5) born November 14, 1847, instead of 1857.
Page 124. No. 437. Asbury W. Hiner (6) married Lena McCalpin, instead of Linnie McGlaughlin.
Page 126. No. 476. Rebecca E. Revercomb (6) born 1884, instead of 1844.
Page 135. No. 282. Anderson F. Stephenson (5) married (1) December 18, 1887, instead of 1883.
Page 135. No. 283. Minnie B.Alexander, born 1858, instead of 1863.
Page 152. No. 905. Richie Lorena Helms, instead of Ritchie.
Page 156. No. 544. William Peter Buchanan Lockridge (6) born September 28, 1897, instead of 1877.
Page 158. No. 616. Bayard Suddarth Stephenson (6) married (1) Annie Mathis, instead of Annie _____.
Page 193. No. 194. James Lightner Gum (6) born 1877, instead of July 1877.
Pages 198 and 213. No. 256. Sadie Irene Lightner (6), born December 11, 1878, instead of December 9, 1878.
Page 211. No. 458. Charles Sheffey McGlaughlin (7), born October 2, 1890, instead of 1880.
Page 232. Line 8. John Warnock makes oath he was not in the county June 10, 1747, instead of 1947.
Page 274. No. 316. William Madison Siple (6), married March 16, 1891, instead of 1921.
Page 290. No. 581. Children: 2 - first marriage, instead of 1.
877. i. Wildred LaRue (8), married Mary Louise Graham, instead of _____ Graham.
ii. Graham (Happy) LaRue (8).

491

Page 306. No. 36. Nancy Ella Kinnear McCown, married (1) in 1821, instead of 1811.
Page 307. No. 85. Georgia Lee Goul Bratton (5) married May 29, 1912, instead of May 26, 1912.
Page 321. Nos. 86 and 87. Mill Gap, instead of Mill Gay.
Page 321. No. 186. May Wade (8), married _____ Hensley, instead of _____ Hesley.
Page 321. No. 88. Walter Price Campbell (7) married (2) Emma McClintic, born 1868, daughter of Andrew Byrd McClintic and Mary Wise.
Page 349. No. 163. Cecil Hull (8), instead of _____ Hull.
Page 323. No. 208. Fern Campbell (8), instead of Feem.

492

LaVergne, TN USA
08 June 2010
185291LV00004B/49/P